D1614924

RADICALISM AND REFORM IN BRITAIN

1780-1850

RADICALISM AND REFORM

IN BRITAIN, 1780-1850

J.R. DINWIDDY

Published by The Hambledon Press 1992

102 Gloucester Avenue, London NW1 8HX (U.K.)
P.O. Box 162, Rio Grande, Ohio 45672 (U.S.A.)

ISBN 1 85285 062 0

A description of this book is available from the
British Library and from the Library of Congress

Printed on acid-free paper and bound
in Great Britain by Cambridge University Press

Contents

Preface

The essays in this book were written by John Dinwiddy over a period of twenty years. They reflect both his early interest in the radicals and reformers of the late eighteenth and early nineteenth centuries, and his subsequent growing absorbtion in the intellectual debates which accompanied and followed the passing of the 1832 Reform Act. A number of the later essays deal with the contributions of Burke and, above all, of Jeremy Bentham, on whose papers John worked extensively in the latter part of his career. He never, however, lost interest in the wider political scene; the comparatively recent essay on Chartism provides a fitting conclusion to the work of a professional lifetime spent studying the conceptual and political aspects of reform in the period 1780-1850.

We would like to thank the editors and publishers of books and journals who kindly gave permission for the various essays and articles in this book to be reprinted. Some of these have been reprinted in their original format, others reset; cross-references have been altered to refer to pages in the present text. The last essay in the book has not been published before; it is the draft of an inaugural lecture to have been delivered in May 1990.

Warm thanks are also due to those friends of John whose help, encouragement and advice led to the publication of this collection of essays; I am particularly indebted to Harry Dickinson, Alice Prochaska, Fred Rosen and Martin Sheppard. In addition to those already mentioned, we would like to thank others who contributed information for the Introduction: Ivon Asquith, James Burns, Tim Card, Ian Christie, Penelope Corfield, Hugh Dinwiddy, Mark Philp, Jonathan Riley Smith, Francis Robinson and Philip Schofield.

Caroline Dinwiddy

Publications of J.R. Dinwiddy
not included in this volume

'Who's who in Trollope's Political Novels', *Nineteenth Century Fiction*, xxi, (1967), pp. 31-46.

'Unsettled Government, 1806-1812', *History of the English Speaking Peoples*, 82 (1971), pp. 2622-27.

'Elections in Victorian Fiction', *The Victorian Newsletter*, 45 (1974), pp. 8-13.

'The "Black Lamp" in Yorkshire, 1801-1802', *Past and Present*, 64 (1974), pp. 113-23; and 'A Rejoinder', *ibid.*, pp. 133-35.

'The Unpublished Recollections of Mary Anne Clarke', *Notes and Queries*, new series, xxi (1974), pp. 328-30.

Confrontation and Reform in England 1790-1832 (Salisbury, Rhodesia, 1975: Central Africa Historical Association, General Series no. 13).

'William Cobbett, George Houston and Freethought', *Notes and Queries*, new series, xxiv (1977), pp. 325-29.

'Party Politics and Ideology in the Early Years of George III's Reign', *Historical Journal*, xx (1977), pp. 983-89.

'The Classical Economists and the Utilitarians', in *Western Liberalism*, ed. E.K. Bramsted and K.J. Melhuish (London, 1978), pp 12-25.

'Bentham's Letters to John Herbert Koe', *Bentham Newsletter*, no. 2 (1979), pp. 30-39.

'Walter Ramsden Fawkes'; 'Charles Hall'; 'Sir John Colman Rashleigh'; 'Robert Waithman'; 'Samuel Whitbread'; 'Henry White'; 'Thomas Holt White', in *Biographical Dictionary of Modern British Radicals*, i, ed. J.O. Baylen and N.J. Gossman (Hassocks, 1979).

'Los circulos liberales y benthamistas en Londres, 1810-1829', in *Bello y Londres: Segundo Congreso del Bicentenario* (2 vols., Caracas: Fundacion La Casa de Bello, 1980-81), i, pp. 377-98. Revised and translated version: "Liberal and Benthamite Circles in London, 1810-1829", in *Andres Bello:*

The London Years, ed. John Lynch (Richmond, 1982), pp. 119-36.

'Jeremy Bentham as a Pupil of Miss Edgeworth's', *Notes and Queries*, new series, xxix (1982), pp. 208-10.

The Correspondence of Jeremy Bentham, vi (Oxford: Clarendon Press, 1984. In *The Collected Works of Jeremy Bentham*).

'The "Influence of the Crown" in the Early Nineteenth Century: a Note on the Opposition Case', *Parliamentary History*, iv (1985), pp. 189-200.

From Luddism to the First Reform Bill: Reform in England 1810-1832 (Oxford: Basil Blackwell, 1986. Historical Association Studies).

The Correspondence of Jeremy Bentham, vii (Oxford: Clarendon Press, 1988. In *The Collected Works of Jeremy Bentham*).

Nationalism in the Age of the French Revolution, ed., with Otto Dann (London, 1988); "England", *ibid.*, pp. 53-70.

Bentham (Oxford: Oxford University Press, 1989. Past Masters Series).

[In Chinese] 'Bentham's Utilitarianism: Modernization in Theory and Practice' in *The Political, Economic and Social Modernization of Britain*, ed. Wang Juefei (Nanjing, 1989).

'Bentham on Invention in Legislation', *Enlightenment and Dissent*, 8 (1989).

'Jeremy Bentham y el mundo Hispanico', in *Estudios en Honor del Profesor Alamiro de Avila Martel* (Santiago de Chile; *Annales de la Universidad de Chile*, 1990).

General Editor of the following volumes in *The Collected Works of Jeremy Bentham:*

Correspondence of Jeremy Bentham, iv and v, ed. A.T. Milne (London: Athlone Press, 1981).

Constitutional Code, i, ed. F. Rosen and J.H. Burns (Oxford: Clarendon Press, 1983).

Deontology, together with A Table of the Springs of Action and Article on Utilitarianism, ed. A. Goldworth (Oxford: Clarendon Press, 1983).

Chrestomathia, ed M.J. Smith and W.H. Burston (Oxford: Clarendon Press, 1983).

a great range of visitors both to the college and to his home (these included Robert Birley, his former headmaster at Eton, and his old nannie), in assisting some Sudanese refugees from a war zone and other African victims of political upheaval, John set an example of professional service and social responsibility that was to characterize the rest of his career.

Although enriched personally and academically by his four years in East Africa, John was anxious to make his mark in the scholarly field of British History; to achieve that, he knew that he needed to return to Britain. In 1967 he was awarded a Research Fellowship at the Institute of Historical Research, in the University of London, and embarked on a Ph.D. on the activities and thought of the constitutional reformers of early nineteenth-century Britain, under the supervision of Ian Christie. By now a little more confident of his intellectual abilities and a thoroughly competent researcher, he appears to have needed little guidance from Professor Christie, though he clearly imbibed from him the precision of thought and language, and the very high standards of scholarship, that were to mark all his subsequent publications. He rapidly completed his thesis in 1971, though he had already been appointed to a Lectureship in History at Royal Holloway College, also in the University of London, in 1969 and had to prepare new lectures for his students. Over the next twenty years he advanced through the ranks of Senior Lecturer (1978) and Reader (1983) to a Personal Chair in Modern History at the combined Royal Holloway and Bedford New College in 1989.

During more than twenty years of service in the University of London, John Dinwiddy demonstrated his wide-ranging talents, his lively concern for teaching and research, his well-developed notions of professional responsibility and his constant readiness to help others. His high standing in the academic world was widely recognized, not only throughout London University but much further afield. He was appointed to external examinerships, awarded prestigious Fellowships abroad, invited to lecture at major conferences across the world, asked to contribute essays to joint volumes and elected to the Council of the Royal Historical Society.

Throughout these years he produced a constant stream of stimulating, seminal, articles in learned journals or sometimes as contributions to collected volumes of essays. His work was accepted by many of the leading historical journals on both sides of the Atlantic and his essays were published across the world. He contributed valuable work on several important political thinkers, including Edmund Burke, James Mill, Charles Hall, and Jeremy Bentham and greatly increased our knowledge of such major radicals and reformers as Christopher Wyvill, Francis Burdett and Charles James Fox. In all of this work he showed a most impressive command of the available sources, an awareness of the current state of the historical debate and of how he could best contribute to it, and a concern to make his arguments clear and accessible to all his readers. Many of his essays reveal that rare blend of a thorough knowledge of the historical context combined with a deep understanding of complex theoretical issues. They also demonstrate an enviable ability to communicate the importance, relevance and excitement of a topic to others. The essays collected here offer fresh perspectives or important re-examinations of major topics, they present a persuasive and well-argued thesis in precise yet lucid prose and, in several cases, entirely transform our understanding of a significant topic. While John's essays range widely, from the campaign against flogging in the army, through studies of English utilitarianism, of early nineteenth-century Luddites and of primitive socialists, to an assessment of the Chartist movement, together they add up to a remarkably coherent volume. As a consequence, *Radicalism and Reform in Britain 1780-1850* makes a spirited, significant and distinctive contribution to our understanding of Britain during the Age of Revolution.

In many of the essays John Dinwiddy engages in debate with other scholars or challenges their interpretations of particular problems. He does so in his distinctively courteous way. Always the serious scholar, but one who pursued excellence in a determined yet urbane, almost disinterested fashion, he attacks the problem and not the author. In his typically civilized manner, he points out error in the most kindly tone or gently rebukes a scholar who, he thinks, has overstated a case. He always expected others to do the same and he was mildly offended when they failed to do so. He well knew that historical understanding develops as the result of serious intellectual disagreements but passionately believed that the debate should always be a courteous and rational discourse between scholars who were ultimately seeking the same goal.

John's unimpeachable scholarship, his scrupulous attention to detail, and his ability to work so well with others, made him a natural choice for the exacting role of general editor responsible for the publication of the *Complete Works of Jeremy Bentham* when that post needed to be filled at University College, London. In 1977 he became joint editor of this massive enterprise, working with Professor J.H. Burns; and in 1979 he took over sole editorial responsibility for the next four years. Appointed during these years to an Associate Research Fellowship at University College, he was remarkably successful in encouraging, organizing and coordinating the work of the international team of Bentham scholars recruited to advance this major scholarly enterprise. Capable of receiving unrealistic suggestions with his usual benign scepticism, he speeded up the whole project and he saw it through its difficult passage from the Athlone Press to Oxford University Press. John also developed an unexpected talent for drumming up the financial support needed for this huge and expensive venture. With his combination of infectious enthusiasm and meticulous attention to detail he saw through the press five volumes prepared for the series by other individual editors. Thereafter he remained on the executive board and the full committee of the Bentham Project and he himself subsequently prepared two expertly edited volumes of *Bentham's Correspondence*.

These volumes (VI and VII) are models of their kind, with notes that are accurate, concise and unobtrusive. There can be no doubt that in undertaking all this editorial and administrative work on such a massive project, John Dinwiddy sacrificed much time and energy that might otherwise have been devoted to producing a major monograph in his chosen field of scholarly enquiry. At least he was able, as a spin-off from his editorial work, to produce the brilliant short study of Bentham in the *Past Masters* series. In happier circumstances, this might well have been the harbinger of the more exhaustive biography of Bentham that is still so clearly needed.

Throughout John Dinwiddy's academic life no call to service went unanswered. He played a major role in the academic affairs of his own college and of London University in general. To every task he brought shrewdness, balance, creative energy and resourceful initiative. From 1978 to 1984 he served on the committee of management of the Institute of Historical Research and on its finance sub-committee. Always a dedicated supporter of the intercollegiate degree programme at London University, he agreed in 1984 to take on the burdensome task of chairing the University's Board of Studies in History. He was the first non-professor appointed to this important post and he discharged his duties for two years with his usual exemplary efficiency. He also played a leading part in setting up a very successful combined degree course in Modern History, Economic History and Politics at Royal Holloway and Bedford New College.

As Dean of the Faculty of Arts in his college, from January 1988 until his death, he gave sterling service at a time when Royal Holloway and Bedford New College was still undergoing the strains of union and when the college was facing particularly difficult administrative and financial problems. For more than two years he served the Faculty admirably, performing a host of tasks to the best of his considerable abilities. He was always tolerant and rational, even in the most difficult of circumstances. He achieved his considerable success at some cost, however, especially as he still had his other teaching and research task to perform. He was in the unenviable position of those leading academics who find themselves committed to the three major tasks of administration, teaching and research. Seeking as always to be fair and judicious and controlling his own emotions in order to display the calm authoritative leadership needed in a difficult situation, he undoubtedly found the task a great strain. Unable always to achieve unanimous support for difficult decisions, yet unwilling to take the easy option of courting popularity, he often found his situation unpalatable and the satisfactory resolution of problems virtually impossible. Invariably genial in manner on the surface, he decided, for good or ill, not to give full vent to his feelings. Since he was a very private person, who often appeared aloof, self-contained and able to keep the world at arm's length, it was not obvious to most of his colleagues or even to those closest to him that his overdeveloped sense of duty was taking its toll.

John Dinwiddy was widely admired as a first-rate teacher who took a close and sympathetic interest in the progress of both his undergraduate and postgraduate students. Despite all his other burdens, he cared deeply about standards of teaching and about the proper care of students' welfare. On this subject he was known to speak out forcefully, even sharply. His own Special Subject on 'English Radicalism, 1790-1820' was a particuarly successful course. His personal kindness, his even temperament, his perceptive understanding of their particular strengths and weaknesses, and his evident love for his subject, were all qualities which combined to encourage the endeavours, improve the abilities and increase the enthusiasm of his students. With new research students, even those he was not supervising, he was extremely approachable and genuinely interested in the work they were doing. He was always ready to listen to any academic problem they might wish to discuss, to talk through any difficulty which they faced in their research, and to offer ideas for further and more fruitful lines of enquiry. He was happy to read through their drafts and make helpful suggestions for improvement. His own work was so meticulous, however, and he was so anxious to encourage the same thoroughness, accuracy and attention to detail in others, that his pursuit of excellence could occasionally be a little inhibiting. His own standards were set so high that few others could attain them. He sometimes feared, unnecessarily, that he himself did not quite match up to his own high ideals in scholarship.

John's qualities as a dedicated teacher and supportive colleague were seen most constantly and frequently in his work at the Institute of Historical Research in London. As one of the main coordinators for many years of the seminar on eighteenth- and early nineteenth-century British History he regularly met other scholars and researchers from many parts of Britain and much further afield. He assisted Professor Ian Christie to run this seminar from the 1970s, took over responsibility for it in 1983, organizing it more recently in conjunction with Penelope Corfield. Punctilious in his attendance, supportive of all the participants and eminently fair in his concluding remarks, he was for years a pivotal figure who strove to make these seminars not only scholarly and professional but spirited and entertaining. He was unobtrusive but unstinting with his advice. He relished a good debate but always sought to create a congenial and supportive atmosphere. No topic of research ever failed to capture his interest and he laboured to offer help on a whole range of subjects outside his main field of research. It was through the Institute's seminar that he made contact with so many other scholars and new research students and built up a wide range of people who respected his abilities and who owed him debts of gratitude, great and small.

Friends and colleagues in many other institutions also found him a firm friend and someone who was ever ready to offer advice or assistance. He was always willing to answer a query, take on the task of external examining, address a conference or contribute an essay to a collective enterprise. The news that he was going to attend a conference was an excellent reason for attending. I was myself with him at conferences in Oxford, Edinburgh, Germany and China. On these occasions he gave excellent papers, made vital contributions to the formal discussions and was a charming companion in the social activities.

John's role in the international conference which I helped to organize in Nanjing in 1987 showed him at his best and demonstrated why he was such a welcome participant at scholarly gatherings. He was uncomplaining during a long and rather trying trip out. On a particularly uncomfortable flight in a Chinese airline a clumsy flight attendant spilt some food over the fine suit he was wearing. To our group's admiration, he put the embarrassed young woman at her ease and made it appear that the accident was somehow entirely his fault. At the conference John gave a very learned, but lively and wonderfully clear, lecture. In seminar discussions and more informal gatherings he did everything possible to support, advise and encourage the young Chinese postgraduates, who were clearly both highly intelligent and enthusiastic, but who had had no chance to visit Britain to consult original sources and who occasionally struggled to express complicated thoughts in English. When one distinguished British academic expressed open impatience with a young Chinese research student, who was making a genuine effort to communicate his views as clearly as possible, John made it very clear that this was a serious breach of manners at a conference where it was the host participants who were making every effort to speak the language of the visiting contributors. John was a great hit with the Chinese, despite the enormous gulf between his background and experience and theirs. I was absolutely delighted that I had made a point of inviting him to join my sponsored group. I was particularly struck by the fact that he showed just as much kindness, courtesy, concern and interest, when discussing a problem with young Chinese students he had never met before and might never meet again, as he habitually did when engaging in historical debate at a rather higher level with his own research students or his closest colleagues back home in Britain.

Tall, slim and distinguished, John Dinwiddy looked every inch the professor. He could often appear rather patrician, slightly distant and self-contained. There were other sides to him, however. He was affectionate, unassuming and modest. He was a fine sportsman and a graceful dancer. He always played a good game of tennis and golf and was such a keen and effective cricketer that he turned out for good club sides such as the Free Foresters and the Old Wykehamists until his late forties. Though widely, and justifiably, respected as being eminently fair, tolerant and judicious, his friends and colleagues also knew him as warm, engaging, amusing and supportive. He was a very social being who loved lively conversation, good food, fine wine, and spirited companions. While on some occasions he was quiet and reserved, at other times he was genial, funny and even hilarious. He was never negative or overly critical in his response to life or to other people. He certainly took his scholarship seriously, but never solemnly.

To some, John Dinwiddy seemed the kind of man whose birth, background and connections made worldly success come easily, naturally and inevitably. A closer look at his career shows that he strove hard for many years before he made his academic mark. Despite his undoubted achievements, he was exceptionally modest and not at all confident of his own abilities. The apparently easy charm and effortless success were hard won. He always had to struggle against his natural reserve, even his innate hesitancy, before opening out to others and he had to labour long and hard before any significant academic rewards came his way. He was never the supremely confident, even aloof, scholar that some thought him to be after only a casual acquaintanceship. To those who knew him better, he was altogether more complicated and more interesting. It was only by the occasional oblique comment that he revealed his innermost doubts about his scholarly worth or his academic reputation. He was never entirely convinced that he had truly earned his success or the admiration of others. He was also more passionate and emotional than he was probably prepared to admit, even to himself, as he usually managed to control or hide this aspect of his character. He was fully aware of the benefits that nature and nurture had bestowed upon him and perhaps excessively conscious of the obligations and responsibilities that these undoubted advantages placed upon him.

In pursuing excellence in everything he did, John Dinwiddy revealed a range of abilities and a depth of quality possessed by few men. The abiding impression he leaves is that of a man of integrity, who brought conscientiousness, scrupulous honesty, great tact, a patient readiness to consider all points of view and unfailing courtesy to all that he did. These are the qualities mentioned repeatedly by those who knew him best. His kindness, his generosity, his 'sheer niceness' would be acknowledged by nearly all those who came in contact with him from the Sudanese schoolboys who needed his help to complete their secondary education to his aged nannie whom he regularly visited and for whom he found her last home. As an academic, John was both a scholar and a gentleman. As a sportsman, he combined the very best of the professional and the amateur approaches to the games he played. These are a fitting tribute to a remarkable man. His death was an enormous shock and it has left many feeling a painful loss. He will undoubtedly be long remembered by his many friends throughout the world, not only for his intellectual integrity but for his liberal, tolerant, kindly and generous spirit.

H.T. Dickinson   University of Edinburgh

Acknowledgements

The articles reprinted here first appeared in the following places and are reprinted by the kind permission of the original publishers.

1 *History*, lv (1970), pp. 342-59.

2 *Historical Journal*, xii (1969), pp. 23-34.

3 Borthwick Papers, no. 39 (1971).

4 *Bulletin of the Institute of Historical Research*, xlvi (1973), pp. 72-94.

5 *International Review of Social History*, xxi (1976), pp. 256-76.

6 *History*, lxv (1980), pp. 17-31.

7 *English Historical Review*, xcvii (1982), pp. 308-31.

8 *Bulletin of the Institute of Historical Research*, xli (1968), pp. 193-211.

9 *The Transformation of Political Culture: England and Germany in the Late Eighteenth Century*, edited by Eckhart Hellmuth (German Historical Institute, London/Oxford University Press, 1990), pp.535-60.

10 'Interpretations of Anti-Jacobinism': *The French Revolution and British Popular Politics*, ed. Mark Philp (Cambridge University Press, 1991) pp. 38-49.

11 *The French Revolution and the Creation of Modern Political Culture*, iii, *The Transformation of Political Culture 1789-1848*, ed. F. Furet and M. Ozouf (Oxford, Pergamon Press, 1989), pp. 447-66.

12 *The Eighteenth Century* (formerly, *Studies in Burke and his Time*), xvi no. 2 (1975), Texas Tech University Press, Lubbock, TX 79409-1037. Used by permission of Texas Tech University Press.

13 *The Eighteenth Century* (formerly, *Studies in Burke and his Time*), xviii, no. 3 (1977), Texas Tech University Press, Lubbock, TX 79409-1037. Used by permission of Texas Tech University Press.

14 *The Eighteenth Century* (formerly, *Studies in Burke and his Time*), xix, no. 2 (1978), Texas Tech University Press, Lubbock, TX 79409-1037. Used by permission of Texas Tech University Press.

15 *Journal of the History of Ideas*, xxxv (1975), pp. 683-700.

16 *Bentham Newsletter*, 8 (1984), pp. 15-33.

17 *Revue Internationale de Philosophie*, xxxvi (1982), pp. 278-300.

18 *Transactions of the Royal Historical Society*, 5th Series, xxxiv (1984), pp.47-69.

19 *Utilitas*, 1 (1989), pp. 283-89.

20 *Social History*, iv (1979), pp. 33-63.

21 Historical Association (1987). New Appreciations in History, 2.

22 This chapter appears here for the first time.

For
Tom and Ruth
Emma and Rachel

1

Charles James Fox and the People

THERE WERE TWO PERIODS in Fox's life from which his claim to be entitled 'the man of the people' derived. Horace Walpole remarked in his journal for 1780 how curious it was 'to see Charles Fox, lately so unpopular a figure, become the idol of the people';[1] and in this year, as a fierce opponent of North's government and the American war, and as chairman of the Westminster Committee and a strong advocate of reform, Fox enjoyed a popularity which secured him one of the most coveted seats in parliament. Enough has been written about his career in the 1780s—about his desertion of reform when he coalesced with North, and his adoption of 'tory' principles at the time of the Regency Crisis—to show that the reputation he acquired at the beginning of that decade was soon largely forfeited. What is less well known is that the revival of his reputation as a man of the people in the decade of the French revolution, when he appeared once more as the friend of peace and reform and stood out against the suspension of civil liberties, was almost equally ephemeral. In the last phase of his life and the period following his death his public image was severely damaged—not so much by Pittites and anti-Jacobins as by the spokesmen of popular radicalism. There were still writers who praised his 'great humanity of heart and liberality of soul',[2] and the Whigs made a cult of his personality both before and after his death, but the spread of political awareness had made the public much more exacting than it had been formerly in its attitude to politicians. There was an increasing acceptance of the view that Fox had never been very interested in the people, except as an occasional ally in his conflict with the Court—a conflict in which he had mainly relied on party combinations in the House of Commons. How Fox's reputation came under attack from the left in the early nineteenth century will be examined in this paper; and particular attention will be paid to his attitude to reform during his later years, as this issue above all others was coming to be regarded as the crucial test of 'patriotism', of whether a politician was on the side of the people or not.[3]

An event which foreshadowed later developments was the Westminster election of 1790, when Fox, hoping to avoid the expense of a contest, arranged a compromise with the Pittites. This was regarded by many people as an

[1] *Last Journals of Horace Walpole*, ed. A. F. Steuart (2 vols., 1910), vol. II, p. 268.
[2] Anon., *The British Cabinet of 1806* (Liverpool, 1807), p. 15.
[3] This paper will offer a different view from that of Fox's most recent biographer, Professor Loren Reid, who has written that Fox 'laid his roots in the people, and it was by what he said in their behalf that the nineteenth century principally remembered him'— 'Charles Fox and the People', *The Burke Newsletter*, vol. VI (1965), p. 429.

attempt to 'disfranchise' one of the country's most democratic constituencies, and Horne Tooke offered himself as an independent reformer in opposition to what he described as the new coalition. Despite his refusal to spend money he won a substantial number of votes; and the Westminster radicals later looked back to this contest as the genesis of a new spirit in the constituency and a notable indication of Fox's lack of consideration for the people.[4] However, in the following years Fox's stock with the reformers rose steadily, owing to his sympathy for the French revolution and his hostility to the government's warlike and repressive policies. It is true that for some time his attitude towards parliamentary reform remained equivocal. He was irritated by the formation of the Society of the Friends of the People in 1792, since his chief aim at that stage was to preserve the unity of his party and keep divisive issues in the background. But as the parliamentary strength of the Opposition declined, Fox moved progressively to the left and began to follow Grey's example in looking outside parliament for support. In November 1795 he could write that while the House of Commons and the higher orders in general were firmly behind the government, the Foxites had 'the popularity', especially among the lower classes. He told his nephew that he did not much like this state of affairs, and he added frankly in a subsequent letter: ' . . . unless the people are prepared to be completely hostile to Pitt, I have no desire for popularity'. But there was no other resource for combating the executive. Since the Whig party on its own was no longer in a condition to assert parliamentary (*scilicet* Whig) control over the Crown, it should, said Fox, 'go further towards agreeing with the democratic or popular party than at any former period'.[5] Consequently in the later 1790s he committed himself more strongly to reform than he had done since early in the previous decade. In his speech on Grey's reform motion of May 1797—which went through at least eleven editions in pamphlet form and appears to have been much the most popular of his printed speeches—he declared his approval of household suffrage; and ten months later, after seceding from the House of Commons, he announced that he would take no part in any administration until there was a radical reform in the representation of the people and a complete and fundamental change of system.[6] These public pledges, reinforced by private assurances,[7] led the veteran reformer Christopher Wyvill to place full confidence in the Whigs. In a published letter to Major John Cartwright, his fellow pioneer, he maintained that Fox merited the trust which the younger Pitt had betrayed:

> There is in him a character formed by time, Experience, and Adversity, to that unbending Firmness which is fitted for the arduous task he has undertaken. With too much penetration to be deceived by a wily Court, with too much philanthropy, too strong a sense of Honour and Justice to betray the Public

---

[4] Place Papers, British Museum Additional Manuscripts (Add. MSS) 27849, fos. 129–35.
[5] *Memorials and Correspondence of Charles James Fox*, ed. Lord John Russell (4 vols., 1853–7), vol. III, pp. 126, 134, 135.
[6] *Cobbett's Parliamentary History*, vol. XXXIII, cols. 725, 1126, 1229.
[7] Christopher Wyvill, *Political Papers* (6 vols., York, 1794–1808), vol. VI, part ii, p. 95.

to its ruin, he possesses that scorn of Power, ill-gotten and ill-employed, that philosophic dignity of mind, that grandeur of consistency, which his inferior Rival never could attain.

Wyvill claimed that the suspicion with which the radicals tended to regard all parliamentary parties should in this instance be relaxed; it would be folly, he said, to reject co-operation with men who had pledged themselves never to accept office without stipulating for reform.[8]

However, before long there were signs that the idea of co-operation with popular elements out of doors was being rejected, after a brief and inauspicious trial period, by the Whigs themselves. The secession from the House of Commons had been a kind of tacit appeal to the public—an attempt to awaken people to the inadequacy of the political system as it was then operating.[9] But perhaps it was not to be expected that the mere withdrawal of the Whigs to their country homes would produce a strong movement of opinion against the government. There was certainly no such response; and Fox, disgusted by the general quiescence, became disillusioned with the idea of a popular alliance. In September 1801 he wrote: 'I begin to think every day more, which even in better times I suspected, that whatever spirit of Liberty there was in this Country it belonged almost exclusively or at least was entirely owing to the Opposition in the two Houses of Parliament'.[10] He was coming to feel that the party would have to rely on its own efforts, in conjunction with whatever allies it could find among the parliamentary politicians. Professor Reid mentions that at the Westminster Election of 1802 Fox was still greeted with shouts of 'No Coalition!'—and he smiles at this popular memory of an event nearly twenty years in the past; it was as if, he says, 'the mature Churchill were rebuked for mistakes made as a Liberal early in the century'.[11] But a historian might well be struck by the timeliness of this cry. Writing to Dennis O'Bryen in the summer of 1803, Fox deprecated attacks on the Grenville party, explaining that though he was 'very far from wishing to make any Coalition at this time', he did not want unnecessary obstacles thrown in the way of any future alliance. In August he was trying to persuade himself and Grey that the Grenvilles were not as incorrigibly warlike as they had the reputation of being; and in December, while he had to admit that they were unpopular, he maintained that they were the only party from which the Whigs could expect cordial and fair co-operation.[12] Early in 1804 direct negotiations were opened, and by March an agreement had been reached whereby the two parties should work together for the purpose of overthrowing the Addington ministry. The great object in Fox's view was to beat the Court; he had spent most of his career struggling with it, and success in this contest was for him an end in itself. What he and his friends would be able to do if they ever succeeded in forcing

[8] *Letter to John Cartwright* (York, 1801), pp. 17–19.
[9] *Parliamentary History*, vol. XXXIII, col. 1260.
[10] Fox to Dennis O'Bryen, 17 Sept. 1801, Fox Papers, Add. MSS 47566, fo. 96.
[11] *Charles James Fox: a Man for the People* (1969), p. 380.
[12] Fox to O'Bryen, 26 June 1803, Add. MSS 47566, fos. 141–2. *Memorials of Fox*, vol. III, pp. 422, 443.

themselves back into power was a matter of less immediate concern.[13] Hence he did not scruple to ally with men whose ideas about policy were different from his own. Looking back in 1804 to the Fox–North coalition, all he could see against it was its ultimate failure; it would be difficult, he said, 'to show when the power of the Whigs ever made so strong a struggle against the Crown, the Crown being thoroughly in earnest and exerting all its resources'. As for the Grenvilles, the great thing about them was that 'among all their faults, they had one good quality, viz., that of being capable of becoming good party men'. Fox was unworried by the fact that the only questions of policy on which they seemed to agree with him were 'the imperfect defence of the country and the affairs of Ireland'.[14]

There were of course a number of other subjects on which the Grenvilles and the Foxites differed widely—especially, in domestic policy, the question of reform. To many people Fox's alliance with 'those hateful villains' (as Sir Francis Burdett called them) was no less reprehensible than his coalition with North—for the Grenvilles were in the eyes of the reformers 'a set of men of the most arbitrary principles', distinguished for nothing but their acumen in 'seeking the sweets of office present and reversionary'.[15] When Wyvill wrote a long letter to Fox expressing his fears about the effect this alliance would have on his commitment to reform, Fox did his best to reassure him.[16] But before long there were signs of a new evasiveness on the part of the Whigs. The Melville affair in 1805 aroused a great deal of anti-ministerial feeling, and both Wyvill and Major Cartwright, believing that popular indignation against corruption in government departments could be directed also against corruption in the House of Commons, thought that the time was ripe for reviving the question of parliamentary reform; but their efforts to secure the co-operation of the Whig leaders were markedly unsuccessful. When Wyvill suggested that reform meetings should be held in and around the metropolis, Fox said that it would be much better for such a movement to originate in 'more distant parts of the kingdom'; and he suggested that Leeds or Manchester should take the lead (though he must have known that both places were firmly dominated by anti-Jacobins). He was clearly anxious to avoid any situation in which a public statement of his views on reform would be expected from him; and Cartwright was still trying to press him into a private declaration on the subject when the Ministry of All the Talents was formed in February 1806.[17] There was then a move to

[13] Fox to Earl of Lauderdale, 30 Mar. 1804, *ibid.*, vol. IV, p. 35: '. . . I say there is a chance of his [Addington's] being forced out. What then? you'll say. Why then there is an inroad upon the power of the real enemy, I mean the Court, happen what may afterwards.'
[14] *Ibid.*, vol. IV, p. 40; vol. III, p. 443. Fox to William Smith, 12 Mar. 1804 (copy), Fox Papers, Add. MSS 47569, fo. 168.
[15] Burdett to Rev. R. N. French, 10 Mar. 1804, Burdett Papers, Bodleian Library, MS Eng. letters d. 97, fo. 123. W. H. Yate, *A Series of Letters on National Subjects* (Gloucester, 1806), p. 31. [F. Place and J. Richter,] *An Exposition of the Circumstances which gave rise to the Election of Sir Francis Burdett for the City of Westminster* (1807), p. 4.
[16] Wyvill to Fox, 27 Apr. 1804 (copy); to Sir John Swinburne, 4 May 1804 (copy), Wyvill Papers, North Riding Record Office.
[17] Frances D. Cartwright, *Life and Correspondence of Major Cartwright* (2 vols., 1826), vol. I, pp. 326–7. Wyvill to Fox, 21 Dec. 1805 (copy); Fox to Wyvill, 23 Dec. 1805, Wyvill Papers. Cartwright to Fox, 4 Feb. 1806, Holland House Papers, Add. MSS 51468.

raise the reform issue at the Westminster meeting that was necessary for Fox's re-election after his appointment as Secretary of State, but Fox having indicated that this would be unwelcome the proposal was staved off with talk of a separate meeting on the subject (which never took place). In his speech to the electors Fox confined himself to estimable generalities.[18]

Of course the Foxite retreat from reform had been carried out in a very discreet manner, and many people imagined that the Whigs—who in terms of parliamentary strength outnumbered the Grenvilles by two to one—would give a reforming tone to the new ministry. But Fox's first public act after being designated as Secretary of State was very disillusioning to such people. In the House of Commons on February 4th he introduced a special bill enabling Lord Grenville to retain the sinecure office of Auditor of the Exchequer at the same time as being First Lord of the Treasury. This was remembered by the radicals as one of the most disgraceful actions in Fox's career—Henry Hunt called it 'a death-blow to the fondly-cherished hopes of every patriotic mind in the Kingdom'. It seemed like a public sacrifice of Fox's professed principles to the arrogant rapacity of the Grenvilles; it was a sign (J. C. Hobhouse wrote later) 'that the Whigs despised all public opinion, and were, for the sake of a ministerial arrangement, quite careless how soon they gave a proof of their contempt'.[19] Hobhouse saw the coalition not as a matter of give and take between the Foxites on one side and the Grenvilles and Addingtonians on the others, but as a complete capitulation by the former. This was an over-simplification; but so far as home affairs were concerned Grenville did call the tune—and it was clear from the beginning that he was not prepared to make any significant move towards the 'entire radical reform in the whole system of our Government' which Fox had once declared to be necessary.[20]

Fox did not attempt a full public explanation of his conduct, but he was ready to explain himself in private to those whose good opinion he wished to retain. He argued that reform, however desirable it might be, was impracticable in existing circumstances and should be given up for the sake of other objects which might possibly be achieved. In particular, he maintained that the chance of obtaining peace should outweigh all other considerations. This was a sound enough argument, and it convinced that exceedingly upright man Christopher Wyvill, who wrote to Fox after a conversation with him early in February, wishing him success in his endeavours to obtain peace and Catholic relief and agreeing that parliamentary reform should be deferred until a more favourable time.[21] Yet what many radicals intuitively felt was that Fox had really sacrificed his reforming principles not so much

[18] Place Papers, Add. MSS 27850, fos. 10–12. *Morning Chronicle*, 14 Feb. 1806.
[19] Hunt, *Memoirs* (3 vols., 1820–2), vol. II, pp. 202–3. Hobhouse, *A Defence of the People in reply to Lord Erskine's 'Two Defences of the Whigs'* (1819), pp. 151–2.
[20] *The Speeches of the Right Hon. C. J. Fox, T. Erskine, etc. etc. at a meeting held at the Shakespeare Tavern on Tuesday, October 10, 1797* (1797), p. 9. Grenville to Fox (on the subject of offices granted in reversion), 28 Feb. 1806, Historical Manuscripts Commission, *The Manuscripts of J. B. Fortescue preserved at Dropmore* (10 vols., 1897–1927), vol. VIII, pp. 44–5.
[21] Wyvill to Fox, 5 Feb. 1806 (copy), Wyvill Papers.

to his desire for peace as to his desire for power. After all, the alliance with the Grenvilles had originated at a time when the most sanguine Francophile could scarcely have imagined that Bonaparte was pacifically inclined. The historian, while conceding that Fox had adequate grounds for shelving reform in 1806, may doubt whether his commitment to the subject had ever been very firm. He had twice taken it up, in the early 1780s and the later 1790s, when he had wanted to secure popular support against the executive; but as soon as the opportunity had arisen of storming the closet in conjunction with other parliamentary factions he had abandoned the idea of a popular alliance and ceased to show any real interest in reform. One suspects that in almost any circumstances Fox would have chosen office in coalition with the Grenvilles rather than fidelity to reform in opposition; and if in 1806 he could produce strong arguments to justify his choice, one feels that their strength was largely fortuitous. In any case, it must be recognized that Fox's conduct in abandoning the position he had so definitely taken up in the previous decade had serious effects on the image of the Whig party and on public confidence in politicians in general. Thomas Creevey, who had at one time summed up his political creed as 'devotion to Fox', could write in 1808: 'With all the adoration I have for the memory of poor Fox, I do firmly believe that the first great blow to the publick opinion of this country respecting its statesmen was given by his coalition with Lord North and that almost its death blow was given by his administration in conjunction with Lord Grenville.'[22]

The Ministry of All the Talents certainly gave, by its limitations, a great stimulus to the emergence of a popular radicalism independent of the Whigs; and the earliest evidence of this development was provided by the press. Henry White, editor of the *Independent Whig*, later told Lord Grey that when he launched his paper at the beginning of 1806 he had been an enthusiastic Foxite. But he was doubtful from the start about an administration 'made up of *avowed Tories* as well as staunch Whigs', and he was shocked by some of its early measures—particularly the bill relating to the auditorship, and the inclusion of the Lord Chief Justice (Lord Ellenborough) in the cabinet.[23] On March 2 he said in an editorial that the new administration had commenced with 'some of the most outrageous violations of the Constitution . . . that ever disgraced the most venal government'. He repeatedly adjured Fox and Grey to honour their pledges; and before long he was accusing them of apostasy, maintaining that there had been a change of men but no change of measures, and that the efforts of the few independent radicals in the House of Commons were more likely to bring about the redress of public grievances than all the party manœuvrings of Fox and his friends.[24] The same alienation from the Whigs can be traced in the pages of *Cobbett's Political Register*. Cobbett had left the ranks of the anti-Jacobins and gone

[22] *The Creevey Papers*, ed. Sir Herbert Maxwell (2 vols., 1904), vol. I, p. 22. Creevey to Whitbread, 11 Dec. 1808, Whitbread Papers, no. 373/6, Bedfordshire Record Office.
[23] *Independent Whig*, 9 Feb. 1806. White to Grey, 27 Sept. 1814, Grey Papers, University of Durham.
[24] *Independent Whig*, 23 Feb., 23 Mar., 4 May, 1 June 1806.

over to Fox some time before. By January 1806 they were on such cordial terms that Fox was undertaking to obtain a dog for him from Coke of Norfolk, and was expressing full agreement with Cobbett's view that this was 'no time for compromise of any sort, the system must be completely destroyed'.[25] But whereas what Fox was determined to avoid was any compromise with the Court, Cobbett (who did not share his hostility to the Crown) had other forms of compromise in mind. Like White, he felt obliged to criticize the early measures of the new ministry, and he showed particular resentment at the change in Fox's attitude to Indian affairs: Paull's motions for an inquiry into Lord Wellesley's administration had been supported by Fox while he was in opposition, but received no encouragement from Fox as Secretary of State. By the end of April Cobbett was writing that he had originally hoped to be able to support the ministry, but had been greatly pained by Fox's failure even to attempt the change of system which he and many others expected from him. After the end of the session he wrote that Pitt himself could not have devised a more effective means of stultifying Fox's party than a coalition with the Grenvilles under the leadership of Grenville himself; Cobbett maintained that the Foxites should never have yielded up the Treasury, but should have held out for the control over the ministry that their superiority in numbers entitled them to claim.[26]

Criticism of Fox was somewhat checked by his illness, which became serious in the summer of 1806; it aroused much public sympathy for him, and reminded his critics of his valuable qualities. Major Cartwright, after hearing rumours in June that Fox's life was in danger, wrote to him that although he lamented his connection with the Grenvilles and greatly deplored its consequences, he was extremely anxious for the re-establishment of his health. 'May it return,' he said, 'and may all the benefit to our country which your influence can produce be the fruit!' An even more impressive tribute came from Cobbett. At the end of July, when he was lacerating the ministry in public, he wrote in a private letter: 'I hope that Fox will live long yet; for I am always afraid, that if he were dead, *tyranny*, sheer unmixed tyranny, would be let loose upon the land.'[27] In the eyes of the radicals Fox's resistance to oppressive rule, especially in the 1790s, constituted his most lasting claim to public gratitude; and Cobbett evidently felt that the danger he had stood out against was not yet over. Also, it was remembered that he had been the champion of reform in the darkest period of Pittite repression, and many still believed that he had it in his power to do more for the people than any other politician could. Hence when he died in 1806 there was a widespread feeling of loss, which was reflected in the attendance at his funeral and in most of the obituaries. Francis Place, recalling in his 'History of general and Westminster politics' the revulsion in Fox's favour at the time of his death, said that by many who should have known better he was held up as everything he ought to have been and 'excused from the unpopular acts of

---

[25] Fox to O'Bryen, endorsed Jan. 1806, Add. MSS 47566, fo. 262.
[26] *Cobbett's Political Register*, 15 Mar., 26 Apr., 16 Aug. 1806.
[27] Cartwright to Fox, 1 July 1806, Holland House Papers, Add. MSS 51470. Cobbett to Wright, 30 July 1806, Cobbett-Wright Correspondence, Add. MSS 22906, fo. 177.

the administration on the pitiful pretence that they did not originate with him'.[28]

However, radical criticism of Fox was not entirely stilled. The *Independent Whig*, for instance, said on 14 September (the day after his death) that while he had earned the character of a disinterested patriot during his thirty years in opposition, the thirty months which covered his three appointments as Secretary of State had been fatal to his reputation. A few weeks later, at the general election, Sir Francis Burdett roused the indignation of the Whigs by coming out strongly against them and aspersing Fox himself. Burdett had been supported by Fox and the Whigs at the Middlesex elections of 1802 and 1804; and on their coming into office he had published an address to the Middlesex freeholders, felicitating them on the change of ministry and assuring them that they could now look forward with confidence to 'a fair and substantial representation of the people'.[29] But in an address after the dissolution of parliament at the end of October he lumped both parties together and attacked them simultaneously: 'The watchword of one party is, "The best of Kings". The watchword of the other is, "The best of Patriots". But neither of these parties will choose to descend to particulars, and inform you what the best of Kings and the best of Patriots have already done, or will hereafter do, for you.' Speaking from the hustings at Brentford on November 20, Burdett said that he had had a very high opinion of Fox's ability, and when he came into power had hoped for 'some of those great schemes of National Reform, which his great mind was calculated to produce'. But when a considerable time had elapsed without any such scheme being brought forward, and without any hint being given that Fox intended to redeem his pledges, he had been forced to abandon his friendly attitude to the ministry.[30] At this Middlesex election, Burdett's attempt to appeal to the independent public against the parliamentary parties was unsuccessful. But his election for Westminster in the following May, brought about by a committee of radical tradesmen in defiance of both the new ministry and the Whigs, was a highly significant sequel to the Grenville–Fox coalition. Lord Cochrane, who was elected along with Burdett, wrote later: 'This election was remarkable as being the first in which public opinion firmly opposed itself to party faction. It had become unmistakably manifest that the two great factions into which the politicians were divided had no other object than to share in the general plunder.' And J. C. Hobhouse, looking back from 1819 to the events of 1806–7, said that Fox's coalition with Grenville and Sidmouth had been 'the signal for the resurrection of the people'.[31]

A striking illustration of the extent to which, within a year or two of his death, Fox's reputation as a man of the people had lost its hold over the minds of popular radicals was provided by an incident at the reform dinner

[28] Add. MSS 27850, fo. 21.
[29] *Independent Whig*, 23 Feb. 1806.
[30] M. W. Patterson, *Sir Francis Burdett and his Times* (2 vols., 1931), vol. I, pp. 182–3, 185–6. For another radical's disillusionment with Fox, see John Gale Jones, *Five Letters to the Right Honourable George Tierney* (1807), p. 20.
[31] Earl of Dundonald, *Autobiography of a Seaman* (2 vols., 1860), vol. I, pp. 219–20. *Authentic Narrative of the Westminster Election of 1819* (1819), p. 340.

organized by Major Cartwright at the Crown and Anchor Tavern on 1 May 1809. When Capel Lofft, who had participated in the reform campaigns of the 1780s and 90s, attempted to propose a toast to Fox's memory, he was shouted down with cries of 'Income tax!' and 'Hanover!'[32] The first of these cries referred to the fact that the income tax, which had been strongly opposed by Fox when it was first introduced, had been increased by the Ministry of All the Talents from six and a quarter to ten per cent; the latter cry referred to a remark said to have been made by Fox when he was Secretary of State to the effect that Hanover should be as dear to Englishmen as Hampshire.[33] But Lofft could not understand how such hostility to Fox could have arisen.[34] He belonged, like Wyvill, to the old school of gentlemen-reformers, and people of this type tended to regard Fox with admiration. Most radicals, however, were much more critical. It is true that William Hazlitt, in an essay on Fox written in 1807, enthusiastically praised him not only for his intellect and eloquence and good nature, but for his 'strength of moral character'. But a few years later, when the aura of Fox's personality had faded, he took a much less favourable view, maintaining that Fox had been *too* good-natured and too flexible: '. . . he made too many coalitions, too many compromises with flattery, with friendship (to say nothing of the baits of power), not to falter and be defeated at last in the noble stand he had made for the principles of freedom.'[35] There were others who had never been admirers of Fox and had always felt that behind his liberal sentiments there was a lack of real concern and constructive purpose. Bentham wrote to Sir James Mackintosh in 1808: 'My expectations of him were never sanguine. He was a consummate party leader: greedy of power, like my old friend Lord Lansdowne—but, unlike him, destitute of any fixed intellectual principles, such as would have been necessary to enable him to make, to any considerable extent, a beneficial use of it.'[36] And Francis Place, writing to John Cam Hobhouse in 1827 when the latter was radical M.P. for Westminster, said that much more was now required from a man of the people than had been in the previous century:

Time was when 'Wilkes and Liberty' and '45' made the silly people mad.

'It was the number 45 O
Set the people all alive O.'

Yet none knew what the words meant, excepting those who in some way expected to profit by them, and the peoples folly. '*The Cause the Cause*' roared Charley Fox; '*the Cause the Cause*', echoed the Whigs, and the people ran after *Fox* and the *Whigs* and '*the Cause the Cause*'.This was playing the game of the factions admirably. *Then* there was no public—now there is a public,—not a good public

---

[32] The incident was vividly described by Crabb Robinson in a letter to his brother Thomas, 4 May 1809, Crabb Robinson Papers, Dr. Williams' Library, London.
[33] *Parliamentary Debates*, vol. VIII, col. 265. W. S. Landor, *Charles James Fox*, ed. Stephen Wheeler (1907), p. 16 & n.
[34] Lofft to Wyvill, 6 May 1809, Wyvill Papers.
[35] *Complete Works of William Hazlitt*, ed. P. P. Howe (21 vols., 1930–4), vol. VII, pp. 313–22; vol. XVII, p. 36.
[36] *Works of Jeremy Bentham*, ed. Sir John Bowring (11 vols., Edinburgh, 1843), vol. X, p. 428.

certainly, but one which will in time become good. 'Wilkes and Liberty', and 'the Cause the Cause' will no longer answer the purpose of the would be 'peoples men'. . . . Would a man have any considerable weight with the people, he must tell them specifically and in words neither likely to be misunderstood nor capable of being perverted, I will endeavour to do so and so, naming particulars seriatim, and then what he says will be canvassed and criticized and pretty fairly appreciated; he must come to the test of utility if he would have consequence now.[37]

It would of course be wrong to assume that the voice of Francis Place was always the voice of the people, or that his hatred of Fox, whom he referred to as 'old Foxey',[38] was universal among the lower classes. Henry Brougham, when standing for Liverpool in 1812, reported that there Fox was remembered with affection even among the Burdettites. But he lamented that this was not the case in other populous places;[39] and there is every reason to think that Place, Cobbett and other radical leaders did speak for a large section of the community. The *Edinburgh Review* admitted in 1807 that Cobbett was merely the mouthpiece for 'a very general spirit of discontent, distrust and contempt for public characters, among the more intelligent and resolute portion of the inferior ranks of society'.[40] As Fox had been largely responsible for this resentment, it was only natural that his reputation should be one of its principal targets. Moreover, the fact that the Whigs went on brandishing his name as if it would 'accomplish all things'[41] exasperated those who felt that he had done little enough for the people while he was alive and (as Burdett had implied in his electoral address of October 1806) was unlikely to do any more for them now that he was dead. Cobbett wrote in April 1809 that at the next meeting of the Whig Club Sheridan was certain to make 'a flaming speech about *Liberty* and *Mr. Fox*. It is too much to tolerate this farce any longer'.[42] As time went on Cobbett's attitude to Fox became more and more hostile.

There was one highly respectable paper, the *Morning Chronicle*, which could be relied upon to stand up for Fox against his radical detractors. But an attempt to establish a weekly paper more specifically devoted to the protection of Fox's reputation and the dissemination of his principles was a marked failure. The projector was none other than Henry White, who along with Cobbett had led the attack from the left on the Ministry of All the Talents. After a number of prosecutions for seditious libel and a three-year spell in Dorchester Gaol, he decided that the vocation of a Foxite journalist might be less arduous than that of a radical one; and in October 1813, having obtained financial backing from several prominent Whigs, he launched a new weekly called *The Charles James Fox*.[43] But it ran for little more than

---

[37] Place to Hobhouse, 19 Dec. 1827 (draft), Place Papers, Add. MSS 35148, fo. 5.
[38] *Ibid.*, 27842, fo. 42: '. . . old Foxey, who was always insincere, always the friend of the people when out of place, always willing to sacrifice them to get into place, and always their enemy when in.' (I owe this reference to Mr. William Thomas.)
[39] Brougham to John Allen, 25 Sept. 1812, Holland House Papers, Add. MSS 52178.
[40] *Edinburgh Review*, vol. X, p. 421.
[41] Place to James Mill, 5 Nov. 1818, Add. MSS 27842, fo. 46.
[42] *Cobbett's Political Register*, 15 Apr. 1809.
[43] There are numerous letters from White, asking for money and explaining his views and objectives at length, in the Grey Papers, University of Durham. There is a prospectus

six months—and it is not surprising that it failed to attract a wide readership. White did try, in a series of biographical articles, to present Fox himself in as popular a light as he could; and once or twice he went so far as to suggest that the contemporary Whig party was not doing all that it might to uphold its hero's 'best principles'.[44] But the basic tone of the publication was inevitably deferential—and this, in the age of Cobbett, was objectionable to 'the more intelligent and resolute section of the inferior ranks of society'. White had appealed very successfully to such people in his heyday as a radical journalist—Thomas Hardy had described the *Independent Whig* in 1807 as the most popular paper in London.[45] But there was little to attract them in a diet of laudatory articles on Fox and earlier Whig leaders, interspersed with letters to the Dukes of Norfolk and Devonshire congratulating them on their adherence to Whig principles. Indeed White not only failed to establish his new paper—he also, by suddenly appearing in Foxite Livery, caused the *Independent Whig* to lose over a thousand readers.[46] Nevertheless in 1816 he made another attempt to commend himself to the Whigs and obtain their financial support by declaring his renewed intention—this time through the medium of the *Independent Whig* itself—'to do justice to the true principles of Whiggism' and 'to protect the memory of such a man as Mr. Fox against the pen and tongue of such vulgar defamers as Mr. Cobbett and Mr. Hunt'. But a few months later he had to report that the circulation of his own paper was dropping, while he calculated that Cobbett, through his cheap editions and the republication of his writings in *The Statesman* and various provincial papers, was reaching a total of three hundred thousand readers a week.[47] In the following years White sent a stream of begging letters to Grey, maintaining that he had a claim on the party because his support for Mr. Fox and Whig principles had caused so many defections from his paper.

Fox was posthumously unlucky in having as a journalistic champion a man who—at least by the time he took up Fox's cause—was more remarkable as a sponger than as a journalist.[48] But White did try, whatever his motives, to extend and popularize Fox's reputation; whereas the Whigs made little attempt to put across their hero to the public, confining themselves (White said) to 'the perpetuation of the memory of Mr. Fox in the occasional public meeting of a particular class of his friends'.[49] The annual dinners held in honour of Fox's birthday were not perhaps so exclusive as this phrase suggests. But they were essentially gatherings of the faithful, presided over by the grandees of the party. H. G. Bennet described a Newcastle Fox dinner chaired by Lord Grey as 'a beat up of political friends—a kind of levee'; and when Joseph Hume was planning a visit to Edinburgh in the winter

of *The Charles James Fox* in the Whitbread Papers (no. 5038); and the complete run of twenty-nine issues, 3 Oct. 1814–17 Apr. 1815, is in the British Museum.

[44] See for instance *The Charles James Fox*, 9 Jan. 1815.
[45] Place Papers, Add. MSS 27818, fo. 64.
[46] White to Grey, 16 June 1816, Grey Papers.
[47] White to Grey, 9 & 17 Sept. 1816, 4 Jan. 1817, *ibid.*
[48] See Brougham to Grey, 1 Sept. 1814, Brougham Papers, University College London; and Place Papers, Add. MSS 35144, fo. 36.
[49] White to Grey, 26 July 1816, Grey Papers.

of 1824-5, Lord Archibald Hamilton told him that a dinner held in his honour would attract a considerably wider attendance than the annual Fox dinner, which was 'a *Party* one exclusively'.[50] That the Whig cult of Fox's memory was not a popular, expansive cult is suggested also by the nature of its literature. Fox's *History of the early part of the Reign of James the Second*, written mainly during the period of his secession from parliament and published by his nephew Lord Holland in 1808, was greeted with enthusiasm by liberal-minded men of letters such as William Roscoe and Capel Lofft;[51] and Lord Holland's introduction, which gave an account of Fox's life at St. Anne's Hill, replaced the picture of him as a gambler and libertine with that of a scholar and a gentleman[52]—which appealed to gentlemen and scholars. But the book (which cost thirty-six shillings) does not appear to have made a wide impact on the public.[53] Fox's correspondence with Gilbert Wakefield, published in 1813, was concerned mainly with questions of classical literature; and Dr. Samuel Parr's *Characters of the late Charles James Fox*—an unwieldy compilation with a mass of notes and notes on notes—was almost equally unfit for popular consumption. There was one work more calculated, in Francis Horner's view, to spread affection for Fox's memory 'among the middle class of people throughout England': John Bernard Trotter's *Memoirs of the latter years of the Right Honourable Charles James Fox* (1811). But unfortunately this publication could not be given the seal of Whig approval, because although it gave a pleasant picture of Fox himself it was full of rancour against his friends and colleagues. (Trotter had been private secretary to Fox while the latter was Secretary of State, and his grievance was that after Fox's death he had not been offered a position of the kind to which he thought himself entitled.) After a lot of discussion in Whig circles as to how the book should be dealt with in the *Edinburgh Review*, it was eventually treated as beneath the reviewers' notice.[54]

It is not perhaps surprising that no 'official' work on Fox was published in the early nineteenth century,[55] for any such work would necessarily have involved some definition of what Fox had stood for, and it was doubtful whether such a definition was desirable. For the Whigs tended (in practice if not in theory) to treat the principles of Charles James Fox less as a gospel to be preached to the unconverted than as a cement for keeping the existing party in one piece. Francis Horner wrote despondently a couple of days after

[50] *Creevey Papers*, vol. I, p. 187. Hamilton to Hume, 1 Nov. 1824, National Library of Scotland, MS 2257, fos. 129-30.
[51] Roscoe to Lord Henry Petty, n.d. (draft), Roscoe Papers, Liverpool Public Library. Lofft to Wyvill, 6 May 1809, Wyvill Papers.
[52] The latter phrase was applied to Fox by J. W. Ward in *Quarterly Review*, vol. IX (1813), p. 328, and by Walter Savage Landor in one of his *Imaginary Conversations of Literary Men and Statesmen* (5 vols., 1824-9), vol. III, pp. 435-6.
[53] Sir James Mackintosh wrote later (to Holland, 6 Aug. 1820, Holland House Papers, Add. MSS 51633) that historical writings did not 'reach low enough for popularity'.
[54] Horner to Lady Holland, n.d. (Oct. 1811), Horner Papers, vol. V, p. 147, London School of Economics. Brougham to Grey, 13 Oct. 1811, Brougham Papers. Holland to Francis Jeffrey, n.d. (Oct/Nov. 1811, draft), Holland House Papers, Add. MSS 51644. Holland to Grey, 7 Nov. 1811, *ibid.*, 51544.
[55] Except for John Allen's largely factual article on Fox written for the Supplement to the 6th edition of the *Encyclopaedia Britannica*.

Fox's death: 'I look upon what has been called Mr. Fox's party, the remains of the old Whig faction, as extinguished entirely with him; his name alone kept the fragments together.'[56] But in fact—there being so little besides devotion to Fox that Fitzwilliam on one wing of the party and the Mountain on the other could profess in common—Fox's ghost was to perform much the same unifying function. The principles of Charles James Fox were useful not only because they had a more up-to-date ring than 'the principles of 1688' or 'the cause for which Hampden bled in the field and Sydney on the scaffold', but also because they could be interpreted in almost as many different ways. Within the party an inconclusive argument was carried on as to how they *ought* to be interpreted. On the question of war and peace, Whitbread maintained that the pacific stand which he took up at the beginning of 1807 would have been approved by Fox—and that if Fox had remained in control of the peace negotiations in the previous year they would not have broken down as they did. Grey, on the other hand, asserted that those who had taken over the negotiation had continued it on the lines laid down by Fox, who had himself, at the time he wrote his last dispatch, considered it to have failed.[57] On domestic issues, also, the left wing of the party frequently claimed Fox's authority for its own policies. When Whitbread came out in favour of reform in 1809, he expressed his conviction that 'that wise man, whose principles he contracted at his outset in political life, would strongly recommend the conduct he was now pursuing'. And when under attack from the more conservative members of the party in the following year, he wrote that many of those who now thought his views 'new fangled' had formerly held the very same views along with Fox and himself in 1793—and had had the very accusation brought against them by the Portland Whigs which they now brought against him.[58] Brougham was another who made great play with Fox's name. He professed his devotion to Fox in order to establish his affiliation to the party, but he interpreted Fox's principles in such a way as to give himself considerable latitude for pursuing popular courses. He said in a speech during the Liverpool election of 1812:

By his principles it is my delight to regulate my conduct—and judging by what he did and said, of what he would have done had he been preserved to our days, I feel well assured, that he would now have followed a course if possible still more popular, because he would have seen, more and more clearly, the vital importance to the country of a strict union between the people and their leaders, against the growing corruptions and augmented insolence of the Court![59]

---

[56] *Memoirs and Correspondence of Francis Horner*, ed. Leonard Horner (2 vols., 1843), vol. I, p. 374.
[57] Roger Fulford, *Samuel Whitbread* (1967), pp. 173–4. Grey to Brougham, 29 Sept. 1908, *Life and Times of Henry Lord Brougham*, written by himself (3 vols., 1871), vol. I, p. 414.
[58] *Parliamentary Debates*, vol. XIV, col. 514. Whitbread to Bedford, 9 May 1810 (draft), Whitbread Papers in the possession of Earl Waldegrave, Chewton House, near Bath.
[59] Brougham to Holland, 8 Oct. 1811, Holland House Papers, Add. MSS 51561. Brougham to Grey, endorsed Nov. 1812, Brougham Papers. *The Speeches delivered during the Election at Liverpool in October 1812, by Henry Brougham, Esq.* (Liverpool, 1813), p. 39.

Brougham told Allen that he wanted to see 'the ancient intercourse between the Whigs and the people' re-established; but there was a limit to how far one could court the people without being disowned by the party. In January 1814 Brougham and other members of the Mountain were excluded from the annual dinner in honour of Fox's birthday. He wrote indignantly to Creevey: 'It is rather good to see the real and best Foxites so treated; us—who stand up for Fox *agt.* Pitt . . . We have lived to see the time when Foxite means Pittite—or something very near it.' In Brougham's view the party was divided into 'those who stand up for Fox *against* Pitt', and 'those who mince the matter as to Pitt's measures'.⁶⁰ By the latter he meant those who abstained from attacking Pitt out of consideration for the Grenvilles—and, partly for the same reason, discountenanced all kinds of reform. Men like Brougham and Whitbread chafed continuously in the ten years after Fox's death against the Grenville alliance and its inhibiting effects on the party. But of course any appeal from the Mountain for more truly 'Foxite' policies could be only too easily countered by a reminder that the Grenville alliance had been Fox's doing. Indeed the Duke of Bedford could tell Whitbread in 1809 that the union of Fox's party with the Grenvilles had been urged by Fox himself 'as his dying hope and left as his last legacy to his surviving friends'.⁶¹

An illustration of the difficulty the Whigs had when it came to defining Fox's principles in a way that would be acceptable to all sections of the party is provided by the story of his epitaph. Westmacott's statue of Fox for Westminster Abbey was finished by 1819, and the sculptor having left a space for an inscription the committee responsible for the monument invited Sir James Mackintosh to compose one. Sir James, despite his radical youth, was by now one of the staider members of the party, and produced what he himself called 'a sober and modest composition . . . I have so laboured to avoid exaggeration that I hope a reasonable opponent will not consider the commendation as excessive proceeding from an affectionate adherent.' He mentioned Fox's efforts in the cause of toleration, his Libel Act, his abolition of the slave trade, the fact that he had 'contended for the rights of the people of America and Ireland', and the rather more dubious fact that he had 'sacrificed power for the hope of bestowing a just government on India'. But there was no reference to reform, and no specific mention of what many people regarded as his chief claim to fame—in Brougham's words, 'his truly glorious career as leader of the patriot band which, during the almost hopeless struggle from 1793 to 1801, upheld the cause of afflicted freedom'.⁶² Such omissions—in the winter when the Six Acts were passed—aroused the indignation of the more militant Whigs. Brougham called on Creevey to help him in suppressing this 'cursed, bad and timid epitaph', and a kind of competition ensued, Brougham putting in a draft of his own. There followed

⁶⁰ Brougham to Allen, 28 Oct. 1812, Add. MSS 52178. Brougham to Creevey, 7 Feb. 1814, Creevey Papers (microfilm), University College London. Brougham to Grey, 24 Oct. 1812, Brougham Papers.
⁶¹ Fulford, *Whitbread*, p. 253, citing Whitbread Papers (Bedford), no. 2462.
⁶² Mackintosh to Holland, 9 Sept. 1819, Add. MSS 51653. R. J. Mackintosh, *Memoirs of the Life of Sir James Mackintosh* (2 vols., 1835), vol. II, pp. 376-8. Brougham, *Historical Sketches of the Statesmen who flourished in the time of George III* (Paris, 1839), p. 108.

several years of discussion and intrigue, but no consensus emerged; and the decision eventually reached was that the monument should simply be inscribed with Fox's names and the dates of his birth and death.[63]

Cobbett would have made something out of this story had he known about it. He enjoyed making the point that so long as the Whig party stood for 'the principles of Charles James Fox' it stood for almost everything and almost nothing. In 1812 when the Prince Regent was being accused by the Whigs of having abandoned the principles of Mr. Fox, Cobbett asked which of Mr. Fox's principles they had in mind:

> The principles he maintained when on the side of Lord North before the American war, at which time I remember a speech of his in support of Ex-Officio Informations; the principles he maintained during the American war against Lord North; the principles he maintained in conjunction with Lord North after the American war; the principles he maintained during the Anti-jacobin war against Lord Grenville and in the present war against Lord Sidmouth; or, the principles he maintained when he came into office with both of those Lords at once.[64]

But although there was certainly a good deal of vagueness and ambiguity about Fox's principles, there was—at least during the last thirty years of his life—one consistent theme: his hostility to the Crown. This orientation may have been largely accidental—Lord Carlisle reckoned that originally (after his quarrel with North in 1774) Fox had adopted the principles of the Whig party 'not from inclination but from resentment';[65] and subsequently it was his personal antipathy to George III that lay at the basis of his anti-monarchism. But he liked to claim an impressive ancestry for his views and to regard himself as in the mainstream of the Whig tradition; perhaps his chief aim in writing his History was to show how close his own political position was to that of the Whig heroes of the 1680s.[66] Thus one might say that although 'the principles of Charles James Fox' sounded more up-to-date in the early nineteenth century than 'the principles of 1688', they amounted in fact to much the same thing: distrust of the crown, and a belief in aristocratic government on behalf, but only to a limited extent under the control, of the people. Henry White took as the motto for *The Charles James Fox* a quotation from one of his speeches: 'I ask you to examine with attention the History of this Country, and to reflect upon it;—you will see that all its calamities have been chiefly owing to that system which tends to increase the Influence of the Crown, and to encroach upon the Rights of the People.' But in the early nineteenth century it was considerably more difficult than it had been earlier to maintain that such a system existed. Although Lord John Russell in the 1820s could still echo Fox's alarm about the increasing influence of the Crown and the approaching euthanasia of the constitution, such language

[63] Brougham to Creevey, n.d., Creevey Papers. *Creevey Papers*, vol. II, pp. 299–300. Memorandum dated 30 May 1823, Holland House Papers, Add. MSS 51472.
[64] *Cobbett's Political Register*, 28 Mar. 1812.
[65] 'Character of Fox' (1806), Carlisle Papers, cited by I. R. Christie, 'Charles James Fox', *History Today*, vol. VIII (1958), p. 114 n.
[66] J. R. Dinwiddy, 'Charles James Fox as Historian', *Historical Journal*, vol. XII (1969), pp. 23–4, 33–4; see below, 19-20, 29-30.

sounded distinctly archaic.[67] For while the Whigs continued to appear in their traditional role as defenders of the people's rights against the encroachments of the executive power, the people themselves were no longer satisfied with the protection of their existing rights, but wanted to extend them—and they felt that their quarrel was not simply with the Court but with the mass of the governing class. Fox's idea of liberty was inadequate at a time when increasing numbers of people were coming to regard self-government through real representatives as the only satisfactory way of securing their interests; and appeals by the Whigs to Fox's principles seemed symptomatic of a backward-looking stance and a lack of sympathy for new ideas and aspirations. John Nicholls, who had been an independent member of parliament at the turn of the century, wrote in 1820:

> Mr. Fox is no more; but they [the Foxites] endeavour to acquire popularity by assuming his name. They find that it is in vain; they feel that the people are not with them... It is well known that the leaders of the Foxite party are among those who are the most averse to Reform. How can they expect that the people should wish to see them in office?[68]

It was not of course necessary for the Whigs to adopt the programme of the extreme radicals; what they needed to do to ensure their own survival was to enlist the support of the 'middling classes' by committing themselves to moderate reform. Francis Jeffrey had said in 1810 that the Whigs stood 'without power or popularity' between two great armies—on the one hand that of Church and King, and on the other that of the democrats; and he had urged the Whigs to abandon their 'cold and repulsive neutrality' and join forces with the more respectable of the latter.[69] For some time, even after the Grenvilles had parted company with the Whigs, the conservative elements in the party remained strong enough to prevent the adoption of such a policy. The party continued to stagnate, and in the 1820s came near to extinction. But eventually reform did supersede 'the principles of Charles James Fox', and gave the Whigs a new lease of life.[70]

After 1832, Fox cannot be said to have had any real influence.[71] In the age of improvement, of classical economics, of democracy, there was less and less to connect the Liberal party with him. Russell, looking back from the 1860s, saw the founders of nineteenth-century liberalism as Grey, Canning and Peel.[72] (After all, of the three great leaders of Victorian liberalism one

---

[67] *An Essay on the History of the English Government and Constitution* (2nd edition, 1823), p. 455.
[68] *Recollections and Reflections, personal and political* (2 vols., 1820–2), vol. I, pp. 212–13.
[69] *Edinburgh Review*, vol. XV (1810), pp. 504–5, 520.
[70] Norman Gash, *Reaction and Reconstruction in English Politics 1832–52* (Oxford, 1965), p. 157.
[71] Thomas De Quincey, writing in mid-century, contrasted the increasing prestige and influence of Burke with Fox's faded reputation; Fox, he wrote, 'is known only as an echo is known, and, for any real effect of intellect upon this generation, for anything but the "whistling of a name", the Fox of 1780–1807 sleeps where the carols of the larks are sleeping that gladdened the spring-tides of those years.' *Collected Writings*, ed. David Masson (14 vols., 1896–7), vol. XI, pp. 35–40.
[72] *An Essay on the History of the English Government and Constitution* (3rd edition, 1865), pp. c–cvi.

had started life as a Canningite and another as a Peelite.) As early as 1838 Fox's reputation was being cut down to size by the *Edinburgh Review* itself:

> Of Mr. Fox it must be said that whilst his political principles were formed upon the true model of the Whig School, and led him, when combined with his position as opposing the Government's warlike and oppressive policy, to defend the liberty of America, and the cause of peace, both in that and the French war, yet he constantly modified these principles, according to his own situation and circumstances as a party chief;—making the ambition of the man and the interest of his followers the governing rule of his conduct.[73]

The author of this article was none other than Lord Brougham. In stressing the force of Fox's ambition he was echoing Bentham's judgement; and there can be little doubt that they were right on this point—indeed Fox had admitted it himself.[74] As for the emphasis on Fox's concern for the interests of his followers, here again Brougham's assessment coincided with that already current in radical circles. The *Newgate Magazine* (published by the Painite Richard Carlile) had said in 1826 in a passage which Francis Place approvingly transcribed into one of his guard-books:

> Party had never a more decided leader than Mr. Fox: no chieftain of banditti was more faithful to his troop than he was to his followers . . . That he should be loved by his friends and enthusiastically admired by his followers, may be easily conceived: but that he should be held up . . . as an object of national gratitude cannot be so easily explained.[75]

There certainly was this feeling that for all Fox's speeches from the hustings at Westminster and the banners that proclaimed him 'the man of the people', he had really belonged less to the people than to his friends. It is true that he had (as Landor said) 'more and warmer friends than any statesman upon record'.[76] Of the amazing potency of his charm there can be no doubt whatever; it captivated many who had no personal contact with him, and to a remarkable extent it retained its power after his death. But there were many who were unsusceptible or out of range. Those on the fringes or beyond the pale of the eighteenth-century political nation could not 'identify' with Fox as they had done with John Wilkes, for there was nothing of the outsider about him. Sir Francis Burdett, on the other hand—wealthy patrician though he was—was more of an outsider in the sense that, at least during the first twenty years or so of his political career, he was more uncompromisingly hostile to 'the system' than Fox had ever been. And he patently relied more on popularity than on friendship; the Westminster radicals could describe him as 'the man indeed of the people, for the people themselves have raised him to the pinnacle on which he stands'.[77]

It would be wrong for the historian to follow Francis Place in maintaining that Fox cared and did virtually nothing for the people. He was courageous

[73] *Edinburgh Review*, vol. LXVIII (1838), p. 217.
[74] Thomas Green, *Extracts from the Diary of a Lover of Literature* (Ipswich, 1810), p. 174.
[75] *Newgate Magazine*, vol. II (1826), p. 467; Add. MSS 27837, fo. 97.
[76] W. S. Landor, *Charles James Fox*, p. xxiii.
[77] *Authentic Narrative of the Westminster Election of 1819*, p. 51.

and impressive in his defence of traditional liberties; and he opposed the war with France partly on the grounds of the hardship which it caused to the people of England.[78] Perhaps Henry White was justified in claiming that Fox deserved more gratitude for what he did than censure for that which he left undone.[79] But this essay has shown that there was in the early nineteenth century a strong reaction, among all but the most gentlemanly radicals, against Fox's claim to be entitled the man of the people. The reaction was partly due to a change in the political climate; the emergence of a politically informed and independent public[80] set up a powerful challenge to the 1688 view of politics which Fox had taken for granted. But the reaction arose also out of a real ambivalence in Fox's career—an ambivalence that became apparent in time even to men who had greatly admired him. One writer argued after Fox's death: 'He was accused of rank democracy; but with much injustice. He entered political life among the aristocracy, and with them closed his career. It was by their prevailing influence against the crown that he twice became a minister; and by them he was supported throughout.'[81] This is no more the whole truth about Fox than the view that he was a 'people's man'. But the element of truth in both views needs to be recognized.

[78] *Parliamentary History*, vol. XXXII, cols. 165–8.
[79] *The Charles James Fox*, 6 Mar. 1815.
[80] Add. MSS 27850, fos. 39–40. *Politics and Public Men for the year 1812* (1813), pp. 28–32.
[81] Extract from *The Epics of the Ton*, in Philopatris Varvicensis [S. Parr], *Characters of the late C. J. Fox* (2 vols., 1809), vol. I, p. 129. In a print of 1802 (by J. T. Smith) Fox is represented with his great paunch inscribed 'Victualled by Subscription of the Nobility'—an allusion to the subscription raised on his behalf in 1793. M. D. George, *Catalogue of Political and Personal Satires*, vol. VIII (1947), p. 91.

2

Charles James Fox as Historian

Several British statesmen have also been historians: Clarendon, Russell, Rosebery, Churchill—and Charles James Fox, although he produced only one volume. His *History of the early part of the Reign of James II* is a fragment of what might have been a much larger work; it was published posthumously, with a preface by his nephew Lord Holland, in 1808. Although it was given a mixed reception by the critics, it was regarded for several decades as something of a classic. It was translated into French, German, and Dutch; and was republished several times in England during the nineteenth century (most recently as a threepenny paperback in Cassell's National Library in 1888). It cannot be claimed that this work is a landmark in the history of historiography —although it is mentioned by writers on that subject.[1] But it is valuable for the light which it reflects on the author. Fox's talents and versatility are almost legendary; he has been taken by G. M. Trevelyan as the representative figure of the eighteenth-century aristocracy[2]—whose ideal (in the words of another scholar) was 'the Renaissance ideal of the whole man.'[3] An article has been written on Fox's literary taste;[4] but his activity as a historian is an aspect of his career which has hitherto been neglected. However, his *History*, together with the correspondence relating to it,[5] is a source which anyone aiming at a full assessment and understanding of Fox should take into account. It was the only considerable piece of serious writing which he attempted;[6] and its publication was welcomed by James Mill as 'affording evidence of the real extent of Mr Fox's abilities and knowledge, more decisive and accurate than anything we have yet received'.[7] It also has political significance in that one of the author's chief motives was to vindicate his own Whiggism, by implicitly demonstrating how close his political position was to that of the Whig heroes of

[1] C. H. Firth, 'The Development of the Study of Seventeenth-century History', *Transactions of the Royal Historical Society*, 3rd series, VII (1913), p. 40, and *A Commentary on Macaulay's History of England* (London, 1938), pp. 56–7; T. P. Peardon, *The Transition in English Historical Writing 1760–1830* (New York, 1933), pp. 195–6.

[2] *English Social History* (London, 1944), pp. 404–5.

[3] Lord D. Cecil, *The Young Melbourne* (2nd edn. London, 1954), p. 6.

[4] J. Dechamps, 'Charles Fox et Racine', *Modern Language Review*, XXXVI (1941), 467–72.

[5] This is mostly to be found in the C. J. Fox and Holland House Papers, British Museum Additional Manuscripts (hereafter referred to as Add. MSS.) 47578 and 51510. The latter bundle is unfoliated. For the original manuscript of the *History*, see Add. MSS. 51508–9.

[6] On Fox's other publications, see Lord Holland's introduction to C. J. Fox, *A History of the early part of the Reign of James the Second* (London, 1808—cited hereafter as *History*), p. xiv n.

[7] Aikin's *Annual Review and History of Literature* (1808), p. 101.

the 1680s; in this sense (as will be suggested below) the *History* can be re-garded as an indirect reply to Burke's *Appeal from the New to the Old Whigs*.

Fox's work as a historian belongs to the quietest, and in some ways the most pleasant, period of his life. In May 1797, when it had been clear for some time that the war with France and the split in the Whig party had made Pitt's position in the House of Commons impregnable, Fox and most of his followers seceded from Parliament. For the next year or two at St Anne's Hill Fox seems to have been happy enough with Homer, Vergil, Ariosto and other favourite authors. But in due course he came to feel the need for some more constructive employment of his time. He might have taken to literary criticism; one of the projects he had in mind during his years of retirement was an edition of the works of Dryden. But Fox, who already felt somewhat uneasy about his with-drawal from Parliament,[8] was too much in the grip of politics to devote him-self to serious literary studies. A historical work, however, would not mean turning his back so completely on politics. It was clear that the political prin-ciples in which he believed were currently out of fashion, and an ephemeral pamphlet expressing these principles would be no more useful than speeches in the House of Commons. But in a history of the Revolution, which is what he planned to write,[9] he could hope to give more lasting and more dignified expression to his constitutional ideas—ideas which he regarded as central to the Whig tradition. As Trotter, his adoring ex-secretary, put it, 'in having recourse to history (still continuing his exertions in favour of liberty), he shewed the generous struggles of a noble mind to serve his country and posterity in the only way left open to him'.[10]

At this period, such motives were not regarded as inconsistent with aspirations to historical scholarship. The eighteenth century was the age of 'philosophical history'. According to Bolingbroke and Voltaire, to study the past for its own sake was mere antiquarianism; history was 'philosophy teach-ing by examples', and it was the business of historians to expound its lessons. Political history was expected to illustrate political principles—the nature of which depended largely on the outlook of the writer; and impartiality was a phenomenon so rare as to be virtually unrecognizable to contemporaries. When Hume tried to write an impartial history of England, he had to throw his weight against the prevalent Whig interpretation[11]—and was inevitably regarded as a Tory. The position at the end of the eighteenth century was that

[8] He admitted that neither Cato nor Brutus would have approved of it—see *Memorials and Correspondence of Charles James Fox*, ed. Lord John Russell (4 vols. London, 1853–7—cited hereafter as *Memorials*), III, 278.
[9] He seems at one stage to have aimed to cover also the reigns of William III and Anne (see an undated letter to the Hon. George Walpole, Add. MSS. 47578, fo. 85); but in January 1804 he told Holland that he did not intend to go beyond the Revolution (*Memorials*, III, 241).
[10] J. B. Trotter, *Memoirs of the latter years of the Right Honourable Charles James Fox* (London, 1811), p. xvi.
[11] See Hume's *History of England* (8 vols. London, 1782), VIII, 323.

Hume's so-called Tory interpretation held the field. As Malcolm Laing, the historian of Scotland, wrote in a letter to Fox in 1800:

his history has certainly contributed, more perhaps than any other cause, to fashion the opinions of the present generation. It is the first, and almost the only history of England ever read, and there is nothing to counter-act the general impression which its fascinating narrative and philosophical researches are calculated to produce, but Mrs Macauley's transcripts of Oldmixon's dull controversial malignity. A historian of England is still wanting, equally remote from the virulence of republican, and the apologetical strain of prerogative writers.[12]

So far as the Stuart period (which was the chief battleground) was concerned, the Tory position had been reinforced by Dalrymple and Macpherson.[13] In setting out to overthrow this Tory predominance in the historiographical field, Fox aimed to do what Macaulay eventually succeeded in doing.

It was an ambitious undertaking for a man who had written almost nothing and had no experience of research; and it has been suggested that Fox merely dabbled in history.[14] But—although he never approached the level of learning attained by Mackintosh, who was the next Whig statesman to embark on a history of the Revolution[15]—he did set about his task in a fairly scholarly way. In a letter to Lauderdale at the beginning of 1800, expressing his intention of becoming a historian, Fox explained that he had been working on an introductory chapter (a 'cursory review' of the historical background to James II's reign), but had not yet 'looked into any manuscript papers, or other documents not generally known'; he was anxious for any information Lauderdale could give him about where such materials could be found.[16] During the next few years Lauderdale and his friend Malcolm Laing gave Fox a considerable amount of help, particularly with regard to Scottish sources. Fox also had two advisers in London: Samuel Heywood, Serjeant-at-law, who subsequently wrote a whole book in defence of Fox's *History*; and William Belsham, a Whig pamphleteer and author of a massive (though undistinguished) history of England since the Revolution.[17] Fox exchanged letters with Belsham on the

---

[12] Add. MSS. 47578, fos. 9–10. Cf. Holland to Fox, 10 September 1800 (Add. MSS. 47574, fos. 115–16): 'the tendency of Hume's History...has certainly led many many people in England to consider their History which ought to be as it were a magazine of proofs and examples against Toryism as the strongest justification for High Church doctrines or at least the strongest satire against the contrary principles'.

[13] Sir John Dalrymple, *Memoirs of Great Britain and Ireland* (2 vols. London and Edinburgh, 1771–3); James Macpherson, *The History of Great Britain from the Restoration to the Accession of the House of Hanover* (2 vols. London, 1775).

[14] J. W. Derry, *The Regency Crisis and the Whigs, 1788–9* (Cambridge, 1963), p. 29.

[15] Forty volumes of historical materials collected by Sir James Mackintosh are preserved in the British Museum (Add. MSS. 34487–526).

[16] *History*, p. xvi.

[17] There are articles on Laing and Belsham in the *Dictionary of National Biography*. For Heywood see H. W. Woolrych, *Lives of Eminent Serjeants-at-Law* (London, 1869), pp. 701–33.

characters of Sunderland and Shaftesbury;[18] and Heywood provided various information, including a lengthy legal opinion as to 'Whether Conspiracy to depose the King or to levy War is a compassing of his Death within the Statute 25 Ed. 3'[19]—which was used by Fox when he considered (in his introductory chapter) the fate of Russell and Sidney. Fox showed a laudable anxiety to check his authorities, and to track down original documents. For instance he tried, though unsuccessfully, to trace the notes written by Argyle in prison before his execution, which Woodrow had apparently seen;[20] and he managed, with the aid of two Roman Catholic friends, Henry Howard of Corby Castle and Charles Butler of Lincoln's Inn, to ascertain the fate of James II's papers which had been in the Scotch College in Paris up to the French Revolution.[21] But his most notable piece of research was carried out in the archives of the French Foreign Office. The correspondence of Louis XVI and Barillon (who was French ambassador in London throughout James's reign) had previously been examined by Sir John Dalrymple, who had published extracts from it in his *Memoirs of Great Britain and Ireland*. But Fox thought a re-examination of the original correspondence would reveal much new material. After the Peace of Amiens he obtained permission from the French Government to study these papers in the Dépôt des Affaires étrangères. He went to France at the end of July 1802; and during the next few months, with the aid of Lord St John, Robert Adair, and John Bernard Trotter, he transcribed most of Barillon's correspondence from the time of James's accession. Trotter has left a description of how this work was carried on:

I shall not easily forget Mr Fox walking upstairs, taking off his hat, and sitting down in our room, oppressed with heat and the fatigue arising from it; taking a few minutes to recover himself and then applying with the same ardour and industry every day, copying, reading aloud the passages leading to any discovery, keeping his friends busily employed, and always cheerful and active.[22]

When he returned from France, Fox proceeded to incorporate the new material he had collected into what he had already written about the months

---

[18] Add. MSS. 47578, fos. 12–13 and 23.
[19] Add. MSS. 51510.   [20] Add. MSS. 47578, fos. 30 and 42.
[21] *History*, pp. xxiv–xxxii. The original Memoirs of James II in his own hand-writing covering the years 1652–60 were burnt at St Omer during the French Revolution; but a French version of these Memoirs has recently been discovered and published in an English translation—see A. Lytton Sells, *Memoirs of James II* (London, 1962). Of the Life of James II, compiled by William Dicconson with the aid of James's papers, there appear to have been two copies extant in the early nineteenth century. One of these was tracked down by Fox and his agents; it was in the possession of Alexander Cameron, Roman Catholic bishop at Edinburgh, and Laing examined it and described it to Fox. The other copy, which had been in the hands of the English Benedictines at Rome, was acquired by the Prince Regent, and an edition by J. S. Clarke was published on his orders in 1816. For Fox's correspondence relating to the papers, Memoirs and Life of James II, see Add. MSS. 47578, fos. 49–52, 58–60, 66–8, 71, 76–7, 80 and 109.
[22] Op. cit. p. 339. See also St John to Holland, 21 April 1808, Add. MSS. 51824.

following James's accession.[23] He also tried to obtain the correspondence of Don Pedro de Ronquillo, who was Spanish ambassador in London during James's reign. Lord Holland, while travelling in Spain, was urged to search for these papers, which Fox said would give him an 'advantage of the greatest consequence over all other historians'. Holland did find and purchase Ronquillo's original letters of the years 1689 to 1691, but could not trace his earlier correspondence.[24]

There are many indications in Fox's letters of his determination to achieve the highest possible standard of accuracy. Writing to Laing he asked for information as to whether Argyle actually addressed the crowd from the scaffold before his execution, or merely handed a written speech to the Dean of Edinburgh who attended him. Fox went on: 'After all, this is all very immaterial, but one becomes sometimes too curious about trifles from a great desire of stating the truth with a minute correctness.'[25] This exactitude was one of the reasons for the rather slow progress of his work. In addition, perhaps surprisingly for such a fluent speaker, Fox found actual composition a great labour. He wrote to Holland in January 1804: 'History goes on, but it goes on very slowly, the fact is I am a very slow writer...I am too scrupulous both about language and facts.'[26] Other retarding factors were the distractions of literature and politics. As to the former, when Lauderdale wrote saying that he hoped Fox had turned his classical books out of the house, Fox replied that he had no intention of doing so, and would give up the whole project if he thought it incompatible with his giving a little time to them.[27] In the years when he was engaged on his history, Fox was carrying on a very learned correspondence with Gilbert Wakefield on matters of classical scholarship; and at the end of his famous letter to Grey on nightingales in literature he said: 'I am afraid I like these researches as much better than those that relate to Shaftesbury and Sunderland, as I do those better than attending the House of Commons.'[28] Between May 1797 and the summer of 1802 Fox appeared very rarely in the House of Commons. But during the session which opened in November 1802 he attended and spoke more regularly, feeling that it was his duty to exert what influence he could in favour of peace; and towards the end of 1803 he became preoccupied with the possibility of creating a strong opposition through a junction with the Grenvilles. With the formation of this alliance, early in 1804, Fox once more devoted his chief energies to politics. His history

[23] When Fox's historical fragment was published, Holland subjoined to it an appendix of documents consisting mainly of the Barillon correspondence between December 1684 and December 1685. The letters of subsequent years which Fox and his friends had transcribed were not published, as being irrelevant to the short period covered by Fox's work; but these copies were later used by Mackintosh and Macaulay.

[24] *Memorials*, III, 219; *History*, p. xxxv n.
[25] Add. MSS. 47578, fo. 46. [26] *Memorials*, III, 232.
[27] Lauderdale to Fox, dated 'Sunday', Add. MSS. 51510; Fox to Lauderdale, 2 May 1800, *Memorials*, III, 301.
[28] Ibid. III, 311. Cf. Fox to Wakefield, 26 January 1801, ibid. IV, 401.

by that stage had been carried up to the execution of Monmouth (he reported Monmouth's death to General Fitzpatrick on 1 January 1804); thereafter he seems to have written only a few paragraphs of his fourth chapter, although he continued (at least during that year) to devote some of his time to historical studies.[29]

Fox died in office in September 1806; and in due course his friends decided that his historical work should be published. Early in 1808 Holland let it be known that he intended to sell the copyright on behalf of Mrs Fox. After some competition it was sold to William Miller for £4,500[30]—an unprecedentedly high price for a single volume (although Robertson had received the same sum for his three-volume *History of the Reign of Charles V*).[31] The work was published in June 1808—the standard edition, of which 5,000 copies were printed, being offered for sale at thirty-six shillings. The book consists of a fifty-page preface by Lord Holland, some 270 pages by Fox, and 150 pages of documents. Fox's introductory chapter is a sketch of the period 1640 to 1685; the second chapter deals with James's measures in the opening months of his reign and the proceedings of his first parliaments in Scotland and England; and the third chapter describes the expeditions of Argyle and Monmouth. Without attempting a minute analysis of Fox's work, I shall try to pick out its main themes and points of interest.

The general tone is, of course, strongly anti-Stuart. The chief preoccupation of Fox's political career was his jealousy of the powers of the crown; and the later Stuart period gave him many opportunities of showing the need for such jealousy. In the passage on the Restoration, Monk was heavily censured for laying the nation prostrate at the feet of the returning monarch, without a single provision in favour of the cause of liberty.[32] Fox went on to describe Charles II's reign as an era of good laws and bad government; and he pointed out 'the inefficacy of mere laws in favour of the subjects, in the case of the administration of them falling into the hands of persons hostile to the spirit in which they had been provided'.[33] When he came to the case of Sidney, Fox criticised Hume for glossing over the king's responsibility for Sidney's prosecution and death. Hume, Fox said, showed 'a spirit of adulation towards deceased princes' which prevented him from fulfilling his moral responsibilities as a historian; as men in situations of unlimited authority need not fear the censure of their contemporaries, it was only 'the dread of posthumous infamy' which might restrain them from crime: but if historians like Hume

---

[29] Ibid. IV, 13 and 65; Add. MSS. 47578, fo. 64.

[30] Miller, determined to outbid Longman, actually offered 4,525 guineas; but as Longman declined to raise his bid from the 4,000-guinea level, Holland agreed to accept £4,500. On the publication of Fox's *History*, see Add. MSS. 47578, fos. 89–103 and 123–4, and T. F. Dibdin, *Bibliographical Decameron* (3 vols. London, 1817), III, 442.

[31] *Dictionary of National Biography*, XVI, 1313.

[32] *History*, pp. 19–20.

[33] Ibid. pp. 20–2 and 36.

apologized for 'their foulest murders' there would be no such deterrent.[34] Fox's conclusion concerning Charles II was that 'his desire of power was more unmixed with the love of glory than that of any man whom history has recorded'. He could find little to say in his favour, except that he was kind to his mistresses (from one of whom, the Duchess of Portsmouth, Fox was himself descended through his mother).[35] In the second chapter, Fox moved on to James II and analysed his aims and measures at the outset of his reign. He maintained that the new king's primary motive at this stage was 'the desire of rendering himself independent of Parliament, and absolute, not that of establishing Popery in England, which was considered as a more remote contingency'. Fox's purpose in insisting on this distinction was made quite clear; he was anxious to refute the view of historians such as Macpherson that it was James's unfortunate religious enthusiasm which cost him his throne. These Tory historians, said Fox,

have taken much pains to induce us to attribute the violences and illegalities of this reign to James's religion, which was peculiar to him, rather than to that desire of absolute power, which so many other princes have had, have, and always will have in common with him.

If this interpretation was accepted, the sole inference would be that no Catholic should be allowed to become king of England. But Fox maintained that James was committed to the system pursued by all the Stuart kings—and that the true lesson of his reign was that Englishmen should never

abate of that vigilant and unremitting jealousy of the power of the crown, which can alone secure to us the effect of those wise laws that have been provided for the benefit of the subject.[36]

The other main point which Fox aimed to establish—though it is only foreshadowed in the fragment he wrote—was that the Tories eventually turned against James II not through any attachment to political liberty, but simply because of the threat to the Church. Bolingbroke, in his *Dissertation upon Parties*, had argued that the Whigs and Tories had co-operated, at the time of the Revolution, on much the same principles:

The Revolution was a fire, which purged off the dross of both parties; and the dross being purged off, they appeared to be the same metal, and answered the same standard.[37]

The Revolution showed, according to Bolingbroke, that when oppression was carried to a certain stage the Tories regarded resistance as justifiable. But Fox

[34] Ibid. pp. 48–50. Cf. Voltaire: 'Le jugement de la postérité est le seul rempart qu'on ait contre la tyrannie heureuse'—*Essai sur les Mœurs*, ch. CLXVI; quoted by J. B. Black, *The Art of History* (London, 1926), p. 32 n.

[35] *History*, pp. 62–4.

[36] Ibid. pp. 101–3.

[37] Bolingbroke, *Works* (5 vols. London, 1754), II, 102–3.

argued that the Tories had shown no hostility to James so long as he contented himself with extending his political power:

Absolute power in civil matters, under the specious names of monarchy and prerogative, formed a most essential part of the Tory creed; but the order in which Church and King are placed in the favourite device of the party, is not accidental... Accordingly as the sequel to this reign will abundantly show, when they found themselves compelled to make an option, they preferred, without any degree of inconsistency, their first idol to their second, and when they could not preserve both Church and King, declared for the former.[38]

In Fox's view the Whigs alone could be credited with 'just notions of liberty'; and of course he believed this to be true not only for the later Stuart period, but also for the reign of George III. To him the chief constitutional danger in the 1790's and in the time of Addington was an excessive increase in the power of the executive; he frequently referred to Hume's remark that absolute monarchy is 'the easiest death, the true *Euthanasia* of the British constitution'.[39] Fox thought that his own times were not very different from the period before the Glorious Revolution. He wrote to Christopher Wyvill towards the end of 1800: 'Is it not to be apprehended that we are verging every day to that situation in which our ancestors would have been, if James II had been a member of the Church of England?'[40] In his *History* he made a number of oblique references to contemporary politics. When he described the 'despondency of good men' caused by Charles II's establishment of despotism, but pointed out that within a few years began 'the brightest æra of freedom known to the annals of our country',[41] he was encouraging the Whigs of his own time not to despair. The Habeas Corpus Act, which Pitt had suspended, was pointedly described as 'the most important barrier against tyranny, and best framed protection for the liberty of individuals, that has ever existed in any ancient or modern commonwealth',[42] and in a footnote he drew attention to the fact that the Bill for the Preservation of the King's Person, introduced into parliament in 1685, had been used as a model in more recent times[43]—the reference being to 36 Geo. III, c. 7, 'an Act for the safety and preservation of His Majesty's person and government against treasonable and seditious practices and attempts'. A further example worth mentioning is Fox's analysis of Whig and Tory views of the prerogative: this arose out of a discussion of the Exclusion Bill, but it contained an implicit justification of the behaviour of the Whigs during the Regency crisis of 1788-9.[44]

---

[38] *History*, pp. 155-6.

[39] *Memorials*, III, 89, 135 and 240; Cobbett's *Parliamentary History*, XXXI, 550. See also Hume's essay 'Whether the British Government inclines more to absolute Monarchy, or to a Republic', *The Philosophical Works of David Hume* (4 vols. Edinburgh, 1826), III, 56.

[40] C. Wyvill, *Political Papers* (6 vols. York, 1794–1806), VI, Part ii, 82.

[41] *History*, pp. 57–8.   [42] Ibid. pp. 35–6.

[43] Ibid. p. 146 n.

[44] Ibid. pp. 38–9. The relevance of this passage was recognized when the Regency question again came to the fore in 1810. See *Morning Chronicle*, 23 November 1810.

The character of Fox's *History* may be further illuminated by a study of the reaction it produced. Despite the fame of the author, no great impact should have been expected from a historical fragment dealing with a very short and not especially significant period. Its reception by the public was certainly less enthusiastic than Miller had hoped, and he barely covered his expenses.[45] However, the book did provoke much discussion and controversy among critics and scholars. The *Monthly Review* gave it unstinted praise in a series of three articles;[46] whereas in the opinion of the *Quarterly* it was 'as great a disappointment as ever occurred in the literary history of the world'.[47] Dr Samuel Parr, in a characteristically discursive 'note' (covering some 180 pages), defended Fox against the charges of the *British Critic*, which had maintained that he was favourable to regicide and hostile to the Church.[48] The fullest attempt to discredit Fox's *History* was made by Pitt's former henchman George Rose, in his *Observations on the Historical Work of the Right Honourable Charles James Fox* (1809)—which Mackintosh justifiably described as 'tedious and inefficient'.[49] Rose accused Fox of inaccuracy and party bias, but his own carelessness and evident partiality laid him open to attack; and Samuel Heywood's *Vindication of Mr Fox's History* (1811) made the most of the weaknesses in Rose's work. The soundness of Fox's facts and arguments was on the whole successfully defended; and Heywood maintained that if Fox was to be condemned for political bias, most other historians of England would have to be condemned likewise.[50]

But it was certainly arguable that Fox's work was marked by an excessive degree of party spirit, and (like Bolingbroke's *Remarks on the History of England*) was more fit to be classified as polemical than as historical literature. Francis Horner, though welcoming the book for the principles expressed in it, was clearly of this opinion; he wrote soon after its publication:

I am rather glad, that the Church and the Tories do not seem to think it worth while to raise a cry against the book; if it were to be stigmatized now as a mere party pamphlet, which would be a plausible criticism, an impression might be given which would last a long while; whereas, if it is suffered to get into every library, and considered, for the present, as curious from the fame of its author, rather than for its own merits, and as the fragment of a history of antiquated times, the day may once more return, when its immortal doctrines will be cherished even in England.[51]

[45] Dibdin, loc. cit.   [46] *Monthly Review*, LVI, 185–200, and LVII, 65–79 and 190–9.

[47] *Quarterly Review*, IX, 314. For another strongly unfavourable judgement, see Walter Savage Landor, *Charles James Fox*, ed. Stephen Wheeler (London, 1907), p. 75.

[48] *British Critic*, XXXII, 209–25; Philopatris Varvicensis, *Characters of the late Charles James Fox* (London, 1809), pp. 584–767.

[49] *Memoirs of the Life of Sir James Mackintosh*, ed. R. J. Mackintosh (2 vols. London, 1835), II, 156.

[50] S. Heywood, *A Vindication of Mr Fox's History of the early part of the Reign of James the Second* (London, 1811), pp. 423–4. Heywood's book was cleverly argued, but very long (nearly twice the length of Rose's *Observations*); for a witty summary, see Sydney Smith's article in *Edinburgh Review*, XVIII, 325–343.

[51] *Memoirs and Correspondence of Francis Horner*, ed. Leonard Horner (2 vols. London, 1843), I, 424.

Jeffrey, reviewing it in the *Edinburgh*, expressed a similar judgement of the work. He said that in recent years anti-Jacobin feeling had been so strong and so much encouraged by the 'favourers of power' that even denunciations of Stuart tyranny and eulogies of the Glorious Revolution had been unfashionable; Fox's book was therefore invaluable for its fresh and unequivocal appeal to 'the old principles of English constitutional freedom'; and, ten years at least after the prostration of Jacobinism in France, it was high time that these principles were revived. But he stated bluntly that he did not think Fox's work had any great value as history.[52]

There were others, however, who treated it with respect as a historical work. Sir James Mackintosh went so far as to say that 'England never sustained a greater loss by the non-completion of a book than on this occasion';[53] and in his *History of the Revolution in England in 1688: comprising a view of the reign of James II* (1834), he paid Fox the compliment of not covering the early months of James's reign: after sketching the characters of James and his ministers, Mackintosh began his narrative with the Bloody Assizes which followed Monmouth's rebellion. Another Whig historian, Lord John Russell, in his life of his ancestor Lord Russell, acknowledged his debt to the introductory chapter of Fox's *History*; and he quoted *in extenso* the passage in which Fox argued that the Rye House assassination plot was a fabrication.[54] By Macaulay's time, however, Fox's work had ceased to carry weight; and in his *History of England* Macaulay mentioned Fox only when acknowledging that he had made use of the materials collected by him.[55] In so far as he set out to make a serious and lasting contribution to history, Fox's success was limited. Today only the appendix to his work is of any value to historians of the Stuart period.[56]

But to historians of George III's reign, and to anyone interested in Fox, the work itself remains of some significance. It is not very well-written or well-constructed;[57] nor is it particularly profound. But it is a book which leaves the

---

[52] *Edinburgh Review*, XII, 271 ff. J. W. Ward maintained that Fox had chosen an unsuitable period, since it was neither sufficiently remote for him to be objective about it, nor sufficiently recent for him to have 'superior means of information' (*Letters to "Ivy" from the 1st Earl of Dudley*, ed. S. H. Romilly, London, 1905, pp. 69–70).

[53] 'Extract from Sir James Mackintosh's letter to R. S.', Add. MSS. 51510. ('R. S.' I take to be Richard Sharp, M.P., a member of the Holland House circle, who was a regular correspondent of Mackintosh while the latter was in India.)

[54] *Life of William Lord Russell* (London, 1819), pp. x and 258–63.

[55] Macaulay, *History of England from the Accession of James the Second* (6 vols. London, 1913–15), I, 289 n.

[56] See the numerous references in D. Ogg, *England in the Reigns of James II and William III* (Oxford, 1955), chapter v.

[57] Jeffrey (loc. cit.) described Fox's style as 'lacking in vivacity' and sometimes awkward; and in a private letter he went so far as to say that is was 'often unequivocally bad'—a judgement which was later echoed by Tom Moore. There is certainly a rather strained and even pretentious quality about Fox's formal prose which is absent from both his letters and his speeches. (See Henry, Lord Cockburn, *Life of Lord Jeffrey*, 2 vols, Edinburgh, 1852, II, 124; *Memoirs, Journal and Correspondence of Thomas Moore*, ed. Lord John Russell, 8 vols. London, 1853–6, v. 306; *Quarterly Review*, IX, 328; and Macaulay's essay on Sir James

reader with a favourable impression of the author: it bears witness to what a recent writer has called 'the liberal bent of his mind and the generosity of his instincts'.[58] James Mill, while criticizing the looseness of Fox's thought, was impressed by the moral character of his work; he wrote:

We fear that Mr Fox's talents were not vigorous and cultivated enough to be very capable of efforts of generalization or analysis. Any reflections of this sort which he hazards are superficial and common. But in the moral department of the philosophy of history, we know no rival to him in the English language. In every part of his valuable fragment, the moral qualities of his actors come home to the bosom of his readers, and call forth their love or their detestation. With regard to public virtue, the love of which it is so peculiarly the business of the historian to inspire, there is scarcely any praise to which he is not entitled.[59]

Even Wilberforce—whose outlook on most political issues was very different from that of Fox—admitted after reading his *History* that he was 'honest in his sympathies with the oppressed and injured, warm in his love of justice and truth'; though he added that Fox was prone to be misled by the ardour of his feelings.[60]

Fox's *History* was also, as Heywood said, 'a most interesting exhibition of the principles of a great political character, not as advanced or supported in debate, but as deliberately written in his closet'.[61] In 1791 Fox and his followers had been accused by Burke, in *An Appeal from the New to the Old Whigs*, of straying from the Whig tradition. In Burke's view the Whig party was essentially aristocratic, and committed above all to defending the old political and social system which gave such a dominant position to the aristocracy.[62] Fox, on the other hand, had said in 1783 that the essential characteristic of a Whig was 'a firm and determined resolution to support the interests of the people against the encroachments of prerogative';[63] and after the French Revolution and the outbreak of war, Fox continued to believe that the chief

Mackintosh, *Edinburgh Review*, LXI, 266–7.) As to the form of Fox's work, Jeffrey said that the narrative was 'too minute and diffusive'; Fox tended to describe insignificant events in excessive detail, and his anxiety to ascertain and demonstrate the exact truth of every particular resulted in the narrative being 'too frequently interrupted by small controversies and petty indecisions'.

[58] J. T. Murley, 'The Origin and Outbreak of the Anglo-French War of 1793' (Oxford D.Phil. Thesis, 1959), p. 338. Jeffrey wrote: 'Nothing, we are persuaded, can be more gratifying to his friends, than the impression of his character which this book will carry down to posterity' (*Edinburgh Review*, XII, 273).

[59] Aikin's *Annual Review* (1808), p. 103. Fox's work abounds in moral judgements—not always favourable to those with whom he sympathized politically; for instance he was outspoken in his condemnation of the proceedings on the Popish Plot (*History*, pp. 33–4).

[60] R. I. and S. Wilberforce, *Life of William Wilberforce* (5 vols. London, 1838), III, 386.

[61] Heywood, op. cit. p. xxxvi.

[62] As Burke told Lord Fitzwilliam in June 1791, anything which tended to disturb 'the recognized ranks and orders, and the fixed properties in the nation' would be fatal to the aristocratic Whigs (*Correspondence of Edmund Burke*, ed. T. W. Copeland et al., Cambridge and Chicago, 1958 –, VI, 272).

[63] Speech to his Westminster constituents, 6 March 1783—quoted in I. R. Christie, *Wilkes, Wyvill and Reform* (London, 1962), p. 177.

danger was not from France and French principles but from the strengthening
of the executive at home.[64] He maintained that the aristocratic Whigs stood for
the constitutional liberties of the people in opposition to the crown[65]—and
that this was the confrontation which mattered. What Burke saw, and Fox did
not see, was that by the 1790s this confrontation between the aristocracy and
the crown was less important than the conflict which was threatening to develop
between the traditional governing class and those hitherto outside the political
nation.[66] In the later Stuart period, and perhaps in the 1770s, the aristocracy
had been threatened from above; in the era of the French Revolution Fox
failed to appreciate the seriousness of the new threat from below. His anti-
monarchism in the latter part of his career has been attributed by one historian
to 'arrested development', and by another to a 'fixation' about George III
and Pitt.[67] There is truth in both these observations. But it should be noted that
Fox was right in thinking that jealousy of the crown was a crucial feature of the
Whig tradition.[68] His historical work was intended to underline the fact that
he had, in the 1790s, taken an authentically Whig stand; and his appeal to the
past was in a sense no less valid than Burke's. Also, his *History* did reflect that
sincere if indefinite concern for liberty which was the saving grace of Fox as a
politician. He may not have been justified in suggesting a parallel between the
rule of James II and that of George III, or in imputing to Pitt sinister designs
against the constitution. But in times when, perhaps necessarily, the powers
of government were being greatly extended, it was salutary that men like Fox
should continue to stress the value of traditional liberties.

[64] H. Butterfield, 'Charles James Fox and the Whig Opposition in 1792', *Cambridge Historical Journal*, XI (1949), 296–8 and 324. As Burke put it in his *Observations on the Conduct of the Minority* (1793), Fox had 'contented himself with defending the ruling factions in France, and with accusing the public councils of this kingdom of every sort of evil design on the liberties of the people; declaring distinctly, strongly and precisely that the whole danger of the nation was from the growth of the power of the crown' (*Works of the Rt. Hon. Edmund Burke*, 6 vols. London, 1887, III, 475).

[65] See, for instance, Fox to Holland, 5 January 1799, *Memorials*, III, 149.

[66] Burke said of the system which the New Whigs had adopted: '...its great object is not (as they pretend to delude worthy people to their Ruin) the destruction of all absolute Monarchies, but totally to root out that thing called an *Aristocrate* or Nobleman and Gentleman' (Burke to Fitzwilliam, 21 November 1791, *Correspondence of Edmund Burke*, VI, 451).

[67] R. Pares, *King George III and the Politicians* (Oxford, 1953), p. 135; I. R. Christie, postscript to 'Charles James Fox', *History Today*, VIII (1958), 283.

[68] Pares, op. cit. p. 57.

3

Christopher Wyvill and Reform, 1790-1820

The Reverend Christopher Wyvill owes his place in history to his achievements as a campaigner for political reform in 1779 and the early 1780's. In those years, Herbert Butterfield says, 'He and his collaborators launched upon the country, and set fairly and squarely on its course, the most important of the movements that have made the modern world'.[1] He continued to play a significant rôle until the defeat of Pitt's parliamentary reform motion of April 1785, and his activities up to that point have been fully examined in Ian Christie's *Wilkes, Wyvill and Reform* (1962). Thereafter his career has not been studied in detail, although historians have used the pamphlets which he wrote in the 1790's and his correspondence during that decade, published in the last two volumes of his *Political Papers*.[2] Virtually nothing has been written about the last twenty years of his life, between 1802 when the printed correspondence ends and 1822 when he died. However, in the collection of Wyvill manuscripts which has been recently transferred from Constable Burton to the North Riding Record Office[3] there is a large amount of material from this period. When volumes V and VI of Wyvill's *Political Papers* appeared, they were recommended by the *Monthly Review* 'as containing the undisguised sentiments, on important subjects, of the most distinguished characters of the time'.[4] The later correspondence, which Wyvill carried on until a few years before his death, is also of great interest. Much of it relates to the campaign for religious toleration, in which Wyvill played a major part.[5] As for the correspondence concerning parliamentary reform (on which this paper is largely based), it is in the

---

[1] *George III, Lord North and the People, 1779-80*, London, 1949, p. 282.

[2] 6 vols., York, 1794-1808 — cited hereafter as *Pol. Papers*. For a brief account of Wyvill's career in the 1790's see N. C. Phillips, 'Country against Court: Christopher Wyvill, a Yorkshire Champion', *Yorkshire Archaeological Journal*, XL, 1962, pp. 601-2.

[3] For a general account of the Wyvill archive, see North Riding Record Office, *Annual Report*, 1967, pp. 35-43. (I am grateful to Professor Christie for suggesting that this archive would repay investigation; to Mr. C. Wyvill, the owner of the Wyvill papers, for permission to quote from them; and to Mr. Michael Ashcroft and his staff at the North Riding Record Office for their kind assistance.) For a description of Constable Burton, the splendid house on the edge of Wensleydale which provides something of a key to Wyvill's politics, see Marcus Binney's article in *Country Life*, 28 Nov. 1968, pp. 1396-1400.

[4] *Monthly Review*, new series, LVIII, Jan. 1809, p. 95.

[5] For a panegyric on Wyvill's efforts in the cause of religious liberty, see Thomas Jervis, *A Speech intended to have been delivered at a General Meeting of the Inhabitants of Leeds*, Leeds, 1813, pp. 23-5. Cf. *Edinburgh Review*, XIX, Nov. 1811, p. 149; and Whitbread's speech in the House of Commons, 17 Apr. 1812, *Cobbett's Parliamentary Debates*, XXII, 418.

first place an important source for the political history of Yorkshire; for Wyvill communicated not only with old members of the Yorkshire Association like William Wrightson,[6] Henry Duncombe[7] and Samuel Shore,[8] but also with younger men who became prominent in the county in the early nineteenth century — notably Walter Fawkes,[9] Daniel Sykes[10] and Sir George Cayley.[11] He also kept in touch with reformers in other parts of the country, including Sir John Swinburne[12] and Thomas Bigge[13] in Northumberland, Dr. J. R. Fenwick[14] in Durham, Joshua Grigby[15] and Capel Lofft in Suffolk, Dr. John Disney[16] (the famous Unitarian) in Essex, and above all Major John Cartwright,[17] dean of the radical reformers (as Wyvill was of the moderates). The letters Wyvill exchanged with these people provide a rare body of evidence about the parliamentary reform movement during the Napoleonic wars (a relatively obscure phase of its history) and about the political views of the liberal gentry in the decades overshadowed by the French Revolution. Furthermore Wyvill corresponded from time to time with leading Whig politicians such as Fox, Grey, Holland, Whitbread and Romilly — and their letters contain valuable information about Whig attitudes to reform.

In the period covered by this paper Wyvill's own influence and achievements were small compared with the contribution he had made in the early 1780's. This was chiefly because — as the Reverend Thomas Jervis

[6] M.P. for Aylesbury, 1784–90; Sheriff of Yorkshire, 1821.
[7] M.P. for Yorkshire, 1780–96.
[8] He actually lived in Derbyshire, but was closely connected with Sheffield. See G. P. Jones, 'The Political Reform Movement in Sheffield', *Transactions of the Hunter Archaeological Society*, IV, 1929–37, p. 57; Lady Stephens, 'The Shores of Sheffield and the Offleys of Norton Hall', *ibid.*, V, 1938–43, p. 7.
[9] M.P. for Yorkshire, 1806–7; Sheriff of Yorkshire, 1823. See R. V. Taylor, *Biographia Leodiensis*, London, 1865, pp. 296–8.
[10] M.P. for Hull, 1820–30, and for Beverley, 1830–1. See *ibid.*, pp. 337–41.
[11] Son-in-law of the Rev. George Walker of Nottingham; M.P. for Scarborough, 1832–4; a distinguished scientist. See *The Times*, 18 Dec. 1857.
[12] M.P. for Launceston, 1788–90; a close friend of Lord Grey. See Richard Welford, *Men of Mark 'twixt Tyne and Tweed*, 3 vols., London, 1895, III, 47–8.
[13] Editor of *The Oeconomist* (published at Newcastle, 1798–9); frequently mentioned in *The Diaries of James Losh*, ed. Edward Hughes, 2 vols., Surtees Society, 1956–9.
[14] See *Durham Directory and Almanack*, 1856, p. 40 (I owe this reference to Dr. J. M. Fewster). There are numerous letters from Swinburne, Bigge and Fenwick in the Grey MSS, University of Durham.
[15] Son of the Joshua Grigby who seconded Henry Flood's parliamentary reform motion of 4 March 1790; member of the committee of the Hampden Club. See *Gentleman's Magazine*, Apr. 1829, pp. 373–4; and a circular dated 2 Nov. 1816, Proceedings of the Hampden Club, Cleary Collection, British Museum.
[16] On Lofft and Disney, see *Dictionary of National Biography*.
[17] The fullest account of his career is Naomi C. Miller, 'Major John Cartwright: a study in radical parliamentary reform, 1774–1824,' Ph.D. thesis, Columbia University, 1963.

said in his obituary of Wyvill[18] — he was to a large extent out of tune with the reformers of a later generation. He remained attached to the principles and methods of the Yorkshire Association in a period when they seemed no longer applicable, and when moderate reform generally was out of fashion. Gwyn Williams has emphasized the polarization of English political society in the 1790's[19] — and this was also a feature of the first twenty years of the nineteenth century. Sir Samuel Romilly wrote in 1807 that the pernicious effects of the French Revolution had by no means worn off: 'Among the higher orders it has produced a horror of every kind of innovation; among the lower a desire to try the boldest political experiments, and a distrust and contempt of all moderate reforms'.[20] The isolation of the moderate reformers was increased by the fact that the Foxite Whigs, who had been firmly committed to reform in the 1790's, tended to shy away from the subject after their alliance with the Grenvilles; and radicals like Burdett and Cartwright faced little competition for the leadership of the renascent reform movement in the country. However, it is arguable that although the position which Wyvill retained throughout this period was unfashionable, it was not as outdated as it seemed. E. C. Black has stressed the similarity between the aims of the Yorkshire Association and the 'brilliant compromise of 1832';[21] and the object of this paper is to throw some light on the survival of moderate reformism in the intervening period. It is natural that the attention of historians should have been concentrated on the radical reformers who were in the ascendant in the early nineteenth century, and who heralded the democratic developments of the Victorian era. But in the pattern of events leading up to the Great Reform Bill the strand of moderate reform is of considerable importance alongside the radical one.

At the time when he had been most active as a political organizer Wyvill had rarely engaged in the abstract discussion of constitutional principles.[22] But between 1792 and 1801 he set out his ideas at length in a series of pamphlets. Comparing these with his earlier political papers, one can see that the French Revolution produced a significant change in

[18] *Gentleman's Magazine*, Apr. 1822, p. 375. Jervis was the son-in-law of John Disney, and had been a tutor at Bowood at the time Priestley was there; in Wyvill's later years he was one of his most regular correspondents.

[19] *Artisans and Sansculottes*, London, 1968, p. 63.

[20] Romilly, *Memoirs*, 2nd edition, 3 vols., London, 1840, III, 399. Cf. *Edinburgh Review*, XV, Jan. 1810, p. 504, where Francis Jeffrey laments that the rising tides of despotism and democracy are eating away the narrow isthmus occupied by the friends of constitutional liberty.

[21] *The Association: British Extraparliamentary Political Organization, 1769–1793*, Cambridge, Mass., 1963, p. 224.

[22] I. R. Christie, *Wilkes, Wyvill and Reform*, London, 1962, p. 188.

his outlook. In the early 1780's he had been fighting on two sides at once, on the one hand against the Court and the opponents of reform, and on the other against reformers more extreme than himself; but at that stage the weight of his offensive had been against the right, against the influence of the Crown and the aristocracy. He had fought a holding action on his left flank against the Society for Constitutional Information; but although he disliked their ideas he had not regarded this small band of intellectuals as a major threat in themselves. His main fear had been that they would thwart his own campaign by propagating ideas so radical as to alarm the upper classes and throw them decisively against parliamentary reform of any kind.[23] In the 1790's and thereafter these strategic considerations remained prominent in his debate with the radical reformers. One of his chief arguments in favour of moderate as against radical reform was always that the former was more practicable, and that the radicals should join in pressing for it rather than obstructing the achievement of *any* reform by insisting on their own specifics. But increasingly Wyvill came to regard radicalism as not only objectionable for reasons of expediency but dangerous on its own account. It became more alarming in the early 1790's partly because it permeated the lower ranks of society to an unprecedented extent.[24] Also, whereas Cartwright and the Society for Constitutional Information had thought (and continued to think) in essentially political terms, Paine's widely circulated writings laid a new emphasis on economic grievances; and thereafter Wyvill was firmly convinced that universal suffrage would entail the invasion of property.[25] Cartwright argued in a printed *Letter to Wyvill* that for possessors of property there would be far less danger in giving the vote to the poor than there would be in withholding it from them:

> Address but the poor in the language of fellow-men and brethren, and render them justice; and from that moment you will have nothing to fear. Once made parties in our elections, and those elections reformed as they ought to be, it will be easy to make them understand, that, then having political liberty in full extent, no other government could possibly better their condition.[26]

Wyvill, however, thought it much more probable that the masses, once enfranchised, would use their power to expropriate the rich. In his view the state had two main functions: 'to protect men in the enjoyment of their personal rights', and 'to protect men in the enjoyment of their

[23] *Ibid.*, p. 131.
[24] *Pol. Papers*, V, 23, 67; and see Wyvill's report to Wilberforce about the disaffected spirit of the lower classes in Durham — R. I. and S. Wilberforce, *Life of William Wilberforce*, 5 vols., London, 1838, II, 2.
[25] *Letter to John Cartwright*, York, 1801, pp. 11–14.
[26] *Letter to the Rev. Christopher Wyvill*, London, 1801, pp. 51–2.

property'. And a balance had to be preserved between these functions, so that neither was accorded such importance as to endanger the other. The protection of property should not be made an excuse for political oppression — and liberty and power should not be so widely extended as to jeopardize property.[27] For Wyvill (as for Cartwright) 'personal rights' had no economic implications. He was prepared to admit that property was too unequally distributed in England; but this fact, far from being an argument in favour of universal suffrage, was a decisive argument against it. For the injustice of economic inequality was by no means equivalent to the 'violence and palpable injustice' of 'Agrarian Laws, and other devices for a more equal distribution of property'. And until, by the operation of natural factors over a long period of time, property had been much more generally diffused, universal suffrage would be inadmissible because it would be wrongfully exploited by the populace.[28] Moreover, since the propertied classes were fully aware of this danger and would resist to the utmost any attempt to establish universal suffrage, such an attempt would provoke a terrible struggle between 'an irritated Democracy' on the one hand, and on the other 'the united power of the Crown and Aristocracy, and their numerous adherents in the most opulent classes of the monied and mercantile interests'. The outcome would be either anarchy and plunder, or the establishment of a much more authoritarian and oppressive system of government than the existing one.[29]

The threat from the left had thus become much more serious since the days of the association movement. But Wyvill did not allow it to force him (as it forced many others) into a conservative position. In his opinion it strengthened the need for a moderate reform of parliament. In the first pamphlet he published in the revolutionary period, his *Defence of Doctor Price and the Reformers of England* (1792), he set out the case for parliamentary reform as a means of forestalling class warfare. At this stage he played down the danger of imminent revolution, but warned the rulers of the country that 'to be safe they must be just'.

Instead of hazarding their dignified privileges and great constitutional powers to preserve their encroachments on the rights of election, prudence and their interest, justly considered, seem to recommend to our great patrician families and to the Crown to secure those powers and privileges, and the Constitution

---

[27] *A State of the Representation of the People of England*, York, 1793, p. 35.
[28] *Letter to Cartwright*, pp. 10–12; *State of the Representation*, pp. 43–4. Wyvill thought that the Americans, having the advantage of a more equal distribution of property, were better fitted for democracy (*A Defence of Dr. Price and the Reformers of England*, London, 1792, p. 68).
[29] *Letter to Cartwright*, pp. 5–6.

itself, by yielding a power unwarrantably gained, before the national resentment be completely roused, and moderate concessions no longer would be accepted with the grateful approbation of the public.[30]

He repeated his warning against intransigence in a pamphlet written early in the following year: he declared, 'It is from the prevalence of Mr Burke's politics alone among the upper classes of society, that the rise of any dangerous disaffection in this country is to be apprehended'.[31] Wyvill and Burke had similar aims to the extent that both wished to safeguard the property and influence of the landowners and to prevent class conflict. But Wyvill regarded Burke's doctrines as even more 'pernicious', even more likely to provoke dissension, than the writings of Paine.[32]

While placing this new emphasis on the need for appeasement, Wyvill did not at this period allow the old objects of reform to fall into the background. He was still very concerned about the dangers of executive tyranny; and indeed this seemed more of a threat during Pitt's war ministry than it had in the time of Lord North. For the fear of democracy seemed to have blinded the propertied classes to the opposite menace[33] — although the war itself was greatly extending the power of the Crown. Under Pitt's direction, wrote Wyvill in 1798, 'the fund of influence has received a rapid extension; the debt and taxes of the public, its establishments, civil and military, have increased in a prodigious degree, and these dreaded instruments of despotism are wielded by the Minister with a skill and ability which double their force'.[34] The fear, which Wyvill shared with Fox, that the constitution was approaching its euthanasia has been disparaged by historians who have been able to see that it was groundless. But one can understand why in the 1790's men who were attached to traditional liberties — viewing the kind of ideological support which the government received from Burke, John Reeves and Arthur Young — should have feared that the suspension of those liberties would be more enduring than it turned out to be.

During this central phase of his political life Wyvill seems to have been more or less equally preoccupied with the threat from the executive and the threat from the demos; and of course he was open to attack from both sides. On the one hand Arthur Young — in a pamphlet which Wyvill described as the most violent assault upon liberty made by any

[30] *Defence of Dr. Price*, p. 87.
[31] *Letter to the Right Hon. William Pitt*, York, 1793, p. 21.
[32] *The Correspondence of the Rev. C. Wyvill with the Right Hon. William Pitt*, Part I, Newcastle, 1796, pp. 73-4.
[33] *Letter to Cartwright*, p. 9.
[34] *The Secession from Parliament vindicated*, 2nd edition, York, 1799, p. 31.

writer since the revolution of 1688[35] — used the floodgates argument against Wyvill's advocacy of moderate reform, accusing him of self-delusion in supposing that the people would be content with it: 'Mr Wyvil, in his late pamphlet, talks of *temperate reformation*, and of *pointing the zeal of the people to a moderate correction of grievances*. As if it was possible . . . that you could draw the line of *moderation*, beyond which the populace should not pass'![36] On the other hand Thomas Cooper of Manchester denounced 'the half-measured Reformers — Men of Rank and Respectability, as they sometimes call themselves; who desire no farther reform than to extend the aristocratic monopoly of power to that circle in which themselves are included'.[37] There was some force in this charge. But although Wyvill thought that political power should not be extended to those without property, and although he believed that the gentry had a stronger claim than any other class to the confidence of the community,[38] one should not overstress the oligarchical nature of his ideas. He wrote in 1793 that Pitt's reform plan of 1785 (which he had helped to frame) had been well adapted to the state of public opinion at that time; but since then the denial of redress, and widespread discussion of the subject, had produced a demand for a more extensive reform. He therefore proposed certain additions to the plan, notably a provision that all tax-paying householders should be enfranchised.[39] However, while he reckoned that a larger section of the people was now supporting reform than previously, he warned the reformers against cancelling this advantage by raising their demands too far: ' . . . if the weight to be moved should be increased in proportion to the power applyed to move it, it is evident, that the utmost efforts of the people will again terminate in disappointment'.[40]

Wyvill was distinguished from most other reformers — who tended to concentrate on ends rather than means[41] — by his more pragmatic approach (deriving no doubt from his co-operation with practising

---

[35] *Pol. Papers*, V, 157.

[36] *The Example of France a Warning to Britain*, 3rd edition, Bury St. Edmunds, 1793, pp. 57–8. For another attack from the right, see George Croft, *Plans of Parliamentary Reform proved to be visionary, in a Letter to the Rev. C. Wyvill*, Birmingham, 1793.

[37] *A Reply to Mr. Burke's Invective*, 2nd edition, London, 1792, p. 74.

[38] *Pol. Papers*, V, 142 n.

[39] I. e. allowed to vote in county elections. *Letter to Pitt*, p. 5; *Pol. Papers*, V, 95–6. It is also noteworthy that Wyvill was opposed to any system of indirect election, although this was advocated by his friend Lord Stanhope. Wyvill maintained that it would give only the shadow of liberty; a parliament so chosen would feel too little sympathy and community of interest with the mass of those whom it was meant to represent. (*Considerations on the Twofold Mode of Election adopted by the French*, York, 1804, pp. 13–14 & 27–8.)

[40] *State of the Representation*, p. 39.

[41] Cf. Caroline Robbins, *The Eighteenth-century Commonwealthman*, Cambridge, Mass., 1959, p. 382.

politicians in the 1780's). This difference emerges clearly from his correspondence with the Society of Friends of the People. He himself did not
join this society, considering such self-constituted organizations greatly
inferior to bodies like the committee of the Yorkshire Association,
which emanated from legal assemblies of the people. But many who
had taken part in the association movement did join the Friends of the
People, and with several of these Wyvill corresponded. He approved of
the basic aim of the society, which was to provide the reform movement
with respectable and moderate leadership. But he did not entirely approve
of its programme, though in many respects it coincided with his own.
The plan of reform submitted by Philip Francis and adopted by the
society in 1794-5 comprised household suffrage, shorter parliaments, and
equal electoral districts.[42] To the first two propositions Wyvill assented.
As for the third, he admitted that given a free choice he would prefer
equal electoral districts to a partial amendment of the current system.
But the superiority of the former 'in a speculative view' was outweighed
by the greater difficulties in the way of its accomplishment. He felt that
a total change in the structure of the representation would be 'too extensive a plan in the present state of the country to be carried by peaceful
efforts'. It would threaten too many vested interests, and there would be
no chance of parliament agreeing to it except under duress. He therefore
preferred a piecemeal improvement of the existing structure on the lines
formerly suggested by Pitt — through the extinction of rotten boroughs
by unforced purchase, and the transference of their seats to counties
and large unrepresented towns.[43] When Francis suggested that it might
be advisable 'to hold up a model, even beyond our expectation of success,
and then endeavour to approach as near to it as we can in practice',
Wyvill replied:

> If a temperate plan might probably be carried into execution, by orderly
> application to Parliament, a less temperate plan should not be proposed, because
> that would load the plan, which really might be carried, with all the difficulties
> and objections which attend the more extensive scheme .... It may be thought
> that holding a model of Reform more perfect than is expected to be carried will
> excite a greater degree of popular support; but then it is to be feared it may also
> excite in a still greater proportion the alarms of quiet men, and the opposition
> of a powerful Aristocracy; and then by what peaceful means can any Reforma-
> tion be effected?[44]

However, the Friends of the People adopted Francis' plan rather than

---

[42] Sir P. Francis, *Plan of Reform in the Election of the House of Commons adopted by the Society of the Friends of the People in 1795*, London, 1817, pp. 25-8.
[43] *Pol. Papers*, V, xvi-xvii, 234, 244–5, 251, 261–5.
[44] *Ibid.*, pp. 260, 267–8.

that submitted by Wyvill — perhaps because at a time when it was fairly clear that no reform could be achieved Wyvill's prudential arguments carried little weight.[45]

In the early days of the society Wyvill had recommended that its measures should be 'taken from the declared sense of the People collected in County Meetings, etc.': the people should first be induced to approve temperate plans of reform, which could then be adopted by the society. But in view of the alarm among the great body of the gentry it was considered very unlikely that county meetings for such a purpose could be held with success.[46] A remarkable illustration of the shift to the right within the political nation was provided by the Yorkshire meeting of December 1795 — an event of great significance in both county and national politics.[47] This meeting was convened by the Yorkshire Whigs and reformers[48] to protest against the Treasonable Practices Bill and Seditious Meetings Bill, which had been introduced into parliament in November and had aroused much indignation among the liberal-minded.[49] Wyvill issued an address to the freeholders calling on the clothiers and yeomen to express their opposition to any abridgement of fundamental liberties. But the ministerialists decided to risk a pitched battle, and energetically mobilized support (Wilberforce being hastily summoned from London). In the event they won a striking victory. First in the Guildhall at York, which was the advertised meeting place, they voted their own candidate into the chair instead of Sir Thomas Gascoigne who was one of the chief promoters of the meeting; and then they carried a motion for an adjournment to the Castle Yard, on the grounds that the Guildhall was not large enough to contain all the freeholders assembled. Although this motion was passed by an indisputable majority, Wyvill and his friends refused to move from the Guildhall; so two separate meetings were held, one petitioning against the two bills, and the other — much the more numerously attended — expressing full confidence in the government and its policies. The West Riding in particular showed itself strongly Pittite — the clothiers, who travelled to York in large numbers, earning the title 'Billy-men' for the rôle they played on this occasion. Wyvill had to admit that he had misjudged the

---

[45] Cf. P. J. Brunsdon, 'The Association of the Friends of the People, 1792–1796', M.A. thesis, University of Manchester, 1961, p. 102.
[46] *Pol. Papers*, V, 9, 56; Brunsdon, *op. cit.*, pp. 221–2.
[47] Cf. E. P. Thompson, *The Making of the English Working Class*, London, 1963, pp. 146–7.
[48] They first sent a requisition to the high sheriff, but he refused to act on it; so Wyvill and his friends decided to convoke an 'unofficial' county meeting.
[49] On the campaign which the Opposition mounted against the 'Two Acts', see *Annual Register* (Otridge), 1796, History of Europe, ch. ii.

sentiments of the county; and for many years the Yorkshire reformers
were inhibited by the memory of this failure.[50]

It was not until the post-war period that Yorkshire was again to throw
its weight against the government (over the income tax and over Peterloo); and almost four decades separate the Yorkshire meetings promoted
by Wyvill in the 1780's from the great county meeting which petitioned
for reform in 1823. However, even in the dark years after 1795 Wyvill
and his friends did not give up hope of reviving the old spirit in Yorkshire. In 1797-8, and again in 1800-1801, efforts were made to rouse the
county. There was even talk in 1798 of resuscitating the old Association
by getting several counties to support a moderate reform programme.[51]
But generally Wyvill recognized that reform had become too much of
a bugbear to be made the principal object of a county meeting; and he
aimed at reactivating the opposition party in Yorkshire through a
campaign for peace or for a change of ministers, in the hope that this
would open the way (as the issue of economical reform had done in
1779-80) to some subsequent move in favour of parliamentary reform.[52]
The chances of the county being induced to petition for peace were
improved around the turn of the century by a change of sentiment in the
West Riding. The manufacturing interest had begun to suffer from the
continuance of the war, and had become much less well-disposed towards
government than it had been in 1795.[53] Leeds, Wakefield and Bradford
petitioned for peace early in 1801; and it was hoped that despite the
backwardness of the landed gentry the county as a whole would follow
suit.[54] However, to Wyvill's disappointment plans for a meeting were
suspended when the news arrived of an impending change of administration;[55] and depressed by a series of false starts, he told Fox that nothing in
favour of liberty could be expected from Yorkshire for some considerable
length of time.[56]

At this period Wyvill's correspondence with Major Cartwright was
particularly intensive, and provided an interesting point of contact

---

[50] *Life of Wilberforce*, II, 117–33; *York Chronicle*, 3 Dec. 1795; *Pol. Papers*, V, xxvii-xxxvi, 303–12; Wyvill to Lansdowne, 6 Dec. 1795, *ibid.*, VI, 353.
[51] *Pol. Papers*, V, 394 n.; Grey to Wyvill, 3 Feb. (1798), Wyvill MSS, North Riding Record Office, Northallerton (all documents cited below whose location is not specified are in this collection).
[52] *Pol. Papers*, V, 372, & VI, 158–9, 232–3.
[53] *Ibid.*, VI, 141–3.
[54] *The Times*, 5 Feb. 1801; Grey to Wyvill, 6 Feb. 1801; Wrightson to Earl Fitzwilliam, n.d. (Feb. 1801), Fitzwilliam MSS, F 41, Wentworth Woodhouse Muniments, Sheffield City Libraries.
[55] *Pol. Papers*, VI, 111 n.; Wrightson to Fitzwilliam, 15 Feb. 1801, Fitzwilliam MSS, F 41, Sheffield.
[56] *Pol. Papers*, VI, part ii, 120–1.

between two largely separate bodies of reformers — Wyvill's connections being mainly with country gentlemen and Whig politicians, while Cartwright was in touch with middle-class and artisan reformers in London and other urban centres. Wyvill understood why the latter were more extreme in their demands than the Yorkshire freeholders; he wrote later in a retrospective note:

> The inhabitants of the metropolis with whom Mr. Cartwright was connected, were more accustomed to speculation; and their zeal for the correction of abuses was more generally felt, better informed, and animated by frequent discussion to a greater degree of warmth and enthusiasm. Hence the promptitude of the citizens of the capital to adopt views of the most extended reform.[57]

But while admitting that the counties erred on the side of caution, and that the gentry were temporarily under the influence of prejudice and delusion,[58] Wyvill maintained that no peaceful reform could ever be achieved by the urban masses alone. Without the concurrence of the gentry, which would guarantee the moderation of the measures pursued and mitigate resistance to them, there would be a head-on collision between the populace and the oligarchy.[59] Since Wyvill believed that any independent movement by the town radicals would be more likely to deter than to encourage similar efforts in the counties, he was anxious that Cartwright should restrain his friends and let Yorkshire take the lead — even if the lead it gave was not immediately directed at reform. In January 1801 Cartwright did reluctantly agree to use his influence to delay urban petitions lest they should prejudice the attempt to rouse Yorkshire.[60] But generally his view was that the towns, being more enlightened and likely to 'take more decisive ground' than the counties, should show the way.[61] He did not share Wyvill's predilection for the gentry and his faith in their ultimate political rectitude. Nothing, he said, short of 'danger to their estates and privileges staring them in the face, could ever call forth an energetic patriotism on their part'.[62] And he maintained in February 1801 that it was owing to the nobility and gentry, who had supported the ministerial policy of repression rather than siding with the people, that many in the lower ranks of society who had formerly been friends to parliamentary reform were becoming totally alienated from the constitution.[63] Thomas Hardy had recently informed

---

[57] *Ibid.*, V, 380 n.
[58] *Ibid.*, VI, 236 n.; Frances D. Cartwright, *The Life and Correspondence of Major Cartwright,* 2 vols., London, 1826, I, 297–8.
[59] *Pol. Papers*, VI, 255 n., 256.
[60] *Ibid.*, VI, 232–4.
[61] *Ibid.*, V, 399, & VI, 229.
[62] *Letter to Wyvill*, p. 7.
[63] *Pol. Papers*, VI, 245.

Cartwright and others that the lower classes, despairing of reform, were being driven to revolution;[64] and in April 1801 Cartwright told Wyvill, who was again anxious that popular petitioning should be delayed, that if the people were denied this outlet for their discontent they would shortly resort to violence.[65] But Wyvill was convinced that a popular campaign for universal suffrage, far from preventing revolution, would be likely to precipitate it — or alternatively would strengthen the hands of government by alarming the propertied classes.[66] When the Committee of Secrecy of the House of Commons reported a recrudescence of seditious practices and recommended the renewal of the Habeas Corpus suspension and the Seditious Meetings Act, Wyvill took the view that it was the rashness of certain reforming societies in adopting the principle of universal suffrage that had made possible this revival of alarm and repression.[67] His interpretation was not entirely correct, since what the authorities were chiefly worried by in 1801 was the activities of more extreme groups outside the 'constitutional' reform movement (to which Cartwright as well as Wyvill belonged).[68] However, it is true that in government eyes — as in Wyvill's own — there was no very clear distinction between radical reformers and revolutionaries. The new emergency legislation was directed against both, and (although underground activities appear to have continued at least into the following year) these measures and the apathy with which they were received by the public reduced overt reformers to silence and despondency.[69]

The next few years were the real dark ages of the parliamentary reform movement. Sir Francis Burdett kept a light burning fitfully in Middlesex, but elsewhere the reformers were sunk in a gloom which was deepened by the events of the period. Sir Cecil Wray (former member for Westminster) wrote to Wyvill that the Irish Union, bringing a hundred *Irishmen* into the House of Commons instead of a hundred county members, was a death blow to reform.[70] Another blow was the exposure of Colonel Despard and his associates; in March 1803 a loyal county meeting was staged in Yorkshire to congratulate the King on his providential escape from this conspiracy.[71] Later in the year the resumption of

---

[64] Hardy to Cartwright, 24 Jan. 1801 (draft), British Museum Additional MSS 27818, fos. 16–18; Hardy to Stanhope, 29 Jan. 1801 (draft), *ibid.*, fos. 20–1.
[65] *Pol. Papers*, VI, 249, 253–4.
[66] *Letter to Cartwright*, pp. 4–5; Wyvill to Fox, 5 Feb. 1801, *Pol. Papers*, VI, part ii, p. 103.
[67] *Annual Register* (Rivington), 1801, Appendix to the Chronicle, pp. 161–2; *Pol. Papers*, VI, 206 n.
[68] E. P. Thompson, *op. cit.*, p. 472 *et seq.*
[69] *Pol. Papers*, VI, 205, 258; Fox to Wyvill, n.d. (June 1801), *ibid.*, VI, part ii, 141–2.
[70] Wray to Wyvill, 25 Jan. 1802.
[71] *York Chronicle*, 31 Mar. 1803.

the war confirmed the climate of loyalism; another Yorkshire county meeting was held in July, at which the freeholders expressed their 'most ardent and entire devotion' to the constitution they had inherited from their forefathers.[72] But most serious of all in its consequences for the reform movement was the behaviour of the Whigs. In 1797 and 1798 Fox had committed himself unequivocally in the House of Commons to parliamentary reform; and in January 1801 he told Wyvill that reform of parliament would be a certain consequence of the Whigs coming into power.[73] Wyvill saw no reason to doubt these pledges (which were doubtless given in perfectly good faith), and though he would never have called himself a Whig he gave his entire confidence to Fox and his party. In 1799 he published a pamphlet in defence of the Whig secession from parliament,[74] and two years later in his printed *Letter to Cartwright* he praised Fox for the 'grandeur of consistency' which 'the conduct of his maturer age' had manifested. He went on to condemn the contempt for party which some reformers professed; it was folly or hypocrisy, he said, to reject co-operation with men who had announced that they would never accept office without stipulating for reform.[75] When at the beginning of 1802 Grey's willingness to negotiate with Addington evoked fears that he was on the point of abandoning the cause of reform, Wyvill refused to believe that this was the case.[76] But the Foxite alliance with the Grenvilles in 1804 was not so easy to disregard.[77] William Strickland wrote to Wyvill that this was even worse than the Fox-North coalition: 'The attempt at bearing down the present administration, by a union of talents, devoid of any union of sentiment or principles, appears to me replete with more political depravity than any struggle for power I have witnessed in my time'.[78] Wyvill expressed his own misgivings in a long letter to Fox. It was clear, he said, that the agreement with the Grenvilles must be confined to the two points of foreign policy and Catholic emancipation, and could not extend to parliamentary reform. He admitted

---

[72] *Proceedings of the County Meeting of Yorkshire, held on the 28th of July, 1803*, York, 1803.
[73] Debrett's *Parliamentary Register*, 3rd series, II, 623–55, & IV, 611–12; *Pol. Papers*, VI, part ii, 95; cf. Lord John Russell, *Memorials and Correspondence of Charles James Fox*, 4 vols., London, 1853–7, III, 305.
[74] Cited above, note 34.
[75] *Letter to Cartwright*, pp. 17–20.
[76] Fenwick to Wyvill, 12 & 16 Jan. 1802; Wyvill to Fenwick, 15 Jan. 1802 (enclosing a copy of Wyvill to Fox, 14 Jan. 1802), Grey MSS, University of Durham.
[77] Though William Smith wrote reassuringly to Wyvill, 24 Mar. 1804: 'It is not a coalition for the purpose of forming a ministry but only a plan of co-operation for displacing one which they (& I) think inadequate to the necessities of the country'. Cf. Fox to Smith, 12 Mar. 1804 (copy), Brit. Mus. Add. MSS 47569, fo. 168.
[78] Strickland (later Sir William Strickland, Bt.; a former member of the committee of the Yorkshire Association) to Wyvill, 29 Mar. 1804.

that no ministry could be formed at present on a reforming basis, but he maintained that Fox would serve the public better by preserving his consistency and reputation than by taking office with the Grenvilles. Although the cause of reform seemed to be defunct, it was 'not in a state of *Death,* but of *Sleep'.* In a few years' time there might be a strong demand for reform; and Fox, if he had retained the confidence of the people, would then be able to prevent revolution and establish freedom on constitutional principles. Wyvill conceded that Fox might justifiably join a coalition ministry in order to conduct peace negotiations — but he added that once these had been concluded he should withdraw from office.[79] Fox did not send a written reply to this letter; instead he had a private conversation with Wyvill, who was then in London. He explained that the possibility of his forming a government with Grenville was not likely to arise for some time; if and when it did, he would very seriously consider the advice which Wyvill had given him. Without making any promises, he expressed his continuing attachment to reform; and Wyvill went away charmed and reassured.[80]

However, the Whigs in the following year showed a coolness with regard to reform which can be attributed at least in part to the inhibiting effect of the Grenville alliance. The Opposition received a considerable boost from the Melville affair, which aroused a greater degree of anti-ministerial feeling than had been expressed for some time and produced indignant resolutions from a number of county meetings.[81] But the Whigs seemed anxious to prevent popular indignation from running to embarrassing lengths. In Yorkshire no county meeting at all took place because Lord Fitzwilliam, having at first appeared keen to promote one, dropped the idea on being advised against it by his political associates; after this, although there was a strong feeling in some circles that a meeting ought to take place, nothing was done.[82] In Middlesex, Cartwright wished to present resolutions to the county based on 'the evident connection between corruption in office, and corruption in Parliament'; but he was dissuaded by Fox and other Whig leaders.[83] Similar proposals were nevertheless made by Wyvill in the following winter. The torpid state of Yorkshire and the absence of any alarming manifestations of extremism in the south[84] seem to have convinced him that an attempt to launch a

[79] Wyvill to Fox, 27 Apr. 1804. (Letters of Wyvill himself cited from the Wyvill MSS are drafts or copies.)
[80] Wyvill to Shore, 30 Apr. 1804; to Swinburne, 4 May 1804.
[81] Henry Jephson, *The Platform,* 2 vols., London, 1892, I, 309–14.
[82] Wrightson to Wyvill, 24 Apr. & 1 May 1805; Bigge to Wyvill, 19 May 1805; *York Herald,* 25 May 1805.
[83] *Life of Cartwright,* I, 323–7; N. C. Miller, *op. cit.,* pp. 268–9.
[84] Earlier in the year respectable meetings on the Melville affair had been held in London, Middlesex and Westminster (*Morning Chronicle,* 19 Apr., 3 & 4 May 1805).

metropolitan reform movement (confined of course to persons of some property) was at least worth considering; and at this time he and Cartwright were sufficiently in agreement to co-operate in trying to counteract the backwardness of the Whigs. In December 1805 Wyvill submitted to Fox an elaborate memorandum suggesting that meetings of taxed householders should be held in districts near London, 'for the joint purpose of expressing their indignation at the gross malversions which have lately been detected in the office of Lord Melville, and of praying Parliament to be admitted to share the Right of Representation'.[85] He followed this up with a detailed 'Plan for a Third Attempt to effect a General Reform of Parliament' — in which Middlesex was to take the lead.[86] Fox argued in reply to the first communication that it would be much better for a petitioning movement to originate in such places as Leeds and Manchester than in the metropolitan area. For one thing, in the vicinity of London 'no precautions could be sufficient to prevent circumstances which would give the Enemy an opportunity of alarming timid Men by the Cry of Jacobinism'. Also, Fox wrote,

> I know from experience that complaints upon constitutional subjects have more effect when they come from more distant parts of the Kingdom . . . . The great object in the present state of things is that in meetings of a publick nature there should not appear too much either of Aristocracy or Democracy, but something between the two. Now near London *both* these extremes would be objected to us, and indeed the probability is that the most active and marked Men would be either what are called Democrats, or great Noblemen and Statesmen or persons immediately connected with or dependent upon such Persons. On the contrary in the towns I have mentioned rich Merchants & Manufacturers, & Tradesmen who, tho' less opulent, are thriving & respectable, would present exactly that sort of middle character which in the present turn of Men's minds, so very susceptible of fear of all kinds, is the most desirable.[87]

This is an interesting attestation of the growing importance of the manufacturing interest as a component of public opinion — although the motive behind Fox's argument was doubtless the desire to prevent the agitation of an embarrassing question within his own political sphere.[88] When Wyvill and Cartwright seemed inclined to go ahead with plans for a Middlesex county meeting, Fox made it clear that he and his friends

---

[86] He sent a copy of the plan to Cartwright on 9 Jan. 1806 and one to Fox on the following day.

[87] Fox to Wyvill, 23 Dec. 1805.

[88] Also he can hardly have been unaware that Leeds and Manchester were renowned for their 'Church and King' loyalism.

[89] Fox to Wyvill, 15 Jan. 1806; Wyvill to Cartwright, 18 Jan. 1806, reporting a conversation he had had with Fox that morning.

would not patronize it.[89] And a fortnight later, after Pitt's death and the formation of the Grenville-Fox ministry, he succeeded in persuading Wyvill to drop his plan, on the grounds that to press reform at that juncture would jeopardize other desirable and more practicable objects such as peace and Catholic relief.[90]

Wyvill was clearly impressed by Fox's arguments, for during the Ministry of All The Talents he showed far more appreciation of the difficulties of the Foxite Whigs than did many of his reforming friends. Capel Lofft for instance took the view that the new ministers should attempt some reform even at the risk of losing their places; the reformers had long been waiting patiently for better times — 'And now that Mr. Fox Mr. Sheridan Mr. Grey are together in office if it be not a better time for Reform in the Representation than when the enemies of that Reform were alone admitted to power, when will it?'[91] But Wyvill held that the Foxite section of the government could not be expected to press the question while the people remained so apathetic towards it. If the change of administration had been effected 'by the authority of public opinion, decidedly favouring Reform', the situation would have been very different; as it was, until a strong popular demand for reform developed, it was only sensible for Fox and his friends to do what they could for the country without raising an issue which would break up the government.[92] In March 1807, after the dismissal of the ministry, Henry Duncombe wrote to Wyvill: 'So there is an end of the administration of all talents & all integrity. They have shewn themselves eminently deficient in both'. But Wyvill replied:

> I honour the late Ministers, for their Negociation with France, conducted with wisdom and broken off on grounds of most substantial solidity. I honour them for having effected an abolition of the infamous trade in Negroes. I am an approver of several other measures of theirs of less importance; and considering all this, & the general apathy on all that concerns Liberty, I forgive their not having attempted to provide fresh securities to Liberty by a reform of parliament.[93]

However, that Wyvill still considered himself an independent reformer

[85] Wyvill to Fox, 21 Dec. 1805, enclosing 'Thoughts respecting the means by which the redress of our Political Grievances at this juncture may be promoted'.

[90] Wyvill to Fox, 5 Feb. 1806, written after another conversation between them; Wyvill to Cartwright, 6 Feb. 1806, *Life of Cartwright*, I, 338; Cartwright to Wyvill, 7 Feb. 1806. At about the same time Fox parried a move to raise the question of parliamentary reform at the Westminster meeting held to propose his re-election after his appointment as Secretary of State (Brit. Mus. Add. MSS 27850, fo. 10).

[91] Lofft to Wyvill, 30 Mar. (& 13 Apr.) 1806.

[92] Wyvill to Lofft, 24 Feb. & 15 Apr. 1806; to Mrs. Barbauld, 2 Apr. 1806.

[93] Duncombe to Wyvill, 25 Mar. 1807; Wyvill to Duncombe, 7 Apr. 1807.

rather than a Whig is clear from his conduct at the Yorkshire elections of
1806 and 1807. He told Walter Fawkes, the Whig candidate at the 1806
election, that he could vote for no candidate who did not express approval
of the principles of reform adopted by the Association of 1780.[94] This
Fawkes was not prepared to do, since he needed on the one hand the
support of Lord Fitzwilliam, and on the other the votes of the West
Riding clothiers — who, although they had turned against the Pittite
member Henry Lascelles for his conduct on the woollen trade committee
of 1806, were still said to 'abhor reform'.[95] Wyvill therefore, while
wishing him success, declared himself unable to vote for him.[96] There was
in fact no contest in November 1806, as Lascelles withdrew before
nomination day. But at the great Yorkshire election of 1807 Wyvill duly
withheld his vote after Lord Milton, the candidate for Fawkes's seat, had
refused to pledge himself to reform.[97]

The one event in the general election of 1807 from which parliamentary
reformers might have derived encouragement was the success of Sir Francis
Burdett in Westminster. But Burdett did not inspire much confidence in
liberal circles in the north. After the militant anti-Whig line taken by
the baronet in the Middlesex election of 1806, William Roscoe of Liverpool had written to Lord Holland:

> I lament with your Lordship the extremes to which ... Sir Francis Burdett
> allows himself to be carried; and fear that a line of demarcation between the
> firm consistent & temperate friends of liberty, & those who allow their feelings
> on this subject to mislead their judgment, must ere long be drawn. That the
> public interest must suffer by this want of union is evident; but it is much better
> that the rational friends of freedom should rely on their own efforts, than that
> they should be led, by the desire of effecting their purpose, to countenance
> measures which they cannot approve, or should even suffer their cause to be
> injured in the public eye by an association with crude, inexpedient or
> injudicious designs.[98]

---

[94] Wyvill to Fawkes, 21 Oct. 1806. Fawkes later became a radical reformer and a henchman
of Burdett, but at this time he was a firm Whig — see Fawkes to Thomas Creevey, n.d.
(3 Feb. 1806), Creevey MSS (microfilm), University College, London.

[95] E. A. Smith, 'The Yorkshire Elections of 1806 and 1807: a study in electoral management',
Northern History, II, 1967, pp. 66–8; Wyvill to John Yorke, 2 Nov. 1806. Wrightson, the
chairman of Fawkes' committee, wrote to Wyvill, 30 Oct. 1806: 'I think you will agree
with me at a popular election, a man must not deprive himself of the means of promoting
his own success, & hazard the loss of his election, by entering into any unnecessary public
declaration'.

[96] Wyvill to Fawkes, 26 Oct. 1806; to Gamaliel Lloyd, 23 Feb. 1807. On the political
differences between Wyvill and Wilberforce (who retained his seat for Yorkshire at this
election), see Wilberforce to Wyvill, 26 Nov. 1806.

[97] Wyvill to Milton, 3 May 1807; Lloyd to Wyvill, 15 May 1807.

[98] Roscoe to Holland, 13 Nov. 1806, Brit. Mus. Add. MSS 51650. The letter is worth quoting
because it was exactly on this principle that Wyvill was to act during the next few years.

As for Westminster, the unsavoury contest between Sheridan and James Paull in November 1806 had been regarded by provincial reformers as damaging to the cause.[99] And the return of Burdett in 1807 through the efforts of a committee of tradesmen which included several former members of the London Corresponding Society was a source of disquiet rather than satisfaction to Wyvill and his friends.[100]

Wyvill's renewed distrust of the metropolitan reformers was very apparent in the winter of 1808–9, when Cartwright was making plans for a new parliamentary reform campaign, to be initiated by a dinner meeting in London and a Middlesex county meeting. The dinner was intended to show that the cause had nation-wide support from men of substance, and gentlemen from all over the country were invited to act (or at least give their names) as stewards. Cartwright hoped that Wyvill would take the chair; and in requesting him to do so he made it clear that although he himself was still privately attached to the principle of universal suffrage, he was now prepared to work for a more limited reform.[101] But despite this important concession Wyvill would have nothing to do with the meeting. He was afraid that the southern radicals would go further than the Major intended, and thought that the Yorkshire reformers should not commit themselves until the nature of the new movement was shown to be 'unexceptionally moderate and constitutional'.[102]

The popular indignation excited by the Duke of York's affair early in 1809 was regarded by Cartwright as a providential aid to his plans,[103] but it made Wyvill more apprehensive than ever. He wrote to Sir George Cayley: '... in one of his late Letters to me Major Cartwright hints at the rage of the People, & seems to think that their voice is on the point of being heard *in Thunder*. I think it an additional motive for wariness & circumspection'.[104] In March 1809 Colonel Wardle's motion to declare the Duke of York guilty of connivance at corrupt practices was rejected by the House of Commons — and this did provoke a strong

[99] Lofft to Roscoe, 9 Nov. 1806, Roscoe MSS, no. 2439, Liverpool Public Library; Roscoe to Paull, 30 Nov. 1806, *ibid.*, no. 2930.
[100] Bigge to Wyvill, 1 July 1807; Wyvill to Bigge, 15 July 1807.
[101] Cartwright to Wyvill, 13 Nov. & 5 Dec. 1808.
[102] Wyvill to Cartwright, 24, 26 & 29 Dec. 1809. Cartwright pointed out that it was in order to ensure such moderation that he wished for the co-operation of men like Wyvill, Wrightson and Strickland; but Wyvill remained convinced that the country gentlemen of Yorkshire should not 'disable themselves from doing the good they may do at some not very distant time, by *prematurely* embarking with Sir Francis Burdett and his friends in London and Middlesex'. (Cartwright to Wyvill, 5 Jan. 1809; Wyvill to Cayley, 4 Feb. 1809.)
[103] Cartwright, *Reasons for Reformation*, London, 1809, p. 3.
[104] Wyvill to Cayley, 22 Feb. 1809.

public reaction, since it was widely believed that the Duke was guilty.[105] Meetings were held in many parts of the country to vote thanks to Wardle for his patriotic efforts, and a considerable number of these passed resolutions in favour of parliamentary reform.[106] Thus the revival of the question was already under way when Cartwright's dinner meeting took place at the Crown and Anchor tavern on 1 May. The dinner was attended by over a thousand people and was regarded by Cartwright himself as a great success.[107] But poor Capel Lofft was shouted down when he tried to propose a toast to the memory of Charles James Fox; and he wrote to Wyvill deploring the lack of sympathy and co-operation between the old and new schools of reformers.[108] Despite Cartwright's efforts to enlist the support of country gentlemen, a striking feature of the agitation of 1809 was its independence of upper-class leadership.[109] The Whigs and many of the reforming gentry, distrusting Wardle, Cartwright and Burdett, remained aloof — and were much alarmed by the success of the so-called Patriots in mounting a popular political movement without them.[110] It had in fact been Cartwright's intention to alarm the Whigs in this way. Disgusted by their repeated refusals to co-operate with him, he had written to Wyvill in February:

> Were the cause of our country left wholly in their hands, the time for reviving the question of reform would not, as I apprehend, arrive till doom's day.... When they see it to be their interest as a party to join us, they will do it, but not one moment before. This we can only do, by shewing them there is a party to which the nation begins to turn a listening ear.[111]

But the rise of a new largely extra-parliamentary party of reformers, instead of inducing the Whig leaders to adopt more popular courses, made them withdraw into their tents, lamenting that the people were being led astray by irresponsible and possibly disaffected men.[112]

---

[105] See for instance *Leeds Mercury*, 25 Mar. 1809.
[106] Several county meetings took place in the south, but no Yorkshire meeting was held. There were however meetings at Sheffield, Hull, Pontefract, Doncaster and Huddersfield. The Huddersfield meeting resolved that 'A radical Reform in the Representation of the Commons House of Parliament is ... become absolutely necessary to the restoration of the Constitution' — which delighted Major Cartwright. (*York Chronicle*, 20 & 27 Apr. 1809; *York Herald*, 29 Apr. 1809; *Cobbett's Political Register*, 20 May & 17 June 1809; Cartwright to Wyvill, 8 June 1809.)
[107] *Life of Cartwright*, I, 392.
[108] Henry Crabb Robinson to Thomas Robinson, 4 May 1809, Crabb Robinson MSS, Dr. Williams' Library, London; Lofft to Wyvill, 6 May 1809.
[109] *Cobbett's Parliamentary Debates*, XIV, 357 (speech of J. C. Curwen, 4 May 1809); Lord King to Lord Holland, n.d. (summer 1809), Brit. Mus. Add. MSS 51572; *Proceedings of the Electors of Southwark, 12th April 1809*, London, 1809, pp. 11–12.
[110] Sir John Swinburne was so disturbed that he wrote to Lord Grey (7 June 1809, Grey MSS): '... the lower & middling classes appear to me more inclined to Revolution than they were even in 1793.'
[111] Cartwright to Wyvill, 15 Feb. 1809.
[112] G. M. Trevelyan, *Lord Grey of the Reform Bill*, 2nd edition, London, 1929, pp. 168–9.

Wyvill, sharing Whig apprehensions, remained on the sidelines of the reform movement during 1809. The Middlesex meeting, which was held after some delay on 9 August, was temperate in tone;[113] but his fears seemed to be justified when the Burdett riots took place in London in April 1810. He wrote to Whitbread on 15 April: 'What dreadful scenes were those we have just witnessed! But those to come may too probably be far more calamitous'.[114] However, Wyvill's reaction was not as negative as that of Grey and the Whig leaders. It was still his view that the best antidote to radicalism was a strong movement for moderate reform; and when towards the end of the month the possibility of a Yorkshire county meeting was mooted, he gave definite support to the idea.[115] He also hoped to arrange in London a private meeting of those friendly to moderate reform (including the Duke of Norfolk, Whitbread, Coke, Brand and Romilly); and he prepared a paper to be submitted to this meeting for the purpose of establishing some agreement and concert between the Yorkshire reformers and the 'friends of rational liberty' in other parts of the country.[116] This paper stressed the need for caution in view of 'the late unhappy violences', but at the same time pointed out that great danger might ensue from 'the continued denial of justice, and the consequent growth of public discontent'. The plan which Wyvill proposed included a number of measures which he expected reformers of all shades to approve: the abolition of sinecures, the repeal of the Septennial Act and the establishment of more polling stations at elections in large counties. In addition he suggested that representation should be given to the taxpaying inhabitants of the London suburbs, Edinburgh, Glasgow, Aberdeen, Birmingham, Manchester, Leeds and Sheffield; and that to obtain the necessary seats without increasing the size of the House of Commons a sufficient number of decayed boroughs should be invited to sell their right of representation to a body of trustees appointed by parliament to treat with them. Also, if possible, the county franchise should be extended to copyholders in England and to holders of property by subinfeudation in Scotland. Wyvill hoped that this plan would 'satisfy numerous Bodies of Men not represented in Parliament, & yet ... be incapable of being carryed to any dangerous extreme in the course of its execution'.

He imagined that the reforming gentry of his own county would

---

[113] Wyvill admitted this in a letter to Fowler Hicks, 5 Oct. 1809.
[114] Whitbread MSS, no. 4297, Bedfordshire Record Office. He went on to 'lament & blame the rashness of our second Wilkes'.
[115] Wyvill to Wrightson, 28 Apr. 1810.
[116] Wyvill to Fenwick, 12 May 1810. There are copies of the paper in the Grey MSS and the Whitbread MSS (no. 4442), as well as in the Wyvill MSS.

favour a limited measure of this kind; but he had not realized that Walter Fawkes, who had originated the move for a county meeting, was now much more radical than he had been three or four years before. When Wyvill sent him a copy of his paper, Fawkes protested against its allusions to those 'who appear disposed to push reformation to a dangerous extreme'; he said there was nothing to suggest that any of the reformers had sinister intentions. He went on to declare his own approval of the reforms advocated by Burdett in the House of Commons on 15 June 1809: the enfranchisement of taxpaying householders, the equalization of electoral districts, and the shortening of parliaments to a 'constitutional duration'.[117] He added that this plan was very similar to that proposed by Grey in 1797. Wyvill admitted that the principle of this plan was constitutional; but, he continued:

in the present temper of the Country, & after the recent proof we have seen of Sir Francis Burdett's great influence over the population of London, & his want of prudence to avoid such resistance to the Speakers warrant as might, & eventually did lead to Commotion & Bloodshed, I think it would endanger the Liberty & Constitution of the Country to support that principle, though constitutional, when attempted by Sir Francis Burdett and his Friends, to be carryed into effect to the extent which he has proposed.[118]

Wyvill withdrew his support from the projected county meeting; and Wrightson, who had been one of its chief promoters, followed his example, declaring that Grey's plan of 1797 was 'objectionable at this moment as having a tendency to throw more power than moderate men would acquiesce in into the hands of the multitude'.[119] The idea of a meeting was then abandoned — and Wyvill shortly afterwards concluded that this was just as well, as the 'rapid growth of Burdettism among the manufacturers [i.e. operatives] in the West of Yorkshire' made it unlikely that 'temperate counsels' would have been adopted by the county.[120]

The Burdett affair certainly had stimulated popular interest in reform, and in the West Riding Sheffield had re-emerged as a centre of radicalism. A meeting there attended by some eight thousand people approved a strong petition condemning the conduct and composition of the House of Commons; and a few weeks later dinners were held at seventeen public

[117] Fawkes said he would regard a triennial term as sufficiently short.
[118] Fawkes to Wyvill, 8 May 1810; Wyvill to Fawkes, 11 May 1810.
[119] Wrightson to Wyvill, 13 May 1810.
[120] Wyvill to Strickland, 4 June 1810. The moderate reformers would also have been faced with opposition from more conservative elements, including Wilberforce and the Fitzwilliam family. (William Smith to Wyvill, 6 May 1810; Wilberforce to Wyvill, 11 May 1810.)

houses in the town to celebrate Burdett's liberation from the Tower.[121] Daniel Sykes, who had himself chaired a reform meeting at Hull in May, wrote to Wyvill about the clash between Burdett and the House of Commons: 'It may have alienated some wise & good men from us, but it has excited now for the first time in all the populous parts of the nation a wish for reform . . . I am more inclined than you seem to be to take our new allies by the hand to make use of their energy & (as I hope) to repress their violence'.[122] But Wyvill still believed that what was primarily necessary was the support of the leading Whigs and a section at least of the upper classes — and that without this, popular enthusiasm was more of a danger than an asset. His private meeting of moderate reformers in London was abandoned at the same time as the county meeting, but he nevertheless sent copies of his paper to those who might have attended. To Thomas Brand he suggested that in present circumstances this more contracted plan might be a likelier basis for a 'union of good and prudent men' than the proposals which Brand had made in the House of Commons on 21 May.[123] However, the leaders of the Whig party were clearly anxious to avoid the subject altogether. Grey, in a letter commenting on Wyvill's plan, expressed reservations even about those parts of it which Wyvill had regarded as uncontentious.[124] Those of the Whigs who had a more positive attitude to reform felt helplessly isolated between (as Thomas Coke put it) 'the wrong-headed violence of some and the total want of zeal on the part of others'.[125] Meanwhile Samuel Shore, who like Sykes was much more in touch with urban radicalism than Wyvill and the Whigs and consequently less afraid of it, defended the Burdettites and lamented the excessive caution of the moderates:

I perceive no more disposition to violence in the friends to the most effectual measure, than in those who only support a shorter & less effectual one. They both profess to proceed by petitions, and by legal and constitutional means alone, and I believe them to be both sincere . . . . If the Gentlemen of Property and Influence who see the dangerous progress of corruption, would come forward with duly tempered zeal in support of a really effectual Reform of the House of Commons, I am satisfied they would have the country with them . . . Major Cartwright I find has given up his Scheme of Universal Suffrage, and I rejoice at it. But if when such a strenuous man as the Major gives up a point to meet other Reformers, such undoubted patriots as yourself shall begin to retreat,

[121] *Statesman*, 11 & 13 June 1810; A. B. Bell (ed.), *Peeps into the Past: The Diaries of Thomas Asline Ward*, London, 1909, p. 163.
[122] Sykes to Wyvill, 21 May 1810.
[123] Wyvill to Brand, 23 Sept. 1810.
[124] Grey to Wyvill, 1 Aug. 1810.
[125] Coke to Wyvill, 14 Oct. 1810; cf. Romilly to Wyvill, 3 Sept. 1810.

instead of advancing, how can the Reformers ever come together, how can those numerous bodies of petitioners be collected, which must take place to have any prospect of success?[126]

In the following year Cartwright made a great effort to bring together the radical and moderate reformers under their respective parliamentary leaders, Burdett and Brand, in order to stage a general dinner meeting of the friends of reform.[127] While making clear to Wyvill his disapproval of half-measures, he expressed the hope that at the proposed dinner reformers of all shades would be able to combine in support of broad resolutions asserting that reform was necessary. 'Let us co-operate,' he said, 'let us reason with each other; let us promote discussion: in short, let us harmoniously yield each to the other as far as possible, without a desertion of principle.'[128] Wyvill approved of this scheme, and asked for his name to be included in the list of stewards.[129] He appears to have understood from Cartwright's letter that the metropolitan reformers were now prepared to 'follow their more cautious brethren of the Counties.'[130] But several of Wyvill's correspondents were much less optimistic about the projected union, fearing that Burdett and Cartwright would not be willing to concede enough to the moderates; Sir Ralph Milbanke wrote nervously, '... experience teaches us that the violent almost always prevail over the moderate, when their interests at first have a mutual dependance.'[131] It was true that a gulf continued to separate the two bodies and that each wanted union essentially on its own terms.[132] The dinner meeting, when it eventually took place on 10 June, did approve general resolutions in favour of reform; but considerable disagreement emerged in the speeches.[133] Dr. John Disney commented: 'We have nothing but the general principle to unite us, — and the moment specific propositions are named, we become a rope of sand.'[134]

---

[126] Shore to Wyvill, 18 Dec. 1810.

[127] Cartwright, *Six Letters to the Marquis of Tavistock*, London, 1812, pp. 3–4; *Life of Cartwright*, II, 1 et seq.

[128] Cartwright to Wyvill, 15 Apr. 1811, *Life of Cartwright*, II, 9.

[129] Wyvill to Cartwright, 18 Apr. 1811, printed in *Morning Chronicle*, 26 Apr. 1811; cf. Wyvill to Stanhope, 22 Apr. 1811.

[130] Wyvill to Duncombe, 19 Apr. 1811.

[131] Fenwick to Wyvill, 29 Apr. 1811; Milbanke (M.P. for Durham County 1790–1812; later to have the misfortune of being Byron's father-in-law) to Wyvill, 30 Apr. 1811. Sir George Cayley was alarmed by the very vagueness of the object for which the meeting was planned; he wished to form an association pledged to certain specific measures of moderate reform. (Cayley to Wyvill, 18 May 1811; Roscoe MSS, no. 773; *York Herald*, 15 June 1811.)

[132] Samuel Shore thought that both sides were somewhat to blame — Shore to Fawkes, 30 Apr. 1811, copy in Wyvill MSS.

[133] *Statesman*, 11 June 1811, Brit. Mus. Add. MSS 27839, fos. 193–4. (Wyvill did not attend.)

[134] Disney to Wyvill, 15 June 1811.

In the summer of 1811 Cartwright laid plans for two associations of reformers: a Society of Friends to Parliamentary Reform (later known as the Union for Parliamentary Reform according to the Constitution), and the Hampden Club.[135] The former was intended to attract a large and diverse membership, while the latter was an exclusive body confined to men of substantial property. Cartwright hoped for a general enlistment of the reforming gentry in the Hampden Club, but at the same time he was anxious that it should not be led astray into the paths of moderation; initially he was afraid that it might be perverted 'by the mock reformers throwing themselves into it for the purpose of counteracting radical reform.'[136] However, it so clearly bore the hallmark of the Cartwright-Burdett party that the moderates regarded it with extreme caution. Sir George Cayley, for instance, wrote that although Burdett's name did not head the list of the club's members he would clearly be its leader and mouthpiece — and since he had hitherto addressed himself to 'the revolutionary class', he could not hope for the support of respectable reformers until he had bound himself and the club not to exceed certain moderate limits.[137] Wyvill took the same view, and submitted to the leading members of the Hampden Club just before its first meeting a number of resolutions which he thought the club should adopt in addition to general declarations about the necessity of reform. He argued that an agitation for parliamentary reform which had no defined and limited objectives would open the way to 'popular tumults, convulsions, and all the excesses of revolutionary rage'; the club should therefore pledge itself to moderation and opt for the programme put forward by Yorkshire and the younger Pitt in the early 1780's.[138] Burdett, however, maintained that 'the mild treatment which might have operated with success upon an incipient malady, will not act upon a confirmed one'; and Wyvill's advice was rejected.[139]

The year 1812 saw an increasing divergence between Wyvill and Cartwright — who previously, despite frequent disagreement, had remained on terms of friendship and mutual respect. Wyvill was even

---

[135] The first printed circular relating to the Hampden Club was dated 1 May 1811, and a further circular dated March 1812 referred to the club as having been instituted in 1811; but it was not publicly launched until April 1812.

[136] Cartwright to Roscoe, 15 May 1812, Roscoe MSS, no. 765.

[137] Cayley to Wyvill, 13 Apr. 1812.

[138] Wyvill to Fawkes, 15 Apr. 1812. For the resolutions he proposed, see Wyvill's *Papers and Letters chiefly respecting the Reformation of Parliament*, Richmond, 1816, pp. 3–6. (The article on Wyvill in the *D.N.B.* does not include this volume in the list of his published works; but for some reason it credits him with *A Serious Address to all the Independent Electors of the United Kingdom*, 1804, and *Political and Historical Arguments proving the Necessity of Parliamentary Reform*, 1811, which were both by the West Countryman Walter Honywood Yate.)

[139] Fawkes to Wyvill, 16 Apr. 1812.

more alarmed by Luddism than he had been by the Burdett riots, and became more and more obsessed by the danger of revolution. Cartwright meanwhile had come to feel (as he had felt in 1801) that no reliance whatever could be placed on the gentry,[140] and that only through enlisting the mass of the people could the cause of reform have any chance of success. He was more outspoken than ever in his denunciation of half measures, and wrote to Wyvill (without any regard for tact) in May: '. . . considering the desperate condition of our Country, the inveterate corruption of parliament, and the extremely agitated and anxious state of the public mind, to propose anything in the style of mere palliative, should now seem to be the dream of a sick man, whose energies were departed, and intellects impaired'.[141] He said later in the same letter that he was in communication with persons in the disturbed counties, and had hopes of 'turning the discontents into a legal channel favourable to Parliamentary Reform'. In the late summer he made his first missionary tour of the manufacturing districts, including the West Riding;[142] and in October he wrote to Wyvill outlining his plans for the promotion of mass petitions, which he hoped would obtain three hundred thousand signatures. The impulsion, he said, must come from below, since the gentry were so inert: 'We must . . . look principally to those who are *ready for the work*. When they appear in great strength the higher orders, if through policy only, *will take their proper station*.'[143] Wyvill was horrified by this appeal to 'the least informed and worst disposed men in the Country, already prone to insurrection'; and he warned Cartwright that to join the working men of the disturbed counties with the populace of London in order to intimidate the propertied classes would have the opposite of the effect he intended — it would consolidate the defensive alliance of the aristocracy and gentry with the Crown and would probably lead to civil war. What was needed, wrote Wyvill to Fawkes, was the union of 'a great body of the nobles and the Men of Property, with the real well-wishers of their Country in every other class, not to compel compliance with the Sword, either drawn or threatened to be drawn, but

---

[140] In a letter to Sir George Cayley, 17 Dec. 1812 (printed in *The Statesman*, 3 Feb. 1814), Cartwright described the series of frustrating attempts he had made to activate the gentry.

[141] Cartwright to Wyvill, 21 May 1812, *Life of Cartwright*, II, 30. Wyvill's reply, 27 May 1812, was understandably cool.

[142] For Cartwright's success in obtaining signatures for reform petitions in the West Riding, see his speech at the Westminster dinner meeting on 14 December, *Statesman*, 15 Dec. 1812.

[143] Cartwright to Wyvill, 31 Oct. 1812. Cf. Cartwright to Roscoe, 3 Nov. 1812, Roscoe MSS, no. 767: 'If the manufacturing Districts break forth in unanimous petitions, the counties, with their gentry and nobility, must as it seems to me join in the cry.'

by constitutional means alone, to effect a moderate but a salutary and substantial Reform'.[144]

In 1813 he was involved with Sir George Cayley, Sir Francis Wood,[145] and William Wrightson in an attempt to form an association of men of property in Yorkshire who shared this point of view. Once again, however, there was little response;[146] and when in October he published in the *York Herald* and *Leeds Mercury* an address to the Yorkshire freeholders entitled 'Reform with Savile and avert a Revolution',[147] this merely drew attacks from both sides. A letter in the ministerial *York Chronicle* defended the character and effectiveness of the existing House of Commons, and described Wyvill's proposals as ill-timed and dangerous.[148] On the other hand Major Cartwright was offended by a reference in Wyvill's address to 'the dangerous innovations which are persisted in by some rash men'. He responded by addressing to Wyvill a series of twenty open letters, published in *The Statesman* between 29 October 1813 and 4 March 1814.[149] While reiterating the arguments he had been using against moderate reform for over thirty years, he now criticized Wyvill with a new freedom and directness. In particular he accused him of aristocratic leanings — here, he wrote, 'is the ground of that difference of opinion which has ever subsisted between us'; and he reproved Wyvill for speaking of the lower orders 'with singular contempt, as prone to nothing but mischief and confusion'.[150] He also maintained that Wyvill tended to think more as a Yorkshireman than as an Englishman — and this in spite of the fact that he no longer represented the reforming opinion of his own county, since sixty thousand Yorkshiremen had already signed the form of petition recommended by Cartwright himself.[151] Cartwright stressed in another letter that this plan of reform which he advocated (comprising

---

[144] Wyvill to Cartwright, 11 Nov. 1812, *Papers and Letters*, pp. 23–4; to Fawkes, 25 Nov. 1812, *ibid.*, p. 29. In his next letter to Wyvill (apparently the last private letter which passed between them) Cartwright maintained that he relied purely on the strength of public opinion, and that Wyvill's fears of revolution were chimerical; surely, he said, the 'borough faction' would follow the examples of King John in 1215 and James II in 1688 rather than stand out against a widely voiced demand for a self-evident right. But Wyvill thought that the changes which Cartwright wished to bring about were such as 'the upper ranks, and the landed interest generally, will never consent to'. (Cartwright to Wyvill, 3 Dec. 1812, printed in *The Statesman*, 30 Dec. 1813; Wyvill to Disney, 8 Aug. 1813.)

[145] Vice-Lieutenant of the West Riding at the time of the Luddite disturbances; Sheriff of Yorkshire, 1814–15.

[146] Wyvill to Whitbread, 4 Aug. 1813; to Swinburne, 19 Oct. 1813.

[147] *York Herald,* 23 Oct. 1813; *Leeds Mercury,* 23 Oct. 1813.

[148] *York Chronicle,* 4 Nov. 1813.

[149] For a summary of Cartwright's lines of argument in these letters, see N. C. Miller, *op. cit.,* pp. 358–60.

[150] Letter IX, *Statesman,* 22 Jan. 1814.

[151] Letter VIII, *Statesman,* 20 Jan. 1814.

annual parliaments, representation co-extensive with direct taxation, and a fair distribution of seats) should not be regarded as

a plan 'of Major Cartwright's'; as that person, although he early exhibited details, whereby a *Constitutional* Reform might be effected, never was so arrogant or ill-advised as to propose, for *reforming the Legislature of his country*, any 'plan', or project, or proposition, of *his*; any conceit of *his own brain*; any arbitrary fancy, resting wholly on *imagined expediency*; but now for nearly forty years, he has invariably called the public attention to the simple, clear, and all-powerful principles of the Constitution, as alone competent to that great object.[152]

It was clear, said Cartwright, that if union was to be achieved one party of reformers would have to concede to the other; and it was equally clear to him which party should make the concessions. For the radical reformers could not make any without abandoning 'principles and self-evident truths' — whereas the moderates would only have to relinquish notions that were arbitrary and erroneous.[153] These passages illustrate the truth of a note once made by Jeremy Bentham imputing to Cartwright's ideas 'a degree of self will and ipse-dixitism that precludes all argument'.[154] However, there was considerable force in some of Cartwright's criticisms of Wyvill. The latter's attitude towards the landless classes does seem (despite the emphasis which some recent historians have placed on the revolutionary or quasi-revolutionary strand in the working-class history of this period) to have been unduly distrustful; while Cartwright's own confidence in the mass of the people was impressive in a person of his class and generation. The other enormously impressive thing about the Major was his stamina and perseverance. Wyvill has been described as dogged and tireless, if sometimes tiresome[155] — but these epithets apply even more forcibly to Cartwright. Wyvill at the end of 1813 decided that the time had come for him, at the age of seventy-three, to retire from political campaigning;[156] whereas the Major, who was almost exactly the same age, had undertaken in that year the second of his strenuous missionary journeys, and was to embark eighteen months later on a third.

Wyvill did not in fact discontinue his political interests and correspondence, although in the post-war period the climate was as unfavourable

---

152 Letter V, *Statesman*, 1 Jan. 1814. (This number of *The Statesman* is missing from the run in the British Museum Newspaper Library; but there are cuttings of the whole series of letters in volume IX of Cartwright's collected political writings in the Houghton Library, Harvard.)

153 Letter VIII, *Statesman*, 20 Jan. 1814.

154 Bentham MSS, box 125, fo. 141, University College, London.

155 N. C. Phillips, *loc. cit.*, p. 589.

156 Wyvill to Disney, 18 Nov. 1813; to Lofft, 28 Dec. 1813.

as ever to moderate reform. In 1816 he published a selection from his political papers of the last few years, in order to reaffirm his dissent from the views of Fawkes and other radical reformers.[157] This work seems to have made little or no impact — while a pamphlet published by Fawkes early in the following year went into a second edition, proving (said Wrightson) how avidly such opinions were received.[158] In the winter of 1816–17 Cartwright's earlier attempts to arouse interest in reform in the manufacturing districts bore spectacular fruit; radical clubs sprang up in profusion, and insisted that nothing would satisfy them short of universal suffrage. In November Wyvill was urging that a Yorkshire meeting should be held to counter the activities of the democrats. At first the reaction of his correspondents was that while the opponents of reform and the ultra-reformers were so implacably arrayed against each other the moderates would have little chance of moving the county with success.[159] But in January 1817 an initiative came from the West Riding which produced a more positive response. Godfrey Higgins of Ferrybridge, a West Riding magistrate, published in the *York Herald* an address to the gentlemen of Yorkshire calling upon them to place themselves at the head of the movement for reform.[160] At the same time a start was made in collecting signatures for a requisition, with motives which Wrightson described as follows:

> 1st: a desire to counteract the false direction which had for some time been given to the popular feeling, and to endeavour to call back those who had been misled by itinerant political missionaries to a respectful and constitutional mode of application to parliament for redress, 2dly to deprecate all those extravagant theories, which in attempting to restore would destroy the constitution. — It is quite impossible to quench the Spirit of Reform in this County. — It is possible to give it a fair direction.[161]

Wyvill strongly approved of this move, which was very much on the lines he had always recommended.[162] By March more than seventy country gentlemen had signed the requisition;[163] but there were

[157] *Papers and Letters*, pp. 30–2; Wyvill to Wrightson, 29 Mar. 1816.

[158] Wrightson to Wyvill, 18 Feb. 1817. Fawkes recommended in his pamphlet Burdett's plan of reform as opposed to 'arbitrary' Whig schemes — *The Englishman's Manual; or, A Dialogue between a Tory and a Reformer*, London, 1817, pp. 83–4.

[159] Wyvill to Cayley, 17 Nov. 1816; Wrightson to Wyvill, 19 Nov. 1816; Wyvill to Swinburne, 14 Dec. 1816.

[160] *York Herald*, 25 Jan. 1817. Lord Eldon wished on account of this publication to erase Higgins' name from the commission of the peace; but he was dissuaded by Lord Fitzwilliam — Fitzwilliam to Higgins (draft), 2 Mar. 1817, Fitzwilliam MSS, F 51h, Sheffield.

[161] Wrightson to Milton, 2 Feb. 1817, Fitzwilliam MSS, Northamptonshire Record Office. (Quotations from documents in this collection are made by kind permission of the Earl Fitzwilliam.)

[162] Wyvill to Henry Peirse (M.P. for Northallerton), 27 Jan. 1817.

[163] *York Herald*, 1 Mar. 1817; Higgins to Fitzwilliam, 6 Mar. 1817, Fitzwilliam MSS, F 51h, Sheffield.

considerable difficulties, as Sir Francis Wood admitted to Lord Milton:
'I think the Moderates have not so bad a chance at York as they would
have in Palace Yard; but of course they will be prepared for the worst
viz: for the violence of the Tories — the Opposition of the Whigs — the
sneers of the Ultras [i.e. the ultra-reformers], & their own 6 or 8 Shades of
Difference in Opinion'.[164] Wrightson (despite his initial enthusiasm)
became even more apprehensive, fearing that the moderates would be
swamped by the extremists from the urban clubs.[165] A meeting of the
requisitionists was held at Etridge's Hotel in York on 13 March — which
as luck would have it was just after the arrest of the leading Lancashire
radicals in St. Peter's Fields and the abortive march of the Blanketeers.
These events had a chilling effect on the gentlemen reformers of Yorkshire. A number of those who had taken a major part in promoting the
requisition (including Wrightson and Wood) withdrew their names from
it; and although Cayley and others were keen to go ahead, it was
eventually not pressed.[166] Wyvill, who on this occasion took a more
intrepid line than many of his old associates, was very disappointed, for
he had hoped 'that moderate measures of Reform recommended by this
great County would be too important to be slighted, and by holding out
to the Public a reasonable prospect of success by peaceful means would
contribute to allay the furious discontent which so generally agitates the
Lower Classes of the People.'[167] To Lord Grey he wrote that the seceders
had been unnecessarily timid.[168] But Grey threw the blame on the radicals
for causing the alarm. The episode was just another proof, he said, that
the violence of the ultra-reformers was more fatal to the cause of reform
than the opposition of its avowed enemies. He concluded: 'I have now no
hope of seeing a moderate & useful reform effected during my life, & we
have to thank Major Cartwright Mr. Cobbett & Co. principally for it.'[169]

This remark shows the despondency which the post-war agitation
produced in the politicians who were to be responsible for the Great
Reform Bill; and it suggests that there was considerable force in Wyvill's
arguments about the counter-productive effects of radical militancy.
Lord Holland went so far as to say in a letter to Wyvill in 1819: 'If Major

[164] Wood to Milton, 24 Feb. 1817, Fitzwilliam MSS, Northampton.
[165] Wrightson to Wyvill, 18 Feb. 1817.
[166] Cayley to Wyvill, 16 Mar. 1817; Wrightson to Wyvill, 19 Mar. 1817; *Leeds Mercury*, 22 Mar. 1817.
[167] Wyvill to Wrightson, 25 Mar. 1817.
[168] Wyvill to Grey, 4 Apr. 1817. He wrote more strongly to Swinburne, 20 Mar. 1817, deploring 'this act of timidity in a few feeble Whigs'.
[169] Grey to Wyvill, 10 Apr. 1817. Cf. Sir G. Cayley, *A Letter on the subject of Parliamentary Reform, addressed to Major Cartwright*, York, 1818, p. 12: '... you who bawl so loudly for an extreme reform, are the most effectual barrier to the accomplishment of any reform whatever, that exists in the kingdom.'

Cartwright and his friends had condescended to follow your advice some years ago, . . . I believe some measures of temperate & useful reform would ere this time have been resorted to by Parliament.'[170] It should be admitted, however, that Cartwright was more realistic than Wyvill in estimating the amount of outside pressure that would be required to induce parliament to reform itself in any substantial way. On the other hand, Wyvill was right in thinking that the reforms demanded should not be so sweeping as to provoke implacable resistance — and that some degree of conversion was necessary before coercion could succeed; for outside pressure to produce a compliant rather than a negative response, a sizable section of the governing and propertied classes would need to be well disposed to reform. Right at the end of Wyvill's life, after the Six Acts had halted radical activity, a significant change of heart did start to become apparent in the upper and middle classes. Several historians have stressed the importance of the period 1820–3 in preparing the ground for the triumph of moderate reform in the following decade. Austin Mitchell has shown that in these years the Whig party associated itself more fully with the demand for reform than it had done at any previous stage; and this was due to the fact that the demand was being strongly voiced by 'respectable' elements in the country.[171] It is to the early 1820's that Peter Fraser assigns the conversion of the middle classes — and Halévy the conversion of the squires.[172] The political docility of the country gentlemen during the French wars had been partly attributable, as Wyvill saw,[173] to the booming state of agriculture. They continued to be relatively well off in the years after 1815; but in 1820 the price of wheat fell sharply, and in the period of agricultural depression which followed the landed interest resented the unresponsiveness of the House of Commons to its demands for relief.[174] In these circumstances that 'attachment to rational liberty' which in Wyvill's imagination had always been a latent characteristic of the gentry revealed itself once more. The reform movement of the early 1820's was exactly of the type which Wyvill had long been hoping to revive. County meetings came back into vogue, patronized by provincial magnates and country gentlemen; and Lord John Russell pointed out in April 1822 that whereas a few years before every petition had prayed for radical reform, at a recent Middlesex meeting 'a venerable advocate of the cause of reform' (Major Cartwright)

---

[170] Holland to Wyvill, 12 Feb. 1819.
[171] A. Mitchell, 'The Whigs and Parliamentary Reform before 1830', *Historical Studies* (Australia and New Zealand), XII, 1965, pp. 32–8 & 42.
[172] P. Fraser, 'Public Petitioning and Parliament before 1832', *History*, XLVI, 1961, pp. 204–6; E. Halévy, *The Liberal Awakening*, 2nd English edition, London, 1949, pp. 146–50.
[173] *Pol. Papers*, VI, 143 n.
[174] E. Halévy, *op. cit.*, pp. 110 & 146.

could find no one to second him when he proposed a petition for universal suffrage.[175] The climax of this new movement of Country against Court was the Yorkshire meeting of January 1823 (unhappily a few months after Wyvill's death). It was the first time Yorkshire had petitioned for reform since 1785, and *The Times* called it 'one of the most important domestic occurrences that have taken place in our time.'[176] Middle-class reformers from the towns of the West Riding co-operated with the liberal gentry in organizing the meeting; the petition was framed in general terms to avoid dissension over specific plans of reform; and it was eventually signed by more than seventeen thousand people.[177] The county thus resumed the rôle which Wyvill had always thought that it should play — and in 1830 (as in 1779) it was to give a lead to the country at large, when Brougham's election for Yorkshire precipitated the course of events which led up to the Great Reform Bill.[178] Brougham of course was regarded as the candidate of the West Riding, and he said in a speech during his election campaign, 'We don't now live in the days of Barons, thank God — we live in the days of Leeds, of Bradford, of Halifax and of Huddersfield.'[179] Yet although in some ways things had changed in the previous fifty years, in other respects there was remarkable continuity. Marmaduke Wyvill, son of Christopher, was chairman of the party meeting which adopted Brougham as one of the candidates for the county.[180] Also Brougham himself was (and always had been except during his brief flirtation with the Westminster Committee) a moderate reformer. The plan of reform which he put forward at a Yorkshire dinner in September 1830 was very similar to that which he had advocated in the *Edinburgh Review* in 1810,[181] — which was in turn very similar to the scheme drawn up by Wyvill in the same year. And speaking from the hustings at York on election day Brougham 'devoted his eloquent

[175] Hansard, *Parliamentary Debates*, new series, VI, 53. Cf. *The Times*, 15 Mar. 1822.
[176] *The Times*, 25 Jan. 1823, quoted by A. Mitchell, *loc. cit.*, p. 37 n.
[177] *Leeds Mercury*, 25 Jan. 1823; R. W. Ram, 'The Political Activities of Dissenters in the East and West Ridings of Yorkshire, 1815–1830', M.A. thesis, Hull University, 1964, pp. 96–8.
[178] Norman Gash, 'Brougham and the Yorkshire Election of 1830', *Proceedings of the Leeds Philosophical and Literary Society, Literary and Historical Section*, VIII, 1956.
[179] *Leeds Intelligencer*, 29 July 1830, quoted by Asa Briggs, *The Age of Improvement*, London, 1959, p. 239.
[180] Marmaduke Wyvill had been elected M.P. for York in 1820, having declared himself in favour of moderate reform. Thomas Jervis wrote in his obituary of Christopher Wyvill: 'It was the good fortune of this revered and excellent father to live to see his own principles revived, like the phoenix rising from its ashes, in the person of his son . . .' (*York Herald*, 11 Mar. 1820; *Gentleman's Magazine*, April 1822, p. 375.)
[181] A. Mitchell, *The Whigs in Opposition 1815–1830*, Oxford, 1967, p. 242; *Edinburgh Review*, XVI, April 1810, pp. 205–11.

peroration to a recall of the great Yorkshire reform tradition of Wyvill and Savile.'[182]

Major Cartwright, in one of his public letters to Wyvill in 1813, had accused him of arrested development — of clinging to ideas 'imbibed in the very cradled infancy of Reform.'[183] But in looking through the discussions of 1830–2 one realizes that from another point of view Wyvill had been ahead of his times rather than behind them. Again and again — in their presentation of reform as the only means of forestalling revolution, and in their insistence on the need to keep within the limits of what the governing class could be brought to accept — the Whig leaders were echoing lines of argument which Wyvill had reiterated in his pamphlets and correspondence.[184] And of course the settlement of 1832 was much more in accordance with Wyvill's ideas than with those of the radicals. He was unfortunate to live through such a long period in which his ideas were undervalued, and to witness only the early stages of their recovery. But his efforts in these unrewarding years deserve to be recorded, constituting as they do a probably unique bridge between the county association movement and the parliamentary reform campaigns of the 1820's and '30's.

---

[182] *Leeds Mercury*, 7 Aug. 1830, quoted by Gash, *loc. cit.*, p. 30.

[183] Letter III, *Statesman*, 25 Dec. 1813.

[184] A. S. Foord writes: 'Grey had originally taken up [reform] as a means to combat the influence of the Crown, but he endorsed it in 1830 "to prevent the necessity for revolution"' (*His Majesty's Opposition, 1714–1830*, Oxford, 1964, p. 464). This was just the transition that Wyvill had made earlier.

4

'The Patriotic Linen Draper':
Robert Waithman and the Revival of Radicalism
in the City of London, 1795-1818[1]

IT IS NOT strictly accurate to call Robert Waithman a radical. The term
came into use after the Napoleonic wars to describe a group that was more
extreme than Waithman and with which he was to some extent in conflict.
He was, however, though never an advocate of universal suffrage, a consistent champion of peace, retrenchment and reform. Moreover, the term
radical has been used so generally by historians to describe the Wilkite
'Patriots' of the seventeen-seventies that it seems legitimate to apply it to
Waithman, whose political standpoint was similar to theirs and who
frequently invoked their principles and example.

The earlier phase of City radicalism had ended in the mid seventeen-
eighties, after which the Corporation, attached to the younger Pitt, had
become with him progressively more conservative. The period covered by
this essay begins in the mid seventeen-nineties when the Corporation was
firmly opposed to Jacobinism at home and abroad, and it ends in 1818 when
for the first time for a generation the City returned three reformers among
its four M.P.s. During this period the City of London did not play quite
such a dominant part in radical politics as it had in the seventeen-seventies:
it was Westminster, at least from about 1807, that tended to set the pace.[2]
Yet the revival of City radicalism was a significant feature of the new reform
movement of the early nineteenth century.[3] It will be examined in this
article with particular reference to Waithman's role, between 1795 when he
first spoke in the Common Hall and 1818 when he was elected to parliament.
Besides his efforts, of course, there were more general factors at work,
which will be mentioned in the course of the essay; and there were other

[1] I am grateful to Mr. William Kellaway for his valuable comments on a draft of
this article, and to Mr. Roland Thorne, Mr. Michael Collinge and Dr. Ivon
Asquith for several useful references.

[2] J. M. Main, 'Radical Westminster, 1807-20', *Historical Studies* (Australia and
New Zealand), xiii (1966).

[3] The fullest treatment of this revival so far published is R. R. Sharpe, *London and
the Kingdom* (3 vols., 1894-5), iii, chs. xli-xliii, which provides a useful survey of
those parts of the Journals of the Common Council and the Common Hall Books
that relate to national politics—though it makes little use of other sources such as
newspapers (in which the debates of the two courts were often very fully reported).
On the subject discussed in this essay the new *History of London* edited by Francis
Sheppard—the relevant volumes being G. Rudé, *Hanoverian London 1714-1808*
(1971) and F. Sheppard, *London 1808-1870: the Infernal Wen* (1971)—draws
heavily on Sharpe and adds little to his account.

individuals who made important contributions, especially the Foxite brewer H. C. Combe (M.P. for London 1796–1817) and Waithman's contemporary Matthew Wood. The latter, indeed, became in some ways a more conspicuous figure than Waithman. He had the advantage of a higher status in the commercial world, being a merchant (a wholesale druggist) while Waithman was a retailer or 'tradesman'; and although elected to the Common Council only in 1802, Wood attained aldermanic rank five years later through a convenient vacancy occurring in his ward.[1] Thereafter he was sheriff in 1809–10, lord mayor for two successive terms in 1815–17, and a member of parliament for the City from 1817 to 1843. He was not by any means, however, a distinguished speaker,[2] and was much less prominent than Waithman in the debates of the Common Council and Common Hall. Nor does he seem to have had Waithman's energy and skill as a political manager. He favoured many causes with his sponsorship and was widely regarded as respectable and well-meaning, but he often seems to have been more of a figurehead than a leader: Francis Place called him 'weak headed' and implied that he was easily imposed upon by men of doubtful character.[3] At least as regards the period covered by this article, Waithman is the person who deserves most credit for the shift to the left in City politics;[4] and an added reason for concentrating attention on him is the fact that he had a well-defined political position which is interesting not only in the context of the City but in that of the reform movement at large.

Robert Waithman was born at Wrexham, Denbighshire, in 1764 and came to London as a young man. After working as a shop assistant he started his own drapery business in about 1786, and this (first in Ludgate Circus and then in a corner house on Fleet Street) became a prosperous concern.[5] He seems to have had his first taste of politics in debates at the Founders' Hall, Lothbury, which was a centre for meetings of the more radical citizens in the early seventeen-nineties.[6] At this time the livery as a body

[1] A vacancy did occur in Waithman's ward, Farringdon Without, on Wilkes's death at the end of 1797, but Waithman was not then in a position to aspire to the bench. A radical candidate, S. F. Waddington, stood for election but was defeated by Charles (later Sir Charles) Price, who lived until 1818—when Waithman succeeded him. See A. B. Beaven, *Aldermen of the City of London* (2 vols., 1908–13), i. 164.

[2] See his obituary in the *Illustrated London News*, 30 Sept. 1843: 'as a public speaker he had very many superiors, his style being as little elevated as can be imagined; he had none of the powers of an orator either to rouse the feelings or rivet the attention of an assembly'.

[3] British Museum, Additional MS. 35144 fo. 38.

[4] The importance of his role has not been recognized by historians of London. In the new *History of London* he is mentioned only once, and then inaccurately (Sheppard, p. 305); and Sharpe (iii, chs. xli–xliii) makes no mention of him before his election to parliament.

[5] For basic biographical information see *Gentleman's Magazine*, 1833, ciii (1), p. 179; *D.N.B.*; J. T. Rhys, 'Alderman Robert Waithman, M.P.', *Handbook of the Denbighshire Society in London*, 1937–8; *Dictionary of Welsh Biography*.

[6] *Gentleman's Magazine*, 1833, ciii (1), p. 179.

was politically quiescent—the records of the Common Hall contain no resolutions relating to national politics during the years 1790–4. It came to life, however, in 1795, petitioning the house of commons in January for peace, and in November instructing the City's representatives in parliament to oppose the Treason and Sedition Bills.[1] A special grievance which provided some of the initial impetus for this revival was the London Militia Act which had been passed at the end of the 1794 session. Whereas the City had previously been responsible for its own militia, the force raised under this act was to be subject to the national authorities and liable for service beyond the City limits—and the measure provoked considerable resentment among the citizens.[2] Also the abnormally high bread prices of 1795 must have helped to create discontent with the war and the ministry. A meeting of Cheap ward in July, while resolving to raise money for the relief of the poor, also called for a City address to the king imploring him to put an end to 'the present ruinous, calamitous, and disastrous war'. And Waithman, at a meeting of merchants, traders and bankers in the same month, protested against the assumption that the distress was due to factors beyond human control.[3] Waithman was clearly one of the moving spirits in the renewal of radical activity in the City. The peace motion in the Common Hall in January 1795 was seconded by him in 'an excellent speech', and his name headed the list of liverymen who signed the requisition for the November meeting.[4] He also figured prominently at a meeting of his ward on 19 November which adopted a petition to the house of commons against the 'Two Bills'; and at the annual elections on St. Thomas's Day he was returned as one of the ward's representatives on the Common Council.[5]

The Common Council at this time was firmly loyalist and Pittite—as it was basically to remain for the next ten years or more. In this body as well as the Common Hall Waithman emerged in the later seventeen-nineties as one of the leading Opposition speakers; but in the Common Council he was almost always heavily outvoted, and on several issues the two courts made contradictory pronouncements, the one approving of government policy and the other denouncing it.[6] At the beginning of 1800 when H. C. Combe, after a protracted struggle between the livery and the Court of Aldermen,[7]

[1] Corporation of London Records Office, Common Hall Book (C.H.) 9, fos. 49–51, 58–59v. 1795 was also the year—not 1793 as Rudé states (p. 242) misconstruing Beaven (ii, pp. xxvi, 202)—in which H. C. Combe was first 'presented' by the livery to the Court of Aldermen in the election for lord mayor.

[2] *Morning Post*, 5, 12, 30 Sept., 23 Dec. 1794. C.H. 9, fo. 49v.

[3] *Morning Chronicle*, 15 July 1795. Place Collection, set 37, p. 42, British Museum. J. Walvin, 'English democratic societies and popular radicalism, 1791–1800' (unpublished D.Phil. thesis, University of York, 1969), pp. 492–3.

[4] *Morning Post*, 25 Jan. 1795. C.H. 9, fo. 58v.

[5] *Morning Chronicle*, 20 Nov., 24 Dec. 1795.

[6] Corporation of London R.O., Journals of Common Council (C.C.) 76, fos. 25–26v; 77, fos. 34r–v, 42–5. C.H. 9, fos. 58–60, 71v–72v, 74r–76.

[7] For Waithman's part in this conflict see C.H. 9, fo. 110v; *Morning Chronicle*, 23 Oct. 1799.

had eventually become lord mayor, the parliamentary Opposition had thoughts of mounting a petitioning movement led by the City of London against the continuance of the war. But Combe told Fox that he saw 'no prospect of doing any thing with the Common Council', though the livery would be likely to approve any motion for peace; and Fox reported to Christopher Wyvill that he thought it scarcely worth while to move the latter body as 'without the Common Council [it] would not be considered as a precedent for other Corporations'.[1] The livery did in fact remain active at this time. Being a municipal body which was unaffected by the repressive legislation of the seventeen-nineties, it was one of the few organs through which popular anti-ministerial sentiment could still express itself—and such sentiment was particularly strong during the renewed distress of 1800-1. A Common Hall approved a petition for peace negotiations in February 1800,[2] and at about the same time a group called the 'Independent Livery'—which included Waithman and Thomas Hardy, former secretary of the London Corresponding Society—began meeting once a month at the Horn Tavern, Doctors' Commons.[3] Early in 1801 (the Seditious Meetings Act having expired) this group was making contact with known 'friends of liberty' in other parts of the country in the hope of organizing a national petitioning movement for peace and a change of ministers. These plans were frustrated, however, by the new alarm about seditious activities which was raised by the government in April.[4]

In fact there was nothing seditious, or even very extreme, about Waithman's politics. The grievances of the petty bourgeois class he represented, and the changes he wished to see made, were set out in a pamphlet which he published late in 1800. His main objection was to the war (whose only apparent purpose was the restoration of the Bourbon family to the throne of France) and the taxation and distress that it entailed. In particular he attacked the expedient of enormously increasing the national debt as a means of paying for the war. 'The accumulation of public debt', he wrote, 'has one uniform tendency, *viz. to enrich the few by impoverishing the many*, to drain from the hard earnings of the industrious by oppressive taxes, the money required for the payment of the interest of this false capital to the idle and indolent creditor'. He complained especially of the oppressiveness of the income tax, pointing out that no distinction was made between earned and unearned income, and that although income from trade was liable to great fluctuations there was no provision for offsetting losses in one year against gains in another. He also maintained that the landowner and stock holder were acquiring far more through increased land values and capital

[1] Fox to Wyvill, Saturday [1 Feb. 1800], C. Wyvill, *Political Papers* (6 vols., York, 1794–1806), VI. ii. 55.

[2] C.H. 9, fos. 116v–119v.

[3] Hardy to Lord Stanhope, 29 Jan. 1801 (draft), and to Major John Cartwright, 23 Feb. 1801 (draft), Brit. Mus., Add. MS. 27818 fos. 20, 28.

[4] See letters cited in previous note, and Hardy to John Foster, 14 Apr. 1801 (draft), *ibid.* fo. 30. *Annual Register* (Otridge), History of Europe, pp. 172–7. Cartwright to Wyvill, 20 Apr., 8 May 1801, Wyvill, VI. ii. 253–4, 258.

gains (the funds, he claimed, had risen in value by thirty per cent when the income tax was imposed) than they were losing through taxation; 'those who have been the loudest', he said, 'in pledging their lives and fortunes for the support of the war, have been the greatest gainers by it'. The remedies he proposed for the distressed condition of the lower orders were the cessation of the war, a reform of corruptions and abuses in every department of the state, the abolition of sinecures, the cultivation of waste lands and the establishment of smallholdings for poor labourers, the abolition or commutation of tithes, the repeal of the income tax, and the transference of the fiscal burden to luxuries such as pleasure horses and livery servants.[1] He did not go so far at this time as to advocate a reform of parliament; and the only action he recommended was the calling of meetings to petition for peace and a change of ministry.[2]

Nevertheless, the role he had played in the City since 1795 had given him the reputation of an *enragé* and made him a target of anti-Jacobin abuse. An amendment which he moved to the Common Council's loyal address of 2 February 1797 following the breakdown of Lord Malmesbury's negotiation had led *The Times* to comment:

An impartial observer would really conclude from the tenor of the Amendment, that this Mr. Waithman was an orator of one of the Jacobin Clubs in Paris, endeavouring to defend the conduct of the Executive Government of France. He could not have made a more Frenchified Amendment.[3]

And the same newspaper had reported with satisfaction in December 1798 that a determined effort was being made by the loyalists in Waithman's ward to prevent 'his Citizenship' from being re-elected to the Common Council—though the effort was unsuccessful.[4] At the general election in 1802 Waithman was nominated as a candidate for the City, but the show of hands went against him and he did not stand a poll. On the two occasions when he tried to speak from the hustings he was greeted with loud hisses and cries of 'Off! Off!' and was unable to obtain a hearing.[5] In general in the opening years of the nineteenth century (though it is true that the Middlesex elections of 1802 and 1804 occasioned strong demonstrations of popular support for Burdett) the prevailing political climate was emphatically loyalist; and in the City the only subject on which Waithman could rouse opposition to the government was the income tax, against which the livery registered protests in 1802 and 1803.[6] It was not until 1805 that an oppor-

[1] R. Waithman, *War proved to be the real cause of the present scarcity and enormous high price of every article of consumption, with the only radical remedies* (1800), pp. 22, 35–44, 53, 57–75.
[2] *Ibid.*, pp. 79–80.
[3] *Times*, 4 Feb. 1797.
[4] *Ibid.*, 11, 22, 24 Dec. 1798.
[5] Anon., *The Picture of Parliament: an impartial account of the general election of 1802* (1802), pp. 71–5.
[6] C.H. 9, fos. 144v–147v, 163v–165. *Morning Chronicle*, 19 March 1802, 30 June 1803.

tunity arose for an anti-ministerial movement of broader political significance. In April of that year, after the tenth report of the commissioners of
naval inquiry and the decision of the house of commons to impeach Lord
Melville, the City gave a lead to the country as a whole—a lead that was
widely followed[1]—in expressing indignation at the abuses which had been
brought to light. At a Common Hall on 18 April Waithman carried a
motion to petition the house of commons for further investigation into the
management of the public money, and a week later the Common Council
approved an address to the king requesting that all necessary measures
would be taken for the 'correction and punishment of proved malversation'.[2]
This address suggested a marked weakening of the Common Council's
allegiance to Pitt—though for another two or three years the court was to
remain more Pittite than Foxite or reformist. After Pitt's death an address
to the king welcoming the formation of the Grenville–Fox ministry was
carried by 91 votes to 79. But fourteen months later, after George III had
made a stand against the Talents ministry and dismissed it over its bill for
opening staff appointments in the army to Catholics, the Common Council
approved by the large margin of 123 votes to 49 a very different address
thanking the king for the protection he had given to the established protestant religion and for 'the firm and constitutional exercise of his Royal
Prerogative to preserve the Independence of his Crown'.[3] In March 1808
a further address was carried assuring the king of 'the unshaken attachment
of this Court to his most sacred Person and Government', and Waithman
said during the debate that

it had been of late years so customary for the Common Council to address his
Majesty in favour of every Administration, that he thought it would...save a
great deal of trouble, both to the Common Council and to his Majesty, if they
would declare at once their determination to support the measures of the present
Administration, as they had of every former Administration, and as they intended
to do of every future Administration.

However, it was notable that a motion proposed by Waithman's colleague
Edward Quin for the insertion of a clause lamenting the recent rejection of
the Reversions Bill by the house of lords was only narrowly defeated.[4]

The tide was in fact on the point of turning. The fervour of loyalism
which had prevailed at the time of the resumption of the war in 1803 had
appreciably diminished. The battle of Trafalgar had removed the threat
of invasion, and the people had become more resentful of the burdens
which the war involved and more critical of the ministerial policies which
their own money financed. The Melville affair had raised doubts about the
way in which public funds were handled; and the return of Sir Francis

[1] H. Jephson, _The Platform_ (2 vols., 1892), i. 312–14.
[2] C.H. 9, fos. 186v–188v. C.C. 82, fos. 252v–254v. _Morning Chronicle_, 19, 26 Apr. 1805.
[3] C.C. 83, fos. 14v–16v, 381–3.
[4] C.C. 84, fos. 194v–198v. _Times_, 26 March 1808.

Burdett at the Westminster election of 1807, after a campaign directed largely against placeholders,[1] had given evidence of strong dissatisfaction with the political establishment. A similar spirit (of which there had been a foretaste in 1805) began to manifest itself strongly in City politics during 1808. The bill to prevent the granting of offices in reversion was not in itself a measure of great importance, but it was the first reform of a constitutional nature which the house of commons had passed for a long time and its rejection by the Lords was understandably regarded as provocative.[2] On 31 March, less than a week after the loyal address, Waithman introduced and carried without a division in the Common Council a pair of strong petitions to the two houses of parliament. These stated that for a number of years the people had submitted patiently to unprecedented burdens; that these burdens had been 'augmented by great abuses in the management and expenditure of the public money', and that 'a profusion of sinecure places and pensions' had not only added to the sufferings of the people but created a pernicious and unconstitutional influence. The petitioners said that having hailed the introduction of a bill to prevent reversionary grants as a first step on the way to salutary reforms, they observed its frustration with grief and disappointment. Finally they expressed the hope that the house of commons would persist in its attempts to carry this measure, and would institute inquiries designed to secure a rigid economy in the public expenditure.[3] The petitions were composed by Waithman,[4] and the *Independent Whig* (a radical weekly of fairly recent origin) commented: 'The language in which they are expressed, and the sentiments which they avow, are worthy of the days of Wilkes and Sawbridge'.[5] In October of the same year the Common Council was quick off the mark in denouncing the Convention of Cintra: an address to the king moved by Waithman, expressing grief and astonishment and praying for an inquiry into 'this dishonourable and unprecedented transaction', was carried unanimously. The *Morning Chronicle* said in an editorial, 'The City of London has done itself great honour by taking the lead in the expression of sentiments which are universally felt through the kingdom'; and several cities and counties followed London's example.[6]

In 1809 and 1810 the leftward trend in City politics continued. The year 1809 was one of revived radical activity in the country as a whole, principally on account of the sensational investigation into the conduct of the duke of York. After the defeat of Colonel Wardle's motion asserting the duke's guilt, the livery was one of the first bodies to protest against the Commons'

[1] See [F. Place and J. Richter,] *An exposition of the circumstances which gave rise to the election of Sir Francis Burdett, Bart. for the City of Westminster* (1807), pp. 11–12, 18–19.

[2] Cf. M. Roberts, *The Whig Party 1807–12* (1939), pp. 192–3.

[3] C.C. 84, fos. 216v–220v.

[4] *Morning Chronicle*, 4 Apr. 1808.

[5] *Independent Whig*, 3 Apr. 1808, p. 523.

[6] C.C. 84, fos. 332–4. *Morning Chronicle*, 5 Oct. 1808. M. Dorothy George, *Catalogue of Political and Personal Satires*, viii (1947), pp. 686–7.

decision: a Common Hall on 1 April voted thanks to Wardle, Burdett, Lord Folkestone and others who had taken a prominent part against the duke. Waithman (as usual on such occasions) initiated the debate,[1] and he was warmly praised by Cobbett in the *Political Register* for his persistent and eventually successful efforts to 'unglue the eyes of the Citizens of London'.[2] The Common Hall was followed up by a meeting of the Common Council, which on 6 April voted Wardle the freedom of the City in a gold box. It also ascribed the recent decision of the house of commons to the 'preponderating influence' of which the court had complained twelve months before, and it called for a 'radical and speedy reform'.[3] The nature of the reform required was not made explicit, but it is clear that Waithman, while taking a cautious view of what the Common Council could be made to swallow,[4] was at this time thinking definitely in terms of parliamentary as well as economical reform. Indeed in the previous August he had supported an attempt by Major Cartwright to raise the question of parliamentary reform at a Middle-sex county meeting, and in the spring of 1809 he placed his name on the list of stewards which Cartwright was compiling in preparation for a general meeting of reformers to be held in the metropolis.[5] On 21 April Waithman presided over a dinner-meeting which he had arranged himself—a dinner of 'independent' liverymen, which was attended by several of the M.P.s who had voted in the minority on Wardle's motion. When Lord Folkestone wrote to Waithman before the dinner saying that he hoped those who attended would not be expected to pledge themselves to parliamentary reform, Waithman said in his reply: 'I am exceedingly sorry any doubt should remain in your mind on a point which I conceive to be the root and source of all our Evils'.[6] At the dinner Waithman proposed a toast to 'Sir Francis Burdett, and a speedy and radical Reform of the Representation of the People in Parliament';[7] and ten days later he was one of the speakers at Cartwright's dinner-meeting at the Crown and Anchor, an occasion which marked the return of parliamentary reform to the surface of politics after more than a decade of virtual submersion.[8] Later in the year the radical

[1] C.H. 9, fos. 229–31. *Morning Chronicle*, 3 Apr. 1809. For an enthusiastic account of the meeting, see Thomas De Quincey to Dorothy Wordsworth, 5 Apr. 1809, J. E. Jordan, *De Quincey to Wordsworth: a biography of a relationship* (Berkeley and Los Angeles, 1962), pp. 139–40.

[2] *Cobbett's Political Register*, 8 Apr. 1809, cols. 521–2.

[3] C.C. 85, fos. 79v–80v.

[4] Cf. W. A. Miles to William Roscoe, 8 Apr. 1809, Roscoe MSS., no. 2714, Liverpool Public Library.

[5] *Morning Chronicle*, 31 Aug. 1808. Holt White MSS., no. 442, The Wakes Museum, Selborne, Hants.

[6] Folkestone to Waithman, 20 Apr. 1809 (draft), and Waithman's reply of the same date, Pleydell-Bouverie MSS., Berkshire R.O.

[7] *An accurate and faithful report of the speeches, songs, &c. at the dinner given by the livery of London to Colonel Wardle, M.P., at the London Tavern* [1809], p. 10.

[8] *A full and accurate report of the proceedings at the meeting held at the Crown and Anchor Tavern, on Monday, the 1st of May, 1809, relative to a reform in the Commons House of Parliament* (1809), pp. 36–9.

feeling which had been roused by the duke of York's affair was fanned by
the Walcheren disaster—and this event provoked an important trial of
strength in the Common Council. On 5 December Waithman proposed an
address to the king which was a thoroughgoing attack on the ministry and
its policies and called for a general inquiry into the failure of recent operations in the Peninsula and Holland. The address was carried, but only by
68 votes to 67;[1] and Waithman's opponents counter-attacked at another
meeting of the court on the 13th, when a much milder address requesting
an inquiry into the conduct of the Walcheren expedition was substituted for
his (the numbers on the critical division being 117 to 100).[2] Cobbett
remarked in a private letter a couple of days later:

The *resinding* of the resolution in the city, or rather, the *altering* it, does not look
so well; but, I should hope, that this desperate attempt of the courtiers will have
the effect of completely rouzing the Wards for Sir [sic] Thomas's Day, which will
be a guarantee for future success.[3]

Although in the last two years the Common Council had to a considerable
extent changed its tune, this had not been brought about by any substantial
change in its personnel: in 1807 and 1808, despite appeals in the press for a
'purging' of the court, there had been little activity among the freemen
householders who voted at Common Council elections.[4] In 1809, however,
political excitement did extend to this level. In late November Waithman
had published in Cobbett's *Register* a letter to the citizens of London
calling on them to prevent the Common Council from being dominated in
future by 'place-hunting canker-worms destitute alike of talents, probity
and shame'.[5] A similar appeal appeared in the *Statesman* at the time of the
elections, and *The Times* reported 'an unprecedented bustle and tumult' in
most of the wards and strong opposition to those councillors who had voted
for rescinding the original address.[6] Fifteen out of the twenty-six wards
were contested, and the outcome was the biggest swing to the left for some
forty years: Waithman claimed a net gain of about thirty seats.[7]

The proceedings in London—including a Common Hall on 9 January
1810 which instructed the City's representatives in parliament to support
any motion for an inquiry into the failure of recent expeditions[8]—may have
had some impact on the house of commons. When on 26 January the House

[1] C.C. 85, fos. 322–325v. *Statesman*, 6 Dec. 1809.
[2] C.C. 85, fos. 349v–351v. *Morning Chronicle*, 14, 15 Dec. 1809 (debate and division list).
[3] Cobbett to John Wright, 15 Dec. 1809, Brit. Mus., Add. MS. 22907 fo. 227.
[4] *Independent Whig*, 20 Dec. 1807, p. 392. *Morning Chronicle*, 17, 22, 24 Dec. 1807, 24 Oct., 22, 23 Dec. 1808.
[5] *Cobbett's Political Register*, 25 Nov. 1809, cols. 799–805.
[6] *Statesman*, 21 Dec. 1809. *Times*, 22 Dec. 1809.
[7] *Times*, 25 Dec. 1809. Waithman to Thomas Creevey, 6 Jan. 1810, Creevey MSS., University College London (microfilm). Cf. I.R. Christie, *Wilkes, Wyvill and Reform* (1962), pp. 33 & n., 57 & n.
[8] C.H. 9, fo. 241.

did resolve on an investigation into the expedition to the Scheldt, Creevey remarked that the City of London and the county of Berkshire (which had also petitioned the king for an inquiry) had 'frighten'd the House of Commons into this vote'.[1] There then followed the series of incidents which resulted in the imprisonment of Gale Jones by the house of commons for protesting against the exclusion of strangers during the Walcheren inquiry, and the imprisonment of Burdett for protesting against the imprisonment of Gale Jones. Waithman was one of the foremost in denouncing the actions and pretensions of the House. On 19 April, ten days after Burdett's arrest, he presided at the second 'Dinner of the Livery of London, Friends to a Constitutional Reform in Parliament', and said in his opening speech 'that all the privileges with which the House of Commons are invested, were intended to fortify them against the encroachments of the Crown, and are privileges to be asserted for the People, and not to be employed against them'.[2] A resolution to the same effect, moved by the veteran Southwark reformer Samuel Favell[3] and seconded by Waithman, was passed at a Common Hall on 4 May. The livery also approved an 'address, remonstrance and petition' to the house of commons condemning the arbitrary imprisonment of Gale Jones and Burdett, demanding the revocation of the proceedings taken against them and calling on the House to adopt an immediate and radical reform.[4] This petition the Commons refused to receive on account of its disrespectful language and its flat denial of the privileges of the House;[5] but a new 'address, petition and remonstrance', though scarcely less strong than the previous one, was eventually accepted.[6]

Meanwhile in the country as a whole there developed the most extensive petitioning movement for parliamentary reform since 1793. From places such as Nottingham, Sheffield and Liverpool, as well as from Westminster, Middlesex and Southwark, petitions came in calling for the release of Burdett and Gale Jones and for a reform of the representation.[7] This revival of reformism in the provinces was of great significance, but perhaps the most notable of all the petitions was that of the Corporation of London. Waithman had been intending for some time to bring forward the question of reform in the Common Council[8]—and thus to put the result of the 1809

[1] Creevey to Mrs. Creevey, 26 Jan. 1810, Creevey MSS.

[2] *Statesman*, 20 Apr. 1810. Cf. Waithman to Creevey, 1 Apr. 1810, Creevey MSS.; and his speech at a Middlesex county meeting, *Statesman*, 27 Apr. 1810.

[3] Cf. *An account of the proceedings of the Electors of Southwark on Wednesday, the 12th April, 1809* (1809), pp. 5–14.

[4] C.H. 9, fos. 245–248v. *Statesman*, 5 May 1810.

[5] *Cobbett's Parliamentary Debates*, xvi, cols. 885–902, 922–44.

[6] C.H. 9, fos. 249v–253v. *Cobbett's Parl. Debates*, xvii, cols. 179–81. Brit. Mus., Add. MS. 27850 fos. 227–8. Sharpe, iii. 277–81.

[7] *Journals of the House of Commons*, lxv. 293, 389, 426, 501. *Cobbett's Parl. Debates*, xvi, col. 780; xvii, col. 616.

[8] Waithman to Creevey, 2 Dec. 1809, 1 Apr. 1810, Creevey MSS.

elections to the crucial test. By the end of May eight of the larger City wards had met to express their approval of the proceedings of the Common Hall and their support for parliamentary reform, and some had instructed their representatives on the Common Council to vote for all resolutions and petitions that had reform for their object.[1] The confrontation in the Common Council took place on 6 June. Waithman himself did not introduce the motion for a petition (it was introduced by Quin), but he supported it in a long though moderate speech. He said that he had been a reformer for twenty years, but had never been in favour of universal suffrage: 'some intemperate men might wish for such a plan, but they were neither formidable for numbers nor talents, so as to create any apprehension or alarm'. The petition to the house of commons was also couched in relatively moderate language, but it contained a formidable list of grievances which were all attributed to the lack of a proper representation of the people in parliament. The reforms which the House was pressed to undertake were disfranchisement of corrupt and depopulated boroughs, an extension of the suffrage, the exclusion of placemen and pensioners (except the 'efficient officers of the Crown') and a shortening of the duration of parliaments. The petition was carried by 87 votes to 81,[2] and the reformers hailed this outcome as a major triumph. The London printer John McCreery wrote to W. S. Roscoe in Liverpool:'The contest in the Common Council here was grand & decisive, the ministry have lost the City, every effort was tried by them but all would not do'. And *The Times* (at this stage going through an anti-ministerial phase) commented likewise: 'Nothing can more strongly indicate the change which has taken place in the sentiments of this body... than a majority thus obtained against all the influence and exertions which ministers and their adherents have been for a long time using'.[3]

The summer of 1810 marks the end of the first stage in the revival of City radicalism. The success of 6 June was not in fact so decisive as McCreery hoped. Though after the events of 1808–10 the tories no longer dominated the Common Council as they had done previously, the balance of forces in the court was to be fairly even for the remaining years of the war (which were generally less conducive to radical activity). Over certain issues the 'Patriots' were able to maintain a majority: for instance in protesting against the restrictions placed on the regent's powers in 1811, in expressing disappointment at the fact that no ministerial changes were made when the restrictions expired, and in taking the side of the princess of Wales in her public quarrel with the prince.[4] However, there were other issues on which the loyalist and conservative element in the Common Council was able to win the upper hand. A notable defeat was sustained by the reformers in

[1] *Statesman*, 17 May 1810. *Alfred and Westminster Gazette*, 31 May 1810.

[2] C.C. 86, fos. 119v–124v. *Alfred and Westminster Gazette*, 7, 8 June 1810 (debate and division list).

[3] J. McCreery to W. S. Roscoe, 9 June 1810, Roscoe MSS., no. 2059. *Times*, 7 June 1810.

[4] C.C. 86, fos. 262v–264v, 290–291v; 87, fos. 193v–196, 506v–509v.

May 1811. Major Cartwright was planning another general meeting of supporters of parliamentary reform, and at Alderman Wood's suggestion (though against Waithman's advice) an application was made to the Common Council for permission to hold the meeting at the Guildhall. This request was considered and granted on 22 May; but the opponents of reform claimed that only those sympathetic to the application had known of it in advance, and they alleged that the grant of the Guildhall for such a purpose would be a most undesirable precedent and would jeopardize the peace of the City. On 31 May the Common Council was convened to reconsider the question and the former decision was reversed, the reformers being defeated by 119 votes to 80.[1] Also, of course, the military successes of the last few years of the war gave a great advantage to the ministerialists. In February 1810 a petition deploring the grant of a pension to Lord Wellington had been carried in the Common Council by 65 votes to 58, but in 1811 the same body voted him the freedom of the City, and after Salamanca it added that the freedom should be conferred in a gold box.[2] In June 1814 after the signing of the peace treaty with France a long congratulatory address to the regent was approved, declaring that the war had been wisely and courageously prosecuted and that the 'astonishing energies' which the nation had displayed in the course of it had been 'called forth by that admirable constitution of government which Britons possess'.[3]

The behaviour of the Common Council showed that the City had not yet gone definitely into opposition—and this was also apparent from the contest in the City at the general election of 1812. Had the election taken place some three years earlier Waithman might well have won a seat;[4] but in October 1812 there was much less anti-government feeling, and three of the successful candidates were ministerialists. Waithman nevertheless maintained that with Combe being returned at the head of the poll and two reformers (himself and Wood) obtaining a respectable number of votes there was some cause for encouragement; it was impressive, he said, that so many liverymen were prepared to vote independently

in the midst of the corruption of this great city—against the influence of the India House, of the Bank, of the South Sea House, of the Post Office, of the Custom House, of the Excise, and all the other powerful interests to which public corruption and an immense taxation gave birth.[5]

[1] Cartwright's printed circular dated 17 Apr. 1811; Roscoe MSS., no. 761. C.C. 86, fos. 386v–387v, 400–5. *Alfred and Westminster Gazette*, 24, 31 May, 1 June 1811.

[2] C.C. 85, fos. 420–422v. Sharpe, iii. 275–6, 286.

[3] C.C. 89, fos. 37–39v. Cf. *Quarterly Review*, xvi (Oct. 1816), 242–4, where this address ('Philip sober') is contrasted with that of Nov. 1816 ('Philip drunk') which described the late wars as 'rash and ruinous,...unjustly commenced and pertinaciously persisted in'.

[4] Cf. Thomas Grenville to Earl Fitzwilliam, 6 Nov. 1809, Fitzwilliam MSS., Northamptonshire R.O.

[5] *Statesman*, 10, 13 Oct. 1812.

How important government influence was in City elections in the early nineteenth century it is not easy to say. According to Francis Place many City electors imagined themselves to be under an influence which they could not resist, when in fact they could have easily defied it.[1] But whether the influence was real or imaginary, it may provide at least part of the explanation for the contrast between the behaviour of the livery in the Common Hall and their behaviour as parliamentary voters.[2] The 'patriotic linen-draper' (as the *Satirist* derisively called him) was still a *bête noire* of the loyalists,[3] and those who wished to avoid giving offence to the authorities were doubtless chary of polling for him. On the other hand a vote for the whiggish and respectable Combe, a former lord mayor and a member of Brooks's, was much less of an act of defiance against the establishment—and this may partly account for the fact that Combe obtained nearly twice as many votes.

It is not the whole explanation, however. While Waithman's supporters at the election were urged to vote for Combe, Combe's were not urged to vote for Waithman, and the latter felt that he had reason to resent the lack of support given him by Combe's whig friends.[4] Waithman's relationship to the whig party is a topic of some importance which needs to be examined, with reference to previous events, in a paragraph of its own. From his early days in politics he seems to have regarded himself as a Foxite.[5] His aims in the seventeen-nineties were clearly in tune with those of the Foxite Opposition, and when the Grenville–Fox ministry was formed in 1806 he seconded the motion in the Common Council for a congratulatory address to the king.[6] He also belonged to the Whig Club, which passed a vote of thanks to him after the Common Council's economical reform petitions of March 1808.[7] However, in 1809 he was much disappointed by the failure of the Opposition leaders to give firm support to Colonel Wardle, and at Cartwright's reform dinner on 1 May he expressed a disillusionment with the whigs that had evidently been growing on him for some time. After an earlier speaker (William Smith, M.P. for Norwich) had warned the meeting not to be too sanguine about the prospects of reform, Waithman deplored this discouraging attitude and asked what had become of the reforming enthusiasm of the erstwhile Friends of the People. When the whigs had come into

[1] Brit. Mus., Add. MS. 27838 fo. 18.

[2] Cf. Waithman's remarks at a meeting of the Common Council after the election, *Statesman*, 30 Oct. 1812.

[3] *Satirist*, 1 June 1810, pp. 539–40; 1 July 1810, pp. 71–2. Waithman had had the windows of his shop broken during the Jubilee celebrations of Oct. 1809 (*Examiner*, 29 Oct. 1809, p. 694).

[4] *Statesman*, 2, 5 Oct. 1812. John Goodwin to Earl Grey, 24 Dec. 1812, Grey MSS., University of Durham.

[5] He later recalled the openness and candour with which he had been treated by Fox himself (Waithman to Lord Holland, 15 Jan. 1818, Brit. Mus., Add. MS. 51829).

[6] *Morning Chronicle*, 15 Feb. 1806.

[7] *Flower's Political Review*, Apr. 1808, p. 237.

power, he said, they had not merely failed to carry any of their great professions into execution but had not even expressed any intention of doing so; and he maintained that their conduct during the last few years had been even more regrettable than that of the Pittites, who had at least acted consistently as the professed lovers of the existing system.[1] Later in 1809, when moving his address of 5 December over the Walcheren expedition, he said that no change of ministers would do the country much good unless the whole system of government was changed; and he asked why men such as Grey, who had called for reform in the seventeen-nineties and had seceded from parliament on account of the apathy of the public, should show so little inclination to pursue their old aims now that public spirit was reviving.[2] This speech produced a reaction from the whig leaders—but essentially a negative one. Lord Holland said in a speech at Nottingham that although a reform of parliament might be desirable it was far from true that no good could be done without it.[3] As for Grey, he inveighed in a letter to Holland against those whose sole aim was 'the degradation of all public characters'; with such people, he wrote,

I cannot consent to an endeavour to keep any terms, & if that policy should be adopted I can hardly look to any other consequence than my separation from those who pursue it. Indeed when I am personally attacked as I have been, particularly by Mr. Waithman, upon ground which was created only by his own misrepresentations, I think I have a right to claim it of my friends as due to me to mark strongly their reprobation of his conduct.[4]

There was an oblique reference here to Grey's brother-in-law Whitbread and the group of whigs known as 'the Mountain', who had shown themselves far more inclined towards popular courses than the whig leaders and had actually fraternized with Waithman, several of them attending his livery dinner in April 1809.[5] Waithman himself had welcomed their co-operation, for although some radicals were so incensed against the whigs that they refused to have anything to do with whiggery or 'party' in any form, he said publicly that he had nothing against party as such and nothing against whig principles as he understood them.[6] He recognized that it was only through the aid of a major party in the house of commons that reform could be peacefully achieved; and he intended to provide what he could in the way of extra-parliamentary backing for those whigs who supported reform, in the hope that the leaders of the party would eventually be

[1] *A full and accurate report of the meeting at the Crown and Anchor*, pp. 31-9.
[2] *Statesman*, 6 Dec. 1809.
[3] *Morning Chronicle*, 27 Dec. 1809. Cf. Holland to Francis Horner, postmarked 10 Jan. 1810, Horner MSS., British Library of Political and Economic Science—which shows that Holland's speech was intended as a reply to Waithman's.
[4] Grey to Holland, 5 Jan. 1810, Grey MSS.
[5] *Morning Chronicle*, 22 Apr. 1809. Cf. Creevey to Samuel Whitbread, 8 Apr. 1809, Whitbread MSS., no. 373/14, Bedfordshire County R.O.
[6] See his speeches reported in *Morning Chronicle*, 7 Apr. 1809, and *Statesman*, 3 Aug. 1809.

induced to take it up again themselves. During the next few years a close association existed between Waithman and the whigs of the Mountain, who wished to push the Opposition leaders in the same direction and regarded him as a useful and sensible ally.[1] However, although he tried both in public and private to make the whig leaders see the error of their ways and to convince them that 'if they declared themselves in favor of reform they would have the City of London and the whole Country at their backs',[2] his efforts were all to no avail. Eventually his impatience with them (exacerbated no doubt by his feelings over the 1812 election) led him into an unfortunate confrontation with Grey. The occasion was a meeting in June 1814 of 'friends to the abolition of the slave trade', there being at that time much public indignation over a clause in the peace terms which allowed France to continue her slave trade for five years. Lord Lansdowne was in the chair and Grey seconded the resolutions (which were moved by Wilberforce). Waithman, from the floor, moved a vote of thanks to those responsible for calling the meeting, and went on to express his gratification at 'the deference which some Noble Lords had to-day shewn for the public opinion'; having 'frequently felt the want of their countenance and support,... he rejoiced in this auspicious change, and he trusted that the example now set would in future be frequently followed'. Such remarks on such an occasion were unwise, and Grey was very cutting in reply, saying that 'a moment when all were unanimous in the cause of justice and benevolence, was not exactly the time for introducing personal animosities'. When Waithman tried to explain his remarks he was shouted down.[3]

While Waithman was mainly occupied during the war years in doing battle on his right against tories and 'high' whigs, there were some indications towards the end of the war of incipient trouble on his left. It was not at this stage over the reform question that disagreement arose. Waithman was correct when he said in the Common Council debate in June 1810 that very few reformers were calling for universal suffrage; Cartwright and Cobbett were both committed to the taxpayers' franchise which Burdett had advocated in the house of commons in June 1809,[4] and universal suffrage being little canvassed, Waithman's avowed hostility to it did not expose him to attack. It was rather his whig connections that aroused suspicion. Cobbett had reproved him in April 1808 for attending the Whig Club;[5] and in 1810–12 there were signs of opposition within the livery from a few people who felt that he was not sufficiently anti-whig and that some of his parliamentary associates, such as Whitbread and George Byng (M.P. for

[1] See for instance Whitbread to Lord Grenville, 25 Apr. 1810 (draft), Whitbread MSS., Chewton House, near Bath (consulted by kind permission of Earl Waldegrave); Henry Brougham to Creevey, Wednesday [28 Apr. 1813], Creevey MSS.

[2] *Morning Chronicle*, 4 May 1811. *Statesman*, 11 June 1811; Brit. Mus., Add. MS. 27839 fo. 194. Waithman to Creevey, 28 March 1812, Creevey MSS.

[3] *Morning Chronicle*, 18 June 1814.

[4] J. Cartwright, *Reasons for Reformation* (1809), p. 13. *Cobbett's Political Register*, 21 Apr. 1810, col. 599.

[5] *Cobbett's Political Register*, 16 Apr. 1808, col. 580.

Middlesex), were not wholeheartedly committed to the people's cause.[1]
Distrust of him on these grounds increased in 1813, when over the affair of
the princess of Wales he co-operated with the princess's personal advisers
Whitbread and Brougham, instead of co-operating (as Wood did) with
Cobbett, who was competing with the Mountain for the credit of champion-
ing her cause and wanted to make her the focus of a great popular campaign.[2]
The affair soon blew over (for the time being); but Cobbett was from now
on to be one of Waithman's fiercest opponents, and Henry Hunt became a
member of the livery specifically in order to 'counteract the tricks and
intrigues of the Whig or Waithmanite faction in the City'.[3]

At the end of the war Waithman thus found himself being regarded by
the whigs (or many of them) as a dangerous radical and by the radicals as a
whig. The post-war period was to see an intensification of internecine
conflict on the left—though first, in the City at least, there was a period of
relative solidarity. Over the Corn Bill and the proposed continuation of the
income tax there was strong feeling in London, and the City (with Waithman
very much to the fore) took a major part in the agitations against both.[4]
Then in the latter part of 1816 attention shifted to parliamentary reform.
One result of the very general and severe distress of that winter was that the
Common Council turned decisively against the ministry and in favour of
reform. At a meeting on 28 November Waithman moved resolutions
attributing the country's troubles to the corrupt state of the representation,
and whereas the reform petition of 1810 had been carried by only a handful
of votes, these resolutions were passed by a very large majority (according to
the *Morning Chronicle* only eight or ten hands being held up against them).[5]
He again received overwhelming support in January 1817 when he proposed
that the court should petition the two houses of parliament for triennial
elections and the enfranchisement of copyholders and taxpaying householders.[6] Meanwhile it was in the Common Hall rather than the Common
Council that serious opposition to his policies developed. Hunt, having
intervened on a couple of occasions to criticize the proceedings of the livery
as too moderate,[7] claimed at the great popular meeting in Spa Fields on
15 November 1816 that he himself was the real champion of the people of

[1] Waithman to Creevey, 26 Apr. 1810, Creevey MSS. Creevey to Whitbread,
Wednesday [9 May 1810], Whitbread MSS. (Bedford), no. 379/2. *Examiner*,
27 May 1810, p. 335; 24 June 1810, pp. 395–6. *Statesman*, 11 May 1812.

[2] Waithman to Whitbread, 22 Apr. 1813, Whitbread MSS., no. 2867. Cobbett,
History of the Regency and Reign of George IV (2 vols., 1830–4), i, paras. 159–97.

[3] H. Hunt, *Memoirs, written by himself* (3 vols., 1820–2), iii. 159–64.

[4] C.C. 89, fos. 2–3v, 171–173v. C.H. 9, fos. 296–9. *Statesman*, 28 May, 10 Dec.
1814. Waithman to Whitbread, endorsed Nov. 1814, Whitbread MSS., no. 5328.
Sharpe, iii. 292–5.

[5] C.C. 90, fos. 377–380v. *Morning Chronicle*, 29 Nov. 1816.

[6] C.C. 91, fos. 9–15. *The speech delivered by Mr. Waithman in the Court of Common
Council on the 23d of January, 1817, upon a motion for petitioning parliament for a
reduction in the public expenditure and a reform in the representation of the people*
(1817).

[7] *Statesman*, 14 Dec. 1814. *Morning Chronicle*, 22 Aug. 1816.

London; the 'City Patriots' of Waithman's ilk, he said, were basically unconcerned about the sufferings of the poor and were 'afraid to appear any where except in their own little conclave and surrounded by their own myrmidons'.[1] In the Common Council on 28 November Waithman said in reply (showing some prescience, in view of the attempted insurrection which emerged from the second Spa Fields meeting on 2 December) that he had no objection to popular meetings,

even in the fields, when other places were denied them; but while every man could meet in his own ward or his own parish, he was not friendly to an assembly which professed to call exclusively upon the lowest order of the people, and which, by being held in the open air, would naturally contain loose and suspicious individuals.[2]

On 29 November the two men came into direct conflict when resolutions in favour of universal suffrage and annual parliaments were moved at a Common Hall, and seconded in a long speech by Hunt. Waithman proposed as an amendment another set of resolutions which recommended in more general terms 'that parliaments may be reduced to a constitutional duration, and that the people may be restored to their fair and just share in the election thereof'. He opposed the original resolutions as calculated to divide the friends of reform; and his counter-resolutions were eventually adopted, though not by a very large majority.[3] He won another victory, this time more decisive, on 31 January 1817 when Hunt made an unsuccessful attempt to substitute annual for triennial parliaments in a petition of the livery to the house of commons.[4] Hunt did achieve one success at Waithman's expense later in 1817. When at the end of May Alderman Combe wrote a letter to the livery regretting that ill health had prevented him from opposing the government's repressive legislation in the Commons, Hunt declared that the City needed a representative who *could* attend and protest against such measures; and he moved and carried (after a stormy debate) a resolution requesting Combe to resign his seat.[5] Matthew Wood was lord mayor, and Hunt calculated—as he explains in his memoirs—that if Combe could be made to resign at this point, Wood (whom Hunt refers to as 'my worthy friend') would be certain to obtain the vacant seat. This is just what happened: Combe took the Chiltern Hundreds, Wood was nominated to succeed him, and Waithman, while reminding the livery that he had obtained more votes than Wood at the last election, offered no opposition.[6] However, this was merely a personal setback for Waithman. In the Common Hall he confirmed his dominance over the extreme radicals in the following February, when he and Favell moved resolutions complaining of the oppressive conduct of ministers during the suspension of the

[1] *Times*, 16 Nov. 1816.
[2] *Morning Chronicle*, 29 Nov. 1816.
[3] C.H. 9, fos. 348v–350v. *Morning Chronicle*, 30 Nov. 1816.
[4] C.H. 10, fos. 6–13. *Morning Chronicle*, 1 Feb. 1817.
[5] *Morning Chronicle*, 31 May 1817.
[6] *Ibid.*, 4, 5, 11 June 1817. Hunt, iii. 484–91.

Habeas Corpus Act. T. J. Wooler, editor of the *Black Dwarf*, objected to these resolutions as insufficiently strong and moved another set of his own, which Hunt seconded. But their proposals were negatived by a large majority, and *The Times* commented:

That party, whose ignorant and disgusting violence has long done so much injury to the cause of the people, and afforded the only pretext for the late inroad on the Constitution, were wholly baffled and disgraced by the more scientific movements of the friends of rational and constitutional reform.[1]

Waithman thus managed to keep the livery as well as the Corporation committed to the moderate position which he favoured—but efforts to build up a movement for moderate reform on a wider stage were less successful. He was involved in such an attempt early in 1817. The leaders of the popular radical agitation had planned for 22 January a meeting in London to be attended by delegates from Hampden and Union Clubs all over the country.[2] Waithman himself had been elected to the original Hampden Club in June 1812 (at the same time as Lord Byron),[3] but he now felt that Cartwright and his friends were going too far.[4] He therefore welcomed the news that some respectable Westminster tradesmen who favoured economy and moderate reform and wished to declare their separation from the extremists were planning a dinner-meeting in London and were hoping to establish some concert with the parliamentary Opposition.[5] He eagerly associated himself with this project, and wrote to Lord Holland on 14 January:

It is to be regretted that there has been so little communication between the leading Members opposed to the present corrupt system of Government, and those who have devoted their labors to the same end in the City of London that they have scarcely ever understood each others views as to the most effective mode of proceeding. The time has now arrived when the circumstances of the Country, and the distresses of the people, will force upon the consideration of Parliament, the question of reform, both with regard [to] the expenditure of the public money and the state of the representation in a manner not to be resisted.—To give to the public opinion a safe temperate and constitutional direction must depend upon the great and leading Characters in Parliament, and men of respectability throughout the Country,— unless they now come forward I fear the business will fall into bad and unskilful hands,—whose folly and violence may lead to mischeivous consequences.—I am glad to find a meeting is to be held, which I mean to attend on Friday next at the free masons Tavern with a view of bringing forward and uniting the leading and respectable part of the community.[6]

[1] C.H. 10, fos. 48–56. *Times*, 25 Feb. 1818.
[2] Minute of 30 Dec. 1816, 'Proceedings of the Hampden Club 1814–22', Brit. Mus., 8135 f. 19.
[3] *Examiner*, 14 June 1812, p. 384.
[4] For his disagreement with 'the indefatigable Major', see Waithman to Holland, 14 Jan. 1817, Brit. Mus., Add. MS. 51828.
[5] On the origins of this plan and the first approaches to the whigs, see George Tierney to Grey, 19, 24 Dec. 1816, Grey MSS.
[6] Brit. Mus., Add. MS. 51828.

When this meeting took place on 17 January Waithman was one of the main speakers and made an earnest and conciliatory appeal to the whigs.[1] A week later he was part of a deputation that waited on Lord Grey to ask his support for the objects of the meeting;[2] and he also requested Grey and Holland to present to the house of lords the petitions for moderate reform which were approved by the Common Council on 23 January and by the livery on the 31st. Writing again to Holland shortly before these were due to be presented, he said that if only the whigs would commit themselves to the people, the latter

would immediately discard all visionary adventurers and your Lordship and your friends might immediately carry the whole country along with you—you may lose a few votes in parliament altho I greatly doubt it, but you will be more than compensated by the affection and support of a grateful nation.[3]

However, these appeals had as little effect as those he had made five or six years before. Holland wrote to Waithman before the Freemasons' Tavern meeting saying that although the Opposition was united on the questions of retrenchment and religious liberty there was no consensus, either inside or outside parliament, on the question of parliamentary reform—which was therefore unlikely, in the foreseeable future, to be a practicable measure.[4] Tierney did apparently feel at this time that the whigs should put themselves at the head of the moderate reformers, but Thomas Grenville thought it would be thoroughly objectionable to 'curry favour with Waithman by voting for triennial Parliaments', and Grey was convinced that the reform question should be left to individuals and excluded from any consideration of what the party stood for.[5] In his interview with the Freemasons' Tavern deputation Grey referred them to the distinctly lukewarm remarks he had made about reform in 1810; and in presenting the City petitions to the house of lords on 18 February he and Holland both spent less time recommending reform than they did explaining why it should *not* be regarded as indispensable.[6] The Freemasons' Tavern group (who called themselves the Friends of Economy, Public Order and Reform) had planned a second meeting to which whig sympathisers in parliament would be invited, but when this was held on 22 February the only M.P.s who attended were Thomas Brand and Sir Francis Burdett.[7]

Waithman subsequently wrote with some bitterness of the frigidity and evasiveness the whigs had shown over the whole episode.[8] No doubt their

[1] *Morning Chronicle*, 18 Jan. 1817.
[2] Lady Holland to Horner, 25 Jan. 1817, Brit. Mus., Add. MS. 51644.
[3] Waithman to Holland, 10 Feb. 1817, Brit. Mus., Add. MS. 51828.
[4] Holland to Grey, 17 Jan. 1817, Grey MSS.
[5] Hist. MSS. Comm., *Fortescue MSS.*, x. 421. Grey to Holland, 17 Jan. 1817, Grey MSS.
[6] Lady Holland to Horner, 25 Jan. 1817, Brit. Mus., Add. MS. 51644. Hansard, *Parl. Debates*, xxxv, cols. 420–8.
[7] Tierney to Grey, 24 Dec. 1816, Grey MSS. *Morning Chronicle*, 24 Feb. 1817.
[8] Waithman to Holland, 15 Jan. 1818, Brit. Mus., Add. MS. 51828.

unresponsiveness could partly be explained as a reaction against radical extremism: Waithman himself said at the Common Hall of 31 January— ten days after Cartwright's meeting of delegates at the Crown and Anchor had approved a resolution moved by Hunt in favour of universal suffrage[1]— that 'he thought the harsh and unaccommodating spirit of those who had led the petitioners of the working classes was one great cause which had prevented the higher ranks also from co-operating in the cause'.[2] But he certainly considered that the whigs themselves were very much to blame in that by failing to commit themselves on the main question that was agitating the country they did nothing to challenge the influence of the extremists and to prevent a possibly dangerous polarization. He also thought that they were misjudging their own interest as a party. Grey's fear was that by making reform into a party tenet he would 'lose the co-operation of many honourable and powerful men';[3] but Waithman may have been right in thinking that the loss of the Grenvilles (who were anyway on the point of separating from the Foxites) and the alienation of one or two powerful whig families would have been more than counterbalanced by the acquisition of a firm basis of support in middle-class opinion—even allowing for the difficulty, under the unreformed system, of translating such support into parliamentary strength. It was significant that at the general election of 1818 almost all the gains made by the Opposition were made by candidates who were avowed reformers—such men as C. F. Palmer, D. W. Harvey, William Williams, Sir Robert Wilson and Waithman himself—rather than by 'high' whigs. John Colman Rashleigh, the Cornish reformer who, like Waithman, had been urging the whigs to take up moderate reform, wrote in 1819:

The issue of the late Election has, it is said, been appealed to by the Whigs, as a triumphant proof of their returning popularity; but where has there been an Election at which the sense of the people was really taken, and at which an opponent of the Ministry was returned, and *the object of the public choice has not been a known Reformer*? and that circumstance, his strongest recommendation?[4]

The contest in the City provided the reformers with the most notable of their successes at this general election. Three of the candidates returned, Wood, Waithman and Alderman J. T. Thorp (who had moved the resolutions at the Freemasons' Tavern meeting in January 1817) were committed to reform.[5] It is true that in the general election of 1820 there was to be a reaction: the election took place soon after the exposure of the Cato Street conspiracy, and the tories—partly it seems through a systematic use of

[1] *Examiner*, 26 Jan. 1817, pp. 57-8.
[2] *Morning Chronicle*, 1 Feb. 1817.
[3] See J. R. Fenwick to Wyvill, 28 Dec. 1816, Wyvill MSS., Yorkshire North Riding County R.O.
[4] *The speech of John Colman Rashleigh, Esq., on returning thanks for the silver vase, voted to him by public subscription, for his exertions in the cause of a parliamentary reform* (1819), p. 57n.
[5] *Statesman*, 6, 17, 18, 23, 24 June 1818.

influence against Waithman[1]—succeeded in ousting both him and Thorp. He was re-elected, however, in 1826 and remained a member for the City until his death in 1833. During the last fifteen years of his life he held several distinguished positions: besides his membership of parliament he was an alderman from July 1818, sheriff in 1820–1, and lord mayor in 1823–4. Yet it was the earlier part of his career that saw his most impressive achievements. For one thing it was a remarkable success-story. It was thought to be unprecedented for a retail trader to become a member of parliament for the City, and it was very rare for a Common Councillor to do so without graduating through the Court of Aldermen.[2] Waithman was not of course the 'mere shopkeeper' that his opponents made him out to be: he was a man of considerable substance who had handed over the running of the business to his sons and owned a house at Winchmore Hill and a hundred acres.[3] But his humble background and lack of education had exposed him to much prejudice and hostility. The whig poet Thomas Moore wrote in June 1811 about a recent fête at Carlton House: 'It was said that Mr. Waithman, the patriotic linendraper, had got a card; and every odd-looking fellow that appeared, people said immediately, "That's Mr. Waithman"'. To Coleridge, Waithman was a typical example of the loquacious but uncivilized radical—as essentially savage (the poet said) as a negro or New Zealander.[4] Others charged him with inflated ambition and self-importance. He did have a tendency towards egotism and self-righteousness;[5] and—although in someone of higher social status this would doubtless have been less remarked on—he was certainly ambitious. When accused at a ward meeting in 1812 of wishing to use the Common Council as a stepping-stone to parliament, he did not deny the charge but asked why such an ambition should be considered wrong. What he did deny was that he had ever made his public conduct subservient to his private aims;[6] and to the historian his personal successes and shortcomings are of less significance than the principles which he consistently represented and did much to revive.

His radicalism was basically of the kind that Engels was to brand contemptuously as 'shopkeepers' radicalism':[7] indeed he might figure in Marxist demonology as the prophet and prototype of the post-1832 shopoc-

[1] *Times*, 26 Feb., 17 March, 13 Apr. 1820. Cobbett's continuous abuse of him as a lukewarm moderate, a 'shoy-hoy', an 'empty insignificant coxcomb', etc., may also have had some effect (*Cobbett's Political Register*, 28 Nov. 1818, cols. 289–96; 14 Aug. 1819, cols. 22–4; 2 Oct. 1819, col. 211).

[2] Cf. *Morning Chronicle*, 13 March, 26 June, 9 July 1818.

[3] *Ibid.*, 23 May 1807, 15 Aug. 1817.

[4] *The Letters of Thomas Moore*, ed. W. S. Dowden (2 vols., Oxford, 1964), i. 153. *The Letters of S. T. Coleridge*, ed. E. L. Griggs (6 vols., Oxford, 1956–72), iv. 714.

[5] Cf. Cobbett, *Regency and Reign of George IV*, i, para. 177; Goodwin to Grey, 24 Dec. 1812, Grey MSS.; Roberts, p. 246n. (quoting from Crabb Robinson's diary).

[6] *Statesman*, 22, 24 Dec. 1812.

[7] F. Engels, *The Condition of the Working Class in England*, introduced by E. Hobsbawm (1969), p. 266.

racy. In 1812, in response to the attempts of his opponents to ridicule his pretensions as a parliamentary candidate, he asked why the shopkeepers of the nation should not be represented in the legislature as well as landowners and merchants;[1] and several of his main political preoccupations—notably his campaign against the income tax and his strong opposition to the Insolvent Debtors Act (which, he said, had 'opened the flood gates of fraud extravagance and dissapation to the loss and ruin of the industrious and honest')[2]—reveal his concern for the interests of this class. Moreover, like Francis Place, whom in many ways he resembled, he seems to have derived from his own experience an unrealistic idea of the value of the 'middle-class virtues' as a prescription for society in general. The nature of his social and economic assumptions can be gathered from two long speeches he delivered at public meetings held in August 1817 to consider Robert Owen's 'Plan for the Employment, Instruction and Re-moralization of the Poor'. He said of Owen's scheme for villages of co-operation:

...the object of Mr. Owen's plan was to ameliorate the condition and character of society. Could, however, such a result be looked for from the adoption of a plan which proposed to isolate a great body of the people—to exclude them from all the prizes that were held out to society at large to excite to exertion and industry? Could any good consequence be expected from a plan, which would operate to suppress the best motives of human action, and to extinguish the warmest feelings of the human heart, by shutting up the people in barracks?

He objected to a system in which parents would no longer be responsible for the care of their own children, and in which 'all distinctions of intellect and industry' would be ignored. The ultimate tendency of Owen's plan, he thought, was 'that all the property of the country should be placed under the management of Government, which, in return, was to supply the people with merely food and raiment'—and in such a state of affairs all feelings of self-reliance would be obliterated. At the second of the two meetings Waithman moved as an alternative to Owen's proposals, and carried by a majority of two to one, resolutions calling for 'such a system of reformation and retrenchment as would tend to restore the happiness and the prosperity of the nation'.[3] Like most radicals of his day (including Hunt and Cobbett) he tended to attribute distress too sweepingly to high taxation; and like them he lacked what E. P. Thompson calls a 'constructive social theory'.[4] Yet the limitations of his outlook and sympathies should not be exaggerated. Though he was a believer in incentives and self-help, he was not an inhumane laissez-faire dogmatist. He advocated the enclosure of common lands to provide smallholdings for the poor, and he expressed himself strongly in favour of legislation to limit the working hours of children—not only in

[1] *Statesman*, 2 Oct. 1812.
[2] Waithman to Whitbread, endorsed Nov. 1814, Whitbread MSS., no. 5328. Cf. Hansard, *Parl. Debates*, xxxix, cols. 180–2.
[3] *Morning Chronicle*, 15, 22 Aug. 1817.
[4] E. P. Thompson, *The Making of the English Working Class* (2nd edn., 1968), p. 862.

factories but in the 'sweated trades' which he knew at first hand.[1] Still, it is certainly in the political field that he has most claim to be regarded as constructive. He led the long campaign which transformed the City of London from a bastion of Pittite loyalism into one of moderate reform; and within the national reform movement (although at times his attitude to the whigs may have been too harsh and antagonistic) he deserves to be remembered as a pioneer of conciliation. He said in 1813 that the intention of his annual dinners of the livery was to remove the mutual suspicions of the aristocratic and plebeian sections of the reform movement, and in the Common Hall in November 1816 he said, 'My wish is to procure a rational and constitutional Reform, and that can only be obtained by conciliating the union of all its friends, by promoting their complete and cordial cooperation'.[2] It was by such means—though the actual proposals he put forward in 1817 were closer to the second Reform Bill than to the first—that the measure of 1832 was to be carried. When this was originally introduced in March 1831 the Common Council led the petitioning movement in its favour,[3] and in the debates that followed Waithman was one of the bill's firmest supporters in the house of commons.

[1] *Morning Chronicle*, 15 Aug. 1817.
[2] *Statesman*, 15 Apr. 1813. *Morning Chronicle*, 30 Nov. 1816.
[3] J. R. M. Butler, *The Passing of the Great Reform Bill* (1914), p. 201. In the Common Council, according to Wood, only one hand was held up against the petition (Hansard, *Parl. Debates*, 3rd ser., iii, col. 14).

5

Charles Hall, Early English Socialist*

Charles Hall's importance has been recognized by a number of scholars. He has been described by C. R. Fay as "the first of the early socialists", and by Mark Blaug as "the first socialist critic of the industrial revolution".[1] According to Max Beer he provided "the first interpretation of the voice of rising Labour", and Anton Menger regarded him as "the first socialist who saw in rent and interest unjust appropriations of the return of labour, and who explicitly claimed for the worker the undiminished product of his industry".[2] Menger, in his book *The Right to the Whole Produce of Labour* (first published in German in 1886), devoted three or four pages to Hall and drew attention to his early formulation of the theory of surplus value. Since then there have been several discussions of Hall's work, but almost without exception they have been quite brief: perhaps the most notable are those provided by H. S. Foxwell in his introduction to the English translation of Menger,[3] and by Beer in his *History of British Socialism*.[4] H. L. Beales, who also wrote a few pages about him in his

---

* I am grateful to Mr John Hooper for his helpful comments on a draft of this article.

[1] C. R. Fay, Life and Labour in the Nineteenth Century, 3rd ed. (Cambridge, 1943), p. 168; M. Blaug, Ricardian Economics (New Haven, 1958), p. 148.

[2] M. Beer, A History of British Socialism, 3rd ed. (2 vols; London, 1953), I, p. 127; A. Menger, The Right to the Whole Produce of Labour, translated by M. E. Tanner, with an introduction by H. S. Foxwell (London, 1899), p. 48.

[3] Ibid., pp. xxxi-xxxviii. In a manuscript note in one of the copies of Hall's The Effects of Civilization in the Goldsmiths' Library of Economic Literature, University of London, Foxwell wrote: "It is a really wonderful statement, in the clearest terms, of the first principles of modern Socialism."

[4] Beer, op. cit., I, pp. 126-32. See also H. L. Beales, The Early English Socialists (London, 1933), pp. 72-75; Alexander Gray, The Socialist Tradition: Moses to Lenin (London, 1946), pp. 262-69; Alexandre Chabert, "Aux sources du socialisme anglais: un pré-marxiste méconnu: Charles Hall", in: Revue d'Histoire Economique et Sociale, XXIX (1951), pp. 369-83. This last piece is enthusiastic about Hall, but is marred by inaccuracy and adds little of substance to earlier accounts.

book *The Early English Socialists*, lamented some twenty years ago that Hall (in common with several other pioneers of socialism and democracy in Britain) had not yet found a biographer.[1] In fact it seems unlikely, owing to the paucity of material, that a biography will ever be possible. But it is nonetheless surprising that Hall has received so little individual attention; and the author of a recent summary of his ideas (again in the context of a general history of socialism) could describe him as "ce précurseur quelque peu oublié".[2] It appears that an essay may usefully be written drawing together what is known about him and attempting a fuller examination of his writings than has been provided hitherto.

Hall was born in 1738 or 1739: so much can be gathered from the records of the University of Leyden which show that "Carolus Hall, Anglus", matriculated there in May 1765 at the age of 26.[3] He obtained the degree of M.D. from that university with a thesis on pulmonary consumption, and he published in 1785 *The Family Medical Instructor*, which was described in the *Monthly Review* as "a compilation from different authors on medical subjects calculated for the general use of country families".[4] The fact that the book was printed at Shrewsbury suggests that Hall was then practising in that area, but twenty years later when he published the work for which he is remembered, *The Effects of Civilization on the People in European States*, he was living and practising at Tavistock.

The chief sources of information about this latter part of his career are two letters which he wrote to Thomas Spence, the advocate of land nationalization, in 1807,[5] and the reminiscences of the Owenite Socialist John Minter Morgan. Hall told Spence in August 1807 that he was a widower of nearly seventy, and that as he found his long rides fatiguing he was intending to retire from his practice before long. He was thinking, he said, of moving to London when he retired, though his family would expect him to live "at little expence", and he asked Spence how much it would cost to rent or purchase a set of chambers

[1] Introduction to R. K. P. Pankhurst, William Thompson (London, 1954), p. viii.

[2] François Bedarida, "Le socialisme en Angleterre jusqu'en 1848", in: Histoire générale du socialisme, I, Des origines à 1875, ed. by Jacques Droz (Paris, 1972), pp. 288-90.

[3] R. W. Innes Smith, English-Speaking Students of Medicine at the University of Leyden (Edinburgh, 1932), p. 105.

[4] Robert Watt, Bibliotheca Britannica (4 vols; Edinburgh, 1824), I, p. 458; Monthly Review, LXXVI (1787), p. 74.

[5] These letters are preserved in the Place Papers, together with two letters from Spence to Hall, British Library (formerly British Museum), Add. Mss 27808, ff. 280-85.

in one of the less frequented Inns of Court.[1] That he did in due course move to London, though not to one of the Inns of Court, is clear from Morgan's memories of him. After praising *The Effects of Civilization*, Morgan goes on to say:

> "The author was in very reduced circumstances, – his work was published without funds to make it known: and as it concerned the poor who could not purchase, no bookseller would incur the risk of advertising. Dr. Hall reached the age of eighty years; but he died in the Rules of the Fleet prison, where I frequently saw him: occasionally when he could obtain a day-rule he dined at my chambers; – his conversation was particularly animated and intelligent: although skilled in the classics, he was more distinguished for attainments in natural philosophy. He had friends who would have released him from prison; but he was confined through a lawsuit, – as he considered unjustly; and rather than permit the money to be paid, he had resolved to remain incarcerated for life."[2]

The records of the Fleet Prison show that the sum involved was small (£157) but that Hall remained in detention for eight and a half years from the time of his arrest in Somerset in December 1816. He did not apparently die in the rules of the Fleet, for there is a record of his being discharged on 21 June 1825, but as he was then eighty-six it is not unlikely that he died soon afterwards.[3]

Hall's one major work, *The Effects of Civilization*, was first published in London in 1805, and reprinted in 1813. Appended to the latter edition, and to some copies of the former, was a shorter work entitled *Observations on the Principal Conclusion in Mr. Malthus's Essay on Population*.[4] A further edition of the main work, omitting the *Observations on Malthus* but otherwise unaltered except for the title-page, appeared in 1820 under the title *An Enquiry into the Cause of the Present Distress of the People*. In 1850 John Minter Morgan reprinted *The Effects of Civilization* in a series called *The Phoenix Library*;[5] and

[1] Hall to Spence, 25 August 1807, ibid., f. 280.
[2] [J. M. Morgan,] Hampden in the Nineteenth Century (2 vols; London, 1834), I, pp. 20-21.
[3] Public Record Office, PRIS 2/118, No 18187; 10/149, f. 4.
[4] Although the shorter work has its own title-page, the pagination continues that of The Effects of Civilization, the pages being numbered 325-49.
[5] This is the only edition held by the British Library, and Beer believed it to be the second edition and the only one extant. But several copies of the 1805 edition survive, for instance in the British Library of Political and Economic

in 1905 a German translation (not of the whole work but of selected chapters) was published in a series of *Hauptwerke des Sozialismus und der Sozialpolitik* edited by Georg Adler.[1]

In the preface to *The Effects of Civilization* Hall says that although the practice of medicine may not at first sight provide a qualification for writing on political subjects, a physician does have unique opportunities for studying the condition of the people, being admitted into their homes, being able to observe them at all stages of life, and often being taken into their confidence on a wide range of subjects.[2] The work itself begins with a neutral definition of civilization: "It consists in the study and knowledge of the sciences, and in the production and enjoyment of the conveniences, elegancies, and luxuries of life." But he goes on to say that the most striking feature of civilized societies – the feature that would most impress a visitor from an uncivilized part of the world – is the contrast between the "great profusion and splendor" of some people and "the penury and obscurity of all the others". He concedes that the people in a civilized state may be divided into many different orders, but he maintains that "for the purpose of investigating the manner in which they enjoy or are deprived of the requisites to support the health of their bodies and minds" only the one horizontal division between rich and poor is of real significance.[3]

The basic fact about the rural poor is that they are insufficiently supplied with the necessaries of life. He points specifically to the inadequacy of their wages, the meagre nature of their diet, and the much higher rate of mortality (especially infant mortality) among them than among the richer classes. As for the manufacturing poor, he maintains that the nature of their employment is generally injurious to their health and stultifying to their minds, and to reinforce the latter point he quotes Adam Smith's famous passage on the mental torpor that

Science and in the Goldsmiths' Library; copies of the 1813 edition exist at Columbia University and in the National Library of Australia; and the Goldsmiths' Library has a copy of the edition of 1820.
[1] C. Hall, Die Wirkungen der Zivilisation auf die Massen (Leipzig, 1905). Adler contributed a twenty-page introduction entitled "Mehrwertlehre und Bodenreform in England im 18. Jahrhundert und Charles Hall"; but this threw little if any new light on Hall and his work.
[2] He adds later that the sufferings of the poor, though they "obtrude themselves on every body's notice", present themselves "more unavoidably and affectingly to a medical practitioner than to any other person". The Effects of Civilization on the People in European States (London, 1805), p. 223.
[3] Ibid., pp. 1-4. Hall did not actually use the word "horizontal", but this was clearly his meaning; cf. Harold Perkin, The Origins of Modern English Society 1780-1880 (London, 1969), p. 209.

results from the division of labour. Hall is in no doubt that the physical
and mental deprivations suffered by the poor do amount to a deprivation of happiness: the attempts of certain writers and preachers to
recommend contentment to the poor by arguing that "the measure of
happiness is much the same in all conditions" he describes as "adding
insult to oppression".[1] Treating the hardships of the poor as too
obvious to require further description, he proceeds in the sections
which follow to analyse the causes of these hardships.

In his opinion scarcity (which he believes to be a chronic condition
in European states, not one confined to years of bad harvest) is
basically due to the fact that too few people are employed in cultivating
the land. The cultivators furnish provisions for themselves, for those
employed in trade and manufactures, and for those who do nothing.
Commerce in itself is unproductive, and international trade only
contributes to the people's sustenance when the goods exported are
exchanged for "articles of prime necessity": Hall does not believe that
this happens to any significant extent since the imports of European
countries consist mainly of various luxury goods, very few of which
"come down to the use of the poor".[2] As for manufacturing industry,
Hall admits the need for what he calls coarse manufactures, producing
articles of "prime and general use"; but he believes that far too many
hands are employed in the "refined" manufactures, which produce
articles that are purchased only by the rich.

The fact that so much labour is diverted from occupations which
produce the necessaries and comforts of life for the people themselves
to other occupations which do not – and which on the contrary sentence
those employed in them to work in offensive and often noxious conditions – can only be attributed in Hall's view to some kind of compulsion; and his analysis of this compulsion leads him on to a radical
interpretation of property. In the hands of the rich, he says, are concentrated all those things which compose wealth: the land, the
livestock and crops raised on it, the raw materials and machinery of
industry, and stocks of manufactured goods ready for sale. The rich
thus control, and the law firmly secures to them, all those things that
the poor man stands in need of; and they can consequently require
from him as a condition of providing for his basic needs whatever

[1] Effects of Civilization, pp. 4ff., 24-26, 28-30. He probably had in mind William
Paley, Reasons for Contentment addressed to the Labouring Part of the British
Public (London, 1793), and Richard Watson, Bishop of Llandaff, Sermon
preached before the Stewards of the Westminster Dispensary (London, 1793) – a
sermon entitled "On the wisdom and goodness of God in having made both
rich and poor".
[2] Effects of Civilization, pp. 36-38, 82-83.

work they please. Hence wealth is definable as "the possession of that
which gives power over, and commands the labour of man". Since the
rich consume only a limited quantity of the necessaries of life the major
part of their income is spent on various refinements and luxuries, and
their demand for such things means that a large section of the labouring
class can only find employment in supplying them. Hume had been
praised by Adam Smith for being the first to observe that manufactures
had freed the people from servile dependence on the feudal barons;
but he failed to recognize, says Hall, "the new species of dependence
of the lower orders on the rich". Although a poor man in a modern
society is not obliged to work for any particular individual, he has to
work for some member of the wealthy class, and "the power of wealth
pervades the whole country, and subjects every poor man to its
dominion".[1]

Next Hall considers some of the lines of argument that have been
used to defend or justify the existing system of property. With regard
to arguments based on natural right, Hall denies that any man can
have a natural, original and exclusive right to any portion of land,
except perhaps to as much as will furnish him and his family with the
necessaries of life; and with regard to prescriptive rights, he maintains
that an unjust appropriation of the land does not "become just by
time" unless time removes the sufferings which the original injustice
produced. As for the incentives doctrine advanced by Hume and Paley
in their utilitarian defence of property, Hall's reply to it is worth
quoting *in extenso*:

> "It has been alleged, that if property were not to be acquired,
> and held out as a reward of labour and industry, mankind would
> be indolent and inactive, having no stimulus to exertion. In my
> apprehension this is directly contrary to what really happens.
> Things of every kind being already appropriated and in the
> possession of certain persons, and firmly secured to them by the
> laws; the prizes, which might be held out to be gained by the
> many, are taken, as it were, out of the wheel; and the chance of a
> man, without education or connexion (which is the condition of
> the great mass of mankind) of bettering his fortune by any efforts
> of his own, is a thousand to one against him; so as utterly to act
> as a discouragement to all attempts of that kind."[2]

In response to Burke's view, expressed in his *Thoughts and Details on
Scarcity*, that the rich are as useful to the poor as the poor are to the

[1] Ibid., pp. 38-52.
[2] Ibid., pp. 55-60.

rich, Hall says that while the poor man produces by his labour almost everything that the rich man eats, drinks, wears and enjoys, the rich do nothing for the poor man except give him access, through money, to a modicum of those goods which poor men have produced, and which he might have provided for himself in much greater quantity if his labour had been at his own disposal.[1] It is to the interest of the rich man to get as much of the poor man's labour, and to give him as little of the produce of that labour, as he can, and the control of the rich over the means of life ensures that they are almost always in a position to dictate terms to those they employ.[2]

Hall tries to calculate statistically – by estimating the average working-class family income, multiplying it by the number of such families, and dividing this figure into an estimate of the total produce of labour in agriculture and industry – how much of the produce of his own labour is actually consumed by the working man and his family; and he concludes that the proportion is only about one eighth.[3] Moreover, Hall believes that because of "the opportunities that wealth gives to acquire more wealth" there is a clear tendency for the rich to get richer; and since the accumulation of wealth in its various forms extends its possessors' claims over the labour of the poor and diminishes the proportion of that labour devoted to producing what the poor themselves require, the condition of the poor tends to deteriorate conversely. This is brought about "not only by those already in a state of subjection being placed in a state of still greater subjection, but also because more people are reduced to that state" – those on the borderline between rich and poor being forced down below it.[4] As the hardships of the poor become more and more difficult to bear, it is likely that a spirit of resistance will begin to show itself – first in a greater frequency of thefts and robberies, and then in open insurrection;

[1] Ibid., pp. 100-03; Edmund Burke, Thoughts and Details on Scarcity (London, 1800), p. 3. Burke and his pamphlet are not specifically named, but the allusion to them seems clear enough.

[2] Effects of Civilization, pp. 111-13. Hall also alludes here to the combination laws; on the so-called freedom of contract, cf. pp. 72-73: "There is no voluntary compact equally advantageous on both sides, but an absolute compulsion on the part of masters, and an absolute necessity on the part of the workman to accept of it."

[3] Ibid., pp. 116-18.

[4] Ibid., pp. 91-95. In a later section (pp. 138-40) Hall describes the dread of poverty felt by those just above the dividing line, and their "continual struggle and jostling" to prevent themselves from sinking below it. He also remarks on the fierce competition produced among the poor themselves by the insufficiency of the means of life: "every man's interest becomes opposite to every man's".

and this in turn will produce an increasingly repressive mode of government.[1]

Hall sees the state and its institutions as instruments of class domination. Almost all civilized states are aristocracies of wealth, he says, since it is in the hands of the wealthy that effective power of all kinds – political, ecclesiastical, military – is lodged. Even in absolute monarchies the authority of the monarch is dependent on the support of the rich, who expect in return for their support that the monarch's power will be used to preserve their wealth. Hall cites Smith's remark that civil government, insofar as it is instituted for the security of property, is in reality instituted for the defence of the rich against the poor; and he adds that the powers requisite for this purpose need to be very extensive.

> "To keep people that are cold, naked, and hungry, from taking fuel to warm themselves, clothes to cover themselves with, and food to satisfy their hunger, when plenty of all those things are before their eyes, [...] requires a magistracy armed with powers indeed; they must have a power of inflicting punishments greater than the sufferings of the poor; which, as these sufferings are continual and unremitting, it is not easy to invent."[2]

However, Hall notes that "artifice" as well as the more naked forms of power has contributed to the subjugation of the poor. He points out that the monopoly of knowledge is a vital aspect of the supremacy of the rich,[3] and he maintains that the realities of exploitation are quite successfully disguised even from the poor themselves. Since exploitation (he does not use the actual word) is carried on "in a regular, orderly, silent manner, under specious forms, with the external appearance of liberty, and even of charity, greater deprivations are submitted to by the poor, and more oppression exercised over them, [...] than force alone was ever known to accomplish".[4] One of the most striking examples, he suggests, of the way in which the poor are made to serve the purposes of the rich is provided by war. Modern warfare arises from competition between the rich of the different civilized countries for the control of trade or territories which will help to supply their inordinate wants; or it can arise merely from the

[1] Ibid., p. 99.
[2] Ibid., pp. 74-75, 115, note, 181-82.
[3] Ibid., pp. 151-52: "Learning, in the unequal shares it is divided among individuals in Europe, is clearly prejudicial; giving some an unfair advantage over others [...]. It is the chief instrument by which the superiority is gained by the few over the many; and by which the latter are kept in subjection."
[4] Ibid., p. 213.

arrogance and ambition of the rich and powerful. While it is the poor who bear the burden of warfare (both in the fighting itself and through a further diversion of national resources away from the production of the necessaries of life), they stand to gain nothing from it: indeed wars are sometimes entered into, as in the case of the war against revolutionary France, for the deliberate purpose of increasing their subjection. Yet so great is the hold of the few over the many that they "can call them out into the field at any time".[1]

Does Hall see any possible remedy for the situation he describes? He recognizes that, strong though the position of the rich may be, it will be endangered when oppression is carried to "a certain point which cannot be borne by the people". But he is not preaching or confidently predicting revolution: on the contrary, he wishes to avoid anything of that nature. The practical proposals he puts forward are much more moderate than his previous analysis would lead one to expect, and he explains his caution by saying that great disorders and even convulsions are apt to be produced, in the political as well as the physical constitution, by "a hasty and indiscreet use of powerful remedies". The redress of political grievances should not if possible be entrusted to those who are aggrieved, as they can hardly be expected to effect it in a cool and temperate manner; "it would be better therefore that the redress of the grievances of the poor should originate from the rich themselves".[2]

One must admit that other sections of his work make this outcome seem rather unlikely. He has shown that the education of the rich leaves them almost wholly ignorant of the condition of the poor, and imbued not with philanthropy but with a love of glory. The history of their country is presented to them as if it were exclusively a history of kings, lords, bishops and generals, and "the books they read treat of little else than of heroes and the exploits of heroes, that is, of bloody warriors and bloody wars". Insofar as political economy is studied, Hall does not believe that it is approached in the same dispassionate way as some other branches of knowledge. Being a complex and abstract subject, it can only be handled by people of education, but these are generally people of some property or members of the learned professions, "for whose interest it is that things should remain as they are". Some of these people will actively discountenance and do

---

[1] Ibid., pp. 166-74. Cf. H. W. Laidler, A History of Socialist Thought (London, 1927), pp. 99-100: "Hall's economic analysis of the causes of war sounds as if it had been made but yesterday." Hall was not thinking in terms of competition for markets or outlets for capital, but he did anticipate Hobson in locating the roots of imperialism in the unequal distribution of wealth in civilized countries.
[2] Effects of Civilization, pp. 190, 215-16.

their best to discredit any attempts to present the truth about social conditions; others, though not wilfully blind to the truth, will tend unconsciously to close their minds to it. "As our interest secretly biasses us in favour of everything that promotes itself, so does it secretly divert us from everything that opposes itself."

Nevertheless, despite his awareness of what Bentham termed "sinister interest" and "interest-begotten prejudice", Hall finds it impossible to believe that once the rich are made fully acquainted with the evils occasioned by their wealth they will resist the reforms necessary to alleviate them.[1] He is particularly sanguine about this because the measures he has in mind will be gradual in their operation and will not substantially diminish the real comforts of the rich. These measures are, first, as a move towards a more equal distribution of property, the abolition of primogeniture and the laws which support it; and secondly the prohibition of, or the imposition of heavy duties upon, the "refined manufactures", with the aim of bringing about a shift of both labour and capital from industry to agriculture.[2]

These proposals are made in a practical spirit as reforms that might actually be effected in current circumstances. Hall goes on, however, to outline in the closing section of the book the social system which in his view would be most productive of happiness – and here he gives full rein to his Utopian ideals. He takes as his starting point Hume's view that happiness flows from a balanced combination of activity and relaxation, and he maintains that in modern civilized societies neither rich nor poor can be truly happy because the former have an excess of leisure and the latter an excess of toil. The right proportions of labour and rest would be achieved, he thinks, if each man worked only as much as was necessary to support his family and if he were able to enjoy the full fruits of his labour. Hall's ideal is a society in which the land would be collectively owned and distributed to families in allotments proportioned to their numbers (with scope for subsequent adjustments to take account of changes in the number and size of families). Though a few people might be selected to devote themselves to the arts and sciences, and a few others might be retained in industrial employment to provide those necessary articles that could not be produced within the family unit, the way of life would be essentially agrarian and families would be as self-supporting as

[1] Ibid., pp. 156, 172, 227-33.
[2] Ibid., pp. 216-19, 316-17. A further measure which he evidently regards as desirable, though he does not include it in the same initial "package", is a reform of the fiscal system; he recommends a graduated income tax, and supports the proposal with a remarkably clear exposition of the diminishing marginal utility of income (pp. 201-08).

possible. "The labour of a father of a family, working a few hours daily on the land, would provide all the food necessary for its comfortable subsistence; and the industry of the other parts of the family would furnish what was necessary for their clothing, etc." Hall calculates that if the land of Britain were shared out equally, there would be as much as thirty-six acres for each family. But he thinks that very much less than this would be sufficient, and he devotes the last pages of his book to showing how a family of five, possessing a spade, a few mattocks, a cow and some poultry, could support themselves in comfort on a holding of three and a half acres.[1]

A strong believer in the virtues of intensive hoeing, weeding and manuring, Hall is inclined to discount the possibility of diminishing returns to labour in agriculture; at least he claims that "the produce of the land would increase in proportion to the number of hands employed upon it, till the whole has arrived at the most complete garden culture".[2] This is one of the positions from which he argues against Malthus in the *Observations* which form an appendix to his main work.[3] He is prepared to concede the possibility of eventual over-population; but he believes that owing to the vastly increased numbers which the land, if properly distributed and cultivated, could be made to support, this prospect is very remote, and could be almost indefinitely postponed by preventive measures such as colonization and the regulation of marriages. Any tendency there has been in European states for population to press on subsistence has been due not to the growth of population, but to the distribution of wealth and the diversion of labour from agriculture. In the prevailing conditions of inequality, even a *decrease* of population would not make food any the less scarce, as the proportion of the working class employed in producing it would not be allowed to increase.[4]

Malthus had proposed in the second edition of his *Essay on Population* that official notice should be given that no child born after a certain date should ever be entitled to poor relief: "He should be taught that the laws of nature had doomed him and his family to starve; that he had no claim on society for the smallest portion of food."[5] Hall protests

[1] Ibid., pp. 259-66, 277-78, 295ff.

[2] Ibid., p. 317.

[3] On Hall's Observations on Malthus, cf. Foxwell, introduction to Menger, op. cit., pp. xxxv-xxxvi, and Kenneth Smith, The Malthusian Controversy (London, 1951), pp. 52-56. Smith credits Hall with being the earliest of Malthus's critics (apart from Godwin), and says that the ideas he put forward were to "appear over and over again in the course of the subsequent controversy".

[4] Observations on Malthus, pp. 327-34, 346-47.

[5] T. R. Malthus, An Essay on the Principle of Population, 2nd ed. (London, 1803), p. 538.

against the attribution to nature of what is attributable to wealth, and against the injustice of the notion that people who produce in their working lives many times more than they consume should have no claim on society for their subsistence. He acquits Malthus of any deliberate malevolence towards the poor, but fears that his general doctrine will encourage those "who were too much before inclined to oppress, to push their tyranny still further". He concludes that what is necessary to relieve the artificial scarcity that currently exists is a more equal distribution of land.[1]

It goes without saying that in an England still very conscious of the French Revolution and still at war with France the educated classes were even less likely than usual to be receptive to radical ideas about property. When *The Effects of Civilization* first appeared more than one reviewer remarked on its resemblance to the *Discourse on the Origin of Inequality* by "the too celebrated J. J. Rousseau".[2] But in general the book was treated as eccentric and paradoxical, rather than dangerous. Facetious remarks were made about "the sage of Tavistock" and his "new political gospel", and the reviews echoed with complacency the fashionable consensus on economic matters. The *Monthly Review*, for instance, observed:

> "It is mentioned by Dr. Hall as a most distressing circumstance, that 'capitals in almost all sorts of businesses are increasing'; and in his view this capital is a mere instrument of tyranny in the hands of the possessors. How vainly has Dr. Smith exquisitely elucidated the important and beneficial operations of this mighty engine!"

The *Critical Review*, commenting on Hall's division of the people into rich and poor and his dismal description of the latter, asked: "Of what country can the author be speaking? Not of England assuredly." And the *Literary Journal* described the book as one that might arouse discontent among the poor and ignorant, but could only "excite ridicule among the well-informed".[3]

If Hall's views were very far removed from the orthodoxies of his

---

[1] Observations on Malthus, pp. 339-41, 349.
[2] Annual Review and History of Literature, IV (1805), pp. 298-99; Monthly Review, LI (1806), p. 15.
[3] Ibid., pp. 15, 18, 21; Critical Review, Third Series, VI (1805), pp. 50-51; Literary Journal, V (1805), p. 706. James Mill (later a strong opponent of Hodgskinite ideas) was probably the author of this last article, see R. A. Fenn, "James Mill's Political Thought" (Ph.D. (Econ.) thesis, University of London, 2 vols, 1972), II, pp. 26, 142.

time, they were not much less remote from the views of the leading advocates of reform. This is clearly shown by two letters of his which appeared in the *Monthly Magazine* in the years following the publication of his main work. The first was written in the spring of 1807, after Whitbread's bill for a reform of the poor laws had been introduced in the House of Commons.[1] The letter was written (as Hall told Spence) partly as a "general answer to the reviewers", and it restated in abbreviated form the central argument of *The Effects of Civilization*.[2] But it also commented adversely on Whitbread's scheme, maintaining that the measures proposed in it for the alleviation of pauperism would be "circuitous, weak, and of inconsiderable effect", and adding that some of them[3] seemed to be "calculated rather for the easing the contributors to the poor-rates, than for the benefit of those who stand in need of their contributions". The second letter, published in October 1811 under the heading "Thoughts on Corruption, and on the Defects of the Representation of the People in Parliament", dealt with a subject which had been in eclipse since the 1790's but had recently returned to prominence. The letter was signed "C.H., Tavistock", and has not previously been noticed by historians; but it is of considerable interest as it tells us something of Hall's views on the political aspects of reform, which he had virtually passed over in his earlier published work.

Hall observes that, although the influence of government on parliamentary elections is generally reprobated, the influence of other descriptions of men is rarely spoken of with disapproval, though its effects in vitiating the representation of the people may be no less serious:

"Whenever any class of people, whether it is that which composes the ministry or government, whether it is that of landed proprietors, whether it is that of master manufacturers, merchants, etc., is able to send a majority of members to parliament, they can enact such laws as they please; and, unless it can be supposed that these members are perfectly upright men, and wholly regardless of their own interest, they will pass such laws as are favourable to themselves, and unfavourable to the rest of the people. Thus for many centuries, the landed interest prevailed; when we find that laws favourable to themselves, were enacted by them;

[1] Cf. J. R. Poynter, Society and Pauperism: English Ideas on Poor Relief, 1795-1834 (London, 1969), pp. 207ff.
[2] Hall to Spence, 9 June 1807, Place Papers, ibid., f. 282; Monthly Magazine, XXIII (1807), pp. 329-31.
[3] For instance the offer of rewards to working men who brought up their families without assistance from the parish.

namely, the laws for distress for the recovery of the rent of land, when no other debts are recoverable in that severe manner; the game laws; the laws excluding all others but themselves from the house".[1]

It has been argued, Hall notes, that since there are now substantial numbers of merchants and manufacturers in the Commons as well as landowners, a sort of balance has been established between the classes and no "overruling interest or influence" prevails. But he maintains that although in a secondary classification these groups may be considered as having different and even opposing interests, in the "grand and primary division" of the people into rich and poor they form but a single class. Under the present electoral system this class alone is represented. No poor man sits in the House of Commons, and although a few of the poor have votes they are rarely if ever able to cast them freely. Those in the House who do support the poor "in cases that materially affect their own interests, must be, if any such there be, men of uncommon degrees of disinterested virtue, and for the poor to depend on these rarae aves is a very precarious situation". Referring to recent debates in parliament, he says that while members have shown some disposition to reduce bribery they have shown no desire to reduce the influence of property, and they have really been aiming at no more than an adjustment of the balance between different kinds of influence. The reforms that have been proposed take no account of the rights and interests of the poor, for whom such measures would mean a "change of masters, not of their condition".[2]

For its time, Hall's exposition of the class-basis of English politics and legislation is remarkably penetrating. It is true that in some publications of the 1790's one can find passages which anticipate the cogency of his treatment.[3] But it is hard to think of any writer who had combined so fully an uncompromisingly radical critique of the political structure with an equally radical critique of the social and economic system.[4] The latter, of course, was the more fully developed by Hall, and this is his contribution to the development of socialism. Two questions that remain to be discussed concerning it are what

[1] He also mentions in a footnote that in some enclosure bills the removal of a piece of fencing has been made a capital crime. Cf. J. L. and B. Hammond, The Village Labourer, 1760-1832 (London, 1919), p. 64.
[2] Monthly Magazine, XXXII (1811), pp. 226-28.
[3] See for example John Thelwall, The Tribune (3 vols; London, 1795-96), II, pp. 59-62, 82, 376.
[4] William Godwin is a possible exception, though he had not applied himself so directly to the criticism of existing political institutions.

sources he may have used in constructing his theory, and how far he in turn exerted an influence on later writers.

Hall told Spence that he had read few books on the subjects on which he wrote,[1] but the range of references given in *The Effects of Civilization* shows this to have been scarcely true, and various influences on his work can be at least tentatively identified. So far as the origins of his economic ideas are concerned, his emphasis on the land as "the basis, the source and substance of all wealth"[2] is clearly in tune with the Physiocrats, though how far he was acquainted with their works at first hand is not clear. He may have known them partly through the writings of John Gray, whose book *The Essential Principles of the Wealth of Nations* (1797) was to earn Marx's commendation for its accurate summary of Physiocratic doctrine and its dexterity in turning that doctrine against the landowning class.[3] Also, although the general tenor of his work was so different from theirs, Hall appears to have taken a certain amount from the English classical economists, especially Adam Smith. Besides the direct citations of Smith noted above, Hall's assumption that the proper measure of exchange-value is "the quantity of the labour employed in making the things exchanged" would seem to reflect Smith's influence.[4] He may even have drawn something from Malthus: at least Malthus had argued – and Hall notes their agreement on this point – that a nation's commercial and industrial wealth may increase greatly without having any tendency to give the poorer classes a "greater command over the necessaries and conveniences of life".[5] Still more striking as an anticipation of Hall's argument is a passage in Lauderdale's *Inquiry into the Nature and Origin of Public Wealth*, a work which was published in 1804 but was evidently read by Hall as he refers to it more than once in *The Effects of Civilization*. Lauderdale pointed out that the distribution of property determines the nature of demand, and thus "regulates and

[1] Hall to Spence, 25 August 1807, loc. cit.
[2] Effects of Civilization, p. 73.
[3] K. Marx, Theories of Surplus Value (3 vols; London, 1969-72), I, pp. 382-86. Hall does not refer to this work of Gray's but does refer (p. 118) to his pamphlet The Income Tax Scrutinized (London, 1802), which applied to a specific issue the principles expounded in Gray's earlier book.
[4] Effects of Civilization, p. 68. It has been suggested that, with the exception of Hodgskin, the so-called Ricardian Socialists of the next generation derived their labour theory of value more from Smith than from Ricardo. See Esther Lowenthal, The Ricardian Socialists (New York, 1911), p. 103; Blaug, op. cit., pp. 148-49.
[5] Hall, Observations on Malthus, p. 325. Malthus, op. cit., pp. 420-25. Cf. also the first edition of the Essay on Population (London, 1798), pp. 312-13, 320-21, where the point is specifically related to Britain.

decides the channels in which the industry of every society exerts itself". Where there is great inequality there is a high demand for the types of labour that produce goods adapted to the taste of the rich, while the rest of the society suffers "from a diversion to the formation of those things that are calculated to flatter the whims of the luxurious, of a part of the labour and capital that would be more advantageously employed in agricultural industry, for the purpose of procuring an ample supply of the necessaries of life".[1]

So far as more general influences are concerned, it has been observed that there is an echo of Locke in Hall's assertion of a man's right to the fruits of his own labour; and Adler firmly located Hall's work "im Banne der naturrechtlichen Auffassung des Staats- und Gesellschafts-lebens".[2] At the same time, Hall seems to have been concerned as much with considerations of "utility" as he was with natural law or natural rights. The proposition that a man should "enjoy the whole fruits of his labour" is advanced not only as a matter of natural right, but as one of the essential conditions of the people's happiness; and Hall says in one of his letters to Spence that the aim of his system is "to produce the greatest possible happiness to mankind".[3] It is unlikely that Hall was influenced, as William Thompson was, by Bentham, but (of writers in what came to be defined as the utilitarian tradition) he had read Hume and Paley,[4] and was probably indebted above all to William Godwin.

Hall does not actually cite Godwin, but echoes of the *Enquiry Concerning Political Justice* – especially Book VIII, "Of Property" – are not infrequent in his work. The notion, described by Foxwell as Hall's "central idea", that wealth is essentially power over the labour of others is to be found not only in Godwin's *magnum opus* but also, very clearly expressed, in his essay "Of Avarice and Profusion" published in *The Enquirer* (1797).[5] Moreover, in the first edition of his *Political Justice* Godwin had hazarded the view that "in civilized countries the peasant often does not consume more than the twentieth

[1] Earl of Lauderdale, An Inquiry into the Nature and Origin of Public Wealth (London, 1804), pp. 281, 329, 341; Hall, Effects of Civilization, pp. 18, 302, note.
[2] R. L. Meek, Studies in the Labour Theory of Value (London, 1958), p. 126 and note; G. Adler, introduction to Hall, Die Wirkungen der Zivilisation, p. 23.
[3] Effects of Civilization, p. 261; Hall to Spence, 25 August 1807, loc. cit.
[4] See Effects of Civilization, pp. 61-62, for a quotation from Paley's Principles of Moral and Political Philosophy (London, 1785).
[5] Foxwell, introduction to Menger, op. cit., p. xxxii; Godwin, Enquiry concerning Political Justice, 2nd ed. (2 vols; London, 1796), II, pp. 427-28; The Enquirer (London, 1797), p. 177.

part of the produce of his labour"[1] – though it was left to Hall to make a more careful attempt at a quantitative assessment of surplus value. Another famous radical whom Hall did not mention (perhaps because he was afraid that to do so would arouse hostile prejudices) was Thomas Paine. Yet the title of Hall's book, and one of its central themes, were surely derived from the opening section of Paine's *Agrarian Justice* (1797), which argues that civilization "has operated in two ways: to make one part of society more affluent, and the other more wretched, than would have been the lot of either in a natural state".[2]

It is also possible that Hall was acquainted with the works of other critics of inequality such as Mably, Rousseau and Brissot on the Continent, and Wallace and Ogilvie in Britain.[3] But he should not be described, as he has been recently in a distinguished work, as a Spencean.[4] From his correspondence with Spence in 1807 it would appear that he had not previously been acquainted with Spence's work, and the letters reveal some significant differences between them. In particular, just as Spence had criticized Paine's *Agrarian Justice* for being insufficiently radical with regard to property, so Hall criticized Spence for imagining that society could be transformed by the abolition of landownership without the abolition of other forms of wealth: such wealth, being power, would continue to be "exercised by the possessors over the non-possessors".[5]

It was in transmuting anti-landlordism into anti-capitalism, and thus redrawing the lines of class antagonism, that Hall moved on from the position of Ogilvie, Spence and Paine. It is true that he regarded inequality as having *originated* in an unequal distribution of landed property, and also that he regarded all wealth, including that of merchants and manufacturers, as ultimately analysable in terms of

[1] Enquiry concerning Political Justice (2 vols; London, 1793), II, p. 792. In subsequent editions this estimate was dropped.
[2] The Writings of Thomas Paine, ed. by M. D. Conway (3 vols; New York, 1908), III, p. 328.
[3] The only one of these writers actually mentioned by Hall is Brissot, and the work referred to is not his Recherches philosophiques sur le droit de propriété, but his New Travels in the United States of America (London, 1792). The historical examples given by Hall (pp. 280-81) of societies which had successfully established equality of property – the Jews, Sparta and Paraguay – were models commonly cited by egalitarian writers of the eighteenth century: see André Lichtenberger, Le socialisme au XVIIIe siècle (Paris, 1895), pp. 29, note, 60-63, 153, 218, 229, 438.
[4] J. F. C. Harrison, Robert Owen and the Owenites in Britain and America (London, 1969), p. 65.
[5] T. M. Parssinen, "Thomas Spence and the Spenceans" (Ph.D. dissertation, Brandeis University, 1968), pp. 111-12; Hall to Spence, 25 August 1807, loc. cit.

claims to the produce of the land.[1] But he imputed exploitation not only to landowners but to property-owners in general (to all whose wealth gave them control, direct or indirect, over the livelihood of others), and he included men of quite modest means among the adversaries of the poor.[2] Asa Briggs has said that Hall "stated clearly for the first time the central proposition of a class theory of society", and indeed his analysis of class divisions can be regarded as superior even to that of the Ricardian socialists who followed him.[3]

The general question of how far he influenced later socialist and radical writers is, as such questions tend to be, difficult to answer. It is easy enough to find parallels between his writings and those of the Ricardian socialists. For instance, Hodgskin resembled Hall in tracing the origins of inequality, and hence of the power wielded by those who had property over those who had none, to the appropriation of the land by the Germanic conquerors of Western Europe in the Dark Ages.[4] John Gray – the author of *A Lecture on Human Happiness*, not the interpreter of Physiocracy mentioned above – calculated by much the same method as Hall's the proportion of the produce of their labour that was consumed by the productive classes (though, using the statistics published by Patrick Colquhoun in 1814, he arrived at a somewhat different answer).[5] Also, Hall's belief that for the labourer and his family to enjoy the whole produce of their labour would be "the highest inducement to industry that could possibly be conceived" was restated with characteristic verbosity by Thompson in a section entitled "The strongest stimulus to production (and that which is necessary to the greatest production) that the nature of things will permit, is security in the *entire use* of the products of labour, to those who produce them".[6]

---

[1] Effects of Civilization, pp. 71-74.
[2] Hall says at one point (p. 203) that riches may be supposed to commence at an income-level of £150 per annum.
[3] A. Briggs, "The Language of 'Class' in early nineteenth-century England", in: Essays in Labour History, ed. by A. Briggs and J. Saville (London, 1960), p. 48; Janet Kimball, The Economic Doctrines of John Gray 1799-1883 (Washington, D.C., 1948), p. 100.
[4] Hall, Effects of Civilization, pp. 53-55, 132-33; [T. Hodgskin,] Labour Defended against the claims of Capital (London, 1825), p. 20; The Natural and Artificial Right of Property Contrasted (London, 1832), pp. 70-73. As Hall pointed out (Observations on Malthus, p. 341, note), these conquests included the Saxon conquest of England; his historical theory of expropriation thus differed from that of the Diggers and Spenceans, who attributed the process to the Norman Conquest, and from that of Marx, who dated it from the sixteenth century.
[5] J. Gray, A Lecture on Human Happiness (London, 1825), p. 20.
[6] Hall, Effects of Civilization, p. 279; W. Thompson, An Inquiry into the Principles of the Distribution of Wealth (London, 1824), p. 35.

Such repetitions are suggestive, but it is not certain how far they represent direct borrowing from Hall. However, some clear evidence does exist to show that his work was known and appreciated in radical and socialist circles. Although he may not have been justified in claiming in 1808 (in a letter to Arthur Young) that Cobbett and William Spence had appropriated his ideas in their recent attacks on commerce,[1] a long extract from his *Observations on Malthus* did appear in *Cobbett's Political Register* in 1817. Cobbett's sons, moreover, in annotating this passage for their father's *Political Works*, mentioned all three editions of *The Effects of Civilization* and described it as a work of "extraordinary merit".[2] The Owenite George Mudie discussed the book in his periodical *The Economist* in 1821, and in the 1830s it was invoked on occasion by the journalists of the Unstamped press.[3] It was approvingly mentioned by Mary Hennell in her *Outline of the various Social Systems and Communities which have been founded on the Principle of Co-operation*, originally published as an appendix to Charles Bray's *Philosophy of Necessity* (1841);[4] and John Goodwyn Barmby, the man responsible for introducing the word "communist" into the English language, regarded Hall as one of his spiritual ancestors.[5]

It does not seem to be possible with Hall – as it is with Thompson, Hodgskin and J. F. Bray – to establish a direct link between him and Marx, but he did anticipate a number of important Marxist-Leninist doctrines. He was not an innovator in terms of vocabulary, and expressions such as expropriation, surplus value, class antagonisms, proletarianization and imperialism are not to be found in his work; but the concepts are definitely there, in a more or less developed form. As to how Hall himself should be classified in Marxist terminology, he clearly has much in common with the category of "critical-Utopian socialists" described in the *Communist Manifesto*. Socialists of this type, say Marx and Engels, address themselves to society at large without distinction of class and hope to achieve their ends without conflict, believing that once their ideas are properly ventilated and understood they will surely gain general acceptance. It is true that

[1] Hall to Young, 29 November 1808, British Library, Add. Mss 35130, f. 128; R. L. Meek, The Economics of Physiocracy (Cambridge, Mass., 1963), pp. 356, note, 358. On William Spence's sources, see his letter in Cobbett's Political Register, 5 December 1807, cc. 923-25.
[2] Ibid., 4 January 1817, cc. 27-29; Selections from Cobbett's Political Works, ed. by J. M. Cobbett and J. P. Cobbett (6 vols; London, n.d.), V, p. 86, note.
[3] The Economist, 17 February 1821, pp. 49-50; Patricia Hollis, The Pauper Press (Oxford, 1970), p. 203.
[4] C. Bray, The Philosophy of Necessity (2 vols; London, 1841), II, p. 657, note.
[5] W. H. G. Armytage, Heavens Below (London, 1961), pp. 198-99.

Hall made some proposals which, as he expressly claimed, could not be described as Utopian; but his ideal society (to which he devoted much more space) was an extreme example of reactionary Utopianism – so extreme that even Thomas Spence regarded it as impracticable.[1] Moreover, it was undoubtedly on the critical rather than the constructive side that Hall's most impressive contribution was made.[2]

However, while the "critical-Utopian" classification fits him well enough in some respects, in others he points the way to socialism of a rather different type. His originality lay in the fact that he approached the phenomenon of exploitation in an analytic rather than a moralistic way, attempting to explain it in terms of the past development and current operation of economic and social forces. It was on this account that Foxwell went so far as to describe his work as "the foundation of the theory of so-called scientific socialism."[3] Inevitably, Hall's insights into the nature of capitalism and the industrial economy were limited to some extent by the time and place at which he wrote. As the following passage shows, when he discussed capital he had in mind that of the merchant capitalist (still the dominant figure in the West Country woollen industry) rather than the fixed capital of the factory owner:

> "The means enabling tradesmen to share a part of the product of the labour of the poor, is their capital, which puts it in their power to furnish materials to the artificers to work on, and to provide them with immediate subsistence; and on that account is supposed to give the tradesmen a just claim to a part of the productions of the workmen's hands."[4]

[1] Hall told Spence (25 August 1807, loc. cit.): "I think what we should aim at should be to go back a good way towards our natural state; to that point from which we strayed; retaining but little of that only (to wit, of the coarser arts) which civilization has produced, together with certain sciences." But Spence considered that Hall was unrealistic in imagining that people would willingly revert to a "state of barbarism" and "give up every elegant comfort of life" (Spence to Hall, 28 June 1807, Place Papers, ibid., f. 284).

[2] R. H. Tawney, indeed, wrote that Hall was "a conservative critic of capitalism rather than a socialist". It is arguable, however, that by virtue of his social ideal as well as his critical analysis Hall does qualify to be regarded as socialist: according to Henry Collins, Hall "crossed the threshold which Paine reached", and "entered, as Paine did not, directly into the mainstream of modern socialist thought". See Tawney, introduction to Beer, op. cit., I, p. x; Collins, introduction to Paine, The Rights of Man (Harmondsworth, 1969), p. 44; cf. Chabert, op. cit., p. 383.

[3] See the manuscript note cited above, p. 87, note 3; and cf. Menger, op. cit., p. 101, note.

[4] Effects of Civilization, p. 70. Hall himself, of course, considered that "the justice of this mode of acquiring wealth is by no means clear".

Also, Hall did not foresee the extent to which machinery might be used to produce goods for mass consumption; nor did he foresee the scale on which an industrial country might import basic foodstuffs in exchange for the articles it sold abroad. Yet despite these limitations to his vision his analyses of the coercive power of capital and the exploitative nature of profit, and of the economic basis and pervasive influence of class divisions, were more sophisticated than any previously made. Engels, in tracing the rise of Utopian socialism, drew attention to the seminal character of the first decade of the nineteenth century, which saw, besides Owen's early years at New Lanark, the publication of Saint-Simon's Geneva Letters and Fourier's *Théorie des quatre mouvements*.[1] Hall's *Effects of Civilization* (which Engels did not mention) adds very substantially to the achievement of that decade.

---

[1] F. Engels, Socialism, Utopian and Scientific (New York, 1901), p. 6.

6

Sir Francis Burdett and Burdettite Radicalism

Nearly 60 years have elapsed since two book-length studies of Sir Francis
Burdett were published, one of them a rather diffuse two-volume biography which contained some valuable material from the Burdett family papers, and the other a doctoral dissertation based almost entirely on printed
sources.[1] In recent years William Cobbett, Major Cartwright and Henry
Hunt, the other leading figures in the early-nineteenth-century reform
movement, have received a considerable amount of attention from scholars,[2] but Burdett has been relatively neglected. He has been treated
briefly, and with particular emphasis on his limitations as a radical leader,
in E. P. Thompson's *The Making of the English Working Class* and in John
Cannon's *Parliamentary Reform 1640–1832* (in which he is described as 'a
Wilkes manqué').[3] Yet he did play an important part in keeping the issue of
parliamentary reform alive, and in inspiring a radical movement independent of the established parties, during the period of anti-Jacobin dominance between the mid-1790s and the end of the French wars. In the
post-war years, although he remained the outstanding advocate of reform
within the House of Commons, working-class radicals in the industrial
areas turned to other leaders. Still, in view of the place he occupied in the
reform movement over two decades or more, his brand of radicalism and
the nature and extent of his influence deserve closer investigation than they
have yet received. This essay will first attempt to show that Burdettite
radicalism was, at least for some years, a movement of greater strength and
scale than historians have commonly supposed; and it will then examine
Burdett's political ideas and *persona* with a view to explaining the extent,
as well as the limitations, of his contemporary appeal. The essay will concentrate on the period up to 1820, and as the facts of this earlier part of his
career are quite well known they will not be rehearsed in detail.

In the metropolitan area, Burdett did acquire a great following during
the first decade of the nineteenth century. When he stood for Middlesex in
1802 he was already a popular figure, having spoken out almost alone
against Pitt's policies during the Foxite secession from parliament, and
having made a special impression by his exposure of the harsh treatment of
political prisoners in the Coldbath Fields prison. The contest of 1802 and
the by-election two years later provided outlets for the anti-ministerial

[1] M. W. Patterson, *Sir Francis Burdett and his Times 1770–1844* (2 vols., London, 1931);
Joseph S. Jackson, *The Public Career of Sir Francis Burdett 1796–1815* (Philadelphia, 1932).

[2] See Naomi C. Miller, 'John Cartwright and Radical Parliamentary Reform, 1808–1819',
English Historical Review, LXXXIII (1968), 705–28; John W. Osborne, *John Cartwright*
(Cambridge, 1972); *idem, William Cobbett: His Thought and His Times* (New Brunswick,
1966); James Sambrook, *William Cobbett* (London, 1973); J. C. Belchem, 'Henry Hunt and
the Evolution of the Mass Platform', *English Historical Review*, XCIII (1978), 739–73.

[3] E. P. Thompson, *The Making of the English Working Class* (2nd edition, Harmondsworth,
1968), pp. 498–9; John Cannon, *Parliamentary Reform 1640–1832* (Cambridge, 1973),
p. 151.

feeling that had been quite effectively suppressed since 1795, and there is plenty of testimony to the degree of support Burdett received from the London 'crowd'. J. S. Copley (the future Lord Lyndhurst) wrote in 1802 that it was 'impossible to describe the enthusiasm of the multitude . . . the people were, to a man, on his side.' One of the police magistrates reported, after the by-election of 1804, that the people had shown themselves 'more hostile and inimical to government' than he could have imagined possible. And the anti-Jacobin pamphleteer John Bowles had to admit that, in both contests, the labouring classes of the metropolis had been 'wrought up to a pitch of fury, which could scarcely have been exceeded, if they had been long subjected to the most severe and wanton tyranny; and they were led to espouse the interests of Sir Francis Burdett as warmly, as if they depended upon him for deliverance from the most galling yoke of oppression.'[4]

It is true that among the freeholders there was not the same clear preponderance of support for Burdett, and that when, in 1806, he renounced the lavish and traditional electioneering methods that he and his agents had used in the previous contests, his third candidature for Middlesex aroused much less excitement. However, his clear breach with the Whigs at this election and his resolve to rely simply on the public spirit and independence of the electors helped to prepare the way for his triumphant return for Westminster in the following year. The latter event reflected the extent to which, at least in the metropolis, 'the progress of public opinion' had 'superseded the influence of party and faction', especially as a result of the Whigs' failure to satisfy while in office the expectations they had aroused in opposition.[5] While the credit for the conduct of the election campaign was mainly attributable to the 'Westminster committee', there is little doubt that Burdett's personal prestige, as the one conspicuous public man who had voiced the popular disillusionment with parliamentary parties, was a major factor in the campaign's success.[6] The chairing of the new member on 29 June, when he was conducted in a procession from his house in Piccadilly to the Crown and Anchor tavern in the Strand, was one of the great political festivals of early nineteenth-century London.[7]

But perhaps the most remarkable demonstrations of London's support for Burdett were to occur in 1810, when he clashed with the House of Commons over its privileges and a motion was passed for his commitment to the Tower. In the tense days between this decision and his arrest, large

---

[4] Sir Theodore Martin, *Life of Lord Lyndhurst* (London, 1883), pp. 93–4; J. Moser to J. King, 14 August 1804, P[ublic] R[ecord] O[ffice], H.O. 42/79; [John Bowles,] *A Letter to the Freeholders of Middlesex . . . By an Attentive Observer* (London, 1804), p. 68.

[5] *Annual Register* (Otridge edition), 1807, p. 235; [F. Place and J. Richter,] *An Exposition of the Circumstances which gave rise to the Election of Sir Francis Burdett, Bart. for the City of Westminster* (London, 1807), pp. 4–6.

[6] Cobbett was later to maintain, when he had broken with Burdett and the Westminster committee, that 'the *real triumph* of freedom in Westminster' had been James Paull's candidature of 1806. But Paull had stood on Burdett's principles and with his backing, and it is clear from letters written by Cobbett in 1807 that he then regarded Paull as of no political consequence without Burdett's support. See C[obbett's] P[olitical] R[egister], 17 January 1818; Cobbet to J. Wright, 28 April 1807 and n.d. (c.30 April 1807), B[ritish] L[ibrary] Add[itional] MSS. 22906, fos. 278 and 279.

[7] Patterson, I, 215–17.

crowds assembled each evening in Piccadilly, passers-by were made to doff their hats and cry 'Burdett for ever!', many windows and lamps were broken, and troops had to be used to clear the streets. The state of popular feeling can to some extent be inferred from the measures taken by the authorities: 10,000 volunteers were paraded under arms on four successive evenings, and detachments of troops, some of them with artillery, were stationed in the principal London squares. On the day of the actual arrest (9 April) the soldiers who conducted Burdett to the Tower were assailed with an 'unremitting' barrage of stones and other missiles on their way back to their barracks, and were eventually provoked into firing on the crowd.[8] An observer wrote to his mother in the country: 'You can have but a faint idea, from merely reading the reports in the papers, of the violence, the fury of the proceedings which have for four days disgraced the metropolis . . . Even the "no popery" riots are said to have hardly come up to these fearful scenes of excitement, in their turbulence and fierceness.'[9]

These events were followed by more constitutional, but none the less emphatic, expressions of public indignation. The meeting of Burdett's constituents that was held on 17 April to petition the Commons for his release was described by Francis Place (who had an unrivalled experience of such occasions) as 'probably the largest meeting ever held in Westminster'.[10] Meetings to petition for Burdett's release and for parliamentary reform were also held by the freeholders of Middlesex and the livery of London, and both adopted such strongly-worded petitions that the Commons refused to receive them—thereby provoking further meetings and petitions from the bodies concerned. Eight of the larger wards of the City held similar meetings; and on 6 June the Common Council, which had been under Pittite dominance for many years, approved its first petition for parliamentary reform since the mid-1780s, protesting at the same time against Burdett's imprisonment.[11] Among other, more impressionistic, evidence of Burdett's popularity in London at this period is a letter from the Swedish historian Erik Gustaf Geijer saying (at the end of April) that 'almost all the lower classes of the people' were partisans of Sir Francis; and this view was corroborated, at least so far as 'journeymen and persons of that class' were concerned, by a report of 14 May from the chief magistrate at Bow Street to the Home Secretary. Dorothy George, the historian of English caricature, has written that although political characters were hardly ever glamorized or hero-worshipped in the prints, Burdett at this time was an exception: not even Chatham or Wilkes, she says, 'had been the subject of such concentrated pictorial eulogy as Burdett in 1810'.[12]

[8] Reports of police magistrates and others, 7–9 April 1810, P.R.O., H.O. 42/106; copy-book entitled 'Secret Correspondence etc. on Sir Francis Burdett's Commitment April 1810', H.O. 42/109; 'Heads of what was observed to have happened on the occasion of Sir Francis Burdett being conveyed to the Tower', P.R.O., P.C.1/3912.

[9] *The Bath Archives: A Further Selection from the Diaries and Letters of Sir George Jackson, 1809 to 1816*, ed. Lady Jackson (2 vols., London, 1873), I, 106.

[10] B.L.Add. MSS. 27850, fo. 215.

[11] *Ibid.*, fos. 219–22, 227–8; *Alfred and Westminster Gazette*, 31 May, 7 June 1810.

[12] E. G. Geijer, *Impressions of England 1809–10*, ed. Anton Blanck (London, 1932), p. 207; J. Read to R. Ryder, 14 May 1810, P.R.O., H.O. 42/107; M. Dorothy George, *English Political Caricature 1793–1832* (Oxford, 1959), pp. 125–6.

It is well known that on his release from the Tower at the end of the parliamentary session he dampened the enthusiasm of many of his followers by refusing to join the procession that his constituents had arranged to escort him to Piccadilly. (He was apparently afraid that such a demonstration would occasion further collisions with the troops and further bloodshed.)[13] But although some people—including Place, who had been one of the organizers of the procession—were very incensed by this incident, his reputation was too great to be destroyed by it. In May 1812, Coleridge, entering a public house in London after Perceval's assassination, heard 'Burdett's health drank with a Clatter of Pots—and a sentiment given to at least 50 men and women—May Burdett soon be the man to have sway over us! . . . he is a Christian Man and speaks for the Poor.' And at the general election later that year, as Place admits, 'it would have been absurd in any man to have opposed him' in Westminster.[14]

While historians have not denied that Burdett attracted wide support in the London area during the early years of the century, it has been suggested that he and his brand of radicalism made little impression during the war on the 'heartlands of the industrial revolution'. E. P. Thompson's contention is that although in London there was some continuity at the 'constitutional' level of activity between the radicalism of the 1790s and that of 1816–20, in the industrial regions the main strand of agitation connecting the two periods was an underground one, 'the illegal tradition'.[15] It is true that in many northern and midland towns it was difficult at this time for radical sentiment to find public expression, and it is also true that in some places, such as Oldham and Sheffield, a local tradition of militancy and even insurrectionism is traceable.[16] However, it is clear that the mass radicalism which emerged after the war was predominantly constitutional; and there is evidence that during the war itself such a movement was already developing, in the north and midlands as well as in the south, with Burdett as its chief national focus.

In the country, this development did take place later than in London. As candidate for Middlesex early in the century Burdett was applauded by what remained of the radical press in the provinces,[17] and his election for Westminster in 1807 drew public expressions of support from groups of reformers and 'low' Whigs in Bristol, Nottingham, Liverpool and Norwich.[18] But it was not until 1809–10 that independent or (in the contemporary sense of the term) 'patriotic' activity occurred on a considerable scale. The initial cause of this was the public indignation aroused by the inquiry into the conduct of the Duke of York and the Commons' refusal to

---

[13] W. J. Burdett to J. Langham, 17 July 1810 (transcript), Bod[leian] Lib[rary, Oxford], MS. Eng. letters d. 97, fo. 216.

[14] *Collected Letters of Samuel Taylor Coleridge*, ed. E. L. Griggs (6 vols., Oxford, 1956–71), III, 410; B.L.Add. MSS. 27850, fos. 232–6, 241.

[15] Thompson, pp. 513–14.

[16] John Foster, *Class Struggle and the Industrial Revolution* (London, 1974), especially pp. 34–41; F. K. Donnelly and J. L. Baxter, 'Sheffield and the English Revolutionary Tradition, 1791–1820', *International Review of Social History*, XX (1975), 405–15.

[17] *Cambridge Intelligencer*, 24 July 1802; *Manchester Gazette*, 7 August 1802.

[18] B.L.Add. MSS. 27838, fo. 205; *Nottingham Journal*, 4 July 1807; Rathbone MSS., 11.4.16, fos. 93 and 105, Liverpool University Library; *Norfolk Chronicle*, 11 July 1807.

declare him guilty of abuse of his military patronage. Colonel Wardle, the instigator of the inquiry, temporarily overshadowed Burdett in terms of popularity. In the spring and summer of 1809, 80 or 90 meetings were held to vote addresses of thanks to him—though his reputation soon afterwards collapsed when Mary Anne Clarke (the chief witness in the investigation) turned publicly against him. In some ways, the meetings of 1809 were more in the nature of a traditional movement of Country against Court—an expression of protest against corruption in high places—than a positive movement for reform. But this year did see, besides the introduction by Burdett of the first general motion for parliamentary reform since 1797, a notable revival of public discussion of this question, which reappeared after a long absence in parts of the provincial press; [19] and, in 1810, there was to be a movement that was centrally concerned with the issue of reform, as well as with that of Burdett's imprisonment by the House of Commons.

The latter event produced a very widespread reaction. In the days following the arrest, Burdettite slogans were chalked up in places as far apart as Carlisle, Newcastle, Birmingham, Exeter and Canterbury.[20] A Fenland farmer wrote on 24 April: 'There is nothing now talked of in the country but the imprisonment of our great and beloved patriot Sir Francis Burdett. I hear my labourers discussing the subject every day.' A month later, Daniel Sykes of Hull wrote that the clash between Burdett and the Commons had 'excited now for the first time in all the populous parts of the nation a wish for reform'.[21] Early in June, a meeting attended by some 8000 people in Sheffield approved a petition to the Commons, which the House in due course rejected on account of its strong remarks about the illegality of Burdett's imprisonment and the unrepresentative nature of the House.[22] The reformers of Liverpool staged a meeting which approved a petition to the Commons and an address of thanks to Burdett for his public conduct, and in Manchester, though no public meeting was held, an address to Burdett was circulated which obtained 17,940 signatures.[23] In Nottingham there were two meetings, owing to a split between the Foxites of the corporation and the local radicals. The former were unwilling, as the town clerk told Lord Holland, to consent 'to Sir Francis Burdett being held up as the great Exemplar and polar Star for every Friend to British liberty to look up to as the Guide and Director of his political Conduct'. They accordingly held a meeting of the mayor, aldermen, common council and livery which petitioned for a change of ministers and for moderate reform. Five days later a meeting of the 'electors and inhabitants' of Nottingham, sponsored by a few middle-class Unitarians but attended chiefly by working men, adopted an address of thanks to Burdett and a petition for 'radical

[19] [*Cobbett's* (later Hansard's)] *P[arliamentary] D[ebates]*, XIV, 1041–58; *Nottingham Review*, 14 April 1809; *Leeds Mercury,* 15 and 29 April 1809; *Manchester Gazette*, 13 May 1809.

[20] Mayor of Carlisle to Earl of Lonsdale, 15 April 1810, P.R.O., H.O. 42/106; reports from postmasters to F. Freeling, 15–18 April 1810, *ibid.*

[21] *Letters to William Frend from the Reynolds Family of Little Paxton and John Hammond of Fenstanton 1793–1814*, ed. Frida Knight (Cambridge, 1974), p. 87; Sykes to C. Wyvill, 21 May 1810, Wyvill MSS., North Yorkshire Record Office.

[22] *Sheffield Iris*, 12 and 19 June 1810; *P.D.*., XVII, 616–24.

[23] *Journals of the House of Commons*, LXV, 389; *Manchester Gazette*, 30 June, 7 July 1810.

reform', which was signed by 4500 people.[24] Other petitions calling for reform and siding with Burdett over the Commons' privileges came from Canterbury, Rochester, Reading, Worcester, Coventry, Hull and Berwick-on-Tweed.[25] A meeting at Carmarthen passed resolutions approving of Burdett's conduct, two sheep were roasted at New Radford on the anniversary of his election for Westminster, and a congratulatory address to him was adopted by a meeting at Lane End in the Staffordshire Potteries.[26] There were also numerous celebrations at the time of his release from the Tower. Ten sheep or lambs were roasted whole in various parts of Nottingham; the Volunteer band of Lenton hired a stage coach and drove through the neighbouring villages playing 'civic airs'; at Melbourne in Derbyshire there were festivities lasting a whole day; and in Sheffield dinners in honour of the event were held at 17 different inns.[27]

Most of these demonstrations of opinion came from towns and industrial villages and were decidedly plebeian in character. Whereas ten county meetings had been held in 1809 over the Duke of York's affair, the only county (apart from Middlesex) which petitioned for reform and voted an address to Burdett in 1810 was Berkshire, where a meeting was sponsored by Sir John Throckmorton and the Berkshire Independent Club.[28] In Yorkshire, a meeting was proposed by Walter Fawkes, a former MP for the county, who had become a supporter of Burdett's plan of reform; but Christopher Wyvill and the moderate reformers were alarmed by Fawkes's views and by the 'rapid growth of Burdettism' among the industrial workers of the West Riding, and no meeting took place.[29] In general (according to Burdett's informants) the Whigs as well as the ministerialists did all they could to prevent meetings, and from several places there were reports that 'the better sort of people' were hostile to Burdett.[30] According to William Lamb, 'The ferment of the public mind . . . was greater than that which had been excited in the foregoing year by the investigation into the conduct of the Duke of York. But the contagion did not creep so far into the sounder parts of the society.'[31] Cobbett pointed out in his *Political Register* of 26 May that it was not easy for the people to meet for the purpose of petitioning when those in influential positions were uncooperative, and lower-class support for Burdett and hostility to the House of Commons may have been considerably more widespread than the number of actual meetings and petitions might suggest.

[24] G. Coldham to Lord Holland, 2 June 1810, B.L.Add. MSS. 51825, fo. 45; *Nottingham Review*, 25 May, 1 June 1810; *Morning Chronicle*, 14 June 1810.

[25] *Commons Journals*, LXV, 389–90, 477–8, 349–50, 389, 488–9, 422, 426.

[26] *Independent Whig*, 29 April 1810; *Nottingham Review*, 25 May 1810; *Alfred and Westminster Gazette*, 22 June 1810.

[27] *Nottingham Review*, 29 June, 13 July 1810; *Peeps into the Past: The Diaries of Thomas Asline Ward*, ed. A. B. Bell and R. E. Leader (London, 1909), p. 163.

[28] *Morning Chronicle*, 6 June 1810; MS. diary of Sir John Throckmorton, under 5 and 8 June 1810, Coughton Court, Alcester.

[29] Wyvill to Sir W. Strickland, 4 June 1810 (copy), Wyvill MSS.; J. R. Dinwiddy, *Christopher Wyvill and Reform 1790–1820*, Borthwick Papers no. 39 (York, 1971), pp. 20–1.

[30] Burdett to Lady Burdett, n.d. (6 May 1810), Bod.Lib., MS. Eng. hist. b. 197, fo. 6; J. Gottwaltz (Birmingham) to Freeling, 15 April 1810, P.R.O., H.O. 42/106; C. Keele (Salisbury) to Freeling, 18 April 1810, *ibid.*

[31] MS. autobiography of William Lamb (later Viscount Melbourne), Panshanger MSS., box 16, Hertfordshire Record Office.

At least for a year or two, Burdettite radicalism remained strong in the provinces as well as in London. The address to the Prince Regent, which Burdett moved at the beginning of the 1812 session of parliament, sold 28,000 copies in pamphlet form within seven weeks[32] (having been defeated in the House of Commons by 238 votes to one). In February of that year, Colonel Fletcher remarked, in a letter to the Home Office, on the Burdettite style of the resolutions of a public meeting at Bolton; in May a dinner chaired by John Payne of Newhill (who had been a prominent figure in the Sheffield Society for Constitutional Information 20 years before) was held in Sheffield to celebrate the fifth anniversary of Burdett's election for Westminster; and, in the following September, Henry Brougham reported from Liverpool that there were 'swarms' of Burdettites there.[33] By this period, the term 'Burdettite' had become a synonym, in the north as well as in the metropolis, for 'radical reformer'.[34]

In the post-war years, however, when the parliamentary reform movement became stronger than ever in the industrial districts, Burdett was to diverge to some extent from other leading radicals and from the working-class agitation in the country. Mr. Thompson attributes this largely to a retreat on Burdett's part: 'Burdett, whose radical enthusiasms were cooling, commenced in April 1816 a campaign for admitting to the suffrage all who paid direct taxes.'[35] But, in fact, this campaign had been initiated several years before, and he had never committed himself to any more extreme programme. Until 1809, he had advocated parliamentary reform without espousing any particular plan, and the scheme which he drew up in consultation with Cartwright and others and put forward in the Commons in June of that year included the equalization of electoral districts, the 'restoration' of annual parliaments and the enfranchisement of those subject to direct taxation.[36] It was in support of this programme that Cartwright endeavoured, with Burdett's support and with considerable success, to organize petitions in the years 1812–15.[37]

What happened after the war was that the popular reform movement, encouraged by Henry Hunt, rejected a tax-paying franchise in favour of universal (or more accurately manhood) suffrage; and this change was endorsed by Cobbett and Cartwright, the latter of whom had been an advocate of universal suffrage until he retreated from it for prudential reasons during the Napoleonic period. Burdett's response was equivocal.

[32] *Sir Francis Burdett's Address to the Prince Regent, as proposed in the House of Commons, at the opening of the Session, on the 7th Jan. 1812* (London, 1812); *C.P.R.*, 19 February 1812.

[33] R. Fletcher to J. Beckett, 25 February 1812, P.R.O., H.O. 42/120; *Sheffield Iris*, 2 June 1812; Brougham to J. Allen, 25 September 1812, B.L.Add. MSS. 52178, fo. 163.

[34] *Diaries of T. A. Ward*, p. 163; Sir F. L. Wood to Sir G. Cayley, 30 November 1812 (copy), Hickleton MSS., A4. 19, Garrowby, York.

[35] Thompson, p. 60.

[36] *The Plan of Reform proposed by Sir Francis Burdett . . . in the House of Commons, June 15th 1809* (London, 1809), p. 18; J. Cartwright, *Address to the Electors of Westminster, April 6th 1819* (London, 1819), p. 20.

[37] Cartwright's printed circular of 11 March 1813, Holt White MSS., no. 464, Gilbert White Museum, Selborne; Hampden Club circular of April 1815, Bod. Lib., G.P. 1987 (7a). For Burdett's warm support for Cartwright's efforts at this time, see J. C. Rashleigh to T. Holt White, 2 April 1815, Holt White MSS., no. 310.

He told a deputation of delegates from provincial Hampden Clubs in January 1817 that he would be prepared to speak in favour of universal suffrage in the House of Commons, though he had little hope of its gaining much support there. However, when he introduced his parliamentary reform motion in May, he did not propose a specific measure but merely moved for a select committee on the state of the representation.[38] In June 1818 he did commit himself to a thoroughly democratic programme by moving in the Commons a set of radical reform resolutions drafted by Jeremy Bentham.[39] But, at a public meeting in August, he said that although he was convinced of the desirability of universal suffrage he despaired of achieving it at present and would be satisfied with 'general suffrage', by which he meant the enfranchisement of all heads of families. At the Westminster by-election in February 1819, he defended himself against the charge of vacillation, saying that he saw 'no inconsistency, and no impropriety, in proposing different plans of Reform, care being taken, that each plan contains in itself sufficient security for the liberty of the country'. And he explained further in March that by 'radical reform' he meant not necessarily universal suffrage but any reform that would 'root out the corruption of the House of Commons'.[40]

It appears that Burdett did not object to universal suffrage as such, but was hostile to any attempt to erect it into a *sine qua non*. He had said in 1812 that 'he was not one of those captious reformists that would take nothing, if they could not get everything they wished for'.[41] In the post-war years, he was more optimistic than he had been earlier about the possibility that the Whigs would commit themselves to a substantial measure of reform; and he said in a speech to the Liverpool Concentric Society in December 1818 that if the Whigs did take up triennial parliaments and household suffrage they would deserve strong public support. He went on:

> As for my own sentiments on the subject, they are, that a far further extent of Reform would be still better: but were such a Reform as I have just mentioned completed, you would be immediately sensible of the benefits of such a check upon the corruptions of the State; you would be conscious that the People were enjoying the great advantages of their natural control: you would feel, and happily feel, that you have a truly national Government . . . I am ready to join all Reformers of every description—to go as far as we can go—to obtain all we can obtain.[42]

This attitude set him apart from those reformers who treated universal suffrage as the touchstone of radicalism and were horrified at any idea of co-operation and 'compromise' with the Whigs. Cartwright criticized him for failing to base his case for reform on the firm ground of natural right,

---

[38] Samuel Bamford, *Passages in the Life of a Radical* (2 vols., London, 1844), I, 21; *P.D.*, XXXVI, 704–29.

[39] *P.D.*, XXXVIII, 1118–49. He actually went beyond Bentham on this occasion, in that he dropped the latter's proposal of a reading qualification for the suffrage: cf. Bentham MSS., box 128, fo. 329, University College London.

[40] *Black Dwarf*, 26 August 1818; *Authentic Narrative of the Events of the Westminster Election of 1819* (London, 1819), p. 111; *Statesman*, 17 March 1819.

[41] *P.D.*, XXIII, 146. Cf. *Times*, 24 February 1817.

[42] *Speech of Sir Francis Burdett to the Liverpool Concentric Society, on the Fourth of December 1818*, printed handbill, B.L.Add. MSS. 27842, fo. 196.

and Cobbett (from the refuge on Long Island to which he withdrew in 1817) attacked him strongly and repeatedly for lack of commitment to the people's cause.[43] Hunt, hero of the Spa Fields meetings and later of Peterloo, became the champion of militant popular radicalism, and was able to claim that the Burdettites had become essentially a party of householders while the 'operative manufacturers, artizans, mechanics and labourers' had transferred their allegiance to him.[44] When he stood for Westminster at the election of 1818 he obtained only 84 votes against Burdett's 5239; but there is little doubt that he and Cobbett did obtain more influence than Burdett among the industrial working classes.

Besides his flexible position on the suffrage question, there were several other features of Burdett's character and outlook that were somewhat incongruous for the leader of a radical reform movement, and which help to explain the partial erosion of his popularity during the second decade of the century. For one thing, there was his personal aloofness—what Place called his 'frigid hauteur'. In Samuel Bamford's autobiography, there is a well-known description of the polite but chilling manner in which he received a deputation of lower-class radicals from the provinces in 1817.[45] Also, he set a high value on his own autonomy. He said when he entered politics that he would be 'callous to every feeling but that of self-approbation',[46] and he was hardly more amenable to direction from below than he was to the influences of Court and party. He told his constituents on more than one occasion that he would be guided by his own judgment rather than theirs, and he claimed in 1820 that 'no man listened less to popular delusions, or even to what is called popular opinions'.[47] Thus, although pledges and instructions had been hallmarks of Wilkite radicalism, Burdett looked back to an older brand of 'patriotism' which had been identified above all with independence.[48]

Also characteristic of the independent country gentleman was the belief, which he shared with Christopher Wyvill among others, that the gentry were the natural leaders of any national political campaign. He often exhorted them to put themselves at the head of the reform movement,[49] and he evidently doubted whether a movement without such leadership would be likely to have beneficial results. In June 1816, when urging country gentlemen to take the initiative in founding local societies in association with the Hampden Club, he warned that if they did not 'stand

[43] Cartwright, *Address to the Electors of Westminster, April 6th 1819*, pp. 13, 23–4; *C.P.R.*, 13 September, 11 October, 20 December 1817, 26 December 1818.

[44] *Memoirs of Henry Hunt, Esq., Written by Himself* (3 vols., London, 1820–2), II, 74–8.

[45] B.L.Add. MSS. 27850, fo. 88; Bamford, I, 21.

[46] *The Journal of the Rev. William Bagshaw Stevens*, ed. Georgina Galbraith (Oxford, 1965), p. 377.

[47] Patterson, II, 420, 482; *The Trial of Sir Francis Burdett, Bart. at Leicester, on Thursday March 23rd 1820* (London, 1820), p. 39. He cited on the latter occasion his public disagreement with his constituents over the Corn Bill of 1815.

[48] Cf. Betty Kemp, 'Patriotism, Pledges and the People', in *A Century of Conflict, 1850–1950: Essays for A. J. P. Taylor*, ed. Martin Gilbert (London, 1966), pp. 40 and 43.

[49] [*Cobbett's*] P[*arliamentary*] H[*istory*], XXXIII, 1157 (3 January 1798); *Morning Chronicle*, 31 July 1804; Burdett to T. W. Coke, 24 October 1812, A. M. W. Stirling, *Coke of Norfolk and His Friends* (London, 1908), p. 343; *P.D.*., XXXVI, 724 (20 May 1817).

forward to act with the people, . . . confusion and disorder may ensue, and the result must be either the establishment of a complete military despotism . . . or some desperate conflict—some scene of blood, which all good men shudder to contemplate'. When the agitation that did develop in the winter of 1816–17 proved to be a predominantly working-class one under the sway of men such as Hunt and Cobbett, Burdett viewed it with some distrust—as he made clear, first by refusing to present to the Regent the address of the Spa Fields meeting of 15 November, and secondly by declining to chair the meeting of delegates from provincial Hampden Clubs on 22 January.[50]

In general, his political ideals and modes of argument were drawn from the past rather than from the contemporary world. He made little use of the doctrine of natural rights; and although he did flirt with Benthamism in 1818 he hardly absorbed it. His favourite justification of reform was always an appeal to the historic 'rights of Englishmen'. Even when introducing Bentham's resolutions in the House of Commons he devoted much of his speech to antiquarian points, maintaining, for instance, that an act of Henry IV's reign had recognized the common-law right of all inhabitants to vote at county elections.[51] He admitted on this occasion that in the eyes of philosophers arguments based on 'antiquity and custom' were of no great weight in establishing the merits of a political measure, but he contended that most men were not philosophers and *were* influenced by such considerations.[52] One suspects, however, that the days when medieval precedents cut much ice in political controversy were coming to an end. Even Major Cartwright, who had frequently appealed to the past himself, criticized Burdett in 1819 for relying too much on historical arguments, and Hazlitt was to write a few years later that Burdett's 'pedantry' in these matters was his main political weakness.[53]

Appeals to the medieval constitution had been a feature of the 'country ideology' of the later Stuart and early Hanoverian periods; [54] and if there was any ideology to which Burdett subscribed, this was the one. As a young man, he was an admirer of Harrington's writings, and he later acknowledged a special debt to Bolingbroke.[55] Several of the preoccupations that were characteristic of both men and of the tradition to which they contributed—in particular, their belief in arms-bearing as an essential safeguard of liberty, and their anxiety about the progress of

---

[50] *A Full Report of the Proceedings of the Meeting, convened by the Hampden Club, which took place at the Freemasons' Tavern . . . on Saturday, the 15th June, 1816, upon the subject of Parliamentary Reform* (London, 1816), p. 33; Patterson, II, 415–18.

[51] *P.D.*, XXXVIII, 1125–6. Himself descended from a companion of the Conqueror, Burdett did not subscribe to the 'Norman Yoke' theory but favoured an interpretation of the 'ancient constitution' that stressed the continuity of English liberties through the Middle Ages.

[52] *P.D.*, XXXVIII, 1121–2.

[53] Cartwright, *Address to the Electors of Westminster, February 4, 1819* (London, 1819), p. 5; *Complete Works of William Hazlitt*, ed. P. P. Howe (29 vols., London, 1930–4), XI, 141.

[54] Cf. J. G. A. Pocock, *Politics, Language and Time* (London, 1971), pp. 135, 229.

[55] Burdett to Lord Stanhope, 24 January 1799 (copy), Bod.Lib., MS. Eng. letters c. 64, fo. 82; *Times*, 24 March 1820.

'corruption'—were shared also by Burdett.[56] Especially reminiscent of Bolingbroke, of course, was the 'Tory' strand that coloured Burdett's radicalism, at least from 1806 onwards.[57] The notion that King and people needed to unite against a corrupt oligarchy that was encroaching on the rights of both may originally have been adopted by Burdett for reasons of policy: partly to forestall anti-Jacobin attempts to equate radicalism with disloyalty, and partly to distinguish his own position from that of the Whigs, who were still trying to direct public hostility against the Court and the influence of the Crown.[58] In any case, this notion was to become a permanent, and somewhat idiosyncratic, part of his political position.[59] The original, gentry-dominated Hampden Club of 1811–12 did espouse the principle that reform was 'alike necessary to the independence of the Crown and to the liberties of the people';[60] but this idea probably had little appeal to radicals in general, especially after the Prince Regent had revealed his true colours.

It is hardly surprising that a wealthy, patrician landowner, who could describe his own political creed (in 1819) as that of a Tory of the reign of Queen Anne,[61] should have been in some ways out of tune with the radical agitation of the post-war period. What needs to be explained, perhaps, is how he ever attracted as much plebeian support as he did.

One of the main reasons for the popularity he acquired during the war was his strong and constant commitment to the cause of parliamentary reform. He emerged as one of its most conspicuous advocates in 1797, when he chaired a large meeting of parliamentary reformers at the Crown and Anchor tavern and delivered a striking speech in support of Grey's reform motion of 26 May.[62] He continued to speak out on the issue during the early years of the nineteenth century, when it had dropped out of the speeches of the Foxite Whigs and virtually disappeared from public debate.[63] When it eventually came back into currency towards the end of the decade, he was plainly its outstanding champion, and was the natural choice as chairman and main speaker at the fresh Crown and Anchor

[56] MS. diary of J. C. Hobhouse, under 28 October 1819, B.L.Add. MSS. 56540, fo. 107; Burdett to Hobhouse, 24 August 1821, B.L.Add. MSS. 47222, fo. 81. (I owe the latter reference to Mr William Thomas.) On the continuity of ideas between Harrington and Bolingbroke, see Quentin Skinner, 'The Principles and Practice of Opposition: the case of Bolingbroke versus Walpole', in *Historical Perspectives: Studies in English Thought and Society in honour of J. H. Plumb*, ed. Neil McKendrick (London, 1974), pp. 113–24.

[57] Burdett's opening address to the Middlesex freeholders at the general election of 1806 contained an ironical reference to 'the best of Kings'; but Cobbett did his best to explain away this phrase in his *Political Register* (1 November 1806), and Burdett may have taken a hint from him, for it was just at this time that he began to strike a new note in his speeches: see *History of the Westminster and Middlesex Elections in the month of November 1806* (London, 1807), pp. 362, 390.

[58] Burdett may also have hoped that the Prince of Wales could be induced to side with the reformers: see 'George Jones' (i.e. James Powell) to J. Read, 31 May 1809, P.R.O., H.O. 42/99.

[59] See, e.g., *P.D.*, XIV, 1046–52 (15 June 1809) and XL, 1455 (1 July 1819).

[60] Hampden Club circulars of 1 May 1811 and March 1812, Holt White MSS., nos. 455 and 456.

[61] *P.D.*, XL, 1455.

[62] *Morning Chronicle*, 19 May 1797; *P.H.*, XXXIII, 681–4. The *Annual Register* (Otridge edition, 1797, p. 257) paid an unwontedly warm tribute to Burdett's speech of 26 May.

[63] *Morning Chronicle*, 28 June, 18 November 1802, 23 February 1806.

meeting of 1 May 1809.[64] During the Napoleonic war, universal suffrage was hardly ever mooted, and in these years before he was outflanked by more extreme reformers Burdett had (as Hunt acknowledged in his *Memoirs*) the general confidence and support of the radical section of the public.[65]

One way in which he gave the reform question a particular relevance to the lives of ordinary people was by arguing that there was a close connexion between the state of the electoral system and the heavy burden of taxation. According to his analysis, a 'borough-mongering oligarchy' had come to dominate the House of Commons and to monopolize official patronage, so that those who voted away the people's money were to a large extent 'interested in the expenditure of it'.[66] In his early years in politics he blamed high taxation on the war as well as on 'corruption'; but during the struggle with Napoleonic France he came to rely more exclusively on the argument that if members of parliament could be made the real guardians of the public purse instead of the 'cut-purses of the public', national expenditure and taxation could be much reduced.[67] To Burdett's critics, this message seemed thoroughly delusive, and even some of his supporters felt it to be simplistic.[68] But its simplicity may have helped it to make an impact. Coleridge overheard among other sentiments expressed in a tavern after Perceval's assassination: 'Every man might maintain his family decent and comfortable if the money were not picked out of our pockets by them damned Placemen.'[69] There was general agreement among political observers in the early nineteenth century that the revival of the demand for parliamentary reform was intimately connected with resentment over taxation;[70] and Burdett, along with Cobbett, did much to link the two issues in the popular mind.

It is true that otherwise in the economic sphere Burdett had little to offer the working classes. So far as industrial matters were concerned, he seems to have accepted the ideas of the political economists. While he did oppose legislation against combinations in 1799, he did so on the grounds that 'it was the wise policy of every well-regulated state to leave trade of every kind to find its own level'; and when Gravener Henson and other framework-knitters' delegates were lobbying parliament in 1812 for legislation to protect the workers in the hosiery trade, Burdett told them that 'Parliament never interfered with Disputes between Masters and Work-

---

[64] *A Full and Accurate Report of the Proceedings at the Crown and Anchor Tavern, on Monday, the 1st of May, 1809, relative to a Reform of the Commons House of Parliament* (London, 1809).

[65] Hunt, II, 77.

[66] Burdett, *A Letter from Oxford to the Electors of Westminster* (Oxford, 1812), p. 5.

[67] *P.H.*, XXXIII, 682–3, and XXXV, 802; *Morning Chronicle*, 4 December 1806; *Statesman*, 6 August 1812.

[68] *P.D.*, XIV, 509–10 (George Tierney, 11 May 1809); Thomas Lee, *White-Lion Club, late Riot, and Dock Tax: An Address to the Public* (2nd edition, Bristol, 1807), p. 34.

[69] *Collected Letters of Coleridge*, III, 410.

[70] *P.D.*, XIV, 754–6 (William Windham, 26 May 1809); Anon., *Politics and Public Men for the year 1812* (London, 1813), pp. 32–3; Lord John Russell, *An Essay on the History of the English Government and Constitution* (London, 1821), pp. 37–8.

men'.[71] His conception of exploitation did not extend to any critique of economic power. However, he was fiercely alive to all forms of *political* oppression. Francis Horner wrote of him: 'That quick sense of indignation which he has against all manner of public injustice and oppression is one of the best elements of the true passion for liberty.'[72] This quality may in fact have been more influential than his reformism in making him a popular hero: according to Southey the campaign over the Coldbath Fields Prison was alone enough to make him 'the most popular man in England'.[73] He continued to speak out on behalf of political prisoners, and was particularly concerned about the persecution of radical journalists. Always a strong defender of the freedom of the press, he denounced the unfairness of the law of libel and the harsh sentences passed on men such as Henry White, John Drakard and Leigh Hunt.[74]

Another way in which his hostility to oppression showed itself was in his opposition to flogging in the army. The three general motions which he introduced on the subject between 1808 and 1812 were all heavily defeated,[75] but the publicity which he and the radical press gave to this practice did have some effect in making it less frequent and severe. Two specific reforms—the empowering of courts martial to substitute imprisonment for corporal punishment, and the prevention of regimental courts martial from inflicting sentences of more than 300 lashes—were introduced in 1811–12; and the general mitigation of the system that occurred in these and the following years was widely attributed to Burdett's efforts.[76]

His concern about flogging was due not only to revulsion at its cruelty, but also to his feeling that it was an intrinsic part of a coercive system of government. He maintained that the soldiery, herded into barracks and subjected to an inhuman type of discipline, lost all fellow-feeling with the people and became 'the passive and unconscious instrument of tyrannical coercion'.[77] Thus opposition to corporal punishment was connected with a broader critique of the use of a 'standing army'. It has been said that for much of the eighteenth century this traditional object of 'patriotic' hostility had been 'little more than a bogey in political reality',[78] but in Burdett's time it could be represented as an issue of some substance. He frequently

[71] *Debrett's Parliamentary Register*, LIII, 687; *Records of the Borough of Nottingham* (9 vols., Nottingham, 1882–1956), VIII, 160, cited by Thompson, p. 590. Cf. also *P.D.*, New Series, XIII, 647–8 (16 May 1825).

[72] Horner to James Loch, 25 June 1810, Horner MSS., British Library of Political and Economic Science.

[73] [Robert Southey,] *Letters from England by Don Manuel Alvarez Espriella* (3 vols., London, 1807), II, 312.

[74] *Speech of Sir Francis Burdett, Bt., delivered in the House of Commons on the 28th March 1811, upon a motion of Lord Folkestone, to examine into the practice of Ex-Officio Informations* (London, 1811); *Purity of Election: Speech of Sir Francis Burdett to his Constituents* [14 November 1812], printed handbill, Bod.Lib., G.P. 1983.

[75] *P.D.*, XI, 1115–22; XX, 698–710; XXI, 1263–92.

[76] Henry Marshall, *Military Miscellany: comprehending a History of the Recruiting of the Army, Military Punishments, etc. etc.* (London, 1846), pp. 180, 184–5; *Manchester Gazette*, 14 March 1812; 3rd Lord Holland, *Further Memoirs of the Whig Party, 1807–1821*, ed. Lord Stavordale (London, 1905), p. 102; Bentham to Burdett, 23 September 1824 (copy), Bod.Lib., MS. Eng. letters d. 97, fo. 5.

[77] Burdett, *Address to the Prince Regent, . . . 7th Jan. 1812*, pp. 14–15.

[78] Pocock, p. 120–1.

drew attention to the spread of barracks over the country, and argued that it was the maintenance of 'corruption' that made repression necessary: the spoils-system and the heavy taxation it entailed would be unable to survive without 'the ever-awing aspect of a military force'.[79] He was particularly outspoken on this theme in 1812. He said on 1 May, shortly after the clashes between troops and machine-breakers at Rawfolds and Middleton, that the government was using the army for 'the subjugation of the people' in defiance of 'the constitutional opinions of our ancestors'.[80] One finds these sentiments echoed in a speech of Gravener Henson at a Nottingham town meeting in January 1813: the army was in part being used, he said, 'to keep down the people at home, rendered desperate by exorbitant taxation'.[81] Burdett himself returned to the theme of government by the sword—and also to the notion that control over the army itself depended on the lash—after the Peterloo massacre, in an outraged public letter which exposed him to prosecution for seditious libel and drew warm praise even from Cobbett and Hunt.[82]

Finally, in explaining Burdett's capacity to win the attachment and confidence of a wide public, one must return to his qualities as an individual. His remoteness from the people has been mentioned above: he never evoked the *warmth* of popular response formerly aroused by Wilkes, whose appeal has been described as 'totally without condescension'.[83] On the other hand, Burdett's elevated and independent position helped him to acquire a reputation for disinterestedness and integrity such as Wilkes never enjoyed. The Manchester journalist William Cowdroy wrote of him in 1802: 'A man of his character, rank and fortune, who devotes himself to the service of the public, can be actuated only by the purest zeal for the good of his country.' And, nearly 20 years later, the veteran radical John Thelwall could praise in similar terms 'the solitary disinterestedness with which, among men of his rank and fortune, he has stood upon all occasions so nobly forward as the advocate of the rights, as the champion of the cause of the humbler classes of the community'.[84] His indifference to material rewards was favourably compared with the conduct of George Tierney, who had been elected to parliament as popular candidate for Southwark in 1796 but had become a placeman under Addington in 1802.[85] Even Burdett's lack of concern about popularity may in some ways have enhanced his reputation and influence. Those radical journalists who took his side

[79] Burdett to Arthur O'Connor, 27 October 1796, Rebellion Papers 620/15/3/22, Irish State Paper Office; *P.H.*, XXXVI, 1107 (9 December 1802); Burdett, *Address to the Prince Regent, . . . 7th Jan. 1812*, p. 16.

[80] *P.D.*, XXII, 1146–8. He wrote in a private memorandum at this time: 'The nation is robb'd till the people have not the means of existence left and the people are shot and killed by soldiers paid by themselves for their defence' (Bod.Lib., MS. Eng. hist. c.294, fo. 55).

[81] *Nottingham Review*, 8 January 1813.

[82] *Patterson*, II, 490–2; *C.P.R.*, 24 December 1819; Hunt, III, 633–4.

[83] John Brewer, *Party Ideology and Popular Politics at the Accession of George III* (Cambridge, 1976), p. 170.

[84] *Manchester Gazette*, 7 August 1802; *Champion*, 18 February 1821. Thomas Hardy wrote to Thomas Paine in New York on 15 October 1807 (B.L.Add. MSS. 27818, fo. 73): 'Sir Francis Burdett . . . is become the popular man and I think very justly he is a worthy man and of the strictest integrity.'

[85] John Gale Jones, *Five Letters to the Right Honourable George Tierney* (London, 1806), pp. 15–16.

against Hunt and Cobbett in the post-war period laid stress on the fact that *he* was no demagogue.[86] And later, when Burdett was playing a leading part in the campaign for Catholic emancipation in the 1820s, Lord Holland drew a comparison between him and Canning, maintaining that the former's straightforwardness was of more value to the cause than the latter's political skills; whereas Canning had never been known to sacrifice power or popularity to principle, Burdett was risking the loss of popular favour for the sake of an object in which he believed, and his 'character' was helping to reduce public hostility to the measure.[87]

It has recently been said that Burdett was essentially a figurehead and 'gave little' to the reform movement 'in terms of ideology or inspiration'.[88] While notoriously unbusinesslike and much less *useful* than Place and others would have liked in furthering various schemes of improvement,[89] he was surely much more than a figurehead. At a time when the threat of prosecution still hung over those outside parliament who ventured to express radical views, Burdett's bold speeches and addresses were widely circulated in pamphlets and newspapers.[90] The contribution he was able to make depended to a considerable extent on the peculiar nature of his style and opinions. In his early years in politics, as the friend of O'Connor and Horne Tooke and even of Despard, he had laid himself open to the charges of Jacobinism that were used so widely and effectively to discredit the cause of reform;[91] he narrowly escaped prosecution for complicity in the schemes of the United Irishmen, and may actually have flirted with revolutionary groups in London.[92] Before long, however, he substantially changed his approach and public image. On his re-election to parliament in 1807 he took a conscious decision not to play into the hands of the establishment by 'acting the savage'; and he became a speaker who, isolated though he was, could command the attention of the House and make an impression on men of very different political views.[93] With regard to agitation outside parliament, he adopted the line that physical force should be clearly discountenanced; however justifiable an appeal to the right of resistance might be in principle, it was not practical for an unarmed people to challenge a standing army.[94] To legitimize his own position, he increasingly reached back beyond the 1790s—even beyond Wilkes—to a set of opposition principles that were unimpeachably English and respectable.

---

[86] *Examiner*, 3 January 1819; *Champion*, 10 January 1819.
[87] 6th Earl of Ilchester, *Chronicles of Holland House 1820–1900* (London, 1937), pp. 65-6.
[88] A. D. Harvey, *Britain in the Early Nineteenth Century* (London, 1978), p. 223.
[89] Cartwright to S. Whitbread, 28 May 1810, Whitbread MSS., no. 448, Bedfordshire Record Office; Graham Wallas, *Life of Francis Place* (4th edition, London, 1925), p. 152; *Memoirs of John Quincy Adams*, ed. Charles Francis Adams (12 vols., Philadelphia, 1874–7), III, 559.
[90] Cf. *C.P.R.*, 20 December 1806.
[91] E.g., *Courier*, 28 July 1804.
[92] *Later Correspondence of George III*, ed. A. Aspinall (5 vols., Cambridge, 1966–70), III, 32; J. Powell to Sir R. Ford, endorsed 25 December 1801, P.R.O., P.C. 1/3535.
[93] Cartwright to Holt White, 25 March 1808, Holt White MSS., no. 358; Patterson, II, 428, 523; *Memoirs of Sir Thomas Fowell Buxton, Bart.*, ed. Charles Buxton (London, 1872), p. 48.
[94] *Proceedings of the Meeting, convened by the Hampden Club . . . 15th June 1816*, pp. 32–3; B.L.Add. MSS. 56540, fo. 107. Cf. J. Ann Hone, 'The Ways and Means of London Radicalism 1796–1821', D. Phil. thesis, University of Oxford (1975), p. 228.

7

The Early Nineteenth-Century Campaign
against Flogging in the Army

THE 'New Liberal' interpretation of early nineteenth-century history offered by J. L. and Barbara Hammond around the time of the First World War laid considerable stress on the role of liberal humanitarians and reformers in parliament – men who could 'break through the prejudices of their class' and campaigned for such causes as penal reform, popular education and the regulation of child labour.[1] In recent general treatments of the period men of this type have figured less prominently. On the one hand, E. P. Thompson has been mainly concerned with working-class consciousness and self-activity, and has shown relatively little interest in patrician and middle-class reformers.[2] On the other hand, there is an influential 'conservative' interpretation of nineteenth-century social reform which attributes the key role in the process not to liberal and radical initiatives and public agitation, but to men in official and ministerial positions who were responding pragmatically to changes in society and social attitudes.[3] The campaign examined in this essay involved, along with Benthamite and other radicals, several of the liberal-minded Whigs whom the Hammonds admired.[4] Also, the issue was one on which the reformers had to face remarkably strong resistance from the authorities. Indeed, within the period covered by this paper – the period up to the Royal Commission on Military Punishments in 1835–6 – the resistance was to some extent successful in that the abolition of flogging was not achieved. Nevertheless, the practice was greatly mitigated and restricted in these years, and it is arguable that although flogging in the army did not cease altogether until 1881, the reforms effected in the pre-Victorian period went much of the way towards this goal. Lord William Bentinck said in 1835 that flogging had diminished 'a hundred, perhaps a thousand fold' since his early years in the army around the turn of the century.[5] The real extent of the reduction cannot be determined, because overall statistics for the first two decades of the century are not available. But there can be no

---

1. J. L. and B. Hammond, *The Town Labourer* (1917), p. 79.
2. The trio of Samuel Whitbread, H. G. Bennet and Sir Samuel Romilly does receive an honourable mention, however: E. P. Thompson, *The Making of the English Working Class* (2nd edn., Harmondsworth, 1968), p. 491.
3. For critical reviews of this interpretation, see Jenifer Hart, 'Nineteenth-Century Social Reform: a Tory Interpretation of History', *Past and Present*, no. 31 (1965); Derek Beales, 'Peel, Russell and Reform', *Historical Journal*, xvii (1974).
4. It also provides an illustration of the gap which the Hammonds emphasized (p. 225) between philanthropists of a liberal or radical cast and those of the evangelical school.
5. Parliamentary Papers [P.P.] 1836, xl. 457.

doubt that a very marked change had taken place. As the course of the early nineteenth-century campaign has not previously been traced in any detail – the most substantial account to date was published in 1846[1] – the first part of the essay will be devoted to a factual account of the agitation and of the official responses to it, and an attempt will then be made to look more analytically at the campaign and at the debate which it provoked. One point should be made about the scope of the essay: it will concentrate on the opposition to *military* flogging and will not cover the related issue of flogging in the navy. The latter practice did attract some attention in the period under discussion – Joseph Hume raised it in parliament in June 1825, and several pamphlets were published against it;[2] but in general it was much less prominent as a public issue, perhaps because it was felt that a stronger case could be made for its retention than could be made for that of military flogging.

Up to the eighteenth century a variety of corporal punishments were used in the army, but during the Hanoverian period flogging with the cat-o'-nine-tails became the stock mode of punishment. By the end of the century military flogging had become an object of intense popular dislike: E. P. Thompson has said that 'next to the press-gang, flogging was perhaps the most hated of the institutions of Old England'.[3] A number of incidents during the first half of George III's reign produced local protests against the practice,[4] and when radical societies and newspapers came into existence in the 1790s this was one of the grievances they occasionally mentioned.[5] It was during the next decade, however, that flogging became a conspicuous issue. One event which helped to bring it into prominence was the trial of Joseph Wall in 1802. This arose out of an incident which had taken place twenty years before, when on the orders of Wall, then lieutenant governor of the settlement at Goree, three men in the Africa Corps had been so severely flogged that they had all died. Wall's trial on a charge of murdering one of these men aroused great interest and feeling: according to Robert Southey, 'the popular indignation had never before been so excited'. Wall was convicted and sentenced to death, and Cobbett, who was at that stage an anti-

---

1. Henry Marshall, *Military Miscellany; comprehending a History of the Recruiting of the Army, Military Punishments, etc. etc.* (1846), ch. vii. For a brief account of the Victorian phase of the campaign, see R. L. Blanco, 'Attempts to abolish Branding and Flogging in the Army of Victorian England before 1881', *Journal of the Society of Army Historical Research*, xlvi (1968).

2. E.g. Thomas Hodgskin, *An Essay on Naval Discipline* (1813); Anon., *An Inquiry into the Nature and Effects of Flogging . . . in the Royal Navy and the Merchant Service* (1826).

3. Thompson, p. 662 n.

4. R. Hamilton, *The Duties of a Regimental Surgeon considered* (2nd ed., 1794), ii. 65–66; E. P. Thompson, 'The Crime of Anonymity', in Douglas Hay, Peter Linebaugh and E. P. Thompson (eds.), *Albion's Fatal Tree* (1975), p. 281.

5. *Argus*, 23 April 1792, 8 March 1793; *Manchester Herald*, 28 April 1792; *Report of the Committee of Constitution of the London Corresponding Society* [1794], p. 3.

Jacobin and objected to the exultation with which the verdict and execution were greeted, recorded in his *Political Register* that 'verses, full of exaggeration and lies, and hideous representations of the punishment of Armstrong, were insultingly bawled in the ears, and held up to the view, of every person of rank or genteel appearance that passed along the principal streets of London and Westminster'.[1] A more general factor that helped to force the issue on public attention was the sheer amount of flogging that took place during the French wars. Although (as has been indicated) statistics are not available to show whether the use of flogging was increasing in proportionate terms, the expansion of the army's total strength almost certainly entailed an absolute increase in its use, and there is much 'literary' evidence to suggest that at this time discipline was particularly severe. Alexander Alexander recorded in his auto-biography that when he was a new recruit in the Royal Artillery at Woolwich in 1801–2 there was 'scarce a day in which we did not see one or more of the soldiers get from three to seven hundred lashes'; and John Shipp, who was a drummer in an infantry regiment at much the same period, had to inflict corporal punishment about three times a week.[2]

The early years of the century were also, by contrast, a time when there was considerable discussion about possible means of raising morale in the army and stimulating recruitment, and in this context criticisms of the system of corporal punishment were publicly expressed by two or three serving officers. The fullest critique was offered in a work of 1804 by Lieutenant-Colonel Robert Wilson (later to become a general and MP for Southwark). The main checks to recruitment, he said, were the system of recruiting for life and the frequency of corporal punishment. He did not suggest that the latter practice should be abolished, but he argued that it was much too commonly and severely used for slight offences, and he proposed several regulations which in his opinion would moderate its use. One was that no officer under the age of twenty-one should be allowed to sit as a member of a court martial, and another was that all witnesses before courts martial should give evidence under oath.[3] These

---

1. *Howell's State Trials* (1816–28), xxviii. 51–178; [R. Southey], *Letters from England, by Don Manuel Alvarez Espriella* (2nd edn., 1808), p. 103; *Cobbett's Political Register*, 6 Feb. 1802.

2. *The Life of Alexander Alexander, written by himself*, ed. John Howell (Edinburgh, 1830), i. 86, cited in T. H. McGuffie, 'Life in the British Army, 1793–1820, in relation to Social Conditions', London University MA thesis (1940), p. 61; J. Shipp, *A Voice from the Ranks; or A Letter to Sir Francis Burdett, on the barbarous and degrading System of Flogging Soldiers and Sailors* (1831), p. 4. Cf. Marshall, pp. 170, 178.

3. Lt.-Col. R. T. Wilson, *An Enquiry into the Present State of the Military Force of the British Empire* (1804), pp. 58–75. For other criticisms of the frequency of corporal punishment, see Lt.-Gen. John Money, *A Letter to the Right Hon. William Windham, on the Defence of the Country at the present Crisis* (Norwich, 1806), pp. 74–75; Brig.-Gen. William Stewart, *Outlines of a Plan for the General Reform of the British Land Forces* (2nd edn., 1806), pp. 33–35.

proposals were followed up during the next session of parliament by General Richard Fitzpatrick, the Foxite MP. He moved the addition of two clauses to the Mutiny Bill, which were both accepted: the first laid down that (as was already the case at general courts martial) oaths should be administered to the members of regimental courts martial and to all witnesses who gave evidence before them; the second laid down that no officer of less than twenty-one years of age should be able to preside over a regimental court martial. It was pointed out during the debate that although these courts were theoretically intended for the trial of small offences, they had come in practice to deal with serious crimes such as mutiny, desertion and theft and sometimes passed sentences of as much as 1000 lashes.[1]

There was no official limit to the number of lashes that could be inflicted. A few years before, after a soldier had died as a result of a flogging at Coventry, the then secretary at war William Windham had suggested to the commander-in-chief (the Duke of York) that some restriction should be placed on the number of lashes that a regimental court martial could award; but a memorandum countering this proposal had been written by the quartermaster general at the Horse Guards (Lieutenant-General David Dundas, later to be commander-in-chief), who held that any such public limitation would have 'the most dangerous military consequences'.[2] In 1806 Windham, as secretary of state for war in the Ministry of All the Talents, brought forward his plan of army reform, the principal object of which was to promote recruitment by replacing enlistment for life by enlistment for a specified number of years. However, apart from a passing suggestion that discipline should be made less rigorous,[3] he did not propose any change in the system of corporal punishment. The only modification that *was* made at this time was a slight and ineffective one. After a general court martial had passed a sentence of 1500 lashes, a General Order was issued on 30 January 1807 stating the King's opinion that an award of 1000 lashes was 'a sufficient example for any breach of military discipline, short of capital offence', and that sentences ought not to exceed that figure; but it is clear that on a number of subsequent occasions this instruction was ignored.[4]

In 1808 public discussion of the question was renewed and very much extended, as a result of its being taken up by Sir Francis Burdett. Earlier, he had denounced the use of flogging to extract information and confessions from civilians in Ireland during 1798; and he had written to Colonel Wilson to congratulate him on his publication of 1804, calling it 'one of the most material services ever

1. Cobbett's (later Hansard's) *Parliamentary Debates* [*P.D.*], iii. 640–1, 857–61.
2. M. Lewis to Col. R. Brownrigg, 18 March 1800, and undated memorandum initialled 'D.D.', Public Record Office [P.R.O.], W.O. 40/13, no. 11.
3. *P.D.*, vi. 666.
4. Marshall, p. 191; Sir Charles Oman, *Wellington's Army 1809–1814* (1913), p. 237.

performed for this country in particular and for humanity in general'.[1] Flogging was one of the first questions he raised after his return to parliament as MP for Westminster, and the initial occasion for his raising it was Castlereagh's Local Militia Bill of 1808. The local militia was to be conscripted by ballot from the population at large, and was to be placed while on duty under martial law. According to Burdett, the implication was that the whole population would be potentially exposed to the lash, and this was no way, he said, 'to inspire the people with enthusiasm and to animate them to general exertion'. He added that he would like to see flogging abolished in the army as a whole, and later in the session, supported by Lord Folkestone, he moved for regimental returns of all corporal punishments awarded and inflicted during the previous ten years; but the motion was defeated by 77 votes to 4.[2] He reverted to the subject in 1811, when he moved an address to the Prince Regent requesting him to issue orders 'calculated to restrain, and finally to abolish, that cruel, unnecessary and ignominious mode of punishment'. This motion, seconded by Brougham, was defeated by 94 votes to 10, and when in March 1812 Burdett moved that a clause enacting the abolition of flogging be inserted in the Mutiny Bill, it was thrown out by 79 votes to 6. Shortly afterwards a further motion for information about corporal punishments, introduced this time by H. G. Bennet (the Whig MP who was subsequently to lead the parliamentary campaign against the use of climbing boys), was strongly supported by Burdett, Brougham and Sir Samuel Romilly but was beaten by 49 votes to 17.[3]

Meanwhile, the campaign in parliament was given strong backing by several radical newspapers, though at considerable hazard to the journalists concerned. In July 1809 Cobbett published an indignant article in his *Political Register* about the flogging of some local militiamen at Ely who had made a concerted protest against a deduction from their pay to cover the price of their knapsacks. This led in July 1810 to his being convicted of seditious libel and sentenced to two years' imprisonment in Newgate and a fine of £1000.[4] In August 1810 John Drakard published in his *Stamford News* an article which included a graphic description of a military flogging and maintained that the lot of French soldiers, who were not subject to such barbarities, was more eligible than that of troops in the British service. The article was reprinted a week later in John and Leigh Hunt's *Examiner*,[5] and both they and Drakard were prosecuted on

1. *Cobbett's Parliamentary History*, xxxvi. 520, 523; Herbert Randolph, *Life of General Sir Robert Wilson* (1862), i. 242–3.
2. P.D., xi. 105–7, 1115–22.   3. *Ibid.* xx. 698–710, xxi. 1263–92, xxii. 374–93.
4. *Cobbett's Political Register*, 1 July 1809 (P.R.O., T.S.11/91/289); G. D. H. Cole, *Life of William Cobbett* (3rd edn., 1947), pp. 150–9.
5. *Stamford News*, 24 Aug. 1810; *Examiner*, 2 Sept. 1810. According to the *Morning Chronicle* (28 Feb. 1811), the *Stamford News* could 'fairly claim the merit of having led the way among country journals in rendering political discussion a principal feature of its arrangement'.

account of it. The Hunts were lucky enough to be acquitted in the court of king's bench, despite a hostile summing-up by Lord Ellenborough; but Drakard, tried before a carefully-packed jury at Lincoln, was convicted and sentenced to eighteen months' imprisonment and a £200 fine. These prosecutions probably had the effect of giving additional publicity to the attack on flogging, and they certainly did not deter the journalists concerned from pursuing the subject further. Drakard published in pamphlet form full accounts of the Hunts' trial and of his own, including the powerful speeches which Brougham delivered as counsel for the defence on both occasions;[1] and two years later he was the printer and publisher of an anonymous pamphlet entitled *The Military Commentator* (actually written by Leicester Stanhope), which was a cogent attack on various aspects of the English military code and on flogging in particular.[2] Also, in June 1811 when Burdett moved his address to the Prince Regent on corporal punishment in the army, articles in support of his motion appeared in Cobbett's *Register*, the *Stamford News* and the *Examiner*; and in June 1812 Cobbett claimed in a further article that the previous two years had seen a significant mitigation of the system of military punishments, which was attributable to the efforts of Burdett and of the press.[3]

One or two concessions had indeed been made. In 1811 the clause in the Mutiny Act that empowered general courts martial to sentence soldiers to corporal punishment for misbehaviour or neglect of duty was slightly altered: the new clause empowered them to inflict corporal punishment 'or imprisonment, as such court shall think fit'. In the following year this provision was extended to cover other grades of court martial as well.[4] There was some doubt as to whether these changes gave courts martial any powers they had not previously possessed,[5] but they did intimate that more use should be made of imprisonment as an alternative to flogging. Another reform made in 1812 may have been more substantial. A confidential circular from the Horse Guards to commanding officers of regiments ordered that in no circumstances should the award of a regimental court martial exceed 300 lashes.[6] Moreover, in 1813 the judge advocate general,

1. *Report of the Proceedings on an Information filed ex officio, by His Majesty's Attorney General, against John and Leigh Hunt, proprietors of The Examiner* (Stamford, 1811); *Report of the Proceedings on an Information filed ex officio, by His Majesty's Attorney General, against John Drakard, proprietor of The Stamford News* (Stamford, 1811). *Cf.* Chester New, *Life of Henry Brougham to 1830* (Oxford, 1961), pp. 52–56.

2. [L. F. C. Stanhope], *The Military Commentator* (1813). The attribution to Stanhope is made in Bentham's hand on the title-page of the copy in the British Library; Stanhope, who later became 5th earl of Harrington, was at this time a captain in the 6th Dragoons.

3. *Cobbett's Political Register*, 22 June 1811, 13 June 1812; *Stamford News*, 28 June 1811; *Examiner*, 30 June 1811.

4. 51 Geo. III c. 8, s. 22; 52 Geo. III c. 22, s. 23.

5. *Cf. P.D.*, xx. 707–8 (Brougham, 18 June 1812).

6. Marshall, pp. 184–5; *Examiner*, 7 June 1812.

Manners-Sutton, told the house of commons that floggings had
become much less numerous of late because in many cases men
sentenced to corporal punishment were being given the option of
commuting the sentence into indefinite service abroad – a procedure
for which provision had been made in the *General Regulations and
Orders of the Army* printed in August 1811.[1] One further concession
that was made to the reformers at the end of the war concerned the
practice of executing sentences of corporal punishment by instal-
ments. If during a flogging the surgeon in attendance decided that
further lashes could not be inflicted without serious danger to 'life or
limb', the punishment was halted; but when the man's wounds had
healed he could be brought out again to receive the remainder, or a
further instalment, of his sentence. A late eighteenth-century work on
the duties of regimental surgeons had protested against this practice,
and Romilly and Bennet raised it several times during the last years of
the war.[2] Manners-Sutton's response was at first equivocal, but in
June 1815 he definitely stated that in his opinion it was illegal to inflict
part of a sentence at one time and the remainder at another, and two
years later he reported that this opinion had been adopted by the
commander-in-chief.[3]

During the post-war years, though the topic was occasionally
raised in the radical press,[4] there was an interlude so far as the
parliamentary discussion of flogging was concerned. But in the
summer of 1822 public concern was aroused by the death of a soldier
after a flogging at Hull, and when the next Mutiny Bill was before the
House in March 1823 Burdett gave notice of a fresh general motion
on the subject.[5] This move led Palmerston, the secretary at war, to
suggest privately to the Duke of York that the maximum number of
lashes which a regimental court martial could inflict should be
reduced from 300 to 200. If Burdett's motion was brought forward,
Palmerston wrote, it would be 'very useful' for him to be able to
announce to the House that an order had been issued to this effect.[6]
But his suggestion drew hostile memoranda from the Duke of York's
military secretary and from John Beckett, the judge advocate

1. *General Regulations and Orders of the Army* (1811), pp. 206–8; *P.D.*, xxv. 128. For
confirmation that this practice was common in the second decade of the century, see
Major-Gen. Sir H. Torrens to H. Alexander, 23 Jan. 1818, P.R.O., W.O. 3/613, p.
248.
2. Hamilton, ii. 31–2; *P.D.*, xxii. 386, xxv. 126. On the frequency of this practice
during the French wars, see Major-Gen. Charles Napier, *Remarks on Military Law and
the Punishment of Flogging* (1837), p. 159.
3. *P.D.*, xxv. 128–30, xxxi. 938–9, xxxv. 273; *Memoirs of the Life of Sir Samuel
Romilly*, ed. by his sons (1840), iii. 183.
4. *Black Dwarf*, 31 March 1819; *Sherwin's Weekly Political Register*, 31 July 1819
(P.R.O., H.O. 42/191).
5. *Traveller*, 30, 31 July 1822; *London Weekly Gazette*, 7 Aug. 1822; *P.D.*, New
Series [N.S.], viii. 616.
6. Palmerston to Major-Gen. Sir H. Taylor, 19 April 1823, British Library,
Additional MSS [BL, Add. MSS] 48419, fo. 90.

general,[1] and no such order was given. Burdett's motion did not materialize, either, in 1823; but in the following session Joseph Hume made the first of a number of attempts to insert clauses into the Mutiny Bill for the purpose of restricting or discontinuing the use of flogging. Though his motions of the mid-1820s were all unsuccessful, the minorities were significantly larger than those on Burdett's motions during the parliament of 1807–12. The most favourable division was that of 10 March 1826, when a clause prohibiting military flogging in the United Kingdom was rejected by 99 votes to 52.[2] Following this debate Sir Henry Hardinge, a major-general and ministerial MP, drew the commander-in-chief's attention to 'the growing feeling in the House of Commons against corporal punishment', and suggested, as a reform which might reconcile many people to the retention of 'this indispensable power', the adoption of the Prussian system of dividing the troops into two classes, only the lower of which (consisting of men 'degraded' by sentence of a court martial) could be subjected to corporal punishment.[3] The Duke of York, however, was opposed to any concession, as he made very clear in a memorandum which he sent to the home secretary on 3 April urging the government not to 'give way to the present cry'.[4] The government did stiffen its resistance. In the spring of 1827 Palmerston made the strongest of his speeches in opposition to the abolitionist case, and a further attempt of Hume's to amend the Mutiny Bill was defeated by a relatively easy margin.[5]

Another interlude followed, but in the early 1830s the situation was altered by the formation of a whig government and, in particular, by the appointment of Sir John Cam Hobhouse as secretary at war in February 1832. Hobhouse recognized when accepting the post that he would be placed in an awkward position, for as Burdett's fellow-member for Westminster he had been a prominent critic of flogging in the parliamentary debates of the 1820s.[6] Indeed, within a few days Henry Hunt was calling on him in the house of commons to put an end to 'this most inhuman practice'. Hobhouse told Grey (who regarded flogging as a necessary evil) that only if he could modify the system of corporal punishment would he feel justified in voting against its immediate abolition; and when Hunt raised the subject again later in the session Hobhouse was able to announce that an alteration had been made in the Articles of War reducing the

1. P.R.O., W.O. 81/62, fos. 138–9, 234–52.
2. *P.D.*, N.S., x. 766–76, 1031–9, xiv. 1292–1305.
3. *Despatches, Correspondence and Memoranda of Field Marshal Arthur, Duke of Wellington*, 2nd series, ed. 2nd Duke of Wellington (1867–80), iii. 198–201.
4. P.R.O., H.O. 50/13, fos. 215–30.
5. *P.D.*, N.S., xvi. 679–80, 1136–9; Jasper Ridley, *Lord Palmerston* (1970), p. 87.
6. BL, Add. MSS 56556, fo. 51. He had said in March 1826 that 'he hoped to live to see the day when those who abetted the continuance of this discipline would be ashamed of their former opinions' (*P.D.*, N.S., xiv. 1371).

maximum award of regimental courts martial from 300 to 200 lashes.[1]
It is clear from his diary that he would have liked to go further but
was faced with stiff opposition from the highest ranks of the army. In
March 1832 the Duke of Wellington sent him via Lord Hill, the
commander-in-chief, a memorandum insisting on the necessity of
corporal punishment, and a year later Hill himself refused his consent
to a proposal by Hobhouse for the abolition of regimental flogging
except in cases of mutiny under arms. An open clash between
secretary at war and commander-in-chief seemed imminent, and was
only averted by a ministerial reshuffle which involved Hobhouse's
transference to the chief secretaryship for Ireland.[2]

A few days later, when the Mutiny Bill of 1833 was before the
House, Hume moved once again the insertion of a clause prohibiting
the flogging of troops within the United Kingdom. At the end of the
debate Burdett proposed, and Hume agreed, that the clause should be
amended to read: 'That flogging should not be applied anywhere
under the Mutiny Act, except in cases of open mutiny, thieving, and
drunkenness on guard.' The whig-liberal ranks were badly split by
this modified motion, and it was only just defeated by 151 votes to
140. Hobhouse, who stayed away from the debate, regarded the
division as 'a very proper lesson for ministers'.[3] When in the
following June a further motion on flogging was due to be
introduced by James Silk Buckingham, radical MP for Sheffield,
Edward Ellice, the new secretary at war, announced that the
government had given serious consideration to the question and had
framed an order restricting the infliction of corporal punishment as
nearly as possible to the offences specified in Burdett's amendment of
2 April. The government's instructions were communicated to Lord
Hill in July, and an order was duly issued from the Horse Guards on
24 August.[4] The order – as the reformers soon pointed out – was not
in fact as restrictive as the formula suggested by Burdett: men could
still be flogged, for instance, for 'insubordination' and 'disgraceful
conduct'. But early in the 1834 session a return was made to the house
of commons showing that since 1831 there had been a marked fall in
the number of corporal punishments inflicted; and it is clear from the
adjutant general's letter-books that after his order of August 1833
Lord Hill made serious efforts to reduce it further.[5]

However, the pressure for reform did not relax. It must have

---

1. *P.D.*, 3rd S., x. 422, xi. 1227; BL, Add. MSS 56556, fo. 80.
2. BL, Add. MSS 56556, fo. 93, and 56557, fos. 122–5.
3. *P.D.*, 3rd S., xvii. 49–70; BL, Add. MSS 56557, fos. 132–3.
4. *P.D.*, 3rd S., xviii. 1229–30; Lord Stanley to Hill, 26 July 1833, P.R.O., W.O. 6/127, pp. 7–8; Marshall, pp. 209–10.
5. *P.D.*, 3rd S., xxii. 223, 243–4; P.P. 1834, xlii. 107; Major-Gen. Sir John Macdonald to Major-Gen. Sir William Nicolay, 9 Nov. 1833, P.R.O., W.O. 3/86, pp. 348–50; Macdonald to Lt.-Gen. Sir R. W. O'Callaghan, 22 Feb. 1834, P.R.O., W.O. 3/542, p. 3.

seemed to the authorities, indeed, that the more infrequent floggings became the more public clamour they aroused. In July 1834 an outcry was caused by a case which not many years earlier would have been too commonplace to attract attention. A private in the Scotch Fusiliers received 300 lashes at Charing Cross Barracks for being drunk on sentry duty and attempting to strike his serjeant. A particularly lurid report of the flogging appeared in a popular radical paper, the *True Sun*, and was reprinted as a leaflet, and the incident provoked several petitions to parliament: 1648 inhabitants of Oxford, for example, signed a petition denouncing 'a disreputable, cowardly, unmanly, unfeeling, brutal, inhuman and bloody mode of punishment'. In view of the state of public feeling the government felt obliged to announce through the secretary at war that it intended to recommend the appointment of a royal commission to inquire into the military code.[1]

The commission 'for inquiring into the system of military punishments in the Army' was actually appointed in the following March, when Peel was in office.[2] Its membership – unlike that of the royal commissions on the poor law and on municipal corporations – was clearly not biased in favour of reform. The chairman was Lord Wharncliffe, a colonel and tory peer, and the other members were three generals, a tory MP, a former chief justice of Calcutta (who had also been a tory MP), and R. C. Fergusson. Fergusson had once been arrested as a speaker at a London Corresponding Society meeting, and had voted for one of Hunt's motions against flogging in 1832, but he had held the office of judge advocate general in Melbourne's first government and he returned to the same post in April 1835. The chief witnesses who gave evidence in favour of reform were Joseph Hume, Major St John Fancourt, Major Aubrey Beauclerk, a liberal MP who had spoken against flogging in the house of commons, Lieutenant-Colonel Thomas Perronet Thompson, proprietor of the Benthamite *Westminster Review* and MP for Hull, and Lieutenant-Colonel George De Lacy Evans, who had displaced Hobhouse as MP for Westminster in 1833. Most of them did not advocate total abolition, but argued that corporal punishment should only be retained for armies in the field. Witnesses who defended the existing practice included the Duke of Wellington, Lord Hill, Major-General Sir Henry Hardinge, General Sir Henry Fane and Major-General Sir John Macdonald, the adjutant general. Some of the arguments employed on the two sides will be considered in due course, but it may be observed here that in the minds of the commissioners (whose general disposition is

1. *True Sun*, 17 July 1834; Hume Tracts 83/8, University College London; *Journals of the House of Commons*, lxxxix. 503, 548, 572, 580; *P.D.*, 3rd S., xxv. 283.
2. The new ministers felt that the appointment of the commission was 'rendered unavoidably necessary . . . by the promises made in that respect by their predecessors': J. C. Herries to Major-Gen. Sir H. Taylor, 26 Feb. 1835, BL, Add. MSS 57442, fo. 48.

apparent from the tenor of the questions posed to witnesses) there can have been little doubt that the weightiest testimony came from the supporters of the system. On the other hand, there was a degree of pressure for reform which could not be ignored; and, as luck would have it, during the period when the commission was sitting two marines died at Woolwich within a short time of being flogged – incidents that were given extensive coverage in the press.[1] The report which the commission eventually produced in March 1836 was not wholly negative. It concluded that it would be unsafe to abolish corporal punishment in wartime or peace-time, at home or abroad, but it recommended that further efforts should be made to render it less frequent and that the extent of the sentences which courts martial could award should be further restricted. It also recommended that more should be done, including the building of military prisons, to facilitate the use of alternative punishments, and that more attempt should be made to promote good conduct by the offer of honorary rewards and adequate pensions to deserving men. Following the publication of the report, a change was made in the Articles of War whereby the award of a general court martial (which had not previously been restricted) was limited to 200 lashes, that of a district court martial to 150, and that of a regimental court martial to 100.[2]

After this narrative account, a more analytical approach will now be adopted in examining the main features of the campaign and the controversy it aroused. First, something needs to be said about the relationship between this campaign and the contemporary process of reform in the British penal system. It has been said with regard to the latter that between 1770 and 1840 there was a shift from a variety of punishments 'directed at the body' to carceral forms of discipline 'directed at the mind'.[3] This development helped the campaign against military flogging in certain concrete ways. The increasing use of solitary confinement in civil prisons and, after the French wars, the widespread introduction of the treadmill, meant that when the army's reliance on corporal punishment came under attack there were current alternatives available; and the Mutiny Acts of the post-war period made increasingly specific provision for the use of such alternatives.[4] Also, the movement for penal reform involved the

1. *Times*, 28 Nov. 1835, 24 Feb. 1836; *Weekly Dispatch*, 29 Nov. 1835, 28 Feb. 1836; *Lancet*, 27 Feb. 1836.
2. P.P. 1836, xxii. 7–23; Marshall, p. 219.
3. Michael Ignatieff, *A Just Measure of Pain: The Penitentiary in the Industrial Revolution* (1978), p. xiii.
4. In 1817 it was declared to be lawful for general courts martial to sentence to solitary confinement, and in 1823 for general and other courts martial to sentence to imprisonment with hard labour. In 1830 it was laid down that regimental courts martial could sentence to imprisonment with or without hard labour for up to thirty days, or to solitary confinement for up to twenty days. (57 Geo. III c. 12, s. 24; 4 Geo. IV c. 13, s. 25; 11 Geo. IV and 1 Wm. IV c. 7, s. 10. See also Lord Hill's confidential circular of 24 June 1830, giving detailed instructions with regard to terms and modes of imprisonment: P.P. 1836, xxii. 334–7.)

rejection of punishments that were somewhat analogous to military flogging. Partly as a result of the efforts of Jonas Hanway, William Eden and others, ritual punishments such as whipping through the streets at the cart's tail, which had much in common with the flogging of soldiers in the presence of their comrades, were becoming discredited. One may add (though here one is moving beyond the sphere of domestic penology) that opposition to savage punishments was a feature of the anti-slavery campaign: there was much concern in the second and third decades of the century about the flogging of slaves in the West Indies, and in the 1820s Lord Bathurst as colonial secretary was pressing the West Indian colonies to adopt regulations that would restrict this practice.[1]

It would be mistaken, however, to regard the campaign against corporal punishment in the army as merely part of a wider movement against corporal punishment as such, for in the early nineteenth century such a movement hardly existed. Although H. G. Bennet did introduce one parliamentary motion for the abolition of whipping, and there were some writers on penology who argued against corporal punishment on general grounds, there was no sustained attack on whipping for criminal offences; and it seems that the abolition of the death penalty for many crimes led to an *increased* use of this form of punishment in the 1820s.[2] It was common for defenders of military flogging to point out how familiar and indispensable corporal punishment was in fields apart from the army (including the schools of the upper classes)[3] – while on the other side of the debate it was usual to treat the military phenomenon as something quite distinct from the milder forms of chastisement used in civilian life.[4]

There was an important international sense in which the British system of military discipline could be represented as anomalous: after the French wars it had virtually no parallel in the other armies of the civilized world. Corporal punishment had been abolished in the French army during the Revolution and in the American one at the beginning of the War of 1812; and in Prussia it had been abolished, for all except 'degraded' soldiers, in the period of reform that followed the battle of Jena. The reformers made much of the comparisons they were able to draw, and in 1835 their case seemed to be strengthened

1. F. J. Klingberg, *The Anti-Slavery Movement in England* (1926), pp. 224 ff.
2. *P.D.*, N.S., viii. 1437–42 (30 April 1823); William Roscoe, *Observations on Penal Jurisprudence, and the Reformation of Criminals* (1819), p. 136; Leon Radzinowicz, *History of English Criminal Law and its Administration* (1948–68), i. 571.
3. *P.D.*, N.S., x. 1034 (Major-Gen. Sir H. Vivian, 15 March 1824); Anon., *Remarks on Military Punishments* (1828), p. 5. Hardinge, in a debate of March 1827, made much of the fact that an attempt to dispense with corporal punishment at the Millbank Penitentiary had ended in a recommendation from the committee of management that this power be restored as a necessary means of dealing with indiscipline. *P.D.*, N.S., xvi. 1140–1; *Seventh Report of the Committee of the Society for the Improvement of Prison Discipline* (1827), Appendix, p. 391.
4. *E.g. P.D.*, N.S. x. 771 (Sir Robert Wilson, 5 March 1824).

further when Lord William Bentinck, as governor general of India, issued an order prohibiting the flogging of troops in the native army.[1] The points that were made about the singularity of British practice drew various responses. One was the assertion that discipline in other armies was much less reliable – a statement that was sometimes illustrated by a reference to the behaviour of the French army during its retreat from the Peninsula in 1813, when the advancing British had allegedly been greeted as deliverers by the population of southern France.[2] Another point was that, instead of flogging, continental armies made much more use of capital punishment and of very severe sentences of confinement: it was stated in the report of the royal commission, for instance, that an offence such as the sale of arms or equipment, which in the British army would be punished by 300 lashes, would be punished under the French code by between two and five years in the galleys.[3] But the most common response of all was that other armies were composed of quite different materials from those which formed the British one. The conscripted armies of the continent, it was alleged, contained a broad cross-section of society and included a large number of men from respectable backgrounds;[4] the rank and file of the British army, on the other hand, were recruited almost exclusively from the lowest strata of the population and were particularly disposed to drunkenness and crime. Wellington's remark that the army was composed of 'the scum of the earth, ... fellows who have all enlisted for drink', is well known. He made similar remarks in papers which he wrote on the flogging question in 1829 and 1832;[5] and the Duke of York said in the memorandum which he sent to the Home Secretary in April 1826: 'Our Regiments are generally speaking composed of the lowest and most thoughtless part of the community who are induced to enlist from some momentary motive mostly arising from the desire to extricate themselves from some scrape. . . . Such people can be restrained by nothing but the strong hand of power.'[6]

This latter argument in defence of flogging had an obvious corollary, which the Dukes of York and Wellington unequivocally endorsed: that the essential purpose of military punishments was deterrence rather than reformation. It was common for opponents of

1. Ten years later, however, Hardinge as governor general revived the corporal punishment of native troops, on the grounds that its abolition had resulted in a great increase in crime and insubordination. P.P. 1836, xl. 450–8; Sir Henry Lawrence, *Essays, Military and Political* (1859), pp. 243–7.

2. *E.g.* P.D., N.S., x. 934 (Palmerston, 11 March 1824).

3. P.P. 1836, xxii. 14.

4. Also, on the high caste and good conduct of the sepoys in the native army in India, see Bentinck's own evidence to the royal commission (*ibid.* p. 304).

5. 5th Earl Stanhope, *Notes of Conversations with the Duke of Wellington 1831–1851* (1888), p. 14; Wellington, *Despatches*, 2nd S., v. 593–4; P.P. 1836, xxii. 345 (where Wellington's memorandum of 4 March 1832 is misdated 1833).

6. Memorandum of 3 April 1826, P.R.O., H.O. 50/13, fo. 224.

flogging to complain that this type of punishment rarely if ever resulted in the reform of those on whom it was inflicted. It tended, according to Wilson, to 'break the spirit without amending the disposition', or as another officer put it, 'to break the honest heart and to render the vicious one callous'.[1] But Wellington, in giving evidence to the royal commission, treated such objections as beside the point. 'The real meaning of punishment, if it means anything,' he said, 'is example – it is to prevent others, by the example of what they see the criminal suffer, from committing the same or a similar offence.'[2] The military authorities disliked the substitution of imprisonment for flogging for a number of reasons – not least, no doubt, because it was more expensive; but the reason that was most often cited was their view that imprisonment was less effective as a deterrent. Wellington claimed that flogging was the only form of punishment that made any impression on anyone, and Hardinge said with regard to solitary confinement that when a man was punished out of sight of his comrades his fate was soon forgotten by those who only heard the sentence read out once on parade.[3] Moreover, one of the strongest arguments of the opponents of change was that a mitigation of the military code not only threatened to produce, but was actually producing, a serious deterioration in discipline and behaviour. The Duke of York complained in 1826 that since 'Liberalism and Philanthropy' had become the order of the day there had been a great increase in the amount of military crime, especially insubordination.[4] And at the time of the royal commission the military authorities were able to present statistics which showed that the marked fall that had occurred during the early 1830s in the number of corporal punishments inflicted had been accompanied by an equally marked and steady rise in the number of men tried by courts martial.[5]

	1830	1831	1832	1833
Number of courts martial held in the British army	5946	7438	8780	9628
Number of men flogged in the British army	1754	1489	1283	1007
Number of courts martial held in the UK	2684	3925	4840	5472
Number of men flogged in the UK	655	646	485	376

1. Wilson, p. 65; Col. F. P. Robinson to Samuel Whitbread, 29 June 1811, Whitbread MSS, Bedfordshire Record Office, W.1/5408.
2. P.P. 1836, xxii. 348.
3. *Ibid.* p. 320.
4. P.R.O., H.O. 50/13, fo. 225. See also Sir H. Taylor to Sir R. Peel, 8 April 1826, P.R.O., H.O. 50/443, no. 3.
5. P.P. 1836, xxii. 338–9.

These figures were difficult to argue with, but the reformers did have a general set of answers to the contention that corporal punishment was indispensable because of the peculiarly coarse materials of which the British army was composed. For one thing, it was argued that it was partly on account of flogging that the army was unable to attract a better class of recruits: self-respecting men would not voluntarily enter a service in which such a brutal and degrading punishment was used.[1] It was argued further that positive steps could and should be taken to raise the quality of recruits through improving rates of pay and terms of service. It was unfortunate, from the point of view of the campaign, that Windham's attempt to effect these improvements had been in large measure abandoned and written off as a failure. Wellington could write in 1829: 'It was the object of Mr Windham's Act to make the army a popular service in England, by rendering service therein profitable as well as honourable, but his measures totally failed.'[2] It was also unfortunate that in the post-war years there was strong pressure for retrenchment – pressure which came to some extent from the same quarter as the pressure for reforms in military discipline. Hume called repeatedly for cuts in military expenditure, and was prepared to argue that these should include a lowering of soldiers' pay; and Hobhouse, while secretary at war, was effecting a reduction in the scale of army pensions at the same time as he was proposing restrictions on flogging.[3] Nevertheless, some of the reformers did argue that it was the system of service for life at very low rates of pay that was the root of the trouble – not only because it discouraged all but the most desperate from enlisting, but also because it meant that once inside the army a man was faced with little better than a life of forced labour. According to Leicester Stanhope, the soldier was 'reduced to a state of servitude in the midst of a nation of freemen'; and Burdett said in 1812: 'Because in that line of life his reward was not adequate to the services he performed, . . . they were obliged to compel him to his duty by torture.'[4] Cobbett made a similar point with reference to the lack of opportunities for promotion to commissioned rank. He said in a memorandum which he wrote for Burdett: 'The soldiers, never being able to hope for anything above the rank of Serjeant (whence they may, any when, be reduced, and flogged) have not a sufficient motive for good behavior; and hence, the lash is used instead of the commissions: *punishments* instead of *rewards*.'[5] The Royal Commission on Military

1. *E.g. P.D.*, N.S., xvi. 1131 (Wilson, 12 March 1827).
2. Wellington, *Despatches*, 2nd S., v. 594.
3. *P.D.*, N.S., xxii. 813–14 (Hume, 22 Feb. 1830); BL, Add. MSS 56557, fos. 67, 104.
4. Leicester Stanhope, p. 74; *P.D.*, xxi. 1265.
5. Bodleian Library (Oxford), MS Eng. hist. b. 197, fos. 2–3. The memorandum is unsigned and undated, but is in Cobbett's hand and appears from Burdett's accompanying notes to have been written in 1812.

Punishments did consider a proposal put forward in his evidence by
Joseph Hume that a certain proportion of commissions should be
reserved for those promoted from the ranks. But Wellington was
strongly opposed to this idea, maintaining that non-commissioned
officers who were promoted to commissions could not 'live in the
society of gentlemen';[1] and the royal commission concluded that, as it
was considered one of the essential requisites of the army that 'its
officers should be of a station and education to fit them for any society
in which they [might] be placed', and as 'ungentlemanly conduct' was
treated in the British military code as a most serious offence, it was
'most imperative that the line should be very strictly drawn between
the officer and the soldier'.[2]

Not surprisingly, some critics of flogging – notably the philosophic radicals, who were very preoccupied with the evils of aristocratic government – treated it as one of the abuses that resulted from
and reflected the hegemony of a particular class.[3] Also, some radicals
went further and argued that it was a crucial instrument of that
hegemony and an intrinsic part of a general system of repression.
Burdett in particular took this view. He believed during the French
Wars that the government, instead of securing the people's support
for the war-effort by redressing their grievances, was relying on a
large standing army to hold the country down, while relying on the
lash to discipline the soldiers. The repressive use of the army seemed
especially obvious in 1812, when regular troops and militiamen were
used against the Luddites, and in that year he was particularly
outspoken both in denouncing the subjugation of the people by
military force and in denouncing military flogging.[4] Later, after the
Peterloo massacre, he explicitly linked the two themes in an indignant
public letter which he addressed to his constituents. After protesting
against this deplorable 'use of a standing army in time of peace', he
recalled that in James II's time the news of the acquittal of the Seven
Bishops had been greeted by the army with cheers, and the king had
shortly afterwards fled; but James II, he went on to say, had not been
able to 'inflict the torture on his soldiers – could not tear the flesh
from their bones with the cat-o'-nine-tails'.[5]

The political aspect of the question of military punishments came
to the fore again during the Reform Bill crisis. In May 1832 Alexander

1. P.P. 1836, xxii. 353. He said in conversation that 'their fault always was, not
being able to resist drink – . . . and you therefore could never perfectly trust them'
(Earl Stanhope, p. 13).
2. P.P. 1836, xxii. 20–21.
3. Perronet Thompson in *Westminster Review*, xx (1834), 495; J. S. Mill in *Monthly
Repository*, viii (1834), 599.
4. *Cf.* J. R. Dinwiddy, 'Sir Francis Burdett and Burdettite Radicalism', *History*,
lxv (1980), 29–30 and nn.; see above, 121-22 and nn.
5. M. W. Patterson, *Sir Francis Burdett and His Times 1770–1844* (1931), ii. 490–2.
The letter led to a prosecution for seditious libel, and Burdett was sentenced to a
£2,000 fine and three months' imprisonment.

Somerville, a young soldier in the Scots Greys, who were then stationed at Birmingham, wrote a letter to the *Weekly Dispatch* in which he said that he and his comrades could be relied upon to defend property against lawless attacks but would never raise their arms against the liberties of their country. Two days after the letter was published Somerville was court-martialled and flogged – ostensibly for refusing to mount an unruly horse, but it was clear from the harangue which the commanding officer delivered to the regiment after the flogging that the letter was the real offence. Somerville subsequently wrote another letter which was published in *The Times*, and the affair became a *cause célèbre*: Hume raised it in parliament, several Political Unions petitioned for an inquiry, and a public subscription was raised for Somerville which enabled him to purchase his discharge.[1] The case encouraged some ultra-radical writers of the unstamped press to argue that the lash was being used to prevent the spread of political awareness in the army – which was something they were anxious to promote. It was claimed in the *Poor Man's Guardian* in March 1833 that copies of the paper were finding their way into several regiments, but that soldiers in the guards, in order to save 'their characters from the black list and their backs from the cat-o'-nine-tails', tore up the paper after reading it, divided the fragments between them, and chewed them into rags.[2] Towards the end of the same year Richard Carlile launched a weekly unstamped paper called *The Political Soldier*, which was intended to create (though in fact it only lasted for five issues) a union of sentiment between the soldiers and the people. Somerville was initially the editor, and the first number contained a report of a speech of his at a public meeting in which he said that the crucial questions were 'whether the aristocracy should be enabled, by means of keeping up a large standing army, to lord it over the industrious classes of the community as they had hitherto done', and 'whether their fellow-men were any longer to be flogged and degraded by the brutal punishment of the lash, until they were themselves rendered fit instruments to be employed against the people, if ever the people chose to resist the acts of a tyrannical government'.[3]

Some of the things that were said by people on the other side did tend to confirm that the question had a political dimension. The Duke of Wellington, in particular, was quite explicit about the importance of the army as the ultimate safeguard against popular disorder and insurrection. In a letter written from the Peninsula at the time of the Burdett riots in 1810 he warned ministers to 'take care that they don't

1. *Weekly Dispatch*, 27 May 1832; *Times*, 10 July 1832; *Journals of the House of Commons*, lxxxvii. 472; [Alexander Somerville], *The Autobiography of a Working Man* (1848), pp. 248 ff.
2. *Poor Man's Guardian*, 9 March 1833; Patricia Hollis, *The Pauper Press: A Study in Working-Class Radicalism of the 1830s* (1970), p. 48.
3. *Political Soldier*, 7 Dec. 1833 (P.R.O., H.O. 64/19).

set fire to the extinguisher, or that the soldiers don't join the Mob'; and twenty-two years later he said in a memorandum on corporal punishment that the dependable conduct of the troops in the face of the popular disturbances of 1831 had demonstrated 'the advantages resulting to the state from the discipline of the army'.[1] Although fear of mutiny and its social implications was not given much prominence in public debate by the defenders of flogging, there can be little doubt that it was an influential factor in the minds of some of them. However, attempts by the opponents of flogging to represent the practice as an aspect of political repression probably did more harm than good to the cause of reform. They could be interpreted as giving substance to allegations such as that of the anti-Jacobin *Courier* that the agitators of the question were intent on 'debauching the army as the readiest way of effecting a Revolution'. And it is worth noting Romilly's remark in the debate of 13 March 1812 that several of those near him, though sympathetic to Burdett's motion, were unwilling to vote for it because they did not wish to be associated with the views he had expressed in introducing it.[2]

In the campaign as a whole – however large the role of radical *instincts* may have been – radical political analysis played a relatively small part. Indeed, to some extent the same thing could be said about analysis and rational argument in general. The reformers did occasionally invoke the penal theories of Beccaria and Bentham;[3] and it has been seen that they made some use of arguments about the inexpediency of flogging. But they tended to be at their least effective in situations, such as the proceedings of the royal commission, where reasoned arguments counted for very much more than appeals to visceral feeling. What they chiefly tried to communicate and arouse was an emotional reaction – not only against the cruelty of a punishment that could be characterized as a form of torture, but also against its degrading effect on both victim and spectators. Drakard wrote that it was a terrible thing 'to tie up a human creature like a dog, and cut his flesh to pieces with whipcord'; and Brougham said that military flogging had 'a direct and inevitable tendency to brutalize the people habituated to the practice of it'.[4] The reformers were inclined to assert as something self-evident that barbarities of this nature simply could not be allowed to continue in a civilized country. Burdett said in 1812 that if floggings took place 'in the face of the

1. Sir Charles Webster (ed.), 'Some Letters of the Duke of Wellington to his brother William Wellesley Pole', *Camden Miscellany*, xviii (1948), 34; P.P. 1836, xxii. 345. *Cf.* also Elizabeth Longford, *Wellington, Pillar of State* (1972), p. 412.

2. *Courier*, 25 Feb. 1811; *P.D.*, xxi. 1285.

3. Wilson, p. 75; Leicester Stanhope, pp. 42, 67, 78–79; *Examiner*, 30 June 1811. Bentham himself did not contribute directly to the campaign, but he was strongly sympathetic to it. See *The Works of Jeremy Bentham*, ed. J. Bowring (Edinburgh, 1844), x. 71–72; Bentham to Burdett, 23 Sept. 1824 (copy), Bodleian Library, MS Eng. letters d. 97, fo. 5.

4. *Stamford News*, 24 Aug. 1810; *P.D.*, xxi. 1204.

public' instead of in military barracks they would very soon have
to be abandoned;[1] and one function of the numerous parliamentary
debates in which the topic was discussed quite literally *ad nauseam* was
to publicize the details of the system. The press too, of course, played
a crucial role in this respect, not only through the publication of
parliamentary debates and editorial comment, but also through direct
reporting. By the early 1830s the reporting of individual instances of
military flogging had become fairly common, and there is evidence
that emotive accounts of this type (such as the report in the *True Sun*
mentioned above) made a great impression on the public mind. F. K.
Hunt, asking in 1835 why it was that so much indignation had been
excited by recent military floggings when there was so much less
corporal punishment than there had been during the French wars,
gave as a reason the fact that the people were now, thanks to the
newspapers, far better informed about these matters than they had
been earlier.[2]

Oliver MacDonagh and other exponents of what has been called
the 'Tory' interpretation of nineteenth-century social reform have
played down the role of political commitment and agitation and have
maintained that there was a benign interaction between public
sentiment and governmental response which brought about the
removal of evils when they came to be regarded as 'intolerable'.
'Intolerability', says MacDonagh, was the trumpet cry that no wall
could permanently withstand, the key that would sooner or later open
any door. This notion has been criticized on the grounds that it rather
blandly overlooks the many years that might elapse, and the amount
of effort that might be necessary, before certain people's view of what
was intolerable came to be generally accepted.[3] With regard to
military flogging, it is clear that in the period covered by this paper
there was a great deal of disagreement about what was tolerable and
what was not. It also appears that divisions of opinion over this issue
– unlike those over some other aspects of social and philanthropic
reform – corresponded quite closely to basic differences in *political*
orientation. The military high command and the bulk of the officer
corps,[4] supported to a large extent by successive ministries and by

1. P.D., xxii. 381.
2. *Times*, 1, 2, 4, 6 Oct. 1830; [F. K. Hunt], *Remarks on Military Flogging, its Causes and Effects, with some Considerations on the Propriety of its entire Abolition* (1835), pp. 3–4. (For the authorship of this pamphlet, see Hume Tracts, 83/8.)
3. O. MacDonagh, 'The Nineteenth-Century Revolution in Government: a reappraisal', *Historical Journal*, i (1958), esp. p. 58; Hart, pp. 48–51.
4. *Cf.* E. M. Spiers, *The Army and Society 1815–1914* (1980), p. 89. It has been argued recently that in the early Victorian period much army reform was inspired by attitudes of 'Tory paternalism' prevalent among officers: see Hew Strachan, 'The Early Victorian Army and the Nineteenth-Century Revolution in Government', *ante*, xcv, esp. pp. 798–801. With regard to the topic and period covered by the present essay, it would doubtless be possible to find *some* evidence to support such an interpretation, but it would be hard to argue that the weight of the evidence was in favour of it.

predominantly 'tory' majorities in parliament, were confronted by what can broadly (if somewhat anachronistically) be called the Left, supported by certain elements within the army. In parliament the most frequent and forceful critics of flogging were either radicals such as Burdett, Hume, Hunt, Buckingham and Daniel O'Connell, or reforming whigs such as Bennet, Romilly, Brougham, Whitbread, Stephen Lushington and Daniel Sykes. As for the officers who gave public support to the cause, it is noteworthy that few of them were of the highest rank and that many of them were inclined to radicalism in politics. Major Charles James, who protested against the excessive use of the lash as early as 1798 (in his *Regimental Companion*), was a member of the Horne Tooke circle,[1] Sir Robert Wilson became an MP on the left wing of the whig party, Leicester Stanhope became a friend and follower of Bentham,[2] Perronet Thompson and De Lacy Evans were radical MPs, and Lord William Bentinck, though in the words of his most recent biographer 'not quite a radical', was certainly a political reformer.[3]

Between these critics of flogging and its defenders there lay – besides the large number of people who preferred not to think about the subject at all – two rather ambivalent groups. One was the main body of the whig party, whose leading members showed themselves more inclined to assist the campaign when they were in opposition than when they were in office. Lords Althorp and Duncannon, for instance, voted for Hume's motion of 15 March 1824 but opposed that of 2 April 1833, when they voted in the majority alongside stern, unbending tories such as Sir Robert Inglis and W. E. Gladstone. Similarly, Lord Grey went so far as to say in a letter to Lord Grenville in 1811 that he was thinking of moving in the house of lords that the awards of regimental courts martial be limited to 50 lashes, and of declaring at the same time that he was 'strongly against this mode of punishment altogether'; but earlier, while a member of the Ministry of All the Talents, he had told Romilly that he considered it 'dangerous, or at least inexpedient' to interfere with military punishments, and later, when he was back in office as prime minister, he took exactly the same line in correspondence with Burdett.[4] The other ambivalent group was the evangelicals. A public comment on

1. Charles James, *The Regimental Companion* (2nd edn., 1800), ii. 361 (I have been unable to trace a copy of the first edition of this work); *P.D.*, xxi. 1266 (Burdett, 13 March 1812, citing James's remarks of 1798); Cyrus Redding, *Yesterday and Today* (1863), i. 247.

2. For Bentham's high estimate of Stanhope's contribution to the campaign against flogging, see Bentham to J.-B. Say, 7 Sept. 1824, D. R. Bentham Collection, Loughborough.

3. John Rosselli, *Lord William Bentinck: The Making of a Liberal Imperialist 1774-1839* (Delhi, 1974), pp. 320–1, 326–35.

4. Historical Manuscripts Commission, *Report on the Manuscripts of J. B. Fortescue, Esq., preserved at Dropmore* (1892–1927), x. 187; *Memoirs of Romilly*, ii. 135; Patterson, ii. 606.

their lack of concern about military flogging was made as early as 1792. Shortly after Wilberforce had introduced a motion for the abolition of the slave trade, a print was published which depicted a flogging in progress, while a gentleman in black (probably representing Wilberforce himself) remarked: 'I and my tribe must look abroad for acts of cruelty and oppression – This is so near home it is beneath our notice. My Duty to my Maker teaches me thus to act.'[1] Later, when the Local Militia Bill of 1808 was before parliament, Wilberforce was urged by his friend James Grahame to introduce an amendment exempting local militiamen from corporal punishment; but he was unwilling to comply, though he told Grahame that he deplored the severity of the military code and wished it to be investigated.[2] In the debates of 1812, Henry Thornton did express disapproval of the flogging of local militiamen, and Wilberforce suggested that it would be a good thing if the power to pass sentences of corporal punishment were confined to general courts martial.[3] But neither of them took any initiative with regard to flogging or even (so far as can be ascertained) voted in favour of any of the motions that were introduced concerning it.[4] Thomas Fowell Buxton did support one or two of the motions of the 1820s and '30s,[5] but the only MP connected with the Saints who played a prominent part in the campaign was Stephen Lushington, who as well as being a member of the Commission for the Building of Churches was a strong political reformer. In general, the evangelicals were politically conservative – Wilberforce is said to have vóted for every single repressive measure proposed by the government between 1795 and 1819[6] – and their attitude to the lower classes was distinctly paternalistic. It is perhaps not surprising that in spite of their support for penal reform and for legislation to prevent cruelty to animals they should have been reluctant to interfere with what may have seemed to them, as it did to other members of the governing class, a necessary though regrettable instrument of control.

One of the points made by the so-called 'Tory' historians is that the opponents of change should not be written off as simply callous or blind. Certainly, it would be facile to present the controversy over

1. M. Dorothy George, *Catalogue of Political and Personal Satires in the British Museum*, vii (1942), 672–3.

2. Wilberforce to Grahame, 12 May and 8 June 1808, National Library of Scotland, MS 3519, fos. 19–22.

3. *P.D.*, xxi. 1287, xxii. 383–4.

4. Wilberforce was reproached by Romilly and Brougham for not supporting the motion of 15 April 1812 for a return of corporal punishments in the army, and Cobbett asked him in 1823 why after the flogging to death of a soldier in his constituency he had not appealed to 'the *religion, justice and humanity* of the nation in behalf of British soldiers'. *P.D.*, xxii. 385, 389–90; *Cobbett's Political Register*, 30 Aug. 1823.

5. *P.D.*, N.S., x. 776, and 3rd S., xvii. 69.

6. Ian Bradley, 'The Politics of Godliness: Evangelicals in Parliament, 1784–1832', Oxford Univ. D.Phil. thesis (1974), p. 228.

military flogging in black-and-white terms, as a conflict between heartless and irrational prejudice on the one hand and disinterested humanitarianism on the other. The men who defended the practice were genuinely convinced that its retention was essential to the welfare of the army and of the country. In the context of the time their arguments had considerable force, and it is worth noting that several men who served as soldiers and non-commissioned officers in the early nineteenth century maintained that the lash was necessary to keep the army in order and to defend the good soldiers against the bad.[1] However, one does feel that there was an excessive tendency on the part of the military authorities to discountenance *any* modification of the late eighteenth-century system. The introduction of oaths at regimental courts martial was opposed by Lieutenant-General Dundas when the idea was mooted in 1800, and it was described by the Duke of Wellington thirty years after its implementation as a regrettable change.[2] Also, it seems clear that the Duke of York personally disapproved of the limitation of the number of lashes that regimental courts martial could award.[3] Nor did he approve of the attempts made by some officers to maintain discipline in their regiments without recourse to the lash. Allegedly successful attempts of this kind were occasionally cited by the reformers to show that flogging was not indispensable;[4] but the Duke of York wrote in his memorandum of April 1826: 'In all those Corps where these new fangled notions of carrying on discipline without flogging have prevailed, insubordination has shewn itself to such a degree as to require the strictest and most severe discipline and punishments to recover the lost ground.'[5]

The defenders of flogging tended to take the view that the men who led the agitation against it were intent on embarrassing the government and exciting discontent inside and outside the army.[6] No doubt there were elements of truth in this charge. Some opposition

---

1. John Stevenson, *A Soldier in Time of War* (1841), pp. 149–67; James Anton, *Retrospect of a Military Life during the most eventful periods of the last War* (Edinburgh, 1841), p. 11; Richard Glover, *Peninsular Preparation: The Reform of the British Army 1795–1809* (Cambridge, 1963), pp. 178. For strong attacks on flogging, however, from men who had served in the ranks, see John Teesdale, *Military Torture: A Letter to the People of England . . . on the use of the Cat-o'-nine-tails in the British Army* (1835); Thomas Morris, *Recollections of Military Service* (1845), p. 45; and the pamphlet of John Shipp cited above at p. 310, n. 2.

2. P.R.O., W.O. 40/13, no. 11; P.P. 1836, xxii. 355.

3. Beckett's memorandum of 19 Dec. 1823, P.R.O., W.O. 81/62, fos. 236–7. Beckett himself described the limitation imposed in 1811 as 'the beginning of error' (*ibid.* fo. 245).

4. *E.g.* P.D., xx. 699 (Burdett, 19 June 1811, citing the record of the whiggish Duke of Gloucester as colonel of the 3rd regiment of footguards).

5. P.R.O., H.O. 50/13, fo. 229. For the case of Colonel Quentin of the 10th Hussars, which lent some substance to the Duke of York's point, see *Military Register*, 19, 26 Oct. 2 Nov. 1814.

6. *E.g.* Duke of York's memorandum, 3 April 1826, P.R.O., H.O. 50/13, fo. 225.

MPs may have hoped to make party capital out of the issue.[1] Some radical politicians may have found it a convenient means of rallying popular support and vindicating their own radicalism, and some ultra-radicals did probably have subversive intentions. Nevertheless, it seems legitimate to suppose that the basic inspiration of the campaign came from simple feelings of compassion and repugnance and concern for human dignity. It has been said recently of Joseph Hume that his pleas for the abolition of flogging reflected 'a deep empathy with the utter degradation that this "soulbreaking, spirit-destroying" punishment inflicted'.[2] And Burdett, although he did incorporate his opposition to military flogging into a broader critique of governmental repression, seems to have been motivated by similar feelings – feelings that were intensified by his first-hand observation of the flogging of some veteran soldiers in the Tower of London in 1810.[3] Lord Holland wrote of him, with particular reference to his stance on this question, that he 'had at all times the great merit of feeling with sincerity and expressing without fear great indignation and horror at all personal cruelty and oppression'.[4] Romilly and Bennet were also well known for their hatred of cruelty – and doubtless this feeling was shared in some degree by all who joined in the campaign. The reformers were helped, of course, by the fact that the public in general was becoming more sensitive about conspicuously cruel practices. Changes in public sensibility, which can be attributed in part to the Enlightenment, the religious revival, the spread of education and 'respectability', help to account for the fact that by the early 1830s flogging in the army had become unacceptable not only to the common people who had long resented it, but also to much of educated 'middle opinion' – as represented, for example, by *The Times*, which joined the agitation around 1830. However, the awakening and diffusion of public concern even to this partial extent had required a generation or so of persistent effort, and in explaining such reforms as were achieved during this period the main emphasis must surely be placed on the exertions of a quite small number of activists. Lord Dudley Stuart (the liberal MP who was to be remembered chiefly as a champion of Polish independence) said in the commons in 1834:

When I look back to the small divisions which formerly enrolled their names against military flogging – when I look to the defence of the system which is

1. Brougham wrote to John Allen of Holland House on 21 June 1811 (BL, Add. MSS 52178, fos. 138–9) that the party should take up questions such as flogging in order to 'regain the estimation of the country', instead of allowing Burdett to take all the credit for raising them.
2. David Roberts, 'The Utilitarian Conscience', in Peter Marsh (ed.), *The Conscience of the Victorian State* (Hassocks, 1979), pp. 49–50.
3. *P.D.*, xx. 702; Sophia De Morgan, *Threescore Years and Ten* (1905), pp. 3–5.
4. 3rd Lord Holland, *Further Memoirs of the Whig Party, 1807–1821*, ed. Lord Stavordale (1905), p. 102.

now put forth, namely, that the practice has materially diminished, to such an extent indeed, that by comparison it can hardly be said to exist at present – I feel that so desirable a result can be attributed to nothing but the fact of the subject having been agitated and re-agitated by the perseverance of a spirited minority.[1]

1. J. H. Barrow (ed.), *The Mirror of Parliament, for the Second Session of the Eleventh Parliament of Great Britain and Ireland* (1834), i. 755. The Victorian phase of the campaign followed very much the same pattern as the earlier one. Again, pressure from radical and liberal elements in parliament and the press, helped by public indignation over particular incidents, produced a series of concessions. In 1846 the death of a soldier after a flogging at Hounslow was ably exploited by Thomas Wakley (West Middlesex coroner, editor of *The Lancet* and radical MP), and in 1847 a limit of 50 lashes was imposed on all courts martial. Another death occurred in 1867, and after a resolution for the abolition of flogging – moved by the liberal Arthur Otway – had been carried in the commons by one vote, it was laid down in 1868 that no soldier could be sentenced to corporal punishment for any offence committed in time of peace. In 1879, with Chamberlain pressing strongly for total abolition, the maximum number of lashes that could be inflicted in time of war was reduced to 25; and the practice was finally abolished two years later. See S. S. Sprigge, *Life and Times of Thomas Wakley* (1897), pp. 404–16; Blanco, pp. 143–5; J. L. Garvin and J. E. Amery, *Life of Joseph Chamberlain* (1932–69), i. 270–3.

For help in directing me to sources relevant to this essay, I should like to thank Mr Michael Collinge, Mr Clive Emsley, Miss Claire Gobbi, Dr Margaret Parnaby, Mr John Pollock, Dr Martin Smith and Mr Keith Sutton.

8

The Use of the Crown's Power of Deportation
under the Aliens Act, 1793-1826

IN THE AUTUMN of 1792 the flow of French emigrants to England reached its climax, and created considerable anxiety in government circles. In September alone, following 10 August and the prison massacres, a total of nearly 4,000 refugees landed in Britain;[1] and J. B. Burges, the Under-Secretary at the Foreign Office, wrote to Lord Grenville on 14 September: 'By what I can learn, the majority of these people are of a suspicious description, and very likely either to do mischief of their own accord, or to be fit tools of those who may be desirous of creating confusion'.[2] It was feared that many of these Frenchmen had been implicated in the Revolution, and that some were Jacobin agents in the guise of *émigrés*. Also it was anticipated that the duke of Brunswick's advance on Paris would create a panic among the revolutionaries, many of whom would try and seek refuge in England. In these circumstances the government began to investigate what measures could be taken to control the influx of foreigners—and in particular whether the executive had the power, without parliamentary sanction, to exclude or expel foreigners from the realm.[3] This latter point was far from clear; and one distinguished lawyer, Serjeant Hill, when consulted by the treasury solicitor, expressed the opinion that although the king did have the power to forbid the entry or order the departure of subjects of a state at war with Britain, he had no such power over the subjects of states in amity.[4] The opinion of the Crown lawyers seems to have been that the king did have a general power to prevent aliens from entering the kingdom or remaining there, but that this power had been so little used that it would be advisable to have recourse to an act of parliament.[5] The need for such a measure was emphasized during the latter part of 1792 by the newspapers, in which the public suspicion of Frenchmen in England and the demand for some control and investigation of them were frequently expressed.[6] In addition, it was well known to the government

[1] *Annual Register* (Otridge), 1792, Chronicle, p. 39.

[2] Hist. MSS. Comm., *Report on the Manuscripts of J. B. Fortescue, Preserved at Dropmore* (10 vols., 1892–1927; hereafter cited as *Dropmore Papers*), ii. 315. Cf. Burges's letters to Auckland in *Journal and Correspondence of William, Lord Auckland*, ed. R. J. Eden (4 vols., 1861–2), ii. 442, 445–6.

[3] Henry Dundas to Lord Kenyon, Lord Loughborough and the lord chief baron, 12 Sept. 1792, Public Record Office, H.O. 43/4.

[4] *Edinburgh Review*, xlii (Apr. 1825), 140–1.

[5] Lord Grenville to marquis of Buckingham, 20 Sept. 1792, Duke of Buckingham and Chandos, *Memoirs of the Court and Cabinets of George III* (4 vols., 1853–5), ii. 217.

[6] E. Wilkinson, 'The French Emigrés in England, 1789–1802: their reception and impact on English life', unpublished Oxford B. Litt. thesis, 1952, pp. 358–60, 363–4.

that Noël, the Dantonist ex-priest who had come to London in September, was the head of a network of French agents and propagandists in England;[1] and the increasingly strained relations between the two countries, together with the fear of internal Jacobinism, made it clearly desirable that the government should have some means of dealing with foreign spies and agitators.

The Aliens Bill was given high priority at the beginning of the parliamentary session, being introduced into the house of lords by Grenville on 19 December. It laid down that when the king, by proclamation, order in council, or order under his sign manual, required any alien to leave the realm, and the alien disobeyed the order, he should be liable to arrest; and one of the secretaries of state might put him into the charge of one of His Majesty's messengers, to be conducted out of the kingdom. The bill also contained detailed regulations concerning the landing of aliens, their registration, the passports they were to carry, and the government's control over their movements and place of residence within the country.[2] In introducing the bill, Grenville said that it appeared to be part of the prerogative of the Crown to forbid foreigners to enter or reside within the realm; and this statement was apparently not challenged. The chief complaints of the Opposition concerned the irresponsible nature of the power claimed by the executive, and the failure of the government to provide evidence for the necessity of the measure. Lord Lansdowne 'considered the bill as a suspension of the Habeas Corpus act, which, though it extended at first only to foreigners, would, he feared, be afterwards extended to all Englishmen'. In the house of commons, Fox expressed the fear that the measure would be used against the French Constitutionalists (he had heard it said by a person of high rank that if Lafayette were in the country he would be a fit person to be deported); and Grey 'did not like to give so much power where there could be no responsibility'.[3] However, the Opposition did not divide either House against the bill, and it became law on 8 January 1793. The act was temporary, but was renewed and revised by a series of subsequent acts; and although the aliens regulations were changed in other respects, the power of deportation[4] was retained by the executive from 1793 until 1826. The purpose of this article is to examine how this

[1] J. T. Murley, 'The Origins and Outbreak of the Anglo-French War of 1793', unpublished Oxford D.Phil. thesis, 1959, pp. 60-2, 214-16.

[2] The original act (33 Geo. III, c. 4) is not printed in the *Statutes at Large;* the bill as amended in the house of commons is to be found in the bound set known as the 'second series', *Parliamentary Papers Printed by Order of the House of Commons* (110 vols., 1731-1800), xxiii, no. 653. An abstract of the act was published in *Annual Register* (Otridge), 1793, Appendix to the Chronicle, pp. 110-13.

[3] Cobbett's *Parliamentary History of England*, xxx. 156, 159, 211, 225 (hereafter cited as *Parl. Hist.*).

[4] The word 'deportation' is almost never used in this period; indeed Lord Holland, one of the leading opponents of the Aliens Act in the post-war period, declared with satisfaction in 1816 that the word was not to be found in any English dictionary, Hansard, *Parl. Deb.*, xxxiv, col. 1069.

power was used, and thereby to throw some light on the security arrangements and political attitudes of the British government during and after the French wars.[1]

The aliens who were deported during the war period can be divided into three basic categories: first, those whose political views were considered objectionable; secondly, those who were suspected of being spies or agents of the French government; and thirdly those who were deported not for political or security reasons but simply because they were regarded as undesirable persons.

The earliest deportee of any note in the first category was Dumouriez. After the failure of his plan to march his army on Paris and restore the monarchy and the constitution of 1791, he went over to the Austrians in April 1793. But he found that, although he was not treated as harshly as Lafayette, he was not welcomed by the enemies of France; and having been turned out of the Electorate of Mainz in May, he landed in England under the assumed name of Peralta on 13 June.[2] He proceeded to London and wrote to Grenville asking to be allowed to live in seclusion somewhere in the country. But Grenville stated firmly in his reply that Dumouriez could not be permitted to remain; and he re-embarked at Dover for Ostend on 22 June.[3] He must have hoped that his attempt to open negotiations with the British government when he was commander of the French army in the Netherlands in late January 1793 would have disposed ministers in his favour; and Lady Wallace, writing to the government on his behalf on 17 June, asked: ' Is he not more worthy of your protection than any Emigrant who fled and abandoned their King and Country he who sacrificed himself for both and only served to repel the invaders & to finally restore the Government [?] '[4] But Dumouriez, who had professed allegiance to the revolution of 10 August, was clearly thought to have involved himself too deeply with the Jacobins; and even his aim of restoring the constitution did not gain him any credit with the British government. Lord Camden,

[1] The Aliens Office, which was set up to administer the Act, was a branch of the Home Office, and the Superintendent of Aliens was subordinate to the Under-Secretaries. The first Superintendent was William Huskisson; and the post was subsequently held by William Wickham (for a short period in 1794), Thomas Carter, C. W. Flint (who had been attached to Wickham's mission in Switzerland) and John Reeves the legal historian. The correspondence relating to aliens for the period 1793–1826 is in the Public Record Office, mostly in H.O. 1/1–5 (unfoliated bundles) and H.O. 5/1–20 (entry-books, from Oct. 1794).

[2] J. Newport (Customs House, Dover) to E. Nepean (Under-Secretary, Home Office), 20 June 1793, P.R.O., H.O. 42/25.

[3] J. H. Rose and A. M. Broadley, *Dumouriez and the Defence of England against Napoleon* (1909), pp. 195–9. The letters exchanged between Dumouriez and Grenville, dated 15 and 16 June, are in P.R.O., F.O. 27/42; they were published, translated into English, in *The Times* of 25 June. Ten years later Dumouriez was allowed to return to England, and was given a pension in return for a political correspondence with the government.

[4] P.R.O., H.O. 42/25; it is not clear to whom the letter was addressed. For Dumouriez's attempt to open negotiations with the British government in Jan. 1793, see Murley, pp. 461–90.

the lord president of the council, in a note approving of Grenville's reply to Dumouriez's letter, said that it was not surprising in view of his conduct that the rest of Europe had refused him an asylum.

Nor [he went on] does his own plan of Government call for our protection or approbation, for as he means to set up the first Constitution establish'd by the Constituent Assembly, he does by no means depart from that accursed principle the sovereignty & equality of all the refuse of the Kingdom. Nor does the name of a King vary the principle, he being only set up as a pageant.[1]

Such a statement from a member of the cabinet might lead one to assume that Fox was justified in anticipating that the powers conferred by the Aliens Act would be used against Constitutionalists; but there was in fact no wholesale deportation of such people. The only member of the Juniper Hall circle to be deported was Talleyrand; and, as will be suggested below, there is reason to think that he was suspected of being an agent of the Republic. Writing to Madame de Staël just before he sailed for America in March 1794, Talleyrand mentioned the fear of Narbonne and his friends that they would all be expelled from England;[2] but the only other French Constitutionalist deported under the Aliens Act was Alexandre de Lameth, two years later. Lameth, after leaving France at the same time as Lafayette, had been imprisoned for over three years in Prussia. He was eventually released in December 1795, and came to England in the following April with the intention of taking the waters at Bath, his health having suffered severely from his confinement; but within a fortnight of his arrival he was ordered to return to the continent.[3] It is not clear why the government should have considered him more objectionable than other Constitutionalists. As Fox said in an eloquent protest against his deportation, Lameth's state of health was such that he could not possibly have been considered dangerous.[4] But it may be worth recalling that two years earlier ministers had opposed a motion of General Fitzpatrick to the effect that the British government should intercede with the Prussian court in order to secure the release of Lafayette, Alexandre de Lameth, La Tour Maubourg, and Bureau de Puzy; and in the course of the debate Pitt had declared that he 'would never admit that the four persons who were the object of the present motion were the friends of true liberty, or deserved well of their country'.[5] So the government was in a sense committed to a hostile attitude towards these individuals who had suffered at the hands of Britain's allies.

Another foreigner who, although he had not been involved in the Revolution, was deported because his political views were disliked by the

[1] 15 June 1793, P.R.O., F.O. 27/42.
[2] Talleyrand to Madame de Staël, 1 March 1794, *Revue d'histoire diplomatique*, iv (1890), 94.
[3] Charles Henry Frazer (British chargé d'affaires at Hamburg) to Grenville, 8 Apr. 1796, P.R.O., F.O. 33/12; Thomas Carter to A. Lameth, 25 and 26 Apr. 1796, P.R.O., H.O. 5/2 pp. 3-4; *Mémoires de Théodore de Lameth*, ed. E. Welvert (Paris, 1913), p. 307.
[4] House of commons, 10 May 1796, *Parl. Hist.*, xxxii. 109-10.
[5] 17 March 1794, *ibid.*, xxxi. 40.

government, was a Venetian nobleman called Count Zenobio. He had for a time been a member of the Society for Constitutional Information, but had found it too jacobinical and had withdrawn from it. He had published a couple of political pamphlets in 1792, in which he had shown his sympathy for Lafayette and the English whigs; he had maintained that France needed a constitution on the English model, and that parliamentary reform was necessary in England because a refusal to correct patent abuses would incense the people.[1] When he was ordered to leave the country in January 1794, at the same time as Talleyrand, he protested that he had always spoken the language of moderation, had never participated in any cabal, and had had no connexion with the French democrats.[2] He was nevertheless deported, and despite frequent applications for permission to take up residence again in England, was not allowed to do so until the whigs came to power.[3]

Also of some interest is the attitude of the British government towards those implicated in the royalist conspiracy which was foiled by the *coup d'état* of Fructidor (September 1797). This conspiracy had had encouragement and financial backing from Britain; but the government was not prepared to welcome indiscriminately those conspirators who were banished from France by the Directory: a circular was sent from the Aliens Office to the ports directing that such persons should not be allowed to land in England.[4] In the following year a number of the leading victims of Fructidor, who had been transported by the Directory to French Guiana, managed to escape; and some of them came in due course to England. Pichegru, who had been one of Britain's main hopes as a leader of counter-revolution in 1795-7, arrived in London in September 1798, and was welcomed and consulted by the government; in December he left to go and play an active role in royalist operations on the continent.[5] In July 1799 two other deportees of Fructidor, the former Director Barthélemy and General Willot, reached England. Had the latter arrived alone, he might have been treated as *persona grata*; but the former had been too deeply implicated in the Revolution to be acceptable. Windham wrote to Pitt on hearing of their arrival at Deal:

[1] See particularly *An Address to the People of England on the Part their Government ought to act in the Present War* (London, 1792), pp. 16-25. On Zenobio, see E. H. Coleridge, *Life of Thomas Coutts* (2 vols., 1920), ii. 130-1, and M. W. Patterson, *Sir Francis Burdett and his Times* (2 vols., 1931), i. 125.

[2] Representation from Count Zenobio, 28 Jan. 1794, forwarded by the Venetian Resident, M. Lavezzari, to Grenville, P.R.O., H.O. 32/4; Zenobio to Dundas, endorsed 31 Jan. 1794, H.O. 1/2.

[3] On 30 Sept. 1805 Zenobio was refused permission to return to England (P.R.O., H.O. 5/10 p. 178); but it is clear from a letter of 24 Sept. 1807 that he was then residing in England with official sanction (H.O. 5/11 p. 390). The inference is that it was under the Ministry of All the Talents that he was allowed to return.

[4] 20 Oct. 1797, P.R.O., H.O. 5/3 p. 104.

[5] E. Daudet, *Histoire de l'émigration pendant la Révolution française* (3 vols., Paris, 1904-7), ii. 256-67.

Willot is a respectable man, and one whom we might be glad to consult, as well
as show attention to. About Barthelemy I hope you retain your opinion, & that
he will not be permitted to come to London, at least not to see any body here. . . .
It would be shocking if the Volunteer Servant of Robespierre, during the time
that Robespierre was travelling with his guillotine through all the highest &
most respectable orders in France, should be received here, as he certainly
would, with more attention than is shown to the best & most distinguished
Emigrants.[1]

The new arrivals were taken to a house on Barnes Common, where they
were kept under close surveillance; and it was made clear to them by the
duke of Portland that they could not be allowed to remain in England.
In August they were taken on a British warship to Cuxhaven—Willot (like
Pichegru) to join in the continental operations against the Republic.[2]
    There were a number of foreigners in the second category of wartime
deportees—those who were suspected of being in the pay of the French
government; but very few of these were actually known to be spies. Noël
and most of the other agents sent over by Lebrun in the latter part of 1792
returned to France before the passing of the Aliens Act;[3] and thereafter it
was not easy for the French to maintain spies in England. After the departure of the French legation from London one man, Restif, remained
behind, calling himself 'agent de la marine et du commerce de France'
and sending reports to Lebrun; but he was deported toward the end of
March.[4] There is a memorandum dated pluviose an II in the archives of
the French Foreign Office which states: 'La difficulté des communications
et la sévérité avec laquelle les Français patriotes sont traités en Angleterre,
ne nous ont pas permis d'y envoyer plus de cinq agens secrets, dont deux
sont Irlandais favorablement connus par les efforts qu'ils ont faits pour
propager en Irlande les principes de notre révolution'. Letters had been
received in Paris from only one of these five; and the silence of the others
gave cause for anxiety.[5] The French government did send a number of
agents to Ireland in the seventeen-nineties, being able to count on co-
operation from the disaffected elements in the country. But in England the
patriotism and vigilance of the population as a whole reinforced the security
measures of the government. The screening process applied to aliens entering the country became quite elaborate. A foreigner wishing to come to
England from the continent had to obtain a passport from the Foreign Office
or from a British diplomatic representative before he embarked; and all
Frenchmen who landed had to give references and 'make themselves well

[1] 2 July 1799, Windham Papers, Brit. Mus., Add. MS. 37844 fo. 191. When J.
Courtenay, M.P., tried to intercede with Windham on Barthélemy's behalf,
Windham replied with a strong attack on Barthélemy's character, *Mémoires de
Barthélemy*, ed. J. de Dampierre (Paris, 1914), pp. 402–3.
[2] *Mémoires de Barthélemy*, pp. 400 *et seq.*; P.R.O., H.O. 5/4 p. 488.
[3] Murley, p. 416.
[4] Paris, Archives des Affaires étrangères [A.A.E.], Correspondance politique,
Angleterre, 587 fos. 23–6, 36–42, 53–4.
[5] *Ibid.*, 588 fo. 142.

known' before they were given passports allowing them to remain.[1] Also, whereas it was easy for royalist agents (who were usually Frenchmen themselves) to land on the west coast of France where help from the local people was assured, it was difficult for French agents to be surreptitiously landed in England. Heavy penalties were imposed by the Aliens Act on masters of vessels who landed foreigners at other than certain specified ports; any foreigner found within ten miles of the coast without a special licence was automatically suspected;[2] and, particularly in the early stages of the war, the government did not hesitate to deport any alien who could not give a satisfactory account of himself.[3]

One would expect the French government to have infiltrated agents into England in the guise of refugees; and a number of suspicious *émigrés* were deported. *The Times* stated on 29 January 1794 that two French Jacobins, concealed under the assumed names of the chevalier de Guienne and the chevalier de Limerac, had joined the emigrants at Cowes who were to serve under Lord Moira; but Moira and the French royalists having no knowledge of them, they had been told that they could not take part in the expedition. They had then tried to return to the continent, but had been arrested at Dover on government orders; and among their papers had been found 'the most convincing proofs of their having carried on a correspondence with the Jacobins in France'. This information was evidently fed to the newspaper by the Home Office; and a few days later the culprits were dispatched to Ostend.[4] Another sinister character amongst the *émigrés* was the *soi-disant* comte de Montgaillard. He came to England in June 1794, and offered his services to Pitt;[5] he also tried to ingratiate himself with other

[1]P.R.O., H.O. 5/2 p. 91. Colonel Oswald, an American officer in the French army who was sent on a mission to Ireland in 1793, found it impossible to cross from Calais to Dover without a passport from the British government, which he could not obtain; he eventually had to make his way to Ireland via Norway and Scotland, L. D. Woodward, 'Les projets de descente en Irlande sous la Convention', *Annales historiques de la Révolution française*, viii (1931), 5–7. The British minister at Hamburg was instructed in July 1798 to grant no passports to *émigrés* wishing to travel to England, until each individual case had been referred to the Foreign Office in London, Grenville to Sir James Craufurd, 20 July 1798, P.R.O., F.O. 158/3.
[2]See for instance the case of Théot, deported after being 'taken upon the coast of Kent under suspicious circumstances' in March 1798, P.R.O., H.O. 5/3 pp. 268, 280.
[3]Carter wrote in Sept. 1796 that the king's order for sending out of the kingdom those who failed to give a satisfactory account of themselves would be 'granted without hesitation upon the requisition of the magistrates', P.R.O., H.O. 5/2 p. 145.
[4]P.R.O., H.O. 43/4 p. 426; Newport to Nepean, 2 Feb. 1794, H.O. 1/2. There is a note in H.O. 42/27 concerning the papers found on Guienne and Limerac when they were arrested; it appears that Guienne had been entrusted by the French consul in Sweden with a trunk for Citizen Maudrée, secretary to the National Convention—but that otherwise nothing obviously incriminating was discovered.
[5]17 June 1794, Chatham Papers, P.R.O. 30/8/160 fos. 231–2.

ministers, and published a pamphlet describing and criticizing the Jacobin régime in France.[1] But he failed to win the confidence of the government, and left England after four months. It is not clear whether he was actually deported; the newspapers announced that he had been sent out of the country—but Montgaillard later denied this in his memoirs, while admitting that he probably would have been deported had he tried to prolong his stay in England.[2] He subsequently became a double-agent simultaneously in the pay of the Directory and the prince de Condé.[3]

A more illustrious figure who aroused the suspicions of the government was Talleyrand. He had been in London as unofficial head of the French embassy between April and July 1792, and had returned in a private capacity in September. It is clear from his letter of 23 September to Lebrun that he had no mission from the French government (despite his later claims to the contrary); he did on his return to London offer his services both to Noël and to Grenville, but neither side was prepared to employ him.[4] During his period as an *émigré* in England he seems to have been genuinely inactive, apart from his being involved in the attempt to bring about negotiations between the British government and Dumouriez in January 1793.[5] He was nevertheless regarded as a dangerous person. When the French Assembly passed a decree of accusation against him on 5 December 1792 (following the discovery in the *armoire de fer* of a document indicating that Talleyrand had offered his services to the royal family), it was rumoured that he himself had arranged this in order to remove the suspicions of the British government and enable him to continue his subversive activities; and in July 1793 Lord Auckland wrote to Grenville suggesting that it would

[1] *Etat de la France au mois de mai 1794* (London, 1794). He sent copies to Grenville (10 July 1794, P.R.O., F.O. 27/43) and to Windham (14 July, Brit Mus., Add. MS. 37856 fo. 95).

[2] J.-G.-M. Roques de Montgaillard, *Mémoires secrets* (Paris, an XII), pp. 36–7. There is a letter from Montgaillard in the Aliens Office papers, dated 5 Aug. 1794, saying he had heard that he was to be deported, and protesting that he had done nothing to deserve such treatment, P.R.O., H.O. 1/2.

[3] H. Forneron, *Histoire générale des émigrés pendant la Révolution française* (3 vols., Paris, 1884–90), ii. 88; and H. Mitchell, *The Underground War against Revolutionary France* (Oxford, 1965), pp. 189–90. Forneron says that Montgaillard came to England as an agent of Robespierre; but he provides no evidence for this. Montgaillard claimed somewhat implausibly in his memoirs (p. 33) that he indignantly refused an offer of a considerable pension from the British government in return for his services.

[4] B. Lacombe, 'Talleyrand émigré', *Revue des deux mondes* (1er juillet 1908), 160–2. In the petition he sent from Philadelphia to the Convention in June 1795, seeking to have his name erased from the list of *émigrés*, Talleyrand stated that he had been sent to London in Sept. 1792 with a mission to prevent a rupture between France and England, *ibid.*, p. 162. In his memoirs he said that his mission was concerned with the equalization of weights and measures, *Mémoires de Talleyrand*, ed. P.-L. and J.-P. Couchoud (2 vols., Paris, 1957), i. 194.

[5] *Dropmore Papers*, ii. 375 and iii. 477–8; C. F. D. Dumouriez, *Mémoires* (London, 1794), p. 78.

be a good thing if the bishop of Autun were sent out of the country.[1] At the time of the passing of the Aliens Act Talleyrand seems to have expected that it would be used against him; he wrote to the grand duke of Tuscany asking for asylum in his dominions, which was refused.[2] He was allowed to remain in England for more than a year, until he was suddenly served with a deportation order on 28 January 1794. It is not certain why the government abruptly decided that he could no longer remain in the country. It has been suggested that the decision was precipitated by the publication in Paris in late 1793 of some forged letters, supposedly from Talleyrand to Lebrun and Madame de Flahaut; these letters are full of plans for inciting sedition in the British Isles and preparing the way for a French invasion—and they appear to have been composed and printed with the deliberate intention of incensing the British government against Talleyrand.[3] But a stronger influence on the government may have been the bulletins concerning affairs in Paris which were at this time being forwarded to Grenville by Drake, the British minister at Genoa. The bulletin dated 25–30 November 1793, which reached the Foreign Office on 13 January 1794, reported that a letter from Talleyrand had been read to the Committee of Public Safety, describing the attitude and plans of the British government with regard to the *émigrés*.[4] The comte d'Antraigues, who was responsible for the final shape in which the bulletins were sent to London, was a thoroughgoing royalist; and his desire to discredit the Constitutionalists in the eyes of the English ministers accounts for the casting of Talleyrand as an agent of the Committee of Public Safety. It has been stated that although Grenville thought the bulletins of sufficient importance to be shown to the king, there is no evidence that they influenced the policy of the British government.[5] But it is possible that ministers were led by this bulletin to decide that the deportation of Talleyrand would be a desirable safeguard. On being ordered to leave the country within five days, Talleyrand wrote off a number of letters to those in authority, defying anyone to prove

[1] Lacombe, *ubi supra*, p. 175; *Dropmore Papers*, ii. 403.

[2] *La mission de Talleyrand à Londres en 1792*, ed. G. Pallain (Paris, 1889), p. xxix.

[3] Lacombe, *ubi supra*, p. 181. There are extensive quotations from the letters in C. M. Catherinet de Villemarest, *Monsieur de Talleyrand* (2 vols., Paris, 1834), i. 64–118.

[4] *Dropmore Papers*, ii. 473. The plausibility of this bulletin was discussed by historians at the time of its publication. J. H. Clapham said that it would not be altogether surprising if Talleyrand should turn out to have been an agent of the terrorists; but he pointed out that Talleyrand's letters to Madame de Staël during the winter of 1793–4 were full of hostility towards the Jacobin government, 'A royalist spy during the reign of terror', *Eng. Hist. Rev.*, xii (1897), 69 and n. H. Glagau said that, there being no other evidence that Talleyrand corresponded with the Committee of Public Safety, the letter described in this bulletin must be regarded as a fiction, 'Achtundzwanzig Bulletins über den Wohlfahrtsausschuss', *Historische Zeitschrift*, lxxviii (1897), 226–7.

[5] H. Mitchell, 'Francis Drake and the comte d'Antraigues: a study of the Dropmore bulletins, 1793–6', *ante*, xxix (1956), 143.

anything against him, and saying that the order he had received must be due either to some mistake or to the machinations of his enemies.[1] But all he obtained from ministers was a brief respite in which to arrange his affairs;[2] and he left for America early in March.

Among the foreigners deported as suspected agents were two well-known figures from the world of the arts—Beaumarchais the dramatist, and the Piedmontese violinist Viotti. Beaumarchais came to London in the summer of 1793, to complete the purchase of a consignment of 50,000 Belgian muskets, which had been bought on his behalf by an English merchant, and which he intended to resell to the French government; but he was denounced to the authorities and ordered to leave the country within three days. He had by then completed his purchase; but the guns were impounded by the British government, which paid Beaumarchais only about a tenth of their value.[3] At the height of the Terror he appealed (through a friend in London) for permission to return to England—if necessary to be committed to prison—in order that he might escape the guillotine; but this request was not apparently granted.[4] Viotti, who had crossed to England from France after 10 August, was denounced in one of the comte d'Antraigues's bulletins, forwarded by Drake to Grenville on 28 October 1793, as the head of the Jacobin agents in London. It was said that he had offered to bring about the assassination of Pitt, but had demanded too large a reward; he had, however, been sent to London with 20,000 livres by Lebrun, and his nationality and musical vocation provided an excellent cover for his activities.[5] There is some evidence that Viotti *had* been in correspondence with an official of the French Foreign Office after the outbreak of war; Maret apparently sent him a packet through W. A. Miles in February 1793—though Miles declined to pass on any further communications.[6] But it was not until years later that Viotti was deported, in February 1798. The manager of the Opera House, where Viotti was performing, was sent an official letter from the Aliens Office stating that 'under the present circumstances of the country an increased degree of vigilance with respect to such people becomes an indispensable duty of Government'.[7] Viotti was presumably listed as a

[1] Talleyrand to Dundas, 29 Jan. 1794, P.R.O., F.O. 27/43; Talleyrand to Grenville, 30 Jan., *ibid.*; Talleyrand to Pitt, 30 Jan., *Catalogue of the Collection of Autograph Letters and Historical Documents formed between 1865 and 1882 by Alfred Morrison* (6 vols., 1883–92), vi. 221.

[2] Dundas to Talleyrand, 4 Feb. 1794, P.R.O., H.O. 43/4.

[3] R. Dalsème, *Beaumarchais 1732–99* (New York, 1929), pp. 366–8, 379, 385–413. On the distrust with which Beaumarchais was regarded by Englishmen, see *Dropmore Papers*, ii. 357, and *The Times*, 7 Jan. 1793.

[4] Two letters from P. Le Cointe, dated 1 and 8 July 1794, P.R.O., H.O. 1/2.

[5] P.R.O., F.O. 95/5.

[6] Miles to Maret, 12 Feb. 1793, W. A. Miles, *Correspondence on the French Revolution* (2 vols., 1890), ii. 70–1.

[7] P.R.O., H.O. 5/3 p. 256.

suspect, and was sent out of the country because of the imminent threat of invasion.[1]

In a number of cases the government acted very expeditiously in dealing with suspicious persons arriving from the continent. For instance the American J. S. Eustace, who appeared in England in March 1797, was promptly ordered to leave. How much the government knew about him is not clear; but there is no doubt that his deportation was a wise move. He had been an officer in the French army and an ardent Robespierrist, and had published a pamphlet entitled *Lettres préliminaires sur les crimes du roi George III . . . par un officier américain au service de la France* (1794). Apparently he had been sent to Holland to prepare the way for the French invasion, and had been imprisoned on the orders of the Stadtholder—but had been released through the intervention of the American minister, and had returned to France.[2] When Eustace was ordered to leave England, the duke of Portland was surprised by his request that he should be sent to France, as he had said on his arrival that he had been banished by the French government. He was made therefore to travel to some other part of the continent; but he did make his way back to France, re-entered the French army, and became a general of division in the Flanders campaign.[3]

Shortly after the resumption of war in 1803 the French government sent over to England the former royalist agent Duverne de Presles. He had been a leading member of the royalist agency in Paris, most of whose members, including Duverne, had been arrested by the French police in January 1797; a month later he had made an extensive confession concerning the activities and organization of the royalists in France, and had thus earned mild treatment from the government. After Fructidor he was released and merely banished from France (instead of being deported to Sinnemary); and after Brumaire he returned, being amnestied in 1803. In June of that year he was sent to England with a secret mission to obtain information about the aims and means of the British government, and the details of its correspondence with dissident elements in France. On his arrival he paid a visit to the comte d'Artois, presumably trying to pass himself off as a genuine royalist; but he was given a cold reception by Monsieur, and very soon afterwards was arrested. He was kept in prison for two months, and deported early in September.[4]

The government was quick to act on information it received throwing any doubts on the bona fides of foreigners. In January 1807 the British

[1] Viotti's biographer states that he was unjustly accused of using 'heinous and sanguinary expressions' about the king, A. Pougin, *Viotti et l'école moderne du violon* (Paris, 1888), p. 77. Viotti was authorized to return to England in 1801, *ibid.*, p. 80.

[2] C. Perroud, 'J.-S. Eustace', *La Révolution française*, xli (1901), 356; *Dictionnaire biographique et historique des hommes marquants de la fin du dix-huitième siècle* (3 vols., London, 1800), ii. 23.

[3] P.R.O., H.O. 5/2, pp. 308, 323, 333. Letter from J. G. Alger in *La Révolution française*, xli (1901), 478–9.

[4] Paris, Archives nationales [A.N.], AF IV 1672 fos. 180–9, and F⁷6372; P.R.O., H.O. 5/8 p. 215.

consul at Altona reported to the Foreign Office that he had been informed that spies had been passing to and fro between England and the French minister at Hamburg; he added that he felt suspicious about two Frenchmen who had recently left for England, Henri de Chapeaurouge and the chevalier de St. Aubin, and he advised that they and their correspondence should be watched.[1] This dispatch was forwarded to the Home Office; and the Under-Secretary, in a letter thanking his opposite number at the Foreign Office for this communication, said that orders had been given for the deportation of both Chapeaurouge and St. Aubin.[2]

One further case worth mentioning in this category is that of the baron d'Imbert. He was a Toulonese emigrant who had come to England from Italy at the end of 1800, and had subsequently been employed by the War Office as a channel of correspondence with royalist agents in France. But in March 1807 he was deported, as it was believed that he had been playing a double game and sending information to the French government. After his deportation he did tell what he knew about the British secret service, first to the French minister at Hamburg and then to Fouché in Paris. But he was evidently not trusted by the French authorities, and was imprisoned for a time in La Force before being placed under police surveillance at Dijon, where he remained until 1813. In several letters which he wrote to the Ministry of Police requesting to be released, he referred to the attempts he had made to supply useful information; but he did not mention any such attempt previous to his deportation—which suggests that the British authorities were mistaken in imagining that he was corresponding with the French government while he was in England.[3] Towards the end of 1814 he returned to England, apparently to try and discover the reasons for his deportation and to claim the arrears of the pension assigned to him for his conduct at Toulon.[4] But he was promptly ordered to leave the country; and having appealed unsuccessfully to the privy council against this order (under a new clause of the Aliens Act which allowed for such appeals), he had to return to France.[5]

[1]Edward Thornton to Viscount Howick, 31 Jan. 1807, P.R.O., F.O. 33/37.

[2]C. W. Williams Wynn to Hon. G. Walpole, 19 Feb. 1807, P.R.O., H.O. 79/1; H.O. 5/11 pp. 134, 149.

[3]A.N., F⁷6459; J. Beckett (Under-Secretary, Home Office) to duke of Wellington, 17 Jan. 1815, P.R.O., H.O. 5/18 pp. 277-8.

[4]*Biographie nouvelle des contemporains* (20 vols., Paris, 1820-9), ix. 315.

[5]P.R.O., H.O. 5/18 pp. 265, 276. Another unsatisfactory agent was the comtesse de Rochechouart. She was sent to France with a mission from the British government, but apparently took the government's money without fulfilling any of her engagements. When therefore she returned to England in 1798, she was ordered to leave. (A.A.E., Mémoires et documents, France 595 fos. 35-56; P.R.O., H.O. 5/4 pp. 104, 178; cf. comte de Rochechouart, *Souvenirs sur la Révolution* (Paris, 1889), pp. 16-18.) Madame de Rochechouart was a *grande dame*, and her deportation was finally decided upon at a cabinet meeting (A.A.E., Mémoires et documents, France 595 fo. 42). Where foreigners of less consequence were concerned, such decisions seem to have been taken by the Home Secretary alone, on the recommendation of an Under-Secretary or the Superintendent of Aliens.

The examples described above will have indicated the range of foreigners who were deported for political and security reasons during the French wars. Occasionally, also, whole batches of aliens were deported for such reasons. In April 1797 it was stated that the duke of Portland had received many complaints from the magistrates about foreigners 'who under a pretence of selling prints, images &c. wander over the country either defrauding the people, or as in many instances dispersing seditious & improper publications'. In the following month ninety-five Italian pedlars were deported; and the British minister at Hamburg was later instructed not to give passports to such people, as there were strong reasons to suspect that they had been the channel for 'a very improper & dangerous correspondence'.[1] After the recommencement of war in 1803 there was a mass deportation of aliens who had come to England during the Peace of Amiens; by a proclamation of 31 August all those who had arrived since 1 October 1801 were ordered to leave.[2]

There remain to be considered those who were deported during the war years for reasons which were basically not political. Such deportations were considerably more frequent before the Peace of Amiens than subsequently. In the seventeen-nineties it seems to have been usual for prison sentences and confinement for debt to be followed, where aliens were concerned, by deportation.[3] The general principle was, as Wickham expressed it, that *émigrés* could not be allowed to 'abuse the protection afforded to them in this country, by flying directly in the face of its laws';[4] and moral offences often incurred the same punishment. A certain sieur Aimé Charles Pierre Mathurin Micault de La Vieuville, who had gone into domestic service and pawned some of his employer's possessions, was deported early in 1799—having previously been deprived of the rank and title of Knight of the Order of St. Louis by a Council of War presided over by the duc d'Harcourt.[5] In November 1797 it was laid down that emigrants who received government assistance through the *comité de secours* should not be permitted to gamble; and in the following July four Frenchmen were deported after being found in a gaming-house.[6] Along with them went a young man called Peter de Pon, who had married an English girl of sixteen and 'compelled her to prostitute herself . . . to maintain him in dissipation

[1] P.R.O., H.O. 5/2 pp. 371, 395; H.O. 5/4 p. 339.

[2] P.R.O., H.O. 5/8 pp. 260–4. The number of reports in the Consular archives from Frenchmen who had visited England during the peace indicates how necessary this measure was (A.N., AF IV 1672 fos. 63–90, 114–42).

[3] Wilkinson, pp. 409–10; P.R.O., H.O. 5/3 p. 298, H.O. 5/5 p. 268.

[4] Wickham (then Under-Secretary, Home Office) to mayor of Bath, 16 March 1798, P.R.O., H.O. 5/3 pp. 281–2.

[5] A.A.E., Mémoires et documents, France 627 fos. 8–17. It was 'l'état de servitude dont le sr. Micaut n'a pas rougi de s'entacher' that seems to have chiefly impressed the Council of War.

[6] C. Greville (Under-Secretary, Home Office) to G. Hughes (secretary to the relief committee), 17 Nov. 1797, P.R.O., H.O. 5/3 pp. 134–5; *Annual Register* (Otridge), 1798, Chronicle, p. 63.

and idleness'.[1] After 1803, when John Reeves became Superintendent of Aliens,[2] deportations of this non-political type did not cease altogether.[3] But the general policy seems to have been that the government's power of deportation should only be used for reasons of national security. Reeves stated in 1805 that he had never proposed to the secretary of state that any alien should be deported merely for a breach of the law; and in the following year he wrote that the powers of the executive under the Aliens Act should not be used 'upon any other cause, or for any other purpose, than such as is national, and concerns the safety of His Majesty's Crown and Government, which were the only reasons for Parliament granting the extraordinary powers that belong to the Alien Regulations'.[4]

During the war period there were very few public complaints about the use of these powers. In March 1794 a whig M.P. named Beilby Thompson vaguely asserted that 'Ministers had ordered some persons to leave the kingdom whom they ought not to have driven away';[5] and protests were made in parliament against the deportations of Talleyrand[6] and Alexandre de Lameth. But in May 1814 Bragge Bathurst pointed out, and Whitbread admitted, that under a series of administrations only two complaints had been brought against the executive for its treatment of aliens; and neither of these complaints related to deportations.[7]

[1]*Annual Register* (Otridge), 1798, Chronicle, p. 63.

[2]Reeves had been the founder, in Nov. 1792, of the Association for the Preservation of Liberty and Property; he is portrayed rather unsympathetically by E. C. Black, *The Association* (Cambridge, Mass., 1963), pp. 233–7. As Superintendent of Aliens (1803–14) he was very conscientious and fair-minded, and earned the praise of men such as Brougham and Holland whose political views were very different from his own (Hansard, *Parl. Deb.*, xxxiv, cols. 971, 1080).

[3]For instance the comte de Butler, who had been an officer in the French army, a royalist agent, and chargé d'affaires to the comte d'Artois at Folly House, Twickenham, was deported towards the end of 1805 for having obtained money from a certain M. de Manneville, under the pretence that he would use it to procure letters of denization for him by bribing the officials of the Aliens Office. (P.R.O., H.O 5/10 pp. 223, 235; letter from Butler, dated 31 Aug. 1803, in which he described himself as 'Charge d'affaires de son altesse royale Monsieur', H.O. 1/4; A.N., F⁷6249.) For the case of Baron Kierrulff, a Swede deported for swindling in 1811, see numerous papers in H.O. 1/4 and 1/5.

[4]Reeves to the magistrates of the Thames Police Office, 4 Jan. 1805, P.R.O., H.O. 5/9 p. 368; Reeves to J. Brown, 14 March 1806, H.O. 5/10 pp. 366–7. Cf. H.O. 5/18 p. 238, and H.O. 5/20 pp. 253–4.

[5]Debrett's *Parliamentary Register*, xxxvii. 630.

[6]*Ibid.*, p. 595.

[7]Hansard, *Parl. Deb.*, xxvii, cols. 999, 1009. The first complaint concerned the treatment of a Portuguese officer named Colville, who was arrested in 1809 on board a British warship off Cuxhaven, brought to England, and imprisoned in Cold Bath Fields until 1814 (*ibid.*, xviii, cols. 1187, 1249–50, and xix, cols. 119–20). The second objection was to the use of a warrant issued by the Secretary of State under the Aliens Act for the arrest of Random de Berenger and the seizure of his papers, after the famous Stock Exchange fraud of Feb. 1814 (*ibid.*, xxvii, cols. 969–89, 997–1010). One further case from the war years was raised subsequently by the Opposition. Whitbread claimed in 1815 that a Portuguese diplomat, the chevalier de Correa, had been deported in 1810 at the instigation of the Portuguese

In the post-war period the number of aliens deported was considerably smaller than it had been during the wars. Between 1816 and 1826 there were only seventeen deportations;[1] whereas in the seventeen-nineties there had usually been more than fifty per year.[2] Nevertheless, the Aliens Act when continued in peace-time aroused far more opposition and controversy than it had while the country was at war. Whitbread declared in the house of commons in April 1815: 'Nothing but the danger which the country was in from French fraternization, could ever have induced the Legislature to entrust such powers to the Government as were given in the first Alien Act; but no one then contemplated that such a measure would be continued in time of peace'.[3] There were lengthy parliamentary debates every two years when the act was renewed. Discussion often centred on the knotty but somewhat irrelevant question of whether or not the Crown had the power to deport aliens without parliamentary sanction; there was much quoting of Magna Carta, Coke and Blackstone, and citing of precedents from the reign of Henry IV. According to Sir William Holdsworth, the Opposition lawyers were justified in asserting that the Crown had no general power to expel aliens from the kingdom.[4] One of the chief arguments against the measure was, of course, that it placed all foreigners in the country at the mercy of the executive. In the view of Sir James Mackintosh,

It was a bill to subject twenty thousand residents of Great Britain to banishment at an hour's warning, on secret information, without knowledge of their offence, without the possibility of proving the clearest innocence . . . To be here in such a state was to live by will and not by law. This was the very definition of slavery.[5]

ambassador in London, who had a personal feud with Correa. Government spokesmen denied that Correa had been deported to satisfy the Portuguese ambassador; but it is clear from the Home Office papers that Whitbread's assertion was substantially correct (*ibid.*, xxix, cols. 1132, 1172, and xxx, cols. 41, 325, 328–30; letters of Feb. 1810 in P.R.O., H.O. 1/4; J. Beckett to attorney-general, 7 Feb. 1810, H.O. 79/1).

[1] *Journals of the House of Commons*, lxxix. 901; Hansard, *Parl. Deb.*, new ser., xv, col. 499.

[2] This is clear from the Aliens Office entry-books. In the early years of the 19th century there were fewer deportations: in the 14 months between June 1807 and Aug. 1808, 11 aliens were deported (P.R.O., H.O. 5/12 pp. 238–9).

[3] Hansard, *Parl. Deb.*, xxx, col. 659.

[4] For learned discussions of this subject, see [William Empson,] 'The alien law of England', *Edinburgh Rev.*, xlii (Apr. 1825), 99–174; W. F. Craies, 'The right of aliens to enter British territory', *Law Quarterly Rev.*, xxi (1890), 27–41; T. W. Haycraft, 'Alien legislation and the prerogative of the Crown', *ibid.*, l (1897), 165–86; W. S. Holdsworth, *History of English Law* (15 vols., 1903–65), x. 393–8.

[5] 10 May 1816, Hansard, *Parl. Deb.*, xxxiv, cols. 476, 479. By the peace-time Aliens Act of July 1814 (54 Geo. III, c. 155), aliens ordered out of the country were given the right to appeal to the privy council against the order. (This concession was withdrawn by 55 Geo. III, c. 54, but renewed by 56 Geo. III, c. 86.) However, when considering the case of Baron d'Imbert, the privy council decided that the alien was neither entitled to know the charge against him, nor to be defended by counsel; and Mackintosh maintained that this decision rendered the concession worthless (Hansard, *Parl. Deb.*, xxxiv, cols. 478, 629–30).

The Opposition also maintained that the Aliens Act was being continued not for reasons of national security, but to gratify Britain's continental allies, which did not want Britain to harbour refugees from their autocratic régimes.[1] Castlereagh said in reply to this charge: 'If the peace of this country depended on the peace and tranquillity of Europe, it was the duty of the government of this country to prevent combinations being formed in this country directed against the tranquillity of other countries'.[2] In fact, however, the act was not used against political refugees from the Holy Alliance states. In 1822 Peel said in the house of commons that in no case had asylum been refused to refugees who had been involved in revolutions or conspiracies in other countries;[3] though he added in 1824 that the Aliens Act did enable the government to warn political refugees against hatching plots while they were in England.[4]

It was largely for use against Bonapartists (particularly those who had rallied to Napoleon during the Hundred Days) that the act was continued after 1815. In February 1816 it was decided that persons excepted from the amnesty recently decreed by the French government should not be allowed to enter British territory;[5] and in the debate on the renewal of the Aliens Act a few months later, Castlereagh asked whether it would be advisable 'to throw open the country to all those violent and troubled spirits who assembled about Buonaparté when he made his last desperate effort to disturb the repose of the world'.[6] *La Minerve française* commented in 1818:

Malgré tout ce que l'alien-bill a de vague dans son énonciation, il est facile de voir qu'au fond son objet est très-précis, et qu'il est dirigé exclusivement contre quelques-uns de nos compatriotes que la tourmente de 1815 a forcés de quitter la France . . . Ainsi, dans un pays où de fougueux démagogues exhaussés sur les tréteaux de Spafields, peuvent haranguer vingt mille malheureux que le besoin dispose à tous les excès, on affecte de craindre la présence d'un petit nombre de Français sans pratique de la langue et des usages de l'Angleterre, et que leur qualité d'étranger rendrait suspect à la plupart de ceux qui l'habitent.[7]

Most of the aliens deported after 1815 were members of Napoleon's entourage at St. Helena who had returned to Europe. It is unlikely that they could have done much harm if they had been allowed to remain in

[1] Romilly claimed in 1816 'that this peace alien bill . . . was designedly in further-ance of that alliance which existed for establishing and forming governments contrary to the will of the people' (Hansard, *Parl. Deb.*, xxxiv, col. 168).

[2] 5 May 1818, *ibid.*, xxxviii, col. 525.

[3] *Ibid.*, new ser., vii, col. 806. This statement was not quite accurate, as a Prussian named Baron Eben had been deported from England in 1818, after being banished from Portugal for his participation in a conspiracy to overthrow the Portuguese government (E. M. Ward, British chargé d'affaires at Lisbon, to Lord Castlereagh, 29 Dec. 1817, P.R.O., H.O. 32/13; H.O. 5/20 p. 252; *The Times*, 4 Nov. 1817).

[4] Hansard, *Parl. Deb.*, new ser., x, col. 1342.

[5] P.R.O., H.O. 5/20 pp. 151, 155.

[6] Hansard, *Parl. Deb.*, xxxiv, col. 456.

[7] *La Minerve française*, ii (1818), 153.

England. But the British government was nervous about the possibility of another escape, and was also sensitive to attacks concerning its treatment of Napoleon, which the Holland House group in particular was loud in criticizing. Ministers apparently assumed that these intimates of Napoleon who returned from Longwood—primed, it was imagined, with plots and propaganda—would be less dangerous and embarrassing on the continent than they would be in England. The first deportee of this type was the comte de Las Cases. In November 1816 he was discovered in an attempt to send clandestine letters to Europe. He was arrested and shipped first to the Cape and thence to England, where he hoped to take up residence; but he was sent on to Ostend, and settled in Germany.[1] The next case was that of General Gourgaud, who told Sir Hudson Lowe in February 1818 that he was desperately anxious to get away from St. Helena, and made some astonishing revelations to him about Napoleon's plans and opportunities for escaping. Lowe was very disturbed and sent Gourgaud off to London, where he made similar revelations to Goulburn (Under-Secretary at the Colonial Office) and to the French ambassador. His aim seems to have been to secure the favour of Louis XVIII's government by a spectacular betrayal of Napoleon. But he realized in due course that he was branded as a Bonapartist and could not hope to be readmitted to the French army. He then made a complete volte-face, and wrote a long letter to Marie Louise (which was published in the newspapers) advising her to attend the Congress of Aix-la-Chapelle in order to make a personal appeal on Napoleon's behalf.[2] In November 1818, a few weeks after the publication of this letter, Gourgaud was served with an order for his immediate deportation. This provoked a nasty scene at his lodgings: according to the general's account, the Aliens Office messenger and his assistants treated him with unwarrantable violence; whereas according to Benjamin Capper of the Aliens Office, Gourgaud refused to come quietly and therefore had to be forcibly removed. In view of Gourgaud's excitable character, it is likely that the latter version of the story is nearer to the truth; but his supposed maltreatment aroused much sympathy and indignation in Opposition circles.[3] Among others of Napoleon's suite who were deported from England on their arrival from St. Helena were the comtesse de Montholon,

[1] P. Ganière, *Napoléon à Ste-Hélène* (3 vols., Paris, 1957–62), ii. 154 *et seq.*; P.R.O., H.O. 5/20 pp. 243–5; unsigned memorandum concerning Las Cases, dated 16 Nov. 1817, H.O. 1/5. Sir Hudson Lowe had made it clear that he regarded Las Cases as a dangerous man; he said in a letter of 29 Dec. 1816 to Lord Charles Somerset (Governor at the Cape): '... there is little doubt of his being very active in his correspondence with all parts of Europe, where he can find means to convey his letters' (Bathurst Papers, Brit. Mus., Loan 57/42; cf. Lowe to Earl Bathurst, 3 Dec. 1816 and 23 Jan. 1817, *ibid.*).

[2] Ganière, ii. 300–15, 352–67.

[3] Debate on General Gourgaud's petition complaining of his arrest, house of commons, 2 Apr. 1817, Hansard, *Parl. Deb.*, xxxix, cols. 1355–80; *A letter to the Right Honourable Earl Grey on the subject of the late arrest and removal of General Gourgaud* (anon., London, 1819); G. Costigan, *Sir Robert Wilson* (Madison, 1932), p. 183n. For Capper's account of the arrest see P.R.O., H.O. 5/20 pp. 281–2.

Napoleon's valet Angelo Gentilini, and his priest the abbé Buonavista; Madame de Montholon returned to Europe in 1819, the others after the emperor's death.[1]

After 1821 there was only one deportation—that of a mad Hungarian count who threatened to assassinate the Austrian ambassador[2]—before the Aliens Act was allowed to lapse in 1826. In that year Peel introduced a new Aliens Registration Bill, which was merely to enable the government to keep a record of the aliens residing in the country. Clearly one reason why the executive relinquished its power of deportation was the small use which had recently been made of that power; but Peel said that he would have no hesitation in calling upon parliament to renew the Aliens Act if political refugees were to 'make this country the scene of cabals or conspiracies against their own governments, while Great Britain was in alliance with them'.[3] Another probable reason for the discontinuance of the act was the stiff resistance which the Opposition had consistently offered to it since the end of the war. It was not an issue which aroused popular interest; nor was it often debated in a full House.[4] But the Opposition regarded it as a matter of constitutional principle over which the government was particularly vulnerable; and each successive Aliens Bill from 1816 onwards was vigorously opposed at every possible stage of its progress through parliament.[5] It may perhaps be regarded as an indication of the bankruptcy of the whigs at this period that they devoted so much energy to opposing a measure of such limited practical importance. But doubtless many whigs and radicals were sincerely offended by a measure which they regarded as more in tune with the principles of the Holy Alliance than with Britain's traditional concern for liberty; and Hobhouse said in 1826 that its abandonment 'would be hailed all over Europe as the principal step (in conjunction with those other liberal measures which had been lately taken by the Secretary for Foreign Affairs) on the part of Great Britain to a return to that policy which had so long made her . . . the great patroness of public liberty all over the world'.[6]

William Windham once said that deporting a foreigner was no worse than drowning a fish;[7] and this would seem to be the assumption of many twentieth-century governments. But in Britain after the Napoleonic Wars the rights and interests of foreigners aroused, in certain circles, a surprising amount of concern and discussion. Earlier, in the seventeen-nineties, there was much public distrust of foreigners, and concern for individual liberties was generally at a low ebb. While the government distributed large sums

[1] P.R.O., H.O. 5/20 pp. 295, 318–20.
[2] *Ibid.* p. 368; Hansard, *Parl. Deb.*, new ser., x, col. 1339, and xv, col. 499.
[3] Hansard, *Parl. Deb.*, new ser., xv, col. 500.
[4] *A Few Thoughts on the Probable Renewal of the Alien Bill, by a Member of Parliament* (London, 1822), pp. 3–4, 36.
[5] On the Opposition's tactics in resisting these Bills, see Hansard, *Parl. Deb.*, new ser., i, col. 780 and xi, col. 113.
[6] *Ibid.*, new ser., xv, col. 501.
[7] *Ibid.*, new ser., xi, col. 144.

to the *émigrés* for their support, it did not hesitate to expel any aliens who seemed at all suspicious or undesirable. Many of the foreigners deported in these years were probably harmless; but as a result of this extensive use of the power of deportation very few Jacobin agents and propagandists from the continent were able to stay long in England.[1] After the turn of the century the fear of Jacobinism to some extent subsided (the Habeas Corpus Suspension Act was allowed to lapse in 1801); and with a very scrupulous lawyer as Superintendent of Aliens from 1803, the executive's power of deportation was used more discriminatingly. But the government was still quick to deport any foreigners who looked as if they might be spies; and in Napoleon's time, as in the seventeen-nineties, few successful missions were carried out by French agents in England.[2] Later, in the post-war years, the Aliens Act was fiercely attacked by the whigs, who proclaimed the principle that 'tyranny shall not be exercised in England over any man, be he native or foreigner'.[3] Faced with a vigilant Opposition, the government made only a sparing use of its power of deportation (chiefly against those who had been closely associated with Napoleon), and eventually relinquished it in the period of Liberal Toryism.[4]

[1] The French were reduced to entrusting Louis Monneron—who was sent over to England to arrange an exchange of prisoners in 1795—with a secret mission for 'l'examen de l'état du pais, des dispositions des esprits, et des vues du gouvernement anglois'. His report was general and contained little of significance (A.A.E., Correspondance politique, Angleterre 588 fos. 468–9; *ibid.*, 589 fos. 46–52; A.N., AF IV 1671 fos. 352–6).

[2] On Perlet's mission to England in 1808, see duc de Castries, *Les Emigrés* (Paris, 1962), pp. 363–4; on that of Sub-Lieutenant Lawless in 1811, see A.N., AF IV 1674 fos. 540–1, 545–61.

[3] J. P. Grant, house of commons, 20 May 1816, Hansard, *Parl. Deb.*, xxxiv, col. 620.

[4] By an act of 1848 the power of deporting aliens was restored to the executive for one year; but the power was not used, and the act was allowed to expire (Haycraft, *ubi supra*, p. 165). In 1852, when foreign powers had been pressing the British government to dismiss political refugees from England, Lord Granville sent a circular letter to the British representatives at Vienna, St. Petersburg, Paris and Frankfurt, stating that 'No foreigner, as such, can be sent out of this country by the executive government, except persons removed by virtue of treaties with other states confirmed by Act of Parliament for the mutual surrender of criminal offenders' (*ibid.*, p. 184). So the position remained for the rest of the 19th century.

9

Conceptions of Revolution in the English Radicalism of the 1790s

Ever since the treason trials of 1794, the most persistently controversial question about the English radicals—or, in the terminology of the late eighteenth century, the 'patriots' or 'Jacobins'—of the 1790s has been how far they were revolutionaries or potential revolutionaries. The purpose of the present paper is to survey the *conceptions* of revolution that were current in radical circles in the 1790s, and to examine what can be learnt from the language and propaganda of the radicals about the strategies of change that they envisaged. The traditions or discourses on which they drew, and to some of which their conceptions of revolution were related, were numerous and diverse. They included 'Commonwealth' or 'Country' ideology, the myth of the ancient constitution, millennial religion, natural-rights theory, American republicanism, French Jacobinism, Irish insurrectionism. Some of them were quite closely linked to one another both historically and conceptually, as American republicanism was to Country ideology. Others, such as historic rights and natural rights, were theoretically more distinct; but none the less they were often treated in practice as mutually reinforcing rather than competing modes of argument, and radicals moved to and fro between them without any great regard for logical consistency.[1] It will be suggested, however, that although the various

For helpful discussion and several useful references, I am indebted to Professor H. T. Dickinson, Mrs Jenny Graham, and Dr Marilyn Morris.

[1] On the ideological eclecticism of the radicals, cf. G. Lottes, *Politische Aufklärung und plebejisches Publikum: Zur Theorie und Praxis des englischen Radikalismus im späten 18. Jahrhundert* (Munich, 1979), esp. ch. 4, sec. 1. For a general survey of radical ideology in the 1790s, see H. T. Dickinson, *Liberty and Property: Political Ideology in Eighteenth-Century Britain* (London, 1977), ch. 7.

influences are often hard to disentangle there *were* shifts in fashion and different concepts of political change were in the ascendancy at different times.

It is well known that in the early stages of the French Revolution the English people who greeted it most enthusiastically were members of the educated classes, many of them associated with the heterodox (anti-Trinitarian) branches of Dissent. The political outlook of such Dissenters was formed by a combination of influences including 'classical–republican' ideas, Enlightenment optimism, and religious millenarianism.[2] In the cases of Joseph Priestley and Richard Price, the last element was particularly important in producing a cast of mind that responded with something like rapture to the events of 1789 and the immediately following years. Even before the Revolution, they had interpreted the moral, political, and scientific progress of their age as a process of preparation for Christ's Second Coming. In a sermon delivered and published two years before the fall of the Bastille, Price said that there were already many signs of improvement in the state of the world, which could be seen as harbingers of a coming 'revolution in favour of human happiness'. Hitherto, he said, the kingdom of the Messiah had been in its infancy. 'The light it has hitherto produced has been like the dawn of the morning. It will hereafter produce a bright day over the whole earth.'[3] Priestley, who had long been deeply interested in the elucidation of biblical prophecies, struck a similar note in a sermon of 1788;[4] and when the French Revolution broke out it seemed to both of them to presage the fall of Antichrist and the approach of the millennium. Price's sermon to the Revolution Society in November 1789, in which he spoke of

[2] The first and third of these are particularly stressed in J. Fruchtman, Jr., *The Apocalyptic Politics of Richard Price and Joseph Priestley: A Study in Late Eighteenth-Century English Republican Millennialism* (Philadelphia, 1983); but for some reservations about the close connection he postulates between the two themes, see the review by Martin Fitzpatrick in *British Journal for Eighteenth-Century Studies*, 8 (1985), 236–8. See also C. Garrett, 'Joseph Priestley, the Millennium and the French Revolution', *Journal of the History of Ideas*, 34 (1973), 51–66; and I. Kramnick, 'Religion and Radicalism: English Political Theory in the Age of Revolution', *Political Theory*, 5 (1977), 505–34.

[3] R. Price, *The Evidence for a Future Period of Improvement in the State of Mankind, with the Means and Duty of Promoting it* (London, 1787), 4–5, 24.

[4] *Sermon on the subject of the Slave Trade*, 1788, in *Theological and Miscellaneous Works of Joseph Priestley*, ed. J. T. Rutt (25 vols.; London, 1817–31), xv. 387.

kingdoms 'starting from sleep, breaking their fetters, and claiming justice from their oppressors', is well known.[5] Priestley said in a sermon delivered in Birmingham in the same month:

Let us, with our prayers and good wishes at least, aid a neighbouring nation, and all who are now struggling for liberty, throughout the world; *that the voice of the oppressor may every where cease to be heard*; that by this means we may see the nearer approach of those glorious and happy times, . . . when the kingdoms of this world shall become the kingdoms of God and of his Christ.[6]

Two years later, when he wrote his reply to Burke's *Reflections*, he was equally sanguine, saying that the French and American Revolutions had effected 'a change from darkness to light, from superstition to sound knowledge, and from a most debasing servitude to a state of the most exalted freedom'; it was only now that one could expect to see what men were capable of being and doing.[7]

There were many other radicals who were not interested in the *direct* association of the French Revolution with the fulfilment of predictions in the book of Daniel or Revelation, but whose enthusiasm reflected a secularized kind of pseudo-millenarianism. They too saw the Revolution as shifting humanity on to a new plane of existence, or at least of potential; and their notions of transformational change were often expressed in a language that was partly borrowed from religious chiliasm. Their language and mode of thinking were also heavily influenced, of course, by the style in which the French themselves conducted and portrayed their revolution. Many historians, one of the most recent being Lynn Hunt, have emphasized that what chiefly distinguished the French Revolution from previous revolutionary movements was a willingness to 'break with the national past' and to treat innovation as something to be embraced rather than avoided or disguised. Whereas the American patriots of the 1770s had largely employed the language of 'Old Whig' and 'Country' opposition groups in England, the French invented a new

[5] R. Price, *A Discourse on the Love of Our Country* (London, 1790), 50.

[6] J. Priestley, *The Conduct to be Observed by Dissenters, in order to Procure the Repeal of the Corporation and Test Acts*, 5 Nov. 1789, in *Works*, xv. 403–4.

[7] J. Priestley, *Letters to the Right Honourable Edmund Burke* (Birmingham, 1791), 251.

language of revolution for themselves.[8] It was a grandiloquent language, characterized by messianic intensity, theatrical bravura, and a heavy reliance on imagery and metaphor; and a similar rhetoric was used by many British supporters of the Revolution. A metaphor that commonly appeared in their writings was that of a sudden and exhilarating illumination. James Mackintosh for instance, in his *Vindiciae Gallicae* of 1791, wrote of 'this flood of light that has burst in on the human race'.[9] Another common metaphor, which again had biblical overtones, was a sudden awakening from sleep or torpor. Such figures of speech were conspicuous in the correspondence of the Revolution Society with the National Assembly and other bodies in France, and in the addresses sent by the English radical societies to the French Convention. An example which brings together several rhetorical devices is the peroration to the address of the Society for Constitutional Information, approved on 9 November 1792:

The lustre of the American republic, like an effulgent morning, arose with increasing vigour, but still too distant to enlighten our hemisphere, till the splendor of the French revolution burst forth upon the nations in the full fervour of a meridian sun. . . . It dispels the clouds of prejudice from all people, reveals the secrets of all despotism, and creates a new character in man. In this career of improvement your example will be soon followed; for nations, rising from their lethargy, will re-claim the Rights of Man with a voice which man cannot resist.[10]

Language of this kind, as has been suggested above, was naturally associated with a conception of political change that was *transformational*, and this meant that the original connotations of the term 'revolution' were very largely eclipsed. The term, having been used initially in astronomy to describe the cyclical movement of celestial bodies around the Earth, had acquired a political meaning in the seventeenth century, and at that time it had usually retained cyclical connotations, being used to denote a circular political process in which there

[8] L. Hunt, *Politics, Culture, and Class in the French Revolution* (Berkeley and Los Angeles, 1984), 27, 50.
[9] J. Mackintosh, *Vindiciae Gallicae* (London, 1791), 345, cit. R. Paulson, *Representations of Revolution (1789–1820)* (New Haven, 1983), 47.
[10] Second Report of the Committee of Secrecy of the House of Commons respecting Seditious Practices, 6 June 1794, *Journals of the House of Commons*, xlix. 691.

was a return to an original point of departure. For some seventeenth-century writers, including Hobbes and Clarendon, the English 'revolution' was associated with the Restoration of 1660.[11] At the same period, however, and especially after 1688, the term was coming to be used in what is now a more familiar sense, to signify a sudden political upheaval such as the overthrow of a regime or dynasty; and by the late eighteenth century the equation of the term with discontinuity and innovation, and with drastic transition from one political situation to another, was common though not invariable practice.[12]

However, although linear conceptions of revolution were fashionable in reforming circles in England in 1789 and the early 1790s, two points should be noted. One, to which we shall return later, is that from 1793 or thereabouts such interpretations became much less widely and positively held. The other is that the enthusiasm for revolution expressed by English preachers and pamphleteers was, in the majority of cases, rather disembodied and vicarious. Despite the sweeping nature of their rhetoric, and their general belief that the French Revolution marked a cosmic advance for the cause of political and religious freedom, very few of them were more than parliamentary reformers in the British context; and it is significant that the most uninhibited condemnations of the British constitution that were expressed in these years came from people who were in one way or another exogenous to the English political scene. Alongside the obvious example of Thomas Paine—that 'transatlantic republican', as one contemporary writer called him[13]—we may cite John Oswald, the Scottish poet, vegetarian, and ex-army officer who settled in Paris, became a vocal member of the Jacobin Club, published

[11] Eugen Rosenstock, 'Revolution als politischer Begriff in der Neuzeit', in *Festgabe der rechts- und staatswissenschaftlichen Fakultät in Breslau für Paul Heilborn* (Breslau, 1931), esp. 90–1. See also V. F. Snow, 'The Concept of Revolution in Seventeenth-Century England', *Historical Journal*, 2 (1962), 167–90; Felix Gilbert, 'Revolution', in *Dictionary of the History of Ideas*, ed. P. P. Wiener (5 vols.; New York, 1973–4), iv. 152–67.

[12] Thomas Paine, it has been suggested, did much to bring this use of the term into currency, and 'to redefine revolution as a phenomenon that looked to the future rather than to the past'. J. P. Greene, 'Paine, America and the Modernization of Political Consciousness', *Political Science Quarterly*, 93 (1978), 91.

[13] I. Hunt, *Rights of Englishmen: An Antidote to the Poison now vending by the Transatlantic Republican Thomas Paine* (London, 1791).

in 1793 a 'plan for the constitution of a universal republic' arguing for a bizarre form of direct democracy, and died in the same year leading a regiment against the rebels in the Vendée. In his *Review of the Constitution of Great Britain*, written in 1790, he said that the emancipation of America and the fall of the Bastille were indications that the human soul was awakening from 'a long lethargy'; that the example of 'the late glorious revolution in France' would sooner or later be followed by every nation in Europe; that in Britain a parliamentary reform might serve for a time to amuse the people but could never 'eradicate the deep-rooted vices of the Government'; and that what was needed there was a National Assembly.[14]

There were others who were excited by first-hand experience of events in France and who might have welcomed a revolution in Britain. Thomas Cooper, the Manchester Unitarian, lawyer, and manufacturer, clearly went through a very militant phase, spending several rapturous weeks in Paris in the spring of 1792. Back in London, he passed on to Thomas Walker in Manchester a report of the events of 10 August, and after recounting that the Swiss Guards had been cut to pieces, the King and Queen forced to take refuge in the National Assembly, and six members of the Assembly beheaded, he concluded: 'Te Deum laudamus'.[15] His friend James Watt, son of the inventor, was prepared to defend the 'absolute necessity' of the September Massacres; and Henry Redhead Yorke, who was in Paris in the same year, confessed later that he and others like him brought back to England 'much of the ferocity of the French character' as well as 'much of the bombast of their style'.[16] However, the great majority of the English middle-class reformers and (in Burke's terminology) 'New Whigs', though they rejoiced at the

[14] J. Oswald, *Review of the Constitution of Great Britain*[3] [?Paris, 1792], 44–5. See the 'Advertisement' in this edn. for the dating of the original version. For an attempt to import 1,000 copies from France in Oct. 1792, and the confiscation of these after Earl Camden had pronounced that the author was 'a most wicked and unprincipled incendiary, and his work diabolical', see Public Record Office, HO 48/2, 365–93. See also D. V. Erdman, *Commerce des Lumières: John Oswald and the British in Paris, 1790–1793* (Columbia, Mo., 1986).

[15] T. Walker, *The Original*, ed. Blanchard Jerrold (2 vols.; London, 1874), i. 86.

[16] E. Robinson, 'An English Jacobin: James Watt, Junior, 1769–1848', *Cambridge Historical Journal*, 11 (1955), 353; M. J. Lasky, 'The Recantation of Henry Redhead Yorke', *Encounter*, Oct. 1973, 73.

downfall of popery and Bourbon despotism, were by no means democrats or revolutionaries themselves. Their views on the practical politics of reform in Britain were conditioned by relatively temperate traditions, such as the Commonwealth ideology or civic humanism which could be traced back into the seventeenth century and beyond. This emphasized, not popular sovereignty and the rights of man, but constitutional balance, the elimination of 'corruption' and executive influence, and the need to confine political rights to those who were 'independent'.[17] Some members of the Society for Constitutional Information, such as Major John Cartwright, were willing to argue strongly for manhood suffrage; and a few, going beyond the rather etiolated strand of so-called republicanism in the eighteenth-century Commonwealth tradition, seem to have shared the hostility of Paine and his fellow-American Joel Barlow towards the hereditary elements in the British constitution. But such opinions were very untypical in propertied and professional circles.

What of the radicalism of the popular or artisan societies, the London Corresponding Society and its provincial counterparts? Was this substantially more militant and thoroughgoing? Republicanism, in the sense of hostility to hereditary monarchy, was probably more widespread among reformers of this class. Francis Place said that the majority of members of the LCS—influenced even more, it seems, by the American than by the French example—regarded a republic as ideally the best form of government, and that many of them hoped that a republican system might be brought into existence in England by a gradual process of change.[18] However, given the laws of treason and seditious libel, and given also the extent of popular attachment to the royal family and the genial public image which George III had acquired by the 1790s,[19] it made

[17] Cf. I. Hampsher-Monk, 'Civic Humanism and Parliamentary Reform: The Case of the Society of the Friends of the People', *Journal of British Studies*, 18 (1979), 70–89. Traces of the same ideology, but with different emphases and concomitants, are to be found in the literature of the popular radical societies; see Lottes, *Politische Aufklärung*, 267 ff.

[18] British Library, Add. MSS 27808, fo. 113ʳ. See also A. Sheps, 'The American Revolution and the Transformation of English Republicanism', *Historical Reflections*, 2 (1975), 22.

[19] L. Colley, 'The Apotheosis of George III: Loyalty, Royalty and the British Nation 1760–1820', *Past & Present*, 102 (1984), 106 ff.

good sense for the society to keep its ulterior republican hopes in the background. In its publications and correspondence it was consistent in maintaining that its only direct political object was a radical reform of Parliament; and Maurice Margarot of the LCS said in a letter to the reformers of Norwich in November 1792 that questions such as monarchy should be avoided, and that once the House of Commons genuinely represented the people, it would be able to take whatever further steps might be necessary.[20]

It was clear that the implications of the programme of manhood suffrage and annual parliaments which the plebeian societies adopted in 1792 were potentially 'revolutionary', in the sense that if it had been possible to achieve such a reform it might have opened the way to other drastic changes. This was true not only in the constitutional field but also in the social one. Paine, in the second part of his *Rights of Man*, had linked political democracy to a redistributive programme of graduated taxation and social reform. One of those who followed up this line was James Parkinson of the LCS, whose pamphlet *Revolutions without Bloodshed* (1794) enumerated twenty-four ways in which a reform of the representation would be likely to increase the happiness of the people. He suggested, among other things, that indirect taxes on the necessaries of life would be abolished; the game laws and laws against workmen's combinations would be repealed; the expense of litigation would be reduced and the severity of the penal code mitigated; a national system of education would be established for the children of the poor; and provision would be made for the aged and disabled.[21]

On the other hand, the democratic societies could justifiably point out that their immediate and overt political objectives fell within the bounds of constitutional reform and had been advocated quite recently by the Duke of Richmond, who had since become one of Pitt's ministers. Also, although the radicals quite often used arguments based on natural rights to enforce the case for manhood suffrage, they frequently

---

[20] Maurice Margarot to United Constitutional Societies at Norwich, 26 Nov. 1792, PRO, TS 24/10/16.

[21] [J. Parkinson], *Revolutions without Bloodshed; or, Reformation preferable to Revolt* (London, 1794).

underlined the constitutionality of their aims by maintaining that they were simply trying to restore the *ancient* constitution. The idea that the constitution had degenerated from an original state of purity was a feature of Commonwealth or Country ideology; but in that context purity was usually associated with balance. The radicals—though they occasionally invoked this concept of balance themselves[22]—harboured a rather different vision of the past, maintaining that a model of free and popular government had existed in Anglo-Saxon times. The notion of the recovery of ancient rights could sometimes be associated with a cyclical concept of revolution: in Charles Pigott's *Political Dictionary*, published by Daniel Isaac Eaton in 1795, the definitions of the term 'revolution' included 'a re-assumption by the People of their long lost rights'.[23] More usually, however, the Anglo-Saxon myth was linked to the idea that the radicals were aiming at restoration *rather than* revolution.[24]

Moving from the aims of the popular radicals to their methods, one may ask by what means they hoped to see their programme realized. As we shall see, they did not generally rule out the possibility of using physical force: in fact towards the end of the decade some of them came to regard this as the only practical option. But in the first two or three years after the first popular societies came into existence in 1792 they seem to have imagined that the force of public opinion might induce the political establishment to concede reform. They did not have much faith in the tactic of petitioning Parliament,[25] which was tried rather half-heartedly in the spring of 1793; but they did pin considerable hopes on the idea of summoning a national convention. This move had been advocated by Paine in his *Letter addressed to the Addressers* (1792), and Joseph Gerrald of the LCS, in a pamphlet called

[22] *Address of the London Corresponding Society to the British Nation, June 14, 1798* (London, 1798), 3.

[23] C. Pigott, *A Political Dictionary: explaining the True Meaning of Words* (London, 1795), 117–18. See also D. A. Lambert, 'The Anglo-Saxon Myth and Artisan Mentality, 1780–1830', unpublished Ph.D. thesis (Australian National University, 1987), 173, 321.

[24] See e.g. *A Narrative of the Proceedings at the General Meeting of the London Corresponding Society, held on Monday, July 31, 1797* (London, 1797), 11, 22, 29.

[25] See LCS to Sheffield Constitutional Society, 4 Mar. 1793, *Commons Journals*, xlix. 705.

A Convention the only Means of Saving us from Ruin (1793), recommended 'the interposition of the great body of the people themselves, electing deputies in whom they can confide'.[26] The Sheffield Constitutional Society used almost the same expression in a letter of 27 May 1793, saying that a reform of Parliament could only be brought about by 'the powerful interposition of the great body of the people themselves'.[27] A convention which was actually held in Edinburgh towards the end of that year was dispersed by the Scottish authorities, but in the following spring the English societies were planning to arrange a sequel in England.

The device was a conveniently ambiguous one. On the one hand, it could simply be portrayed as a means of bringing reformers together to decide on a generally acceptable plan of reform and on the best means of campaigning for it. On the other hand, there was the possibility that, with the delegates being elected in a democratic fashion all over the country, the convention might claim to be a more genuinely representative body than the House of Commons, and might actually challenge the authority of Parliament. The government decided to assume that what was being planned in the spring of 1794 was a revolutionary anti-parliament, and this was the chief pretext it gave for arresting the radical leaders and suspending the Habeas Corpus Act in May. The Commons Committee of Secrecy alleged in its report of the same month that the radical societies had been engaged in 'an open attempt to supersede the House of Commons in its representative capacity'.[28] Among the radicals themselves there seems to have been some real uncertainty about what the role of a convention would be. It appears that at least a few of them, including Henry Redhead Yorke, were thinking in terms of an anti-parliament; but others such as Thelwall referred rather vaguely to 'the force of collective opinion' and seem to have envisaged a convention as a means of bringing *moral* pressure to bear on Parliament and the governing class.[29] It is significant that although the Committee of Secrecy did its best

[26] J. Gerrald, *A Convention the Only Means of Saving us from Ruin* (London, 1793), 85.
[27] *Commons Journals*, xlix. 716.   [28] Ibid. 609.
[29] T. M. Parssinen, 'Association, Convention and Anti-Parliament in British Radical Politics, 1771–1848', *English Historical Review*, 88 (1973), 514–15.

to make out that arming had been going on in conjunction with the planning of a convention, it was able to find very little evidence of this. Nevertheless, the convention strategy was probably the most challenging one that the radicals seriously contemplated before the late 1790s.

After the repressive measures of 1794 and 1795, the LCS stuck for some time to a collective policy of attempting to sustain constitutional agitation. When John Binns and John Gale Jones were sent as deputies to Birmingham in March 1796, they were instructed to state that the sole aim of the society was parliamentary reform and that all that was needed to obtain it was a 'strict union' of those who were convinced of its necessity.[30] Six months later the LCS said in a letter to a society at Leicester: 'Our Association renounces every thought of Revolution it is alone friendly and zealous in a Reformation of the House of Commons.'[31] It is clear, however, that at this time some radicals were consoling themselves with the hope that the existing system would somehow collapse of its own accord. In particular, there were hopes that this would occur as a result of financial failure. The notion that the financial system, with its growing national debt and its growing volume of paper money, was fundamentally unsound, was an idea that Price among others had expressed at an earlier date; but it was popularized in 1796 by Thomas Paine's tract *The Decline and Fall of the English System of Finance*, originally published in Paris and reprinted in the same year by Thomas Williams of Blackfriars. Paine did not in fact prophesy an *immediate* national bankruptcy: he merely said that such an event was bound to occur within the next twenty years. But there were others who maintained that financial breakdown was likely to take place at any moment. William Williams, a law student who belonged to the London Corresponding Society, claimed in a pamphlet of 1796 that the funding system was 'on its deathbed';[32] and when the Bank of England suspended cash

[30] Report of the Committee of Secrecy relating to Seditious Societies, 15 Mar. 1799, *Reports from Committees of the House of Commons, reprinted by order of the House* (15 vols.; London, 1776–1806), x. 809.

[31] LCS to Leicester, 6 Aug. 1796 (draft), BL, Add. MSS 27815, fo. 117ʳ.

[32] W. Williams, *Rights of the People or Reasons for a Regicide Peace* (London, 1796), 62. Cf. G. Gallop, 'Ideology and the English Jacobins: The Case of John Thelwall', *Enlightenment and Dissent*, 5 (1986), 6.

payments in February of the following year it seemed that such predictions were being fulfilled.[33]

Some radicals adopted in this situation a rather passive or fatalistic attitude. Writing to the LCS in March 1797, the Friends of Liberty at Sheffield said that it was only necessary to wait for the collapse of the whole system of corruption operated by the 'Treasury Panders, Loan Jobbers and Borough Mongers'.

Let them [Ministers] go on then, till the roots themselves decay—till the very enormity of the corruption (as it shortly must) works its own cure. . . . This is the state of things to which the present Administration are hastening forwards, with unparalleled rapidity: by adding Loan to Loan, and profusion to profusion. . . . Let us wait then with patience for the approaching crisis.[34]

Francis Place indicated in his autobiography that he and his closest associates in the LCS were of much the same opinion. They believed, he wrote, that abuses would go on increasing until 'corruption had exhausted the means of corrupting'; at that point 'an explosion would be caused' and 'the whole system of Government would break up'. But those who anticipated this sequence of events, he added, were 'strenuous in their exertions to have the people well instructed in the principles of Representative Government', in the hope that these principles could be implemented when the crisis came.[35]

Political education had always been a principal concern of the Society for Constitutional Information and the corresponding societies, and this concern was often associated with the idea that it was only on the basis of a transformation of attitudes that a successful transformation of political institutions and machinery could be achieved. Indeed, it was sometimes held that a change of attitudes would necessarily *entail* political change. The most important exponent of this

[33] See *Moral and Political Magazine of the London Corresponding Society*, Mar. 1797, 135–6, for a warning that the English currency would suffer the same fate as the *assignats* in France. Cf. R. Dinmore, *An Exposition of the Principles of the English Jacobins*[2] (Norwich, 1797), 36.

[34] Friends of Liberty at Sheffield to LCS, 15 May 1797 (printed), BL, Place Collection, set 38, iii. 67–8.

[35] *The Autobiography of Francis Place (1771–1854)*, ed. M. Thale (Cambridge, 1972), 197; BL, Add. MSS 27808, fo. 114^r.

idea was William Godwin, whose *Enquiry concerning Political Justice* had a great influence on many educated and self-educated radicals. He wrote in the first edition (1793) that 'the revolutions of states, which a philanthropist would desire to witness, . . . consist principally in a change of sentiments and dispositions in the members of those states'; and he said in the second edition (1796) that imperfect institutions could not long survive once they had come to be generally disapproved of: at a certain point 'they may be expected to decline and expire almost without an effort'.[36] Such ideas were often expressed by the members of radical societies. The Sheffield Constitutional Society said in an address of 1794: 'People of Britain, cultivate Reason! . . . Let revolution of sentiment precede reformation in government.'[37] When the LCS launched its *Moral and Political Magazine* in mid-1796, Godwin's influence was apparent in the emphasis that was placed on the need to bring about a *general* process of education and enlightenment. The aim of the periodical, in the words of its prospectus, was 'to form a pure channel of instruction to the peasant, the artificer, and the labourer: of instruction, as well concerning the natural and proper duties and rights of men in general, as respecting the temporary posture of their public concerns.'[38] And the LCS said in a letter to Perth in the following autumn that the society's objective was the propagation of political knowledge, in order to effect 'a Revolution in the Minds of [the] Nation . . . An enlightened nation immediately becomes free.'[39] What remained very unclear, of course, was *how*—or at least how *soon*—far-reaching political change could be expected to result from this process of enlightenment.

The outstanding question still to be considered about the radicals' conceptions of 'revolution' is what their attitudes were towards physical force. In the early years of the French Revolution it was possible to take the view that huge and

[36] W. Godwin, *Enquiry concerning Political Justice*, 1st edn. (2 vols.; London, 1793), i. 202; 2nd edn. (2 vols.; London, 1796), i. 276.

[37] *Proceedings of the Public Meeting, Held at Sheffield, in the Open Air, on the Seventh of April, 1794; and also an Address to the British Nation* (Sheffield, 1794), 44.

[38] *The Political and Moral Magazine of the London Corresponding Society. Prospectus,* printed sheet dated 30 May 1796, John Rylands University Library of Manchester, R 94736.   [39] BL., Add. MSS 27815, fo. 130ʳ.

beneficent changes had been achieved in France at the cost of surprisingly little bloodshed. Early in 1792 Joel Barlow could write in his *Advice to the Privileged Orders* of 'that mildness and dignity which have uniformly characterized the French, even in their most tumultuous moments'; and in Paris in the following November, when presenting an address from the Society for Constitutional Information to the National Convention, he said that as a result of the French example 'les révolutions vont devenir faciles'.[40] Even Godwin, in the first edition of his work, was prepared to view the French Revolution and its effects in a quite favourable and sanguine light. He said that the American and French Revolutions had both evinced 'a general concert of all orders and descriptions of men, without so much (if we bear in mind the multitudes concerned) as almost a dissentient voice'; and there was reason to hope, he added, that before very long France, 'the most refined and considerable nation in the world', would 'lead other nations to imitate and improve upon her plan'.[41] After the Terror and the Thermidorean reaction, however, the view of revolution as a basically benign, consensual, linear process obviously became hard to sustain. In his 1796 edition, Godwin put a strong emphasis on the *costs* of revolution, on its tendency to replace one tyranny by another, and on its capacity for interrupting rather than advancing the course of improvement.

None the less, there were some radicals in the mid-1790s who showed a tendency to glorify political violence or to hark back to violent episodes in the past. In Pigott's *Political Dictionary* there were entries expressing approval of tyrannicide, and 'Citizen' Richard Lee, in one of the cheap tracts he published from 'The British Tree of Liberty', Soho, in 1795, included the following passage on 'King-Killing':

If an individual believes that an act of seasonable violence on his part will operate as a salutary example to his countrymen and awaken them to the energy and dignity of their characters by breaking the wand whose magic power lull'd them into sloth and

[40] J. Barlow, *Advice to the Privileged Orders in the Several States of Europe, Resulting from the Necessity and Propriety of a General Revolution in the Principles of Government* pt. i (London, 1792), 8; *Gazette nationale ou Le Moniteur universel*, 29 Nov. 1792.
[41] Godwin, *Political Justice*, 1st edn., i. 203, 225.

inaction, does he not in committing that act of violence perform his duty as a member of the community whose interests are closely connected with his own.[42]

There *was* a plot of a kind to assassinate George III in 1794: the so-called 'Pop-Gun Plot', whereby a poisoned dart was to have been fired at the King from an airgun in the form of an imitation walking-stick. But the person who organized the plot seems to have done so with the deliberate intention of betraying it to the government. Generally speaking, the radicals seem to have thought that demystifying satire was a better way of striking at the monarchy then melodramatic violence. An example of such satire is a poem that was occasioned by this very episode, and which played on the King's reputation for being intellectually dense:

> But sure your hair will stand on end when once I do begin, sir,
> The dreadful story to relate of our most gracious King, sir;
> How that a *poison'd arrow*, by some base *plebeian hand*, sir,
> In his most *sacred guts* was intended to be cramm'd, sir.

> But, ah, the dark design!—what a blessing for the nation!—
> Was happily discover'd while 'twas in contemplation:
> For had it pierced his *Royal paunch*, he surely had been dead, sir,
> Tho' possibly he'd not been hurt if it had struck his head, sir.[43]

So far as *collective* violence was concerned, the contexts in which the radicals were most inclined to contemplate it were those of 'self-defence' and 'resistance'. Thelwall wrote in *The Tribune* in 1795 that he was not in favour of 'violence and massacre' but that every man should defend himself and his principles when attacked; and in a speech delivered at an LCS public meeting in the same year he said: 'Let us cultivate our reason; and, if violence comes, let it come from our oppressors; and that, in so barefaced and unprovoked a way, that all moderate men shall be compelled to cry out against them.'[44]

---

[42]Pigott, *Political Dictionary*, 3, 12–13; PRO, TS 11/837/2832, *R. v. Richard Lee*, draft indictment.

[43] *The Pop-Gun Plot Found Out, or Ministers in the Dumps*, printed broadside (n.d.), BL 806. k. 16 (120); cit. Marilyn A. Morris, 'Monarchy as an Issue in English Political Argument during the French Revolutionary Era', unpublished Ph.D. thesis (University of London, 1988), p. 137.

[44] *The Tribune* (3 vols.; London, 1795–6), i. 241; J. Thelwall, *Peaceful Discussion, and not Tumultuary Violence, the means of redressing National Grievance* (London, 1795), 18.

The distinction between 'resistance' and 'revolution' was a common one: Godwin, indeed, devoted separate chapters to the two concepts in his *Political Justice*. In fact it was not always easy to differentiate between them, in either historical or theoretical terms, for the 'right of resistance' was often thought of as the basic justification for revolutionary action. But through the emphasis on 'resistance' the blame for political violence could be firmly pinned on the regime. 'Resistance', by definition, was *provoked*, by an oppressive or authoritarian trend on the side of government, and the concept was usually linked to an explicit or implied con-tractarianism: the subjects' duty of obedience lasted only as long as the ruler respected their rights and liberties. The praiseworthiness of resistance to arbitrary and oppressive government was a time-honoured theme which had a very wide appeal to oppositionist and radical groups, from the Foxite Whigs to the plebeian corresponding societies. Heroes and episodes from the national past could be invoked as precedents: Hampden and the resistance to Charles I, Algernon Sidney and the resistance to Charles II, and (though this was regarded with less favour by many radicals) the Glorious Revolution of 1688. There was also a wealth of literary authorities, including not only Locke but Blackstone and William Paley, who could be cited in support of an ultimate right of resistance.

The emphasis on this right, however, carried with it certain problems. For one thing, it was very difficult to be specific about the circumstances in which a resort to the sanction of revolt would be justified and advisable. John Baxter of the LCS wrote in 1795 in his *Resistance to Oppression, the Constitutional Right of Britons* that any act which was subversive of the constitution was 'a just ground of Resistance'; but he went on to say: 'How far it may be expedient for a nation to exercise this Right, or what particular circumstances shall determine them to it, are questions which I will not take upon me to resolve.'[45] Similarly, the LCS itself said, in a circular of December of the same year, when the Treasonable Practices Act and the Seditious Meetings Act had just passed into law:

[45] J. Baxter, *Resistance to Oppression, the Constitutional Right of Britons* [London, 1795], 4.

'We pretend not to say at what degree of depravity on the part of Government actual insurrection becomes the duty of the People.'[46] When the possibility of resistance was mentioned, it was almost always in a conditional sense: *if* oppression and corruption increased, or *if* the government persisted in refusing to redress grievances, revolution would become necessary and legitimate. It is true that some quite militant things could be said behind the shelter of conditional clauses. Hazlitt said of Horne Tooke that he used to 'talk treason with a saving clause',[47] and this syntactical device was certainly useful as a means of avoiding charges of treason or seditious libel. But it also had the inevitable effect of blunting the urgency of the rhetoric by postponing the need for action until some ill-defined future contingency.

The fact was, of course, that a resort to arms by the radicals seemed to offer no more, or hardly more, chance of success than constitutional agitation, at a time when the bulk of articulate opinion seemed to be either hostile or indifferent to the radical cause, and when revolution on French lines had been deeply discredited. For most of the 1790s, the threat of revolution was more of a political stratagem, more of a feint, than a matter of serious intention or conspiracy;[48] and affirmations of the people's right to overthrow an oppressive government were more often interpretable as warnings to those in authority than as efforts to foster a rebellious disposition in the people.[49] In the later years of the decade, however, a more purposeful and pragmatic attitude to revolution did become apparent in some ultra-radical circles in Britain. There was a considerable amount of undoubtedly seditious activity, which was associated with the so-called 'United Societies' and which lasted—with something of a lull in 1799–1800—until the arrest of Colonel Despard and his fellow-conspirators in Lambeth in November 1802. There has

[46] *Selections from the Papers of the London Corresponding Society*, ed. M. Thale (Cambridge, 1983), 332.
[47] *Complete Works of William Hazlitt*, ed. P. P. Howe (21 vols.; London, 1930–4). xi. 52. [48] Cf. M. J. Lasky, *Utopia and Revolution* (London, 1977), 518.
[49] But T. Spence may have had the latter purpose in mind when he serialized in his *Pigs' Meat, or Lessons for the Swinish Multitude* in 1795 a 17th-cent. account of a popular rebellion in Naples. Cf. O. Smith, *The Politics of Language 1791–1818* (Oxford, 1984), 104–7.

been much controversy about the scale and seriousness of the agitations,[50] and we shall not in this paper have space to tackle such major questions directly. Our attention will be focused on the concepts and models of revolution which the United Societies articulated.

One of the principal schemes being canvassed in 1797-8 was that a revolution might be staged in conjunction with a French invasion of the British Isles; and a subsidiary plan, often associated with hopes for an invasion, was that attempts should be made to subvert the armed forces. Earlier, the idea of invoking French help had not had much currency among English radicals. Even the British Club in Paris, which was heavily stocked with militants, rejected in January 1793 (though by the narrowest of margins) an address calling for a French invasion to rescue England from slavery;[51] and when the Reverend William Jackson came over from France in 1794 to investigate what the likely response to a French invasion would be, he was told by his informants that in England it would be generally resisted. He was told that in Ireland, on the other hand, an invasion would be welcomed. Wolfe Tone, a leader of the United Irishmen, said in a memorandum written for Jackson that the situations of England and Ireland were fundamentally different, in that the English system of government was a 'national' one, while the Irish government was 'provincial' (i.e. colonial, or imposed from outside). Tone went on: 'The prejudices of the one country are directly favourable, and those of the other directly adverse, to an invasion.'[52]

In Ireland by the mid-1790s the 'Defender' tradition of secret societies, oath-taking, and sectarian rancour had fused to some extent with an advanced radicalism which was heavily influenced by French revolutionary ideas as well as by long-standing resentments against British political control; and in 1795-6 the Society of United Irishmen adopted a secret oath-

[50] The fullest account of them is R. Wells, *Insurrection: The British Experience 1795-1803* (Gloucester, 1983).

[51] J. G. Alger, 'The British Colony in Paris, 1792-3', *English Historical Review*, 13 (1898), 676.

[52] *Life of Theobald Wolfe Tone*, ed. W. T. W. Tone (2 vols.; Washington, 1826), i. 277-8. On Jackson's mission, see A. Goodwin, *The Friends of Liberty: The English Democratic Movement in the Age of the French Revolution* (London, 1979), 322-4, 424-6.

bound system of organization, and a policy of seeking French support for an Irish rebellion against British rule.[53] Soon afterwards, societies of United Englishmen, United Scotsmen, and United Britons were being formed, on the same secret, oath-bound model, in the parts of Britain where there were large numbers of Irish immigrants, especially in the north-west and London. Irishmen played important parts in creating these organizations: Robert Gray and James Dixon in Manchester, the Binns brothers and Dr R. T. Crossfield in London (all of whom had been prominent in the LCS), and Father O'Coigley, a priest from county Armagh who had studied at the Irish College in Paris and who travelled to and fro between Ireland, Manchester, London, and France in 1797–8, providing some of the main links in a chain of international conspiracy against the British government. Another Irishman who was involved was Colonel E. M. Despard, and plans were apparently laid for an insurrection to be attempted under his leadership in London as soon as the French landed in Ireland.[54]

The oaths and addresses of the United Societies used a language which was more explicitly revolutionary and republican than that of any other kind of radical propaganda in Britain in the 1790s. An oath administered to soldiers in the local garrisons in Lancashire contained a promise to obey the committee of the United Englishmen, 'and to assist with arms, as far as lies in my power, to establish a republican form of government in this country and others, and to assist the French on their landing to free this country'.[55] An 'Address of the Secret Committee of England to the Executive Directory of France', written by Crossfield and found on O'Coigley when he was arrested at Margate on his way to France in February 1798, said that Englishmen were no longer 'the dupes of an imaginary Constitution' and recognized that 'in order to possess a Constitution they must *make* one'. The address went on:

---

[53] See M. Elliott, *Partners in Revolution: The United Irishmen and France* (New Haven and London, 1982), chs. 1–4.

[54] W. J. Fitzpatrick, *Secret Service under Pitt* (London, 1892), 293; J. Ann Hone, *For the Cause of Truth: Radicalism in London 1796–1821* (Oxford, 1982), 54.

[55] *Reports from Committees*, x. 815–16.

United Britain burns to break her chains. . . . We now only wait with impatience to see the hero of Italy, and the brave veterans of the great Nation. Myriads will hail their arrival with shouts of joy; they will soon finish the glorious campaign! Tyranny will vanish from the face of the earth, and, crowned with laurel, the invincible army of France will return to its native country, there long to enjoy the well earned praise of a grateful world.[56]

One of the questions that such documents pose is how far they represented the views of *British* radicals as well as those of Irish expatriates. There were certainly *some* pro-French extremists in radical circles in England who were not themselves of Irish origin. One notable example was in fact a Scotsman: Robert Watson, a doctor of medicine and former secretary of Lord George Gordon. He wrote in the *Moral and Political Magazine* of the LCS in the spring of 1797 that the people would soon 'have recourse to steel'; shortly afterwards he went down to Portsmouth during the naval mutiny with the apparent intention of turning it in a political direction; and later in the year he was sending information to Léonard Bourdon, French agent at Hamburg, to the effect that 50,000 men in Scotland and 200,000 in England were ready to rise when a French landing occurred.[57] He subsequently fled to Paris in 1798, following the example of John Ashley, a former secretary of the LCS who had taken the same step shortly before. Ashley submitted a memorandum to Talleyrand in April 1798 claiming that 30,000 'active and decided' Londoners were ready to act against the government when the opportunity arose; and Watson published in a French newspaper a highly rhetorical address in which he urged the patriots of England to co-operate with the French in liberating their country.[58]

Some prominent English democrats, on the other hand, undoubtedly had serious misgivings about how far the French could be trusted as 'liberators'. Thelwall had written in a pamphlet of 1796 that foreign interference could 'only, at best, produce a change of masters', and he said in a letter to

[56] Ibid. 813.

[57] *Moral and Political Magazine*, Mar. 1797, 114–15; Examinations of Henry Hastings [May 1798], PRO, PC 1/43/A.152; Elliott, *Partners in Revolution*, 141–2.

[58] Goodwin, *Friends of Liberty*, 437; R. Watson, 'Au peuple de la Grande-Bretagne', *La Clef du Cabinet*, 2 frimaire an VII: copy in PRO, PC 1/43/A.152.

Thomas Hardy in May 1798 that the French Directory seemed determined to *extinguish* liberty, both in France and elsewhere.[59] Also, when in April 1798 the General Committee of the LCS debated what the society's attitude to an invasion should be, Richard Hodgson (the president) said that liberty was currently 'at a lower ebb' in France than in England, and the general opinion seems to have been in favour of resistance.[60] There is little doubt that support for the idea of a French invasion was less common among English radicals than it was among Irish nationalists in 1797–8.

It should be added, however, that the idea of encouraging disaffection in the armed forces seems to have had attractions for the first group as well as the second. While the evidence concerning attempts to spread political discontent in the navy suggests that most of the moving spirits were United Irishmen, it is probable that English ultra-radical networks were used for the distribution of subversive propaganda to the troops in May and June of 1797, when seditious handbills were found in army barracks as far apart as Carlisle, Newcastle, Bristol, and Chichester.[61] The prosecutions of Henry Fellows of Maidstone (who was shown to have corresponded with John Bone of the LCS) and Richard Fuller of London for distributing such material were mentioned in the Report of the Commons Committee of Secrecy of 1799.[62] Moreover James Powell, a normally reliable spy, stated in a subsequent report that several leading London radicals had been involved, including Ashley, Hodgson, Bone, and (believe it or not) Francis Place.[63] Underground agitation in Britain was checked by a number of arrests that were made in Manchester and London in the spring of 1798, and by the

[59] J. Thelwall, *The Rights of Nature, against the Usurpations of Establishments* (2 parts; London, 1796), pt. i, 45; J. Holland Rose, *William Pitt and the Great War* (London, 1911), 352 n.

[60] *Papers of the London Corresponding Society*, ed. Thale, 429–35; BL, Add. MSS 27808, fo. 90ʳ.

[61] Wells, *Insurrection*, 95–104, 145–51; C. Emsley, 'Public Order in England 1790–1801', unpublished M. Litt. thesis (Cambridge, 1970), 286–93.

[62] *Reports from Committees*, x. 794, 809–11.

[63] PRO, PC 1/3490: unsigned report in Powell's handwriting, dated 20 May 1800, and endorsed in the hand of Richard Ford of Bow Street, 'The within Account comes from a very confidential person who can be depended on.' On Powell, see C. Emsley, 'The Home Office and its Sources of Information and Investigation 1791–1801', *English Historical Review*, 94 (1979), 553–4.

...pression of the Irish Rebellion in June. But spies' reports indicate that later that year attempts were still being made by the remnants of the United Englishmen in London to administer the oath to soldiers at Woolwich.[64]

In the years 1800–2 there was a revival of agitation, and this second phase was similar in some respects to the first: there was again, for example, a strong Irish component, and oath-taking, including the swearing-in of soldiers, was again an essential feature of the movement. On the other hand, there were also some significant differences. For one thing, economic hardship—though it had certainly been stressed in earlier seditious literature—was an even more insistent theme at the turn of the century, when there was exceptional distress as a result of the bad harvests of 1799 and 1800. A printed pamphlet, embodying a clear call for revolution, which was circulating in 1801–2, enquired:

Would not a speedy and honourable Death be a salutary refuge from accumulated horrors of the more protracted and lingering one by fatigue and famine? . . . Is not the present system precipitating all ranks to the Abyss of *Distress and Despair?* . . . Look around to the situation of your fellowcreatures numbers of whom are *pining in the most abject misery* beneath the scourge of *Hunger and Oppression.*[65]

The Committee of Secrecy of 1801, in making a case for continued repression, alleged that the disaffected were seeking drastic economic change as well as political revolution.[66] Place subsequently claimed that the Committee had exaggerated this element in the agitation in order to heighten the alarm; and he maintained, in particular, that the Committee's second report (15 May 1801) had given an unwarranted prominence to the ideas of Thomas Spence.[67]

Spence did advocate a kind of social revolution. He believed that private ownership of land should be abolished, and he thought that a take-over of the land could be carried out by the people acting in unison. In his pamphlet *The Restorer of*

[64] Reports of John Tunbridge and William Gent, 6 Aug. 1798, PRO, PC 1/42 A.144; cf. Wells, *Insurrection*, 152.

[65] Pamphlet headed 'Countryman', Wentworth Woodhouse Muniments, Sheffield City Libraries, F. 45/71–1; *Reports from Committees*, x. 830–1, 836–7.

[66] *Reports from Committees*, x. 830–1.

[67] BL, Add. MSS 27808, fos. 201ʳ–207ᵛ.

Society to its Natural State, published early in 1801, he held up the naval mutinies of 1797 as a model: the landowners would be no more able to resist united action on the part of the people than the officers had been able to prevent the seamen from taking over their ships.[68] Place's point, however, was that Spence's whole approach was so open and naïve, and his following so paltry, that the Committee of Secrecy had no real grounds for suggesting in its report that his ideas were a significant strand in the current agitation. Place wrote that Spence was 'a simple honest harmless creature' and that no one could have doubted his harmlessness; and Spence himself may well have been justified in declaring, when he was put on trial for seditious libel in 1801: '. . . notwithstanding any insinuations of the said Report, I stand alone unconnected with any party, and except by a thinking few am looked on as a lunatic.'[69] None the less, there *is* some evidence that ideas about the people's right to the land—whether or not they were traceable to Spence's influence—were featuring in the propaganda of the United Societies in the opening years of the century. A printed *Address to United Britons* which came into the hands of a West Riding magistrate in the summer of 1802 said that mankind, using the knowledge acquired from previous revolutions, should carry out one further revolution of 'permanent utility', whereby 'every principle of monopoly' and 'every badge of usurped power' would be extinguished. The tract built up to a closing attack on 'the great monopolists of the soil, . . . the tyrannic class that supports all other classes of oppressors'; and it said that the people at large had been disinherited of their natural right to the surface of the earth: 'God produces an earth for man in common, to whom he gives an equal right.'[70]

Another respect in which the agitation of 1801–2 differed from that of 1797–8 was that there was less talk of reliance of French help. The possibility of an invasion had indeed receded, and from September 1801, when preliminaries of

[68] *The Political Works of Thomas Spence*, ed. H. T. Dickinson (Newcastle upon Tyne, 1982), 78.
[69] BL., Add. MSS 27808, fo. 221ʳ; *The Important Trial of Thomas Spence* (London, 1803), in *Political Works*, 93.
[70] *Address to United Britons*, sent by R. Walker to Earl Fitzwilliam, 28 June 1802, and by Fitzwilliam to the Home Secretary, 1 July 1802, PRO, HO 42/64, fos. 2ʳ–9ᵛ.

peace were signed, Britain and France were no longer at war. Both of the printed tracts mentioned above called for revolutionary action without making any reference to foreign assistance. It has been suggested that in 1802 Colonel Despard was reluctant to let his more impetuous associates plan an insurrection in London and would have preferred to wait until it could be combined with an Irish rebellion and a French invasion.[71] But it seems none the less that an insurrection was planned at this time, independently of French help. The conspirators included a number of Guardsmen, and the intention was to seize the King on his way to the state opening of Parliament, to occupy the Houses of Parliament and the Tower, and, by stopping the stage-coaches from leaving London, to give the rest of the country a signal which would have precipitated a general rising.[72] There is evidence that an organization of United Britons did exist in Yorkshire in the autumn of 1802, and that some pike-making had been going on there.[73] But few traces of similar preparations have been found elsewhere, and so far as most of the country was concerned hopes for a rising in response to a *coup d'état* in London seem to have rested largely on faith. When John Nichols, a London ultra-radical who escaped prosecution, made a tour of the provinces to collect money for the defence of the prisoners arrested with Despard, he returned with only a few pounds and reported that the London conspirators had been 'much deceived' about the number of 'patriots' in the country.[74]

This paper has reviewed the main ways in which the term 'revolution' was used and in which the possibility of revolution was envisaged by radicals in England between 1789 and 1802. Some of the conceptions surveyed were associated with rather bombastic forms of rhetoric and others with scenarios of

[71] M. Elliott, 'The "Despard Conspiracy" Reconsidered', *Past & Present*, 75 (1977), 46–61.

[72] See the examinations of John Emblin and John, alias Patrick, Connell, Nov./Dec. 1802, PRO, PC 1/3553. Connell, because of a technicality, was not able to give evidence at Despard's trial: see *Howell's Complete Collection of State Trials* (33 vols.; London, 1809–28), xxviii. 418.   [73] Wells, *Insurrection*, 238 ff.

[74] M. W. Patterson, *Sir Francis Burdett and His Times* (2 vols.; London, 1931), i. 169; J. R. Dinwiddy, 'The "Black Lamp" in Yorkshire 1801–1802', *Past & Present*, 64 (1974), 121.

varying degrees of plausibility. There is no doubt that there was more direct incitement to revolution towards the end of the period than there had been earlier, and it is also likely that the actual danger of revolution was considerably more serious in the later years. Under the impact of sustained repression and wartime hardship some radical activists came to the view that pursuit of parliamentary reform was neither a feasible nor an adequate strategy. Thomas Hardy, founder of the LCS, said in a letter to Major Cartwright in January 1801 that this was the clear lesson to be drawn from ministerial policies:

They have been terrified at the word *reform* least [*sic*] it should tend to a *revolution* and terminate in a republic—they have efected [*sic*] such a *revolution* in the country which the most violent reformer never had the most remote idea of. The word reform may *now* be blotted out of the vocabulary—repeatedly and honestly have the rulers of this country been told within these forty years of the necessity of a reform in the democratic part of the constitution in order to *save* the Crown but the die is cast!!![75]

Moreover, there is much evidence to show that attitudes of alienation and disaffection were far more widespread at the popular level in the years round the turn of the century than they had been in the early 1790s, when radicals, even in most industrial areas, had been an embattled minority subject to loyalist persecution.[76]

Whether an autonomous revolution would have been likely may be doubted: although occasional reports of arming reached the authorities, this does not appear to have taken place on a large scale, and the problems of organizing a co-ordinated 'general rising' would have been formidable. On the other hand, if a French invasion had occurred, perhaps in association with an Irish rebellion, parts of the English population might well have risen in support of it, especially if

[75] Hardy to Cartwright, 24 Jan. 1801 (draft), BL., Add. MSS 27818, fos. 16ʳ–17ᵛ. Cartwright, however, replied: 'I do not agree with many, who think it is even now too late so to compose the public mind as to be able to stop at *Reform*, instead of driving on to *Revolution* . . . The example of France would certainly operate, to prevent our thinking of settling things on a wholly new bottom.' F. D. Cartwright, *Life and Correspondence of Major Cartwright* (2 vols.; London, 1826), i. 290–3.
[76] Cf. E. P. Thompson, *The Making of the English Working Class*² (Harmondsworth, 1968), 662–3, 937–8; id., 'The Crime of Anonymity', in Douglas Hay *et al.*, *Albion's Fatal Tree* (London, 1975), 278–82.

the moment had been one of acute distress. It was fortunate from the point of view of the regime that it was never faced with such a conjunction of events. One of the most dangerous moments was the early part of 1798, when Ireland was preparing for rebellion and before Bonaparte shifted his attention away from the English Channel towards Egypt. But wheat prices at that point were relatively low. In the early months of 1801 they were nearly three times as high; but the harvests of 1801 and 1802 were good, and when the threat of invasion returned in 1803 food prices were again at moderate levels and the underground societies had virtually ceased to operate.[77]

[77] Data on monthly wheat prices in *Annual Register*; W. Smart, *Economic Annals of the Nineteenth Century* (London, 1910), 47, 56.

10

Interpretations of Anti-Jacobinism

During the last dozen years, something which looks rather like a consensus has developed, to the effect that in the political debates of the 1790s the conservatives or anti-Jacobins had the better of the argument. Harry Dickinson, for example, says that it can be argued quite strongly that the radicals were defeated, at least in part, 'by the force of their opponents' arguments'.[1] This remark has been cited by Ian Christie, who has described the intellectual defences of the Hanoverian regime as 'formidable', and by Jonathan Clark; while Philip Schofield has endorsed another remark of Dickinson's about the appeal and intellectual power of late eighteenth-century conservative ideology.[2] Faced with this phalanx, one feels rather as Horne Tooke must have felt in about 1800; and I have no intention of making a frontal assault on it. Nor do I favour a reversion to an earlier consensus, which Harry Dickinson has quite rightly criticized: the consensus among historians operating in the Whig tradition of English radical and labour history, who regarded the intellectual case for extensive political reform in the late eighteenth century as unanswerable, and who treated the case *against* reform with facile neglect.[3] All I want to do is to ask some questions about the new Dickinsonian consensus: to ask, for example, what assumptions and contentions are being made by the various members of the phalanx, and in what senses it can really be said that the arguments of anti-Jacobins were stronger than those of their opponents.

1. H.T. Dickinson, *Liberty and Property: Political Ideology in Eighteenth-Century Britain* (London, 1977), p. 272.
2. Ian R. Christie, *Stress and Stability in Late Eighteenth-Century Britain: Reflections on the British Avoidance of Revolution* (Oxford, 1984), p. 159; J.C.D. Clark, *English Society 1688-1832: Ideology, Social Structure and Political Practice during the Ancien Regime* (Cambridge, 1985), pp. 199-200; T.P. Schofield, 'Conservative political thought in Britain in response to the French Revolution', *Historical Journal*, 29, 3 (1986), p. 604.
3. P.A. Brown's *The French Revolution in English History* (London, 1918) contains a couple of pages on Burke's thought, but nothing else on the intellectual reaction except a single quotation from Hannah More's *Village Politics* and a remark that Burke's arguments were 'parodied by the host of anti-Jacobin writers'; G.S. Veitch's *The Genesis of Parliamentary Reform* (London, 1913) paid even less attention to the ideological response to radicalism, though it included several chapters on repression.

In his chapter – or lecture – on 'The intellectual repulse of revolution', Ian Christie gives some attention to the Burke-Paine controversy; and he claims that while Paine's perception of what was happening in France was superficial, Burke's 'penetrated to the heart'.[4] Burke discerned, or claimed to discern, in 1790, elements or tendencies within the Revolution, and especially within its ideology, that were leading ineluctably towards social breakdown and lawless tyranny. In 1792-4, much of what he had predicted did actually occur; and for Christie the events of these years are a vindication of Burke's analysis and of his perception of a 'destructive, murderous' element at the heart of the Revolution. In support of this kind of interpretation Christie can cite some formidable authorities – especially François Furet, or at least the Furet of *Penser la Révolution française*,[5] as well as earlier writers such as Talmon; and the ideological determinism that infuses Furet's interpretation still seems to be fashionable in French Revolution scholarship. It has met with some opposition lately, however;[6] and there is another tradition of interpretation which does not see the Terror as the predetermined outcome of developments that had taken place in the opening year or two of the Revolution. This alternative tradition goes back as far as Mallet du Pan, who argued in his *Considérations sur la nature de la Révolution de France* in 1793 that the increasing violence of the Revolution was attributable largely to the counter-revolutionaries, whose desperate attempts at reaction gave strength and opportunity to extremists on the opposite side.[7] Also, of course, the alternative tradition has put much emphasis on the impact of invasion and total war; and one can add that Furet Mark I – the Furet who published *La Révolution* with Denis Richet in 1965 – belonged to a large extent to that tradition, explaining the *dérapage* (the skidding off course) of the Revolution principally in terms of counter-revolution and war.[8] If this interpretation is regarded as more right than wrong, then the Terror cannot be plausibly construed as the natural fruit of the doctrine of popular sovereignty and as the culmination of trends manifest to Burke in 1790. Much of what Burke predicted may have occurred – but for reasons which lay *outside* his analysis.

Christie goes on to say in his lecture: 'To contemporaries then, and to us now, the clash between Burke and Paine over the French Revolution

---

4. Christie, *Stress and Stability*, pp. 170-1, see also Roger Scruton, 'Man's second disobedience: a vindication of Burke' in Ceri Crossley and Kay Small (eds.), *The French Revolution and British Culture* (Oxford, 1989), pp. 187-222.
5. (Paris, 1978); Eug. trans. *Interpreting the French Revolution* Cambridge, 1981).
6. See, for example, Norman Hampson, *Prelude to Terror: The Constituent Assembly and the Failure of Consensus, 1789-1791* (Oxford, 1988).
7. Jacques Mallet du Pan, *Considérations sur la nature de la Révolution de France* (London, 1793), pp. 17-18, 50; cf. Robert R. Palmer, 'Reflections on the French Revolution', *Political Science Quarterly*, 67 (1952), p. 76.
8. François Furet and Denis Richet, *La Révolution* 2 vols., (Paris, 1964-5), vol. 1, ch. 5.

epitomized the confrontation beween conservatism and revolution.'[9] That is certainly one way of seeing the Burke-Paine controversy. But it seems to me that there is another way of seeing it: as a confrontation, not between conservatism and revolution, but between conservatism and redistributive radicalism. The essence of Paine's critique of the late eighteenth-century government machine in England was that it was mainly a device for raising money from the consuming population at large and transferring it into the pockets of placeholding members of the oligarchy; whereas it *could* operate, he believed – if it was turned into a genuinely representative government – to transfer resources in the opposite direction, raising money by progressive taxation and using it to finance such things as old-age pensions and popular education. In 1800, nettles were selling at Oldham for tuppence a pound (according to William Rowbottom's diary), while Parson Woodforde was sitting down one day to 'a boiled rabbit and a goose', the next day to 'boiled pork and a roast pheasant', and the next day to 'cod-fish and oysters and shrimp-sauce and a couple of partridges roasted, etc.'[10] A few years earlier, Paine had published his *Agrarian Justice*, in which he said that the current state of civilization presented a horrifying contrast of affluence and wretchedness; and he went on to say, in explaining that the problem could never be solved by private charity: 'It is only by organizing civilization upon such principles as to act like a system of pullies, that the whole weight of misery can be removed.'[11]

Burke, at much the same time, was formulating one of the most extreme arguments for economic *laissez-faire* that has ever been written. During the crisis of 1795 he was deeply alarmed by the arguments being expressed by Samuel Whitbread and others to the effect that the authorities should interfere at least temporarily with the labour market or the market for provisions by fixing minimum wages or maximum prices. It was vitally important, Burke maintained, to resist any idea that it was 'within the competence of government, taken as government, or even of the rich, as rich, to supply to the poor those necessaries which it had pleased Divine Providence for a while to withhold from them'. And he went on to say, in words that Marx not surprisingly picked up later, that the people should be made to realize that their hardships could not be alleviated by any breach of 'the laws of commerce, which are the laws of Nature, and

---

9   *Stress and Stability*, p. 170.
10. MS Diary of William Rowbottom, under 20 April 1800, Oldham Public Library; *The Diary of a Country Parson: the Reverend James Woodforde, 1758-1802* ed. J. Beresford, 5 vols., (London, 1924-31), V, p. 282.
11. M.D. Conway (ed.), *The Writers of Thomas Paine*, 4 vols. (New York, 1894-6), vol. III, p. 337. See also Gregory Claeys *Thomas Paine: Social and Political Thought* (London, 1989) pp. 196-208.

consequently the laws of God'.[12] He opposed any measure of a redistributive tendency – and he included the fixing of minimum wages in this category, as being tantamount to an 'arbitrary division' of the employer's property among those he employed – on the grounds that once the sanctity of property suffered any infringement the way would be open to wholesale levelling. He went so far as to argue in the *Reflections* that it was good for vast accumulations of property to exist and to be rigidly protected, for they then formed 'a natural rampart about the lesser properties in all their gradations'. Paine, on the other hand, maintained that some degree of redistribution would make property *more* secure by reducing the resentments it aroused. He said in arguing for the introduction of a death duty to finance old age pensions: 'To remove the danger [to property], it is necessary to remove the antipathies, and this can only be done by making property productive of a national blessing, extending to every individual.'[13]

It seems to me that there are dimensions of the Burke-Paine confrontation or comparison which those who side with Burke are inclined to ignore; and I feel also that those who emphasize the strength of conservative thought in general in the 1790s are apt to show a similar selectiveness. Philip Schofield, in his very interesting study of conservative 'high theory', shows how quite sophisticated lines of argument were developed on the basis of different traditions of eighteenth-century British thought: theological utilitarianism, social contract theory, and the natural-law tradition. What one does not get from his work, it seems to me – aside from a brief summary of some of Paine's more vulnerable arguments – is a sense of the range of *dialogue* that was in progress in the 1790s, and a recognition that although in some areas the conservatives were able to counter radical arguments quite cogently, there were other areas where they had to resort either to evasiveness, or to misrepresentation, or to some fairly transparent special pleading. Before the emphasis on the strength and superiority of conservative argument in the late eighteenth century is endorsed, one would do well to compare (for example) William Paley's arguments against parliamentary reform with Thomas Holt White's *Letters to William Paley . . . on his Objections to a Reform in the Representation of the Commons* (1796), a pamphlet in which much of the nineteenth-century utilitarian case for representative government was adumbrated, and which was to be described by John Colman Rashleigh in

12. *Thoughts and Details on Scarcity*, in F.W. Rafferty (ed.) *The Works of the Right Honourable Edmund Burke*, 6 vols. (Oxford, 1907), vol. VI, p. 22; cf. Karl Marx, *Capital*, trans. E. and C. Paul (London, 1974), p. 843n.
13. Edmund Burke, *Reflections on the Revolution in France and on the Proceedings in Certain Societies in London Relative to that Event*, ed. Conor Cruise O'Brien (Harmondsworth, 1968), p. 140; Conway, *Writings of Paine*, vol. III, p. 341.

1820 as perhaps the ablest work published on the side of constitutional reform.[14] In combating Paley's view that no new mode of election to the House of Commons promised 'to collect together more wisdom, or produce firmer integrity' than the existing system, Holt White wrote: 'Something more than large property, external eminence, and shining talents are requisite in an assembly of Legislators . . . because these qualities do not necessarily involve an IDENTITY OF INTEREST between the Governed and their Governors.'[15] Similar points were made by Thomas Cooper in 1792 and by John Thelwell in 1795:

I have always thought that it will be found on examination (whether pursued with a view to mere Theory, or the evidence of past facts) that every Government has been and will be conducted for the advantage in the first instance of the *Governors*, whoever they are: and the whole secret lies in making those the *actual* Governors, whether directly or indirectly, whose Interests and Welfare are intended to be the main object of the Government.[16]

The plain and simple fact is, that . . . the great body of the people are neglected, because the great body of the people are not represented in the legislature; and those who make the laws are not at all dependent upon their favour or approbation.[17]

It was in this line of argument, rather than in the more easily contestable doctrines of natural and historic rights, that the core of the radical case lay.

A work of Paley's which Schofield wisely treats as beneath his attention is *Reasons for Contentment, addressed to the Labouring Part of the British Public*. Jonathan Clark does mention it, however. He says that because radical historians hold such texts up to derision, we lack scholarly studies of them; and he himself characterizes the pamphlet as a 'classic and lasting formulation of the Anglican argument for the rule of law and social subordination in an inegalitarian, Christian society'.[18] But the only evidence he adduces for awarding it this status is the fact that the tract was reprinted in a Manchester newspaper two days before Peterloo; and I personally find it hard to believe that anyone with any critical sense, or indeed, sensibility, could ever have read the work without objections

14. Cf. J.R. Dinwiddy, 'White, Thomas Holt (1763-1841)', in Joseph O. Baylen and Norbert J. Gosman (eds.) *Biographical Dictionary of Modern British Radicals, 1770-1830*, (Hassocks, 1979), vol. I, pp. 528-9.

15. [Thomas Holt White], *Letters to William Paley, M.A., Archdeacon of Carlisle, on his Objections to a Reform in the Representation of the People* (London, 1796), p. 30.

16. Thomas Cooper, *A Reply to Mr Burke's Invective against Mr Cooper and Mr Watt, in the House of Commons, on the 30th of April, 1792* (Manchester, 1792), p. 27.

17. John Thelwell, *The Tribune* 3 vols., (London, 1795-6), vol. II, p. 82.

18. Clark, *English Society*, p. 262.

crowding into his mind. A sample of such objections expressed by a
contemporary can be found in *A Letter to William Paley . . . in Answer to his
Reasons for Contentment* (1793). The anonymous author protested not only
against the insultingly specious comparisons between the 'cheerfulness
and serenity' associated with a life of labour and the satiety and worry
associated with a life of wealth. He also protested – much as Bentham did
in his devastating critique of Mr Justice Ashhurst's *Charge to the Grand Jury
of Middlesex*[19]– against the airy assertions that were made about the
English legal system. According to Paley, 'it is rather more the concern of
the poor to stand up for the laws than of the rich; for it is the law which
defends the weak against the strong, the humble against the powerful, the
little against the great.' For Paley's critic, the Combination Laws were a
standing refutation of any such pretence.[20]

What I have been suggesting is that to assert that the anti-Jacobins had
the better of the argument simply in terms of argument involves value-
judgements which are questionable – or at least involves a tendentiously
selective approach to the debate. It has to be said, however, that there was
one level of conservative ideology – exploited by Paley among others –
which the radicals had some difficulty in coping with directly. Clark says
that in his *Reasons for Contentment* Paley saved his trump card till the end: 'If
in comparing the different conditions of social life we bring religion into
the account, the argument is still easier. Religion smooths all inequalities,
because it unfolds a prospect which makes all earthly distinctions
nothing.'[21] This quotation recalls, of course, Burke's admonition in the
Reflections: 'The body of the people . . . must labour to obtain what by
labour can be obtained; and when they find, as they commonly do, the
success disproportioned to the endeavour, they must be taught their
consolation in the final proportions of eternal justice.'[22] (It also recalls
Mary Wollstonecraft's response to Burke: 'It is, Sir, *possible* to render the
poor happier in this world, without depriving them of the consolation
which you gratuitously grant them in the next.')[23] However, it is argued by
Clark that Anglican 'political theology' was a major element in the
strength of conservative thought in general in the 1790s and of Burke's
thought in particular. 'Burke's achievement in his later works,' he says,
'was to give eloquent but unoriginal expression to a theoretical position

19. *Truth* versus *Ashhurst*, in John Bowring (ed.) *The Works of Jeremy Bentham*, 11 vols.
     (Edinburgh, 1843), vol. V, pp. 231-7.
20. *Reasons for Contentment, addressed to the Labouring Part of the British Public*, in *The Works of
     William Paley, D.D.* (London, 1835), p. 568; Anon., *A Letter to William Paley, M.A.,
     Archdeacon of Carlisle, from a Poor Labourer in answer to his Reasons for Contentment* (London,
     1793), pp. 12-13.
21. Paley, *Reasons for Contentment*, p. 571.
22. Burke, *Reflections*, p. 372.
23. Mary Woollstonecraft, *A Vindication of the Rights of Men* (London, 1790), p. 136.

largely devised by Anglican churchmen.'[24] Earlier writers, of course, such as the New Conservatives of the Cold War period, have argued that the essence of Burke's thought was religious, thereby, in C.B. Macpherson's words, putting the basis of his thought 'beyond the reach of criticism, which is no doubt where Burke intended it to be'.[25] But Clark's interpretation is distinctive in that he sees the Burke of the 1790s not as a defender of all religion, but as a defender of trinitarian religion; he had come to the view, says Clark, that 'Anglican Christianity was established not merely because it was expedient but because it was true.'[26]

This raises some interesting questions, but also doubts. What is beyond doubt is Burke's belief that an established church – indeed a union of church and state which 'consecrated' the latter – was highly desirable for a number of reasons: among others, so that those who contemplated any reform of the state should do so with reverence and caution, approaching (he says) 'to the faults of the state as to the wounds of a father, with pious awe and trembling solicitude'.[27] Also, to maintain the credibility and value of the state religion, it was necessary that those in positions of political authority should subscribe and be seen to subscribe to its doctrines. 'They would find it difficult', Burke says, 'to make others to believe in a system to which they manifestly gave no credit themselves.'[28] Yet there is little to suggest that he was interested, for their own sake, in the *doctrinal* differences which separated the Church of England from Dissent. He explicitly disowned, in the *Reflections*, those 'miserable bigots . . . who hate sects and parties different from their own, more than they love the substance of religion'; and in his speech of 11 May 1792 on the issue of toleration for the Unitarians, he said that he regarded the question *not* as a theological one but as 'a question of legislative prudence upon a point of policy'.[29] It is also noteworthy that at much the same time as he was defending the Church of England as essential to the English state he was stressing the value of the old Catholic church in France and the value of the Hindu religion to the society of India.[30] It is true that Burke had a clear perception that any notion of a 'double truth' in John Burrow's sense of the term, implying a disjunction between the truth of a belief and its social value,[31] should not if possible be allowed to surface. This perception

24. Clark, *English Society*, pp. 200, 249.
25. C.B Macpherson, 'Edmund Burke and the New Conservatism', *Science and Society*, 22 (1958), p. 238.
26. Clark, *English Society*, pp. 251-2.
27. Burke, *Reflections*, p. 194.
28. *Ibid.*, p. 200.
29. *Ibid.*, p. 257; W. Cobbett (ed.), *Parliamentary History of English from the Norman Conquest in 1066 to the Year 1803* (London, 1817), vol. XXIX, p. 1382.
30. C.P. Courtney, *Montesquieu and Burke* (Oxford, 1963), pp. 135-6.
31. J.W. Burrow, *Whigs and Liberals: Continuity and Change in English Political Thought* (Oxford, 1988), p. 57.

is evident in a fascinating passage in his early notebook:

> If you attempt to make the end of religion to be its utility to human society . . .
> you then change its principle of operation, which consists on views beyond this
> life, to a consideration of another kind, and of an inferior kind; and thus, by
> forcing it against its nature to become a political engine, you make it an engine
> of no efficacy at all. It never can operate for the benefit of human society but
> when we think it is directed quite another way . . .[32]

However, in spite of this perception, and in spite of Burke's
grandiloquence on the subject of religion in his later writings, I agree with
Victor Kiernan that the importance he attached to the social and political
value of religion was clearly discernible through his rhetoric. And
Kiernan may be right in suggesting that Wilberforce's 'vital Christianity'
was of greater utility from a hegemonic point of view *because* its priorities
were more patently spiritual. Wilberforce (in Kiernan's words) 'did not
appear to set up religion for the sake of the State: religion made its own
infinite demands, and wholesome political consequences followed merely
as a by-product.'[33] One can see how Burke's emphasis on the threats to
religion and the established church could have added to the cogency of his
work in the eyes of those who had an interest in the preservation of the
existing order. But his remarks on religion leave an erastian after-taste
that probably restricted their appeal, as compared with the headier
impact of Evangelicalism.

A similar point can be made more broadly, in regard to the Anglican
political theology that Clark so much esteems. He emphasizes – as
Dickinson and Schofield do in relation to secular political theory – that the
writers of the nineties were drawing on a longstanding eighteenth-century
tradition. Much the same thing was said nearly forty years ago by Bernard
N. Schilling. He quoted an array of passages from both mid-eighteenth-
century and late-eighteenth-century writers, contending that religious
belief was vital to the welfare of society and that an established church was
vital to the stability of the state.[34] But he did not see the reiteration of these
well-worn themes as indicative of the *strength* of conservative argument in
the 1790s. Nor, one may add, does Nancy Murray, author of the most
impressive study of the Church of England in that decade. It is true, of
course, that the French Revolution unleashed an unprecedented quantity
of Anglican tracts and published sermons in which traditional political
theology was deployed for anti-Jacobin purposes. But while the scale of

32. M.V.F. Somerset, (ed.) *A Notebook of Edmund Burke*, (Cambridge, 1957), p. 67.
33. V. Kiernan, 'Evangelicalism and the French Revolution', *Past and Present*, (1952), pp. 47-9.
34. Bernard N. Schilling, *Conservative England and the Case against Voltaire* (New York, 1950), especially chapter 9, 'Religion as the support of government'.

this output was very large, Murray attributes this in part to the fact that such publications seemed 'the most likely road to preferment';[35] and she sees the content of this body of work as stale and repetitive, and as limited in its impact on uncommitted opinion by its failure to engage in any but a crudely negative way with the criticisms that were being levelled against the established order. Most orthodox defenders of the alliance or union between church and state were unreceptive to criticism of either the secular or the ecclesiastical hierarchy, and justified both in terms of their combined roles in promoting a well-ordered and harmonious society. For writers on the evangelical wing of the church, on the other hand, this sort of complacent analysis, even when combined with fierce denunciations of French atheism and barbarity, seemed unlikely to carry widespread and lasting conviction.

Their message was not that everything was as it should be, but that *moral* reform was required among the higher orders as well as among the lower; that too much of the established Church was marked by a 'barren formality' (Hannah More's phrase for the religion of the *Anti-Jacobin Review*); that religion should bind all classes together in a common pursuit of salvation; and that, in the words of one of the reports of the Society for Bettering the Condition of the Poor, 'rank, power, wealth, influence, constitute no exemption from activity, or attention to duty; but lay a weight of real, accumulated responsibility on the possessor.'[36] The *Anti-Jacobin Review* may have been shocked by evangelical attacks on the moral and spiritual shortcomings of the opulent and privileged, but it seems likely that Murray and Kiernan are right in suggesting that the brand of religion which did most to counter political radicalism was the evangelical brand:[37] and it did so more by *outflanking* the radical case, or by diverting the discourse from political into spiritual and moralistic channels, than by confronting radical argument directly. It is not of course necessary to suppose that this was a deliberate maneouvre, or that there was anything insincere about the beliefs of the Evangelicals. What Bentham called 'interest-begotten prejudice' works in a variety of oblique and unselfconscious ways; and 'hegemonic' ideas – ideas which help to sustain the position of an elite or superior class, or to deflect threats to it – do not

35. Nancy U. Murray, 'The Influence of the French Revolution on the Church of England and its rivals, 1789-1802', unpublished D.Phil. thesis, Oxford University (1975), p. 316.
36. *Ibid.*, pp. 290 and 367, and chs 7-9 in general; Hannah More to William Wilberforce, 11 September 1800, R.B. Johnson (ed.), *Letters of Hannah More*, (London, 1925), p. 177; *Reports of the Society for Bettering the Condition and Increasing the Comforts of the Poor* 7 vols. (London, 1798-1817), vol. II, pp. 27-8.
37. See also Richard A. Soloway, 'Reform or ruin: English moral thought during the first French Republic', *Review of Politics*, 25 (1963), pp. 110-28; Robert Hole, 'British counter-revolutionary propaganda in the 1790s', in Colin Jones (ed.) *Britain and Revolutionary France: Conflict, Subversion and Propaganda*, (Exeter, 1983), pp. 64-8.

need to be adopted deliberately for 'hegemonic' purposes in order to be so described: indeed it is arguable that the less consciously they are used for such purposes, the more effective they are likely to be.

It has to be admitted, of course, that there were important senses in which the conservatives did prevail over the radicals in the debate of the French revolutionary period. For one thing, this was clearly the case in terms of *volume*. As Gayle Pendleton has conclusively shown, the conservatives produced and sold many more publications. It is also plain, however, that many writers on the conservative side were either place-holders or place-hunters. Of the attributable publications classified by Pendleton as having substantial political content of a conservative kind, well over half – nearly three-fifths – were written by people who were identifiably part of the patronage network, either as recipients of government money or as clergymen of the Church of England.[38] As for the volume of sales, it needs to be remembered that many conservative tracts, especially at the popular end of the spectrum, were purchased in bulk for free distribution, and that their extensive circulation said far more about upper-class anxiety to instil anti-Jacobin views than about the lower-class appetite for them. Francis Freeling reported from the General Post Office to the Crown and Anchor Association that 'vast quantities of Judge Ashhurst's Charge' had been sent 'to every Post Town in the Kingdom' for circulation.[39] But how many people reacted to the work like Bentham? Or like the author of *Justice to a Judge*, who in response to Ashhurst's claim that the law only laid such restraints on the actions of individuals as were necessary for the safety and good order of the community, asked whether the game laws were necessary for this purpose?[40] Or like the anonymous correspondent of Reeves, who wrote: 'Poor Ashhurst's Weakness and Folly has damned him and his Understanding for ever, such time-serving pimps are a disgrace to any professional character whatever.'[41]

Even when such points have been taken into account, it doubtless remains true that the great majority of these defined by Burke in *Letters on a Regicide Peace* as 'the people'[42] – a great majority (shall we say) of the pamphlet- and newspaper-reading public – *was* more conservative than radical. But how far the same could be said of the rest of the people – of the

38. Gayle Trusdel Pendleton, 'English conservative propaganda during the French Revolution, 1789-1802', unpublished Ph.D thesis, Emory University (1976), pp. 56-7, 185-6. See also Emily Lorraine de Monthuzin, *The Anti-Jacobins 1798-1800* (London, 1988).
39. Francis Freeling to [? John Reeves], 28 December 1792, British Library [BL], Add. MSS 16923, fo. 146.
40. Anon., *Justice to a Judge: An Answer to the Judge's Appeal to Justice, in Proof of the Blessings enjoyed by British Subjects* (2nd edition, London, 1793), p. 7.
41. 'Equality' to John Reeves, 16 December 1792, BL, Add. MSS 16923, fo. 4.
42. Rafferty, *Works of Burke*, vol. VI, p. 128.

labouring classes who made up two-thirds of the population – is another matter. There is much evidence to suggest that in the earlier 1790s the popular mood was predominantly anti-Jacobin, and that radicals (outside one or two places such as Sheffield and Norwich) were conscious of being a minority which faced either apathy or hostility from the bulk of the community. However, E.P. Thompson has rightly emphasized the major shift which took place in what he calls the 'sub-political attitude of the masses' in the course of the French wars; and there are clear indications that the years 1795-1802 were an important phase in this important change.[43] Whether a serious danger of revolution developed is a problem that lies beyond the scope of this chapter. But it seems that there was at least a great deal of *passive* disaffection among the labouring population in these years of economic distress and political and economic repression (even if this was offset to some extent by the patriotic feeling – patriotic in the modern sense – that was periodically excited by the threat of invasion). It is sometimes suggested, for example by Robert R. Dozier, that by 1794 the loyalists had definitely won the battle for the minds of the people. This seems an unfounded assumption, arising perhaps from the blinkered view that 'the people' in Burke's limited sense was *really* the people. And even in regard to the politically articulate classes, one should bear in mind that the petitions sent to parliament against the Treason and Sedition Bills in late 1795 carried four times as many signatures as the loyalist counter-petitions: a fact which Dozier completly ignores, saying that the Two Acts were passed 'with relative ease'.[44]

In so far as it can be said that the anti-Jacobins were 'victorious' in the debate of the 1790s, this was due less to the superiority of conservative over radical arguments about the merits or demerits of reform, than to *circumstances*: circumstances which enabled conservative polemicists to misrepresent English reformers as French-style Jacobins,[45] to maintain that French models and experience were more relevant than the American ones which most English radicals preferred,[46] and to assert (as Arthur Young did in 1794) that 'what is *reform* in the commencement becomes *massacre* in the conclusion'.[47] It may be objected that the force of an

---

43. E.P. Thompson, *The Making of the English Working Class* 2nd edition, (Harmondsworth, 1968), pp. 85, 202-3, 662-3; John Dinwiddy, 'England', in Otto Dann and John Dinwiddy (eds.), *Nationalism in the Age of the French Revolution*, (London, 1988), pp. 66-7.
44. BL, Add. MSS 27808, fo. 52; Robert R. Dozier, *For King, Constitution and Country; The English Loyalists and the French Revolution* (Lexington, Ky., 1983), pp. 169-70.
45. For a spirited response to this mode of attack, see Richard Dinmore, *An Exposition of the Principles of the English Jacobins* 2nd edition, (Norwich, 1797).
46. Cf. Arthur Sheps, 'The American Revolution and the transformation of English Republicanism', *Historical Reflections/Réflexions Historiques*, 2 (1975), pp. 7-10, 17-18, 22-3, 26-8.
47. Arthur Young, *The Example of France a Warning to Britain* 4th edn, (London, 1794), p. 219.

argument cannot be gauged in abstraction from the context in which it is expressed. That may be largely true: and it is in fact part of my point. Some scholars seem to me to have written about the conservative ideology of the 1790s in ways that suggested that this ideology had an intrinsic strength and superiority which was *not* dependent on the particular circumstances which the conservatives were able to exploit. If they were merely saying that conservative publicists helped to raise an alarm, I should not disagree with them (any more than Schilling would have done). There is no doubt that a great many members of the educated and propertied classes were turned against reform. But how far was it the intellectual cogency of the arguments of Richard Hey, or William Cusac Smith, or Paley, or even Burke, that was *responsible* for turning them against it? The evidence suggests that when Burke's *Reflections* appeared it had a very mixed reception,[48] and that its main effect in the first year or two after its publication was to stimulate the articulation in England of the very ideas that he was trying to counteract. It was only after the September Massacres and the outbreak of war and the onset of the Terror that he came to be widely regarded as a sage.

48. Cf. F.P. Lock, *Burke's Reflections on the Revolution in France* (London, 1985), chapter 5.

11

English Radicals and the French Revolution, 1800-1850

MUCH has been written about the impact of the French Revolution on English radicalism in the 1790s. There was considerable disagreement at the time about how far French principles and practices should be adopted by the English democratic societies, and there has been a long-running debate among historians about how far such principles and practices *were* actually adopted. There is no doubt that the early phase of the Revolution aroused enthusiastic though ephemeral interest among intellectuals and Dissenters, and that the events of 1792 gave an important stimulus to the artisan radicalism that was then emerging. Some of the democratic reformers—such as Maurice Margarot, Henry Redhead Yorke, John Thelwall—identified very closely, at least at times, with the French jacobins. However, the ideology of English radicalism in the 1790s was highly variegated, and it is doubtful whether French elements can be said to have predominated. Much was carried over from the "real whig" and "country" traditions of the eighteenth century; and the myth of an Anglo-Saxon phase of truly popular government, which enabled the reform movement to be represented as a campaign for the recovery of "lost rights," was a powerful source of legitimation.[1] Also, of course, Paine was a major influence; but despite his fervent defence of the French Revolution against Burke it was arguable that the basic tenets of his republicanism were more American than French. As the September Massacres, the execution of Louis XVI, and the Terror succeeded one another, the American example became increasingly important for those in England who wished to emphasize the virtues of republican government.[2] It is true that around the end of the decade, constitutional agitation having been virtually ruled out by repressive legislation, those radicals who remained active did often appear strongly Francophile. Many of them expatriate Irishmen, they saw their best hope of success as lying in an Irish rebellion, co-ordinated with a French invasion and a rising or *coup d'état* in

1. Günther Lottes, *Politische Aufklärung und plebejisches Publikum. Zur Theorie und Praxis des englischen Radikalismus im späten 18. Jahrhundert* (Munich, 1979), especially chap. 4; D.A. Lambert, "The Anglo-Saxon Myth and Artisan Mentality, 1780–1830", unpublished Ph.D. thesis, Australian National University (1987).
2. Cf. Arthur Sheps, "The American Revolution and the Transformation of English Republicanism", *Historical Reflections/Réflexions Historiques* 2 (1975), 3–28.

England. However, although these ultra-radicals attracted a considerable amount of working-class support in areas of Irish immigration such as south Lancashire, their aims and methods appealed only to limited segments of the population; and developments in France, which seemed to carry the country further and further away from the ideals of the Revolution and in the direction of an aggressive nationalism, were making it increasingly difficult for most English reformers to see the French republican regime in a positive light.[3]

This paper will not attempt to reassess the influence of the French Revolution on the English radicalism of the 1790s.[4] It will be concerned with the less familiar question of how the French Revolution was seen by English radicals during the first half of the nineteenth century. For this purpose, it will be convenient to distinguish between the first and second quarters of the century, since prevailing attitudes towards the Revolution differed markedly as between the two periods.

During the first twenty-five or thirty years of the century, attitudes were generally reserved and often defensive, and it was common for reformers to steer clear of the episode in their speeches and publications. Between the mid-1790s and the latter part of the French wars, the whole question of political reform featured very little in public discussion, partly because of official repression but more fundamentally because of a strong reaction among the politically articulate classes against "French" principles. When reform resurfaced as a subject of debate towards the end of the first decade of the century, its proponents were careful to avoid positions which could be stigmatized as jacobin, and the conservative Whig MP William Windham commented on this in a speech of May 1809. The new agitation was fuelled, he said, not by the "metaphysical reasoning" and "grievances of theory" which had been prominent during the French Revolution, but by discontent over taxes and "abuses". The agitators of the day were exciting popular opinion against "the wasteful expenditure of the public money in jobs and corruption"; and these alleged abuses provided a focus for the resentment produced in the first instance by wartime taxation, and filled the place of "the abstract rights of a few years ago".[5] He doubtless had Cobbett chiefly in mind, and it was certainly the case that the brand of radicalism purveyed by Cobbett and Henry Hunt in the 1810s and 1820s put a strong emphasis on taxation and corruption in supplying a political explanation for popular distress. In so far as they and their associates argued that the people at large had a *right* to the vote, they tended to appeal to the historic "rights of Englishmen", maintaining for example (as Major Cartwright did) that the Anglo-Saxon witenagemot had been elected annually by the people at large, or (as did Sir Francis Burdett) that a statute of the early fifteenth century had

---

3. Cf. J. R. Dinwiddy, "Conceptions of Revolution in the English Radicalism of the 1790s", forthcoming in E. Hellmuth, ed., *The Transformation of Political Culture: England and Germany in the Late Eighteenth Century* (Oxford, 1990). See above, chapter 9, 169-94.
4. For a valuable survey of recent research and discussion, see H.T. Dickinson, *British Radicalism and the French Revolution 1789–1815* (Oxford, 1985).
5. *Cobbett's Parliamentary Debates*, 14: 733–6.

recognized the common law right of all Englishmen to vote at county elections.[6] Some reformers did make explicit use of natural right concepts, but although Thomas Paine's authority was sometimes invoked in support of these (notably by Richard Carlile), they were not usually associated in any explicit way with the French Revolution.[7]

In regard to symbols, also, the tendency of postwar radicals was to avoid those with a jacobin resonance. The distinctive headgear sported by radicals in the years around Peterloo, especially in the north west, was the tall white hat habitually worn by the gentleman-farmer Henry Hunt; and a periodical entitled *The White Hat* was published during the latter months of 1819.[8] Another periodical was appearing at much the same time called *The Cap of Liberty*, but this title did not refer directly to the *bonnet rouge* which had come into fashion in Paris during 1792.[9] It referred to a symbol which, imported originally from Holland, had been part of the English "patriot" tradition well before the French Revolution. The periodical itself has been described as "full of the old rhetoric" about the ancient constitution and historic liberties of England; and an article published in the paper in September 1819 on "The origin and properties of the Cap of Liberty" emphasized the cap's Phrygian and Roman provenance, described it as "whitish, the native colour of the wool undyed," and included no mention of France. At the trials of Hunt and Sir Charles Wolseley in the following year, it was stated that the cap was an ancient symbol of British constitutional liberty, and by no means a symbol of revolution.[10]

If the inclination of reformers was to say as little as possible about the French Revolution, the tendency of their opponents was to do quite the opposite. The multiplicity of purposes for which they turned it to account was satirized by Lord John Russell in an anonymous pamphlet of 1820:

6. John Cartwright, *The English Constitution Produced and Illustrated* (London, 1823), pp. 85, 191; Hansard, *Parliamentary Debates*, 38: 1125–6.
7. A work of French Revolutionary provenance that *was* popular in English radical circles in the early nineteenth century was Volney's *Les Ruines*, first translated into English in 1795 and reprinted in 1796, 1801, 1807, 1811, 1822, 1826, 1833, 1835, and 1840. Carlile estimated in 1820 that it had sold at least 30,000 copies in English, though he added that Paine had been much *more* influential, having "applied himself more particularly to the English nation, and the English people". *The Republican*, 18 February 1820, p. 148; and cf. Iorwerth Prothero, "William Benbow and the Concept of the 'General Strike' ", *Past and Present* 63 (1974), 161–2.
8. Cf. P.A. Pickering, "Class without Words: Symbolic Communication in the Chartist Movement", *Past and Present* 112 (1986), 154–5; Louis James, *Print and People 1819–1851* (London, 1976), pp. 62–69.
9. Jennifer Harris, "The Red Cap of Liberty: A Study of Dress worn by French Revolutionary Partisans, 1789–1794", *Eighteenth-Century Studies* 14 (1981), 283–312.
10. Lambert, op. cit., pp. 63, 305; *Cap of Liberty*, 29 September 1819, p. 64; Robert Walmsley, *Peterloo: The Case Re-opened* (Manchester, 1969), p. 68n. Recently James Epstein, in a well-researched and interesting article, has argued that the cap of liberty did have strong Jacobin as well as "patriot" connotations: "Understanding the Cap of Liberty: Symbolic Practice and Social Conflict in Early Nineteenth-Century England", *Past and Present* 122 (1989), 75–118.

If a book is written containing new opinions on subjects of philosophy and literature, we are told to avoid them, for to Voltaire and Rousseau is to be ascribed the French Revolution. If an ignorant cobbler harangues a ragged mob in Smithfield, we are told that the state is in danger, for the fury of a mob was the beginning of the French Revolution. If there is discontent in the manufacturing towns, we are told that discontent of the manufacturing towns in France was the great cause of the French Revolution. Nay; even if it is proposed to allow a proprietor of land to shoot partridges and hares on his own ground, we are told that this would be to admit the doctrine of natural rights, the source of all the evils of the French Revolution.[11]

At times, radicals felt constrained to produce some rejoinder to the reiteration of this theme. One response was that the situation of late eighteenth-century France was so different from that of early nineteenth-century Britain that analogies between them were meaningless. Cartwright wrote in 1812 that although France had had men of genius at the outset of the Revolution, the people as a whole had had no tradition of town and country meetings for political discussion, and no familiar landmarks such as Magna Carta and the Bill of Rights: "The national mind of France, when called to the great work of political regeneration, was in utter darkness, forming a complete contrast to the public mind of England."[12] Cobbett made a similar point in his *Political Register* in 1816, and the Burdettite reformer Walter Fawkes wrote of the French in the following year:

They had been governed by the *sword*, and only knew how to resist by *violence*. They had *no law*, no *ancient Constitution*, the proud legacy of their forefathers, to appeal to. They were misled by *metaphysics* and *imaginary* good. We bow to the *accumulated wisdom* and *experience* of ages. When they had *curbed* their *old* government, they had a *new* one to make; when we get rid of our "virtual representation," we shall fall into the *old current*, and feel ourselves *at home* again.[13]

The view that the French example was basically irrelevant to English conditions was sometimes accompanied by the idea that much more pertinent lessons were to be drawn from the experience of America. Jeremy Bentham was influenced by considerations of this kind when he took up a radical position in politics in 1809. Events in France in the 1790s had turned him against political reform; but by 1809 he had come to see the American example as closer, in a cultural sense, to the Britain of his day than the example of France in 1792—or, indeed, than that of the English themselves in the 1640s. What the recent history of the United States showed was that when men with "English-bred minds" and an advanced level of civilization adopted a democratic system of government they were able to stop at that point and were not carried on into anarchy.[14]

A different and rather more positive line of argument, which was used quite widely in the early years of Louis XVIII's reign, was that whatever "horrors" the

11. [Lord John Russell], *Essays and Sketches of Life and Character. By a Gentleman who has left his Lodgings* (London, 1820), pp. 141–42.
12. Cartwright, *Six Letters to the Marquis of Tavistock, on a Reform of the Commons House of Parliament* (London, 1812), p. 24.
13. *Cobbett's Political Register*, 2 November 1816, col. 568; Walter Fawkes, *The Englishman's Manual; or, A Dialogue between a Tory and a Reformer* (London, 1817), p. 76.
14. University College London, Bentham MSS, cxxvii. 38–42. Cf. D.P. Crook, *American Democracy in English Politics 1815–1850* (Oxford, 1965), chap. 2.

French Revolution had involved, it *had* brought substantial improvements. In his journal *The Republican* in September 1819, Richard Carlile printed an item headed "BENEFITS OF THE REVOLUTION IN FRANCE. Concerning which it is assumed few will disagree". The list included the abolition of arbitrary and partial imposts, the extinction of venal hereditary offices of justice, the abolition of *lettres de cachet*, and "the establishment of a representation of the people: full, free and equalized in a very high degree".[15] Another artisan radical, John Wade, wrote in his journal *The Gorgon* that in spite of the "transitory evils" associated with the Revolution, the state of France was far better since that event than it had been before it; and he drew attention to improvements in agriculture and communications, the abolition of tithes and of the privileges of the nobility, reforms in the law and the administration of justice, and "the general liberty that has been extended to all classes".[16] A radical of a different kind, Shelley, said much the same thing in his *Philosophical View of Reform* (1820). Adapting Shakespeare, he wrote that the good the revolutionaries had done lived after them, the evil lay interred with their bones.[17]

Yet another line of response to the use made of the French Revolution by anti-reformers was to look more closely at the actual history of the Revolution, putting the "horrors" into perspective and explaining them as the outcome of a particular set of circumstances rather than as the natural consequence of revolution *per se*. John Stuart Mill wrote in 1826 that the conception most English people had of the Revolution was a confused but horrible vision of mobs, massacres, and guillotines, derived from what the Tory press chose to tell them about this period of history.[18] In fact he may have been overstating the point, for considerable efforts to bring the educated public to a more balanced and understanding view had already been made—notably by the Whig writers of the *Edinburgh Review*. The general explanation which they offered for the Revolution was that the old political regime had failed to adjust itself to the progress of civil society. The emerging middle ranks had been confronted by an inflexible system in which the avenues to both political power and social prestige were monopolized by the court and aristocracy. A new political élite had broken through in the years after 1789, but its failure to achieve a peaceful transition to constitutional government was a predictable consequence of the conditions which had previously excluded its members from all political experience.[19]

Mill did carry on the work of the desensationalizing of the Revolution and of engaging sympathy for elements within it. The first generation of Edinburgh

---

15. *The Republican*, 24 September 1819, p. 78. Cf., *ibid.*, 11 February 1820, p. 110; Henry Weisser, *British Working-Class Movements and Europe 1815–48* (Manchester, 1975), pp. 11–13.

16. *The Gorgon*, 14 November 1818, p. 201; 26 December 1818, p. 256.

17. *Shelley's Prose*, ed., David Lee Clark (London, 1988), p. 236.

18. J.S. Mill, *Essays on French History and Historians*, ed., J.M. Robson and J.C. Cairns (Toronto, 1985), in *Collected Works of John Stuart Mill*, 20, pp. 4–5.

19. Biancamaria Fontana, *Rethinking the Politics of Commercial Society*: The Edinburgh Review *1802–1832* (Cambridge, 1985), pp. 11–38; J. W. Burrow, *Whigs and Liberals: Continuity and Change in English Political Thought* (Oxford, 1988), pp. 29, 39–44.

reviewers was too much linked with an aristocratic party to identify closely with the Girondins; their sympathies and connections—notably through Étienne Dumont, whom they encountered at Holland House—were more with the constitutional monarchists. But for Mill and other middle-class radicals, the Girondins embodied much of the virtue of the Revolution. Reviewing Sir Walter Scott's *Life of Napoleon* in 1828, Mill went so far as to describe them as "the purest and most disinterested body of men, considered as a party, who ever figured in history".[20] He also argued in this and other articles that the excesses of the Revolution were principally attributable to the "dogged resistance of the privileged classes" to political reform, and that the essential object of those who perpetrated the excesses was to *defend* the Revolution against "its irreconcilable enemies, within and without".[21]

William Hazlitt went further along the same lines in the chapters on the Revolution which he included in the first volume of his own *Life of Napoleon* (1828). Dating the horrors of the Revolution from the Brunswick Manifesto, he interpreted the Terror as a necessary evil which enabled France to "weather the storm" of foreign and domestic hostility. He did not approve of Robespierre and Marat: in fact he was extremely damning about their dogmatism and insensitivity. But he maintained that the "humane and accomplished" Girondins,

> The true representatives of liberty, . . . necessarily gave place to those men of violence and blood, who, rising out of the perilous situation in which the Republic was placed, were perhaps alone fitted, by their furious fanaticism and disregard of all ordinary feelings, to carry the Revolution triumphant through its difficulties, by opposing remorseless hatred to the cold-blooded and persevering efforts of tyranny without, and cruelty and the thirst of vengeance to treachery and malice within.[22]

By the late 1820s the crude use of the French Revolution as a blanket argument against any kind of change was no longer very compelling. Hazlitt, indeed, wrote in 1826: "The cant about the horrors of the French Revolution is mere cant—every body knows it to be so . . . There were none in the American, and have been none in the Spanish Revolution."[23] The years of social calm since the Cato Street conspiracy, and the relatively moderate nature of the European revolutions of 1820, had allayed the fears that had been first aroused in the 1790s and then revived by the working-class discontent and agitation of the postwar period. The July Revolution of 1830 underlined the message, for middle-class reformers, that revolution was not such a terrible thing and that political change need not be uncontrollable. It also carried other messages, of course—notably the one that intransigent conservatism of the kind displayed by Polignac was more likely to jeopardize stability than to preserve it.

In the debates on the Whig Reform Bill, T.B. Macaulay derived the same moral

20. *Essays on French History and Historians*, p. 99.
21. *Ibid.*, pp. 58, 121.
22. *Complete Works of William Hazlitt*, ed., P.P. Howe, 21 vols. (London, 1930–34), 13: 144–5. See also pp. 110–11, 119, 123, 127–28, 137, 153–55, 163–68.
23. *Ibid.*, 12: 51–52.

from the first French Revolution, maintaining that the nobility provoked its own destruction through its obstinate resistance to reform. J.W. Croker, his principal opponent so far as historical interpretation was concerned, claimed that this was nonsense: the French nobles had made a whole series of concessions, and their downfall was attributable to their weakness in granting them.[24] But although Croker had a historical case here that was not satisfactorily answered, the realities of the contemporary situation gave a formidable thrust to the practical lesson which Macaulay drew from the French precedent. In the years after the Reform Bill was passed, Croker's line lost favour even in Tory circles. In Disraeli's *Coningsby*, the speeches of Rigby (a character based on Croker) at the Darlford election of 1837 are described as being so loaded with tedious digressions on the French Revolution that "the people at last, whenever he made any allusion to the subject, were almost as much terrified as if they had seen the guillotine".[25]

So far, this paper has been concerned with those who engaged in open political debate, and it has said little about the *ultra*-radical strand in early nineteenth-century politics. (The last paragraph, indeed, has strayed away from radicalism altogether.) There was, however, an extreme wing of the radical movement which engaged spasmodically in conspiracy and insurrectionism, and it is in this environment that one would most expect to find French Revolutionary myths and symbols being kept alive and cherished. As E.P. Thompson and others have noted, by the end of the eighteenth century the language of popular protest had acquired a distinct jacobin tinge. Anonymous threatening letters sent to magistrats or employers, and the handwritten notices that were passed around or posted on trees during food riots, showed a belief that the French Revolution, if not an example to be actually followed, at least provided means of intimidation and incitement for local purposes. During the famine of 1800 a sketch of the guillotine appeared on a handbill advocating *taxation populaire* at Maldon in Essex, and posters elsewhere carried messages such as "Peace and Large Bread or a King without a Head," and "Bread or Blood . . . Have not Frenchmen shewn you a pattern to fight for liberty?"[26]

Traces of the same practice are to be found in the early nineteenth century. During the Luddite disturbances of 1812, a manuscript handbill was circulated at Huddersfield which proclaimed: "All Nobles and Tyrants must be put down, come let us follow the noble example of the Brave Citizens of Paris . . . above 49,000 Heroes are ready to break out, to crush the Old Government and establish a New one."[27] Also it is clear that in a few places groups of committed "jacobins" remained in existence through the years of the war, a notable example being the

---

24. Hedva Ben-Israel, *English Historians on the French Revolution* (Cambridge, 1968), pp. 102–6.
25. Benjamin Disraeli, *Coningsby* (London, 1844), Book V, chap. 3.
26. Roger Wells, *Wretched Faces: Famine in Wartime England 1793–1801* (Gloucester, 1988), p. 144; W.F. Galpin, *The Grain Supply of England during the Napoleonic Period* (New York, 1925), p. 19. Cf. E.P. Thompson, "The Crime of Anonymity", in Douglas Hay et al., *Albion's Fatal Tree* (London, 1975), pp. 282, 333.
27. Public Record Office [PRO], HO 40/1, fo. 228.

Oldham–Royton–Chadderton district to the north-east of Manchester. Captain William Chippendale, a local mineowner, complained repeatedly about the restless spirit of jacobinism, "the true French revolutionary mania," which activated these people and led them to seize every opportunity of exciting popular disaffection.[28] He was not simply an alarmist: other records testify to the militancy of this neighbourhood, and a spy's report of August 1816 indicates that the Royton leaders had some acquaintance with the history of the Revolution. According to the report, they argued at a radical meeting at Hollinwood that

> if they would but establish Hampden Clubs in all the great Manufacturing Districts of the Kingdom, it would enable the Hampden Club in London to raise its head above the Government, and that it was practicable was certain, from the success of the Jacobin Club in France, which rose from small beginnings, and under more unfavourable Circumstances.[29]

However, indications of this kind were more the exception than the rule. Provincial risings were attempted at Pentridge and Huddersfield in 1817 and at Barnsley in 1820; but although it has been suggested that the concept of a popular seizure of power on French Revolutionary lines was in the minds of these insurgents, it is not easy to find firm evidence of this.[30] Rather more evidence exists in relation to London. The Spa Fields insurrection of December 1816 was launched by a group of conspirators which had at least tenuous links with the United Societies of the years round the turn of the century. The group talked of setting up a Committee of Public Safety, and used a tricoloured flag of red, white, and green to symbolize the future British Republic.[31] On other occasions members of the ultra-radical underworld meeting in London taverns were reported as singing *Ça ira* and drinking outrageous toasts such as "May the guillotine be as common as a pawnbroker's shop and every tyrant's head a pledge"; and the Spencean agitator Allen Davenport said in October 1819, two months after Peterloo: "I compare the present time to the crisis of the French Revolution, we must arm ourselves as they did."[32] Yet even in the metropolis it appears that jacobin influences were not the dominant strain in the mentality of the far left, which embraced a bizarre mixture of Saxon constitutionalism, seventeenth-century republicanism, agrarian socialism, pseudo-

28. Chippendale to Ralph Fletcher, 29 January 1806, PRO, HO 42/87, and 25 December 1807, HO 42/91; Chippendale to Richard Ryder, 22 May 1812, HO 42/123.
29. Donald Read, "Lancashire Hampden Clubs: A Spy's Narrative", *Manchester Review* 8 (1957–58), 84. Cf. John Foster, *Class Struggle and the Industrial Revolution: Early Industrial Capitalism in Three English Towns* (London, 1974), pp. 39–40, 138–43.
30. K.J. Kaijage, "Working-Class Radicalism in Barnsley, 1816–1820", in Sidney Pollard and Colin Holmes, eds., *Essays in the Economic and Social History of South Yorkshire* (Sheffield, 1976), pp. 126–27.
31. J. Ann Hone, *For the Cause of Truth: Radicalism in London 1796–1821* (Oxford, 1982), p. 264. The fact that "the intended Insurrection assumed the symbols of the French Revolution" was stressed by the Commons Committee of Secrecy which endorsed the need for repressive legislation (19 February 1817, *Journal of the House of Commons*, 42: 86).
32. Iain McCalman, *Radical Underworld: Prophets, Revolutionaries, and Pornographers in London, 1795–1840* (Cambridge, 1988), pp. 151, 122; Malcolm Chase, *The People's Farm: English Radical Agrarianism 1775–1840* (Oxford, 1988), pp. 90–91.

religious millenarianism, and sheer saturnalian ribaldry.[33]

It was not until the 1830s that a serious and positive interest in the first French Revolution became a marked feature of English popular, or populist, radicalism. Hedva Ben-Israel says in a book on the English historiography of the Revolution that after 1832 there was an increasing separation of history from politics, and that the obsession with drawing polemical analogies between Revolutionary history and English political developments went out of fashion.[34] This is true up to a point at the level of Whig-Tory debate, and Thomas Carlyle's determination to get away from historiography as party-political propaganda is the outstanding illustration of the new trend. But among radicals it was the 1830s and 1840s that saw the most notable attempts (after the 1790s) to treat the Revolution as a source of inspiration.

The July Revolution of 1830 was certainly one cause of the revival of interest in the French Revolutionary tradition. The enthusiasm it aroused in England was at first fairly widespread and undifferentiated: even Sir Walter Scott claimed to have been turned into a jacobin by the conduct of the French ministry.[35] But before long a division took place between those who welcomed the moderate and controlled nature of the Revolution, and those who regarded this outcome as a betrayal of the Parisian artisans who had actually manned the barricades. The latter view was held by the National Union of the Working Classes and by the "unstamped" press. In 1831, 1832 and 1833 the NUWC held meetings to celebrate the anniversary of the July Revolution, and speakers lamented that although it was the artisans who had overthrown Charles X, the republic they wanted had not been proclaimed and the fruits of victory had been wrested from them by the "crafty middlemen".[36]

At the same time, of course, in the period before and after the passage of the Reform Bill, convinced democrats were becoming increasingly disgusted with whig and middle-class reformism in England. It was a period of excitement when revolutionary and republican possibilities were in the air, and some activists, no longer feeling any need to avoid postures which might alarm middle-class allies, reached back to the 1790s for the symbols and strategies of an uncompromising jacobinism. The journalist J.H.B. Lorymer was a conspicuous example. From March 1831 he edited a weekly paper called *The Republican*, and the leading article in the first issue, addressed to "Fellow Citizens," asserted that the whole of Europe was on the verge of being "revolutionized" and that both France and England would be "republicanized" within thirty years. When reproved by the *Morning Chronicle* for using the term "Citizen," he responded that it was "the most honourable

33. See McCalman, op. cit., part II, for a fascinating account of these circles.
34. Ben-Israel, op. cit., p. 109.
35. Henry, Lord Cockburn, *Memorials of His Time* (London, 1856), p. 468; cit. Michael Brock, *The Great Reform Act* (London, 1973), p. 110.
36. *Poor Man's Guardian*, 3 August 1833, p. 248. Also *ibid.*, 6 August 1831, pp. 38–39, and 4 August 1832, pp. 482–83.

appellation by which a man can be designated".[37] For several weeks in 1833 his paper substituted for its original title the even more challenging one of *Le Bonnet Rouge*; and an article headed "Fraternization," addressed to the French inhabitants of England, began: "We are thus led to address you because the symbol, under which our lucubrations are ushered into the world, is the same that figured so conspicuously, during the annals of your first grand Revolution."[38]

One of Lorymer's favourite themes was the need for the summoning of a "national convention". This was a device that had a long history in English radical strategy, and one of its attractions was that it was neatly ambivalent: it could either be presented as a mere assembly of reformers for purposes of consultation, or it could be conceived as a body which, being far more representative of the people than the established authorities, would be able to supersede them and set up a new constitutional system. Partly as a result of the French Convention of 1792, the latter conception had been strong in the 1790s; but the convention of Hampden Club delegates held in London in January 1817 had been closer to the former. Lorymer clearly had the French model in mind. He sometimes wrote of a "National Convention," sometimes of a "National Assembly," and one of the articles in which he mooted the idea (in August 1831) was signed "TRICOLOR".[39] When the House of Lords resisted the Reform Bill in the following May, he published a handbill entitled *A National Convention the Only Proper Remedy*, in which he argued that the hereditary elements in the constitution should be eliminated, and that delegates should be elected to a national convention "to sit and legislate" in place of the present parliament: ". . . nothing could be more feasible than for the real Representatives to turn out the mock-Representatives."[40] In the period of sharp disillusionment that followed the passage of the Reform Bill and the Irish Coercion Act of 1833, the National Union of the Working Classes tried to turn the idea into a reality, calling a public meeting "to adopt preparatory measures for holding a National Convention". One of the Union's leaders, Richard Lee, said it was quite clear that "the people were the source of political power, and they had a sacred right to remodel and alter any form of Government so as to make it meet their wants".[41] The government was sufficiently alarmed first to ban the meeting, and then to use the police to disperse those who nevertheless assembled.[42]

At a more analytic level, the political conditions of the 1830s gave rise, in England as in France, to interpretations of the French Revolution that put a new emphasis on the role of social class. In the radicalism of the early nineteenth

---

37. *The Republican*, 26 March 1831, pp. 1–3; 2 July 1831, p. 8. The best account of Lorymer's career is that by David Large in J.O. Baylen and N.J. Gossman, eds., *Biographical Dictionary of Modern British Radicals*, vol. 2, *1830–1870* (Brighton, 1984), pp. 295–99.
38. *Le Bonnet Rouge*, 16 February 1833, p. 1.
39. *The Republican*, 16 April 1831, p. 13; 6 August 1831, p. 2.
40. PRO, HO 64/19, fo. 728.
41. British Library [BL] Add. MSS 27797, fo. 8.
42. T.M. Parssinen, "Association, Convention and Anti-Parliament in British Radical Politics, 1771–1848", *English Historical Review* 88 (1973), 516–17; Prothero, op. cit., pp. 139–40.

century, class feeling had been strong, but it had been directed in a general way against those classes perceived as parasitic, among which aristocratic landowners and placeholders were conspicuous. In the years after 1832, though anti-aristocratic feeling continued, hostility towards the *middle* classes became much stronger and more specific than it had been previously: partly because the anti-capitalist theories broached in the previous decade by Thomas Hodgskin and others had become an important strand in popular radicalism, and partly because the middle classes, having been helped by the working classes to obtain the Reform Bill, were thought to be monopolizing its benefits and supporting a regime that was *more* oppressive towards working people than the governments of the 1820s. François Furet, in his book *La Gauche et la Révolution française*, has noted how the July Revolution helped to produce new perspectives on the *first* French Revolution, driving a wedge between its liberal interpreters, the men of 1789, and its socialist or social-democratic interpreters, the men of 1793.[43] Under the combined impact of 1832 and of Orleanism in France, much the same thing was happening in England. Indeed, the articulation of a new anti-bourgeois interpretation of the Revolution was taking place as early on the English side of the Channel as on the French, and the man responsible for this was the outstanding radical journalist of the 1830s, the Irishman Bronterre O'Brien. Especially famous for his association with the *Poor Man's Guardian*, which he edited between September 1832 and 1835, he expressed more vividly and memorably than any of his contemporaries the notion that capitalists and "middlemen" were the principal exploiters of the working class and that profits rather than taxes should be the prime focus of the latter's resentment.

The book which fired his interest in the French Revolution was Buonarroti's *History of Babeuf's Conspiracy*, though curiously it was on the right rather than the left that this conspiracy first attracted attention in England. Robert Southey devoted several pages to it in an article on "Lives of the French Revolutionists" in the *Quarterly Review* for 1812, but he remarked that it had been little noticed in England at the time when it occurred.[44] Buonarroti's account was first published in Brussels in 1828, and Southey reviewed it at some length in the *Quarterly* three years later, at the height of the Reform Bill crisis. He maintained that it was the most important book about the French Revolution that had yet appeared, because in explicitly recording the aims of the conspiracy it disclosed the immanent trend of revolutionary politics—the kind of politics that Southey associated with the unstamped press.

> The object was to subvert the existing system, not of government alone, but of society in France, and to introduce an absolute community of goods . . . To this principle it is that the course of revolution is tending in the present state of the old world . . . The most inflammatory of those papers which openly defy the laws profess that principle; and they accompany it with excitement to insurrection little less direct than those which Babeuf addressed in his journal to the people of Paris.[45]

43. François Furet, *La Gauche et la Révolution française au milieu du XIXe siècle: Edgar Quinet et la question du Jacobinisme* (Paris, 1986), pp. 8-19.
44. *Quarterly Review*, 7 (1812), 417–22.
45. *Ibid.*, 45 (1831), 207–9.

O'Brien, who had had a university education in Dublin and spoke French, drew attention to Buonarroti's book in an article in the *Poor Man's Guardian* on 24 November 1832. The article broached several themes which were to be found in Buonarroti: the glorification of the Constitution of 1793, the rehabilitation of Robespierre, and the attribution to him of a thorough-going policy of socio-economic as well as political egalitarianism.[46] These themes were to be reiterated in O'Brien's subsequent writings on the French Revolution, which included, besides many newspaper articles, an extensively annotated translation of Buonarroti's *History* (1836), the first volume of an uncompleted biography of Robespierre (1838), and *A Dissertation and Elegy on the Life and Death of the immortal Maximilian Robespierre* (1859).

O'Brien paid several visits to Paris in the mid-1830s to collect material on Robespierre, and on one of these occasions he actually met Buonarroti. The latter had communicated with him shortly before, having seen an advertisement of the forthcoming translation of his own book; and he had sent O'Brien an essay in defence of Robespierre which he himself had recently written but had not yet published.[47] The 500-page volume of biography which O'Brien completed went only as far as the end of the Constituent Assembly. (The reason why the work was never finished was recounted in the *Dissertation*: soon after the appearance of the first volume, a prosecution for debt—which O'Brien attributed to middle-class malignity—led to the forced sale of all his property, his family being "stripped of books, furniture, and every essential convenience of life" and being "literally turned into the streets".[48]) His most important source was the great *Histoire parlementaire de la Révolution française* compiled by Buchez and Roux, the first volumes of which appeared in 1834. Buchez, though the Saint-Simonian ideas he had absorbed in the 1820s were fused with Catholicism, had anti-bourgeois views which accorded to a large extent with those of O'Brien; and, as he made very clear in the prefaces to the *Histoire parlementaire*, he too was an admirer of Robespierre.[49] Other sources sympathetic to Robespierre which O'Brien used, though with some recognition of their shortcomings as historical evidence, were the fictitious autobiography entitled *Mémoires authentiques de Maximilien de Robespierre*, of which the first two volumes appeared in 1830–31, and Laponneraye's *Mémoires de Charlotte Robespierre sur ses deux frères* (1835).

He rightly emphasized, however, in the introductory chapter of his biography, that the overwhelming weight of the historiography of the Revolution up to that point had been highly critical of Robespierre. Much of it, he said, had been totally

46. *Poor Man's Guardian*, 24 November 1832, pp. 617–18.
47. Alfred Plummer, *Bronterre: A Political Biography of Bronterre O'Brien 1804–1864* (London, 1971), chap. 4; Alessandro Galante Garrone, *Filippo Buonarroti e i rivoluzionari dell'Ottocento (1828–1837)* (Turin, 1951), pp. 410–27.
48. James Bronterre O'Brien, *A Dissertation and Elegy on the Life and Death of the immortal Maximilian Robespierre* (London, 1859), pp. 4–5.
49. Roger Reibel, "Les idées politiques et sociales de P.-J.-B. Buchez", *Travaux et recherches de la Faculté de droit et de sciences économiques de Paris, série "Science politique"*, 5 (1966), 1–60.

and extravagantly damning, while the so-called "liberal" histories of Mignet and Thiers had "said all the bad that it was possible to say of Robespierre with the chance of being believed, and omitted all the good that it was possible to omit with the chance of appearing impartial".[50] As for works in English, he mentioned the two biographical sketches of Robespierre which had been published in the late 1790s by John Adolphus and Richard Phillips. While the former writer was manifestly anti-jacobin, the latter was a radical publisher and bookseller who had suffered a spell of imprisonment for selling Paine's *Rights of Man*. But he was no ultra-radical, and in his sketch, which O'Brien described as "a cross between whiggery and sham-radicalism," the Girondins were praised while Robespierre was vilified.[51] As further evidence that even radicals in England were generally inimical to the latter, O'Brien might have cited Cobbett's famous postwar "Address to the Journeymen and Labourers," in which Robespierre was described as a "monster" who was "exceeded in cruelty only by some of the Bourbons". And O'Brien himself, in fact, had written in 1831 about "the Robespierres, the Marats, the Dantons, and other such demons of the day as were thrown up to the surface in the seething of the revolutionary cauldron".[52] When he first started *praising* Robespierre in the *Poor Man's Guardian* in the following year, he drew a protest from the radical journalist William Carpenter, who pointed out that Robespierre had imprisoned Thomas Paine and might well have had him executed if he had remained longer in power. Since Paine was a "real philanthropist," Carpenter asked, how could one admire Robespierre, who attempted to crush such a man? O'Brien's answer was that Paine, though "a very able man for his day," was not a true radical, and "his views fell immeasurably short of the exalted destiny intended by Robespierre for mankind".[53]

The main features of O'Brien's own interpretation of the Revolution will be unsurprising to those familiar with the work of later socialist historians, though the novelty of the interpretation at the time when he was writing should not be lost to view. His heroes are few: Robespierre and Saint-Just; Marat, though his character is said to have contained "a strand of cynicism"; and the *Égaux* of the Year IV, though as we shall see O'Brien was not wholly in agreement with them.[54] His villains are numerous. The constitutional royalists of the Constituent Assembly were representatives of the wealthy, of aristocrats and usurers; and the Constitution of 1791, through the distinction it drew between active and passive citizens, "converted all France into one huge monopoly for the rich," placing the

---

50. O'Brien, *The Life and Character of Maximilian Robespierre*, vol. 1 (London, [1838]), p. 7.

51. *Biographical Anecdotes of the Founders of the French Republic*, 2 vols. (London, 1797–98), 1: 260–72.

52. *Cobbett's Political Register*, 2 November 1816, cols. 568–59; Plummer, op. cit., p. 68.

53. *Poor Man's Guardian*, 8 December 1832, pp. 637–38. The republican writer W.J. Linton, in his *Life of Thomas Paine* (London, 1840), pp. 25–26, was to reconcile an admiration for Robespierre with an admiration for Paine by attributing the latter's regrettable association with the Girondins to his previous acquaintance with Brissot, and to his poor knowledge of French, which prevented him from really understanding what was going on in the Convention.

54. *Dissertation*, p. 13.

lives, fortunes and liberties of the mass of the people "at the utter mercy of the upper and middle classes".[55] The Girondins were "lawyers, bankers, and babbling literati, who, jealous of the nobility and privileged orders, sought to swindle the Government, and all the advantages derivable from it, into their own hands," chiefly by means of an alliance with the "small middlemen". Equally bad was "the sham-Radical portion of the Mountain party," which included "the chief terrorists of the Convention" and other self-seeking desperadoes, and which conspired to overthrow Robespierre when his unflinching commitment to virtue, democracy, and social equality came to be seen as a threat by those who were less disinterested and philanthropic.[56] Those who then substituted the Constitution of 1795 for that of 1793 performed one of the most hideous acts of treason in the history of the world, and France was "never so infamously governed as it was by the middle classes under the Directorial government they installed over the grave of Robespierre".[57]

The episodes in Robespierre's career which O'Brien highlighted also seem quite predictable from a later perspective. They include his opposition to the property qualifications incorporated in the Constitution of 1791, his opposition to the Le Chapelier law of the same year, the declaration of rights which he presented to the Convention in April 1793, his famous report of 17 Pluviôse (5 February 1794) on the principles of public morality, and the laws of Ventôse proposed by him and Saint-Just a few weeks later.[58] His views on property were of special interest to O'Brien. Buonarroti had criticized the Declaration of Rights incorporated in the Constitution of 1793, on the grounds that it consecrated the right of property "in all its appalling latitude". O'Brien took the opportunity of drawing attention to the clauses which Robespierre had proposed but the Convention had rejected. Here the right of property had been defined as the right of every citizen to dispose of whatever goods were guaranteed to him by the law; and this left the law open, O'Brien said, "to unlimited change at the will of the sovereign people" and "to any or to every social order that the most enlarged and comprehensive benevolence can contemplate".[59] He also admired Babeuf and his fellow *Égaux*, whose conspiracy he regarded as the only one in history that was genuinely designed for the benefit of the human race; but he did not consider that they were justified in attempting to establish communism by force. "Without the people's consent," he said, "we have no right to thrust systems upon them (be they ever so perfect in our view), but with their consent all systems should be equally accessible to them." These, he claimed, were the principles implicit in Robespierre's declaration.[60]

55. *Robespierre*, pp. 519–22.
56. *Buonarroti's History of Babeuf's Conspiracy for Equality*, trans. and ed., O'Brien (London, 1836), pp. xiv–xv.
57. *Ibid.*, pp. xix–xx; *Dissertation*, p. 36n.
58. *Robespierre*, pp. 477–96, 512–13; *Babeuf's Conspiracy*, pp. 72n., 79n.; O'Brien, *An Elegy on the Death of Robespierre* (London, [? 1857]), p. 15.
59. *Babeuf's Conspiracy*, p. 72n.
60. *Ibid.*, pp. 72n., 218n.

It will be evident that in O'Brien's view Robespierre was virtually incapable of error. In August 1838, when the *Northern Star* reported Thomas Attwood as saying at a Chartist meeting in Birmingham that he would never be an English Robespierre and that no blood would be shed with his concurrence, O'Brien wrote to protest against this aspersion on his hero, and offered to prove "not only that he was not the author of all, or any, of the horrors committed in the French Revolution, but that he laboured harder than any other Frenchman of his day to prevent such horrors".[61] O'Brien's adulation reached its peak, or *reductio ad absurdum*, in the *Elegy on the Death of Robespierre* which he published in the 1850s. The verse is bad, apart from a few lines borrowed verbatim from Milton's *Lycidas*; and the author's accompanying remarks are about as far over the top as Burke's famous passage on Marie Antoinette.

> The words of this Elegy are supposed to be spoken by a small group of brave, sorrowing workmen of the Faubourg St. Antoine, in Paris, a few days after the fatal 9th Thermidor, when they saw the last hopes of the Revolution extinguished in the blood of its most illustrious chief and his most devoted friends. They are represented in the act of plucking laurel, myrtle, and ivy berries, to strew the bier of their murdered apostle . . . All that was great and glorious in the Revolution originated with him and a few other master-spirits; and amongst his innumerable acts, discourses, and proposed reforms at that epoch, there is not a single one that does not reflect honour upon his memory, and glory upon his country.[62]

What were the motives that led O'Brien to become a historian, or hagiographer? One motive arose from his belief that history, and indeed literature in general, were almost invariably written by "rich men or their tools" and were very powerful engines of delusion.[63] In a footnote to his translation of Buonarroti, he said, in announcing his forthcoming biography of Robespierre:

> If there be one duty which, more than another, an intellectual man owes to his country, it is to blast the existing literature of the world, and to damn its authors in the eyes of posterity. This literature is, from beginning to end, a mass of fraud and misrepresentation, designed and encouraged to perpetuate the present cannibal state of society; and is, perhaps, the most formidable and fatal of all existing obstructions to human progression.[64]

He claimed that even before he had read Buonarroti's book, his interest in Robespierre had been aroused by the violent and constant abuse that was directed at him. He attributed this treatment to the fact that Robespierre's levelling projects were seen as an appalling threat by the upper and middle classes; and he believed that a vindication of Robespierre would not only "shake the credit of 'history'," but would help the cause of political and social regeneration in Britain by showing how that cause had been frustrated and calumniated in France.[65]

61. *Northern Star*, 25 August 1838, p. 4.
62. *Elegy*, pp. 2, 14.
63. *Poor Man's Guardian*, 22 December 1832, p. 639.
64. *Babeuf's Conspiracy*, p. 36n. Cf. *Robespierre*, p. 284: "The pulpit, the press, the stage, the universities and public seminaries, the literature of the country, in short, every avenue to knowledge, every channel and vehicle of information, . . . all are preoccupied and conducted in the interests of the upper and middle classes."
65. *Robespierre*, p. 4.

In the course of his historical writings, he found many opportunities for inserting contemporary analogies and observations. For instance, the men who were responsible for the Constitution of 1791 were compared to the supporters of the July monarchy and to the perpetrators of the 1832 Reform Bill; the *Tiers État* was said to have used "pressure from without" to overawe the privileged orders in France in just the same way as middle-class reformers used it to intimidate the borough-mongers in England; and "Swing"—the mythical leader of the agricultural riots in southern England in 1830, whom O'Brien treated as the quintessential spirit of popular revolt—was declared to have been the real hero of 4 August 1789.[66] Also, a comparison which Buonarroti himself had drawn between the ideas of Babeuf and those of Robert Owen led O'Brien to explain that in regard to property he differed from both of them. In his own view, so long as the means of acquiring and retaining wealth were equally available to everyone "in proportion to the respective industry and services of each," private property was unobjectionable; what one needed to eliminate was usury—the practice which enabled a rich man to use his wealth as "a sort of sucking-pump or thumbscrew for sucking and screwing other people's produce into his possession".[67]

The impact of O'Brien's writings about the French Revolution is hard to gauge; but one prominent radical who shared his interest in this period of history, and who seems at least in part to have derived this interest from him, was George Julian Harney. A young man in his early twenties when he became a conspicuous figure in the opening phase of the Chartist movement, Harney called O'Brien in 1838 his "guide, philosopher, and friend"; and one finds him, at a dinner in September 1845 to celebrate the anniversary of the establishment of the French Republic, purveying an interpretation of the Revolution which closely resembled O'Brien's in its disparagement of Lafayette and the Girondins and its praise of Robespierre and Babeuf.[68] However, in the early and most militant phase of his career, the aspects of the French Revolution which appealed to him were rather different from those that appealed to O'Brien: it was the insurrectionary strand that particularly excited him.

O'Brien was prepared to write positively about violent revolution in some contexts. He applauded, for example, the negro rising of 1791 in Saint Domingue and went so far as to add:"May their example be one day followed by the oppressed of all nations!"[69] But in relation to England he tended to write more cautiously. In the *Poor Man's Guardian* in July 1833 he said that although the French had achieved many triumphs in their first revolution through "the irresistible energy of popular action," the English should not imitate them by taking up arms.

> Could we, indeed, accomplish a successful insurrection as readily as we could wish it, our admonitions might be different; but as we know that it is one thing to will a general rising, but quite another

66. *Babeuf's Conspiracy*, p. xiv; *Robespierre*, pp. 281, 219.
67. *Babeuf's Conspiracy*, p. 216n.
68. *The Operative*, 11 November 1838, p. 19; *Northern Star*, 27 September 1845, p. 5.
69. *Robespierre*, p. 510.

to succeed with it, we must (at least for the present) be content to leave to our gallant neighbours, the French, all the glories of that species of struggle.[70]

Three years later, he wrote that his admiration for the political and social principles of Buonarroti should not be taken to imply that he wished "to instruct the British people in the arts of conspiracy and insurrection".[71] For Harney, on the other hand—at least in 1838–39—the insurrectionary aspect of the French Revolution had a much stronger and more immediate attraction. At a meeting at Norwich in October 1838, speaking with a tricolor ribbon round his neck, he said that when the French petitioned for a redress of grievances on 20 June 1792 they backed their petition with 30,000 pikes and muskets; and when their wishes were still unfulfilled several weeks later, they rose *en masse* on 10 August and overthrew the monarchy. He went on to tell the Norwich Chartists that "if their present peaceable petition failed, if the National Petition should be trampled upon, then he should ask them for a 20th of June, and, if needs be, for a 10th of August, against the present abominable system of representation".[72]

A jacobin style also characterized the London Democratic Association, of which Harney was a leading member, and its organ the *London Democrat* which he helped to launch in April 1839. The LDA was formally inaugurated (having previously been the East London Democratic Association) on 10 August 1838; and at a meeting in the following December to commemorate the Polish Revolution of 1830, Harney said that just as the French Convention of 1793 had required a Jacobin Club to "look after it," so the forthcoming Chartist Convention in London would need the "watchful support" of the LDA.[73] Of the great figures of the Revolution, it was Marat with whom he specially identified. In a series of articles he wrote for the *London Democrat* he styled himself "The Friend of the People," and he declaimed in the first of these:

Hail! spirit of MARAT! Hail! glorious apostle of Equality!! Hail! immortal martyr of Liberty!!! All hail! thou whose imperishable title I have assumed; and oh! may the God of Freedom strengthen me to brave, like thee, the persecution of tyrants and traitors, or (if so doomed) to meet, like thee, a martyr's death![74]

He also contributed a number of "Scenes and Sketches from the French Revolution," in order, as he put it, that in the approaching revolution in England his countrymen might learn "to avoid the errors, and to imitate the heroic, god-like deeds of the sons of republican France".[75] After a few weeks, owing to the pressure

70. *Poor Man's Guardian*, 6 July 1833, p. 213.
71. *Babeuf's Conspiracy*, p. 214n.
72. *The Operative*, 11 November 1838, p. 21.
73. Jennifer Bennett, "The London Democratic Association 1837–41: A Study in London Radicalism", in James Epstein and Dorothy Thompson, eds., *The Chartist Experience: Studies in Working-Class Radicalism and Culture, 1830–1860* (London, 1982), p. 87; A. R. Schoyen, *The Chartist Challenge: A Portrait of George Julian Harney* (London, 1958), p. 50.
74. *London Democrat*, 13 April 1839, p. 5.
75. *Ibid.*

of other engagements, Harney passed on the "Scenes and Sketches" to J.C. Coombe, principal editor of the paper; and Coombe ended an account of the storming of the Bastille and the march on Versailles by asking: "Englishmen, how many more examples of energy, courage, and success, will you require before YOU commence the battle?"[76] It was Harney's view, expressed in the *London Democrat*, that there was only one way of obtaining the Charter, and that was "by INSURRECTION";[77] and at the LDA meeting which he chaired at the end of February—and at which he was alleged to have waved a naked dagger above his head—some strongly worded resolutions were passed and ordered to be presented to the General Convention when it assembled a few days later. The resolutions declared that if the Convention did its duty the Charter would be the law of the land within a month, that all acts of oppression should be met with immediate resistance, and that the Convention should "impress upon the people the necessity of an immediate preparation for ulterior measures".[78]

How far did this style of politics gain sympathy and support within the Convention itself and within the Chartist movement as a whole? The answer is that it was widely deprecated. When the LDA resolutions of 28 February were presented to the Convention, three members who had been present at the meeting—Harney, William Rider, and Richard Marsden—were called upon to disclaim them. A succession of speakers—including R.J. Richardson of Salford, John Taylor of Glasgow, James Whittle of Liverpool, Hetherington, Carpenter, and O'Brien—deplored the threatening language of the resolutions; and when the three militants refused to dissociate themselves from the transactions at the LDA meeting a motion of censure upon them was passed by 16 votes to 9.[79] In the paper called *The Operative* which he was then editing, O'Brien printed a letter in support of Harney and his colleagues by J.H.B. Lorymer, whom he described as "a well-known democratic writer of the French republican school". But he commented in his leading article that the London Democrats should not express suspicion of the Convention until it had been tried and found wanting, and that most people were inclined to be more suspicious of the LDA than of the Convention.[80]

Further discussion of jacobin postures was to follow later in the Convention debates, when Harney provoked criticism for having appeared at a public meeting in Smithfield on 22 April wearing a red cap of liberty. He defended himself stoutly, saying that in his opinion all members of the Convention should attend its meetings in red caps of liberty; and in response to the laughter which greeted this remark, he went on to say that the *bonnet rouge* was "the emblem under which mankind had won the most glorious victories over tyranny, and the most glorious triumphs of democracy". William Lovett, however, commented that "all the talk of daggers, and all the swagger of persons who decorated themselves with the cap of liberty"

---

76. *Ibid.*, 1 June 1839, p. 59.
77. *Ibid.*, 4 May 1839, p. 29.
78. BL Add. MSS 34245A, fo. 76; *London Despatch*, 10 March 1839, p. 1036.
79. *The Charter*, 10 March 1839, p. 108.
80. *The Operative*, 17 March 1839, pp. 8–9.

were "unworthy of the cause";[81] and a few days later W. S. Villiers Sankey, delegate from Edinburgh and Midlothian, gave notice of the following motion:

> That this present Movement being essentially English and not having in view any theoretic Innovations but a recurrence to the first principles of the original Saxon Constitution this Convention do deprecate all language or expressions which would appear to assimilate our objects to those of the French Revolution or having in view to take it as our model.

The motion, though seconded by John Collins, was withdrawn at the suggestion of Dr. Fletcher of Bury, on the grounds that it would give rise to unnecessary dissension and "personal observations".[82] But there is little doubt that it did reflect the predominant tone of the assembly, and indeed of the movement at large.

While in the Convention's correspondence one finds some use of the word "Citizen" as a form of address, few people seem to have regarded the body itself as a reprise of the French Convention of 1792.[83] It is true that there was much talk of physical force in 1839, and a belief in some areas that it might actually succeed. In south Wales and south Lancashire a considerable amount of arming took place, and at the end of the year there was the famous Newport Rising, followed by insurrectionary plotting in Yorkshire and the north east. Few traces are to be found in the provincial agitations, however, of French Revolutionary concepts and models. The example of the Parisian *sans-culottes* had some relevance in the metropolitan setting, but much less in the manufacturing districts of the north and midlands. Even in London, the jacobin brand of militancy did not win general support. Recent research has underlined the fact that London Chartism at the end of the 1830s was dominated neither by the moderation of the London Working Men's Association nor by the extremism of the LDA, but by the O'Connorite element which formed the mainstream of the national movement.[84]

Feargus O'Connor himself, in one of the debates in the Convention when the LDA came under fire, did say that he had no objection to so-called Jacobin Clubs or Democratic Associations if they managed to infuse energy into the Convention, and that there was quite enough discretion in that body to counteract any excess of zeal.[85] But although he wanted the movement to be menacing enough to intimidate parliament and the governing classes, he always stopped short of inciting physical confrontation; and in spite of being the nephew of Arthur O'Connor, who had promoted co-operation between the United Irishmen and republican France in the 1790s, he had a political style that was distinctively English and consciously patterned on that of Henry Hunt. As Paul Pickering has shown, what symbolism he used was directly aimed at the everyday class perceptions of English working people—as when, on his release from York Castle in August 1841, he appeared in

81. *Northern Star*, 27 April 1839, pp. 1, 8; *The Charter*, 28 April 1839, p. 221.
82. BL Add. MSS 34245B, fo. 255; *Northern Star*, 4 May 1839, p. 5.
83. BL Add. MSS 34245A, fos. 124, 134, 154, 368.
84. David Goodway, *London Chartism 1838–1848* (Cambridge, 1982), pp. 26–27.
85. *Northern Star*, 27 April 1839, p. 1.

a fustian suit, thereby (gentleman though he was) placing himself firmly on the working-class side of the sartorial divide between fustian and middle-class broad-cloth.[86] During the earlier 1840s, the jacobin strand in the Chartist agitation was far from conspicuous. The emphasis at this time was on organization—the building up of the National Charter Association—and on co-operation with trade unions; and the climactic moment was the general strike of August 1842. Although the concept of a general strike had not been unknown in late eighteenth-century France, it was not one that was commonly associated with the French Revolution, and the strike movement in the west midlands and the north west owed little or nothing to jacobin inspiration.

In the Chartism of the mid-1840s two different currents of interest emerged into prominence. One, associated principally with O'Connor, was the Land Campaign. The other, with Harney much to the fore, was an international dimension which was chiefly apparent in London and especially embodied in the society of Fraternal Democrats; and this element did involve a recurrence to the mythology of the 1790s, which lay at the foundation of the European revolutionary inheritance. Although the Chartist press (Harney being editor of the *Northern Star* from 1845 to 1848) gave substantial coverage to both elements in the movement, relations between them were uneasy. In September 1846, O'Connor came to speak at a meeting arranged by the Fraternal Democrats to celebrate the anniversary of the proclamation of the first French Republic, but he used the occasion to highlight one crucial particular in which the Chartist movement was superior to the French Revolution. The French had waged war on an oppressive system but had not been prepared with a substitute for it; the Chartists, on the other hand, *were* prepared, because they had devised the Land Campaign.[87] Others present at the meeting, such as Harney and the German exile Karl Schapper, were also interested in the land question, influenced by a tradition of ideas which could be traced back to Spence and Babeuf.[88] But this was not a tradition that appealed to O'Connor. The Land Campaign, as he made clear on a number of occasions, had nothing to do with agrarian socialism, its aim being to transfer as many people as possible from industrial employment to the position of independent agricultural smallholders.

At the anniversary celebration which took place a year after the one attended by O'Connor, one of the toasts proposed was: "May the society of Fraternal Democrats, founded to propagate the principles of the French Revolution, pro-gress triumphantly, and advance in this and every other land the principles of Equality, Liberty, and Fraternity."[89] The revolution in Paris five months later produced (at least for a time) a heightened enthusiasm for the slogans and incan-

86. James Epstein, *The Lion of Freedom: Feargus O'Connor and the Chartist Movement, 1832–1842* (London, 1982), pp. 90–91; Pickering, op. cit., pp. 158–60.
87. *Northern Star*, 26 September 1846, p. 7.
88. Schoyen, op. cit., pp. 14, 135. At an equivalent meeting a year earlier, Harney had praised Babeuf for his attempt to institute a republic in which "the selfishness of individualism should be known no more" (*Northern Star*, 27 September 1845, p. 5.)
89. *Northern Star*, 25 September 1847, p. 5.

tations of the French revolutionary tradition. Not only in London, but in Glasgow and elsewhere, people were singing the Marseillaise and shouting *"Vive la République!"*[90] Harney was in his element, and proposed to the Fraternal Democrats an "Address to the People of Paris" which urged them to introduce a republican system based on the central principles of the Constitution of 1793: "Universal Suffrage in the choice of the Legislative Deputies, and the adoption of the laws by the direct vote of the people in the primary assemblies."[91] (This element of direct democracy in the Constitution of 1793 had earlier been applauded by O'Brien in his notes on Buonarroti.[92]) The address, engrossed on parchment and surrounded with a tricoloured border, was also approved by the executive committee of the National Charter Association and by a large metropolitan demonstration in Lambeth, and Harney was one of the delegates chosen to present it to the Provisional Government in Paris.[93]

On his return, he contributed a series of letters to the *Northern Star* under the pen-name "L'Ami du Peuple", and further echoes of the French Revolution are to be found in the papers he edited from 1849 to 1851—the *Democratic Review*, the *Red Republican*, and the *Friend of the People*. The *Democratic Review* for May 1850 carried a report of a "social supper" held by the Fraternal Democrats to celebrate Robespierre's birthday. Harney, who presided, proposed a toast to "the Incorruptible" and to his inspiring example in promoting the cause of democratic and social equality; and "Citizen Bronterre O'Brien" followed this up with a dissertation on Robespierre's career.[94] When he launched the *Red Republican* a few weeks later, Harney began his first issue with a quotation from Saint-Just: "Those who make half revolutions, dig a grave for themselves!" And to encapsulate the aims and principles of his paper, he simply quoted two paragraphs from Robespierre's report of 17 Pluviôse Year II.[95] He did say in his leading article that the tricolor had lost its authenticity as the flag of the people, because it had been "thrice polluted": by the despotism of Napoleon, the corruption of Louis Philippe, and the treason of Lamartine. Henceforth the red flag, "dyed in the life-stream of the martyrs of June," should be the flag of European democracy. But although the June Days had become a more immediate reference point, it is clear that, at least for Harney and O'Brien, the first French Revolution retained its potency as a source of principle and inspiration.

O'Brien and Harney, as two of the outstanding publicists of the "Unstamped" and Chartist periods, were in positions to ensure that their own enthusiastic interest in the French Revolution was widely ventilated in radical circles. But one would hesitate to say that this preoccupation of theirs was of great significance for radical culture: to put it in perspective one should note that at public meetings and in

90. Schoyen, op. cit., p. 160; Henry Weisser, *April 10: Challenge and Response in England in 1848* (Lanham, Maryland, 1983), p. 14.
91. *Northern Star*, 4 March 1848, p. 1.
92. *Babeuf's Conspiracy*, p. 215n.
93. *Northern Star*, 4 March 1848, p. 1; 11 March 1839, p. 1.
94. *Democratic Review*, May 1850, p. 463.
95. *Red Republican*, 22 June 1850, pp. 1, 5.

the press American models were cited much more frequently than French ones.[96] O'Brien's interest in the French Revolution reflected a kind of politicized antiquarianism, and one doubts whether many readers of the *Poor Man's Guardian* shared his concern for the rehabilitation of Robespierre; those with any critical sense, indeed, may well have felt that his interpretation was as unbalanced as those he attacked. His attempt to revise the history of the Revolution was an idiosyncratic by-product, rather than an essential feature, of his role in popularizing anti-capitalist ideas. As for Harney, he came much closer than O'Brien to thinking of *himself* as a revolutionary. His style contained a strong element of theatricality, but so of course did the style of his French prototypes; and in 1839, as well as deploying the trappings and rhetoric of revolution, he may have genuinely hoped that a revolutionary situation would develop. However, in a candid letter to Engels in 1846 he admitted that he was not the sort of person to take the lead in such a situation, as he lacked the "animal courage" and "physical energy" required. He also said in the same letter that his countrymen in general were so unmilitary—even anti-military—that to try to achieve a revolution in England by "organized combat" would be foolish and indeed culpable.[97]

Fostered by O'Brien and Harney, and by others such as Lorymer and Coombe, a jacobin strand did figure in the radicalism of the 1830s and 1840s—principally in the capital, where it was fertilized by contacts with revolutionary movements in Europe, and rooted in a social milieu of alienated journalists and sub-professional men. But in the country as a whole popular radicalism had a different tone. Less exposed to disaffected and freethinking intellectuals, it was more strongly coloured by religious nonconformity; and it was more parochial and pragmatic in its emphasis on the specific grievances of labour against capital. The English labour movement was never very receptive to foreign influences; but in so far as Harney and his circle made a memorable contribution to it they did so less by their jacobinism than by providing the original conduit through which new socialist doctrines were introduced from the Continent in mid-century.[98]

96. Cf. G. D. Lillibridge, *Beacon of Freedom: The Impact of American Democracy upon Great Britain 1830–1870* (Philadelphia, 1955).
97. *The Harney Papers*, ed., F.G. Black and Renée M. Black (Assen, 1969), pp. 240–41.
98. It was in Harney's *Red Republican* that the first English translation of the *Communist Manifesto* appeared in 1850.

12

Utility and Natural Law in Burke's Thought: A Reconsideration

The term utilitarianism as Bentham understood it means an ethical theory which treats the maximization of pleasure or the greatest happiness of the greatest number as the proper end of human action and the criterion of right and wrong. Utility, in the context of this theory, means conduciveness to happiness or pleasure. On the other hand, utility can have a wider meaning and philosophical application and may be regarded as a basic component of any teleological theory,[1] and the term utilitarianism is sometimes used in the same broad sense to describe a mode of thought in which utility plays a crucial part—a mode of thought which bases moral rules and judgement on considerations of usefulness (or, where motives are to be judged, of intended usefulness). Utility in this second sense does not have any necessary connection with hedonism. Usefulness, Hume said, is "only a tendency to a certain end,"[2] and even Bentham could give a definition of utility which on the face of it allowed for some latitude in the choice of ends: "By utility is meant that property in any object, whereby it tends to produce benefit, advantage, pleasure, good or happiness" (though he of course believed that all these terms signified the same thing).[3] Moreover, utilitarianism as a historical classification, a term denoting membership of a particular school or tradition, has not been applied exclusively to thinkers who subscribed to a hedonistic teleology. Within the tradition as it is usually conceived, definitions of ultimate good vary considerably, and hedonism shades into eudaimonism and even perfectionism. For instance, Richard Cumberland, whom Sidgwick agreed with Hallam in regarding as the founder of English utilitarianism, did not adopt a hedonistic interpretation of good: in laying down that "the common good of all rationals" was

---

[1] *Cf.* C. D. Broad, *Five Types of Ethical Theory* (London, 1930), pp. 220-221.

[2] David Hume, *Essays Moral, Political and Literary*, ed. T. H. Green and T. H. Grose (London, 1882), II, 207.

[3] Jeremy Bentham, *Works*, ed. J. Bowring (Edinburgh, 1838-43), I, 1-2.

the supreme end and standard by, reference to which all other rules and
virtues were to be determined, he included in his notion of good not only
happiness in the ordinary sense but perfection.[4] Similarly Francis Hutcheson, the originator of the formula of "the greatest happiness of the greatest
number," equated "our supreme and complete happiness" with Aristotle's
eudaimonia and used as the moral criterion by which actions should be
judged their conduciveness to the "happiness and perfection" or "happiness and virtue" of mankind.[5] J. S. Mill's concept of utility was also linked
to a teleology which can be seen as Aristotelian rather than hedonistic:
"I regard utility as the ultimate appeal on all ethical questions; but it must
be utility in the largest sense grounded on the permanent interests of man
as a progressive being."[6] And some more recent writers, anxious to dissociate their own concept of utility from the particular meaning which Bentham gave to the term, have called themselves "ideal utilitarians" in con-
tradistinction to hedonistic ones.[7] Insofar as Burke has been interpreted
as a utilitarian, this interpretation has not involved (so far as I am aware)
the ascription to him of purely hedonistic values but has rested on the argument that his mode of thought was basically teleological or consequentialist: that he regarded utility in the broad sense or conduciveness to the
general well-being as a better criterion of moral and political judgement
than any code of absolute rights or laws. This is the general burden of the
passages from earlier writings on Burke which Peter J. Stanlis, in his book
Edmund Burke and the Natural Law, cites in a section entitled "Burke's
Supposed Utilitarianism,"[8] and this is the interpretation which he proceeds
in that work to attack.[9]

[4] Henry Hallam, *Introduction to the Literature of Europe in the Fifteenth, Sixteenth and Seventeenth Centuries* (Paris, 1839), IV, 185. Henry Sidgwick, *The Methods of Ethics* (7th ed., London, 1907), p. 423 and note; *Outlines of the History of Ethics* (6th ed., London, 1931), p. 174.

[5] Francis Hutcheson, *A System of Moral Philosophy* (Glasgow, 1755), I, 1, 221-222, 252. On the utilitarianism of the final version of Hutcheson's thought as embodied in the *System,* see W. R. Scott, *Francis Hutcheson: His Life, Teaching, and Position in the History of Philosophy* (Cambridge, 1900), p. 272; W. T. Blackstone, *Francis Hutcheson and Contemporary Ethical Theory* (Athens, Ga., 1965), pp. 31-40.

[6] J. S. Mill, *Utilitarianism: Liberty: Representative Government,* introduced by A. D. Lindsay (London, 1910), p. 74. *Cf.* A. W. Levi, "The Value of Freedom: Mill's Liberty (1859-1959)," *Ethics,* LXX (1959), 41.

[7] See particularly Hastings Rashdall, *The Theory of Good and Evil* (Oxford, 1907), I, 216-218.

[8] Peter J. Stanlis, *Edmund Burke and the Natural Law* (Ann Arbor, 1958), pp. 29-34, 264.

[9] For the view that this interpretation has been "completely reversed," see Edmund Burke, *Selected Writings and Speeches,* ed. Peter J. Stanlis (New York, 1963), p. 37; Peter J. Stanlis (ed.), *The Relevance of Edmund Burke* (New York, 1964), p. 50.

The present essay will attempt to show that utility played a more important part in Burke's thought than Stanlis seems to allow, and it will question his view that the natural law "as a normative code of ethics" can be regarded as the basis of Burke's political philosophy.[10] But before Burke's thought is directly discussed, there are one or two further points that should perhaps be made about utility and utilitarianism. Stanlis says with reference to the passage in the *Tract on the Popery Laws* where Burke designates equity and utility as the two foundations of law, that had Burke's utilitarian critics read this work with greater care they would have found that "he expressly rejected the principle that utility is the sole source, test, and ultimate foundation of all thought."[11] But one wonders whether any utilitarian thinker could have maintained that in Burke's philosophy, or any one else's, utility *per se* was "the sole source, test, and ultimate foundation of all thought." Utility is an empty concept unless it is related to certain ends, and those ends and the supposition that men ought to promote them can only be posited by some ultimate intuition or value judgement or act of faith. This was expressly recognized by such thinkers as Hutcheson and Sidgwick;[12] and Bentham and J. S. Mill, despite their so-called "proof" of the principle of utility, saw that in every ethical system there must be some initial and unprovable assumption concerning what is good.[13] Some utilitarians believed that their basic teleological assumption was in the last analysis a human value judgement; others, theistic utilitarians such as Gay and Paley, took it for granted that the end, and the means whereby it was to be promoted, were willed by God. There is nothing foreign to utilitarianism in the recognition that morality must have some absolute basis. Nor, one may add, is there any necessary incompatibility between utilitari-

---

[10] Stanlis, *Edmund Burke and the Natural Law*, p. 123. This article will concentrate on responding to Stanlis's arguments, not because his is the only book which presents a "natural law" interpretation of Burke's thought, but because it is the one that does so most uncompromisingly. Moreover, it can still be described as "the most complete discussion of the subject." Frank O'Gorman, *Edmund Burke: His Political Philosophy* (London, 1973), p. 149.

[11] Stanlis, *Edmund Burke and the Natural Law*, p. 45. Stanlis does not come to terms with Sir Leslie Stephen's remark that in treating equity as one of the foundations of law and saying that it "grows out of the great rule of equality, which is founded upon our common nature," Burke is simply expressing "the axiom which must lie at the base of all utilitarian, as well as of all metaphysical systems." Leslie Stephen, *History of English Thought in the Eighteenth Century* (2nd edition, London, 1881), II, 226; cf. Sidgwick, *Methods of Ethics*, pp. 416-417.

[12] Hutcheson, *System of Moral Philosophy*, I, 38. Sidgwick, *Methods of Ethics*, pp. xvi-xix.

[13] Mill, *Utilitarianism*, p. 4: "Whatever can be proved to be good, must be so by being shown to be a means to something admitted to be good without proof." Cf. E. W. Hall, "The 'Proof' of Utility in Bentham and Mill," *Ethics*, LX (1949), 6-18.

anism and natural law. Hutcheson, for instance, believed in the existence of natural laws, defining them as the rules of conduct which tended most effectually to promote "the greatest happiness and perfection" of mankind.[14] John Austin (who seems, incidentally, to have been the first significant thinker to draw attention to the importance of utility in Burke's thought[15]) maintained that there were two species of natural law theory, the intuitional and the utilitarian. Where they differed, he said, was over the question of how the laws of God (those that are not directly revealed through God's word) are to be recognized as such by man. According to the former theory, men are endowed with a faculty—variously described as moral sense, practical reason, common sense—which enables them to apprehend directly what actions are enjoined and what actions are forbidden by God. According to the latter theory, the theory of utility, the laws of God which are not revealed "must be gathered by man from the goodness of God, and from the tendencies of human actions." The theory is summarized in a paragraph:

> God designs the happiness of all his sentient creatures. Some human actions forward that benevolent purpose, or their tendencies are beneficent or useful. Other human actions are adverse to that purpose, or their tendencies are mischievous or pernicious. The former, as promoting his purpose, God has enjoined. The latter, as opposed to his purpose, God has forbidden. He has given us the faculty of observing; of remembering; of reasoning: and, by duly applying those faculties, we may collect the tendencies of our actions. Knowing the tendencies of our actions, and knowing his benevolent purpose, we know his tacit commands.[16]

The tendency of an action, Austin goes on to say, is the whole of its tendency—the sum of its probable consequences, remote as well as direct, insofar as any of its consequences may influence the general happiness. Furthermore, to estimate the true tendency of an action we must not consider the action as if it were single and insulated but must look at the *class* of actions to which it belongs and ask ourselves what, if acts of this class were generally or frequently done, the effect on the general happiness would be. He concludes:

[14] Hutcheson, *System of Moral Philosophy*, I, 1.

[15] John Austin, *The Province of Jurisprudence Determined* (London, 1832), pp. 57-59.

[16] John Gay had propounded substantially the same argument a hundred years before. See his *Concerning the Fundamental Principle of Virtue or Morality* (1731), in L. A. Selby-Bigge (ed.), *British Moralists* (Oxford, 1897), II, 273.

If this be the ordinary test for trying the tendencies of actions, and if the tendencies of actions be the index to the will of God, it follows that most of his commands are general and universal. The useful acts which he enjoins, and the pernicious acts which he prohibits, he enjoins or prohibits, for the most part, not singly, but by classes: not by commands which are particular, or directed to insulated actions; but by laws or rules which are general, and commonly inflexible.[17]

As this argument shows, the idea of the existence of a body of moral rules or natural laws which men ought to obey should not be regarded as necessarily inconsistent with utilitarianism. Where natural law theory is disparaged in utilitarian writings, it is the idea of self-evident natural laws to which objection is taken. Stanlis quotes Bentham's remark in the *Introduction to the Principles of Morals and Legislation*: "A great many people are continually talking of the law of nature: and then they go on giving you their sentiments of what is right and what is wrong: and these sentiments, you are to understand, are so many chapters and sections of the law of nature." Stanlis comments that "Bentham could not even distinguish between what Natural Law was in fact, and derivations or violations of Natural Law made in its name."[18] Indeed, this was very much Bentham's point: that so long as no criterion was laid down by which natural laws could be recognized in terms of the good which they were calculated to produce, neither he nor anyone else could determine by reference to any external standard what should qualify to be regarded as natural law and what should not, and assertions about the law of nature were mere "ipsedixitism."

Stanlis' interpretation places Burke (by implication) in the first of the two schools of natural law as defined by Austin. It is true that Stanlis distinguishes between Shaftesbury's "moral sense" and Ciceronian "right reason" and maintains that Burke's moral principles were centered in the latter.[19] It is also true that Hutcheson used the term "right reason" to denote the rational faculty which enables men to perceive what conduct is conducive to the general good.[20] If Stanlis understood the phrase in the same

---

[17] Austin, *The Province of Jurisprudence Determined*, pp. 33-39.

[18] Stanlis, *Edmund Burke and the Natural Law*, pp. 14-15.

[19] *Ibid.*, p. 284.

[20] Hutcheson, *System of Moral Philosophy*, I, 269-271. Bentham, on the other hand, regarded "right reason" as one of those phrases appeals to which "are but so many ways of intimating that a man is firmly persuaded of the truth of this or that moral proposition, though he either thinks he *need not*, or finds he *can't*, tell *why*." *Works*, I, 269.

sense, there would be no argument: to say that natural laws could be perceived by right reason would be the same as to say that natural laws were
deducible from considerations of utility. But that Stanlis does not understand the phrase in this sense is clear from his statement that "to Burke a
law or action was not good because it was useful, but utility was merely one
of several positive social consequences of morality."[21] The morality of a
law or action, we are to understand, was to be perceived in Burke's view
by some other means than by reference to a criterion of utility.

In opposition to this interpretation, it will not be argued that Burke subscribed systematically and exclusively to a teleological theory of ethics in
which utility was the sole criterion of moral judgement. He was an unsys-
tematic thinker, and he certainly appealed on occasions to other criteria.
What *will* be suggested is that he tended to use intuitional and *a priori* concepts as the outer defenses of his position, while its inner defenses were (in
the broad sense of the word) utilitarian. He did not like, admittedly, to be
forced back on utilitarian arguments. "What would become of the world,"
he asked in the preface to his *Vindication of Natural Society,* "if the practice of all moral duties, and the foundations of society, rested upon having
their reasons made clear and demonstrative to every individual?"[22] The
question implies that moral duties and social conventions do have a rationale, but one that is often not easily grasped. Burke wanted people as far as
possible to regard such duties and conventions as axiomatically right; and
he thought that for most people most of the time "inbred" sentiments and
preconceptions (he spoke of the moral sentiments as being "so nearly connected with early prejudice as to be almost one and the same thing") were
a more reliable guide to moral conduct than the individual reason.[23] But
to treat sentiment as a valuable guide to moral conduct is by no means the
same thing as to say that the ultimate validity of moral propositions can be
tested by their conformity to sentiment. Francis P. Canavan, while he draws
attention to Burke's "frequent recourse to natural feeling as a criterion of
moral and political judgement," goes on to point out that "Burke was very
far from thinking sentiment a sufficient criterion of morals": he thought
that our moral feelings might conceivably "mislead our judgement" and

---

[21] Stanlis, *Edmund Burke and the Natural Law,* p. 122.

[22] Edmund Burke, *The Works of the Right Honourable Edmund Burke* (London, 1899),
I, 6-7.

[23] Edmund Burke, *Reflections on the Revolution in France, Works of . . . Burke,* III,
345. *Appeal from the New to the Old Whigs, ibid.,* IV, 205.

must therefore be kept "under the direction of reason."[24] Since Burke gave this directing role to reason, it is necessary to ask on what principles he thought reason should operate. Stanlis might simply say on *moral* principles, as he believes that such principles were (in Burke's opinion) self-evident to right reason,[25] and that intellectual calculations of utility are somehow antithetical to genuine moral judgement.[26] But I would take the view that for Burke it was essentially on teleological or consequentialist principles that reason should operate in the formation of moral judgements. Burke himself said in a speech of 1792: "It is the direct office of wisdom to look to the consequences of the acts we do; if it be not this, it is worth nothing"—a remark on which John MacCunn commented, "If this be not utilitarian, what is?"[27] It is true that the remark related—as, inevitably, did most of the similar evidence that will be produced below—more directly to the public than to the private sphere. Burke was a politician rather than a moral theorist, and the scantiness of his recorded statements on private ethics means that his position on this subject must be largely a matter of inference or conjecture. The relationship between his views of public and of private morality, and the possibility of a divergence between them, will be considered at the conclusion of this essay.

Of course, to show that Burke's mode of thought was basically teleological, it is necessary to demonstrate that there were certain ultimate ends in which he did believe and which could have provided general criteria for moral judgement. Here again the evidence does not make for straightforward treatment, partly because Burke took the view that the definition of ends was the business of the "speculative philosopher" rather than of the politician,[28] and partly because in the statements which he did make on the question there would seem at first to be some inconsistency. At

[24] Francis P. Canavan, *The Political Reason of Edmund Burke* (Durham, N.C., 1960), pp. 56-59. *Cf.* Bentham, *Works*, I, 412: "I reject sentiment as an absolute judge, but under the control of reason it may not be a useless monitor."

[25] "To Burke moral insight could come to man through divine revelation, or more commonly through natural right reason." Stanlis, *Edmund Burke and the Natural Law*, p. 118.

[26] Stanlis contrasts "the expediency of the utilitarian calculator" with Burke's principle of prudence, which was "not an intellectual but a moral discretion." *Ibid.*, pp. 47, 120.

[27] Edmund Burke, *The Speeches of the Right Honourable Edmund Burke* (London, 1816), IV, 66. John MacCunn, *The Political Philosophy of Burke* (London, 1913), p. 46. Burke also wrote: "Proper action is an action directed to an end—and is tried by that end"; notes for a speech, undated, cited from the Fitzwilliam MSS, Sheffield, by Canavan, *The Political Reason of Edmund Burke*, p. 6.

[28] Edmund Burke, *Thoughts on the Causes of the Present Discontents, Works of . . . Burke*, I, 530.

times, especially early in his career, he was satisfied to define the function
of the state in terms of the protection of Lockean natural rights, thus apparently subscribing to an *a priori* theory such as Bentham would have condemned. He wrote in the *Tract on the Popery Laws*: "Everybody is satisfied that a conservation and secure enjoyment of our natural rights is the
great and ultimate purpose of civil society; and that therefore all forms
whatsoever of government are only good as they are subservient to that
purpose."[29] He declared in 1772 that men's lives, liberty, and property were
"those things for the protection of which society was introduced"; and as
late as the 1780's he more than once treated security of life, liberty, and
property as a test of the effectiveness of a constitution.[30] However, he does
seem to have become dissatisfied with the Lockean trinity as a definition of
what men in society had a right to and what governments had a duty to
secure for the governed. In the *Reflections* he argued that whatever natural
rights men might be supposed to possess in a state of nature, in civil society these were bound to be severely modified and did not therefore provide a very useful—provided in fact a positively misleading—concept. In
entering civil society, he said, man "in a great measure abandons the right
of self-defence, the first law of nature"; and as for the second of his natural
rights, "that he may secure some liberty, he makes a surrender in trust of
the whole of it."[31] What Burke adopted in place of the Lockean formula
was a less specific and more flexible concept of natural right: "If civil society be made for the advantage of man, all the advantages for which it is
made become his right. . . . Government is a contrivance of human wisdom
to provide for human *wants*. Men have a right that these wants should be
provided for by this wisdom."[32] Though Burke did list—both in this passage and in a speech delivered in the same year—some of the advantages
which society and government might be expected to provide,[33] he was evidently not trying to formulate a new theory of specific rights. The idea that
men had a corpus of clear-cut and absolute rights might, he wrote, be meta-
physically true, but it was "morally and politically false."[34] What men in
society essentially had a right to was to be governed for their benefit; and,

[29] Burke, *Works of . . . Burke*, VI, 333.

[30] Burke, *Speeches of . . . Burke*, I, 109. *Speech on the Representation*, Burke, *Works
of . . . Burke*, VII, 101. Thomas Copeland (ed.), *The Correspondence of Edmund Burke*
(Cambridge and Chicago, 1958-70), VI, 42-43.

[31] For a discussion of Burke's treatment of the right to property, which raises problems of its own, see below.

[32] Burke, *Works of . . . Burke*, III, 308-310.

[33] *Ibid.*, 308-309. Burke, *Speeches of . . . Burke*, III, 476.

[34] Burke, *Reflections, Works of . . . Burke*, III, 313.

conversely, their benefit was the basic end which governments were to promote. This generalized conclusion harmonizes with a number of other statements made by Burke concerning the ends of government. He said in the 1770's that government was "instituted for the ease and benefit of the people"; it was "a practical thing, made for the happiness of mankind."[35] His essential duty as a legislator, he said, was "that of promoting the common happiness," and he added more fully in 1792:

> The object of the state is (as far as may be) the happiness of the whole. . . . The happiness or misery of mankind, estimated by their feelings and sentiments, and not by any theories of their rights, is, and ought to be, the standard for the conduct of legislators towards the people.[36]

In these quotations—particularly the last, where the general happiness is explicitly treated as the standard by which political conduct is to be judged—there is nothing to suggest that Burke's criteriology was substantially different from that of the Benthamites. However, there are some other statements of his which suggest a further dimension. He wrote in the *Reflections* that society was "not a partnership in things subservient only to the gross animal existence of a temporary and perishable nature" but was "a partnership in every virtue and in all perfection." And he went on to say that without civil society "man could not by any possibility arrive at the perfection of which his nature is capable. . . . He who gave our nature to be perfected by our virtue willed also the necessary means of its perfection: He willed, therefore, the state."[37] Here the idea of perfection as an end has been introduced alongside happiness as an end; and one may perhaps conclude that Burke shared Hutcheson's view that human "happiness and perfection" were the ends for which society was established.[38] Admittedly there are certain difficulties in such a view. For one thing, there is the possibility of clashes between the two goals;[39] but is not clear that either Hutcheson or Burke would have seen this as a serious problem, since

---

[35] Burke, *Speeches of . . . Burke*, I, 61. *Letter to the Sheriffs of Bristol, Works of . . . Burke*, II, 227.

[36] Copeland, *The Correspondence of Edmund Burke*, III, 438. Burke, *Speeches of . . . Burke*, IV, 58.

[37] Burke, *Works of . . . Burke*, III, 359, 361.

[38] *Cf.* Edmund Burke, *A Notebook of Edmund Burke*, ed. H. V. F. Somerset (Cambridge, 1957), p. 72: "In disputed questions those notions that tend to make [man] better and happier . . . are true rather than the contrary."

[39] *Cf.* A. L. Macfie, *The Individual in Society: Essays on Adam Smith* (London, 1967), p. 56.

they both appear to have followed Aristotle in believing that the highest form of happiness involved and to a large extent consisted in the full employment of human faculties and the practice of virtue.[40] Secondly, there is the argument put forward by Sidgwick that in a teleological theory of ethics moral perfection cannot be treated as a part of ultimate good without "an obvious logical circle."[41] But this point was contested from the "ideal utilitarian" position;[42] and it does not seem impossible that Hutcheson and Burke, while treating right conduct as basically definable in terms of the promotion or intended promotion[43] of human welfare, could have believed that virtue was good, and willed by God, for its own sake.

Now it is clear that an interpretation which treats utility as crucial to Burke's thought must come to terms not only with his references to natural rights but also with the appeals which he certainly did make to natural law. It has been suggested above that his notion of natural right seems to be largely reducible (in the maturer expressions of his thought, at any rate) to the belief that men have a right to be governed for their own benefit. Similarly, in many of his most eloquent appeals to natural law he seems to be appealing not so much to the specific injunctions of a "normative code of ethics" as to this more general principle—or to the complementary principle that all governments are obliged to rule for the welfare of the governed. It was in relation to cases where this rule was in his opinion flouted—Ireland under the Protestant Ascendancy, India under Hastings—that his appeals to transcendental principles were chiefly made; and in such appeals it is difficult to see anything more specific than solemn affirmations of the absolute and divinely ordained status of a rule which utilitarian thinkers would equally have regarded as mandatory (and which some of them would also have regarded as willed by God). In his denunciation of the penal laws in Ireland, it was the making of "a law prejudicial to the whole community" that he declared to be "against the principle of a superior law, which it is not in the power of any community, or the whole race of man, to alter." Later in the same tract he invoked natural rights in a general fashion, but they were apparently subsumed in his striking remark that even the truth of Christianity was not so clear as the proposition "that all men, at

[40] Burke spoke of "the happiness that is to be found by virtue in all conditions." *Reflections, Works of . . . Burke*, III, 279; cf. Hutcheson, *System of Moral Philosophy*, I, 226.

[41] Sidgwick, *Outlines of the History of Ethics*, p. 174.

[42] *Cf.* H. Rashdall, "Professor Sidgwick's Utilitarianism," *Mind*, X (1885), 206-207, 221-226.

[43] *Cf.* Hutcheson's distinction between "material" and "formal" goodness. *System of Moral Philosophy*, I, 252-253.

least the majority of men in the society, ought to enjoy the common advantages of it."[44] Again, in his speeches denouncing Hastings he invoked "the primeval, indefeasible, unalterable law of nature and of nations" and "those eternal laws of justice which are our rule and birthright"; but the essence of his argument was, as summarized by Burleigh Taylor Wilkins, "that Hastings was bound by the eternal laws of justice . . . to protect the rights of Indians."[45] In other words (the rights of men in government being their advantages) he was reiterating as impressively as he could the principle he had laid down in speaking on Fox's India Bill: that "all political power which is set over men . . . ought to be some way or other exercised ultimately for their benefit."[46] That when he appealed to natural law he often had this principle in mind rather than any more particularized code is suggested by the fact that one of his most famous appeals of this kind—an appeal to the House of Commons to reject a bill which it had the power but not the right to pass, because the bill was "contrary to the eternal laws of right and wrong, laws that ought to bind all men, and above all men legislative assemblies"—was made in 1772 against an attempt to encroach on the lawful sphere of the East India Company;[47] whereas a decade later he was to make similar appeals to natural law in order to *justify* Parliament's interference in the company's domain. The difference was that the interference of 1772 proceeded in his view from sinister purposes and was not legitimized by concern for the welfare of the subject peoples of India, whereas the protection of their welfare was, he believed, the fundamental purpose and justification of Fox's India Bill.

There were occasions, however, when Burke did appeal to natural right or natural law in a more specific way to reinforce a particular rule or principle. The most frequent of these specific appeals were made in relation to property. Indeed, Burke's defense of property throws special light on his methods of argument, in that in the course of it he employed all his resources: appeals to natural right, natural law, and moral sentiment—and also, it will be suggested, arguments of a basically utilitarian kind. If Burke did recognize any absolute and inviolable natural right (apart from the

[44] Burke, *Tract on the Popery Laws, Works of . . . Burke*, VI, 321-322, 333-334.

[45] Burleigh Taylor Wilkins, *The Problem of Burke's Political Philosophy* (Oxford, 1967), p. 37.

[46] Burke, *Speeches of . . . Burke*, II, 411. *Cf.* Stephen, *English Thought in the Eighteenth Century*, II, 226: "He is protesting against the right of a minority to govern Ireland or India exclusively for its own interest; and to assert the rights of man in this sense is simply to lay down the principle . . . that the happiness of the governed, and not the happiness of any particular class, is the legitimate end of government."

[47] Burke, *Speeches of . . . Burke*, I, 151.

general right to be well governed) it would seem to have been the right to property. In the passage in the *Reflections* where he describes how natural rights are modified by civil society, he says that men in society to a large extent abandon their right of self-defense and their right to liberty: but there is no suggestion of their surrendering their property rights. Indeed, having early in his career treated property as merely one of the fundamental rights which society was instituted to protect, he subsequently on more than one occasion echoed Cicero in treating its preservation as the *main* function of the state. He said in a speech in 1794 that the first principle of any government must be the security of property, "because for the protection of property all governments were instituted";[48] and in the following year, in arguing against any attempt by the state to relieve distress in time of famine by effecting some transfer of means from the propertied classes to the poor, he went so far as to say that such an interference by the magistrate would be "a violation of the property which it is his office to protect."[49] He also believed that "the ascertaining and securing *prescription*" was a primary cause of the formation of states. Prescription, he wrote, was "rooted in its principle in the law of Nature itself, and [was] indeed the original ground of all known property"; and he believed that it gave "right and title" irrespective of how the property concerned had been originally acquired: "that which might be wrong in the beginning is consecrated by time and becomes lawful."[50] Now on what grounds did Burke claim that the rights of property and "long possession" were part of the law of nature?[51] He did so partly by appealing to the natural law tradition[52]— though it has been argued that his interpretation of prescriptive rights, and of property rights in general, could find little real support in that tradition.[53] He also invoked moral sentiment, maintaining that the rights of ownership were evident to men's "natural rude unplanted sense of justice." He said in a letter to a French correspondent in 1791: "The fury which arises in the minds of men on being stripped of their goods, and turned out

[48] *Ibid.*, IV, 166. *Cf.* Copeland, *Correspondence of Edmund Burke*, VII, 389; *Reflections, Works of . . . Burke*, III, 370; Cicero, *De Officiis*, II, 21.

[49] Burke, *Thoughts and Details on Scarcity, Works of . . . Burke*, V, 146. On this particular point there was certainly a sharp contrast with Bentham; *cf.* Bentham's *Works,* I, 316.

[50] Copeland, *Correspondence of Edmund Burke*, VI, 95. Burke, *Letter to Richard Burke, Works of . . . Burke*, VI, 412.

[51] *Sir Henry Cavendish's Debates of the House of Commons* (London, 1841-43), II, 318.

[52] Burke, *Reflections, Works of . . . Burke*, III, 433.

[53] Paul Lucas, "On Edmund Burke's Doctrine of Prescription," *Historical Journal,* XI (1968), 35-63. C. B. Macpherson, "Edmund Burke and the New Conservatism," *Science and Society*, XXII (1958), 236.

of their houses by acts of power, and our sympathy with them under such wrongs, are feelings implanted in us by our creator."[54] However, he may have realized that neither of these lines of defense—neither the appeal to authority nor the appeal to self-evident rights and natural justice—could be relied upon beyond a certain point. Since he was well acquainted with the natural law tradition, he must have known that conclusions very different from his own could be drawn from it. As for the idea of self-evident natural rights, that was even more likely to be turned against him. Locke's theory of property, proclaiming man's natural right to the fruits of his labor and extending this natural right to cover property of all kinds, had won widespread acceptance in his own time and society because it had provided philosophical backing for an already existing consensus: it had embodied "one of those truths which express so exactly what men feel that they seem self-evident."[55] But by Burke's later years the notion of natural rights or laws was being widely invoked by *opponents* of the existing system of property. Burke noted in the *Reflections* that the French peasants were being encouraged to believe that "by the laws of Nature, the occupant and subduer of the soil is the sole proprietor—that there is no prescription against Nature."[56] Moreover, in view of the conception of justice being popularized by men like Godwin and Paine, it could no longer be asserted as self-evident that redistributive measures were wrong simply because of the injustice of any infringements of property. As John Thelwall wrote in 1795: "It is one thing to place a barrier round property; another to put property in the scale against the welfare and independence of the people."[57] Even a contemporary of Burke's who was no less conservative than he was, William Paley, could concede in his famous parable of the pigeons that the current system and distribution of property were thoroughly unnatural; in his view it was only through a close examination of the *consequences* of the system that its advantages could be perceived and its existence justified.[58] Burke himself was equally aware that on the face of it the system could seem far from just. In his early parody of Bolingbroke he had shown how plausibly it could be argued that in civil or "artificial" society the many are sacrificed to the few:

---

[54] Copeland, *Correspondence of Edmund Burke*, VI, 108, 266.

[55] Richard Schlatter, *Private Property* (London, 1951), p. 151.

[56] Burke, *Works of . . . Burke*, III, 529.

[57] John Thelwall, *The Tribune* (London, 1795-96), III, 256.

[58] William Paley, *Principles of Moral and Political Philosophy* (London, 1785), pp. 91 ff.

> The most obvious division of society is into rich and poor; and it
> is no less obvious, that the number of the former bear a great
> disproportion to those of the latter. The whole business of the
> poor is to administer to the idleness, folly, and luxury of the rich;
> and that of the rich, in return, is to find the best methods of con-
> firming the slavery and increasing the burdens of the poor. In a
> state of nature, it is an invariable law, that a man's acquisitions
> are in proportion to his labors. In a state of artificial society, it is
> a law as constant and invariable, that those who labor most enjoy
> the fewest things.[59]

When such arguments came to be seriously used, when the existing system
came to be attacked in the name of natural rights, it was clear that to defend it by appealing to another set of supposedly self-evident rights would
seem less than conclusive. Consequently Burke was forced back on arguments based on utility—arguments drawn from considerations of public
welfare. *Prima facie,* his extreme concern for the rights of property and
his assertions that a government's principal duty must be the protection of
those rights are difficult to reconcile with his statements that all governments were instituted "for the ease and benefit of the people" and that the
basic duty of a legislator was "that of promoting the common happiness."
However, it is arguable that his defense of property rested in the last resort
not simply on a belief that the right to property was a natural and sacred
right which was inviolable in any circumstances, but rather on a reasoned
conviction that the protection of property was essential to the stability and
prosperity of society and that any interference by the state for the purpose
of redistributing property would do more harm than good to the general
welfare. The reasons he gave for this belief may not seem altogether convincing. But we must surely assume that Burke himself was persuaded of
their cogency; and from the pains he took to elaborate arguments showing
that total security of property was in the interests of everyone, it may surely be inferred that he regarded such a rationale as essential to the justification of the system he was defending.

As has been suggested above, Burke liked as far as possible to rely on
direct appeals to men's inbred sentiments and prejudices and on authoritarian rules to which they could be expected to respond (and which he
genuinely believed to embody the profoundest wisdom). He fell back on
utilitarian arguments (on the exposition of that wisdom) only when these
other methods no longer seemed to work—and he did so with reluctance
because he was afraid that the appeal to reason was unlikely to work any

---

[59] Burke, *Vindication of Natural Society, Works of . . . Burke,* I, 57-58.

better. He doubted its effectiveness not because of any fear on his part that
the institutions he wished to defend would not bear looking into, but because he feared that most people were incapable of seeing far enough to
perceive what was really for their benefit. It was especially difficult, of
course, to convey the rational basis of the current system of property to
men seduced by the egalitarian visions of Jacobinism—so difficult, in fact,
that Burke was inclined to think that Jacobin doctrines must be silenced
by state authority rather than confuted by argument. He wrote in 1791:

> They indeed who seriously write upon a principle of levelling
> ought to be answered by the magistrate—and not by the specu-
> latist. The people whom he [that is, they] would corrupt, and who
> are very corruptible, can very readily comprehend what flatters
> their vices and falls in with their ignorance; but that process of
> reasoning, which would shew to the poorest, how much his poverty
> is comparative riches in his state of subordination, to what it
> would be in such an equality as is recommended to him, is quite
> out of his reach . . . because it involves in it a long and labourd
> analysis of society.[60]

Still, the implication was that it *could* be shown by a "long and labourd
analysis of society" that the present state of economic and political inequality was beneficial to all classes of the community; and to a considerable extent Burke's writings of the 1790's can be regarded as having put
forward such a case. So far as his treatment of property is concerned, his
reasons for presenting it as inviolable were partly of an economic and
partly of a broader social and political nature.

The economic arguments are chiefly to be found in his *Thoughts and
Details on Scarcity,*[61] written at a time when Burke thought that there was
a real threat of redistributive measures. He set out to show that it was not
in the power of government, or of the rich as a class, to provide for the
subsistence of the poor. The ultimate source of all wealth, he said, was
the labor of the people, and it was therefore the government and the rich
who had to depend on the working population: to suggest that this dependence could be reversed did not make sense. Moreover there was simply
not enough wealth in existence to effect a significant mitigation of poverty,
however equally it was shared out.

[60] Copeland, *Correspondence of Edmund Burke,* VI, 304.

[61] But see also *Tract on the Popery Laws, Works of . . . Burke,* VI, 351-352, on the
disincentive effects of any curtailment of the normal rights of property.

> In a fair distribution among a vast multitude none can have much. That class of dependent pensioners called the rich is so extremely small, that, if all their throats were cut, and a distribution made of all they consume in a year, it would not give a bit of bread and cheese for one night's supper to those who labor, and who in reality feed both the pensioners and themselves.[62]

If any such plundering of the rich did take place, it would seriously damage the prosperity of all; for the rich, said Burke, "are trustees for those who labor, and their hoards are the banking houses of these latter. . . . When the poor rise to destroy the rich, they act as wisely for their own purposes as when they burn mills and throw corn into the river to make bread cheap." He presumably had in mind the need for capital accumulation (which Smith had so much emphasized); and he went on to say that the effect of any compulsory equalization of wealth would be to "depress high and low together beneath the level of what was originally the lowest." The particular measure which aroused his anxiety was not directly of a levelling nature, but he believed that it had that tendency. It was a bill introduced by Samuel Whitbread in the winter of 1795 to enable magistrates to fix minimum wages for agricultural laborers. Burke said that the fixing of wage rates at a level higher than the market price of labor would be tantamount to an "arbitrary division" of the employer's property among those he employed. But he did not concentrate his attack on the *injustice* of the measure: the essence of his case was that it would be contrary to the real *interests* of both employer and employed. He argued that the interests of farmer and laborer were fundamentally the same and that free contracts between them would not be prejudicial to either party. It was to the interest of the farmer that his work should be done efficiently, and therefore that the laborer should be well fed and kept in "good condition." At the same time it was in the interest of the laborer that his wages should be kept low enough for the farmer to make a sufficient profit. For "if the farmer ceases to profit of the laborer, and that his capital is not manured and fructified, it is impossible that he should continue that abundant nutriment and clothing and lodging proper for the protection of the instruments he employs." To fix wages at a level higher than the farmer would pay if left to himself would simply force him to employ fewer laborers; and if the state then intervened further and prevented him from reducing his labor force, he would have to put up the price of his corn, which would affect the labor-

---

[62] Burke, *Works of . . . Burke*, V, 133-134. *Cf. Reflections, Works of . . . Burke*, III, 298: "The plunder of the few would . . . give but a share inconceivably small in the distribution to the many."

er as consumer and leave him (Burke maintained) no better off. If the farmer was unable to raise his prices sufficiently to cover his increased labor costs, the destruction of agriculture itself could be expected to follow and a state of equality would indeed be produced—"equal want, equal wretchedness, equal beggary."[63] After some further argument designed to show that government interference in the market for provisions would be as counter-productive as interference in the labor market, Burke concluded that it was vitally important to resist any idea that it was "within the competence of government, taken as government, or even of the rich, as rich, to supply to the poor those necessaries which it has pleased the Divine Providence for a while to withhold from them."[64] To those who argued that at least some special provision could be made for the poor during brief periods of distress, he replied that "years of scarcity or plenty do not come alternately or at short intervals, but in pretty long cycles and irregularly." Once such a policy was adopted it would probably have to be continued; the poor, having quickly become habituated to it, would "never be satisfied to have it otherwise"; and the government would have embarked on a policy whose continuance would bring economic ruin, and whose cessation would convulse the state.[65]

Whatever one may think of the merits of this line of argument, it was patently consequentialist, and the same can be said of Burke's social and political case against any encroachment on the rights of property. Aware that property was particularly vulnerable in countries like France and England where it was very unequally divided,[66] he believed that once the sanctity of property suffered any infringement—once confiscatory policies were introduced in any form—then all property would be seriously endangered and so would ordered society along with it. Hume had stressed the need for rules of justice to define and stabilize possessions, because the

---

[63] Burke, *Works of ... Burke*, V, 134, 138-143.

[64] The people must be made to realize, Burke continued, that their hardships could not be alleviated by any breach of "the laws of commerce, which are the laws of Nature, and consequently the laws of God." Stanlis comments that here Burke "explicitly stated his belief that economics rests upon Natural Law." But Alfred Cobban surely had the emphasis right when he interpreted Burke as thinking: "Obedience to the rules which determine commercial prosperity is a condition of the public well-being, and since it is the desire of God that his people should be happy, the laws conditioning that end may be taken as divinely decreed." Stanlis believes that writers such as Halévy and Laski who "thought they found utilitarianism at the heart of Burke's economic principles" were mistaken; Cobban, on the other hand, considered that Burke's economics did rest on the principle of utility, and that he merely conferred on it "a divine halo." Stanlis, *Edmund Burke and the Natural Law*, pp. 55-58; A. B. C. Cobban, *Edmund Burke and the Revolt against the Eighteenth Century* (2nd ed., London, 1960), p. 191.

[65] Burke, *Works of ... Burke*, V, 156-157.

[66] Copeland, *Correspondence of Edmund Burke*, VI, 96.

chief cause of contention between men was human acquisitiveness, of all passions the most "directly destructive of human society."[67] For such men as Burke the French Revolution seemed to confirm in a palpable and horrifying way that without fixed laws of property and a constant respect for them, such lusts could get out of control and make social existence impossible. He wrote that in France a set of banditti had been "butchering hundreds of men, women and children, for no other cause than to lay hold on their property."[68] However cautious and limited the National Assembly's first encroachments on property rights had been, they had opened the way to a *general* disrespect for such rights and to general insecurity; the principles adopted had led first "to ecclesiastical pillage, thence to a contempt for *all* prescriptive titles, thence to the pillage of *all* property, and thence to universal desolation." Now not even grocers' and bakers' shops possessed "the smallest degree of safety," and "no laborer knew whether he should enjoy for a day his earnings, or even his personal liberty or his life."[69] It will be apparent from these quotations that the main emphasis of his argument was not on the defense of rights *qua* rights, but on the social utility (or rather necessity) of a stable system of property. He explicitly said in a speech of 1794 that it was not property for its own sake that he was primarily concerned to defend, but property as the basis on which civilized life was founded.[70] He referred in his *Letter to a Noble Lord* to "the great stable laws of property, common to us with all civilized nations"; and he wrote at the end of his life with regard to Ireland that if a war should be fought out there between "property and no property—between the high and the low, the rich and the poor," a victory for the latter in alliance with Jacobinism would mean "the utter subversion of human society itself, of all religion, all law, all order, all humanity, as well as of all property."[71]

It has been submitted in the two preceding paragraphs that Burke defended the laws of property (which he regarded as part of the natural law) with the same kind of arguments as one might find—indeed does find—in the writings of Hume and Paley. But whatever may be *suggested* by the degree of his reliance on such arguments, the fact that adherence to certain

---

[67] David Hume, *A Treatise of Human Nature*, ed. L. A. Selby-Bigge (Oxford, 1888), pp. 489-492.

[68] Burke, *Letters on a Regicide Peace, Works of . . . Burke*, VI, 87.

[69] Copeland, *Correspondence of Edmund Burke*, VII, 389-390. Burke, *Letter to a Noble Lord, Works of . . . Burke*, V, 203. Burke, *Speeches of . . . Burke*, IV, 167.

[70] Burke, *Speeches of . . . Burke*, IV, 166.

[71] Burke, *Works of . . . Burke*, V. 209. Copeland, *Correspondence of Edmund Burke*, IX, 188-189.

natural laws could be shown by Burke to have good consequences does not *prove* that in his view it was on account of their good consequences that such rules qualified to be regarded as part of the law of nature. To show that utility was for Burke the governing principle, the ultimate test of the validity of natural laws, it is necessary to show that it was only so far as such laws coincided with utility that he regarded them as binding. He clearly believed that the rules of justice and natural law almost invariably did coincide with utility. In the *Reflections,* in reply to the argument that the confiscation of Church property in France was "a great measure of national policy" undertaken to remove an extensive evil, he said that it was only with the greatest difficulty that justice and policy could be separated. Justice itself, he said, was "the great standing policy of human society." However, in adding that justice could be overridden only where "the policy of the measure, that is, the public benefit to be expected from it," was "at least as evident and at least as important" as the injustice caused, Burke surely implied that justice in the ordinary sense did not always accord with utility and that where they came into conflict the latter should prevail.[72] He made a similar point, more explicitly, with regard to the basis and ultimate validity of law in a speech of 1780. He began by saying that interference with property rights, even on grounds of public convenience, should be avoided: "What the law respects shall be sacred to me. If the barriers of law should be broken down, upon ideas of convenience, even of public convenience, we shall have no longer any thing certain among us." Stanlis ends the quotation at this point and comments: "In any conflict between merely utilitarian convenience and law, his stand was clear."[73] However, Burke immediately went on to say:

> There are occasions, I admit, of public necessity, so vast, so clear, so evident, that they supersede all laws. Law being only made for the benefit of the community cannot in any of its parts resist a demand which may comprehend the total of the public interest. To be sure, no law can set itself up against the cause and reason of all law.[74]

What Burke was saying in this passage was that a system of law which

[72] Burke, *Works of . . . Burke,* III, 438-439.

[73] Stanlis, *Edmund Burke and the Natural Law,* p. 121.

[74] Burke, *Speeches of . . . Burke,* II, 62-63. He said in another speech in the same year (though in a rather different context) that it was "to the last degree absurd to . . . separate the private rights of an individual, or any description of men, as held for any other end but for the good of the whole community." *Ibid.,* p. 119.

protected property was vital to general security, and that although such a system might incidentally provide protection for certain abuses, to damage the sanctity of the law for the sake of removing such abuses would be to take a very shortsighted view of the public interest; on the other hand, there might, very rarely, be cases in which the interest of the community required that the law should be set aside. A similar line of argument, though it relates to natural rather than positive laws, is to be found in Hutcheson's *System of Moral Philosophy* (of which there was a copy, incidentally, in Burke's library).[75] Hutcheson says that although the precepts of the laws of nature are commonly deemed immutable and eternal (and it is good that they should be so regarded), they are not so immutable as they are generally represented to be. "As the precept is no more than a conclusion from observation of what sort of conduct is ordinarily useful to society, some singular cases may happen in which departing from the ordinary rule may be more for the general interest than following it." The fundamental precept of promoting the general good is the one in which all exceptions from the "special" laws of nature are founded; and such exceptions are only justifiable

> where the whole good effects of receding from the ordinary rule, whether immediate or remote, are so great, and the evils ensuing upon our adhering to it . . . so pernicious, as will in all probability over-ballance all the evils to be apprehended from our counteracting the rule. . . . The more important any law is for the internal or external happiness of mankind, the greater must that utility or necessity be which in any singular cases can justify an exception from it.[76]

When Stanlis says that Burke stood up for law against "merely utilitarian convenience," he implies that for the utilitarians mere convenience could take precedence over law. Yet the utilitarians were always anxious to stress that utility or expediency as they understood it should be clearly distinguished from short-term or partial advantage; and J. S. Mill stated directly that "that which is expedient for some immediate object, some temporary purpose, but which violates a rule whose observance is expedient in a much higher degree," must be regarded by a utilitarian as harmful rather than useful, wrong rather than right.[77] That Burke attached as broad a meaning

---

[75] *Catalogue of the Library of the late Right Hon. Edmund Burke* (London, 1833), p. 15.

[76] Hutcheson, *System of Moral Philosophy*, I, 273-274; II, 122, 138. *Cf.* Austin, *The Providence of Jurisprudence Determined*, pp. 53-54.

[77] Mill, *Utilitarianism*, pp. 20-21.

to the terms utility and expediency as did the utilitarians is clear from his own statements;[78] and it also seems beyond question that like them he regarded the benefit of the community as the touchstone, the "cause and reason," of law. He had written early in his life in the *Tract on the Popery Laws:* "The essence of law . . . requires that it be made as much as possible for the benefit of the whole. If this principle be denied or evaded, what ground have we left to reason on?" And he wrote more epigrammatically in the *Reflections,* "Law itself is only beneficence acting by a rule."[79] In the face of these quotations it would be difficult to maintain that in Burke's view the validity of a law was deducible from its conformity to some *a priori* code rather than from its conduciveness to the general good.

Evidence can also be adduced to show that Burke's judgements of political and social systems—and of political conduct—were ultimately based on the same criterion. C. B. Macpherson has argued that Burke made use of the natural law in order to buttress the traditional subordination of ranks.[80] But perhaps it would be fairer to say that it was because Burke believed this traditional order to be for the benefit of the whole community that he regarded it as "natural," as in accordance with natural law.[81] Hume said that writers on the law of nature, whatever principles they set out with, always terminated by giving the needs and convenience of mankind as the ultimate reason for every rule which they established;[82] and although Burke's view of human needs would seem to have been more exalted than Hume's, with that qualification the remark can be seen to have some application to him. Burke said of his own *Reflections on the Revolution in France*: "The foundation of government is there laid, not in imaginary rights . . . but in political convenience, and in human nature." He took issue with those who built their politics "not on convenience, but on truth" —for, he said, political problems "do not primarily concern truth or falsehood. They relate to good or evil. What in the result is likely to produce evil is politically false: that which is productive of good, politically true."[83]

---

[78] He said that utility should be understood not as partial and limited, but as general and public utility *(Tract on the Popery Laws, Works of . . . Burke,* VI, 323); and he explained that by expediency he meant that which was good for the whole community. Burke, *Speech on the Reform of the Representation, Works of . . . Burke,* VII, 98.

[79] Burke, *Works of . . . Burke,* VI, 324; III, 308.

[80] C. B. Macpherson, "Edmund Burke," *Transactions of the Royal Society of Canada,* LIII (1959), 19-26.

[81] For assertions of Burke's belief that social inequality and aristocratic government were for the benefit of all, the humble as well as the highly placed, see Burke, *Reflections, Works of . . . Burke,* III, 279-280; *Appeal From the New to the Old Whigs, Works of . . . Burke,* IV, 174; Copeland, *Correspondence of Edmund Burke,* VII, 53.

[82] Hume, *Essays,* II, 187-189.

[83] Burke, *Appeal From the New to the Old Whigs, Works of . . . Burke,* IV, 169, 206-207.

It would be hard to find a clearer statement of the consequentialist principle, but two passages from other places can be cited to reinforce it. Burke wrote to a French correspondent in 1792: "Je ne suis pas fanatique pour les Rois. Je mesure mon attachement par l'utilité de leurs fonctions à jamais augustes et sacrés."[84] It was on account of their utility, we must infer, that these functions should be regarded as sacred; and he wrote in the *Reflections* with reference to traditional institutions in general: "Old establishments are tried by their effects. . . . We conclude that to be good from whence good is derived."[85] But what of political behavior—was this, at least, to be judged by its compliance with some "normative code of ethics"? It does seem that in purely abstract terms Burke was prepared to entertain a deontological view of ethics, just as he was willing to conceive that in the realm of metaphysics a doctrine of natural rights might be tenable. But he apparently did not consider that abstract speculations of this kind had anything to do with real life, with practical morality or practical politics. At any rate such an interpretation accords with the following remarks which he made in 1792 when speaking on a petition from the Unitarians:

> Whether any thing be proper to be denied, which is right in itself, because it may lead to the demand of others which it is improper to grant;—abstractedly speaking, there can be no doubt that this question ought to be decided in the negative. But as no moral questions are ever abstract questions, this, before I judge upon any abstract proposition, must be embodied in circumstances; for since things are right and wrong, morally speaking, only by their relation and connexion with other things, this very question of what it is politically right to grant depends upon this relation to its effects.[86]

This passage belongs in a political context and relates primarily to what is "politically right." Yet the remarks about morality seem intended to apply to morality in general, not simply to morality in politics. It is true that Burke never directly explained *private* ethics in utilitarian or consequentialist terms. But perhaps, for other reasons besides his preoccupation with politics, this is not surprising. He may well have been influenced by considerations which have worried a number of utilitarian thinkers: that a utilitarian theory of ethics, however much it may insist on the utility of moral rules, cannot treat them (or at least cannot treat rules of any sim-

---

[84] Copeland, *Correspondence of Edmund Burke*, VII, 263.
[85] Burke, *Works of . . . Burke*, III, 460.
[86] Burke, *Speeches of . . . Burke*, IV, 66.

plicity) as invariably binding; and that an absolute, authoritarian system of morals may be more efficacious, and therefore more desirable on utilitarian grounds, than a utilitarian theory.[87] Burke thought that the mass of mankind were destined to "live on trust." "It would be impossible that civil society could subsist long if we were all philosophers," he said. And he wrote in the *Appeal from the New to the Old Whigs* that the finer points of moral science should only be handled by men of "a very solid and discriminating judgment," for in general it was wrong "to turn our duties into doubts. . . . Our opinions about them ought not to be in a state of fluctuation, but steady, sure, and resolved."[88] It is not surprising that someone holding these views should have avoided the public exposition of a theory of ethics which might have made ordinary moral rules seem less than absolute.[89] Yet it is hard to believe that Burke could really have combined a consequentialist view of public morals with a deontological view of private morals. To the passage quoted at the end of the last paragraph, in which public morality was apparently assimilated to morality in general, one can add his statement that "nothing universal can be rationally affirmed on any moral or any political subject"[90] (a statement which his natural law interpreters have had considerable difficulty in explaining away). Moreover, his much-quoted remark that "the principles of true politics are those of morality enlarged" surely carries the inference that the principles of private morality can be construed as those of public morality contracted.[91] In any case, it is obviously as a political thinker that Burke is important. What this essay has tried to show is that utility played a more fundamental part in his political thought than did natural law (unless by natural law one simply means some primary belief or intuition about the right ends of hu-

---

[87] *Cf.* R. F. Harrod, "Utilitarianism Revised," *Mind*, XLV (1936), 150. Anthony Quinton, *Utilitarian Ethics* (London, 1973), p. 108.

[88] Burke, *Reflections, Works of . . . Burke*, III, 360. Edmund Burke, *Extracts from Mr. Burke's Table-Talk, at Crewe Hall, Written Down by Mrs. Crewe*, reprinted in *The Burke Newsletter*, V (1963-64), 291. Burke, *Appeal from the New to the Old Whigs, Works of . . . Burke*, IV, 168.

[89] Burke would have been quite aware that one could not rest an absolute code of ethics on a utilitarian rationale—just as he was always conscious that however socially useful one might consider religion to be, to defend it on the grounds of its utility would be to undermine the very qualities from which its efficacy derived. *Notebook*, pp. 67-68; Burke, *Tract on the Popery Laws, Works of . . . Burke*, VI, 338.

[90] Burke, *Appeal From the New to the Old Whigs, Works of . . . Burke*, IV, 80.

[91] Copeland, *Correspondence of Edmund Burke*, II, 282. *Cf.* Bentham, *Traités de Législation civile et pénale*, ed. E. Dumont (Paris, 1802), I, 27: "Ce qui est politiquement bon ne sauroit être moralement mauvais, à moins que les règles d'arithmétique, qui sont vraies pour les grands nombres, ne soient fausses pour les petits."

man life in society); and it is submitted therefore that the natural law "as a normative code of ethics" cannot rightly be regarded as the basis of his political philosophy.

13

James Mill on Burke's Doctrine of Prescription

The place of utility in Burke's thought, and his relationship both
to the broad utilitarian tradition of moral and political philosophy
and, more narrowly, to Benthamism, are subjects which have attracted considerable attention.[1] I have myself argued, in an earlier
contribution to this journal, that Burke's ideas had marked affinities
with those of certain eighteenth-century thinkers who (although not
"Benthamites") are generally classified as belonging to the utilitarian tradition—and that the assignment of Burke (by Peter J. Stanlis) to an aprioristic natural law tradition contraposed to the utilitarian one is misleading, since his moral and political principles can
be seen to have rested largely on consequentialist foundations.[2]
However, it was not my intention to suggest that the differences between him and the utilitarians were unimportant. Indeed, if one
equates utilitarianism with the "philosophic radicalism" of the
school of Jeremy Bentham, the differences must clearly be regarded
as more important than the similarities: and it is with some of these
differences that the present paper is concerned. As Benthamism did
not become a democratic creed until the early nineteenth century,[3]
there could be no such direct confrontation between Burke's conservatism and philosophic radicalism as there was between Burke
and Paine. What Burke would have thought of Benthamite radicalism must be a matter of inference and conjecture. But there is, as one
would expect, some evidence concerning Benthamite reactions to
the works of Burke; and the purpose of this paper is to draw attention to certain evidence of this nature in the hope that it will throw
some light on the relationship between two important species of
political thought.

1. See for example Elie Halévy, *The Growth of Philosophic Radicalism*, trans. Mary
Morris, 2d ed. (London: Faber and Faber, 1934), pp. 155-164; Peter J. Stanlis, *Edmund
Burke and the Natural Law* (Ann Arbor: University of Michigan Press, 1958), pp. 29-34.
    2. "Utility and Natural Law in Burke's Thought: A Reconsideration," *Studies in Burke
and His Time* 16 (1974-1975): above, 229-52.
    3. See my paper "Bentham's Transition to Political Radicalism, 1809-10," *Journal of the
History of Ideas* below, 273-90 ; Halévy, *Philosophic Radicalism*, pp. 258-264. In the
1790s the political differences between Bentham and Burke were less marked: see J. H.
Burns, "Bentham and the French Revolution," *Transactions of the Royal Historical Society*
5th ser. 16 (1966):110-112.

It is well known that Bentham himself wrote in 1810 and published in 1817 a "Defence of Economy against the Late Mr. Burke"—a detailed critique of Burke's speech of 11 February 1780 on economic reform.[4] It set out to show that the real object of the plan of reform which Burke was proposing was not to attack corruption and extravagance in earnest but to gain credit for his party at the cost of a minimal reduction in the patronage which it could hope to take over when it returned to office. The work contains some hostile comments both on Burke's oratorical technique—on his expertise in "the use of those phrases by which the imaginations of men are fascinated, their passions inflamed, and their judgments bewildered and seduced"[5]—and on his ideal polity: "a government in the quondam *Venetian* style—a government in which, under the guidance of upstart Machiavelism, titled and confederated imbecility should lord it over king and people, and behind the screen of secrecy, waste, oppression, and peculation, should find themselves for ever at their ease; such was the Utopia of Edmund Burke."[6] But for the most part the pamphlet is of more significance in the history of administrative reform than it is in the broader history of political ideas: its purpose was to expose the speciousness of Burke's pretensions as a reformer rather than to examine the main tenets of his political philosophy.

There survive in addition to this work some manuscript comments which Bentham made in his own copies of several of Burke's early pamphlets, now bound together in the British Library;[7] but his remarks are fragmentary, and the pamphlets are not those which gave Burke his reputation as a theorist of conservatism. On Burke's writings of the 1790s, direct comments by Bentham are hard to find, though there is one interesting passage in his manuscripts (written in 1795) which refers to Burke's *Reflections on the Revolution in France*:

> The system of the democrats is absurd, and dangerous: for it subjugates the well-informed to the ill informed *classes* of mankind. Mr. Burke's system though diametrically opposite is absurd and mischievous for a similar reason: it subjugates the well-informed to the ill-informed *ages*. Of all Tyranny the most relentless is that of the dead: for it can not be mollified.

---

4. *The Pamphleteer* 9 (1817):3-47; *The Works of Jeremy Bentham*, ed. John Bowring, 11 vols. (Edinburgh: William Tait, 1843), 5:278-301.

5. Bentham, *Works*, 5:283. Cf. ibid., 10:510.

6. Ibid., 5:297.

7. The British Library shelf mark is 08138.dd.50. An article has been written about the marginalia in these pamphlets: Jeffrey Hart, "Bentham and Burke," *Burke Newsletter* 6 (1964-1965):347-359. But it is flawed by a failure to observe that, although the pamphlets did belong to Bentham, most of the marginal comments are not in his handwriting but in that of James Mill.

Of all Folly the most incurable is that of the dead: for it can not be instructed. Mr. Burke's pamphlet on French politics, a strange mixture of
salutary reason and mischievous absurdity.[8]

This passage shows that even during the anti-Jacobin phase of his
career Bentham was critical of the line of argument which he was
later to describe as the "wisdom-of-our-ancestors" fallacy.[9]

Among Burke's arguments in favor of established institutions his
use of the concept of "prescription," which appears more than once
in the *Reflections*, drew hostile comments from several of his critics
in the 1790s.[10] But his fullest exposition of this concept belongs to a
work which, although written before his anti-Jacobin pamphlets of
the 1790s, was not published until it was found among his papers after his death. This was his "Speech on a Reform of the Representation of the Commons in Parliament," probably composed in 1784
and first published in 1812 in volume 5 of the first edition of his collected works.[11] A few years after it appeared in print the speech attracted the critical attention of James Mill; and in one of Mill's unpublished commonplace books there is an attempt to provide a
direct refutation of the theory of prescription as advanced in this
work. The theory of prescription has long been recognized as an important feature of Burke's thought: indeed it has recently been described as his "key and characteristic doctrine."[12] Mill's attempted
refutation can thus be seen as an assault on strategically central
ground.

To introduce the passage itself, something needs to be said about
its location and context. James Mill's commonplace books survive
in five volumes, four of them at the London Library (to which they
were presented by John Stuart Mill) and the fifth in the Mill-Taylor
Papers at the British Library of Political and Economic Science.
They consist mainly of extracts from the works of other writers, but
they also include a few passages of sustained argument or commentary by Mill himself. There is, for example, an extended critique of
the speech delivered by Burke's friend and follower William Wind-

8. Bentham Papers, box 44, fo.5, University College, London. For a column of jottings on
Burke's *Reflections*, see ibid., box 108, fo.105.

9. Bentham, *Works*, 2:398-401.

10. See Paul Lucas, "On Edmund Burke's Doctrine of Prescription; or, an Appeal from
the New to the Old Lawyers," *Historical Journal* 9 (1968):45n., 51n.

11. Burke's literary executors originally assigned the speech to May 1782, but in the 1816
edition of his collected speeches it is dated June 1784. It was reissued as a pamphlet during
the Reform Bill crisis of 1831. See William B. Todd, *A Bibliography of Edmund Burke*
(London: Rupert Hart-Davis, 1964), pp. 271-272.

12. Lucas, "Burke's Doctrine of Prescription," p. 36. See also Russell Kirk, "Burke and
the Philosophy of Prescription," *Journal of the History of Ideas* 14 (1953):365-380; Francis
Canavan, "Burke on Prescription of Government," *Review of Politics* 35 (1973):455-474.

ham on 26 May 1809 against Curwen's Bribery Bill; and it is interesting to have Mill's point-by-point reply to a speech which was described at the time by Henry Brougham as "a full statement . . . of the
arguments which the most powerful enemy of reform could urge
against it, in the most general form of that important question."[13]
But in the passage on Burke, Mill was addressing himself to a conservative text of still greater significance, and this passage is probably the most valuable piece of original writing which the commonplace books contain. Mill's commentary cannot be dated exactly, but it falls between two entries in the same volume for which approximate dates can be inferred. The earlier entry is headed "Rules
for discrediting a book, the argument of which cannot be safely
meddled with; as Bentham on Parl. Ref.," and it appears to have
been provoked by the review of Bentham's *Plan of Parliamentary
Reform* in the *Edinburgh Review* for December 1818. The later entry is a quotation from a newspaper report of Lord Grey's speech at
the Newcastle Fox Club dinner of 6 January 1819.[14] It would seem
that the passage on Burke belongs to the period when Mill was collecting background material for his articles in the *Encyclopaedia
Britannica*, including the famous article on "Government."[15]

Immediately preceding the passage on prescription there are
three pages of extracts headed "Maxims & Dicta of Burke, pro & con
Parl. Ref.";[16] these are taken from Burke's "Speech on the Duration
of Parliaments" and his "Speech on a Reform of the Representation,"
and the "con" quotations have short comments appended to them by
Mill. The last and longest of the extracts, taken from the second of
the two speeches, is transcribed by Mill as follows:

> In favour of the constitution, as it stands, "what have you to answer but
> this?—Our constitution is a prescriptive constitution, it is a constitution
> whose sole authority is, that it has existed time out of mind. . . . Prescrip-
> tion is the most solid of all titles, not only to property, but, which is to
> secure that property, to government. They harmonize with each other, &
> give mutual aid to one another. It is accompanied with another ground
> of authority in the constitution of the human mind, presumption. It is a
> presumption in favour of any settled scheme of government against any
> untried project, that a nation has long existed & flourished under it. It is
> a better presumption even of the *choice* of a nation, far better than any
> sudden & temporary arrangement by actual election. . . . It is a deliber-
> ate election of ages & of generations; it is a constitution made by what is

13. James Mill's Commonplace Books, 2: fos.17-22, London Library; *Edinburgh Review*
17 (1810-1811):255.

14. Mill's Commonplace Books, 1: fos.27v. and 163v.

15. See Alexander Bain, *James Mill: A Biography* (London: Longmans, 1882), pp. 187-
189.

16. Mill's Commonplace Books, 1: fos. 32v.-33v.

ten thousand times better than choice, it is made by the peculiar circumstances, occasions, tempers, dispositions, & moral, civil, & social habi-
tudes of the people, which disclose themselves only in a long space of
time. It is a vestment which accommodates itself to the body. Nor is prescription of government founded upon blind unmeaning prejudices—for
man is a most unwise & a most wise being. The individual is foolish. The
multitude for the moment is foolish, when they act without deliberation;
but the species is wise, & when time is given to it, as a species it almost
always acts right."[17]

Mill then embarks on his commentary, which covers two and a
quarter closely written pages:

The following observations are to be applied. "Good by prescription." The
things that are said to be good by prescription, would have been either
good or bad without prescription. If good without it, i.e. *per se*, nothing
more in any case can possibly be desired. We must suppose that things
that are said to be good by prescription would have been bad without it.
They are things that can be defended on no other ground, than that of old
existence. They are *mala per se*, good only by reason of certain other
things, which are connected with them. If prescription renders bad things
good; it would have been still better if good things had been chosen at the
beginning, & prescription had been had in favour of them. So, if we resolve
upon good things now, time will give us prescription in favour of them.
But time, it will be said, has made an adaptation of all things to all things.
If you alter some things in the system, you must alter all. To this argument
many answers may be returned. In the first place, allowing that bad
things, by a long operation, form adaptations between other things & themselves, it does not follow, that substituting good things to the bad things,
would require any such changes in other things as would be very difficult to introduce. Suppose by the long operation of some thing a man's leg
has been held in a bad posture, till the muscles are contracted. There is
no doubt, that not only the contiguous muscles, but all the muscles in the
body are adapted to the bad habit; yet if by any operation of the healing
art, the contraction of these muscles can be redressed, the other muscles
are easily brought from the bad habit to the good one. Another answer is,
if it be taken as a general objection to the removal of all old evils, that
they have adapted other things to themselves, it is undeniably & conspicuously condemned & scouted by the reason & practice of mankind, by
whom on so many occasions old evils have been removed without any regard to this argument of the adaptation: if it is notoriously unworthy
of regard as a general answer to all removal of old evils, it is only good,
if it is ever good, where it applies to the particular circumstances of
some particular case, when in the particular circumstances of that particular case, the removal of the evil things would by the other changes
which it would require, produce more inconvenience than the object is
worth. For a third answer, we may consider, what is the sort of adaptations which bad things make of other things to themselves. They may be
first, things to correct the bad effects of the bad things. Get rid of the bad

17. The passage is taken from *Works of the Right Honourable Edmund Burke*, 8 vols.
(London: J. Dodsley, 1792-1827), 5:389-390.

things, & you no longer need them. They may secondly be things which co-operate with the bad things to produce bad effects. The sooner you get rid of them the better. Thirdly, they may be things which produce good effects, acting along with the bad things; but could not be made to concur in useful operation with good things. The things, however, which would concur in useful operation with the good things, would produce still more good effects. All then, which you have to include in the account is the inconvenience of change; & about that no general rule can be given, it must in every case be decided by the circumstances of that very case. Upon the whole, it is plain, that this argument about prescription is nothing but the common fallacy of "No innovation." As a general argument against all improvement, this is exploded by the general reason & general practice of mankind. Innovation never is or can be bad, but on the particular merits of the particular case, when the benefit sought is less than the benefit abandoned.

But Burke's argument further is, that prescription, that is long usage, is a *proof* of goodness. If his rule is held in obedience, that bad things, if once established, are to be held to for ever because they are established, antiquity of usage is no proof of goodness at all. Observe the mental process of this arguer. You are to keep to bad things, if they are once introduced: and if you keep to them long, your very keeping to them will prove that they are good. Prescription, says Burke, is a presumption of choice. True: but choice, by *whom?* Nothing in government, or in human affairs, ever took place but by choice. The point of importance is, who were the chusers? If the people were the chusers, Burke's argument is conclusive, "the species is wise," & the choice would be right. If the choice never has been by the people, but always by the peoples oppressors, then, it is clear, the choice would be wrong. Good government would give to the people the choice, & then as "the species is wise," the choice would be sure to be good.

Burke talks of prescription to government & prescription to property, as things of the same sort. They are intrinsically different. Prescription to government means antiquity of the institution. Property as an institution exists always & without dispute; it is only the title of an individual to some portion of it, that gets the name of prescription. The title of an individual to some portion of the powers of government is not what Burke means by prescription to government. To make good prescription to property, that is to maintain the title of an individual to some particular portion of it, is a very different thing from maintaining that a bad institution of government ought not to be changed.

The constitution [is] good as it is; & such as it is, it has experience on its side. This [is] Burke's argument, in pp. 391-3 of the same speech. That is to say, you have experience of the good effects which it actually does produce, & no other. But you have also experience of the evil effects which it produces. And is any body ready to declare it an impossibility, looking at a frame of government, to determine with certainty whether a better could not be made? There is no government of which you may not say, it produces good effects, & we have had experience of it. Would it therefore be a right conclusion, let no bad government ever be changed? May not experience go, & go with absolute certainty, beyond the results of any particular machine. Suppose as perfect a piece of machinery as any that has yet been in play, will it be pronounced impossible for mechanical knowledge looking at this machinery to say, exaggerate as you please the good effects which it produces, there are other contrivances which would produce them in greater abundance, & this which I now present to you is to an absolute certainty one of that description. Would it be endurable to say, we have had experience of the other machine: we have had none of yours. Would not the intelligent contriver say, this is a mere perversion of the word experience. Is there one single power in this machine of which the most ample experience has not been had? Is there a single combination of those powers in it of which the experience has not been had? Add the effect of one combination to another, & can you not tell the result? If 100 men eat 70 lbs of beef to [sic] dinner, cannot you tell what 1000 men will eat? Or would it be necessary for you to make the experiment, & would you deny in such a case that you had experience to guide you.— You have had *Experience*: & the good of it is—you are never to profit by that experience. To profit by experience is to observe defects & correct them. According to Burke, if you do observe defects, you are to go on repeating them for ever!

A favourite fallacy of Burke, as of most of the antireformers is—that any change in the government, so as to make it true to its ends, instead of being false to them, is the same thing as a proposal to dissolve all the bonds of government, & leave society in confusion. They present to you this alternative: Either keep to your present government; Or have none at all. They make an assumption contrary to experience; & on that they build their conclusion. It is established by the experience of the human race in all ages & all countries, that nothing is so difficult to be dissolved as government; that after it has been once established, there is no instance of its having been dissolved, or any thing like dissolved. A temporary relaxation in some of its parts is all that history gives us an instance of. This, then, is all that is ever to be apprehended. The bonds of society are strong & vigorous. Let the idea of anarchy then be always scouted.[18]

It is not my intention in presenting this document to set myself up as an adjudicator of the respective positions adopted by Burke and Mill; but a few comments may be offered on the piece itself. Perhaps the most obvious thing about it is that it is a characteristic passage, illustrating Mill's predilection for pursuing lines of logical argument. Macaulay, in his celebrated article on "Utilitarian Logic and Politics," was to criticize Mill for his a priori method of reasoning and his neglect of the inductive method.[19] Yet although it may be true that as a means of constructing a science of politics Mill's reliance on axioms and syllogisms was unsatisfactory, as an instrument for dissecting what he regarded as myths and mystifications his severe logic was more appropriate. His approach had something in common with Bentham's treatment of the theories expounded by Blackstone and others;[20] and there was a tacit reference to

18. Mill's Commonplace Books, 1: fos.33v.-34v.
19. *Edinburgh Review* 41 (1829):161-162.
20. Mill's method was more austere: he did not imitate Bentham's touches of facetiousness.

Bentham's *Book of Fallacies* near the end of the first paragraph of Mill's critique, where he declared that Burke's argument about prescription was "nothing but the common fallacy of 'No innovation.' "[21]

A question of obvious importance is how far Mill interpreted Burke's views correctly: how far his criticisms were based on a full understanding and fair presentation of Burke's position. The line of argument pursued through most of the first paragraph might be regarded (given Mill's point of view) as a legitimate response to Burke, though Mill seemed to be addressing himself less directly to the quoted extract from the speech on reform than to another passage in Burke's writings: the passage in the *Reflections* where he maintained that there was a great difference between "what policy would dictate on the original introduction of . . . institutions, and on a question of their total abolition, where they have cast their roots wide and deep, and where by long habit things more valuable than themselves are so adapted to them, that the one cannot be destroyed without totally impairing the other."[22]

However, it is more doubtful whether Mill's interpretation of the actual concept of prescription as used by Burke was entirely fair. The concept is admittedly one that has been variously interpreted by students of Burke's thought; but there does at present seem to be widespread agreement that when he described the British constitution as "a prescriptive constitution, . . . a constitution whose sole authority is, that it has existed time out of mind," he did not mean quite what he said (or appeared to be saying).[23] About what he did mean by prescription, there is less agreement; but he seems to have meant, at the least, that where institutions or regimes had been established for a long period of time their validity could not be challenged by any questioning of their original legitimacy or of the principles on which they were founded. Prescription ruled out any objection to an old institution on the grounds that it had been established by force rather than by contract or consent, and it precluded any supposed right of the present generation to condemn such an institution for failing to conform to some modern theory of how it should be constituted. Further, Burke meant—though this was not strictly a part of his doctrine of prescription, since he spoke of

---

21. Bentham, *Works*, 2:418. *The Book of Fallacies* was not published in English until 1824, but a French version edited and translated by Dumont was published in 1816.

22. Burke, *Works*, 3:208.

23. See B. T. Wilkins, *The Problem of Burke's Political Philosophy* (Oxford: Clarendon Press, 1967), pp. 228-229; David Cameron, *The Social Thought of Rousseau and Burke* (London: Weidenfeld and Nicolson, 1973), pp. 151-153, 221-222; Canavan, "Burke on Prescription of Government," p. 464.

"another ground of authority"—that the very fact of an institution having long been in existence created a strong presumption in its favor. He did not, however, maintain that age was a guarantee of an institution's worth. In fact he conceded later in the same speech on reform that "to say your constitution is what it has been, is no sufficient defence for those who say it is a bad constitution"; and he said in the *Reflections*: "Old establishments are tried by their effects. . . . We judge that to be good from whence good is derived."[24] It would seem, therefore, that Mill was not justified in saying in his second paragraph that for Burke "prescription, that is long usage, is a *proof* of goodness." Still, it should be remembered that others besides Mill have interpreted Burke in this way;[25] and Burke himself may have been partly to blame for his ideas being misconstrued. He was at times so anxious to stress the value—meaning the presumptive value—of tried practices and inherited institutions that the moral criteria by which the legacies of the past were ultimately to be tested were allowed to fall into the background.

In any case, the fact that Mill put too "hard" an interpretation on Burke's theory of prescription does not affect the pertinency of most of his arguments. When he went on in his second paragraph to answer Burke's statement that long usage was "a presumption of choice" by asking who was presumed to have done the choosing, he was making a particularly germane point; and his suggestion that the choice had always been made by the people's oppressors reflected the Benthamite conviction that traditional institutions and conventions, far from deserving any presumption in their favor, had been shaped to serve the interests of a dominant minority. Mill said in a letter to Dumont in December 1819: "The government of England has hitherto been, like that of all other countries, a government actually and in fact aristocratical—the whole powers of government have always been in the hands of the aristocracy—government has therefore been, and is an aristocratical engine, wielded by the aristocracy for their own benefit."[26]

The point made in Mill's third paragraph—that the legal concept of prescription could not be directly translated into a political concept—needs little comment, though mention should be made of

24. Burke, *Works*, 5:391; 3:227-228.

25. See for example Robert M. Hutchins, "The Theory of Oligarchy: Edmund Burke," *Thomist* 5 (1943):73: "Prescription means that whatever is old confers a right, and nothing confers a right unless it is old." Cf. Basil Willey, *The Eighteenth Century Background* (London: Chatto and Windus, 1940), p. 244; Leo Strauss, *Natural Right and History* (Chicago: University of Chicago Press, 1953), p. 319.

26. Mill to Etienne Dumont, 13 December 1819, MS Dumont 33/III, fo.42, Bibliothèque publique et universitaire, Geneva. Cf. Bentham, *Works*, 10:511.

Burke's own remark in *An Appeal from the New to the Old Whigs*
that to invoke the notion of "rights" in the political sphere involved
"a confusion of judicial with civil principles."[27] In his fourth paragraph Mill broadened the focus of his argument and considered
Burke's general case for relying on experience rather than specula-
tion. According to Halévy, the essential difference between the utilitarian radicals and Burke was that the former regarded politics as a
demonstrative and deductive science, while for the latter it was
(in Burke's own words) an "experimental science, not to be taught
a priori."[28] Judging from what he said in this paragraph, Mill may
not have been as indifferent to the value of experiment as the abstract approach of his essay on "Government" has led people to
suppose.[29] But there was certainly a very wide (indeed a classic) difference between his conception of a political system as a machine
which could be superseded by one of more efficient design, and
Burke's idea of the state as something organic and delicate which
needed to be treated by the legislator with great caution and sensibility.[30] Burke's view did not, as Mill suggested, exclude one's profit-
ing by experience to the extent of observing defects and correcting
them; but it did exclude any attempt to dismantle the political
structure and reassemble it on new lines. Burke preferred a medical
image to a mechanical one: he said that one "should approach to the
faults of the state as to the wounds of a father, with pious awe and
trembling solicitude"; and he expressed horror at "those children of
their country, who are prompt rashly to hack that aged parent in
pieces, and put him into the kettle of magicians" in the hope of re-
generating the paternal constitution.[31]

In his final paragraph Mill contested the argument that any political change would inevitably lead to the dissolution of all the bonds
of government.[32] He did not suggest, as Paine had,[33] that gov-

---

27. Burke, *Works*, 3:511-512.
28. Halévy, *Philosophic Radicalism*, p. 158; Burke, *Works*, 3:92.
29. See Fred Kort, "The Issue of a Science of Politics in Utilitarian Thought," *American
Political Science Review* 46 (1952):1140-1152.
30. Burke, *Reflections*, in *Works*, 3:223. Cf. David Hume, *Philosophical Works*, ed. T. H.
Green and T. H. Grose, 4 vols. (London: Longmans, Green and Co., 1874-1875), 3:480: "It
is not with forms of government, as with other artificial contrivances; where an old
engine may be rejected, if we can discover another more accurate and commodious." See
also Michael Oakeshott, *Rationalism in Politics and Other Essays* (London: Methuen, 1962),
p.4.
31. Burke, *Reflections*, in *Works*, 3:135.
32. Here again there was an implicit reference to Bentham's *Book of Fallacies*. Bentham's
other name for the "no innovation" fallacy was "the hobgoblin argument"—the hobgoblin
being "*anarchy*, which tremendous spectre has for its forerunner the monster *innovation*"
(Bentham, *Works*, 2:418).
33. *Writings of Thomas Paine*, ed. M. D. Conway, 4 vols. (New York: G. P. Putnam's
Sons, 1894-1896), 2:407-408.

ernment itself was scarcely necessary (he could hardly have done so in view of his Hobbesian assumptions about human nature); but his optimism about the durability of government contrasted sharply with Burke's belief in its extreme fragility. It is worth noting, however, that Mill's confidence seems to have applied only to the consequences of *political* reform: he was to write some years later that if socialist ideas were to gain acceptance the result would be "the subversion of civilised society; worse than the overwhelming deluge of Huns and Tartars."[34] However much Mill disagreed with Burke about political systems, they were alike in believing that the existence and complete security of private property were essential to economic prosperity and social peace. Mill was echoing Burke as well as Locke when he wrote in his article "Government": "it is for the sake of property that Government exists."[35]

Mill's critique of Burke did not bring out the similarities between them. Nor did it reveal all their important differences. It said nothing directly, for example, about their fundamental difference of opinion over the educability of the people at large. It was Mill's faith in the power of education that enabled him to combine a belief in democracy (or at least in a much extended franchise) with a belief in an economic system which was inherently inegalitarian;[36] Burke, on the other hand, considered that knowledge, in being diffused, was "weakened and perverted,"[37] and he shared the fear of most conservatives that an extension of political power to the nonpossessing classes would result in spoliation and anarchy. However, though Mill's critique may not cover every aspect of the relationship between Benthamite radicalism and Burkean conservatism, it does constitute a piece of evidence which any student of this relationship should take into account. Alan Bullock and Maurice Shock remarked in their introduction to *The Liberal Tradition from Fox to Keynes*: "In an iconoclastic frame of mind which was totally indifferent to Burke's argument of prescription, the Philosophical Radicals demanded the submission of all institutions—legal, constitutional, ecclesiastical—to the rationalist criterion of utility."[38] Mill's

34. Bain, *James Mill*, p.364.

35. [James Mill], *The Article Government, Reprinted from the Supplement to the Encyclopaedia Britannica* (London: Traveller Office, 1821), p. 5. Cf. *Speeches of the Right Honourable Edmund Burke*, 4 vols. (London: Longman, 1816), 4:166.

36. In the letter quoted above Mill went on to say that, provided he had the opportunity of combatting them by means of rational instruction, he would not fear the propagation of doctrines hostile to property: "I have seldom met with a labouring man (and I have tried the experiment upon many of them) whom I could not make to see that the existence of property was not only good for the labouring man, but of infinitely more importance to the labourers as a class, than to any other" (Bain, *James Mill*, p. 365).

37. Burke, *Letter to William Elliot*, in *Works*, 4:245.

38. (London: Adam and Charles Black, 1956), p.xxvi.

piece explains in a considered fashion why the philosophic radicals were not merely indifferent, but positively hostile, to Burke's theory of prescription.

14

Burke and the Utilitarians: A Rejoinder

The purpose of my article "James Mill on Burke's Doctrine of Prescription"[1] was to present an unpublished document in the hope that it would be of interest to students of the political ideas of the late eighteenth and early nineteenth centuries. The comments offered on this document were not intended to be controversial, though I did suggest (or at least imply) that both points of view, Mill's as well as Burke's, deserved consideration. Peter J. Stanlis, in his "Reflections on Dinwiddy on Mill on Burke on Pre-scription,"[2] does not express any serious disagreement with my comments. But he does make it clear that in his opinion the Benthamite position has little or nothing to be said for it. He describes the Benthamites, accurately enough, as "men who were constantly digging at the roots of established institutions in order to compel them to justify their existence." For him, evidently, this is a presumptuous and noxious activity. Yet, it is arguable that in the late eighteenth and early nineteenth centuries such an approach was in many ways salutary—that institutions and practices inherited from the past did need critical reexamination at a time of rapid social and economic change—and that one of the most important achievements of Benthamism was the exposure of various contemporary abuses and of the "fictions" and special pleading that had been used to support them. John Stuart Mill called Bentham "the great *critical* thinker of his age and country" and wrote: "It is by the influence of the modes of thought with which his writings inoculated a number of thinking men, that the yoke of authority has been broken, and innumerable opinions, formerly received on tradition as incontestable, are put upon their defence, and required to give an account of themselves."[3] In presenting the extract from James Mill's commonplace book, I observed that the approach he adopted was comparable with

---

1. *Studies in Burke and His Time* 18 (1977): 179-190.
2. Ibid., pp. 191-198.
3. *Dissertations and Discussions,* 4 vols. (London: J. W. Parker, 1859-1875), 1:332, 334. Cf. J. H. Burns, "Bentham's Critique of Political Fallacies," in *Jeremy Bentham: Ten Critical Essays,* ed. Bhikhu Parekh (London: Frank Cass, 1974), p. 154.

that of Bentham in *A Fragment on Government* and *The Book of Fallacies.* I did not claim that the passage was a particularly distinguished specimen of Benthamite critical reasoning; but I cannot agree with Stanlis that its only significance is to reveal "the rigid cast of Mill's own mind and temper."

Stanlis is less than fair to Mill and the point of view he represents. He says, for example, that Mill's arguments are "pitched on an abstract level of 'good' and 'evil,' with no attempt to specify the content of either." But one would hardly expect Mill, in a passage in his own commonplace book, to restate the first principles of utilitarian theory and to explain that what he meant by calling something good was that it was conducive—and by calling something bad or evil that it was inimical—to the aggregate happiness of the members of the community. So much could surely be taken for granted; and it was of course the contention of the utilitarians that by defining good and evil in this way they had given the terms a *more* distinct and substantial content than they usually had in political discourse.[4]

The central point that Mill was making in the passage under discussion was that when one was considering the value of an old institution and the question of whether or how far it needed reform, the antiquity of the institution should not in itself be regarded as a bar or obstacle to change. All that should be taken into account was how effectively the institution in question was promoting the ends of government and whether the benefits to be derived from a reform were likely to outweigh any damage or inconvenience it might involve. Even where an institution or system of government could be shown to have had good effects, this was not a decisive argument against reform, because it might well be possible to envisage changes which, judging from the way in which such arrangements operated elsewhere, could be expected with a fair degree of confidence to make the institution or system still more beneficial. It is worth nothing that Burke himself had made similar points, though more briefly, in opposing what he regarded as an unjustified appeal to "the sanction of custom and prescription" in 1772. The relevant passage begins with a remark which brings to mind Bentham's concept of "interest-begotten prejudice": "How weak an argument prescription is in this case, they [ministers] do not seem to feel;

4. See *The Works of Jeremy Bentham,* ed. John Bowring, 11 vols. (Edinburgh: William Tait, 1843), 2:441; 3:214.

for, where interest is concerned, what will men not think an argument?" Burke then goes on to say: "*Stare super antiquas vias* is their political creed. What then! is the maxim to preclude every improvement, however obvious and necessary, in the constitution? The first enquiry, before we proceed to walk upon this old road, is, whether we can be said to *star bene*, and the next is, whether, if this be the case, we cannot *star meglio*."[5] By contrast, Burke's "Speech on a Reform of the Representation" tended, in Mill's view, to obscure the need for this kind of inquiry or at least was calculated to instill a predisposition so hostile to change as to rule out an evenhanded assessment of the likely costs and benefits of any proposed reform.

It is true that Burke did not, in the passage on which Mill was commenting, altogether discard the criterion of effectiveness. He said: "It is a presumption in favour of any settled scheme of government against any untried project, that a nation has long existed and flourished under it."[6] The phrase "and flourished" is there; but (like the qualification "just" which appears in the last sentence of the famous passage on prejudice in Burke's *Reflections*[7]) it is not very conspicuous, and from the Benthamite angle it must have seemed in need of definition. Elsewhere one can find some amplification of what Burke had in mind. He wrote in the *Reflections*, for instance: "Old establishments are tried by their effects. If the people are happy, united, wealthy, and powerful, we presume the rest. We conclude that to be good from whence good is derived."[8] But there was room for more than one opinion about how happy and united and wealthy and powerful the people actually were. Stanlis rightly points out that the Benthamites' conception of "the people" differed from that of Burke: "Mill's discussion assumes a conception of 'the people' that is purely numerical: he shows no awareness of Burke's principle of the *corporate* people." The Benthamites did think of the people more in quantitative terms—more in terms of the individuals who composed the community, with each person's happiness being considered of equal weight—than as a fictitious entity; and their approach meant that in evaluating the English system of government they needed to ask how far,

5. *The Speeches of the Right Honourable Edmund Burke*, 4 vols. (London: Longman, 1816), 1:140.
6. *The Works of the Right Honourable Edmund Burke*, 8 vols. (London: J. Dodsley, 1792-1827), 5:390.
7. Ibid., 3:124-125.
8. Ibid., 3:227-228.

to what proportion of the people, its benefits really extended.[9] To them, Burke seemed too inclined to evade this kind of test by using vague phrases and lofty assertions.[10]

They regarded him, in fact, more as a rhetorician than as a philosopher. According to Bentham he was a master of "the art of misrepresentation,"[11] a purveyor of "aerial generalities" rather than of solidly grounded arguments, a man of "brilliant talents" who had made himself "the agent and spokesman of *the ruling few*."[12] This view is patently one-sided; but there are elements of truth in it which ought to be recognized. However much one admires the wisdom that Burke's pamphlets and speeches contain, one has to remember that he *was* an orator and polemicist rather than a philosophical writer.[13] One needs to be on the watch for the devices commonly used in these genres of composition—the evasion of a difficulty, for example, by a bland assumption or an emotive phrase; and one also needs to be constantly aware of the party-political and class position he represented. On the part of James Mill, it was surely legitimate to consider that there were facile and tendentious aspects of Burke's thought which could and should be identified by means of close critical analysis. The passage in which he examined Burke's doctrines of prescription and presumption did, as my article suggested, misinterpret Burke on certain points,[14] but it also drew attention to some obscurities and questionable assumptions in the

9. For example, in response to Mr. Justice Ashhurst's assertion that "no man is so low as not to be within the law's protection," Bentham maintained (*Works*, 5:232-233) that in practice ninety-nine men out of every hundred were excluded from such protection by considerations of expense and that this was likely to remain true until the system of government was reformed.

10. As when he declared in the *Reflections* (*Works*, 3:87) that "our representation has been found perfectly adequate to all the purposes for which a representation of the people can be desired or devised."

11. Bentham wrote in his memorandum book (*Works*, 10:510): "*Logic*, alias *Metaphysics*, is the art and science whereby clearness, correctness, completeness and connexity are given to ideas.... 'I hate metaphysics,' quoth Edmund Burke in his pamphlet on the French Revolution. He may safely be believed. He had good cause to hate it. The power he trusted to was *oratory—rhetoric*—the art of misrepresentation—the art of misdirecting the judgment by agitating and inflaming the passions."

12. Ibid., 5:297, 301; Bentham Papers, box 166, fo. 257, University College, London.

13. For the view that Burke's mode of argument was essentially that of an orator rather than of a philosopher, see a suggestive book review by Donald C. Bryant in *Quarterly Journal of Speech* 47 (1961):202.

14. Mill assumed (understandably, I think) that Burke was putting forward a prescriptive theory of government. But I agree with David Cameron that in fact "Burke did not hold a prescriptive theory of political obligation, although he sometimes appeared to": i. e., he did not subscribe to "the view that a government can be legitimized by virtue of its longevity alone." See *The Social Thought of Rousseau and Burke* (London: Weidenfeld and Nicolson, 1973), pp. 153, 221.

piece concerned: for example, the uncertain import and pertinence of the legal term prescription when applied to politics, and the disputable supposition that long usage is a presumption of choice by the nation at large rather than by its rulers. One may add that with regard to the substantive issue that lay behind the disagreement between Burke and Mill, the question of parliamentary reform, even commentators sympathetic to Burke are disinclined to defend the rigidly conservative position he took up[15] (though it should in fairness be said that the need for reform was less palpable in the 1780s than it was to be at the time of Mill's critique).

Peter Stanlis in the latter part of his article moves on to consider views I have expressed regarding his own interpretation of Burke as a natural law thinker; and here he disagrees with me more sharply than he does with my comments "on Mill on Burke on prescription." In particular, he rejects my use of the term "aprioristic" to describe the natural law tradition to which he assigns Burke. In using this term I had in mind Stanlis's own statement that "Burke regarded the Natural Law as a divinely ordained imperative ethical norm which, without consulting man, fixed forever his moral duties in civil society."[16] In his "Reflections on Dinwiddy" Stanlis says that, according to Burke, "the moral natural law was ... anything but a priori, because it was perceived by men out of their divinely created moral nature in the empirical events of history, in the fulfilment or violation of ethical norms in human affairs." But it is surely not Stanlis's contention that in Burke's view the ethical norms themselves were *derivable from* history; indeed he quotes a letter in which Burke specifically denied that his principles were "formed out of events ... either present or past," and Stanlis himself has written elsewhere: "The ultimate basis of Burke's political conservatism is not to be found in history, but in his moral principles. ... History is descriptive, not normative. ... Burke drew his absolute ethical principles from the natural law."[17] In view of these quotations it is hard to see how he can object to my inference that the ethical tradition to which he claims Burke's adherence is an aprioristic one.[18] The fact that it is only

15. See Francis P. Canavan, *The Political Reason of Edmund Burke* (Durham: Duke University Press, 1960), p. 166: "Burke's fear of the consequences of constitutional change verged upon morbidity and cannot be taken with full seriousness."

16. *Edmund Burke and the Natural Law* (Ann Arbor: University of Michigan Press, 1958), p. 73.

17. "The Basis of Burke's Political Conservatism," *Modern Age* 5 (1961):265, 268.

18. I may add that I am not the only person who has been led by Stanlis's own writings to apply the term "aprioristic" to his conception of natural law. See C. P.

in the context of "empirical events" that one can judge human conduct does not alter the fact that the principles on which such judgments are based—"the infinitely fixed moral norms of the Natural Law," as Stanlis has called them[19]—are regarded as having an existence and validity anterior to the events themselves.

It is true that the substance of these principles is, in Stanlis's interpretation, undefined. He claims that Burke's faith in the natural law gave his political ideas an order and cohesion which they would otherwise have lacked.[20] But what the ethical norms of natural law actually were is not explained (or not explicable), and C. B. Macpherson has made the point that it is not difficult for Stanlis to present Burke as consistently loyal to the natural law when that law is "stripped of any specific moral principles."[21] Macpherson—a scholar, one need hardly say, who is far from sympathetic to Burke—accepts that he relied heavily on the concept of a divine law but considers that he used this concept as an obscurantist device to sanctify the traditional order and to place his own ideology beyond the reach of rational criticism.[22] I should contend, however, that although Burke did believe in God and did believe that religion was necessary to society, the case he made for political conservatism was less dependent than either Stanlis or Macpherson suggests on transcendent, or obscurantist, appeals to an unspecific law of nature.

While he did make occasional and allusive references to a higher law, his contribution as a political thinker surely lies in the realm of what he called "practical wisdom." The function of politics, he recognized, was "to find out proper means" towards the ends of government and "to employ them with effect." The political institutions and practices that he favored were defended less on the grounds that they accorded with natural law than on the grounds that they were conducive to the "social ends" which "political

Courtney, "Edmund Burke and the Enlightenment," in *Statesmen, Scholars and Merchants: Essays in Eighteenth-Century History Presented to Dame Lucy Sutherland,* ed. Anne Whiteman, J. S. Bromley, and P. G. M. Dickson (Oxford: Clarendon Press, 1973), pp. 305-306.

19. *Burke and the Natural Law,* p. 208.

20. "The Basis of Burke's Political Conservatism," p. 270.

21. "Edmund Burke and the New Conservatism," *Science and Society* 22 (1958): 235.

22. Ibid., pp. 231-239; Macpherson, "Edmund Burke," *Transactions of the Royal Society of Canada* 53 (1959): 19-26. Another scholar sees Burke's appeals to the natural law as essentially a polemical or rhetorical device to "reinforce the status" of the principles he was enunicating. See Frank O'Gorman, *Edmund Burke: His Political Philosophy* (London: George Allen and Unwin, 1973), pp. 19, 104-105.

arrangement" should promote.[23] It is true that his conception of the ends of government was less well defined than (for example) Bentham's. When he said in the "Speech on a Reform of the Representation" that "that which is good for the community, and good for every individual in it . . . is the *desideratum,*" it was not clear exactly what he meant by "good." Still, it *was* by reference to the good of the community—even if this was not something that he defined precisely—that his political judgments were apparently made: as he wrote in the *Appeal from the New to the Old Whigs,* "What in the result is likely to produce evil, is politically false: that which is productive of good, politically is true."[24]

I have argued in a previous article that Burke's mode of evaluating institutions and policies was not as different from that of the Benthamites as Stanlis has suggested, however different his conclusions were from theirs.[25] And although they regarded him as a partial and evasive thinker, many of his ideas did have at the empirical level a cogency for which, by their own criteria, they should have shown more respect: for instance, a more receptive reading of Burke's theory of presumption would have given Bentham and James Mill a more realistic appreciation of the difficulties and dangers of political change.[26] Stanlis misunderstands me, however, when he says at the end of his "Reflections" that in my earlier article there was little or nothing to convince him that "Burke was a utilitarian in his political philosophy." I could have wished that instead of focusing his attention mainly on my piece about Burke and James Mill, he had confronted my earlier article more directly and had addressed himself to the arguments there presented. Had he done so he would have realized that that article did not maintain "Burke was a utilitarian." Burke *has* at times been described as a utilitarian, but the scholars who so described him used the term in a somewhat loose sense.

23. *Works,* 3:58; 1:498-499; 3:224.
24. Ibid., 5:393; 3:477. My argument does not, of course, imply that Burke's political thought lacked a moral basis. He did regard politics as inseparable from morals; but so does any thinker—such as Bentham—who judges what is politically right and wrong by reference to a moral standard. Stanlis appears to argue (*Burke and the Natural Law,* p. 120) that Burke's "principle of prudence" was "moral" while "utilitarian expediency" was merely "intellectual." But the Benthamites *were* normative thinkers, and the fact that Burke claimed divine sanction for his moral views while the Benthamites made no such claim for theirs should not be taken to mean that his political thought had a moral basis while theirs did not.
25. "Utility and Natural Law in Burke's Thought: A Reconsideration," *Studies in Burke and His Time* 16(1974-1975):105-128.
26. See J. S. Mill, "Remarks on Bentham's Philosophy," in E. L. Bulwer, *England and the English,* 2 vols. (London: Richard Bentley, 1833), 2:243.

According to a recent definition, utilitarianism in its classic (Benthamite) form can be expressed as the combination of two principles, the hedonist principle and the consequentialist principle.[27] Hardly anyone, so far as I know, has contended that Burke was a hedonist—that he believed that the only thing that was good in itself was pleasure. He *has* been interpreted, however, as someone who judged institutions and policies essentially in terms of their consequences (or expected consequences) for human welfare; and this was the view which—without maintaining that he was a sufficiently systematic or consistent thinker to be easily classified—I attempted to support in my "Reconsideration." Until the case presented in that article is directly challenged, it would be gratuitous to enlarge on it further in this journal.

27. Anthony Quinton, *Utilitarian Ethics* (London:Macmillan, 1973), p. 1.

15

Bentham's Transition to Political Radicalism, 1809-10

It is known that in 1789-90 Jeremy Bentham, having previously been more or less uncritical of the existing forms of government in European states, was briefly converted to democratic views. In the opening year of the French Revolution he decided that the Bourbon régime could not be renovated by any but the most sweeping reforms, and he wrote an essay for the National Assembly arguing that the French should adopt a system of representation based on a wide suffrage and the secret ballot.[1] He did not at this time regard such radical measures as necessary in England; but shortly afterwards, as Mary Mack has shown, his examination of English institutions revealed so many abuses and inadequacies that he came to see parliamentary reform as the indispensable prelude to other changes, and in 1790 he sketched out a treatise on this question which anticipated many of the points he was to make in his first published work on the subject twenty-seven years later. Mrs. Mack says that Bentham's conversion to democracy in 1790 was "the climactic change in his thought," and she refutes the "fiction"—repeated, as she says, by Bain, Halévy, Bertrand Russell, Crane Brinton, Sabine, and Plamenatz—that James Mill converted Bentham to democracy in 1809.[2] Yet she admits that owing to the alarming course taken by the French Revolution the original conversion was very ephemeral; three or four years later Bentham was writing *against* parliamentary reform,[3] and he subsequently forgot that he had ever written the fragment of 1790 in support of it.[4] So the fact surely remains that the really fruitful turning-point in the development of his political thought came in 1809, when he began the process of drafting and redrafting that was to culminate in the works on parliamentary reform published in 1817 and 1819.[5] Some attention has been paid to this turning-point by Halévy and Michael Roberts, but neither of them used the unpublished notes and drafts in Bentham's papers which throw much light on the evolution of his ideas.[6] Professor Roberts' section on the *Parliamentary Reform Catechism* uses the pamphlet of 1817

[1] E. Halévy, *La Formation du Radicalisme philosophique* (3 vols., Paris, 1901), I, 455ff.

[2] Mary Mack, *Jeremy Bentham: an Odyssey of Ideas 1748-1792* (London, 1962), 17, 416, 432-40.

[3] *Works of Jeremy Bentham*, ed. Sir John Bowring (11 vols., Edinburgh, 1838-43), X, 293. University College, London, Bentham MSS, box 44, fos. 2-5. Cf. J. H. Burns, "Bentham and the French Revolution," *Transactions of the Royal Historical Society*, 5th series, **16** (1966), 110-12.

[4] Bentham MSS, box 44, fo. 1. Mack, *op. cit.*, 441.

[5] *Plan of Parliamentary Reform, in the form of a Catechism* (London, 1817). *Bentham's Radical Reform Bill, with extracts from the Reasons* (London, 1819).

[6] Halévy, *The Growth of Philosophic Radicalism*, trans. Mary Morris (2nd ed., London, 1934), 256 *seq.*; and M. Roberts, *The Whig Party 1807-1812* (London, 1939), 259 *seq.* Nor are these papers made use of in K. M. Adams, "How the Benthamites became Democrats," *Journal of Social Philosophy and Jurisprudence*, 7 (1942), 161-71.

and discusses it in the context of the reform movement of 1809; but although the catechism itself (which covers only about a dozen pages in Bentham's collected works) was written in 1809,[7] the long introduction[8] to which Roberts' points chiefly refer was written considerably later, in 1816–17. What Bentham did write (in addition to the catechism) in the twelve months or so after August 1809 was a total of some thousand pages of draft material[9] for a projected work on parliamentary reform, plus five hundred pages on the subject of sinecures.[10] This last group of papers may originally have been intended as part of the work on reform of parliament,[11] but came to form a separate study. The other papers carried the general heading "Parliamentary Reform" and were ranged under three principal sub-headings: "Necessity," "Influence," and "Plan." Bentham apparently designed the work in three main sections, one on the reasons why reform was necessary, another on the various kinds of influence that could be exerted over voters and representatives and which of these were legitimate, and another on the actual measures of reform which he wished to see effected. The more detailed arrangement of the work will not be discussed in this article, nor can any attempt be made here to provide a general analysis of the whole body of papers. But the reasons for Bentham's conversion—or return—to political radicalism will be examined, together with the main features of the new doctrine he was shaping in these lengthy drafts of 1809–10.

The extent of James Mill's influence over Bentham in 1809 is not directly deducible from the latter's manuscripts; but some new evidence can be produced to confirm Halévy's inference that Mill's entry into his life in 1808 was a crucial factor in turning Bentham into a radical. The one piece of evidence that Halévy gave for this supposition was a passage in an article on Spanish American politics which Mill wrote for the *Edinburgh Review* of January 1809—a passage in which he made a novel attempt (Halévy said) "to base the theory of representative government on the principle of utility."[12] In fact there is a somewhat earlier and perhaps more striking adumbration of the Utilitarian argument for representative government in an article Mill wrote for the same review in October of the previous year. He maintained in this essay ("Leckie on the Foreign Policy of Great Britain") that the condition of Sicily showed the inevitable effects of a political system which allowed one order of the citizens to pursue its own ends without any check or control from the rest. "The natural feelings of men impel them to be much more solicitous for their own interests than for the interests of others," he wrote.

Whenever the joint affairs of a community are not managed by the joint influence, fairly compounded of all the orders of which it consists—whenever the small number acquire the whole, or the greater part of the direction of the common interests, they are sure to draw towards themselves the advantages, and thrust upon the multitude the burdens of the social union, to the utmost of their power.

---

[7] Bentham, *Works*, III, 435, 458.

[8] Drafts in Bentham MSS, boxes 125, 129(a), 129(b).

[9] Interspersed with later material in Bentham MSS, boxes 125–30. [10] *Ibid*., box 147.

[11] Some of the early pages (e.g., fos. 109–16) were re-headed "Sinecures" after being initially headed "Parliamentary Reform." [12] Halévy, *op. cit.*, 257.

He went on to say that even in England since the Revolution of 1688, despite the existence of more safeguards for the people's interests than had ever been established in any other government, there had been a tendency for the aristocracy to increase its power and exploit its position. He argued that the system of taxation, to a much greater extent than was generally supposed, favored the higher orders and threw the main burden onto the middle and lower; that the composition of the House of Commons had become less dependent on the voice of the people; and that the enormous revenue of the government, which was mostly taken from the pockets of the people, mostly found its way into the pockets of members of the higher ranks by whom so many of the lucrative offices were held.[13] He was also convinced, as is clear from other passages which he wrote in the years 1808–09, that the preponderance of landowners in parliament had produced legislation which favored the landed interest at the expense of other sections of the community.[14] Of course his ideas were not wholly novel. The Manchester radical Thomas Cooper had written in 1792: "It will be found on examination (whether pursued with a view to mere theory, or the evidence of past facts), that every government has been, and will be conducted for the advantage in the first instance of the *governors,* whoever they are: and the whole secret [of good government] lies in making those the actual governors, whether directly or indirectly, whose interests and welfare are intended to be the main object of the government."[15]

Similarly Bentham had written in 1790 that "the stricter the dependence of the governors on the governed, the better will the government be."[16] In 1808–09, however, it seems that Mill led the way in formulating, or reformulating, the basic argument on which the Utilitarian case for democracy was to be built. Bentham himself did not start writing about parliamentary reform until the summer of 1809—and here there is a notable coincidence of dates that tends to confirm the theory of Mill's influence. Bentham had rented a house at Oxted as a summer residence, and James Mill and his family joined him there for a two-month visit at the end of July. It can be seen from the dated sheets on which Bentham wrote his drafts that it was just at this time, in the first half of August, that he began applying himself intensively to the reform question.[17]

Another factor which may have been important in changing the character of Bentham's politics was the impact of events in Spain and Spanish America. Brougham and Jeffrey, in the famous "Don Cevallos" article in the *Edinburgh*

[13]*Edinburgh Review,* 13 (Oct. 1808), 196–98. The article is only tentatively attributed to Mill in *The Wellesley Index of Victorian Periodicals,* vol. I, ed. Walter E. Houghton (Toronto, 1966), 444; but a comparison between the passage quoted above and that quoted by Halévy from Mill's article of Jan. 1809—together with a reference to "his [i.e. Mill's] Leckie" in a letter from Jeffrey to Brougham (19 Oct. 1809, University College, London, Brougham MSS)—leaves no doubt as to the authorship.

[14]James Mill, *Selected Economic Writings,* ed. Donald Winch (Edinburgh, 1966), 9–10, 96. *Eclectic Review,* 5 (Jan. 1809), 51.

[15]Thomas Cooper, *A Reply to Mr. Burke's Invective against Mr. Cooper and Mr. Watt, in the House of Commons, on the 30th of April, 1792* (Manchester, 1792), 27. George Dyer, *The Complaints of the Poor People of England* (London, 1793), 12.

[16]Mack, *op. cit.,* 455.

[17]Alexander Bain, *James Mill* (London, 1882), 72–73, 99–101. Bentham MSS, box 104, fo. 78; box 126, fos. 406 *seq.;* box 127, fos. 168ff.

Review (Oct. 1808), maintained that the Spanish rising against Bonapartist rule had decisively shifted the balance of political sentiment in England away from anti-Jacobin alarmism and in the direction of liberal sympathies; "the cause of freedom and reform," they wrote, was now on a better footing than it had been even at the beginning of the French Revolution.[18] James Mill and Bentham's friend Dumont were both enthusiastic about the liberation of Spain and the Spanish colonies. Dumont began revising his translation of Bentham's *Political Tactics* in the hope that it would be of use to Spanish statesmen, and Mill wrote a spirited article in January 1809 called "The Emancipation of Spanish America." At the same period Bentham himself seriously considered going to live in Mexico, and there was even a wild idea that his American friend Aaron Burr would set up an independent empire there with Bentham as his legislator. In 1809 Bentham was in contact with Don Gaspard de Jovellanos, a leading member of the Spanish Junta, and with General Francisco de Miranda, soon to become the first ruler of an independent Venezuela; indeed in August Mill wrote to Miranda at Bentham's request inviting him to join them at Oxted.[19] The drafts on parliamentary reform which Bentham was composing at this time do not show a direct connection between his new interest in this subject and his interest in constitutional renovation in Spain and the establishment of new states in Spanish America. But it is likely that such a connection existed—just as in 1789–90 his concern with the remodeling of political institutions in France had made him look with a more radical eye at English institutions.

In England, in 1809, there was a marked revival of radical feeling, but this was due less to events abroad than to a sensation at home—the investigation into the conduct of the Duke of York as Commander-in-Chief. The inquiry ended in a storm of indignation against the House of Commons when the House acquitted the Duke of corruption in spite of a widespread popular belief that he was guilty. Bentham was not particularly stirred by this affair—in fact he described the instances of corruption and misgovernment which it revealed as "comparatively trifling."[20] He did pay some attention to current controversy on reform,[21] but on the whole the domestic events and abuses which affected him were different from those which lay behind the radical agitation in the country. This is clear from some jottings he made, before he settled down to elaborate his ideas on reform, in June and July 1809: especially from a list dated 4 July setting out the grievances which in his view made political reform necessary.[22] He included sinecures, which were a subject of public and parliamentary interest at that period;[23] but most of the grievances he mentioned

[18] *Edinburgh Review, loc. cit.,* 221–23.

[19] Dumont to Bentham, 15 Apr. and 26 Aug., 5 Sept. 1808, British Library Additional MSS [Add.MSS] 33544, fos. 356, 368, 375, 384–85. *Edinburgh Review,* 13 (Jan. 1809), 277–311. Bentham, *Works,* X, 432–48. W. Spence Robertson, *Life of Miranda,* 2 vols. (Chapel Hill, 1929), II, 63.   [20] *Works,* X, 449.

[21] See the short list of recent publications on the subject which he made out on 25 June, Bentham MSS, box 127, fol. 116. Note also his copy of Curwen's Bribery Act of June 1809, and his dismissive remarks about it (*ibid.,* box 125, fo. 411; box 127, fo. 62).

[22] *Ibid.,* box 127, fo. 117.

[23] Roberts, *op. cit.,* 183–90. Bentham's unpublished work on sinecures, written in the Spring of 1810, consisted partly of an extended critique of the third report of the Com-

were more idiosyncratic and more specifically related to the law: e.g., "Virtual Outlawry of the bulk of the people. Preference given by the Laws to the superior to the prejudice of the middle and inferior ranks. . . . The statute law in a state of chaos. . . . On the occasion of Scotch Reform among Commissioners not one who had manifested any signs of his having applied his mind to the subject."

This last point referred to the commission on the judicature of Scotland, a subject in which Bentham was deeply interested. Since June 1806, when Grenville had introduced resolutions in the House of Lords as a preliminary to a legislative reform of civil justice in Scotland, Bentham had devoted much of his time to working out proposals of his own for Scottish legal reform;[24] and the treatment of this question by the legislature had become for him something of a test case, a trial of parliament's goodwill and effectiveness. In the three years or so *before* 1806, Bentham's chief concern had been his analysis of the law of evidence, and in the course of this study he had become more than ever convinced that the obscurities, complexities, delays, and inordinate expenses which characterized English legal procedure were the outcome of the "sinister interest" of the legal profession. The reason, in his view, why the system was so bad was that "the *power* found itself in company with the *interest,* and consequently the *will,* to produce as bad a system as the people, with the legislature at their head, could in their primeval, and as yet but little ameliorated, state of relative ignorance and helplessness, be brought, by the utmost stretch of artifice, to endure."[25] Bentham had long regarded it as axiomatic that individuals or groups, if entrusted with irresponsible power, could only be expected to use that power for the promotion of their own interests. He noted in 1805 that this axiom applied to government as well as to any other branch of human activity; but at that stage he still regarded the legislature as a body sufficiently identified with the public to moderate in some degree the exploitation which the public suffered at the hands of lawyers: it provided some protection by "interfering for the benefit of the people, and removing more or less of the mountain of abuse and injustice which the fraternity of lawyers were so constantly employed in raising up in the pursuit of their own sinister ends."[26] In reaching the very different view of parliament which he expressed in 1809, he was definitely influenced by its behavior over the Scottish judicature question. His pamphlet on *Scotch Reform* (1808) had been intended as a contribution to parliament's consideration of the subject,[27] but no official, and little unofficial,

---

mons select committee on public expenditure (presented in June 1808 and considered in a committee of the whole house in June 1809); and partly of Bentham's own more rigorous analysis of the issues which the committee had discussed. See Bentham MSS, box 147; Parliamentary Papers 1808, III, 257 *seq.*; *Cobbett's Parliamentary Debates,* XIV, 862–81, 957–60.

[24] *Parliamentary Debates,* VII, 730–36. Bentham MSS, boxes 82, 91–94, 168. *Scotch Reform* (1808), *Works,* V, 1–53. [25] *Works,* V, 4.

[26] Bentham MSS, box 47, fos. 176–77.

[27] *Works,* V, 3. He had wished, through Sir Samuel Romilly, to offer the House of Commons his gratuitous services in preparing a code of law for Scotland; but Romilly had told him that—the temper and principles of the House of Commons being what they were—such a disinterested offer would be "absolutely incredible" and would excite nothing but ridicule (*ibid.,* X, 432).

notice had been taken of it.[28] Lord Eldon had carried a small measure of reform in 1808, but Bentham regarded it as nugatory;[29] and although a commission had been appointed to investigate the need for further reforms it appeared from discussions in parliament in 1809 that this body had not yet got down to business.[30] Bentham was shocked by the general perfunctoriness of the proceedings—and particularly by the threadbare arguments which Perceval and Robert Dundas were able to get away with in the House of Commons in replying to Francis Horner's criticisms of abuses in the Court of Session.[31] By the summer of 1809 he was convinced that what he had seen as a marvellous opportunity of purifying and rationalizing the law of Scotland would in fact produce no improvement of consequence. The legislature, he now saw, habitually deferred to the lawyers within it on any legal question, and would carry no measure relating to the law without the lawyers' sanction.[32]

This realization had major implications for Bentham's whole strategy as a reformer of the law. He had always believed that what was necessary to reduce English law to order and simplicity was codification—the conversion of jurisprudential or "judge-made" law (i.e., common law) into enacted or statute law.[33] He had recognized that statute law was itself unsatisfactory in its present state,[34] but he had assumed that its imperfections were remediable. By 1809, however, he had lost any hope he may have had that parliament would one day embark on the task of codification; and he had decided that the chaotic state of statute law arose endemically from the fact that the unreformed parliament had no more interest than the judges did in making the law intelligible to the public.[35] For the notion that the legislature had provided some check to the growth of legal abuses, he now substituted the theory that abuses in the law and abuses in parliament were symbiotic. Members of parliament were themselves beneficiaries of abuses and were united in one "confederated sinister interest" with others who benefited from abuses in other shapes.[36] This partnership he saw as deriving from the fact that those who profit from a particular species of abuse will naturally join in the protection of other abuses from which they draw no direct profit—both "on account of the mischief done in the way of precedent to their interest in any instance in which abuse in any shape receives correction, and in consideration of the assistance they may expect to secure in return, for the eventual protection of abuse in that special shape in which they possess their special interest."[37] Thus parliament and the legal profession (directly linked by the lawyers who had seats in parliament) were allied against the people, and so

---

[28]But cf. James Mill's enthusiastic review in *Annual Review and History of Literature*, 7 (1808), 198–203.   [29]48 Geo. III, c. 151. *Works*, V, 47.

[30]*Parliamentary Debates*, XIV, 405–08, 889–95.

[31]*Ibid.*, XIV, 1016–18. Bentham MSS, box 127, fo. 114.

[32]Cf. *Rationale of Judicial Evidence, Works*, VI, 207.

[33]See, for instance, Bentham MSS, box 49, fos. 291–95.

[34]*A Comment on the Commentaries*, ed. C. W. Everett (Oxford, 1928), chaps. x and xii.

[35]For further remarks about the "disorderliness" and other imperfections of English statute law, see *Nomography, Works*, III, 238–41.

[36]Bentham MSS, box 126, fo. 304.   [37]*Ibid.*, box 125, fo. 30.

long as this alliance was allowed to subsist the law would remain a mystery which only lawyers could penetrate and justice would remain too expensive for any but the rich to obtain. This brings one back to Bentham's remark about "outlawry," which he amplified in a passage dated 14 August 1809:

By the systematical improbity of the governing part of the fraternity of lawyers on all benches and in both houses, the factitious expense of an appeal to justice has been swollen to such an amount as to have placed the great body of the people—including not only all day labourers and journeymen in husbandry and other occupations but classes even superior to these—in a state of perpetual outlawry.[38]

The fact that ninety-nine men out of a hundred were too poor to obtain the protection of the law was something he had been aware of for many years;[39] what he now perceived was that the evil had its roots in parliament as well as in the courts.

The other aspect of the partnership, clinching for Bentham the theory of the mutual reinforcement of sinister interests, was the support given by the lawyers to the political establishment in its resistance to political reform. The lawyers had an obvious interest in the survival of a political régime that was remote from popular control and hostile to the spirit of inquiry; and their important contribution to the suppression of criticism of the system was brought forcibly to Bentham's attention by his study of the law of libel in the spring of 1809. This study, provoked by the numerous prosecutions for libel which were set on foot in the winter of 1808–09 by the Attorney-General Sir Vicary Gibbs,[40] resulted in a work entitled *The Elements of the Art of Packing, as applied to Special Juries, particularly in cases of Libel Law.*[41] In the course of writing it Bentham became convinced that the lawyers had done all they could, through the authoritarian interpretation of the law of libel and the packing of special juries, to make the system of government effectively despotic. It only required a Prime Minister and Attorney-General who were determined to make full use of the weapons thus provided, for the freedom of the press to be completely extinguished: "by law there exists no more liberty of the press in England than in Morocco."[42] Earlier, Bentham had regarded a free press as one of the essential instruments whereby existing (undemocratic) régimes might be induced to govern in the general interest,[43] and there can be no doubt that his fears about the undermining of this sanction formed another major cause of his conversion to parliamentary reform.[44]

There is one passage in Bentham's papers, headed "J. B.'s quondam opinions concerning reform" (28 Jan. 1810), which explains his conversion in

---

[38] *Ibid.*, box 127, fo. 186.   [39] *Truth versus Ashurst, Works*, V, 233.

[40] *The Times*, 20 Feb. 1809; G. P. Stout, *The Political History of Leigh Hunt's Examiner* (St. Louis, 1949), 6–7.

[41] *Works*, V, 61–186; Bentham MSS, box 26, fos. 66–136. Because of the danger of exposing both author and bookseller to prosecution, the work was not published until 1821.

[42] Bentham MSS, box 128, fo. 123; and box 126, fos. 56–57.   [43] Mack, *op. cit.*, 315–17.

[44] For direct links between *The Elements of the Art of Packing* and Bentham's work on parliamentary reform: Bentham MSS, box 129(a), fos. 5, 26; *Works*, V, 182–86.

more general terms. He wrote here (apparently without any recollection of his earlier conversion) that he had had no very definite ideas on the subject until he recently applied his mind to it. If anything, his inclination had been against reform because of the inadequacy of the arguments he had heard advanced in its favor. It had been alleged that the Crown could maintain through influence a constant majority in the House of Commons, but this had been contradicted by certain changes of administration that took place in opposition to the King's wishes; confidence in the King's ministers was from time to time withdrawn when some serious mischief or danger jolted members of parliament out of their customary acquiescence in the measures of government. However, Bentham had come to realize that although "ruinous mischiefs" might be thus prevented those that were not ruinous were allowed to abound, and he concluded that while it was not in the power of the King and his ministers to carry everything that was bad, it *was* in their power to prevent everything that was good.[45] No doubt the frustration of his Panopticon scheme was one of the main things he had in mind. Indeed John Plamenatz has gone so far as to state that "his experiences in this matter converted Bentham to democracy."[46] This would seem to be an oversimplification, in that the scheme had fallen through several years earlier (soon after the turn of the century) and as has been suggested above there were various other factors that were more immediately responsible for convincing him of the need for political reform in 1809. However, it has been shown by L. J. Hume that the affair did in some important respects prepare his mind for this reorientation. He felt that the project had been killed by the personal influence of the King and of certain aristocrats, and that in failing to bring the Panopticon into being in accordance with the Penitentiary Act of 1794 the executive had blatantly defied the authority of parliament.[47] The elimination of sinister influence and the real subordination of the executive to the legislature were to be among the chief objectives of his parliamentary reform programme.

Moving on from the causes of his conversion to the actual measures he proposed, one finds these set out in the *Parliamentary Reform Catechism*. He divided them into two categories. First, he listed the measures required to ensure that members of parliament had the necessary probity (i.e. devotion to the public interest), intellectual aptitude, and assiduity. These measures were: the disqualification of placemen from voting in the House of Commons (though official persons from each department should be allowed to sit in the House and participate in debates); annual elections; the prompt and authentic publication of parliamentary debates; and regulations to ensure the constant and universal attendance of members. Secondly, he listed the means of obviating the "inconveniences" of elections and election judicature: a "uniformly large" electorate in each constituency; a suffrage conferred on those who paid certain taxes to a certain amount; secret voting; and the establishment of two classes of constituency, those for "territory" and those for "popu-

---

[45] Bentham MSS, box 126, fos. 98–104.

[46] John Plamenatz, *The English Utilitarians* (2nd edition, Oxford, 1958), 63. Cf. Gertrude Himmelfarb, *Victorian Minds* (London, 1968), 73.

[47] L. J. Hume, "Bentham's Panopticon: an administrative history—II," *Historical Studies*, **16** (1974), 39–40, 50–54. I am grateful to Dr. Hume for his helpful comments on a draft of my paper.

lation," with the latter (i.e., urban constituencies) accounting for a third of the total number of seats.[48] Halévy makes a great deal of the fact that the extension of the suffrage and the redistribution of seats were included in the secondary list, and were apparently recommended more as measures of electoral convenience than as essential moves towards democracy.[49] It is true that in 1809 Bentham's ideas were not as positively democratic as they later became: in 1817 the remedies he proposed were placed in an entirely different order, and by then he had rejected the notion of a property or fiscal qualification and favored "virtual universality of suffrage."[50] However, it is clear from his unpublished writings that even in 1809 he regarded an extension of the franchise as one of the crucial means of ensuring that "the greatest happiness of the greatest possible number shall be the object really and constantly aimed at" by the state.[51] The reason for the priority which he gave in the catechism to measures such as the exclusion of placemen and annual elections was his particular mistrust of the influence of the Crown. He was so concerned about the ability of the Crown to corrupt the representatives of the people that he laid special emphasis on measures designed to counteract that corruption. As he wrote in a passage on "Influence," he thought that the most effective safeguard would be "dependence of agents for their situation on their principals, dependence secured by annual re-elections";[52] the exclusion of placemen, though important, would not by itself be sufficient because "a member is capable of being as effectually corrupted by a place or pension or other object expected by him for another as by the like object of desire expected by him for himself."[53]

Bentham's attitude towards the Crown was one of the respects in which he differed most significantly from the contemporary reform movement. Sir Francis Burdett and his followers (partly it would seem in order to safeguard themselves from charges of Jacobinism and disloyalty, and partly to differentiate themselves from the Whigs, whose reformism generally took the shape of attacks on the influence of the Crown) had adopted certain ideas that were reminiscent of Bolingbrokean Toryism. Burdett's speeches in 1809 developed the theme that it was not the Crown but the "borough-mongering oligarchy" that was threatening to subvert the constitution; indeed the borough-mongers were encroaching on the rightful prerogative of the Crown as well as on the rights of the people, and King and people should join forces in order to rid the constitution of this incubus.[54] Bentham, on the other hand, attributed great malignancy to the Crown, asserting that by means of its influence, plus the support of those who had a common interest with the King in the protection of abuses, the monarch could generally impose his will on the House of Commons.[55] That in any matter of importance the King's will *ought* to prevail Bentham strongly denied. He denied it partly on principle, on the grounds that the "irremediable unfitness of the King, as King, to govern" was the funda-

[48] *Works*, III, 540–41.
[49] Halévy, *op. cit.*, 259.
[50] *Works*, III, 425, 459–64.
[51] Bentham MSS, box 127, fo. 185.
[52] *Ibid.*, box 126, fo. 405.
[53] *Ibid.*, box 127, fo. 121.
[54] *A Full and Accurate Report of the Proceedings at the Crown and Anchor Tavern, on Monday, the 1st of May, 1809, relative to a Reform in the Commons House of Parliament* (London, 1809), 12. *Parliamentary Debates*, XIV, 1046–52.
[55] Bentham MSS, box 125, fos. 22 *seq.*

mental tenet of English limited monarchy,[56] and partly on the grounds that the present King could be no more relied upon than the general run of monarchs to pursue the public interest. In a caustic passage he drew attention to the danger inherent in the current practice of eulogizing the "good old King" and claiming special respect for his wishes. The danger, he said, lay in "disposing men to take the supposed personal will of the Monarch . . . for the rule of action and the standard of propriety"; and as an example of the pernicious consequences he maintained that over the question of Catholic Emancipation the interests of five or six million people in Ireland were being chronically sacrificed to the prejudices of one man.[57] Bentham may in fact have exaggerated the King's power, and his preoccupation with the "separate and sinister interest" of the King[58] may have somewhat obscured for him the broader conflict of *class* interests which Mill had recognized as the basic one. For Bentham the current political system was bad not so much because it concentrated legislative power in the hands of the representatives of a particular economic and social class, as because it concentrated influence and emoluments in the hands of the King and "his servants in all departments and ranks"—the partnership Bentham was later to describe as "C[orrupto]r-General & Co."[59] However, one should add that there was a certain element of class analysis in his concept of the "partnership interest":

the partnership interest, which the profiter by each abuse has in the maintenance of every other—the general bond of union by which all the members of the government together with the opulent members of the different classes of the community in the character of persons unduly favoured by the laws and habits of government in various parts of it are bound and linked to one another.[60]

Bentham's mistrust of monarchs was to lead him in due course to a firmly stated belief in republican government;[61] but in 1809, perhaps because he too wished to avoid being associated with revolutionary Jacobinism, he was anxious not to give the impression that his proposals for a reform of the representation had any republican motive or tendency. David Hume, in his essay "On the Independency of Parliament," had argued that if it were not for the fact that a considerable proportion of the members of the House of Commons were dependent on the Crown the House would overwhelm the other branches of the legislature and become absolute.[62] But Bentham said that this result would be likely only if the House of Commons were wholly independent of the people as well as of the Crown. He admitted that it would be easy enough for the *people,* if they wished, to destroy the monarchy and establish a

[56] *Ibid.,* box 128, fo. 81.
[57] *Ibid.,* box 128, fos. 78–92.   [58] *Ibid.,* box 125, fo. 36; box 129(a), fos. 158–69.
[59] *Ibid.,* box 129(a), fo. 55. *Works,* III, 442. Of the extent of this partnership Bentham wrote in Sept. 1809 (Bentham MSS, box 128, fo. 125): "So numerous is become the body of those dependents whose sinister interests are connected with and united to the sinister interest of the King, that the voice of this part of the people is become capable of raising itself to such a pitch as to be scarcely distinguishable from that of the whole."
[60] *Ibid.,* box 126, fo. 304.   [61] *Constitutional Code, Works,* IX, 127–45.
[62] David Hume, *Essays Moral, Political and Literary,* ed. T. H. Green and T. H. Grose, 2 vols. (London, 1882), I, 120–21.

commonwealth, but he claimed that in spite of the provocation caused by corruption they showed no disposition to do so; and he considered that the elimination of corrupt influence would be far more likely to increase popular attachment to the existing constitution than to diminish it.[63] However, what Hume had really been afraid of was less a change in the outward form of the constitution than an internal imbalance that would mean the constant prevalence of the will of the people over that of the King and the aristocracy: and this was precisely what Bentham was advocating. The kind of monarchy the latter envisaged in his reformed system of government seems to have been a largely formal one: the King's function should not be to govern, he said, but only to appoint from time to time such ministers as were "indicated to him . . . by the voice of the people faithfully represented in parliament."[64] Moreover, Bentham wrote that although he had no wish to do away with monarchy if it could be properly controlled, he would very much prefer a democratic commonwealth of the American type to the "mixt despotism composed of Monarchy and Aristocracy" which seemed to be approaching in England.[65]

It is clear from Bentham's papers that an important background factor in facilitating his transition to radicalism was the example of the United States. He had criticized the natural-rights basis of the American Declaration of Independence as he had the French Declaration of the Rights of Man; but the actual experience of America helped him to get over what had actually happened in France. It has been shown that his revulsion against popular government in the early 1790s was deeply felt, and far more than a "Fabian retreat": he could denounce Jacobinism with almost Burkean vehemence.[66] And yet by August 1809 he could see the anti-Jacobin reaction which the French Revolution had produced as one of its most unfortunate consequences. His friend and fellow law-reformer, Sir Samuel Romilly, wrote in 1807 of the pernicious effect the Revolution had had and was still having on all projects of reform;[67] and Bentham himself wrote two years later:

In the endless catalogue of calamities and mischiefs of which the French revolution has been the source not the least is that which consists in the severe and hitherto paralizing check given to reform—to peaceable and rational reform in every shape imaginable. . . . Scared out of our wits by distant anarchy we have been driven into the ever open arms of domestic despotism. . . . The genealogy of despotism is in this wise. The Marats and the Robespierres begat our Percevals and our Ellenboroughs. The blood of these martyrs was the seed of this our Church.[68]

Bentham now took the view that the example of the French Revolution was not really relevant to English conditions, at least was much less relevant than the American example. It was less relevant because when political reform was

[63] Bentham MSS, box 126, fos. 408–13.

[64] *Ibid.*, box 128, fo. 97. As for the House of Lords, he thought it worth retaining only if its powers were exercised "in maturing measures not in crushing them: in securing and not in obstructing the conformity of the will of the elected part of the trustees of the people to that of the body of their constituents" (*ibid.*, fo. 99).

[65] *Ibid.*, box 126, fos. 408–09.   [66] Burns, *loc. cit.*

[67] Sir S. Romilly, *Memoirs* (2nd ed. 3 vols., London, 1840), III, 399.

[68] Bentham MSS, box 127, fo. 47. Ellenborough was Lord Chief Justice, and notoriously severe in cases of seditious libel.

first attempted in France the people there were far less familiar with political matters, and were exposed to far greater oppression and provocation, than either the Americans in the 1770s or the British in 1809. Moreover the experience of the Americans was more pertinent because they were essentially Englishmen, men bred up in English traditions and habits of thought. The basic lesson of their history over the last quarter of a century was that when such men adopted a democratic system they were able to stop at that point— they did not allow themselves to be carried on into anarchy.[69] In 1789, when recommending representative government to the French, Bentham had conceded that one of the most cogent arguments against democracy was that by giving political power to "non-proprietors" it would undermine the security of property; and in 1791 it had been the growing danger to property that started to turn him against the Revolution.[70] In 1809, however, he invoked American experience to show that democracy did not necessarily involve expropriation, any more than it need involve conflagrations and massacres.[71] Furthermore, Bentham argued that if popular government could function in America without getting out of hand, it was even more likely to work smoothly in England as English society was more stratified, and "the unexceptionable species of influence, the influence of understanding on understanding possessed and exercised by the few over the many," was stronger than in America and provided a built-in safeguard against popular excesses.[72]

Besides these empirical arguments there was a more theoretical process of reasoning whereby Bentham superseded his earlier objection to popular government as tending to "subjugate the well informed to the ill informed classes of mankind."[73] When he began to write about parliamentary reform in August 1809 he still attached at least as much importance to the level of intelligence (or presumptive intelligence) in the electorate, as to its fidelity to the community at large. The problem, he wrote, in a section entitled "Qualification of Electors," was how to strike the right balance between intelligence and probity. In securing the latter, disposition to pursue the general interest, he did not feel that any reliance could be placed on altruism: men could only be relied upon to pursue their own interest. Thence he argued that the more widely the franchise was extended the more closely the agglomerated self-interest of the electors would approximate to the interest of the whole community, and the more probity could be expected in the electorate. On the other hand, he said, the further down one went "in the scale of wealth, and thence of mental culture," the more one would have to sacrifice in terms of intelligence, and the more danger there would be that through too many people

[69] *Ibid.*, box 127, fos. 38–42. One should add that there were others at this time, with more direct knowledge of American politics than Bentham had, who regarded the American experience as a strong argument *against* popular government. E.g., Earl of Selkirk, *A Letter to John Cartwright, Esq., on the subject of Parliamentary Reform* (London, 1809), 6–8.   [70]Mack, *op. cit.*, 17, 452–53. Burns, *ubi supra*, 109 and n.

[71]Bentham MSS, box 127, fos. 41–42.

[72]*Ibid.*, box 126, fo. 148. For Bentham's distinction between legitimate influence, the influence of understanding on understanding, and illegitimate influence, the influence of will on will, see Mack, *op. cit.*, 436, 441, and Bentham MSS, box 126, fos. 179–92.

[73]*Ibid.*, box 44, fo. 5. Cf. Himmelfarb, *op. cit.*, 72.

failing to understand what was in their own interest, measures would be adopted that were prejudicial to the interest of the whole. Indeed he considered that want of intelligence might result in the adoption of measures more noxious, and perhaps even destructive to the state, than any which "deficiency in the mere article of probity" could produce. He concluded that

supposing the right of suffrage to have received in respect of the number of the possessors of it such an extension as to embrace all the different interests of the community in such sort as to preserve the interest of the majority, if not from being at any time sacrificed to that of the minority, at any rate from continuing to be so for any considerable length of time—that in such a state of things, any ulterior extension would be productive of no advantage, but of considerable hazard and inconvenience.[74]

However, nine months later he took a substantially different view, maintaining that more weight should be given to probity than to intelligence. For, he said, if political power were placed in the hands of the few, the misgovernment that was likely to result, through the subjection of the joint interest of the many to that of the governors, was an evil that would not admit of any remedy. But the "intellectual imperfection" which would result from power being placed in the last resort in the hands of the many was "a weakness which not only admits of, but is every day enjoying the benefit of a remedy," through the spread of political information and understanding.[75] This tension between the respective claims of intelligence and probity is a theme that can be traced through the subsequent writings of the Philosophic Radicals. Bentham was to admit in December 1819 that he for his part (whether on grounds of practicability or because of his doubts about the political judgment of the lower classes, he did not say) would gladly "compound for householder suffrage"; but, he went on,

I do not see how those who on this plan would be excluded from the right of suffrage, and also would perhaps constitute a majority of male adults, should be satisfied with such exclusion; and being myself unable to find what appears to me a reason in favour of it, I must leave the task to those who consider themselves able to accomplish it.[76]

James Mill was considering the same problem, at much the same time, in composing his *Essay on Government*. In practice, he was prepared at the Westminster election of 1819 to support a moderate reform candidate in preference to one committed to universal suffrage.[77] But in examining in the *Essay* the question whether "there is any qualification which would remove the right of suffrage from the people of small, or of no property, and yet constitute an elective body, the interest of which would be identical with that of the community," he felt obliged to conclude that only if the qualification were such as to embrace a majority of the adult male population, and to exclude therefore only a minority, would there be a "tolerable security" for good government.[78]

[74] Bentham MSS, box 127, fos. 181-85.

[75] *Ibid.*, box 126, fos. 145–47. Cf. the very similar argument in James Mill, *An Essay on Government*, introduced by Ernest Barker (Cambridge, 1937), 63–65.

[76] Bentham MSS, box 137, fo. 78; *Works*, III, 599.

[77] William Thomas, "James Mill's Politics: a Rejoinder," *Historical Journal*, **14** (1971), 741–42.   [78] *Essay on Government*, 49–50.

Bentham, somewhat later, decided in the *Constitutional Code* that no such exclusions from the franchise were reconcilable with Utilitarian principles.[79] On the other hand, John Stuart Mill, repelled by "the ignorance and especially the selfishness and brutality of the mass"[80] was to react against the logic of this doctrine and to put the emphasis back where Bentham had originally placed it in August 1809, on intelligence and education.

Another problem which was to exercise the Philosophic Radicals, and one which they are thought to have helped significantly in resolving, was the problem of how reform was to be achieved. It has been argued by Joseph Hamburger that James Mill was responsible for evolving a strategy whereby the "threat of revolution" could be used to extort peaceful constitutional change by convincing the ruling class that it was in its own interest to concede fundamental reforms.[81] Hamburger notes that Mill's views about public pressure on the authorities had been to some extent anticipated by Bentham in a letter which he addressed to the people of Spain in 1820.[82] But in fact ten years before that, in July 1810, Bentham had given fuller consideration to the strategy of peaceful coercion under the chapter-heading "Course to be taken by the friends of Reform" and in a section entitled "Sole means of conversion, popular pressure." The problem, he saw, was how to convert the possessors of borough and county influence into supporters of efficient reform; and he argued that, leaving aside the few who might be prepared to sacrifice parliamentary interest for the sake of gaining office with popular support, and the still smaller number who valued personal reputation more highly than the power and status conferred by parliamentary interest, this could only be done by inculcating a belief that resistance was hopeless.[83] In considering how such a belief could be induced, Bentham invoked three different lessons which he regarded as pertinent. First, he mentioned the importance attached by Locke to "uneasiness" as a motive for action. Secondly, he referred to the parable of the importunate widow and the unjust judge in St. Luke's Gospel: it was by her importunity that the widow prevailed upon the judge and (unjust though he was) obtained justice from him. Thirdly, he recalled the episode of Antient Pistol and the leek in Henry V. Pistol did eventually eat the leek, and actually claimed to enjoy it—after the Welshman had shown him his fists. Bentham concluded:

If fists be shewn let them, at any rate in the first instance, be open and not closed. If Locke's be the principle employed let it rather be not the Antient's instrument but the old woman's instrument: that instrument which was found so efficient when employed in the application of Locke's principle to the breast of the unjust Judge.[84]

The treatment of the question was characteristically discursive, but the message was clear enough. Bentham believed—indeed he explicitly said in a

---

[79] *Works*, IX, 107–08.

[80] J. S. Mill, *Autobiography*, ed. J. Stillinger (Oxford, 1971), 138.

[81] J. Hamburger, *James Mill and the Art of Revolution* (New Haven, 1963), esp. 23–24.

[82] *Ibid.*, 24n., citing *On the Liberty of the Press, and Public Discussion* (*Works*, II, 287).   [83] Bentham MSS, box 127, fos. 84–87.   [84] *Ibid.*, box 127, fos. 88–90.

parenthesis on Pistol and pistols—that in England weapons would not be necessary and words would suffice (provided they were "strong enough and to the purpose"). But it was only through the realization that these words repre- sented a force to which resistance was ultimately impossible, that the possessors of parliamentary interest could be brought to capitulate.

In examining the early development of Philosophic Radicalism, it is difficult if not impossible to distinguish between the respective contributions of Bentham and Mill. From the summer of 1809 they were in frequent contact with each other, and the lines of thought which Bentham pursued and elaborated in his drafts probably owed a good deal to joint discussion, just as Mill's later essays for the *Encyclopaedia Britannica* owed much to Bentham's cogitations on the same problems.[85] But how, if at all, did Queen's Square Place fit into the contemporary reform movement, and what if anything did Bentham draw from it? It has been noted that he showed no sympathy for the Tory proclivities of Burdett. Nor, though he was prepared to defend the re- formers against the charge of "innovation,"[86] did he share Burdett's preoccu- pation with the "ancient constitution" as the prototype for modern reform. Yet for the actual program of reforms which he adopted he does seem to have been indebted, in part at least, to the Burdettites. He wrote in November 1809 that in the plan of reform for which he had recently been making out a detailed case he had seen "little reason to go in quest of novelty"[87]; he subsequently indicated that it was Burdett's lead that he had followed.[88] In fact, though Bentham's program in the *Parliamentary Reform Catechism* did coincide in several respects with that which Burdett had put forward in the House of Commons in June 1809,[89] it bore a more striking resemblance to one which Major John Cartwright had set out in a pamphlet published earlier in that year. Cartwright advocated not only a taxpaying suffrage,[90] an equalization of constituencies, and annual parliaments, the three main features of Burdett's plan, but also the ballot and the disqualification of office-holders from voting in the House of Commons.[91] As Bentham later denied having read any of Cartwright's publications before drawing up his own plan,[92] the resemblance would appear to have been accidental. But it is noteworthy that once the catechism was written it was submitted to Major Cartwright for his com- ments.

Among Bentham's papers there is an unsigned (and hitherto unnoticed) group of about a dozen pages in Cartwright's handwriting, consisting of a proposed introductory section to be prefixed to Bentham's catechism, plus a

[85] *Essay on Government, op. cit.,* xiii-xiv.   [86] Bentham MSS, box 127, fos. 169–74.

[87] *Elements of the Art of Packing, Works,* V, 186; Bentham MSS, box 129(a), fo. 26.

[88] *Works,* III, 458.

[89] *The Plan of Reform proposed by Sir Francis Burdett in the House of Commons, June 15th, 1809* (London, 1809), 18.

[90] For most of his career he was a strong advocate of universal suffrage, but during the Napoleonic War he temporarily retreated from this position. See Naomi C. Miller, "John Cartwright and Radical Parliamentary Reform, 1808–1819," *English Historical Review,* **83** (1968), 711.

[91] J. Cartwright, *Reasons for Reformation* (London, 1809), 7, 12–13.

[92] *Works,* III, 458n.

few notes on the work itself.[93] The fragment is undated (the watermark dates, for what they are worth, being 1806 and 1808), and it is not known when the two men first became acquainted; but in August 1811 in their earliest recorded exchange of letters Bentham mentioned "a person whom you once met at my house,"[94] which suggests that they had then known each other for some time. One may perhaps infer that it was soon after the catechism was written that Bentham sent it to the Major and the latter made his suggestions. These few pages among Bentham's manuscripts represent, a third of a century after the publication in 1776 of Cartwright's *Take Your Choice!* and Bentham's *Fragment on Government,* a notable intersection between the theory of democracy based on natural rights and the political theory of Utilitarianism. Bentham's short catechism did not include any discussion of first principles, and Cartwright evidently felt this to be a weakness; hence the "preliminary explanation" which he drafted. It is full of assertions about "rights" and "justice," "immutable principles" and "self-evident truths." Question 1 asks "What is meant by *Parliamentary Reform?*" and the answer begins "A correction of all those deviations from justice which have more or less destroyed the political right of the Nation to be represented in the Legislature." When he comes to comment directly on Bentham's catechism the contrast between his style of argument and Bentham's is particularly obvious. Bentham having said that he saw no reason in principle why women (if they had the proper qualification) should not be able to vote, Cartwright observes: "The objection to women being electors is this—that election is an essential part of dominion, and that the female is by a law of nature put under the dominion of the male." Similarly on Bentham's provision that (as a matter of convenience in preserving secrecy of voting) no one should qualify for the vote who could not write his name, the Major comments: "Political liberty being a sacred right of nature, the disqualification here introduced seems unwarrantable." Bentham's counter-comment pencilled in the margin evinces the difference between them: "In my view rights of nature are a mere lawyerlike fiction invented for a mask to the fallacy called Petitio Principii, and a degree of self will and ipse-dixitism that precludes all argument."[95] Bentham was the author of what a great scholar has called "the most complete exposure of the logical absurdity of the doctrine of natural rights which has ever been written."[96] Yet one should not, perhaps, for all the superiority of Bentham's ratiocinative powers over those of the "worthy Major," assume that his ideas were in every respect superior to Cartwright's. One further extract from the latter's commentary is worth quoting:

By a law of nature, political liberty is a necessary *mean* to the *end* in view, when the Creator made man in his own image, and with the faculties he bestowed upon him; namely reason, a sense of right and wrong, sensibility to good and evil, and a capacity (as he makes a progress towards excellence) of discerning and feeling the dignity of his nature. . . . Let me than appeal to your own bosom, and ask, if in your own case a deprivation of political liberty would not dissatisfy your reason? would not shock your sense of right and wrong?

---

[93]Bentham MSS, box 125, fos. 138–41.   [94]*Works,* X, 463–65.
[95]*Works,* III, 540–41. Bentham MSS, box 125, fo. 141.
[96]Sir William Holdsworth, *History of English Law* (16 vols., London, 1903–66), XIII, 56, referring to *Anarchical Fallacies.*

would not cause you to feel the absence of a good and the presence of an evil? as well as that it were uncongenial with the dignity of your nature as a man?[97]

Bentham left the question unanswered[98] and must indeed have regarded it as virtually meaningless. But it reminds one of John Stuart Mill's subsequent feeling that Bentham's indifference to such concepts as "personal dignity" and "self-respect" was a major blind-spot in his philosophical outlook.[99] One should also bear in mind the opinion of Lord Bryce (expressed fifty years ago) that in terms of effectiveness the "transcendental" doctrine of natural rights had done far more to commend democracy to mankind than had the carefully reasoned arguments of the Benthamites.[100] However, perhaps these differences, and the relative merits of each approach, are less important than the fact that Bentham and Cartwright were and remained allies. As has been seen, they differed remarkably little in their aims in 1809; and six or seven years later Bentham moved to "virtual universality of suffrage" at much the same time that Cartwright reverted to his earlier belief in manhood suffrage.[101] Whatever Bentham may have thought of Cartwright as a thinker, he approved of him as an intrepid campaigner, and in the introduction to the *Plan of Parliamentary Reform* published in 1817 he referred to him as "the worthy father of radical reform."[102]

Towards some other radicals Bentham was less well disposed. Cobbett he admired for the force of his journalism, and in November 1810 he offered him the Parliamentary Reform Catechism for publication in the *Political Register*.[103] But Cobbett sent it back after a fortnight, and thereafter Bentham seems to have regarded him with some hostility.[104] He seems also to have felt some distrust of Burdett, at least after the riots of April 1810 for which the baronet could to some extent be held responsible. Bentham admitted, in a draft dated 17 June, that there was a close similarity between his own opinions on reform and "those of some persons to whom designs of a pernicious tendency, and in some instances possibly not altogether without reason, have been imputed." A marginal précis of the passage indicates the person Bentham had in mind: "J. B.'s measures the same nearly as Burdet's &c. . . . ."[105] By the

[97] Bentham MSS, box 125, fos. 139–40.

[98] But for a brief "Enquiry how far the word right is applicable to the subject of parliamentary reform," see *ibid.*, box 127, fo. 142; and for some criticisms of the rights-of-man "fallacy," written in June 1810, see box 105, fos. 17–20.

[99] J. S. Mill, *Dissertations and Discussions* (2 vols., London, 1859), I, 359–60.

[100] James, Viscount Bryce, *Modern Democracies* (2 vols., London, 1921), I, 51; cited by Holdsworth, *op. cit.*, XIII, 24.

[101] Sir James Mackintosh pointed out in *Edinburgh Review*, **31** (Dec. 1818), 173, that the plan of reform proposed by Bentham in 1817 was in essence the same as Cartwright's.

[102] *Works*, III, 481n. Cf. Bentham to Cartwright, 9 Apr. 1821, *ibid.*, X, 523.

[103] Add. MSS 33544, fo. 482. *Works*, X, 458–59. Bentham may also have submitted it to *The Times*. He said in the published introduction to the catechism that soon after it was written it was rejected by "one of the time-serving daily prints" (*ibid.*, III, 435); and he appears to refer to this incident in a draft letter to *The Times* dated 18 June 1811 (Bentham MSS, box 125, fo. 144).

[104] *Works*, X, 471. J. Colls, *Utilitarianism Unmasked* (London, 1844), 20.

[105] Bentham MSS, box 127, fo. 20.

following May, however, Bentham was in friendly contact with Burdett, and in 1812 was prepared to say that he was on the whole well-intentioned and had done a considerable amount of good though he still considered him much inferior "in real worth" to Romilly and Brougham.[106] With Romilly Bentham had been on close terms for some time, and Brougham he had met more recently through James Mill.[107] He described them both as "more democratic than the Whigs,"[108] but his views coincided more closely with theirs over law reform than over the reform of parliament. Brougham did provide Bentham with copies of the replies he received to a circular letter on parliamentary reform which he sent out in the spring of 1810.[109] But the moderate, piecemeal plan of reform which Brougham put forward in this letter was not one that Bentham could approve;[110] he was more impressed by the reply sent to Brougham by William Roscoe, arguing for more radical measures such as Burdett had proposed in 1809.[111]

It is clear that in the years before he emerged as a public champion of parliamentary reform Bentham did have various contacts with other reformers. In addition to those mentioned above, he became friendly with Thomas Northmore, founder of the Hampden Club,[112] and he came to exercise a strong influence over the leading Westminster radical Francis Place, who was introduced to him in 1812.[113] It is true that between 1811 and 1816 he was writing mainly on subjects other than political reform (notably education and the Church),[114] and it was not until 1818, when a popular edition of the *Plan of Parliamentary Reform* was produced by T. J. Wooler of the *Black Dwarf*, and when Burdett moved in the Commons a series of resolutions drafted by Bentham,[115] that he can be said to have made a real impact on the national reform movement. Still, despite the shift in Bentham's programme from a tax-paying franchise to virtually universal suffrage, there is a clear continuity of thinking between the unpublished writings of 1809–10 and the post-war publications on reform. The former are thus significant as the foundations of an important political doctrine; and the incisiveness and modernity of the ideas developed in them provide a striking contrast with most constitutional theorizing of the time.

[106] *Works*, X, 460–61, 471.

[107] Chester New, *Life of Henry Brougham to 1830* (Oxford, 1961), 151.

[108] *Works*, X, 472.

[109] Bentham MSS, box 127, fos. 195–215. *The Satirist* (June 1810), 567–75.

[110] *Book of Fallacies, Works*, II, 458.

[111] Brougham to Roscoe, 14 July 1810, Add. MSS 34079, fo. 83. Roscoe's letter was published as *A Letter to Henry Brougham, Esq., M.P., on the subject of a Reform of the Representation of the People in Parliament* (Liverpool, 1811).

[112] *Works*, X, 484–85. Northmore to Bentham, 1 Oct. 1814, attached to Sir John Bowring's own copy of his *Memoirs of Jeremy Bentham*, British Library, call-mark C.61 c.15, vol. VI.

[113] Graham Wallas, *Life of Francis Place* (4th ed., London, 1925), ch. 3.

[114] But he did not lose sight of the political question: Bentham MSS, box 125, fos. 64–67; box 129(a), fos. 55–81, 86–88; box 130, fos. 92–93.

[115] Halévy, *op. cit.*, 262–63.

16

Bentham and the Early Nineteenth Century

In July 1832, a month after Bentham's death, Thomas Babington Macaulay published an article in the *Edinburgh Review* about a work by Etienne Dumont, the Genevan who had devoted much of his life to editing Bentham's works and translating them into French. Macaulay said in this article:

> If M. Dumont had never been born, Mr Bentham would still have been a very great man. But he would have been great to himself alone. The fertility of his mind would have resembled the fertility of those vast American wildernesses, in which blossoms and decays a rich but unprofitable vegetation ... His speculations on laws would have been of no more practical use than Lord Worcester's speculations on steam-engines. Some generations hence, perhaps ... an antiquarian might have published to the world the curious fact, that in the reign of George the Third, there had been a man called Bentham, who had given hints of many discoveries made since his time, and who had really, for his age, taken a most philosophical view of the principles of jurisprudence.[1]

There are, perhaps, two Benthams (excluding the auto-icon). One of them survives in the 176 boxes of manuscripts in the library of University College, London. This is, if you like, the *esoteric* Bentham, many of whose speculations do resemble in some respects those of the seventeenth-century Earl of Worcester on steam-power or those of Bentham's near-contemporary Charles Babbage on mechanical computing. These speculations of Bentham – unpublicized in his own time, but receiving attention from scholars in the twentieth century – include his great work on what he called the 'metaphysics' of law, *Of Laws in General*, which he regarded as too abstract and abstruse to be worth publishing in his own time. They also include works on logic and language, and those in which Bentham attacked the current laws and prejudices against homosexuality and other forms of 'sexual nonconformity'. The other Bentham is what might be called the *historic* Bentham: the one whom people actually read,

1. *Edinburgh Review*, lv (1832), 553-4.

and who influenced the contemporary climate of ideas; and it is on this Bentham that, as a historian, I wish to concentrate, looking at the ways in which his ideas circulated, the places they reached, and the sort of impact they made, in the early nineteenth century.

At the beginning of the century Bentham was little known, in England or abroad. Of the people who had then heard of him, a high proportion would probably have associated him with his Panopticon prison scheme, for his efforts to get this implemented had attracted a certain amount of public attention. But in fact his central preoccupation had been – and was to remain for the rest of his life – legislation and the codification of law. What he wanted above all to do (though he often got side-tracked onto peripheral or topical matters) was to produce a 'pannomion' or complete body of laws – a comprehensive code, or set of codes, which he thought would be applicable (with a certain amount of modification and filling-in of detail) to virtually any society. In most of his writings in the 1770s and 80s he had been trying to lay the foundations of this pannomion; and he had actually published, in 1789, a preliminary exposition of its underlying principles, called *An Introduction to the Principles of Morals and Legislation.* This is of course the work by which he is best known today in the English-speaking world. But it was little read in his own time. Only 250 copies of the original edition were printed, and half of those were destroyed by rats or damp at the printers;[2] and references to the work in contemporary literature are very sparse. It was Dumont who, by taking over and digesting Bentham's writings (most of them in manuscript), presented the fruits of his work to an international public, and was thereby largely responsible for giving Bentham the reputation in the early nineteenth century of being the greatest living expert on legislation.

It is worth saying a little about Dumont, as Bentham's debt to him was so great. He started life as a pastor in the Calvinist church, but he found himself at odds with the political regime in Geneva in the 1780s, and went abroad. He came in due course (via St Petersburg) to England, and was engaged as tutor to a son of Lord Lansdowne, who had formerly been Prime Minister as Lord Shelburne in 1782-3. Within a few years, a sinecure was found for him as a nominal clerk in the office of the Clerk of the Pells, who was then Lansdowne's friend Isaac Barré. This was strictly speaking irregular, as Dumont was not a British subject, and he appears in the official lists as Stephen Dumont. The post, and the pension he received after its abolition, brought him four or five hundred pounds a year for the rest of his life and (ironically, as Bentham was a strong opponent of sinecures) it was an important factor in enabling him to

---

2. *Correspondence of Jeremy Bentham (in Collected Works of Jeremy Bentham,* ed. J.H. Burns and others (London/Oxford, 1968-[CW])), iv. 34-5.

devote so much of his time to editing Bentham.[3] Dumont and Bentham first came into contact with each other as members of the Lansdowne circle on the eve of the French Revolution. Dumont was directly involved in the revolution for a time, as an associate or assistant of Mirabeau. But by 1793 he was back in England, disillusioned with revolutionary politics, and he lived mainly in this country during the French wars. He was a very sociable and agreeable person, and the novelist Maria Edgeworth, who knew him very well, wrote after his death: 'I think he was, take him all in all, the man of the coolest judgment and of the warmest heart I ever knew, and therefore he had the most attached friends who loved him with all their souls'.[4] His wide circle of friends included a number of people in aristocratic whig society, and he spent a considerable amount of time at great houses like Bowood and Holland House. Meanwhile, he occupied himself with editing and translating Bentham's chaotic manuscripts.

The first major publication which he based on these manuscripts – and which always remained the most important of his recensions – was the *Traités de législation civile et pénale*, published in three volumes in Paris during the Peace of Amiens in 1802. There were second and third editions in 1820 and 1830, and it was translated into Russian in 1805, Italian in 1819, Spanish in 1821-2, German in 1830. Dumont also produced four further publications based on Bentham's writings, which were all translated into Spanish and other languages; and a collected edition of Bentham's works as edited by Dumont appeared at Brussels in 1829-30. One should add that even in the English-speaking world it was largely through Dumont's versions that Bentham came to be read. For one thing, these publications were quite extensively reviewed in British periodicals – especially in the *Edinburgh Review*, the great liberal periodical of the day. Also, several of Dumont's versions were translated back into English. For example, the *Traité des preuves judiciaires*, published in 1823, appeared in an English translation as *A Treatise on Judicial Evidence* two years later; and this remains in many ways the clearest and most useful presentation of Bentham's views on evidence. Similarly, there were two American translations of the *Traités de législation*, and it was primarily through these that Bentham's ideas circulated in the United States in the nineteenth century.

By contrast, the works which Bentham himself brought out in England

---

3. Etienne Dumont, *Principles of Legislation: from the MS. of Jeremy Bentham*, translated, with notes and a biographical notice of Jeremy Bentham and of M. Dumont, by John Neal, Boston, 1830 [cited hereafter as Neal], pp. 151-7.
4. Maria Edgeworth to Mrs. Marcet, 25 Oct. 1829, in H.W. Häuserman, *The Genevese Background*, London, 1952, p. 153. Lord Brougham wrote of Dumont: 'His manners were as gentle as they were polished and refined. His conversation was a model of excellence; it was truly delightful.' *Speeches of Henry Lord Brougham* (4 vols., Edinburgh, 1838), ii. 303-4.

tended to be published in a haphazard and often restricted way. It is extraordinary that someone as vain and concerned about his own reputation as Bentham was should have been so casual about the way in which his works were made available to the public. What he really liked doing was following trains of thought on paper; the business of revising his own material and seeing it through the press was something he found extremely tiresome, and whenever he could he left it to other people. Also his attention tended to veer about from subject to subject, and he rarely managed to complete anything before moving onto something else that had caught his interest. Consequently one finds that some of his works were printed, or partially printed, but never published. Some of those that *were* published appeared in very small editions: the 'in-letters' in Bentham's correspondence in the early nineteenth century contain many complaints about how difficult his works were to get hold of. One can say quite confidently that none of his works sold at all extensively in English during his lifetime; and one may add that the collected edition of his works in eleven volumes, which his disciple and literary executor John Bowring produced in the early 1840s, did not do much to disseminate his work further. The *Edinburgh Review* said of these volumes when they were published that they were 'incomplete, incorrect and ill-arranged', and that with their close print, small type and double columns they had 'typographically interred' the opinions of the author; and Bowring's son admitted in the 1870s, in a memoir of his father, that the publication 'did not attain extensive popularity'.[5] Yet Bentham has been described recently – by the author of a book on Benjamin Constant, his only possible rival in this respect – as 'the most widely-read liberal thinker of his time'.[6] Whether he was a liberal or not is debatable: but he *was* widely read, thanks to Dumont. A Paris bookseller estimated near the end of Bentham's life that 50,000 copies of the *Traités de législation* had been sold in Europe, and that another 40,000 volumes of Bentham's works edited by Dumont had been sold in South America.[7] There was some truth in what William Hazlitt wrote in the essay on Bentham which he published in 1824: 'The lights of his understanding are reflected, with increasing lustre, on the other side of the globe. His name is little known in England, better in Europe, best of all in the plains of Chili and the mines of Mexico'.[8]

Before examining Bentham's influence in the Iberian world, it may be worth making one or two general points about the differences between what one may call 'Bentham-Dumont' and the unprocessed Bentham of

5. *Edinburgh Review*, lxxviii (1843), 516; L.B. Bowring (ed.), *Autobiographical Recollections of Sir John Bowring* (London, 1877), p. 14.
6. G.H. Dodge, *Benjamin Constant's Philosophy of Liberalism* (Chapel Hill, 1980), p. 143.
7. John Bowring (ed.), *The Works of Jeremy Bentham* (11 vols., Edinburgh, 1843), xi. 33, 80.
8. P.P. Howe (ed.), *Complete Works of William Hazlitt* (21 vols., London, 1930-4), xi. 5.

the early nineteenth century. One very obvious difference is in regard to style. Bentham's style had at one time been rather good, and Henry Brougham and Sir James Mackintosh both commented on the lucidity and even elegance of some of his early works (such as his *Defence of Usury*, published in 1787), in contrast to the obscurity and ungainliness of the style he had since developed.[9] Paradoxically it was partly as a result of his efforts to be completely unambiguous that his style became so convoluted and opaque. A former secretary of his, Walter Coulson, wrote in the *Examiner* in 1817: 'He seems every where to have laboured to express his opinions with a degree of accuracy, and a number of reserves, quite inconsistent with fluency. He has parenthesis within parenthesis, like a set of pill-boxes; and out of this habit have grown redundancies which become tiresome to the reader'.[10] A specimen of his later style is a 260-word sentence from a letter of his to the *Examiner* in 1814:

And now, Sir, if you would wish to understand *how* and *why* it is, that for the same sort of thing *one* man is reprimanded and ordered to *refund, another* man *whipped* or *pilloried* or *transported* or *hanged*, it may be time for you to call to mind, that to the purpose of *depredation* – not to speak of delinquency in other *shape* – a general principle fully established and steadily acted upon under our excellent Constitution in Church and State, is – that the population of the country is composed of *two* classes or casts of people, viz, *one* in whose instance, in case of misfortune or want of dexterity, the *obligation of refunding*, with or without reprimand (for in the case of the *Steeles*, the *De Lancys*, the *Villerses*, the *Chinnerys*, &c. &c. there was nothing of reprimand), or at any rate *an invitation* to *refund*, to wit, *with* or, as in the present case, *without* interest (the interest consequently secured to them) – is, in case of detection and prosecution and conviction, regarded as a sufficient check – conviction, in fact, being by a tissue of regulation and construction and complication rendered next to miraculous: *the other*, for whose reformation, as far as by experience upon experience the otherwise unimaginable possibility of the several forms of delinquency shall have been demonstrated, the operation of *hanging by the neck* is to be provided, and for whom, in the mean time, nothing less than *whipping* or *pillory* or *transportation*, or the recently devised improvement of putting into chains, and cramming into a *hulk*, can suffice.

Cobbett described Bentham's style in 1818 as 'puzzling and tedious beyond mortal endurance', and William Empson, professor of law at Haileybury, wrote in a review of Bentham's *Rationale of Judicial Evidence*:

9. *Edinburgh Review*, xxvii (1816), 339; Sir James Mackintosh, *Dissertation on the Progress of Ethical Philosophy* (Edinburgh, 1836), pp. 288, 311-12.
10. *The Examiner*, 19 Oct. 1817. For the authorship of the article, see Francis Place to James Mill, 20 Oct. 1817, British Library, Add. MSS 35153, fo. 22.
11. *The Examiner*, 20 Feb. 1814; J.R. Dinwiddy, 'Jeremy Bentham as a Pupil of Miss Edgeworth's', *Notes and Queries*, New Series, xxix (1982), 208-10.

'Even the cabinets of diplomacy can scarcely ever have witnessed so successful an employment of words for the concealment of thoughts, as is here exhibited'.[12] Even Dumont sometimes had difficulty in understanding what Bentham wrote. On the manuscripts which Bentham passed on to him there are occasional comments in Dumont's hand such as 'J'ai lu dix fois le MS sans le comprendre': 'J'ignore pour quelle planète l'auteur a écrit'; and on one occasion the single word 'Hébreu'![13] But in general Dumont did a remarkable job in understanding Bentham and making him comprehensible – and readable – by others. This involved a certain amount of pruning and simplification. Bentham, for example, had a passion for classification. He was a great admirer of Linnaeus and believed that his method of classifying botanical phenomena by division and sub-division could be fruitfully applied to human behaviour in order to produce an exhaustive classification of, for example, the offences which people might commit and which the author of a penal code would have to consider and provide against. There was a lot of this sort of classification in *An Introduction to the Principles of Morals and Legislation*, and Bentham himself recognized that it could be very tedious to the reader.[14] Dumont included a certain amount of it in his recensions, but he explained in his introduction to the *Traités* that he had tried to avoid the things that had hampered the success of Bentham's own work: 'les formes trop scientifiques, les subdivisions trop multipliées et les analyses trop abstraites'.[15]

There were also important ways in which Dumont's recensions differed in tone and content from the work that Bentham himself was producing in the early nineteenth century. The versions of Bentham's thought, in fact, which circulated most widely in the early nineteenth century represented the *eighteenth*-century Bentham. The *Traités de législation* was based mainly on manuscripts written in the 1780s. The Bentham of the late eighteenth century *was* radical in his approach to law reform, and in his hostility to various widely accepted theories such as those of natural law and social contract. But he was not, except for a brief period in 1789-90, a radical in politics. Dumont was able to say correctly enough in his introduction to the *Traités* that Bentham was not exclusively attached to any particular form of government, and that he considered that if a people had good laws

12. *Cobbett's Political Register*, 12 Dec. 1818, cit. Wiliam Thomas, *The Philosophic Radicals: Nine Studies in Theory and Practice, 1817-41* (Oxford, 1979), p. 29; *Edinburgh Review*, xlviii (1828), 460.
13. Bernard Gagnebin, 'Jeremy Bentham et Etienne Dumont', in *Jeremy Bentham: Bicentenary Celebrations* (London, 1948), p. 46.
14. Bentham, *An Introduction to the Principles of Morals and Legislation* (*CW*), ed. J.H. Burns and H.L.A. Hart (London, 1970), p. 196n.
15. Dumont, *Traités de législation civile et pénale; ouvrage extrait des manuscrits de M. Jérémie Bentham.* (3 vols. Paris, 1802), i, p. ix.

it could achieve a high degree of happiness without possessing any political power.[16] During the early years of the nineteenth century, however, Bentham became convinced that the vested interests of lawyers, which were the most immediate obstacle to any reform of the English legal system, were closely linked with the vested interests of other sections of Britain's ruling elite, and that a whole range of abuses, in the governmental system and the established church as well as in the law, were being sustained and protected by a corrupt and unrepresentative legislature. From 1809 onwards he was developing a set of arguments in favour of parliamentary reform, and in his first published work on the subject in 1817 he called for annual elections, secret voting, and the enfranchisement of all adult males capable of passing a literacy test.[17] Privately he seems to have believed at this time that a *revolution* might be desirable. In 1817 he was in the habit of going for walks in Hyde Park and Kensington Gardens with John Quincy Adams, then American minister in London and later President of the United States; and Adams in his diary, recorded Bentham as saying on one of these occasions: 'Upon the whole, it was likely that no great and real reform could be effected in England without a civil war. Corruption had so pervaded the whole mass of the Government, and had so vitiated the character of the people, that he was afraid they could be purified only by fire'.[18] While he never displayed this degree of militancy on paper, he did insist on the need for 'democratic ascendancy'; and this distanced him to some extent from people who might have been regarded as his natural allies, such as the whig law reformers Sir Samuel Romilly and Henry Brougham, who were liberals but not democrats.

Such people disapproved not only of the substance of Bentham's radical views, but also of the strident and vituperative tone which he adopted in attacking the legal and political and religious establishment. Romilly, who was a personal friend of both Bentham and Dumont, wrote to the latter in 1817 saying that the 'asperity' with which Bentham was attacking tne English system of government was 'very injudicious';[19] and indeed the conservative *Quarterly Review* was able to write dismissively of his 'rancorous abuse' and 'vulgar scurrility' and 'indiscriminate railing'.[20] Dumont never adopted this sort of style, and Empson wrote in 1828 that he obtained a hearing for Bentham's ideas by adopting 'the tone of

16. *Ibid.*, p. xvi.
17. Bentham, *Plan of Parliamentary Reform, in the form of a Catechism* (London, 1817), pp. lvi-ci (Bowring, iii. 451-65).
18. Charles Francis Adams (ed.), *Memoirs of John Quincy Adams* (12 vols., Philadelphia, 1874-7), iii. 539.
19. *Memoirs of the Life of Sir Samuel Romilly*, edited by his sons (3 vols., London, 1840), iii. 317n.
20. *Quarterly Review*, xxi (1819), 176; xxvii (1822), 379.

civilized debate'.[21] One or two of the volumes Dumont produced in the post-war period did draw on *recent* writings of Bentham – that is to say, on writings of Bentham in his radical phase. But Dumont tended to soften or qualify Bentham's most provocative statements. For example in presenting his views on codification in a volume published in 1828, Dumont reproduced a remark of Bentham's to the effect that those who opposed the codification of law could be divided into two classes: they were either imposters, or dupes. But Dumont added a footnote saying that in his opinion this classification was not complete, as there were some men of intelligence and good faith who opposed codification on the grounds that it was difficult if not impossible to do it satisfactorily.[22]

Dumont also differed, more fundamentally, from the later Bentham in that he himself was never a democrat. When Bentham published his parliamentary reform pamphlet in 1817, he knew Dumont would not like it and did not send him a copy: Dumont had to write and ask for one, saying that although he himself did not believe in universal suffrage he wanted to see Bentham's views on the subject fully set out.[23] But those views were not reproduced in any of Dumont's recensions: his volumes contained nothing about Bentham's ideas on representative government and constitutional law; and Bentham went so far as to say in a letter to his Spanish disciple and interpreter Toribio Nuñez in 1821 that in knowing only such works of his as had found 'a French elaborator and editor in Dumont', Nuñez scarcely knew half of him.[24] However, as Dumont himself pointed out in a letter to Bentham in the following year, the fact that constitutional matters were *not* discussed in the work was one of the reasons why the *Traités de léglisation* had been able to circulate so widely and exert an influence under *various* political regimes.[25]

That is not to imply that the *Traités* was an uncontroversial book. It was, in fact, despite its avoidance of politics, highly controversial and from a certain point of view very *subversive*, because it challenged the basis of most accepted systems of morality. Bentham himself was fundamentally anti-religious, partly because he believed that in practice religion had proved to be on balance damaging to human happiness, and partly because he was an empiricist who did not see any substantial evidence for the existence of God. He refers in one of his early manuscripts to 'Religion,

21. *Edinburgh Review*, xlviii (1828), 462.
22. Dumont, *De l'organisation judiciare, et de la codification, extraits de divers ouvrages de Jérémie Bentham* (Paris, 1828), p. 380.
23. Dumont to Bentham, 1 Oct. 1817, Bentham MSS, box x, sheet 120, University College London [UC x. 120].
24. Pedro Schwartz (ed.), *The Iberian Correspondence of Jeremy Bentham: A Provisional Edition* (2 vols., London and Madrid, 1979), 1. 515.
25. Dumont to Bentham, 28 Nov. 1822, UC clxxiv. 70.

or if the term please better Superstition'.[26] Dumont, in the *Traités*, was careful not to present Bentham as explicitly *hostile* to religion. But he did not conceal the fact that Bentham's utilitarianism was basically secular: that it was a system of morality which depended not on God-given notions of right and wrong, but on the simple principle (which, in Bentham's view, nobody who really thought about it could deny) that society should be organized in such as way as to maximize the happiness of its membrs. It followed from this that the basic moral criterion by which all institutions and policies and human conduct should be judged was their conduciveness to the maximization of happiness – and this criterion provided, according to Bentham, an external, non-mystical standard such as was *not* provided by other moral systems which purported to be derived from natural law, or divine ordinance, or intuitive moral senses. Such arguments being set out in the *Traités de legislation*, it was clear that the work could not be reconciled with traditional Catholic theology, and in 1819 it was placed on the papal index of prohibited books.[27] It is also worth noting that two of the fullest attempts to criticize and refute Bentham's doctrines in the early nineteenth century were written by Spanish ecclesiastics. (One of them, José Vidal, was a theologian at the University of Valencia; the other, Martínez Marina, was a liberal in politics and a member of the Cortes in the period of constitutional goverment in the early 1820s, but he was also a firm believer in natural law.)[28]

One of the main reasons, of course, why two of the major attacks on Bentham's philosophy were written in Spain was the great impression his ideas had made there. I want to examine his influence in the Peninsula and Latin America, because this is one of the most striking features of his impact – or rather the impact of Bentham-Dumont – on the early nineteenth-century world. In early nineteenth-century Spain there were two periods of liberal or constitutional government – one in 1808 to 1814 and the other in 1820 to 1823. By the time of the first of these, Bentham's works had *begun* to circulate in Spain. Three hundred copies of the original edition of the *Traités de législation* had been sent by the Paris publisher to Spain, and Nuñez first obtained a copy in 1807, when be bought one from a pedlar who was travelling with the French army through Spain on its way to fight the English in Portugal.[29] Between 1810 and 1814 several articles on Bentham's ideas appeared in *El Español*, a periodical edited in

26. UC lxxi. 40, cit James Steintrager, 'Morality and Belief: The Origin and Purpose of Bentham's Writings on Religion', *Mill News Letter*, no. 6 (1971), p. 7.
27. Joseph Hilgers, (ed.), *Der Index der verbotenen Bücher* (Freiburg, 1904), p. 456.
28. José Vidal, *Orígen de los errores revolucionarios de Europa, y su remedio* (Valencia, 1827); F. Martínez Marina, *Principios naturales de la moral, de la política y de la legislación*, ed. Adolfo Posada, (Madrid, 1933).
29. Bowring, iv. 572, x. 395.

London by the Spanish expatriate Blanco White, which had a considerable circulation in the Peninsula. But it was in the second period of
liberal government, the 'triennium' of 1820-23, that Bentham's ideas were
most widely and warmly discussed. Nuñez, who was librarian at the
University of Salamanca, produced in this period two volumes which
were not so much translations of Bentham as attempts (based on the
materiasl published by Dumont) to present the essence of his ideas in a
systematic way; and Ramón Salas, professor of law at the same university,
was responsible for the first Spanish translation of the *Traités de législation*.
Nuñez and Salas both became members of the Cortes and another leading
propagator of Bentham's ideas, the Madrid journalist José Joaquín de
Mora, wrote in an article for an English newspaper in 1821: 'I have been
delighted with the enthusiasm and the reverence with which the most
illustrious men in this country speak of Bentham'.[31] In that year Bentham
was consulted by the Minister of the Interior about trial by jury, and the
President of the Cortes, Count Toreno, sent him the draft of a new penal
code which had been drawn up by a committee of the Cortes and asked for
his comments on it.[32] The *Portuguese* Cortes went one better than that.
Bentham was always hoping that some head of state or sovereign body
would invite him to draw up a complete code of laws for the state
concerned, for he felt that such an invitation would give him the stimulus
he needed to settle down to the very onerous task of substantive
codification. When Portugal (like Spain) had a revolution in 1820,
Bentham sent over a collection of his works and an offer to draw up and
submit a code of laws for the new regime. The Cortes responded by
ordering that his works should be translated into Portuguese and by
accepting his offer to submit a code of laws.[33]

    In fact, Benthamic codes did not materialize in either Portugal or
Spain. The encouragement from the Portuguese Cortes did lead Bentham
to start serious work on his constitutional code (which was intended to be
one of the component parts of his pannomion).[34] But in 1823 the liberal
regime in Portugal was overthrown. Meanwhile, in regard to Spain,
Bentham responded to Toreno's invitation by writing him a series of
letters, amounting in all to a pamphlet of 120 pages.[35] But this work is an

---

30. For information concerning these writers and their works, see Courtney Kenny, 'A
     Spanish Apostle of Benthamism', *Law Quarterly Review*, xi (1895), 175-84; Pedro
     Schwartz, 'La Influencia de Jeremías Bentham on España', *Información Comercial
     Española*, Sept. 1976, pp. 43-7.
31. *The Traveller*, 27 Oct. 1821; Bentham, *Iberian Correspondence*, i. 586.
32. *Ibid.*, i. 416, 563.
33. *Ibid.*, i. 497, 506-10, 600-2, 623.
34. Bentham, *Constitutional Code*, vol. i (*CW*), ed. F. Rosen and J.H. Burns (Oxford, 1983),
     pp. xi-xii.
35. Bentham, *Letters to Count Toreno on the proposed Penal Code* . . ., (London, 1822) (Bowring,
     viii. 487-554).

example of the later Bentham at his worst. It is a very polemical and destructive critique, unnecessarily caustic and even facetious about the draft code and those responsible for it; and the essence of his argument is that the whole thing should give way to a code of his own making. Not surprisingly, although parts of the pamphlet were translated into Spanish and published in Madrid, little or no attention was paid to it in practice;[36] and in any case, in Spain as in Portugal, the restoration of absolutist government in 1823 put a stop to projects of legal reform. Nevertheless, Benthamism had become, and was to remain for some decades, a major strand in Spanish liberalism: a Spanish scholar has written that between 1820 and 1845 no other foreign author exercised so great an authority in Spain.[37] In 1837 (after constitutional government had been again restored) George Borrow, the novelist, was travelling in the north-west corner of Spain as an agent of the British and Foreign Bible Society, distributing copies of the New Testament. At Finisterre he was arrested as a suspected Carlist (a supporter of the absolutist pretender to the Spanish throne), and was even suspected of being the pretender Don Carlos himself. He was taken before the *alcalde*, the local mayor, who on finding that he was an Englishman became very friendly. This according to Borrow, is how the conversation went:

Alcalde Allow me to look at your passport. Yes, all in form. Truly it was very ridiculous that they should have arrested you as a Carlist.

Myself Not only as a Carlist, but as Don Carlos himself.

Alcalde Oh! most ridiculous; mistake a countryman of the grand Baintham for such a Goth!

Myself Excuse me, sir, you speak of the grand somebody.

Alcalde The grand Baintham. He who has invented laws for all the world. I hope shortly to see them adopted in this unhappy country of ours.

Myself Oh! You mean Jeremy Bentham. Yes! a very remarkable man in his way.

Alcalde In his way! in all ways. The most universal genius which the world ever produced . . .

Myself I have never read his writings . . .

Alcalde How surprising! . . . Now here am I, a simple *alcalde* of Galicia, yet I possess all the writings of Baintham on that shelf, and I study them day and night.

Myself You doubtless, sir, possess the English language.

Alcalde I do, I mean that part of it which is contained in the writings of Baintham. I am most truly glad to see a countryman of his in these Gothic wildernesses.

36. Courtney Kenny, 'A Spanish View of Bentham's Spanish Influence', *Law Quarterly Review*, xi (1895), 60-3; Schwartz, 'Influencia . . .', p. 48.
37. *Discursos leídos ante la Real Academia de Ciencias Morales y Políticas en la recepcion publica del excmo. Señor Don Luis Silvela*, Madrid, 1894, p. 46.

The *alcalde* set Borrow free and found a lodging for him for the night, though on discovering that his mission was to distribute copies of the New Testament, he expressed surprise that 'the countrymen of the grand Baintham should set any value upon that old monkish book'.[38]

Even more remarkable than the diffusion of Bentham's writings in Spain was their diffusion over Latin America. Bentham corresponded personally with a number of the great figures of the age of liberation, including Bernadino Rivadavia, the first president of what was to become Argentina, Francisco de Paula Santander, vice-president of Gran Colombia in the 1820s and later president of New Granada, and the great Simón Bolívar. But it was through his works (via Dumont's recensions translated into Spanish), rather than through his letters, that his influence was mainly disseminated.[39] A civil servant who worked under Santander records that even in the days before he had any contact with Bentham, Santander always had a copy of the *Tratados de legislación* open on his desk.[40] Several scholars working independently on the history of different parts of Latin America, from Chile to Mexico, have commented on how frequently Bentham's work was cited in newspapers and debates.[41] Members of the Colombian Congress in the mid 1820s were quoting Bentham at each other much as eighteenth-century Englishmen had quoted classical authors in the House of Commons; and one remarkable member of the Mexican Congress (José María de Jáuregui) claimed to have started reading Bentham at the age of eight.[42] Such precocious Benthamism was rare even in Latin America, but there were a number of places in which Bentham's works were adopted as texts at university level. For example, the man appointed by Rivadavia as first professor of civil law in Buenos Aires, Pedro Somellera, produced in 1824 a course-book on the principles of civil law which was entirely founded on the *Tratados*; and in Chile the great humanist and jurist Andrés Bello, when he started teaching 'universal legislation' at the Colegio de Santiago in 1829, used the *Tratados* as the basic text for three-quarters of his course.[43]

In Colombia a major controversy developed over the use of Bentham's

38. George Borrow, *The Bible in Spain* (London, 1843), chap. xxx.
39. Theodora McKennan, 'Jeremy Bentham and the Colombian Liberators', *The Americas*, xxxiv (1978), 460, 475.
40. Theodora McKennan, 'Santander and the Vogue of Benthamism in Colombia', Ph.D. thesis, Loyola University, Chicago, 1970, p. 172.
41. E.g. Simon Collier, *Ideas and Politics of Chilean Independence 1808-1833*, Cambridge, 1967, p. 171; Mario Rodriguez, *The Cádiz Experiment in Central America, 1808 to 1826* (Berkeley, 1978), p. 198; C.A. Hale, *Mexican Liberalism in the Age of Mora* (New Haven, 1968), pp. 155-60.
42. McKennan, 'Santander . . .', pp. 164-5; Hale, p. 155.
43. Ricardo Piccirilli, *Rivadavia y su tiempo* (2 vols., Buenos Aires, 1943), i. 322-4; Alamiro de Avila Martel, 'Londres en la formación jurídica de Andrés Bello', in *Bello y Londres: Segundo Congreso del Bicentenario* (2 vols., Caracas, 1980-1), ii. 212-16, 229-42.

work as a prescribed text. In 1825 Santander, who was ruling Gran Colombia in Bolívar's absence, issued a vice-presidential decree ordering that professors of law in the republic should teach the principles of legislation from Bentham. Some churchmen and conservatives saw this as a very provocative move, and as part of a general plan to undermine Catholicism in Colombia; several priests publicly attacked the work, and some educational authorities followed suit. For instance, the departmental *subdirección* for Panama (which was then part of Gran Colombia) said in a report to the Director-General of Studies in Bogotá, with regard to Bentham's denial of the existence of natural law:

> The doctrine involves, in the opinion of this *subdirección*, the ruin of the foundations upon which the science of law rests, and the complete subversion of morality as well. Pernicious and melancholy doctrine, against which the human species raises a cry of indignation! His false philosophy has invented for the present generation a system improperly called moral, based upon the ignoble and disreputable base of interest or individual pleasure – well or ill understood. It is capable of engendering in the hearts of Colombians a sad egoism.[44]

Bentham also had enthusiastic defenders – such as Vicente Azuero, a lawyer, journalist and public servant who wrote that the *Tratados* was more valuable than thousands of other volumes, and that from it one could learn 'at one time the elements of public law, private law, and international law, and of the purest morality, most conformable to the principles of the Gospel'.[45] However, Bolívar, when he returned to Bogotá from Peru at the end of 1826, had become convinced that what post-liberation conditions required in South America was strong, authoritarian government; and he was anxious not to antagonize the Church and the landowners. In 1822, he had written flatteringly to Bentham (from what is now Ecuador) saying that 'the name of the preceptor of legislators is never pronounced, even in these savage regions of America, without veneration nor without gratitude'.[46] But in 1828 he put a stop to the public debate over the use of Bentham's work, by issuing a decree saying that the *Tradados* should no longer be used as a prescribed text in universities. Later in the year, after an assassination attempt on Bolívar in which a number of liberal intellectuals were involved, the plan of studies in universities was completly revised, and (by an irony of history which Bentham would not have relished) the funds formerly used to finance courses in the principle of legislation were transferred to finance new compulsory courses in the Roman Catholic religion. A few years later, however, when Santander was elected president of New Granada

44. McKennan, 'Santander . . .', p. 212.
45. *Ibid.*, p. 180.
46. Bentham, *Iberian Correspondence*, ii. 777.

after the disintegration of Gran Colombia, he reinstated Bentham in the university curriculum.[47]

What sort of function, one may ask, did Benthamism perform in Latin America? Bentham cannot in general be said to have had a major substantive influence on the institutions and legal systems of the new Latin American states, though one such case is worth mentioning. His *Political Tactics*, a work on the procedure of legislative assemblies written at the time of the French Revolution and published by Dumont in 1816, was used by Rivadavia as the basis for the rules he drew up for the Chamber of Deputies in Buenos Aires in 1822; and these rules, with amendments, have continued ever since to govern the proceedings of the Argentinian legislature.[48] For the most part, however, what Bentham did was to provide a source of legitimation for liberals in their conflict with various conservative forces: with the Church and utlramontanism, in particular, but also with other privileged groups and vested interests surviving from the colonial period. As Professor John Lynch has put it: 'Seeking an alternative authority to absolutism and religion, liberals seized upon utilitarianism as a modern philosophy capable of giving them the intellectual credibility they wanted'.[49] Most of them were not democrats or egalitarians, and in this sense the *moderate* brand of Benthamism available to them in Dumont's volumes, with its strong emphasis on the need for order and security, suited them well. At the same time, they liked Bentham's uncompromising rejection of prescription and his determination to subject all institutions and practices to the test of public utility. Also, whereas Montesquieu and Savigny regarded laws as largely a product and reflection of the societies in which they were found, Bentham had a basic belief in the power of legislation to *alter* society, and to change people's attitudes and promote progress. One feels that his main contribution to Latin America was to encourage, in those who paid close attention to his works, a modernizing, innovatory spirit, impatient – perhaps too impatient – of what they regarded as outmoded views and practices. It is certainly arguable that men such as Rivadavia and Santander tried to modernize too fast, and that this largely accounts for their frustration and limited success.

I should like to describe briefly Bentham's impact on some other parts of the early nineteenth-century world, though it will not be possible to cover all the countries in which he had a significant influence. The country

47. For published accounts of this controversy, see Armando Rojas, 'La Batalla de Bentham en Colombia', *Revista de Historia de América*, xxix (1950), 37-66, and Theodora McKennan, 'Benthamism in Santander's Colombia', *Bentham Newsletter*, no. 5 (1981), pp. 29-43.
48. Piccirilli, i. 321-2; Pedro Schwartz, 'Work in Progress: Bentham's Influence in Spain, Portugal and Latin America', *Bentham Newsletter*, no. 1 (1978), p. 34.
49. John Lynch, book review, *ibid.*, no. 5 (1981), pp. 59-60.

he himself most admired was undoubtedly the United States: he described the American political system, in a letter to Dumont in 1817, as a 'species of government in comparison with which the least ill-conducted of all other governments are but nuisances'.[50] But one great *blemish* on the American system in his view was its retention of the common law. There were various reasons why Bentham disapproved so much of case law; but perhaps the most basic one was that it did not tell people in explicit, unequivocal terms what they ought not to do. It was the judge who, in the light of the precedents, pronounced on the legality of an action after the action had taken place; and according to Bentham this was how a man made laws for his dog: 'When your dog does anything you want to break him of, you wait till he does it, and then beat him for it'.[51] Moreover, the volume and complexity and uncertainties of the common law meant that it could not possibly be comprehended by the layman in the way that codified law might be; and this of course very much favoured the interests of the legal profession at the expense of the community at large: Bentham said that the lawyers loved the common law for the same reason that the Egyptian priests loved hieroglyphics.[52] In the years after 1815, Bentham did his best to get his ideas on codification, and his criticisms of the common law, publicized in the United States.[53] There *was* a considerable codification movement in North America in the early nineteenth century, and one of its leading figures, Edward Livingston, who drew up a remarkable set of codes for the state of Louisiana, told Bentham in 1829 that many years earlier Dumont's volumes had helped to stimulate his interest in the subject; also he referred to Bentham (in one of his own works) as 'a man to whom the science of legislation owes the great attention that is now paid to its true principles, and to whom statues would be raised if the benefactors of mankind were as much honoured as the oppressors of nations'.[54] In general, however, the ideas that Bentham was trying to put across were rejected by the legal establishment in North America, and his name was mentioned surprisingly little in the debates that took place on codification. It appears that legal reformers in the United States, although they did make some use of Bentham's arguments, were anxious to dissociate themselves from his sweeping radicalism; and an article in the whiggish *North American Review* in 1825, while cautiously

50. Bentham to Dumont, 14 Dec. 1817, MS Dumont 33/V, fo. 15, Bibliothèque Publique et Universitaire, Geneva.
51. Bentham, *Truth versus Ashhurst; or Law as it is, contrasted with what it is said to be* (London, 1823), p. 11 (Bowring, v. 235.
52. Bentham, 'A General View of a Complete Code of Laws', Bowring, iii. 206.
53. H.L.A. Hart, *Essays on Bentham: Jurisprudence and Political Theory* (Oxford, 1982), pp. 76-7.
54. Bowring, xi. 23; *The Complete Works of Edward Livingston on Criminal Jurisprudence* (2 vols., New York, 1873), i. 209n.

recommending codification, referred disparagingly to Bentham as a visionary foreign philosopher who was as much distinguished for his zeal in politics as for his learning in jurisprudence[55]

In continental Europe, much more attention was paid to Bentham's ideas in France than in Germany. In Germany the main currents of thought were dominated either by Kant's ideas – and Kantian ethics was and has remained one of the most powerful systems of moral philosophy opposed to utilitarianism – or by the 'historical school', whose approach to jurisprudence was quite different from Bentham's analytical approach.[56] In France, on the other hand (as Bowring put it in his *Autobiographical Recollections*) Bentham's name was 'universally known to the learned through Dumont's translations of his writings'.[57] He had some notable French followers, including the economist Jean-Baptiste Say and the historian and politician Félix Bodin; the *Revue Encyclopédique*, the equivalent in France of the *Edinburgh Review* in Britain, reviewed his work almost as extensively as the *Edinburgh* did; and when he paid a visit to France in 1825 (at the age of 77) he was very flatteringly received. A bust of him – a copy of which stands by the issue-desk in the University of London Library – was sculpted by David of Angers, and when he was taken to see the law courts all the advocates present stood up in his honour.[58] The experience went to his head somewhat, and he said in a letter to Peel shortly after his return to England: '. . . for one disciple (so to speak) in this country, I have fifty at least in France.'[59] One should add that his ideas also provoked a lot of criticism there. France – unlike Latin America – had developed its own liberal ideology in the eighteenth century; and compared with the doctrine of natural rights, to which the French were attached, Benthamism seemed to many people a rather uninspiring philosophy. Many French and French-speaking intellectuals, such as Constant and Madame de Staël, disliked the emphasis on calculation and prudence in utilitarianism, and favoured an ideology which was more uplifting and more capable of producing what Madame de Staël called *dévouement*.[60]

There are three other places I should like to mention before returning to

55. Maxwell Bloomfield, 'William Sampson and the Codifiers: the Roots of American Legal Reform 1820-1830', *American Journal of Legal History*, xi (1967), 245; *North American Review*, xx (1825), 414.
56. On the obstacles to the spread of Bentham's ideas in Germany, see L. Meynier, 'Principles de législation', *Annales de Législation et de Jurisprudence*, ii (1821), 20-7.
57. *Autobiographical Recollections of Sir John Bowring*, p. 338.
58. Evert Schoorl, 'Bentham, Say and Continental Utilitarianism', *Bentham Newsletter*, no. 6 (1982), pp. 8-18; Bowring, x. 551, 600; Bentham to Dumont, 1 Nov. 1825, MS Dumont 74, fo. 56.
59. Bentham to Robert Peel, 8 May 1826, Harvard Law School Library.
60. Norman King, '"The airy form of things forgotten"; Madame de Staël, l'utilitarisme et l'impulsion libérale', *Cahiers Staëliens*, no. 11 (1970), pp. 5-26. See also pp. 00.

England. The first is Greece.[61] During the struggle for independence Bentham was invited by representatives of the Greek provisional government to submit codes for the use of the new state; this encouraged him to press on with his constitutional code, and he actually dispatched a draft of it to Greece in 1823-44. The Greek Senate thanked him in a very complimentary letter, saying among other things: 'The children of friendly Greece, gathering flowers from the flowery meadow of your works, are continually soaring to a height which they have not as yet been able to attain'.[62] That may have been a tactful way of saying that Bentham's code, envisaging as it did the creation of an extremely elaborate bureaucracy, was hardly suitable for a not very developed country in the throes of a war of independence. Certainly Bentham's offerings in the field of constitutional law were shelved; and in *civil* law, although a Greek translation of Dumont's *Traités* was published in Athens after Bentham's death, the new Greek state opted for traditional Byzantine law, with some borrowing from French codes.[63]

The other two places, in both of which Bentham's influence was more substantial, are the tiny republic of Geneva, and the great Indian subcontinent. In the former, after the fall of Napoleon and the restoration of Geneva's independence in 1814, there was a notable period of reform, and Dumont, returning from England, played a crucial role in this as a leading liberal in the Representative Council. Indeed Geneva became a sort of laboratory or testing-ground for the application of Bentham's ideas. Dumont, in the first place, was responsible for drawing up a set of rules for the proceedings of the Representative Council; these rules, like those drawn up by Rivadavia in Buenos Aires, were largely derived from Bentham's work on 'Political Tactics', and (again like Rivadavia's) they have remained substantially in force ever since in Geneva's cantonal parliament.[64] Secondly, a new code of civil procedure was adopted in Geneva in 1819 which was drawn up by Dumont's friend Pierre-François Bellot, who made use of both published and unpublished writings of Bentham on procedure.[65] Thirdly, Dumont himself drew up a code, or regime, for the Geneva penitentiary, which was adoptd in 1825. The prison itself was not built on the architectural model of Bentham's Panopticon, but Dumont's prison regime was closely based on that recommended by Bentham, with its emphasis on constant surveillance,

61. Frederick Rosen, *Bentham, Byron and Greece* (forthcoming, Oxford 1992).
62. Bentham, *Constitutional Code*, vol. i (*CW*), pp. xvi-xxi; Bowring, iv. 583.
63. P.J. Zepos, 'Jeremy Bentham and the Greek Independence', *Proceedings of the British Academy*, lxii (1976), 297-300, 304.
64. Gagnebin, pp. 50-1.
65. Dumont to Bentham, 27 Sept. 1820, Brit. Lib., Add. MSS 33545, fo. 438; Pierre-François Bellot, *Exposé des motifs de la loi sur la procédure civile pour le canton de Genève*, 1821, Avertissement' and pp. 20, 95n., 141n.

regular work, the reform of character, and the separate treatment of different classes of prisoners.[66] Lastly, Dumont tried to introduce a new penal code in Geneva. But this ran into considerable difficulties, and the episode throws some interesting light on the problems of Benthamic codification in a democratic political system. Pierre-François Bellot went so far as to say, shortly after Dumont's death: 'The construction of codes is almost incompatible with the forms of a representative government. Experience proves that almost everywhere where codes exist, they have been passed by bodies which did not have the right to amend, and sometimes not even the right to discuss, and which were forced to obey a strong impulse issuing from a single, all-powerful will'.[67] Bentham indeed believed that the sort of systematic, comprehensive, internally consistent code he envisaged would have to be the product of a single mind, and would then have to be either accepted or rejected by the sovereign legislative power. But Dumont's projected code had to be considered and debated in detail by a succession of committees and commissions and councils;[68] he had to accept a series of modifications and compromises; and when he died in 1829 the project was still some way from final acceptance, and it died with him.

As for Bentham's influence in India, or on British policy in India, this was through James Mill, who had a key post in the East India Company's administration in London – through Macaulay, who was law member of the Governor-General's Council between 1834 and 1838 – and through lesser-known Benthamites such as Alexander Ross and Holt Mackenzie, who served in important judicial and administrative posts in India. Macaulay, though a sharp critic of the utilitarian theory of democracy, was a very well-informed devotee of Bentham's ideas on law. He wrote in the article I quoted from at the beginning of this lecture: 'Posterity will place in the same rank with Galileo and with Locke, the man who found jurisprudence a gibberish, and left it a science'; and in 1835 he wrote in a private letter from India: 'I have immense reforms in hand . . . such as would make old Bentham jump in his grave'.[69] In fact, Macaulay's attempt to introduce a new system of judicial organization and procedure on Benthamic lines was frustrated; but he did succeed (unlike Dumont, and of course in different circumstances) in producing a new penal code for India, which reflected Bentham's influence in a number of ways: for instance in the abandonment of 'technical' terms such as felony and

66. Robert Roth, *Pratiques pénitentiaires et théorie sociale: L'exemple de la prison de Genève (1825-1862)* (Geneva, 1981), pp. 164-7, 171-4.
67. Cited (in French) by Roth, p. 109.
68. For some of the problems he faced, see Dumont to Bentham, 12 Aug. and 1 Oct. 1817, UC x. 107-8, 119-20.
69. *Edinburgh Review*, lv (1832), 553; Eric Stokes, *The English Utilitarians and India* (Oxford, 1959), p. 213n.

misdemeanour, and the substitution of what Bentham called a 'natural' classification of offences; in the precise definition and consistent use of terms; and in the clarity of the arrangement, particularly in the way in which each law was initially stated as a simple command, and then followed by a subsidiary matter such as explanations and exceptions.[70]

Finally I turn to Bentham in his early nineteenth-century English context. Probably the happiest period of his life was his last twenty years or so. He was comfortably off, especially after parliament voted him £23,000 in 1813 to compensate him for the non-implementation of his Panopticon scheme. Also, in contrast to his frailty as a child, he enjoyed a vigorous old age, still playing fives and badminton at the age of 70, and jogging for the sake of his health. (In this respect as in several others he was a pioneer: John Neal, a young American who was staying with him in 1826, recorded in his diary one day in August of that year that Bentham, then 78, had just 'trotted' all the way from Fleet Street to his house in Queen's Square Place on the edge of St James's Park.[71]) Also, as we have seen, Bentham had acquired an international reputation, which gratified him very much; and he had attracted a circle of devoted followers in England. In these latter years he was light-hearted, whimsical and egocentric. He had a favourite walking-stick called Dapple (after Sancho Panza's mule) and an ancient cat called the Reverend Dr John Langborn; and he had a joky vocabulary for use in his own circle, which was a sort of parody of the style in which he wrote. Lady Romilly, staying at Forde Abbey (the country house Bentham had rented) in the autumn of 1817, marvelled at some of the expressions current in his household: 'post-prandial vibration' (stroll after dinner), 'circumgyration' (a walk round the grounds), and 'the grandmother-egg-sucking-principle.'[72]

Some people, at this stage of his life, found him very engaging and regarded him with great affection – as did John Neal, for example;[73] others found him tiresome and even unattractive. He certainly had considerable faults. He was extremely vain; and he could be ungenerous and ungrateful to individuals – as he was towards Dumont, who applied to him for help over the proposed penal code for Geneva, but found him very unresponsive, because he apparently regarded Geneva as too small and unimportant to claim his attention when he was busy with other schemes of greater potential scope.[74] Brougham, in an assessment of Bentham

70. Stokes, pp. 203-17, 219-33.
71. Neal, p. 95.
72. *Ibid.*, p. 64; Bowring, xi. 80; S.H. Romilly (ed.), *Romilly-Edgeworth Letters 1813-1818* (London, 1936), p. 176.
73. Neal described him (p. 22) as 'a man whom it were impossible to know without loving and revering him'. Cf. [William Bridges Adams], 'Jeremy Bentham', *New Monthly Magazine*, July 1832, pp. 49-52.
74. Bentham to J.J. de Mora, 19 Sept. 1820, *Iberian Correspondence*, i. 211-12; Dumont to [?], 6 Feb. 1821 (copy), UC x 43.

published in 1838 which did full justice to his greatness as a legal philosopher, wrote: 'His impatience to see the splendid reforms which his genius had projected, accomplished before his death ... made him latterly regard even his most familiar friends only as instruments of reformation, and gave a very unamiable and indeed a revolting aspect of callousness to his feelings towards them'.[75] Still, there was something rather splendid about Bentham's egotism; about his pride in the range and importance of his efforts to increase human happiness, and his ambition to be remembered as the 'most effectively benevolent' person who had ever lived.[76]

In any case, whatever his shortcomings as a man in his later years, one can say with confidence that few people, between the ages of 54 and 84, have shown as much intellectual vigour and creativity as Bentham did beween 1802 and 1832. In the early years of this period he wrote the work which was to be edited by J. S. Mill and published in five volumes in 1827 as the *Rationale of Judicial Evidence* – a work which was described by Elie Halévy as 'without doubt the most important' of all Bentham's works.[77] In the years after 1808 he developed a whole new utilitarian theory of democracy; and he also developed along with it a sophisticated analysis of the structure and operation of Britain's ruling elite, and anticipated to a large extent the modern Marxist notion of ideological hegemony. He showed how the elite maintained itself not only by relatively crude means such as coercion and corruption, but also by 'delusion' – by using education and various kinds of propaganda to instil into the mass of the people ideas and beliefs that were not in tune with their real interests.[78] Also, in the second decade of the century, Bentham did intensive and original work on logic and language;[79] and in the 1820s he produced his massive *Constitutional Code*, which is a quite remarkable intellectual achievement and (in Dr Rosen's words) a 'classic text of liberal democracy'.[80]

How much impact was made in early nineteenth-century England by this later work of Bentham's? It must be said that much of it either belongs

75. Brougham, *Speeches*, ii. 297.
76. UC xv. 108, cit. Mary Mack, *Jeremy Bentham: An Odyssey of Ideas 1748-1792*, London, 1962, p. 8.
77. Elie Halévy, *The Growth of Philosophic Radicalism*, trans. Mary Morris (2nd ed., London, 1934), p. 383.
78. Cf. L.J. Hume, 'The Political Functions of Bentham's Theory of Fictions', *Bentham Newsletter*, no. 3 (1979), pp. 22-3.
79. For some remarks by C.K. Ogden (co-author with I.A. Richards of *The Meaning of Meaning*, 1923) about the importance of this work, see his articles 'Why Bentham?', *Psyche*, viii, no. 4 (Apr. 1928), p. 2, and 'Forensic Orthology: Back to Bentham', *ibid.*, pp. 3-6.
80. Frederick Rosen, *Jeremy Bentham and Representative Democracy: A Study of the Constitutional Code* (Oxford, 1983), p. 236.

to the esoteric Bentham, or had a very limited circulation. We have seen what Empson wrote about the style of the *Rationale*; and he went on to say: 'Writings, in order to be useful, must be such as people will consent to read'.[81] As for the *Constitutional Code*, only the first volume was published in Bentham's lifetime, in 1830 – and by the end of 1831 only thirteen copies had been sold.[82] The *Plan of Parliamentary Reform* did have a wider circulation, largely because the radical journalist T. J. Wooler of the *Black Dwarf* brought out a cheap edition which was a sort of translation into ordinary language.[83] The most popular of Bentham's later works was *The Book of Fallacies* (in which he cleverly exposed the various types of specious argument that were used by opponents of reform); but probably most people who knew of the book were acquainted with it at second hand through the amusing review or précis of it which Sydney Smith wrote for the *Edinburgh Review*.[84] In general, one feels that it was less through the *direct* impact of his writings, than through the dissemination of his ideas by a limited number of followers and sympathizers, that his influence was exerted in England. To some extent this was done through the press: the *Morning Chronicle*, the *Examiner*, the *Westminster Review*, the *Spectator*, the *Philanthropist* and the *Jurist* were all edited by people who were committed (or at least friendly) to Benthamism, and they all included quite frequent citations of Bentham's work. Also, as is well known, men who were avowed followers of his, such as Edwin Chadwick and Southwood Smith, got into important positions on commissions of inquiry and in government departments in the 1830s and 40s, and played a major role in publicizing abuses and framing legislation to remove them – in fields such as public health, poor relief, and the restriction of child-labour in factories.[85]

It was unfortunate for Bentham's posthumous reputation that by an accident of history one of the principal measures that can be associated with his influence was the New Poor Law of 1834: Chadwick, who was largely responsible for shaping this measure, had worked on Bentham's published and unpublished writings of the 1790s on poor relief, in which the famous (or infamous) principle of 'less eligibility' was clearly expounded.[86] The Benthamites believed, as Joseph Hume told the

81. *Edinburgh Review*, xlviii (1828), 460.
82. Rosen, p. 8n.
83. Thomas, p. 41n.
84. *Edinburgh Review*, xlii (1825), 367-89.
85. Cf. S.E. Finer, 'The Transmission of Benthamite Ideas 1820-50', in G. Sutherland (ed.), *Studies in the Growth of Nineteenth-Century Government* (London, 1972), pp. 11-32; J.W. Flood, 'The Benthamites and their Use of the Press, 1810-1840', Ph.D. thesis, University of London, 1974; Jenifer Hart, 'Nineteenth-Century Social Reform: A Tory Interpretation of History', *Past and Present*, no. 31 (1965), pp. 39-61.
86. J.R. Poynter, *Society and Pauperism: English Ideas on Poor Relief 1795-1834* (London, 1969), pp. 326-7.

Commons, that a generous Poor Law was an evil because it tended to destroy 'that habit of self-dependence and that spirit of self-reliance, upon which alone they could depend for the well-being of the people'.[87] But the harshness of the Act of 1834 did more than anything else to give rise to the conception of Benthamism which one finds in the works of Dickens and Disraeli – the conception that Disraeli summed up in the word 'Brutilitarianism'.[88] However, this should not overshadow the other more beneficial measures of social reform which Bentham's followers helped to bring about; nor should it overshadow the long series of legal reforms in which his influence has been traced.[89]

Of course, the total reconstruction of the English legal system which he would like to have seen never occurred. Nor were the *political* changes of the early nineteenth century such as to produce the sort of 'democratic ascendancy' which, acording to his analysis, was the only thing that could break down the entrenched position of the 'ruling few' and open the way to extensive reform in every field.[90] What in fact happened was a process of infiltration and piecemeal improvement, and much of Bentham's influence in England was of a general and rather intangible kind. John Stuart Mill wrote in a famous essay published in 1838:

> Bentham has been in this age and country the great questioner of things established. It is by the influence of the modes of thought with which his writings inoculated a considerable number of thinking men, that the yoke of authority has been broken, and innumerable opinions, formerly received on tradition as incontestable, are put upon their defence, and required to give an account of themselves.

The *Westminster Review* had said ten years earlier that Bentham's influence was extending itself 'silently and gradually', and was affecting people who hardly knew the titles of his works. And the radical MP John Arthur Roebuck wrote similarly in 1847 of the 'silent revolution' that Bentham had produced in the mode of treating political and moral subjects. 'The whole body of political writers', Roebuck said, 'without the most part

87. Cit. David Roberts, 'The Utilitarian Conscience', in Peter Marsh (ed.), *The Conscience of the Victorian State* (Hassocks, 1979), p. 59.
88. William Hutcheon (ed.), *Whigs and Whiggism: Political Writings by Benjamin Disraeil* (London, 1913), p. 50.
89. For a list of these, see Sir William Holdsworth, *History of English Law* (16 vols., London, 1903-66), xiii. 132-4.
90. For some disparaging remarks about the Great Reform Bill which Bentham made to a visiting foreign jurist in October 1831, see Eduard Gans, *Rückblicke auf Personen und Zustände* (Berlin, 1836), pp. 210-11.

knowing where the inspiration came from, were full of the new spirit'.[91]

A great deal has, of course, been written about the impact of Benthamism in England. This survey, however, has been largely concerned with its impact in other parts of the world; and I should like to finish by recalling a tribute which was paid to Bentham by a foreigner who (as we have already seen) was *not* one of his followers. Madame de Staël once said that the early nineteenth century would be remembered not as the age of Bonaparte or the age of Byron, but as the age of Bentham.[92]

91. John Stuart Mill, *Essays on Ethics, Religion and Society*, ed. J.M. Robson (Toronto, 1969), p. 78; *Westminster Review*, ix (1828), 198-9; R.E. Leader (ed.), *Life and Letters of John Arthur Roebuck* (London, 1897), p. 217, cit. H.L.A. Hart, introduction to paperback edition of Bentham, *An Introduction to the Principles of Morals and Legislation*, ed. Burns and Hart (London, 1982), p. lxix.
92. *The Atlas*, 27 Jan. 1828.

17

Bentham on Private Ethics and the Principle of Utility

At present, any discussion of Bentham's ideas about ethics must take account of the reinterpretation of the subject offered by David Lyons in the first hundred pages or so of his book *In the Interest of the Governed : A Study of Bentham's Philosophy of Utility and Law* (¹). This work, which has cast doubts on many of the received assumptions about this important area of Bentham's thought, has been called 'a major new interpretation', and 'an essential book for students of historical utilitarianism' (²). Most of Lyons' argument is based on a close analysis of certain parts of *An Introduction to the Principles of Morals and Legislation* (³) (particularly the early paragraphs of chapter I and the first twenty paragraphs of chapter XVII), though he does refer from time to time to other writings of Bentham's. He maintains that his concentration on *An Introduction to the Principles* is justified by the fact that it contains the most systematic and celebrated exposition of Bentham's ideas. The main points of Lyons' interpretation can, with the aid of his own summary on pp. 18-20 of his book, be sketched as follows. First, Bentham assumed that interests naturally harmonized. Secondly, he did not embrace psychological egoism ; his view of man as motivated by desire for pleasure and aversion to pain did not have egoistic implications, and for most of his life he did not even think that selfishness was predominant in human motivation. The third and most

---

(1) Oxford, 1973.

(2) J. Brenton Stearns, 'Bentham on Public and Private Ethics', *Canadian Journal of Philosophy*, v (1975), 583 ; Jan Narveson, review in *Philosophical Review*, lxxiv (1975), 425.

(3) First printed in 1780, and published in 1789 ; edited, for *The Collected Works of Jeremy Bentham*, by J. H. Burns and H. L. A. Hart (London, 1970). Referred to in subsequent footnotes as *IPML*, followed by chapter and paragraph numbers.

important point, or set of points, is that Bentham's principle of utility was not 'universalistic,' and that he embraced a 'dual standard,' with community interest as the test within the public or political sphere, while self-interest was to rule in 'private' matters. Lyons goes on to say (pp. 82, 95) that these two standards were conceived by Bentham as resting on a more fundamental principle of utility, which laid down that one ought to serve the interests of the persons (or person) subject to one's governance or 'direction'.

Lyons' book has stimulated a considerable amount of discussion. Some scholars have been unable to accept his main contentions, and two or three interesting critiques of his work have been written [4]. However, although several of the points I wish to make in this essay have been anticipated in some degree by other scholars [5], I believe that some of the important questions that Lyons raised have not yet been as fully examined and as satisfactorily resolved as they might be. My aims will be, first, to provide a thorough refutation of many (though not all) of Lyons' arguments, and secondly to provide an alternative interpretation of Bentham's ideas which is more plausible and firmly based than his, and which improves on other interpretations put forward in the course of the controversy over his book. These aims, I believe, can largely be accomplished on the basis of the work of Bentham's on which Lyons has chosen to focus ; but I shall also, like him, draw on other writings of his when they seem to illuminate passages found in *An Introduction to the Principles*. In particular, reference will be made in the latter part of the essay to the writings on 'deontology' [6], in which, towards the end of his life, Bentham returned in a more direct fashion to some of the themes which had been treated in passing in *An Introduction*. An eminent reviewer of Lyons' book, D. D. Raphael, has said that whether one accepts his

---

(4) See in particular Stearns' article cited above, pp. 583-94 ; Rolf SARTORIUS, review in *Journal of Philosophy*, lxxi (1974), 779-87 ; L. J. HUME, 'Revisionism in Bentham Studies', *Bentham Newsletter*, no. 1 (1978), 3-20 (especially 5-11).

(5) Particular instances will be acknowledged in the footnotes below.

(6) I am much indebted to Professor Amnon Goldworth, who is editing the *Deontology* (exclusively from Bentham's manuscripts) for *The Collected Works of Jeremy Bentham*, for allowing me to make use of his transcripts. I am also grateful to Miss Claire Gobbi, Dr. Douglas Long and Dr. José de Sousa e Brito for drawing my attention to relevant sources, and above all to Professor Herbert Hart for his valuable comments on a draft of this paper.

interpretation or rejects it, it is difficult, without forced readings of one kind or another, to make anything really coherent out of what Bentham said. 'On ethical theory', says Raphael, 'he writes loosely, and it is hard to resist the conclusion that his thought lacks rigour' [7]. It is not my intention to argue that there was no inconsistency in what Bentham wrote about ethics. But I hope to be able to provide a better explanation of what he meant than has been offered hitherto.

The first point that Lyons makes at any length in his book is that Bentham's criterion of right and wrong within the public or political sphere was one of 'parochial' rather than 'universalistic' hedonism. He says that more often than not, when Bentham gave a considered definition of his standard, he referred not to the maximization of happiness in general, but to the maximization of the happiness of the community in question. This may well be true. But it should not be taken to imply that Bentham *rejected* universalism, or that there was anything inherently restricted or parochial about his criterion. In an unpublished 'Constitutional Catechism' written in 1817 and intended as a theoretical preface for a work on parliamentary reform, he explicitly stated that for the purposes of the work in question he was assuming the position not of a 'philanthropist' but of a 'patriot' – of a patriot who regarded the proper end of government as 'the production of the greatest quantity of happiness on the part of the greatest number of the members of the community in question'. But he added that he did not wish to disclaim altogether the character of a 'general philanthropist' ; he was putting it aside on the present occasion for the sake of simplifying the discussion [8]. In most of his writings, the standpoint he adopted was that of a writer on legislation, concerned with the laws that could be made by a sovereign ruling over a particular community ; and he wrote in a manuscript of the 1780s : 'The end of the conduct which a sovereign ought to observe relative to his own subjects, – the end of the internal laws of a society, – ought to be the greatest happiness of the society concerned' [9]. This statement by no means

---

(7) D. D. RAPHAEL, 'The Jurisprudence of Bentham', *Times Literary Supplement*, 27 September 1974, p. 1036.

(8) Bentham MSS, University College London, box cxxv, sheets 185, 192 (cited below in the form : UC cxxv. 185, 192).

(9) 'Principles of International Law', *Works of Jeremy Bentham*, ed. John Bowring (11 vols., Edinburgh, 1838-43), ii. 537.

rules out the possibility that if a different standpoint were adopted the principle of utility could be given a wider application, and more will be said about this possibility later in the essay. For the time being, however, it may be accepted that in *An Introduction to the Principles of Morals and Legislation* Bentham regarded the criterion appropriate to his purpose as being the happiness of the community to which the legislation was to apply.

The next point in Lyons' argument is that while this 'parochial' standard applied to the field of public ethics or the art of government, Bentham embraced a different standard for the field of *private* ethics or the art of *self*-government : under this art, according to Lyons, 'only the interests of the single, *self*-directing agent who is concerned are to be promoted, by himself' (p. 31). The most explicit piece of textual evidence cited in support of this interpretation is drawn from paragraph 20 of chapter XVII :

> Private ethics teaches how each man may dispose himself to pursue the course most conducive to his own happiness, by means of such motives as offer of themselves : the art of legislation (which may be considered as one branch of the science of jurisprudence) teaches how a multitude of men, composing a community, may be disposed to pursue that course which upon the whole is the most conducive to the happiness of the whole community, by means of motives to be applied by the legislator.

This passage is a crucial one, and Lyons' critics have admitted that it does appear to give strong support to his dual standard hypothesis ([10]). But before we consider the passage and its interpretation directly, we may examine some of the difficulties which, as Lyons recognizes, his hypothesis presents, and the ways in which he attempts to resolve them.

One such difficulty arises from the possibility of conflict between the two standards. How could Bentham have said that in the private sphere one should maximize one's own happiness, while in the public sphere one should maximize the happiness of the members of one's community ? How could he have combined an egoistic standard in private ethics with a community standard in public ethics ? Lyons has various answers to offer to this objection, but perhaps the most basic one, and the one which has the largest implications for the develop-

(10) Sartorius, p. 784 ; Hume, p. 9.

ment of his argument is that 'Bentham, when he embraced the dual standard, did not entertain the possibility of a real conflict between the long-term interests of a single individual and the interests of his community' (p. 42). Lyons concedes that it is apparent from some of Bentham's later writings that he did not *retain* a belief in the natural harmony of human interests. He refers to the passage in the prefatory section of the *Constitutional Code* which says that 'on every occasion, the happiness of every individual is liable to come into competition with the happiness of every other', and that two people may find themselves in a situation in which 'not merely the happiness of each, but the existence of each, stands in competition with, and is incompatible with the existence of the other' [11]. Lyons is convinced, however, that at the time when he wrote *An Introduction to the Principles* Bentham would have denied the possibility of such conflicts of interest ; and he considers that textual evidence to this effect can be found in *An Introduction* itself.

The passage to which he draws attention – in chapter XVII, paragraph 8 – looks on the face of it rather unpromising from the point of view of his general interpretation of Bentham's thought. The passage contains the following statements :

> There is no case in which a private man ought not to direct his own conduct to the production of his own happiness, and of that of his fellow creatures ... Every act which promises to be beneficial upon the whole to the community (himself included) each individual ought to perform of himself ... Every act which promises to be pernicious upon the whole to the community (himself included) each individual ought to abstain from of himself ...

Lyons recognizes that in saying that a 'private man' ought to do what was beneficial on the whole to the community and ought to abstain from doing what was pernicious to it, Bentham was apparently treating community interest as a standard applicable to private as well as public affairs. But, Lyons argues, Bentham also said that a man ought always to pursue *his own* happiness, as well as to benefit his community. The only way of making sense of the paragraph, according to Lyons, is to suppose that Bentham assumed that the interests of a private man converged, at least in the long run, with those of his community :

(11) Bowring, ix. 6.

Lyons interprets him as saying in effect that 'a man who serves his own happiness will always serve the happiness of his fellow creatures' (p. 54).

However, there is another way of interpreting the passage, which does not entail the assumption by Bentham of this sort of convergence or harmony. According to this interpretation, he was not saying or implying anything here about the *relationship between* an individual's promotion of his own happiness and his promotion of the happiness of others. What he was indicating was that, in assessing a man's conduct by the criterion of utility, one should take into account the effects of that conduct *both* on his own happiness *and* on that of his fellow creatures. Bentham was saying that a private man 'ought' to — because it was in accordance with the principle of utility that he should ([12]) — direct his conduct to increasing the combined stock of his own happiness and that of his fellow creatures (i.e. the happiness of the community, himself included). Bentham should not, one may add, be understood as saying in this passage that *every action* a man performed ought to be directed to increasing the happiness of other people as well as his own ; for he had said two paragraphs earlier that 'a man's happiness will depend, in the first place, upon such parts of his behaviour as none but himself are interested in : in the next place, upon such parts of it as may affect the happiness of those about him'. Clearly, in those parts of his behaviour which concerned only himself a man would, by promoting his own happiness, increase the stock of happiness in the community without increasing the happiness of other people. But in those parts of his behaviour which did affect others, the extent to which his actions conformed to the principle of utility would depend on their impact on the aggregated happiness of himself and the others affected. It will be apparent that this interpretation of the passage involves a view of Bentham's basic principle that is at odds with the hypothesis put forward by Lyons. More will need to be said later in exposition and defence of the view advanced as an alternative to his. But first there are some further aspects of his argument that need to be considered.

One consequence of his view that Bentham believed in a natural harmony of interests is that Lyons is brought up against the usual

(12) *IPML* I para. 9.

interpretation of Bentham's theory of legal punishment. According to this interpretation, as Lyons summarizes it (p. 62),

> Bentham's rationale for legal punishment ... presupposes that the interests of an individual often conflict with those of his community ... Punishment is needed to *create* an *artificial* harmony, so that individuals while serving their own interests will be obliged to serve the overall interest of the community too. The threat of punishment is added to *change* the interests of those who come under the laws.

Lyons maintains that this interpretation is unfounded – or at least has no foundation, expressed or implied, in *An Introduction to the Principles*. His own counter-interpretation of Bentham's theory of punishment is rather briefly sketched. But what he suggests is that the function of punishment, in Bentham's view, was not to change our long-term *interests* but to adjust our *motives* – our motives, Lyons says, being 'no simple function of our long range interests' (p. 63). He seems to be saying that according to Bentham punishment, or the threat of punishment, was necessary to adjust people's motives in instances where the people concerned misconceived their long-term interests and imagined, wrongly, that they stood to gain from conduct which would damage the interests of others : i.e. punishment was necessary to prevent one individual from harming another in cases where their interests '*appear[ed]* to conflict without actually doing so' (p. 64).

In claiming that around 1780 Bentham did *not* regard legal punishment as necessary to create a harmony of interests, Lyons relies less on positive evidence in support of his own interpretation than on what he regards as the absence of evidence against it. He claims that Bentham's actual pronouncements on punishment and human psychology in *An Introduction to the Principles* 'are all compatible with the view that there is a natural harmony of human interests in the long run' (pp. 63-4). However, there are passages in *An Introduction* which seem hard to reconcile with this claim. In paragraph 8 of chapter XIV (the chapter on punishments and offences) Bentham did apparently assume that, if punishment were left out of the account, men *could* profit from offences against others – and that punishment was necessary to eliminate the possibility of such profit. 'The value of the punishment', he wrote, 'must not be less in any case than what is sufficient to outweigh that of the profit by the offence'. And he explained in a footnote that what he meant by the profit of an offence was 'the pleasure or advantage, of whatever kind it be, which a man reaps, or expects to reap, from the gratification of the desire which prompted him to engage in the offence'. There was no suggestion here that, because of a *natural* harmony of interests, any such advantage must be illusory [13]. Moreover, as L. J. Hume has pointed out, there is clear evidence in other writings of Bentham's that both before and after the time when he wrote *An Introduction to the Principles* he regarded legislation as necessary (at least in many instances) to adjust and harmonize people's *interests*, not simply to adjust their motives. He said, for example, in *A View of the Hard-Labour Bill* (1778) that it was the function of law, by the administration of punishments or rewards, to connect a man's interest with his duty (a theme to which he was often to return); and he wrote in his 'Scotch Reform' manuscripts thirty years later: '... it is the endeavour of the legislator, so far as he understands his business, to bring the interest of each individual separately taken into a connection and coincidence as close and intimate as possible with the interest of the public' [14].

After his attempt to show that Bentham's theory of punishment was not inconsistent with a belief in a natural harmony of interests, Lyons goes on to say (p. 64):

> ... the main error in the received interpretation of Bentham's rationale for punishment is that it pictures Bentham as a 'psychological egoist', one who holds that we all try to serve our own interests without a thought for others (except as we think that they are obstacles to or instruments for reaching our own private ends). It is dogmatic that Bentham conceived of human nature as selfish. But this dogma, like many others, is ill-founded.

Lyons admits that in the latter part of his life Bentham did expound a 'principle of self-preference' which affirmed that human nature was predominantly selfish. But he reckons that this principle could hardly have been combined with a belief, such as he supposes Bentham to have held earlier in his career, in a natural harmony of interests – for if such harmony existed what occasion would there be for self-preference

---

(13) Cf. also the passage in *IPML* XII para. 17 where Bentham says that if justice ceased to be administered 'the weak would presently be oppressed and injured in all manner of ways by the strong'.

(14) BOWRING, iv. 12 (cf. Hume, pp. 10-11); UC xciv. 281.

to operate ? So he suggests (pp. 68-9) that Bentham's adoption of a belief in human selfishness accompanied his recognition, late in his career, that the interests of different individuals might conflict.

In the passage quoted above Lyons identifies, in effect, psychological egoism with the belief that human nature is selfish. In my view it is easy enough to show that Bentham did not believe that human nature was wholly 'selfish' in the usual sense of the word – but less easy to show that he was not a psychological egoist. A question posed, as Lyons recognizes, by his denial that Bentham was a psychological egoist is how this denial can be made compatible with Bentham's 'psychological hedonism', his belief that all human action is determined by the desire for pleasure and the aversion to pain. A line of argument that Lyons suggests in answer to this question is that Bentham's 'hedonic theory of goals' can be reconciled with his 'acceptance of non-egoistic motivations and desires' if we assume him to have thought that although our desires are always for pleasures and our aversions are always to pains, those pleasures and pains need not be *our own*. The prospect of bringing pleasure to another might attract us for its own sake, says Lyons : 'it need not be the case that one wants to serve others *because of the pleasure one gets from it*' (p. 71). The weakness of this line of argument is that it simply does not square with the argument of chapter X, 'Of Motives', in *An Introduction to the Principles*. It is clear from this chapter that when Bentham said that every act was motivated by a prospective pleasure or pain, he meant a pleasure or pain for the agent himself. For instance, when he listed the pleasures and pains to which the different motives corresponded, he said that the motive termed good-will or benevolence corresponded to 'the pleasures of sympathy' (paragraph 25) (¹⁵).

There is a real sense, therefore, in which Bentham did have an egoistic theory of motivation. But his view that all actions were motivated, directly, by a desire to obtain some pleasure or to avoid some pain on the part of the agent did not by any means imply that he considered human nature, or human conduct, to be wholly 'selfish'. In *An Introduction to the Principles* and elsewhere, he clearly maintained

---

(15) Cf. STEARNS, p. 589. The point that benevolent actions arose from a desire on the part of the agent to obtain the pleasures or to avoid the pains of sympathy was very clearly made in a manuscript of Bentham's dated September 1814 : UC xiv. 140.

that men had (at least to a certain extent) social or sympathetic affections which led them to take pleasure in, and hence social motives which led them to promote, the happiness of others ([16]).

Lyons, while somewhat misconstruing (as it seems to me) Bentham's theory of motivation, correctly recognizes that the view of human nature presented in *An Introduction* allowed for what may loosely be termed 'unselfish' conduct. But he pushes his argument considerably further than this. He suggests (p. 18) that for most of his life Bentham 'did not even think that selfishness is generally predominant' in human nature. It was only in his later years, Lyons maintains, that he was '*converted* to the opinion that human beings are generally selfish' (p. 70). It has been argued above that the view that Bentham first held, and then abandoned, a belief in a natural harmony of human interests is unfounded. Similarly, there seems to be little foundation for the view that in the course of his career Bentham radically changed his opinions about human selfishness. The main piece of direct evidence that Lyons adduces for such a change (p. 68) is a passage of reminiscence, recorded by Bowring, in which Bentham said that until he was sixty or so he was at a loss to know why his proposals for promoting the greatest happiness of the greatest number met with such a negative response from those in authority. All this time, said Bentham, the field of politics was a mystery to him ; but eventually he found a clue to the labyrinth, and that clue was 'the principle of self-preference' ([17]). Lyons interprets Bentham as saying that it was at this point that he first became properly aware of the existence of the principle. It would be equally possible, it seems to me, to interpret the passage as meaning that it was at this point (around 1809, the date of his definitive conversion to political radicalism) that he recognized the way in which the principle operated on the conduct of politicians. In any case, Bentham's exercises in intellectual autobiography are not always very reliable, and too much weight should not be attached to the passage. What is more important is to inquire whether the concept of self-preference − i.e. the notion that, in general, self-regarding interests and motives predominate over social ones − is to be found in Bentham's earlier as well as his later writings.

(16) *IPML* V para. 10, VI para. 21, X paras. 34-6 ; *A Table of the Springs of Action*, Bowring, i. 202.
(17) Bowring, x. 80.

In chapter X of *An Introduction to the Principles* Bentham suggested that there was one motive, good-will, which could be described as 'purely social' ; this was the motive that corresponded to the pleasures of sympathy — the pleasures that an individual derived from the contemplation of the happiness of others, without his being influenced by any ulterior view with respect to his own self-regarding interest. There were also motives — the love of reputation, the desire of amity, and the motive of religion — which could be described as semi-social, meaning that they had a social tendency but were 'self-regarding at the same time'. Thirdly, there were the self-regarding motives : physical desire, pecuniary interest, love of power, and self-preservation (the last embracing the fear of pain, the love of ease, and the love of life). Some pages later (chapter XII, paragraph 33), Bentham wrote unequivocally that 'the motives, whereof the influence is at once most powerful, most constant, and most extensive, are the motives of physical desire, the love of wealth, the love of ease, the love of life, and the fear of pain : all of them self-regarding motives'. One may add that in 1790 he could write even more explicitly that 'the predominance of the self-regarding affections over the social' was a 'universal' property of human nature [18].

We must now turn our attention to the central question of 'private ethics' and how Bentham's view of it should be interpreted. In chapter XVII, paragraph 20, of *An Introduction to the Principles* he undertook to 'recapitulate' his account of the distinction between the art of private ethics and the art of legislation, and he said (as we have already seen) that private ethics 'teaches how each man may dispose himself to pursue the course most conducive to his own happiness'. One of Lyons' critics, L. J. Hume, has argued that in fact this statement did not accurately summarize what Bentham had said earlier in the chapter —

---

(18) UC cxxvi. 12 ; printed in Mary P. MACK, *Jeremy Bentham : An Odyssey of Ideas, 1748-1792* (London, 1962), p. 455, and cited by Hume, p. 7. Just as the notion — if not the explicitly formulated 'principle' — of self-preference can be found in Bentham's earlier writings, so can sympathy be found playing a substantial part in his later writings. Indeed, far from attaching *less* importance to sympathy in the latter part of his life, he actually gave it in a significant respect more prominence. In *IPML* III he had enumerated four 'sanctions' (or sources of pain and pleasure, and thus of motives) : the physical, the political, the moral and the religious ; in his later writings, the 'sympathetic sanction' was added to the original list. See particularly 'Logical Arrangements, or Instruments of Invention and Discovery', BOWRING, iii. 291-2.

notably in paragraph 6, where he wrote about the role of ethics in leading a man to discharge his 'duty to his neighbour'; and Hume suggests that in his definition of private ethics in paragraph 20 Bentham simply made a mistake [19]. However, this explanation seems unsatisfactory in view of the fact that Bentham made several other statements to the same effect. For instance, in a passage which was apparently a draft for part of chapter XVII of *An Introduction to the Principles*, he described 'the business of Ethics' as being 'to teach a private person how to compass his own happiness by ordering his own actions' [20]. And there are similar statements in his later writings on 'Deontology' or 'Deontology Private'. He wrote in 1819, for example : 'Deontology, or *Ethics*, ... is that branch of art and science which has for its object the learning and shewing for the information of each individual, by what means the net amount of his happiness may be made as large as possible' [21]. It seems likely that Bentham meant what he said about private ethics in chapter XVII, paragraph 20. If one accepts that Lyons is correct in making this assumption [22], a question one must ask is how far he is right in deducing from what Bentham said that he intended private behaviour to be judged by the standard of self-interest and not by that of community interest.

The first point that needs to be made – or argued further, for it has been adumbrated above in the discussion of chapter XVII, paragraph 8 – is that several passages in *An Introduction to the Principles* seem clearly to indicate that the standard of community interest was meant to apply to the private as well as the public sphere of conduct. One such passage occurs in chapter XI ('Of Human Dispositions in General'), paragraph 2, where it is said that a man's disposition can be judged good or bad 'according to the effects it has in augmenting or diminishing the happiness of the community'. Another passage, to which Lyons devotes some attention (pp. 74-8), occurs in the 'explicit and determinate account' of the principle of utility early in chapter I. Paragraphs 6 and 7 read as follows :

(19) HUME, p. 9.
(20) UC c. 24.
(21) UC xiv. 215.
(22) The assumption does involve certain difficulties with regard to the consistency of Bentham's argument, and these will be considered below.

6. An action then may be said to be conformable to the principle of utility, or, for shortness sake, to utility, (meaning with respect to the community at large) when the tendency it has to augment the happiness of the community is greater than any it has to diminish it.

7. A measure of government (which is but a particular kind of action, performed by a particular person or persons) may be said to be conformable to or dictated by the principle of utility, when in like manner the tendency which it has to augment the happiness of the community is greater than any which it has to diminish it.

Lyons admits that these paragraphs seem to leave no room for a dual standard ; they appear to say that community interest is the single, basic standard of utility by which any action, private or political, should be judged. He tries to reconcile the passage with the dual standard reading by suggesting that Bentham was referring in paragraph 6 not to actions in a general sense but to a particular type of political action, 'the ordinary things done by real government functionaries in their official capacities', whereas in paragraph 7 he was talking about 'measures of government, or the things done by the state as a whole'. Lyons admits that this reading of paragraph 6 appears forced. Indeed, there is nothing in the text to indicate that by 'an action' in that paragraph Bentham meant a political action performed by a government official, or that in the two paragraphs together he was drawing a rather fine distinction between two different kinds of political action. And it is surely implausible to suggest that if Bentham found it necessary to explain in paragraph 7 that a measure of government was 'a particular kind of action, performed by a particular person or persons', he would have found it unnecessary to explain in paragraph 6 that by 'an action' he meant not any action but another particular kind of action. Moreover, that by 'an action' in paragraph 6 Bentham did in fact mean *any* action is strongly indicated by paragraph 9 of the same chapter (which Lyons does not quote) : 'A man may be said to be a partisan of the principle of utility, when the approbation or disapprobation he annexes to any action, or to any measure, is determined by, and proportioned to the tendency which he conceives it to have to augment or to diminish the happiness of the community'.

Bentham thus held, it seems, *both* that each person should be taught how to maximize his own happiness, *and* that each person's conduct could be judged by the standard of community interest. To see how this apparent inconsistency may be resolved, we need to return to the beliefs about motivation which underlay Bentham's treatment of both legislation and private ethics. As indicated above, he had an egoistic theory of motivation in that he believed that all actions were directly motivated by a desire on the part of the agent to obtain some pleasure or to avoid some pain (or by a combination of such desires). Furthermore, he thought it not only psychologically inevitable, but also consonant with the principle of utility, that each person should pursue his own happiness [23]. Indeed, he believed that the basic drive of each individual to maximize his own happiness was the most important mechanism whereby the maximization of happiness in the aggregate was promoted ; and it could to a large extent be relied upon to achieve this object for reasons stated in chapter XVI, paragraph 44, of *An Introduction to the Principles* : '... as there is no man who is so sure of being *inclined*, on all occasions, to promote your happiness as you yourself are, so neither is there any man who upon the whole can have had so good opportunities as you must have had of *knowing* what is most conducive to that purpose.'

However − and this is a crucial point in relation to Lyons' dual standard hypothesis − the fact that Bentham approved of this basic drive did not mean that he set up the promotion of the agent's own happiness as the one standard by which all his private (or non-political) actions should be judged : he did not suggest that *anything* a private individual could do that was conducive to his own happiness was, in utilitarian terms, right. For he recognized that although there were many ways of promoting one's own happiness that were either innocuous or actually conducive to the happiness of others, one *might* derive pleasure [24] or advantage from actions that *damaged* other people's happiness. The individual's pursuit of his own happiness thus needed, for the sake of the general happiness, to be regulated to a certain extent ; and the basic means of doing this − of adjusting the individual's pursuit of his own happiness to the requirements of utility − was legislation. In a draft of chapter XVII of *An Introduction to the Principles*, Bentham wrote :

(23) He wrote in a draft of *IPML* I that it would be 'without any foundation' to suppose that 'any other than his own happiness ought to be the end of any individual' (UC c. 114).

(24) He wrote in *IPML* VI para. 22 that as well as 'sympathetic sensibility' there was such a thing as 'antipathetic sensibility' − 'the propensity that a man has to derive pain from the happiness, and pleasure from the unhappiness, of other sensitive beings'.

... a private man has need of the legislator for two purposes : to give him information about what acts are beneficial, what pernicious : and to furnish him with what motives he may stand in need of to induce him to perform the one and abstain from the other, in addition to any motives which he may chance to be furnished with by any other means (²⁵).

Legislation was not the only means of influencing behaviour in such a way as to promote happiness : as Bentham made clear in *An Introduction* itself, private ethics was another (²⁶). Now according to Lyons' interpretation of the term, 'private ethics' must be concerned essentially with moral *judgements* − with saying what private individuals ought and ought not to do. In his view, whereas legislation is concerned with regulating behaviour, private ethics 'simply judges acts of ordinary individuals in their concrete circumstances' (p. 57). He therefore finds it puzzling that Bentham should refer (in chapter XVII, paragraph 9, of *An Introduction*) to 'cases in which ethics ought, and in which legislation ought not (in a direct manner at least) to interfere' ; and Lyons suggests that when Bentham spoke thus of private ethics 'interfering' in private behaviour he was speaking 'in a loose and misleading way' (p. 56). However, it is evident from what Bentham said that he did not regard private ethics as simply a matter of enunciating moral principles and judgements. It was an 'art' of a more practical nature, and the exponent of this art was not a detached theorist or arbiter of morals, but someone committed, like the legislator, to the promotion of happiness.

In chapter XVII of *An Introduction* Bentham outlined the respective spheres of legislation and private ethics. In doing so, he indicated that it was primarily the business of legislation to block those channels of behaviour in which a man's pursuit of his own happiness would cause injury to other people (²⁷), while the distinctive sphere of private ethics − the sphere in which it operated more or less independently of legislation − consisted very largely of those areas of behaviour in which a man's pursuit of his own happiness either would not affect, or would actually promote, the happiness of others. His main concern was to

(25) UC c. 24.
(26) *IPML* XVII para. 8. A third, intermediate, mode of influencing behaviour − indirect legislation − was not explicitly mentioned in the original text of *IPML*.
(27) Cf. *IPML* XVII para. 18 : 'There are few cases, if any, in which it would *not* be expedient to punish a man for injuring his neighbour'.

define how far the role of *legislation* should extend, and he did not embark on a direct examination of the art of private ethics itself. None the less, one or two points were brought out clearly enough about the differences between the ways in which private ethics and legislation respectively operated. The former was a mode of influencing behaviour by teaching or instruction [28] rather than by legal constraint. Also, whereas legislation dealt with people in the mass, private ethics was concerned with individuals ; and it was defined as the art of teaching each individual how to maximize his own happiness 'by means of such motives as offer of themselves' [29]. While legislation was capable of influencing behaviour by creating *new* motives, private ethics had to operate with whatever motives were available – i.e. those that arose from the individual's own temperament or sensibility, and from the circumstances in which he found himself [30].

In paragraph 7 Bentham asked what motives a man could have, apart from those furnished by legislation (and, he added, by religion), for consulting the happiness of others. He said in reply that while 'the only interests which a man at all times and on all occasions is sure to find *adequate* motives for consulting, are his own' [31], men did have *some* motives for consulting the happiness of others : and he specifically mentioned the 'purely social' motive of sympathy or benevolence and the 'semi-social' motives of love of amity and love of reputation. But it followed from his own theory of human nature that a man could only be motivated to consult the happiness of others to the extent that he himself expected, directly or indirectly, to obtain pleasure or to avoid pain by so doing. It therefore made sense for Bentham to say in paragraph 20 that the purpose of private ethics was to teach each individual how to maximize his *own* happiness, and not to say that one of its purposes was, as an end in itself, to teach him how to promote the happiness of others.

(28) Cf. *IPML* XVI para. 46 : '... to instruct each individual in what manner to govern his own conduct in the details of life, is the particular business of private ethics'.

(29) *IPML* XVII para. 20.

(30) *IPML* XVII, para. 7.

(31) In *Of Laws in General* (ed. H. L. A. Hart, London, 1970, p. 70n.) Bentham said that if the word 'interest' was understood 'in a large and extensive sense ... as comprehending all sorts of motives', it was undoubtedly true that a man was 'never governed by any thing but his own interest'. Cf. *Rationale of Judicial Evidence*, Bowring, vi. 257n.

Bentham did evidently believe that teaching the individual how to maximize his own long-term happiness (at any rate within a framework of law which made most forms of 'pernicious' behaviour unprofitable) would in many ways have the effect of promoting or protecting the happiness of those with whom that person came into contact. Thus from the legislator's point of view private ethics could be regarded as a valuable adjunct of legislation in ensuring that each man consulted the happiness of his neighbour. Moreover, Bentham said (in paragraph 15) that the legislator could increase the efficacy of private ethics in this respect by 'giving strength and direction to the influence of the moral sanction' : in other words, by influencing the climate of opinion he could alter the circumstances in which private ethics had to operate, and could increase the extent to which the motive of love of reputation prompted people to act in ways that were conducive to the general happiness ([32]). However, it remained true that the exponent of the art of private ethics, as a teacher of individuals, could only induce those individuals to consult the happiness of others to the extent that he could show them that they would maximize their own happiness by doing so.

Now it is true that there are some passages in chapter XVII which seem to conflict with this interpretation of Bentham's view of private ethics. At times in that chapter – for example in paragraph 12, where he said that it was the business of private ethics to 'endeavour to prevent' pernicious acts which could not be effectively dealt with by legislation – he was apparently suggesting that private ethics could be governed by the same moral principle as legislation. It may be that at the time when he wrote the chapter he was only in the process of realizing that he could not, consistently with other parts of his theory, treat the direct object of private ethics as being identical with the proper end of legislation. In paragraph 20, however, Bentham *does* seem to have recognized this ; and that my interpretation is the right way of elucidating what he said here about private ethics is strongly suggested by some later remarks of his in the *Deontology*. We have already observed that in 1819 he defined 'deontology or ethics' in terms very

(32) In his unfinished work on 'Indirect Legislation', written shortly after *An Introduction to the Principles*, Bentham suggested various ways in which the legislator could 'cultivate' the moral sanction : see especially UC lxxxvii. 18.

similar to his definition of private ethics in *An Introduction*. In the same year, in explaining the purpose of his treatise on deontology, he wrote :

> For its ultimate and practical result this work has for its object the pointing out to each man on each occasion what course of conduct promises to be in the highest degree conducive to his happiness : to his own happiness, first and last : to the happiness of others no farther than in so far as his happiness is promoted by promoting theirs, than his interest coincides with theirs : for that in the case of man in general regard should any further be had to the happiness of others will be shewn to be neither possible nor upon the whole desirable [33].

One implication of the interpretation I have been offering is that there *was* a certain dualism in Bentham's thinking on ethics. This, again, emerges clearly from the *Deontology*. In a passage written in 1814 he said that the answer to the question of *whose* happiness a man ought to promote 'will be liable to be different, according to [whether] the party whose interest, i.e. whose well being, is considered as the preferable object of regard is the individual alone, or the society of which he is considered as a member' [34]. Bentham clearly believed that if one considered matters from the standpoint of the individual it made no sense to say that he *ought* to seek anything other than he was psychologically bound to seek. The only judgement that could be made from this standpoint was how *effectively* the individual was pursuing his own happiness : how far the behaviour determined by his current conception of his own interest was in fact calculated to promote his own greatest happiness in the long term. On the other hand, a man's conduct could also be considered from a *social* standpoint, and judged by how far it was conducive to the welfare of the community − or to the welfare of those members of it (not excluding himself) whose interests his conduct affected. In so far as his behaviour, judged from this point of view, was in conflict with the dictates of utility, the principal implication for Bentham was not, one imagines, that the individual himself should be held to be personally responsible and culpable, but that the social arrangements and other factors that had conditioned his behaviour were at fault, and should as far as possible be adjusted so as to supply him with motives to behave otherwise.

(33) UC xiv. 233.
(34) UC xiv. 46.

Bentham regarded as futile the sort of moralizing that simply consisted in telling people that they ought to behave differently from the ways in which they were disposed to behave. He wrote in the *Deontology* : 'By no other means with any rational prospect of success can you endeavour to cause a man to do so and so, otherwise than by shewing him that it is, or making it to be, his interest so to do' ([35]).

Of the two basic modes of influencing behaviour in Bentham's scheme of things, legislation and private ethics (or private deontology), it was the former that could *make* it to be a man's interest to behave in one way rather than another, by providing him with *inducements* to do so ([36]). And the legislator could and should give direct application to the principle of utility : as Bentham put it in chapter III, paragraph 1, of *An Introduction to the Principles*, 'the happiness of the individuals, of whom a community is composed, ... is ... the sole standard, to which each individual ought, as far as depends on the legislator, to be *made* to fashion his behaviour'. But the exponent of private ethics had to adopt the standpoint of the individual, and operate within the limits set by the individual's pursuit of his own interest in the given circumstances : he could only *show* the individual what his real interest was ([37]). There is a sense, therefore, in which the object or 'standard' of private ethics or deontology *was* necessarily different from that of legislation. However, while this shows that Lyons was not entirely on a false scent, it does not validate the dual standard hypothesis as he presents it. As I have tried to show, Bentham did not divide behaviour into public behaviour, which should be judged by the standard of community interest, and

(35) UC xiv. 186.

(36) Laws, wrote Bentham in the *Deontology*, 'have for their endeavour to cause it to be for a man's interest to do that which they make it his duty to do' (UC xiv. 232). See also the distinction between nomography and private deontology in Bentham's 'Nomography ; or the Art of Inditing Laws', Bowring, iii. 235.

(37) It would seem to follow from this that if the circumstances were such that an individual could maximize his own happiness by conduct which damaged the happiness of others, the exponent of private ethics (or the deontologist) should point to such conduct as the most expedient course. How far Bentham faced and accepted this implication is not clear. He did say, in describing the purpose of the section of his *Deontology* that concerned the 'dictates of extra-regarding prudence', that it was intended not only to show 'how far on each occasion it will be conducive to a man's self-regarding interest to have regard to the interest of others', but also to show, 'so far as the regard for his own general and ultimate interest allows of his pursuing his particular and immediate interest at the expense of theirs, what course of conduct is most conducive to his purpose' (UC xiv. 235).

private behaviour, which should be judged by the standard of self-interest. The distinction he drew was between two different modes of influencing behaviour, and between the different standpoints and objectives which were appropriate for the exponents of these respective 'arts'. In so far as he made normative judgements regarding policy and behaviour within a particular community, these were based on the utilitarian standard of community interest, and actions of all kinds, private as well as public, could be judged good or bad by this criterion [38].

A matter that remains to be considered is Lyons' contention that the two standards he attributes to Bentham were both derived from an underlying 'differential' principle of utility. According to Lyons, 'Bentham defines and divides ethics ... in terms of those being directed rather than those affected' (p. 82) ; the standard for public ethics, or the sphere of government and legislation, is the happiness of the community − the standard for private ethics, or the art of self-government, is the happiness of the self-directing agent − and both these standards can be understood as being derived from a basic principle of utility which says that one ought to promote the happiness of those under one's governance or direction. Lyons admits that this formulation of the principle of utility, and the derivation of the dual standard from it, are not explicitly set out in Bentham's work ; and he admits also that his own 'reconstruction' of Bentham's argument raises a number of problems (which he considers in chapter V of his book). However, he maintains (pp. 25-6) that there is no evidence to support the alternative view that in Bentham's opinion those whose interests one should take into account in judging human actions were those whose interests were *affected* by the actions concerned.

In fact, Bentham did on occasion explicitly define his basic normative principle in these terms. In 1810, for example, he wrote that the term 'principle of utility', 'when employed to designate the standard of reference to which the merit or demerit of a human act is referred and by which it is to be judged of, indicates as the criterion and measure of such merit or demerit the influence of such act on the

---

(38) Cf. A. J. AYER, 'The Principle of Utility', in G. W. Keeton and G. Schwartzenberger, eds., *Jeremy Bentham and the Law* (London, 1948), p. 249 : 'The standpoint from which he considered all questions of right and wrong, justice and injustice, and so forth, was not personal but social'.

welfare of as many human beings on whose welfare it is capable of exercising any influence' ([39]). Also, in a manuscript of 1816 he suggested that the term 'principle of utility' might be understood as having two senses, an 'exegetic or expository' one and a 'deontological or censorial' one.

> In its expository sense, the compound appellative 'principle of utility' contains in it the essence of a proposition to this effect, viz. : Of every human being the conduct is on every occasion at every moment determined by the conception which at that moment he has of his individual interest ... Very different from, howsoever connected with, the expository sense is the deontological sense of the appellative 'principle of utility'. The proposition of which it contains the essence is to some such effect as this : It is desirable — fit, right, proper, desirable, any one of these words may be employed — that on every occasion the course taken by every man's conduct should be that which will be in the highest degree conducive to the welfare of the greatest number of those sensitive beings on whose welfare it exercises any influence ([40]).

These definitions do not seem to me to be in conflict with the account of the principle of utility given in *An Introduction to the Principles*. There are several passages in that book which seem to demonstrate that in Bentham's view actions, and the dispositions that gave rise to them, should be assessed in terms of their influence on the welfare of those members of the community whose interests they affected. For instance, in chapter X, paragraphs 36-7, and chapter XI, paragraph 31, Bentham wrote that if the dictates of a confined benevolence were allowed to eclipse those of a more enlarged benevolence, and led a man to promote the interests of a particular set of persons to which he was attached at the expense of the interests of another and more extensive set, he would be contravening the dictates of utility through 'not taking into contemplation the interests of all the persons whose interests [were] at stake'.

There are also passages in Bentham's works which indicate that the principle of utility could be given a wider application than the one he usually gave it, and that the interests which it might require to be taken into account could extend well beyond the membership of a particular

(39) UC cxxx. 187.
(40) UC xviii. 173-4.

community. He wrote in his unpublished 'Article on Utilitarianism' in 1829 : 'Of the greatest happiness principle, application can not be made upon too large a scale : it can not be carried on too far' [41]. Generally, in dealing with the principles on which the internal affairs of a community should be conducted, he seems to have adopted the political and moral equivalent of a closed-economy model, and to have assumed that the interests of people outside that community could be treated as extrinsic to his analysis. But he evidently believed that if one adopted the broader perspective of a 'citizen of the world' [42] and concerned oneself with international relations, a universalistic standard would have to be adopted instead of a standard of community interest. He wrote in his manuscripts of the 1780s on the 'Principles of International Law' :

> Expressed in the most general manner, the end that a disinterested legislator upon international law would propose to himself, would ... be the greatest happiness of all nations taken together ... He would regard as a positive crime every proceeding − every arrangement, by which the given nation should do more evil to foreign nations taken together, whose interests might be affected, than it should do good to itself [43].

It is true that in these manuscripts (as Lyons points out on pp. 103-5) Bentham was concerned to argue as far as he could that it was in the interest of the sovereign of any particular state to respect the interests of other states. He evidently felt that the sovereign of a particular state could not, generally speaking, be expected to observe the norms of utility in the universalistic sense unless it could be shown to be in the interest of his state to observe them. But he nevertheless seems to have held that in the case of a conflict of interests it would be *meritorious* for the sovereign to sacrifice the interests of his own state to those of some other state or states, if the latter weighed more heavily in the scales of general felicity [44].

Elsewhere, Bentham maintained with regard to human beings in general that the more widely their sympathies, and the effects of the

(41) UC xiv. 354.

(42) 'Principles of International Law', Bowring, ii. 537.

(43) *Ibid.* 538. Cf. Bentham's distinction, in his 'Division of Arts and Sciences', Bowring, viii. 289, between the national and international branches of public deontology.

(44) Bowring, ii. 537.

operation of their sympathies, extended, the better these should be judged to be. Even in *An Introduction to the Principles* (as Rolf Sartorius has pointed out), one finds him arguing that the sympathetic biases of the female are generally less 'conformable to the principle of utility' than those of the male, because they are 'apt to be less enlarged : seldom expanding themselves so much as to take in the welfare of her country in general, much less that of mankind, or the whole sensitive creation' ([45]). Similarly, in analysing the effects of the operation of sympathy in *A Table of the Springs of Action*, he said that the *goodness* of these effects depended on the extent to which they reached – their potential range having at one end 'unity', and at the other 'the number of the whole human race, – or rather of the whole sensitive race, all species included, – present and future' ([46]). It seems clear that Bentham regarded the standpoint of a 'general philanthropist' or 'citizen of the world' as ultimately superior in the moral scale to that of a 'patriot'. Although it is true that he was mainly preoccupied throughout his life with legislation and other matters affecting a state's *internal* affairs, and did not concern himself much with the analysis of policies and activities that had a wider impact, one cannot accept Lyons' contentions that it is 'extremely difficult to regard Bentham as a universalist' (p. 25) and that his basic principle of utility required one simply to consult the welfare of those subject to one's governance or direction.

(45) *IPML* VI para. 35 ; Sartorius, pp. 783-4.
(46) Bowring, i. 216.

18

Early-Nineteenth-Century Reactions to Benthamism

IN 1965 a very distinguished Bentham scholar read a paper to this society on 'Bentham and the French Revolution'.[1] During the period dealt with by that paper Bentham became an honorary citizen of France (largely through his friendship with Brissot), but he remained little known either in Britain or on the Continent. Thirty years later, he was world-famous. In 1825 members of the Colombian Congress in Bogotá were quoting Bentham at each other much as eighteenth-century Englishmen had quoted Cicero in the House of Commons; and among the leaders of the Decembrist mutiny of the same year in St Petersburg were men who confessed to having been influenced by Bentham's works.[2] In 1829 a weekly newspaper was appearing at Boston, Massachusetts, which carried his phrase 'the greatest happiness of the greatest number' as its motto,[3] while a journal called *L'Utilitaire* was being published at Geneva to propagate his ideas.[4] This paper will not tackle the large and controversial subject of the extent and significance of Bentham's influence. It will address itself to questions that are more limited, though they have some bearing on the larger topic. These questions are: how did those outside the circle of his followers react to his ideas, and what attempts were made to challenge or refute them?

Given the limited circulation of his work before the publication of the *Traités de législation*, edited and translated by Etienne Dumont, in 1802,[5] the opening years of the century provide a natural starting-point for this investigation. The terminal date I have chosen—1832, the year of Bentham's death—is more arbitrary, as the posthumous

---

[1] By J.H. Burns, *Transactions*, 5th series, 16 (1966), 95-114. I should like to thank Professor Burns, Dr Fred Rosen, and above all Mr William Thomas, for helpful suggestions regarding my paper.

[2] Theodora McKennan, 'Santander and the Vogue of Benthamism in Colombia', Ph.D. thesis, Loyola University, Chicago, 1970, 164-5; E. Salkind, 'Die Dekabristen in ihrer Beziehung zu Westeuropa', *Jahrbücher für Kultur und Geschichte der Slawen*, Band iv, Heft iv (1928), 537-8.

[3] *The Yankee and Boston Literary Gazette*, edited by John Neal, 1828-9.

[4] Edited by Antoine-Elisée Cherbuliez, 1829-30.

[5] *Traités de législation civile et pénale*, ed. E. Dumont (3 vols, Paris, 1802).

impact of his thought and the many responses to it after the early
1830s were of great interest and importance; but to have included
these within the scope of the paper would have made it very unwieldy. So it will deal with Bentham's early critics, stopping short of
the well-known essays about him that were published by John Stuart
Mill in 1833 and 1838. As for the term 'Benthamism' in the title of
the paper, this may be somewhat misleading. For Benthamism could
be seen as to some extent the product of other minds besides Bentham's, and some of the sharpest reactions to it were provoked either
by James Mill's reductionist presentation of the doctrine or by the
arrogance and dogmatism of the young intellectuals who formed the
Utilitarian 'sect' of the 1820s and wrote for the *Westminster Review*.
But this paper will be essentially concerned with responses to the
ideas expressed in Bentham's own writings and in the recensions of
his work produced by Dumont.

If one looks first at the broad category of 'conservative' writers
and their attitudes to Bentham one finds that many of them paid
little or no attention to him. In particular, there was little in the
way of direct response to his ideas from conservative writers of the
Romantic school. The distance between them and Bentham may
have seemed too great for meaningful debate to be possible, and in
general in the early nineteenth century the characteristic response
of Romantic writers to utilitarianism was an affirmation of other
values rather than a resort to argument. Bentham and Walter Scott,
it has been suggested, represented antithetical viewpoints,[6] but Scott
seems to have ignored Bentham just as Bentham ignored Scott. As
for Wordsworth, Coleridge and Southey, they had all reacted earlier
against the Godwinian version of utilitarianism that had originally
attracted them, and they may have felt that Bentham did not require separate treatment. Coleridge did write a critique of Paley's
consequentialism for his journal *The Friend*,[7] but he very rarely mentioned Bentham and did not show any close acquaintance with his
works; and Southey seems to have confined himself to some anti-
Benthamite jokes in his private correspondence, where the *Westminster Review* appeared as the 'Jerry-bedlamite review', Bentham's
jurisprudence as 'Jerrysprudence', and the Utilitarians as 'Futili-
tarians'.[8]

In public as well as in private, ridicule was one of the most
common responses of conservative writers and organs of opinion:

[6] Russell Kirk, 'Scott and Bentham', *Fortnightly Review*, New Series, clxxii (1952),
397-403.

[7] *The Friend*, ed. Barbara Rooke (2 vols, 1969), I. 313-25.

[8] Southey to Henry Taylor, 31 Dec. 1825, 19 Apr. 1828, Bodleian Library, Oxford,
MS Eng. letters d. 6, ff. 42, 204; *Life and Correspondence of Robert Southey*, ed. C.C.
Southey (6 vols, 1849-50), V. 290.

and it has to be said that Bentham himself almost courted this sort of of treatment. The image he cultivated as the 'hermit' of Queen's Square Place may have been useful in protecting him against unwanted intrusions, but it also gave a handle to his critics by creating the impression that he was much more cut off from the world than he actually was, and his apparent isolation and undoubted eccentricities made it easy to portray him as the quintessential comic philosopher. One such portrayal, which featured his habit of jogging for the sake of his health, appeared in a book called *The Last Days of Lord Byron* by William Parry. The author, before leaving England to serve with Byron in Greece, was asked to accompany Bentham on a visit to Alexander Galloway's factory in Smithfield, where the stores intended for the Greek expedition were being kept. They set out with a secretary of Bentham's from Queen's Square Place, and as soon as they got into St James's Park (Parry writes) 'he let go my arm, and set off trotting like a Highland messenger. The Park was crowded, and the people, one and all, seemed to stare at the old man; but heedless of all this he trotted on, his white locks floating in the wind.' Later, Parry found himself running after Bentham and his secretary down Fleet Street. 'I was heartily ashamed of participating in this scene, and supposed that every body would take me for a mad-doctor, the young man for my assistant, and Mr Bentham for my patient, just broke adrift from his keepers.'[9] Parry's book needs to be treated with caution by historians;[10] but the whole passage about Bentham was reprinted in many journals and newspapers, including *The Times*, which commented that although he was regarded by some retired tradesmen (an allusion to Francis Place) as the equal of Bacon or Locke, he was 'too elaborately odd for a great man: a great man may be occasionally odd by accident, or from the circumstances of education; but he never doggedly sets about doing every thing differently from other men, in order to be thought a genius because he is eccentric.'[11] The *North American Review* said it was convinced by Parry's account of Bentham that he was suffering from 'a partial aberration of intellect' and that his ideas were consequently unworthy of detailed examination.[12]

The eccentricities of his behaviour, however, were far less damaging to his influence and reputation than those of his literary style. Broadly, he had two somewhat different styles in the latter part of his life, one for his theoretical or constructive writings, the other for his more polemical ones. The former style is found in its most ex-

[9] William Parry, *The Last Days of Lord Byron* (1825), 155–9.

[10] See William St. Clair, 'Postscript to *The Last Days of Lord Byron*', *Keats-Shelley Journal*, xix (1970), 4–7.

[11] *The Times*, 19 May 1825.

[12] *North American Review*, xxvi (1828), 188–9.

treme form in his 'Essay on Nomenclature and Classification' in *Chrestomathia* (1817), which is studded with grotesque terms formed out of combinations of Greek words. Neologisms such as 'catastatico-chrestic physiurgics' and 'coenonesioscopic noology' may have been justified up to a point by his desire to develop a new vocabulary that would be scientifically neutral and precise. But there was less excuse for the fact that much of his polemical writing in his latter years was hardly more readable.[13] In his *Plan of Parliamentary Reform*, for instance—his most important radical pamphlet, published in 1817—the sentences are self-indulgently loaded with subordinate clauses and parentheses, grammatical inversions, and cumbrous compound terms such as 'the universal-interest-comprehension principle'. Maria Edgeworth, who was sent a complimentary copy, said in contrasting Bentham's own work with Dumont's recensions of it that when he wrote for himself Bentham seemed to be 'half a madman and half a pedant—and he writes in such an uncouth disorderly style that it is really impossible to understand him or to wish to read his book'.[14] The defects of his style (or styles) were much played upon by his opponents. William Gifford of the *Quarterly Review*, for instance, said in 1819 how singular it was that the man who complained so much about what he called the 'uncognoscibility' of English law should use a language that was quite as impenetrable as any legal jargon.[15] Similar points were made in a light vein by *Blackwood's Magazine*. The first of John Wilson's sketches called 'Noctes Ambrosianae' in that journal included a ballad in which Bentham was invited by a Scotsman visiting London to sup at the Jolly Bacchus, but refused on the grounds that

> I'm writing a word three pages long,
>   The Quarterly dogs to rout,
> A word that never will human tongue
>   Be able to wind about.

Bentham did offer to read the Scotsman his treatise on special juries, but drew the response

> Jeremy, not for a gallon of ale
>   Would I stay that book to hear . . .[16]

[13] Mary Mack has said—*Jeremy Bentham: An Odyssey of Ideas 1748-1792* (1962), 198—that his political writings are all 'popular and easy'; but this is far from being the case.

[14] Maria Edgeworth to Mrs Marcet, 21 Jan. 1818, in H.W. Häuserman, *The Genevese Background* (1952), 88.

[15] *Quarterly Review*, xxi (1819), 175.

[16] *Blackwood's Edinburgh Magazine*, xi (1822), 365-7. For a fine parody of Bentham's style by F.D. Maurice, see *Metropolitan Quarterly Magazine*, i (1826), 353-77.

It is hard to escape the conclusion that Bentham himself was largely to blame for the fact that many conservative writers regarded his work as too bizarre and esoteric to be worth the trouble of responding to.

Outside England, where his ideas were circulated in volumes that were much less idiosyncratic than his own unedited productions, ridicule was a less common mode of response. And whereas in his own country he was never prosecuted for seditious or blasphemous libel,[17] in other parts of the world his work was sometimes seen as dangerous enough to require suppression. Although Dumont was careful not to present him as explicitly hostile in religion, he did not conceal Bentham's psychological hedonism and his dismissal of innate moral sense and natural law. It was clear that the *Traités de législation* could not be reconciled with orthodox Catholic theology, and in March 1819, soon after it was translated into Italian, the work was placed on the index of prohibited books.[18] Political authority, also, was exerted against the work—for instance, ironically enough, by the Liberator Simón Bolívar in Colombia. In the new states of South America Bentham was widely regarded by liberals as the greatest modern expert on the principles of legislation, and in 1825 Francisco de Paula Santander, as vice-president of Gran Colombia, decreed that the *Traités* should be a prescribed text for all law students in the republic. Santander was anxious to curb the power and autonomy of the Church, and may have regarded Bentham's work as an antidote to religious fanaticism as well as a good vehicle of legal education. But in installing Bentham in the curriculum he seems to have moved ahead of public opinion. There were strong protests from clerics and conservatives, and when Bolívar returned from Peru to resume his presidential functions and wished to institute a more authoritarian régime, he banned the teaching of the *Traités* in March 1828. During the controversy of these years, which has been called 'la batalla de Bentham en Colombia', a number of ephemeral publications appeared attacking his ideas as dangerous to religion, morality and social order.[19]

The most sustained critique of this kind, however, was published in Spain in 1827. Entitled *Orígen de los errores revolucionarios de Europa, y su remedio*, it was written by José Vidal, a Dominican theologian at the University of Valencia. As is well known, Bentham's ideas had

---

[17] Bentham was inclined to attribute this to his being a bencher of Lincoln's Inn, but a more basic explanation can perhaps be found in the remark of 'Timothy Tickler' of *Blackwood's*—xv (1824), 146—that his 'absurd peculiarities' rendered him harmless.

[18] *Der Index der verbotenen Bücher*, ed. Joseph Hilgers (Freiburg, 1904), 456.

[19] McKennan, 'Santander', 170-216; Armando Rojas, 'La Batalla de Bentham en Colombia', *Revista de Historia de América*, xxix (1950), 37-51.

circulated widely in Spain in earlier years, especially during the liberal triennium of 1820-23; but as the main medium was Dumont's *Traités*, which had been written before Bentham's conversion to political radicalism around 1809, his work was more of an inspiration to moderates than to the so-called 'Liberales exaltados'.[20] One man who had absorbed Benthamite ideas when a moderate reformer during Joseph Bonaparte's régime, and subsequently became a supporter of the absolutism of Ferdinand VII, was José Gomez Hermosilla; and his work *El Jacobinismo*, published in Madrid in 1823, was the main precipitant of Vidal's assault on Bentham. Gomez Hermosilla cited Bentham's *Anarchical Fallacies* in the course of attacking the natural-rights doctrines of the revolutionaries, and he also declared his belief that general utility should be the criterion for judging the goodness or badness of laws.[21] In Vidal's opinion, the doctrines of Bentham were just as pernicious in tendency as the doctrine of natural rights, and his book was intended to demonstrate this. It contains long quotations from the Spanish version of the *Traités*, followed by passages of indignant commentary. Vidal himself took for granted the truth of traditional natural law thinking. The only true principle of morals and legislation, he asserted, and the surest road to felicity, lay in the observance of natural law, understood and applied to particular cases in accordance with the dictates of right reason. Honesty and justice were not derived from utility, but vice versa: utility was a species of reward or blessing, with which the most wise Creator and Provider of all things had seen fit to approve and sanction the honesty and justice of human actions. And what dangerous consequences for moral behaviour were likely to ensue if one set up utility as the sole criterion of morals and then went on to tell people (as the *Traités* did) that each man was the best judge of his own utility! With regard to politics, Vidal cited a footnote in the *Traités* which said that in deciding whether to obey or resist laws which were contrary to the principle of utility one should weigh the probable evils of obedience against those of disobedience. In Vidal's view, as revolutionaries would naturally consider that the evils of obedience to laws which they disliked were greater than those likely to result from resistance, to leave such a question to their judgment was equivalent to providing a justification for revolution. If the principle of utility were generally adopted, he said, it would not merely undermine the foundations of a healthy morality but would threaten the very existence of government and society.[22]

[20] See Pedro Schwartz, 'La Influencia de Jeremías Bentham en España', *Información Comercial Española*, Sept. 1976, 39, 44, 50.
[21] José Gomez Hermosilla, *El Jacobinismo* (3 vols, Madrid, 1823), I. 217, 281.
[22] José Vidal, *Orígen de los errores revolucionarios de Europa, y su remedio* (Valencia, 1827), 254n., 268, 274, 279-80, 288-9, 307. Another Spanish Catholic who criticised Ben-

In England, natural law doctrine of this absolute type had for the most part lost its hold, and the principle of utility in some form had come to be fairly widely accepted. Bentham himself noted in 1814 a speech in the House of Lords in which the Lord President of the Council referred to 'general utility' as 'the test of all public law'; and C.P. Cooper, one of Bentham's leading critics in the field of jurisprudence, said that he had no objection to Bentham's basic principle.[23] Attacks on the principle were certainly made, several of them by people whose political stance was not very different from Bentham's; and some of these attacks will be examined later in the paper. But it will be convenient at this point to look at reactions to his views on the codification of law, for it was in this area more than any other that a considered conservative (or liberal-conservative) response to his ideas was developed in his own time.

One is touching here on what can be regarded as the central preoccupation of Bentham's life. From the 1770s onwards his great ambition was to produce a pannomion, or comprehensive body of laws. He told an American correspondent in 1818 that his 'grand object' was 'Codification, and that rationalized',[24] and he liked to think of himself as the seminal thinker on the subject. But although he invented the word 'codification' (which passed into use in several other languages), he did not, of course, invent the practice. The debate on whether or not the practice was desirable was an international one, and the extent to which his ideas entered into this debate varied considerably from one part of the world to another. In some places the controversy was carried on with little or no reference to his writings; and this was largely the case, for example, in the United States. It is true that Edward Livingston, whose codes drawn up for the state of Louisiana were among the most remarkable examples of substantive codification in the nineteenth century, said that the *Traités de législation* had 'fortified him in a design to

---

tham at length from a natural law position, though he was a liberal in politics, was F. Martínez Marina; but the work in which he did so was not published until a hundred years after his death. See his *Principios naturales de la moral, de la política y de la legislación*, ed. Adolfo Posada (Madrid, 1933), esp. 74–9, 138–53, 168–83.

[23] Bentham, *Deontology, together with A Table of the Springs of Action and The Article on Utilitarianism*, ed. Amnon Goldworth (Oxford, 1982), 49 & n.; C.P. Cooper, *Lettres sur la Cour de la Chancellerie d'Angleterre*, ed. P. Royer-Collard (third edn., Paris, 1830), 372n.

[24] Bentham to William Plumer jr., n.d. [c. Dec. 1818], Plumer MSS., New Hampshire State Library. His arguments in favour of codification were set out in the *Traités de législation*, in *Papers relative to Codification and Public Instruction* (London, 1817), in *Codification Proposal addressed to all Nations professing Liberal Opinions* (London, 1822), and in another volume edited by Dumont, *De l'organisation judiciaire et de la codification* (Paris, 1828).

prosecute the subject'.[25] But most critics of the common law and advocates of codification, such as William Sampson of New York and Thomas Grimké of South Carolina, referred hardly at all to Bentham, perhaps from a conscious desire to dissociate themselves from the radicalism and abrasiveness of his approach.[26] Consequently, American opponents of codification did not find it necessary to give extended consideration to his theories.

In Germany, also, little attention was paid to his ideas, although the debate there was particularly lively. At the end of the Napoleonic wars, Thibaut of Heidelberg wrote a pamphlet proposing that a written code of laws should be constructed for the whole of Germany,[27] and this provoked Savigny's classic reply of the same year *Vom Beruf unsrer Zeit für Gesetzgebung und Rechtswissenschaft*. In 1815 Savigny and others launched the journal which became the principal organ of the German historical school, *Zeitschrift für geschichtliche Rechtswissenschaft*, and Savigny himself wrote an article for it in 1817 which surveyed the controversy among German jurists over the desirability of new codes.[28] In none of the writings just mentioned was there any discussion of Bentham's work. Although a German translation of the *Traités* was published in 1830 and a few reviews of his writings were appearing by that time in German periodicals,[29] the jurists of the historical school were in general too fully occupied in combating the schools of legal philosophy inspired by Kant and Hegel to have much time for Bentham.

In Western Europe much more interest was shown in his ideas, partly, no doubt, because Dumont's recensions of his work first appeared in French. In France the battle for codification had been more or less won, and the principal division among jurists was between an established school which concerned itself mainly with the exegesis of the Napoleonic codes, and another which was inclined to be more critical of them. Some members of the latter school—such

[25] Livingston to Bentham, 10 Aug. 1829, in *The Works of Jeremy Bentham*, ed. John Bowring (11 vols, Edinburgh, 1843), XI. 23.

[26] Maxwell Bloomfield, 'William Sampson and the Codifiers: the Roots of American Legal Reform 1820-1830', *American Journal of Legal History*, xi (1967), 245-6; G.M. Hezel, 'The Influence of Bentham's Philosophy of Law on the Early Nineteenth Century Codification Movement in the United States', *Buffalo Law Review*, xxii (1972-3), 255.

[27] *Über die Nothwendigkeit eines allgemeinen bürgerlichen Rechts für Deutschland* (Heidelberg, 1814).

[28] 'Stimmen für und wider neue Gesetzbücher', *Zeitschrift für geschichtliche Rechtswissenschaft*, Band iii (1817), 1-52.

[29] E.g. *Kritische Zeitschrift für Rechtswissenschaft und Gesetzgebung des Auslandes*, Band i (1829), 252-70; Band iii (1831), 88-97. For earlier remarks about how little known Bentham's works were in Germany, see *Hermes oder kritisches Jahrbuch der Literatur*, Band xv (1822), 331, and *Kritische Zeitschrift für Rechtswissenschaft*, Band i, Heft iii (1827), 1.

as Hyacinthe Blondeau, who was to become dean of the Paris law faculty after the July Revolution—were avowedly influenced by Bentham,[30] who regarded the French Codes as a considerable achievement but as insufficiently systematic and complete.[31] Others—such as Athanase Jourdan, founder in 1819 of a journal called *Thémis, ou Bibliothèque du Jurisconsulte*—were influenced by the German historical school.[32] It was by French-speaking jurists that the ideas of Bentham and those of Savigny were first juxtaposed and contrasted. Pellegrino Rossi, a former professor of law at Bologna who had moved to Geneva after the restoration, launched there in 1820 a journal called *Annales de Législation et de Jurisprudence*; and in a long article on the state of jurisprudence in Europe which he wrote for the first issue, he posited a basic division between the historical school on the one hand and several philosophical schools on the other, singling out from the latter what he called the 'analytical' school as the one most worthy of attention. This was the school of Bentham. According to Rossi, it resembled the historical school in certain respects, especially in that both wished to avoid vague abstractions and to take into account 'la manière actuelle de voir et de sentir du peuple'.[33] But he recognised that there were fundamental differences over the nature and role of law, one school treating it as an endogenous product and reflection of the society in question, while the other saw it as created by the will of the sovereign, who could *use* legislation to influence and correct the people's outlook and sentiments.[34] Six years later an article in the *Revue Encyclopédique* drew a similar comparison, saying that Bentham's approach and that of the historical school were the only ones that deserved serious study, and regretting that the two schools had hitherto remained isolated from one another instead of engaging in a fruitful debate.[35]

One French lawyer who drew on the ideas of the historical school, Eugène Lerminier, devoted a chapter to Bentham in a general introduction to the history of law which he published in 1830, and censured him for his ignorance and neglect of legal history; and in a chapter on codification in another book published in the following year he said that Bentham had drawn too sharp a contrast between

---

[30] Hyacinthe Blondeau, *Essais sur quelques points de jurisprudence* (Paris, 1819), esp. 47-56, 61-2; Dumont to Bentham, 10 Aug. 1821, Bentham MSS., X, 124-5, University College London.

[31] Bentham, *Papers relative to Codification and Public Instruction*, Supplement, 130-1 (*Works*, ed. Bowring, IV. 500).

[32] Julien Bonnecase, *La 'Thémis' (1819-1831): son fondateur, Athanase Jourdan* (Toulouse, 1912), 54-5, 96-7.

[33] He referred on this point to Bentham's *De l'influence des temps et des lieux en matière de législation*, which formed part of the *Traités de législation*.

[34] *Annales de Législation et de Jurisprudence*, i (1820), 1-66.

[35] *Revue Encyclopédique*, xxxi (1826), 626-41.

custom and reason.[36] The fullest critiques along comparable lines, however, were written by English lawyers. In England in the 1820s a considerable amount of interest was being shown in partial codification, or at least in the consolidation of certain branches of the law. But although Bentham's writings doubtless helped to spread an awareness of the deficiencies of the existing law, his ideas do not seem to have been the main inspiration of leading advocates and practitioners of this mode of reform such as Antony Hammond,[37] James Humphreys[38] and Robert Peel. Nevertheless, his arguments in favour of thorough codification, having been largely endorsed by Sir Samuel Romilly in an article in the *Edinburgh Review* in 1817,[39] were widely disseminated in the 1820s by newspapers and periodicals such as the *Morning Chronicle*, the *Examiner*, the *Westminster Review* and the *Jurist*;[40] and these arguments provoked critical responses, which made some use of ideas imported from Germany.

The first English edition of Savigny's *Vom Beruf unsrer Zeit*—translated by Abraham Hayward, a young barrister who was a Tory opponent of the Utilitarians at the London Debating Society[41]—did not appear until 1831. But in 1828 a Scottish advocate who had a doctorate from Göttingen, James Reddie, published a *Letter to the Lord High Chancellor of Great Britain, on the Expediency of the Proposal to form a new Civil Code for England*. Without citing Savigny, he borrowed freely from his work, as in the following passage:

> As circumstances, habit, or inclination happen to prevail, each nation involuntarily and insensibly adopts different, but appropriate, and according to her own situation, necessary views of national justice. As manners change, laws change with them. ... From the people, taken in the aggregate, of any state, all law emanates.... It is the genius of the people that gives birth to, and animates the system, which is elucidated, and technically

[36] Eugène Lerminier, *Introduction générale à l'histoire du droit* (Brussels, 1830), 240-5; *Philosophie du droit* (Paris, 1831), 312-13.

[37] Hammond's proposals for the consolidation of the criminal law helped to prepare the ground for Peel's statutes of 1827-30; see Leon Radzinowicz, *History of English Criminal Law and its Administration from 1750* (4 vols, 1948-68), I. 574-7.

[38] Humphreys, after the publication of his *Observations on the Actual State of the English Laws of Real Property, with the Outlines of a Code* (London, 1826), was hailed by Bentham as an unavowed disciple of his (Bentham to Peel, 19 Aug. 1826, Bentham MSS., XI, 201-3); but he appears to have been inspired by Continental civil codes rather than by Bentham.

[39] 'Bentham on Codification', *Edinburgh Review*, xxix (1817), 217-37.

[40] See J.W. Flood, 'The Benthamites and their Use of the Press 1810-1840', Ph.D. thesis, University of London, 1974, chap. iv.

[41] J.S. Mill, *Autobiography and Literary Essays*, eds. J.M. Robson and J. Stillinger (Toronto, 1981), 133.

arranged by lawyers, and, through their labours, becomes a science.

The arguments which Savigny had used to defend the customary law of Germany were applied by Reddie to the defence of the English common law, and he included in his pamphlet a sharp attack on Bentham, whose insistence on codification was said to involve sacrificing the lessons of the past while attempting to 'throw fetters on the future'.[42] A further attack that was partly inspired by Savigny appeared two years later in the third edition of a learned but somewhat bizarre work, written by the chancery barrister C.P. Cooper and published in Paris under the title *Lettres sur la Cour de la Chancellerie d'Angleterre*. The work was critical of Eldon, the ultra-conservative Lord Chancellor, which may help to expain why the original edition of 1828 was published anonymously and in French. But while Cooper himself favoured some degree of reform, he was firmly opposed to codification, and in an appendix to the third edition Bentham's views on this subject were controverted at length. Cooper argued that in an advanced commercial society such as existed in England Bentham's belief that the law could be codified so comprehensively that unwritten law could be dispensed with was chimerical; and he maintained that in other countries where such attempts had been made—France, Prussia, Austria—it had proved necessary in practice to supplement the new codes by frequent reference to Roman-law jurisprudence and case-law. Secondly, he said that Bentham's complaints about the uncertainty of the common law and the power that it gave to judges would apply far more strongly to a new code, whose generalities and inevitable lacunae would leave much to judicial discretion. Thirdly, he said that Bentham was quite wrong in holding that codified law was more favourable to liberty than common law, and here he drew particularly heavily on the ideas that Savigny and others had developed in reaction against the codes that Napoleon had imposed on much of Germany. No code, he maintained, could be regarded as deriving so directly from the will of the people, or as being so susceptible of being modified by it, as the common law. In a system such as the English one, the lawyers did constitute a distinct group, but they none the less *represented* the mass of the people, and the decisions of the courts were no less founded on the usages and requirements of the society at large than if they had been pronounced by the people themselves.[43]

A third legal writer who attacked Bentham at some length, in a pseudonymous pamphlet published in 1830, was J.J. Park (who

[42] James Reddie, *Letter to the Lord High Chancellor* ... (1828), 5–7, 44–52.
[43] Cooper, *Lettres*, 350–72.

shortly afterwards became the first professor of jurisprudence at King's College, London). But although Park did cite Savigny in this work, his attack relied more on rhetoric and *ad hominem* points than on theoretical argument. He accused Bentham of building up a reputation for himself by exploiting the peculiar ignorance of his countrymen on legal and jurisprudential matters. Though himself familiar with legal developments on the Continent, Bentham had concealed from his English readers the fact that recent attempts at codification had proved the impossibility of supplanting the functions of the judge in the interpretation of law; and his unrelenting assault on the common law as 'judge-made' and 'uncognoscible' had been 'one of the most unfounded, fallacious, and therefore mischievous attacks, which ever was made on any existing system of jurisprudence'. Park went on to say that Bentham's practical experience of law was much too limited to qualify him to act as the architect of any legal system.[44] He had made the same point in a pamphlet two years before, saying that for Bentham to undertake such a task would be 'like a man who never was inside of the Horse-Guards composing a plan for the reform and regulation of the Army'.[45]

Bentham was not without defenders in the English legal world. C.S. Cullen, for example, a commissioner of bankrupts, included in a pamphlet of 1830 a eulogium of Bentham which was quite as rhetorical as Park's indictment;[46] and the *Jurist*, a journal run by a group of young lawyers who were friendly to reform,[47] carried an article in January 1829 which defended Bentham against Reddie and maintained that Savigny's arguments lost most of their force when taken out of their German context.[48] Bentham himself seems to have had little or no acquaintance with the works of the historical school.[49] But this did not deter him from drafting a reply to what he assumed them to have said. In his manuscripts there is a five-page piece dated April 1830 and headed 'On the Anti-Codification, alias the Historical School of Jurisprudence'. The essence of his argument (which shows how impossible he found it to envisage laws as anything other than emanations of the sovereign's will) is summed up in the following passage:

[44] 'Eunomus', *Juridical Letters; addressed to the Right Hon. Robert Peel, in reference to the present Crisis of Law Reform. Letter I* (1830), 4, 12-24.

[45] J.J. Park, *A Contre-Projet to the Humphreysian Code* (1828), 229.

[46] C.S. Cullen, *Reform of the Bankrupt Court; with a Letter to John Smith, Esq. M.P.* (2nd edn., 1830), iii-xi.

[47] Cf. *Sutton Sharpe et ses amis français*, ed. Doris Gunnell (Paris, 1925), 13, 99; *Thémis*, x (1831), 372.

[48] *The Jurist*, ii (1828-9), 181-218.

[49] For an anecdote which illustrates his vagueness about it, see Eduard Gans, *Rückblicke auf Personen und Zustände* (Berlin, 1836), 201-6.

According to the jurists of the Historical School when the Sovereign of a country wants anything to be done by his subjects, the most effectual course that can be taken by him for that purpose is—not to tell them and let them know what it is that on the occasion in question he wants to be done, but to put it to them to enquire what it is that on occasions which appear to be similar he has ordered to be done, or judges appointed by him and acting under his authority have punished men for their not having done without having ever been bid to do it. Apply this notion to domestic life—to expression of will operating on the smallest scale ... Occasion suppose, that of providing for dinner: say a sirloin of beef, and a plum pudding. What is the most suitable course for the master or mistress to take? To call up the Housekeeper or Cook and say to her, Let me have a sirloin of beef today with a plum pudding? Oh no. What then? Answer, this: Look over the Housekeeper's book as far back as is necessary, and then tell me what the dinner is that I have a mind for.[50]

Bentham used the same analogy in a letter to Edward Livingston, and added: 'Not that the Cook would have any great objection to this substitute for a command, if his wages were to go on increasing in proportion to the number of housekeeping books in which the search was made, and the length of time occupied in making it.'[51] Bentham's critique of the historical school was only (as he himself called it) a squib,[52] and apart from a few sentences which appeared in a pamphlet of his on bicameral legislatures later in 1830[53] it remained unpublished.

A much more substantial critique of Savigny was produced at about the same period by Bentham's pupil John Austin. He was well informed about the historical school,[54] having spent six months studying law in Germany; and as professor of jurisprudence at University College London he included in his lecture course of 1829–30 a sharp and detailed rebuttal of Savigny's arguments about codification. However, this hardly counted as a contribution to the early-nineteenth-century debate, as it did not appear in print until it was published forty years later from notes taken at the original lectures by John Stuart Mill.[55] In the latter years of Bentham's life the ideas

[50] Bentham MSS., LXXXIII, 157.
[51] Bentham to Livingston, 23 Feb. 1830, Livingston MSS., John Ross Delafield Foundation, New York.
[52] Bentham to Adolphe Hauman, 4 Aug. 1831, Osborn Collection, Yale University.
[53] *Jeremy Bentham to his Fellow-Citizens of France, on Houses of Peers and Senates* (1830), 10 (*Works*, ed. Bowring, IV. 425).
[54] A.B. Schwarz, 'John Austin and the German Jurisprudence of his Time', *Politica*, i (1934–5), 178–99.
[55] John Austin, *Lectures on Jurisprudence*, 3rd edn., ed. Robert Campbell (2 vols, 1869), II. 689–704.

of the historical school were very much in vogue. They provided a convenient legitimation for defenders of the common law, and the conservative *Law Magazine* could assert in 1830 that the debate was virtually concluded in England and that codification had become 'a dead letter'.[56] The magazine did go on to say, however, that the debate was continuing on the Continent, and C.P. Cooper conceded that Bentham's ideas might be advantageously adopted in some parts of the world outside Britain.[57] A distinguished Continental jurist who sided with Bentham against Savigny in a book published in 1830 was J.D. Meijer of Amsterdam,[58] author of a massive work on the judicial institutions of Europe. At the same period Andrés Bello, who was later to produce a civil code for Chile, was using Bentham's *Traités* as the basic text for the course on legislation which he taught at the Colegio de Santiago.[59] Also, codification was high on the agenda for India, and Bentham would have been gratified by the role which his ideas played in attempts to reconstruct the Indian legal system in the 1830s.[60]

There remain to be considered the reactions that Bentham aroused from whigs and liberals and non-Benthamite reformers. One thing that has to be said of the contributors to the great liberal periodical of the day, the *Edinburgh Review*, is that they were far from under-valuing his importance. The *Quarterly Review* devoted only three short and disparaging articles to Bentham during the second and third decades of the century, but in the *Edinburgh*'s consolidated index for the years 1813 to 1830 the references to Bentham fill six columns, placing him only half a column behind Napoleon and well clear of any other rival. The *Edinburgh* gave particular support to Bentham's ideas on law, notably through Romilly's article on codification and through an article of Brougham's in 1813 which provided a lucid and appreciative summary of Bentham's theory of punishment.[61] Other articles contained some striking compliments. Francis Jeffrey described Bentham in 1807 as 'by far the most profound and original thinker' that English jurisprudence had produced, and Brougham wrote in 1830 that his exposure of the faults of the English legal system was 'the greatest service ever rendered to

---

[56] *Law Magazine*, iv (1830), 244.

[57] Cooper, *Lettres*, 370, 396.

[58] J.D. Meijer (*alias* Meyer), *De la codification en général, et de celle de l'Angleterre en particulier* (Amsterdam, 1830), pp. ix, xii, 126n.

[59] Alamiro de Avila Martel, 'La Filosofía jurídica de Andrés Bello', in *Actas del Congreso Internacional 'Andrés Bello y el Derecho'* (Santiago de Chile, 1982), 41-62, esp. 48-9. One should add that Bello subsequently came under the influence of Savigny, and the code he drafted in the 1840s and '50s was an eclectic one which drew only to a limited extent on Bentham's ideas.

[60] Eric Stokes, *The English Utilitarians and India* (Oxford, 1959), 184-233.

[61] *Edinburgh Review*, xxii (1813), 1-31.

the country by any of her political philosophers'.[62] Yet the *Edinburgh* could by no means be described as Benthamite. Even in regard to legal matters, it was not uncritically admiring. For one thing, the reviewers felt that he had a tendency to push his ideas to impractical and even risible extremes. Brougham gave as an example the suggestion (in a passage recommending that punishments be made analogous to the crimes committed) that the tongue of someone convicted of slander should be publicly pierced with a sharp instrument, and that in order to minimise the pain inflicted while maximising the deterrent effect on the spectators, the pointed part of the instrument which actually penetrated the tongue should be very thin while the part of it visible to the spectators should be alarmingly thick.[63] Fifteen years later William Empson, professor of law at Haileybury, wrote a long review of the *Rationale of Judicial Evidence* in which he expressed agreement with much of the substance of the work but lamented that Bentham's 'eccentricities and impracticableness ... put such a fatal drag on the progress of his philosophical opinions'. The greater part of the article, indeed, was concerned with what Empson regarded as the weaknesses of Bentham's work—such as the style of writing (which was described as 'the Sanskrit of modern legislation') and the exaggeration with which he attributed all the faults of the English legal system to the grasping self-interest of the legal profession.[64] Also, the whigs generally adopted a more cautious and gradualist approach to law reform than the one favoured by Bentham. Sir James Mackintosh, while expressing admiration for Bentham's work on the principles of jurisprudence, wrote that 'the sudden establishment of new codes can seldom be practicable or effectual for their purpose' and that legal reforms 'ought to be not only adapted to the peculiar interests of a people, but engrafted on their previous usages'.[65]

However, it was in politics, once Bentham had extended his attack on the legal system into a general assault on the country's institutions, that the gap between him and the *Edinburgh* reviewers was most apparent. Both Romilly and Brougham, though supporters of a moderate reform of parliament, expressed their disapproval of his *Plan of Parliamentary Reform*,[66] and Mackintosh wrote a long review of it in the *Edinburgh*. The article did not in fact discuss Bentham's pamphlet very directly, but it argued strongly against universal suf-

---

[62] Ibid., ix (1807), 483; li (1830), 481-2. Cf. Macaulay's tribute, ibid., lv (1832), 553.

[63] Ibid., xxii (1813), 10-11.

[64] Ibid., xlviii (1828), 457-520.

[65] Sir James Mackintosh, *Dissertation on the Progress of Ethical Philosophy* (Edinburgh, 1836), 290. (This work was written in 1828-30 for the *Encyclopaedia Britannica*.)

[66] Hansard, *Parliamentary Debates*, xxxvi, 784; xxxviii, 1164-5.

frage[67] and vote by ballot. Universal suffrage, said Mackintosh, would give a perpetual majority to the labouring classes, and no other section of the community would have any means of securing its interests. Greatly preferable to this—or to any uniform franchise—was a heterogeneous electoral system which gave representation and protection to all social groups and united and balanced 'the principles of property and popularity'. Also, as the great object of popular elections was to 'inspire and strengthen the love of liberty' and it was desirable for this purpose that men should exercise their political rights 'with pleasure and pride', voting should be open rather than secret: the inevitable consequence of the ballot would be public apathy.[68] Bentham's usual practice was to avoid reading articles about his work, for the sake (as he once explained to John Herbert Koe) of 'saving present time, and saving attention from being needlessly called off'.[69] But he did read this article, or at least part of it, and he wrote an extensive (though never published) response to its arguments against the ballot.[70] He never produced a direct reply to the more basic charge—later to be echoed by Macaulay in his critique of James Mill's *Essay on Government*[71]—that his proposals would lead to a tyranny of the majority; but he was sufficiently aware of the objection to adopt the phrase 'the greatest happiness' as signifying the proper end of government, instead of his earlier formula 'the greatest happiness of the greatest number', in case the latter might be taken to imply that the happiness of minorities was of little or no account.[72]

In addition to the difference of opinion over politics, there was some disagreement between Bentham and the *Edinburgh* reviewers over ethical questions. The reviewers did not deny—indeed Mackintosh and Macaulay explicitly agreed—that utility was the appropriate test for political institutions.[73] But most of them had been reared in the 'common sense' tradition of eighteenth-century Scottish philosophy and were admirers of Dugald Stewart, and they had objections to utilitarianism as a general system of morality. One major statement of such objections was the first article the journal devoted to Bentham, a review of the *Traités de législation* written by Jeffrey in 1804. Even here, the notion that general utility was the

---

[67] Bentham had actually recommended a somewhat less comprehensive franchise, which he called 'virtually universal suffrage': see his *Plan of Parliamentary Reform, in the form of a Catechism* (1817), pp. lxxx-c (*Works*, ed. Bowring, III. 458-64).

[68] *Edinburgh Review*, xxxi (1818), 165-203.

[69] Bentham to John Herbert Koe, 1 Feb. 1818, Koe MSS., Wilbraham Temple, Cambridge.

[70] Bentham MSS., CXXXI, 27-183.

[71] *Edinburgh Review*, xlix (1829), 180-3.

[72] 'Article on Utilitarianism', in *Deontology*, ed. Goldworth, 309-10.

[73] *Edinburgh Review*, xxxi (1818), 174; xlix (1829), 292.

ultimate basis of distinctions between right and wrong, in both morals and legislation, was not contested. Where Jeffrey differed from Bentham was over how these distinctions were in practice to be recognised. As against the view that moral feelings were mere sympathies and antipathies which varied from one individual to another and could provide no reliable standard for moral judgments, Jeffrey maintained that 'the common impressions of morality' provided much more dependable guidance than one could obtain from calculations of utility. These common impressions might be, as he described them, 'summaries of utility', in that they were derived from long experience of what rules of conduct were conducive to human welfare. But to suggest that one should regulate one's conduct by estimating the good and evil likely to result from every particular action was to expect far too much wisdom and impartiality from individuals.[74] Similar points were made twenty-five years later by Mackintosh in the 'Dissertation on the Progress of Ethical Philosophy' which he wrote for the *Encyclopaedia Britannica*. He said that although the principle of utility formed a necessary part of every moral theory, it ought not to be made the immediate regulator of human conduct. Utility itself required that men should cultivate those habitual sentiments and dispositions that were known by experience to be the source of beneficial actions, and virtuous conduct could be most confidently expected to result from 'that state of mind in which ... the moral sentiments most strongly approve what is right and good, without being perplexed by a calculation of consequences'.[75] It is rather strange, however, that Mackintosh should have presented this criticism of act-utilitarianism as a criticism of Bentham, for he had written in 1813 (in an article on Madame de Staël): 'The most specious objections to Mr Bentham have arisen from losing sight of his object, which is to present a calculation of pleasures and pains ... as the basis of general rules of law, not as a guide in the deliberation of an individual concerning the morality of each single action.'[76]

Another basic criticism of Bentham's ethics which appeared in the *Edinburgh Review* was made by Macaulay in the course of his controversy with James Mill and the *Westminster Review* in 1829. In the second of his articles on utilitarianism in that year, Macaulay anticipated many later critics in drawing attention to the apparent

[74] Ibid., iv (1804), 10–15.
[75] Mackintosh, *Dissertation on the Progress of Ethical Philosophy*, 292–3.
[76] *Edinburgh Review*, xxii (1813), 234n. Dumont had written in a detailed reply to Jeffrey, which he never published: 'L'objet de Mr. B. n'est ... point de rejeter les règles générales, mais de les vérifier par le principe de l'utilité.' (MS. Dumont 55, f. 127, Bibliothèque publique et universitaire, Geneva.)

inconsistency between Bentham's psychological egoism and his 'greatest happiness principle'. Bentham said both that every man inevitably pursued his own happiness or interest, and that every man ought to promote the general happiness; and (to state the objection in Macaulay's words) 'he can give no reason why a man should promote the greatest happiness of others, if their greatest happiness be inconsistent with what he thinks his own'.[77] This criticism, like Jeffrey's, assumed Bentham to be saying that the greatest happiness principle ought to be taken by each individual as the principle that should govern his conduct. But in fact, although Bentham thought that every reasonable person would accept that the greatest happiness principle was the principle on which society as a whole should be *managed*, he did not expect each individual to aim at anything other than the maximisation of his own happiness. The best way of promoting the maximisation of the general happiness, in his opinion, was for those responsible for the management of the society to ensure as far as possible, by manipulating the sanctions at their disposal, that people pursued their own happiness in ways that were innocuous or actually conducive to the happiness of others.[78]

While it would probably be true to say that few of Bentham's contemporaries fully understood the role of social and moral engineering in his system, the general importance of this element was made fairly plain in the *Traités de législation*. It was stated there that the object of the legislator was to 'determine' the conduct of the citizens, and that ethics was the art of 'directing' people's actions in such a way as to produce the greatest possible happiness.[79] Also, many contemporaries associated Bentham with his Panopticon plan, which helped to create the impression—in which there was a substantial amount of truth—that his general approach to society was an authoritarian and manipulative one. It was not only people on the left of the political spectrum who saw Bentham in these terms. The Panopticon image aroused revulsion and distrust from John Wilson Croker of the *Quarterly* as well as from the radical William Hazlitt.[80] Similarly, Bentham's theory of sovereignty, which represented the supreme legislative authority as the source and creator of *all* laws and rights, was criticised by writers as far apart from each other as the French legitimist Bonald and the English proto-socialist

---

[77] *Edinburgh Review*, xlix (1829), 294. Cf. *Utilitarian Logic and Politics*, eds. Jack Lively and John Rees (Oxford, 1978), 261-3. This was also to be the central argument in one of the main attacks made on Bentham's moral philosophy in the 1830s: Théodore Jouffroy, *Cours de droit naturel* (2 vols, Paris, 1834-42), I, Leçon xiv.

[78] Cf. my paper 'Bentham on Private Ethics and the Principle of Utility', *Revue Internationale de Philosophie*, xxxvi (1982), 278-300 ; see above, chapter 17, 315-37.

[79] *Traités de législation*, I. xxx, 93.

[80] *Quarterly Review*, x (1814), 489; *New Monthly Magazine*, x (1824), 74.

Thomas Hodgskin. Bonald said that this theory could not be applied even to God himself, 'dont la volonté est réglée par les lois immuables de l'éternelle raison'.[81] Hodgskin maintained that the doctrine was even less acceptable than that of the divine right of kings; it left the individual with no defences against the state, and was equivalent to saying that men could be 'experimented upon' in any way the legislator pleased.[82]

One of the most eloquent protestors against Bentham's tendency to treat individuals as human materials to be conditioned and manipulated by the managers of society was another contributor to the *Edinburgh Review* (though a rather different one from the whig contributors we have previously considered), Thomas Carlyle. Although he once contemplated writing a whole essay on Bentham for the *Edinburgh*,[83] he never did so; but comments on utilitarianism, which are impressionistic but suggest some knowledge of Bentham's works, are scattered through the articles he did publish in the late 'twenties and early 'thirties. From the utilitarian viewpoint, he suggested, good conduct was a matter of prudence rather than virtue, and something that was contrived by the legislator rather than something that depended on the will and merit of the individual. Under this system of ethics, he wrote, goodness had to 'seek strength from sanctions', and necessity usurped the throne of free will.[84] The wise men of the day were constitution-makers and code-builders, who believed that human welfare depended on 'mechanism'—on outward circumstances such as political and legislative arrangements. These sages, said Carlyle, occupied themselves in 'counting-up and estimating men's motives', and strove 'by curious checking and balancing, and other adjustments of Profit and Loss, to guide them to their true advantage'; but they ignored the vital and spiritual elements, 'the inward primary powers of man', which were the chief sources of human worth and happiness.[85]

Carlyle had some knowledge of Kant's ideas—and so had Hazlitt, another of Bentham's critics. One of the formulations of Kant's

---

[81] Vicomte de Bonald, *Législation primitive, considérée dans les derniers temps par les seules lumières de la raison* (3rd edn., 2 vols, Paris, 1829), I. 113.

[82] Thomas Hodgskin, *The Natural and Artificial Right of Property Contrasted* (1832), 21. There were other contributors to early socialist thought, the Saint-Simonians, who had no objection to the *dirigiste* element in Bentham's system, though they differed from him on other points: see [J.-B. Duvergier], 'De la législation', in *Opinions littéraires, philosophiques et industrielles* (Paris, 1825), 199–212; [B.-P. Enfantin *et al.*], *Doctrine de Saint-Simon. Exposition. Première année, 1829* (2nd edn., Paris, 1830), 241–5.

[83] *Collected Letters of Thomas and Jane Carlyle*, eds. C.R. Sanders and K.J. Fielding (Durham, North Carolina, 1970-), V. 211–12.

[84] *Edinburgh Review*, xlvi (1827), 348; liv (1831), 357.

[85] Ibid., xlix (1829), 447–52. *Cf.* J.B. Schneewind, *Sidgwick's Ethics and Victorian Moral Philosophy* (Oxford, 1977), 166–8.

categorical imperative declared that one should not use individuals as means to an end without treating them at the same time as ends in themselves; and it has been said that respect for persons, as embodied in Kant's analysis, 'presents perhaps the greatest challenge to dogmatic Utilitarianism'.[86] Hazlitt suggested that Bentham's calculus might be used to justify the slave trade, on the grounds that the sufferings of the slaves were outweighed by the pleasure derived from the sugar they produced.[87] Another writer who thought that Bentham's theory allowed people to be treated essentially as instruments was the Genevan liberal Pellegrino Rossi. He wrote in his *Traité de droit pénal* (1829): 'Dans le système de l'utilité générale, l'individu n'est rien. ... Lorsque vous punissez un homme uniquement pour le plaisir des autres hommes et pour inspirer de la crainte à leur profit, le condamné n'est qu'un moyen matériel employé pour faire peur.' If the man were to complain that he had done nothing *wrong*, a sufficient answer would be that his punishment suited the interests of the greatest number.[88]

Rossi founded his penal theory on a doctrine of natural right, and there were several other writers who held that only a doctrine of this kind could offer the protection for individuals which utilitarianism did not provide. Bentham himself had written a destructive critique of the French Declaration of the Rights of Man, and when this was published by Dumont in the post-war period it drew an indignant response from the liberal *Revue Encyclopédique*, which usually dealt sympathetically with Bentham's works. The reviewer (Avenel) declared:

> Les droits naturels ne sont pourtant pas une chimère: le Créateur n'a point jeté l'homme sur la terre sans aucune protection; son éternelle providence a mis dans la conscience de l'homme un sentiment intime de ces droits, et ce sentiment de tous est en effet une sauvegarde pour chacun.[89]

Another, more prominent, liberal writer who upheld natural rights against utilitarianism was Benjamin Constant, though in his case the divergence from Bentham was not very substantial.[90] He conceded that if the word utility were appropriately defined, the rules that

---

[86] R. Wellek, *Immanuel Kant in England 1793-1838* (Princeton, 1931), 164-71, 183-202; Roy Park, 'Hazlitt and Bentham', *Journal of the History of Ideas*, xxx (1969), 373.

[87] William Hazlitt, *The Plain Speaker* (2 vols, 1826), I. 112-15.

[88] Pellegrino Rossi, *Traité de droit pénal* (3 vols, Paris, 1829), I. 176, 178.

[89] Bentham, *Tactique des assemblées législatives, suivie d'un Traité des sophismes politiques*, ed. Dumont (2nd edn., 2 vols, Geneva, 1822), II. 255-369; *Revue Encyclopédique*, xix (1823), 578-85.

[90] He admitted this to Dumont at a dinner party in Paris in 1817: MS. Dumont 16, f. 9.

one would erect on the basis of that principle would be the same as those which would be erected on the basis of natural-right doctrine. But whereas Bentham held that natural right was a vague notion that anyone could define in his own way, Constant maintained that the notion of utility opened the way to even more uncertainties and differences of opinion. He considered that although the idea of rights and the idea of utility were not really in conflict, they ought to be kept as far apart as possible. To tell someone that he had a *right* not to be put to death or arbitrarily despoiled would give him a much greater feeling of security than if he were told that it was not *useful* that he should be put to death or arbitrarily despoiled. In speaking of a right one was expressing an idea that was independent of calculation; in speaking of utility one appeared to suggest that the matter was always open to verification.[91] Moreover, Constant believed that in regard to politics the idea of rights was more *inspiring* than that of utility: it was worth conserving because (as he wrote in 1829) 'elle réveille ces passions généreuses dont les temps de calme et de bonheur peuvent se passer, mais qu'il est bon de retrouver au besoin dans les temps d'avilissement et de tyrannie'.[92] A similar point was made by Auguste de Staël, the son of Constant's celebrated friend. He wrote in 1825 that Bentham and his followers were not justified in appealing to the example of the United States in response to conservative critics of their radicalism, for the Americans had fought for their independence not in the name of the arid dogma of utility, which had never evoked heroism, but in the name of the rights of man.[93]

The charge that utilitarianism was an uninspiring, and even ignoble, doctrine—in morals as well as in politics—was common among liberal writers. The roles of egoism and calculation in Bentham's system were found particularly distasteful, and to some contemporaries the system seemed to be founded on, and to endorse, a view of human nature as thoroughly selfish. Auguste de Staël, for example, said that the basic dogma of Benthamite utilitarianism was 'l'intérêt personnel, quelquefois déguisé sous le nom de *principe d'utilité*'.[94] Bentham, in fact, when he said that all actions were determined by what the agent believed to be his interests, intended the latter term to embrace what he called 'social interests' as well as 'self-regarding' ones, and his defenders often insisted that sympathy and benevolence

[91] Benjamin Constant, *Principes de politique applicables à tous les gouvernements*, ed. E. Hofmann (Geneva, 1980), 59–60. The passage appears to have been written in 1802; it was published in the *Mercure de France*, Nov. 1817, 248–9.

[92] Constant, *Mélanges de littérature et de politique* (Paris, 1829), 148.

[93] Auguste de Staël, *Lettres sur l'Angleterre* (Paris, 1825), 323–5.

[94] Ibid., 310.

were significant elements in his system.[95] Dumont went so far as to suggest at one point that the term 'principle of utility' should be replaced by 'principle of benevolence'.[96] This, however, would have been to *exaggerate* the importance of benevolence in Bentham's system, for he believed that as a general rule self-regarding interests and motives predominated over social ones and that little reliance could be placed on the latter. John Stuart Mill, who was more thoroughly acquainted with Bentham's thought than any of his earlier critics, considered that he had put an undue emphasis on the selfish aspect of human nature. One of the functions of ethical writing, he wrote soon after Bentham's death, was to inspire people with a belief in man's capacity for virtue; but the effect of Bentham's works on those who read and absorbed them 'must either be hopeless despondency and gloom, or a reckless giving themselves up to a life of that miserable self-seeking, which they are there taught to regard as inherent in their original and unalterable nature'.[97] Twenty years earlier Madame de Staël had argued rather similarly that the propagation of Bentham's doctrines would tend in practice to encourage selfish behaviour. Someone, she wrote, who was told that his own happiness should be the goal of all his actions could only be diverted from a wrong action which appeared to suit his convenience by the danger of punishment—a danger which a bold and cunning person might think he could escape. She maintained that true goodness could only result from the cultivation of virtue for its own sake, without regard to consequences; and she called for a morality of *dévouement* rather than one of utility.[98] The Genevan economist Sismondi was another contemporary who held that Bentham's system was unconducive to altruism,[99] and J.S. Mill was probably right in saying that it was above all by giving rise to this belief that Bentham had prejudiced 'the more enthusiastic and generous minds' against his whole philosophy.

The foregoing survey of early-nineteenth-century reactions to Benthamism cannot claim to be comprehensive. Moreover, by focusing on the aspects of his thought which contemporaries found objectionable or absurd, it may have given a misleadingly one-sided impres-

[95] E.g. *L'Utilitaire*, i (1829), 399-401.

[96] Dumont to Bentham, 21 Aug. 1822, Bentham MSS., X, 128. Dumont added (to Bentham, 28 Nov. 1822, ibid., CLXXIV, 70) that the main objection to the word 'utility' was 'le malheureux liaison vulgaire établi entre ce mot et l'intérêt personnel'.

[97] 'Remarks on Bentham's Philosophy', in E.L. Bulwer, *England and the English* (2 vols, 1833), II. 339-41.

[98] Germaine de Staël, *De l'Allemagne* (3 vols, Paris, 1813), III. 181n. Cf. Norman King, '"The airy form of things forgotten"; Madame de Staël, l'utilitarisme et l'impulsion libérale', *Cahiers staëliens*, no. 11 (1970), 5-26.

[99] *Revue Encyclopédique*, xliv (1829), 263-4.

sion of the reception of his ideas: this paper needs to be balanced by one describing what many people found to *admire* in his work. It is hoped, however, that the paper has indicated the aspects of his thought that attracted most attention from critics, and the main quarters from which attacks were made. Many of the points which were to be reiterated through the nineteenth century, and indeed in the twentieth, by opponents of utilitarianism were already being expressed in his lifetime. Indeed, towards the end of his life there was a crescendo of criticism, and in 1829 the French utilitarian Jean-Baptiste Say was urging Dumont to write a full defence of the principle of utility against the *Edinburgh Review*, Rossi, Constant and other assailants. Dumont died in that year, and although Say himself drafted such a defence he was dissatisfied with it and it was not published until after his death.[100] Bentham, as we have seen, was not generally interested in replying publicly to critics, and those of his followers who attempted to do so, such as Antoine Cherbuliez of *L'Utilitaire* and Colonel Perronet Thompson of the *Westminster Review*, do not seem to have made much impact on opinion. Moreover, a further barrage of hostile comment was to follow in the eighteen-thirties and 'forties when Benthamism became closely associated in the public mind with the harsher aspects of political economy. Hazlitt had complained in the eighteen-twenties about the lack of compassion in Bentham's philosophy, and had described the Utilitarian reformers as men who exulted in the idea of 'plucking the crutch from the cripple'. But it was the New Poor Law of 1834, above all, which gave currency to the notion of what Disraeli called 'Brutilitarianism'.[101]

---

[100] J.-B. Say to Dumont, 10 Aug. 1829, MS. Dumont 77, f. 9; Say, *Mélanges et correspondance d'économie politique*, ed. Charles Comte (Paris, 1833), 362-74, 406-41.

[101] Hazlitt, *The Plain Speaker*, I. 114-15, 438; *Morning Post*, 24 Aug. 1835, reprinted in *Whigs and Whiggism: Political Writings by Benjamin Disraeli*, ed. William Hutcheon (1913), 50.

19

Adjudication under Bentham's Pannomion

Gerald J. Postema's monograph *Bentham and the Common Law Tradition* (1986) is the most sophisticated and challenging book yet published on Bentham's jurisprudence—with the possible exception of H. L. A. Hart's *Essays on Bentham* (1982), which as its title indicates is a different type of publication.[1] Among the stimulating lines of argument that run through the book is the notion that the importance, in Bentham's legal theory, of social *control* by means of penal legislation has been over-emphasized by most commentators as compared with the importance of social *co-ordination* via the definitional and distributional functions of civil law. Postema stresses, most helpfully, the weight that Bentham attached to 'security' and expectation utilities.[2] He also argues cogently that 'utilitarian positivism' is not, as it might seem to be, a contradiction in terms: Bentham did not attempt to separate the conceptual and the normative aspects of jurisprudence to the extent that Austin and the 'Analytic Jurists' did subsequently, for he saw the dispassionate analysis and definition of legal concepts as an integral part of the utilitarian juristic enterprise. However, although Postema does not see any contradiction here, he does build up to a conclusion in his final chapter that there *is* a crucial incoherence in Bentham's theory of law. The present paper is an attempt to examine this contention.[3]

The argument which leads Postema to his conclusion can be summarized, baldly but I hope fairly, as follows. On the one hand, Bentham was a legal positivist, who believed that public and determinate laws were necessary to focus expectations and 'to define and maintain a secure framework for social interaction' (p. 448); case-law was in-

---

[1] Gerald J. Postema, *Bentham and the Common Law Tradition*, Oxford, 1986; H. L. A. Hart, *Essays on Bentham: Studies in Jurisprudence and Political Theory*, Oxford, 1982.

[2] For similar arguments in a somewhat different context, see Frederick Rosen, *Jeremy Bentham and Representative Democracy: A Study of the Constitutional Code*, Oxford, 1983, especially chaps. iv and vi.

[3] I am grateful to Gerald Postema for friendly discussion of our differences of interpretation. In my *Bentham* (Oxford, 1989) I have given a brief account of Bentham's theory of adjudication, which differs markedly from Postema's; but there was insufficient space in that book to confront his arguments directly, and this paper is an attempt to explain on what grounds my account diverges from his.

capable of providing the certainty and security that were required for the maximization of happiness. On the other hand (Postema maintains) Bentham had a 'direct-utilitarian' theory of adjudication. He expected judges *not* to adhere strictly and mechanically to the enacted law, but to apply the principle of utility to each case, departing from 'the line marked out by pre-established law' if in any particular case such deviation seemed to be requisite on utilitarian grounds. But these two positions, the positivist conception of law and the direct-utilitarian conception of judicial decision-making, are incompatible, in Postema's opinion: in his own words, 'Bentham's theories of law and adjudication, far from fitting together into an organic unity as he supposes, are in fact in deep conflict' (p. 453). For codified law can only serve the purpose of securing expectations and co-ordinating social interaction so long as the citizens in general are convinced that the laws embodied in the code correspond closely to the laws applied and enforced by the courts. When judges (for what they see as compelling utilitarian reasons) depart from the code, these departures are bound to become public knowledge; and public expectations, instead of being fixed on the code, 'will inevitably shift back to focus on the activities of the courts and the patterns that emerge from them'. In consequence, 'a system of precedent-based case-law will inevitably arise', as happened in France after the introduction of the Napoleonic codes (p. 454).[4] Thus Bentham's attempt to combine consistency on the one hand with flexibility on the other was doomed to failure.

Of the two elements in Postema's interpretation that make up the conflict he postulates, the view that Bentham was a convinced believer in positive, codified law is beyond question. But the other element—the argument that Bentham's theory of adjudication required the direct application of the utilitarian criterion rather than a strict application of the code—is more problematic. This argument is set out in the penultimate chapter of *Bentham and the Common Law Tradition*, where Postema says that according to Bentham's theory 'the judge will treat the code as a guide setting out the relevant (utilitarian) considerations to be taken into account, ... but he will not regard it as a set of fixed rules determining his decision in a mechanical way' (p. 405). More specifically, Postema maintains that a 'model' of Bentham's theory of adjudication is to be found in his theory of evidence and in his view of the role of the judge in procedural matters generally. He is able to produce several quotations from Bentham's *Principles of Judicial Procedure* and his *Rationale of Judicial Evidence* to show that in regard

---

[4] Postema does consider one or two rather subtle arguments that Bentham might putatively have produced to counter the objection raised; but as they are not arguments that Bentham actually used for this purpose, and as Postema does not regard them as constituting a very effective rebuttal, we may leave them aside.

to procedure and evidence he clearly was opposed to the laying down of inflexible rules. One may add that William Twining, in his *Theories of Evidence: Bentham and Wigmore* (1985) has argued rather similarly that in this particular field Bentham was an 'anti-nomian': he considered that the judge, in arriving at the facts necessary to enable him to make a fully informed decision on the case, should be as little restricted by formal rules as possible.[5] The question is, how far can one regard Bentham's 'anti-nomianism' as applying not only to what he called 'adjective law' but to substantive law as well? While Twining (understandably in a book focused on theories of evidence) does not attempt to answer this question, Postema does contend that the 'model' that Bentham advocated in relation to procedural matters was intended to be applicable to judicial decision-making in general. The main empirical support he finds for this view is in Bentham's writings of 1829–30 proposing the establishment of an 'Equity Dispatch Court'.

It was recommended in this work that the judge in the proposed court should base his judgments on the 'disappointment–prevention principle'—i.e. on the principle that disputes over titles to property should be decided in favour of whichever party would suffer greater disappointment from the loss of the property concerned. Postema, reasonably enough, treats the disappointment–prevention principle as a 'deputy' of the principle of utility, and says that what Bentham is in effect doing is recommending the direct application of a utilitarian criterion rather than the application of rules. It is not quite clear, however, that he is correct in holding that the Equity Dispatch Court can be treated as a pattern for Bentham's general theory of adjudication. He quotes Bentham as saying in his *Equity Dispatch Court Proposal* (published in 1830) that 'a much better chance for prevention of disappointment will be obtained, by aiming at that object *immediately*, than by aiming at it through so unconducive, and in every respect unapt a *medium*'.[6] But it is evident from the context that what Bentham meant in this passage by the word '*medium*' was not rules *per se* but the rules which currently operated in the English Equity Courts—rules which he regarded as unsatisfactory and in many instances mutually contradictory. Postema is not able to show that from the indifference to rules which Bentham recommended to the judge in the proposed Equity Dispatch Court (which would have been dealing with titles acquired under a legal system that was intrinsically unable to provide certainty and definition), one can deduce that he would have

---

[5] William Twining, *Theories of Evidence: Bentham and Wigmore*, London, 1985, pp. 66–75.

[6] Postema, p. 416, quoting *The Works of Jeremy Bentham*, ed. John Bowring, 11 vols., Edinburgh, 1838–43, iii. 312. (In the text below, this edition is cited in the form: Bowring, iii, 312.)

recommended a similar attitude, in regard to enacted substantive laws, to judges operating under the Pannomion—i.e. under a complete system of codified law explicitly founded on utilitarian principles.

Bentham's fullest and most mature discussion of the role to be played by judges under the Pannomion is to be found in his *Constitutional Code*. He was quite prepared to recognize that although the Pannomion as he envisaged it would be *intended* at every point to be conducive to the greatest happiness, legislators were not infallible and could not be expected to provide satisfactorily for every contingency that might arise within the legal sphere. Any judge might well be faced at times with a situation in which a strict application of the law as it stood would not, in his opinion, produce the optimal outcome in utilitarian terms. In the sections of the *Constitutional Code* on what are called the 'emendative' and 'sistitive' (or suspensive) functions of the judge (B ix. 504–11), Bentham described what action a judge should take in such a situation. The emendative function was the role of the judge in proposing any alteration to the Pannomion which he regarded as necessary in order to bring its provisions into line with the dictates of utility. The sistitive function was one whereby the judge suspended execution of the law on a particular case, pending the legislature's decision on a proposed emendation. It is the latter of the two functions which, as Postema recognizes, presents a problem for his interpretation of Bentham's theory of adjudication.

He describes the function, and the problem, as follows (p. 435):

The main idea is that the judge in exercising this power simply suspends execution of the existing law—which is under consideration for alteration or amendment—*until* the legislature decides regarding ... the alteration proposed by the judge.... The decision of the legislature will not only affect the law or provision of the code but also will apply to the case which occasioned the proposed amendment. The judge apparently has no power to decide the case before him, but must wait on the decision from the legislature, and the decision of the legislature automatically determines the disposition of the particular case before the court. This, of course, would pose a challenge to my interpretation of Bentham's view of adjudication. For on this view the judge appears to be justified in *questioning* the application of the law to a particular case (on utilitarian grounds) *only when* there is apparent utilitarian justification for *alteration* of the law. Moreover, the power to decide even particular cases according to the principle of utility is taken from the judge and placed in the hands of the legislature.

As Postema goes on to acknowledge, Bentham's account of the sistitive function might well be taken to imply that the judge is *denied* the power to appeal directly to the principle of utility to determine the case before him, and that what is being asserted is 'an extreme form of judicial subordination to the legislature'. In place of such a construction of the passage, which would plainly controvert his own thesis about Bentham's view of adjudication, Postema puts forward an alternative reading. He suggests that what Bentham is doing is providing the judge with a set of *optional* courses from which he may choose when faced with a case in which a simple application of the law would appear to produce a less than optimal result. To quote Postema again (p. 439):

The judge may decide to set aside the law, making his decision by direct appeal to the principle of utility, *or* he may decide to submit a proposal for amendment to the legislature. If he chooses that latter course, he must decide *further* whether, on utilitarian grounds, he ought to decide the present case (either in accord with the existing law, or with the law as he thinks it should be amended) or to suspend decision until the legislature has decided.

This interpretation, however, seems to me strained, and is hard to reconcile with the actual text of the *Code* (as edited by Richard Doane for the Bowring edition of Bentham's *Works*).

So far as the latter pair of supposed options is concerned, what Bentham says in the section on the sistitive function is that where the judge believes there is an imperfection in the law which, if put into execution, will produce injustice,[7] and he consequently proposes an amendment to the legislature, 'it is not only allowable to him, but on his responsibility, rendered incumbent on him, to stay execution accordingly' (Bowring ix. 508). He should issue, in such a situation, three decrees: one giving execution to the law as it stands, the second giving execution to the law as it will stand if his amendment is adopted, and the third stopping the execution of both 'until the will of the legislature shall have been made known'. It seems clear that whenever the judge makes use of his emendative function with a view to correcting an imperfection in the law which would produce injustice in the conclusion of a particular case, he is *obliged* to make use of his sistitive function also. What of the first pair of postulated options? In his section on the emendative function, Bentham does not explicitly say that in *every* case in which the application of the existing law would in the judge's view produce injustice he is *obliged* to propose an amendment. But elsewhere in the *Constitutional Code* there are passages which make it clear that the judge should *not*, in any such case, deliver and order the execution of a final judgement which *contravenes* the existing law. The most striking such passage is in the 'Judges' Inaugural Declaration' (Bowring, ix. 533). It is here laid down that the judge must undertake to give execution and effect to every part of the law, 'not presuming on any occasion to substitute any particular will of my own, to the will of the Legislature, even in such cases, if any, where the provisions of the law may appear to me inexpedient: saving only the

---

[7] i.e., an outcome that conflicts with the dictates of utility.

exercise of such discretionary suspensive power, if any, with which the Legislature may have thought fit to entrust me'. The judge, in other words, may *suspend* the execution of the law, in the manner explained above (pending the decision of the legislature on a proposed amendment). But he *cannot*—as Postema suggests he can—'decide to set aside the law, making his decision by direct appeal to the principle of utility'.

Let us return to the conclusions of Postema's book and to his contention that, because of a basic incoherence, 'Bentham's mature theory of laws and adjudication ... is self-defeating' (p. 454). So far as the theory of adjudication is concerned, Postema is in one important sense right in his interpretation. Bentham did *not* consider that judges should apply the codified laws of the Pannomion in a mechanical and uncritical fashion. They were to address themselves directly to the principle of utility, in the sense of considering what the balance of utilities in each particular case was, and checking that the provisions of the code did not dictate a judgement that went against this. At the same time, however, Bentham was anxious to *prevent* judges from delivering judgements that contravened the Pannomion, and he devised an elaborate machinery for ensuring that this would not be necessary or permissible. Moreover, he was anxious to ensure that *within* the boundaries laid down by the Pannomion, differing *interpretations* of the law should be unequivocally resolved. Consequently, he assigned another function to the judiciary which he called the 'contested–interpretation–reporting function' (Bowring, ix. 502–4). On any appeal that was grounded on a matter of law rather than a matter of fact, an appeal judge was to give his opinion of the correct interpretation of the law, and a report setting out the points at issue was to be channelled, via the Justice Minister and the Legislation Minister, to a standing committee of the legislature called the Contested Interpretation Committee, which would make the final decision on the matter of law and on any amendment or refinement of the code which seemed necessary in order to elucidate the relevant provision.

In designing the machinery we have described—the emendative, sistitive, and contested–interpretation–reporting functions—one of Bentham's purposes was to obviate the very danger that Postema accuses him of failing to guard against: the danger that 'a system of precedent-based case-law' would arise alongside the codified law. The functions concerned were intended, Bentham explicitly says,

to preserve the Pannomion from being infested, and its usefulness impaired, by masses of that very sort of spurious and excrementitious matter, which it was originally employed to take the place of: matter composed of masses of the so called *common law*, in the shape of Reports of judicial decisions, professed to be grounded on the law, together with dissertations, grounded partly on the genuine text, partly on this spurious matter, and succeeding one another without end. (Bowring, ix. 512.)[8]

The other purpose of these functions of the judiciary—along with the provision in the *Constitutional Code* that amendments to the law could be proposed by members of the legislature—was to ensure that the Pannomion was open to continuous *improvement*. The judges' emendative function was considered particularly important in this respect, as 'giving to the Pannomion at all times, the benefit of such experience, information, and correspondent skill, as cannot, in any other situation, in an equal degree, have place' (Bowring, ix. 431). A standard objection to codified law has always been that it tends to be inflexible, and Postema seems to assume that the objection is applicable to Bentham's Pannomion as to other codes of law. 'The demands for "flexibility" ', he asserts (p. 458), 'are not met by his code even in its most ideal form'; according to him, it was through a direct-utilitarian theory of adjudication that Bentham tried to meet these demands—and this theory was incompatible with the nature and purposes of his positivist conception of law. I hope I have shown, however, that in the *Constitutional Code* Bentham was trying to get over the problem that Postema identifies, by constructing a system of positive law which combined *within itself* determinacy with flexibility. He was insistent that judges should not have the latitude to deliver judgements, on their own authority, which deviated from the provisions of the Pannomion. He recognized that such decisions might sometimes be desirable, in order to implement what was presumed to be the real purpose of the legislature, the optimal application of the utilitarian criterion; but he laid down that whenever such a decision was required, it had to receive the sanction of the legislature, and the Pannomion had to be adjusted in order to make it clear that similar cases would be similarly treated in future. How far his elaborate system would have been *practicable* may be open to question; but it was not open to the charge of *incoherence* which Postema levels against it.

[8] He goes on to cite the same example as Postema cites: 'It is for want of such an institution, that in this respect the condition of France, since the prodigious improvement received from Buonaparte's Codes, has been continually growing worse and worse. Not more than a dozen years have those five codes been in authority, and already the field is crowded, the conception of the people perplexed, and uncertainty continually rendered more uncertain by swarms of commentaries.'

20

Luddism and Politics in the Northern Counties[1]

During the eighteenth century machine-breaking was common as a way of putting pressure on employers or of resisting the introduction of machinery which threatened to create unemployment.[2] The 'Luddism' of 1811–12 – machine-breaking and associated disturbances in the East Midlands, the area round Manchester, and the West Riding – had much in common with earlier episodes in the three trades concerned: the hosiery, cotton and woollen industries.[3] But it was distinguished by the fact that it was widely suspected of having political as well as industrial motives. Luddism has been examined in several scholarly works,[4] and this essay will not try to tackle the subject as a whole. It will not attempt to break new ground, for example, with regard to the industrial grievances and general economic distress that lay behind the disturbances, and it will take for granted much of the information that is available on these topics elsewhere. It will concentrate on the particular problem of the relationship between Luddism and political agitation. This emphasis is not intended to imply that the industrial and economic background to Luddism requires no further elucidation. On the contrary, it is very likely that further research will extend our knowledge of the changes that were taking place in the technology and structure of the trades concerned. But it is also true that there has been much less disagreement among historians about the economic and industrial causes of discontent in the disturbed counties than there has been about the form the agitation took.

The question of whether, or how far, the Luddite troubles had a political dimension *has* provoked considerable controversy, and the conclusions of the twentieth-century historians who have examined the subject can be briefly summarized. J. L. and B. Hammond and F. O. Darvall decided that political motives played little or no part in

[1] I am grateful to Michael Collinge and John Styles for their advice on aspects of this paper.

[2] E. J. Hobsbawm, *Labouring Men* (1964), ch. II, 'The machine breakers'.

[3] Cf. M. I. Thomis, *Politics and Society in Nottingham 1785–1835* (Oxford, 1969), 77; A. G. Rose, 'Early cotton riots in Lancashire, 1769–1779', *Transactions of the Lancashire and Cheshire Antiquarian Society*, LXXIII–LXXIV (1963–4), 60–100; W. B. Crump (ed.), The *Leeds Woollen Industry 1780–1820*, Thoresby Society Publications, XXXII (Leeds, 1931), 46.

[4] J. L. and B. Hammond, *The Skilled Labourer 1760–1832* (1919), chs. IX–XI; F. O. Darvall, *Popular Disturbances and Public Order in Regency England* (Oxford, 1934); E. P. Thompson, *The Making of the English Working Class* (2nd ed., Harmondsworth, 1968), ch. XIV; M. I. Thomis, *The Luddites: Machine-Breaking in Regency England* (Newton Abbot, 1970).

the disturbances. Darvall went so far as to say that 'there was no movement, or even tendency, of revolt against the established [political or social] system as such; no disposition to see in the system the cause of the very many grave evils from which great bodies of the people were suffering'. François Crouzet followed the same interpretation, concluding: ' Il est à peu près certain que le mouvement luddite n'avait absolument aucun aspect politique.'[5] E. P. Thompson, on the other hand, in *The Making of the English Working Class*, attacked the 'limited industrial interpretation' of Luddism and argued that both in Lancashire and the West Riding the disturbances displayed 'revolutionary features' which could not be ignored or explained away.[6] Malcolm Thomis then mounted a counter-attack, arguing that although Luddism (at least in Lancashire) had some of the elements of a 'general protest movement' the Luddites could not be regarded as revolutionaries: 'political revolution was too sophisticated a concept for the Luddites', who 'had only vague notions of social amelioration, and no concept of this as a consequence of political action and the use of political power'.[7]

In the face of such differences of opinion Duncan Bythell has taken the view that the dispute about the revolutionary element in the disturbances of 1812 is 'incapable of final resolution', because the validity of the evidence on which it turns – especially the reports of spies – cannot be definitely tested: 'in the last resort, those who want to believe that England came near to revolution at this time will find support for their belief in these papers, whereas those who do not wish to believe this will find little difficulty in discounting the records'.[8] Yet this conclusion may be too pessimistic. It is true, perhaps, that recent protagonists in the debate have each been concerned to make out a case and have tended to take, from their respective positions, a rather one-sided view of the evidence. But the present essay is written in the hope that a re-examination of the sources (though much of the ground it covers will be familiar) may result in some progress towards the probable truth.

It is necessary at the outset to indicate how the term 'political' is to be used in this essay. Briefly, 'political agitation' will be defined as any agitation aimed at producing changes in the political system, whether by revolution or by reform. Several of the strategies used by sections of the working class to advance or protect their interests did not involve, in themselves, any direct challenge to the political system (although, of course, the control of that system by the propertied classes might crucially affect the context in which such strategies had to operate and their chances of success). For example, working-class groups could try in spite of the combination laws to obtain concessions from employers through collective bargaining and, if necessary, strike action. Another possibility was to take the employers to court – to bring actions against them for contravening laws that regulated industrial practices. And a third approach was to

[5] Darvall, *op. cit.*, 317; F. Crouzet, *L'Economie britannique et le Blocus continental* (2 vols., Paris, 1958), II, 801–2.

[6] Thompson, *op. cit.*, 642, 648. Another recent historian of Marxist persuasion, John Foster, refers to the Lancashire agitation as 'the guerilla campaign',

but without explaining what he considers its aims to have been: *Class Struggle and the Industrial Revolution* (1974), 40, 139.

[7] Thomis, *The Luddites*, 78, 95.

[8] Duncan Bythell, *The Handloom Weavers* (Cambridge, 1969), 209.

appeal to parliament in the hope of securing either the reinforcement of existing statutes or the enactment of new ones for the protection of particular working-class interests (for instance, the introduction of minimum-wage legislation applying to a specific trade). In cases of this third type the *method* might in one sense of the term be described as political, in that any such campaign involved an attempt to influence and gain concessions from the legislature. But since the direct objectives were still, as in the courses of action previously mentioned, industrial, and as such campaigns were conducted within the framework of the current political system, this type of movement will not be treated as 'political agitation' for the purposes of this essay. A fourth possible line of attack was 'collective bargaining by riot' – an attempt to coerce employers by machine-breaking or other forms of direct action. Prima facie, this would seem to be another form of *industrial* action – though one must bear in mind the possibility that once working men were mobilized for violent practices of this kind they might find themselves in direct confrontation with the state, and might conceivably be led to broaden the conflict with their employers into a wider challenge to the existing structure of authority. This brings us to a mode of action that clearly *was* political – namely, seditious activity intended to undermine or overthrow the political régime. One further option, also political, was to campaign for the *reform* of the political system. Most of the controversy over Luddism and politics has centred on the question of whether, or how far, machine-breaking merged into revolutionary activity. But the present essay, while devoting much of its space to that problem, will also pay some attention to the role of reformist agitation in the popular ferment of 1812.

It will not be suggested here that any sharp line can be drawn between those types of action classed as 'industrial' and those classed as 'political'. Often, as will be observed, the two types were very closely associated, and they might feed to a large extent on the same grievances. Activities of the industrial type – or rather their failure – might lead on quite logically to the adoption of either (or both) of the political strategies. Moreover, the ulterior purpose of the latter might remain in a basic sense economic: to secure a political system that would be more responsive to the economic and industrial demands of working men. However, despite these interconnections, there does seem to be a significant difference between, on the one hand, types of activity that were essentially sectional, being devoted to the amelioration of conditions in a particular trade or group of trades, and, on the other hand, activities designed to bring about a change or changes in the general system of government. As E. P. Thompson has said, for most of the eighteenth century overt popular antagonism rarely extended as far as the political structure; though the period saw various kinds of plebeian self-assertion the 'larger outlines' of power and political authority were rarely questioned.[9] The process whereby discontent became 'politicized', in the sense of being turned against the political régime, seems an important one,[10] which a study of the 1812 crisis may help to illuminate.

---

[9] E. P. Thompson, 'Patrician society, plebeian culture', *Journal of Social History*, 1 (1974), 388, 397.

[10] On the 'politicization of discontent', see T. R.

Gurr, *Why Men Rebel* (Princeton, 1970), 178 *et seq.* Cf. also R. Quinault and J. Stevenson (eds.), *Popular Protest and Public Order* (1974), 19.

One point about which there is fairly general agreement is that the Nottinghamshire Luddism of 1811–12 had little political content. The main phase of frame-breaking in Nottinghamshire, between November 1811 and February 1812, was preceded by persistent attempts on the part of the stockingers to secure their interests through negotiation or legal action, and it was followed by an unsuccessful campaign for parliamentary legislation to protect them from the 'abuses' of which they complained. Historical controversy over this branch of Luddism has focused on the relationship between violent and non-violent strategies in pursuit of industrial objectives, rather than on the relationship between industrial and political militancy.[11] On the latter topic there are questions of interest to be asked – for example, about the degree of continuity in the East Midlands between Luddism and the postwar political agitation which culminated in the Pentrich rising.[12] But the present essay will concentrate on the northern counties. Here, both in Lancashire and Yorkshire, there had been underground political activity – the agitation of the United Englishmen and United Britons – in the years around the turn of the century;[13] and these counties provide stronger evidence than the hosiery district of a connection between machine-breaking and politics in 1812.

For the weavers in the Lancashire cotton industry the underlying problem was one of overcrowding.[14] The high wages of the late eighteenth century, combined with the lack of restrictions on entry to the trade, had brought too many people into weaving, and the results were widespread under-employment and falling wages.[15] In addition there was the threat to handloom weaving posed by powered machinery. The steam loom, owing partly to mechanical imperfections, had not yet established a decisive cost advantage over traditional methods. By the time of the Luddite disturbances it had been introduced in only a small number of establishments and its effect on employment was marginal; but it had none the less become an object of fear and resentment to the handloom weavers. In the early years of the century the weavers' object was to find some means of checking the fall in wages. They did obtain the Cotton Arbitration Act of 1800, which established rudimentary machinery for the arbitration of wage disputes, but after an amending Act of 1804 the procedure was largely inoperative. In 1807–8 the

[11] See Thompson, *The Making of the English Working Class*, 582–91, 924–34; R. A. Church and S. D. Chapman, 'Gravener Henson and the making of the English working class', in E. L. Jones and G. P. Mingay (eds.), *Land, Labour and Population* (1967), 131–45; Thomis, *Politics and Society in Nottingham*, ch. v.

[12] Cf. on this question A. Temple Patterson, 'Luddism, Hampden Clubs and trade unions in Leicestershire, 1816–17', *English Historical Review*, LXIII (1948), 170 *et seq.*; E. Fearn, 'Reform Movements in Derby and Derbyshire, 1790–1832', M.A. thesis, University of Manchester (1964), 128 *et seq.*

[13] Thompson, *The Making of the English Working Class*, 515–22, 923–4; J. Walvin, 'English Democratic Societies and Popular Radicalism, 1791–1800', D.Phil.

thesis, University of York (1969), 663–88; J. R. Dinwiddy, 'The "Black Lamp" in Yorkshire 1801–1802', *Past and Present*, LXIV (1974), 113–23; J. L. Baxter and F. K. Donnelly, 'The revolutionary "underground" in the West Riding, myth or reality?', *ibid.*, 124–32.

[14] For detailed treatment of the problems and developments sketched in this paragraph, see Bythell, *op. cit.*, chs. IV, VII and VIII; Crouzet, *op. cit.*, II, chs. XV and XVI; M. M. Edwards, *The Growth of the British Cotton Trade 1780–1815* (Manchester, 1967), 18–19, 60–1, 72.

[15] John Foster has also drawn attention (*op. cit.*, 21) to the downward pressure on wages exerted by competition from cheap weaving labour on the continent.

weavers applied to parliament for minimum-wage legislation covering their trade. An Act of 1773 had sanctioned the fixing of wages in the Spitalfields silk industry, but in the Smithian climate of the early nineteenth century such measures were regarded with disfavour, and although a bill for the regulation of handloom weavers' wages was rather half-heartedly introduced by George Rose, it was soon dropped in the face of general criticism. A large-scale weavers' strike which then took place in Lancashire and Cheshire in May–June 1808 did gain a small rise in wages, and trade was relatively good during 1809 and most of 1810. In 1811, however, depression returned more severely than ever. This was primarily due to international factors: the last and tightest phase of Napoleon's Continental System coincided (as a result of friction over the Orders in Council) with an interruption of trade with the United States, and Britain's textile industries were seriously affected by the restriction of foreign markets. The situation was worsened by a bad harvest in 1811 and a steady rise in food prices, which continued until the late summer of 1812. Although Luddism did not appear in Lancashire until the spring of 1812, there was a considerable amount of working-class activity in the previous year or so; and the nature of this activity – particularly the extent to which it already had a political content – requires some attention.

In February 1811 the weavers of Bolton issued a printed address drawing attention to their 'frightful situation' and stating their intention of petitioning the Prince Regent for some means of relief. In March a petition was duly presented to the Regent and was referred to the Privy Council's committee for trade, but the committee, apart from expressing the hope that some benefit might be derived from the Bill then before the House of Commons for aiding commercial credit, could not suggest any measure that would be likely to provide effective help.[16] In April a teacher who had been acting as treasurer of the petitioning committee at Bolton alleged in a letter to a local manufacturer that the leadership of the campaign was being taken over by men whose design was 'if possible to raise tumult and disturbance in the country'.[17] There were other signs of agitation among the weavers, and in May the Bolton magistrate Colonel Fletcher obtained permission from the Home Office to employ agents at public expense (as he had done a decade earlier) for the purpose of gathering information about the movements that were afoot.[18] In fact the accent was still at this stage on petitioning. In Manchester at the end of April a public meeting was held, chaired by William Washington, a book-keeper in a Manchester factory, and it was agreed that a petition to parliament asking for relief should be circulated for signatures.[19] On 30 May petitions from Manchester and Bolton, signed by 40,000 and 7,000 people respectively, were

---

[16] Printed address dated 11 February 1811, enclosed in T. Fosbrooke to Home Office [H.O.], 12 February 1811; petition from inhabitants of Great and Little Bolton, n.d., enclosed in J. McMahon to R. Ryder, 15 March 1811; Viscount Chetwynd to H. Goulburn, 21 March 1811, Public Record Office [P.R.O.], H.O. 42/110.

[17] J. Hamill to T. Ainsworth, 19 April 1811, H.O. 42/115.

[18] W. Chippendale to R. Fletcher, 21 February 1811, H.O. 42/114; M. Dawes to H.O., 1 May 1811, H.O. 42/115; J. Beckett to Fletcher, 17 May 1811, H.O. 79/2, fo. 100.

[19] *Cowdroy's Manchester Gazette*, 4 May 1811. For Washington's occupation, see John Bent's report endorsed 10 October 1811, H.O. 42/117.

presented to the House of Commons by the members for Lancashire. The petitions described the extreme distress caused by lack of employment and the high price of provisions, and called on the legislature to provide some remedy. A select committee was appointed to consider the petitions (together with some from Scotland) but the report which it produced on 13 June was a classic statement of laissez-faire principles.[20] James Nisbet wrote on behalf of the Bolton committee to Samuel Whitbread: 'Surely, sir, the wisdom of the legislature can devise some means to help us. We will do our duty, as loyal, as peaceable subjects but grant us existance, otherwise who shall fight the battles of our countrey.'[21]

During the summer of 1811 Fletcher's agents discovered little that he considered of sufficient importance to be transmitted to the Home Office, but in the autumn he began forwarding fairly regularly the reports sent to him by John Bent. Bent was a dealer in cotton waste at Manchester,[22] and had been employed as a spy by Fletcher ten years before. Most historians of Luddism have treated his reports as too sensationalized to be of much historical value, but Thompson has argued that although (being a stupid and credulous man) he may have passed on inflated ideas about activities and organizations beyond his immediate knowledge, his descriptions of events in which he participated himself can be regarded as trustworthy.[23] The reports which Bent was sending in before the commencement of Lancashire Luddism have been little studied, but they have some bearing on his interpretation of the 1812 crisis.

One thing that emerges from these reports, and also to some extent from other sources, is that in the latter part of 1811 another application to parliament was being considered – this time a petition for peace and parliamentary reform. A committee in Manchester, probably a continuation of the body which had organized the petition in May, tried in July to obtain the support of 'several persons of property who had been in the habit of expressing opinions hostile to government'; but although sympathetic, these men were reluctant to participate in any public measure.[24] This discouraged activity for a time, but early in October some of the weaving towns to the east and north-east of Manchester sent urgent requests that Manchester itself should again give some kind of lead, and the committee reassembled.[25] Later that month it distributed a printed address which forcefully pointed out the connection between the weavers' recent failure to obtain redress from parliament and the need for parliamentary reform – the address being written in part (according to Bent) by John Knight, a small cotton manufacturer who had been the moving spirit behind an address of congratulation sent

[20] *Journals of the House of Commons*, LXVI, 383; Parliamentary Papers 1810–11, II, 389–90; Bythell, *op. cit.*, 155.

[21] Nisbet to Whitbread, 19 July 1811, Whitbread MSS., no. 3663, Bedfordshire Record Office.

[22] *Pigot's Manchester and Salford Directory, for 1811* (Manchester, 1810), 15; statement of H. Yarwood, 22 June 1812, H.O. 40/1, fo. 47.

[23] Hammonds, *op. cit.*, 274–5; Darvall, *op. cit.*, 279; Thomis, *The Luddites*, 90–2, 99–100, 115; Thompson, *The Making of the English Working Class*, 649–50.

[24] Fletcher to H.O., 12 October 1811, H.O. 42/117.

[25] Bent's report endorsed 10 October 1811, *ibid.*

from Manchester to Sir Francis Burdett in the summer of 1810.[26] On 6 November at a general meeting of representatives of the Manchester trades the committee was formally reconstituted and instructed to draw up resolutions; and another general meeting a week later, to which delegates from places outside Manchester were invited, agreed to the committee's proposal that a requisition should be sent to the Borough Reeve for a town meeting to petition for peace and parliamentary reform.[27] But although the committee met several times during the next few weeks, the presentation of its requisition was for one reason or another repeatedly postponed.[28]

In January 1812 similar preparations were being made at Bolton. The committee there wrote again to Whitbread asking for advice about what line of action it should take, and he wrote back suggesting that it should petition both parliament and the Prince Regent for peace.[29] The Borough Reeve of Bolton refused to comply with a requisition for a town meeting, but a meeting called by public advertisement was held on 21 February and petitions to the House of Commons and the Regent were approved. The petition to the House of Commons maintained that the extreme distress prevailing in Bolton was due to the war, and that the continuance of the war was attributable to the inadequate representation of the people in parliament:

> It is the humble opinion of the petitioners, that if the House consisted of representatives of the people only, it would not, for any doubtful prospect of benefit to our Allies, consent to expose the people of this country to the certain misery, ruin and starvation, which the continuance of the war must bring upon them.[30]

Whitbread presented this petition on 18 March, and a few days later Lord Stanley presented a petition from Preston, which also asked for an early restoration of peace and a reform of the representation. But there was no debate on either petition, and the one from Bolton was mistakenly described in the press as a petition from Yorkshire.[31] Meanwhile the committee in Manchester had still not taken any public action, and cannot have been encouraged by the outcome of the Bolton petition. By the end of March its own plans seem to have been suspended.[32]

For the activities of the Manchester committee during the winter of 1811–12 we are

[26] Printed address dated 21 October 1811, quoted in L. S. Marshall, *The Development of Public Opinion in Manchester 1780–1820* (Syracuse, N.Y., 1946), 133; Fletcher to H.O., 21 November 1811, H.O. 42/117; Knight to Whitbread, 16 June 1810, Whitbread MSS., no. 2519. On Knight's career, cf. Foster, *op. cit.* 139–40.

[27] Bent's reports headed 4 and 11 November, H.O. 42/117.

[28] Bent's reports headed 2, 9 and 30 December, H.O. 42/119.

[29] James Lomax to Whitbread, 14 January 1812, Whitbread MSS., no. 3838; Whitbread to Lomax, 25 January 1812 (copy), H.O. 42/120. Fletcher received

a transcript of Whitbread's letter from Bent, who reported that a copy had been sent by the Bolton committee to the committee at Manchester: Fletcher to H.O., 6 February 1812, *ibid.*

[30] Fletcher to H.O., 25 February 1812, H.O. 42/120; *Cowdroy's Manchester Gazette*, 7 March, 2, 16 May 1812; *Commons Journals*, LXVII, 207–8.

[31] Hansard, *Parliamentary Debates*, XXI, 29–30, 108–10; *The Times*, 19 March 1812; Lomax to Whitbread, 4 April 1812, Whitbread MSS., no. 4212.

[32] Bent's reports headed 17 February, H.O. 42/120, and 25 March, H.O. 40/1, fo. 87.

largely dependent on Bent's information; but there seems to be no reason to question this, as it fits in with the other evidence available and provides a plausible background to the petitioning attempt of May–June 1812.[33] There is less corroboration for the reports he was sending in at the same period on activities and organizations of a different nature. According to these reports in the weaving towns and villages around Manchester there was a much more militant spirit than in Manchester itself and serious doubts prevailed about the usefulness of petitioning. He recorded early in November, for instance, the view of a Royton man named Taylor[34] that the people of his neighbourhood were 'worne out with petitioning' and wished instead to 'demand of the Prince Regante and if he would not do it then to shake them off all together and by that mains the business would be completed in a short time'.[35] It appears from Bent's accounts that in the latter months of 1811 there were already organizations on the eastern side of Manchester which were administering oaths, holding meetings of delegates, and forming contacts in Yorkshire and elsewhere.[36] He also recorded meetings of his own with men from outside the Manchester region – from Chesterfield and Sheffield, for example – who told him of revolutionary preparations that were under way;[37] and he learnt at third hand (via 'a Jack from Stockport' and a delegate who had been sent from Mottram in Longdendale to Yorkshire) that in Leeds 5,000 people had been sworn to the cause and that Wakefield and all the nearby villages were 'on the Revolutionne sistom'.[38] He had visitors from Nottingham as well, who said that the people of that area were sworn not only to assist in the destruction of machinery but also to join a revolution: the Nottingham men were in correspondence with Scotland and Ireland and most parts of England, and some 40,000 people had taken the oath.[39] Several of Bent's English informants mentioned the need to co-ordinate their efforts with an expected Irish rising,[40] and he apparently had a number of visits from Irish delegates who described the plans of the disaffected in Ireland and their efforts to sound popular feeling in England.[41]

This material, if accepted at face value, would indicate that well before the outbreak of northern Luddism extensive revolutionary plans were being laid. If one is to regard Bent's information about the committee of trades at Manchester as authentic one might seem obliged to accept the rest of his information also. Yet it is conceivable that, while giving fairly accurate accounts of proceedings in Manchester about which his employer might be suspected of having other intelligence, he should have been less scrupulous in covering more shadowy and remote spheres of activity on which no such check was likely

[33] See below, pp. 384-85.
[34] Perhaps the Caleb Taylor who had been active in the underground agitation of 1801: cf. F. K. Donnelly and J. L. Baxter, 'Sheffield and the English Revolutionary Tradition, 1791–1820', *International Review of Social History*, xx (1975), 408-9.
[35] Report headed 4 November, H.O. 42/117. Cf. the views of Waterhouse of Shaw, recounted in Bent's report headed 30 December, H.O. 42/119.
[36] Report postmarked 5 October 1811, H.O. 42/117; reports headed 9 and 23 December, H.O. 42/119.
[37] Report endorsed 10 October 1811, H.O. 42/117; report headed 23 December, H.O. 42/119.
[38] Report headed 30 December, H.O. 42/119.
[39] Reports headed 6 January, H.O. 42/119, and 17 February, H.O. 42/120.
[40] E.g. Taylor of Royton, Bent's report headed 4 November, H.O. 42/117; Williamson of Nottingham, Bent's report headed 17 February, H.O. 42/120.
[41] Reports headed 11 November, H.O. 42/117, and 2 December and 14 January, H.O. 42/119.

to exist. It would also be understandable if, anxious to magnify the need for his services, he had wished to compensate for the rather unexciting nature of the Manchester proceedings by giving an impression of much more threatening developments elsewhere. It will be suggested below (on the basis of his later bulletins) that he *was* subject to the 'occupational bias' of which Thompson and Richard Cobb have written – the informer's tendency to exaggerate the scale and seditious character of the activities on which he reported.[42] With regard to the reports described above, one would certainly hesitate before accepting what he said about Nottinghamshire Luddism, as the mass of other evidence that survives on that subject suggests that little or nothing in the way of political motivation or secret oath-taking was involved. On the other hand, there is less apparent reason to question what he said about the weavers of south Lancashire and Cheshire. It is quite conceivable that in the conditions of 1811–12, when industrial action was virtually out of the question and appeals to parliament had recently failed, there should have been moves to resume the kind of underground activity that had existed in this area in 1797–8 and 1801.[43] We have the independent testimony of William Rowbottom, an Oldham man who was *not* a Jacobin, that the workers' situation was desperate and that trouble was in the air. He wrote in January 1812:

> There is nothing to be seen but misery and want... To all appearances if there be an alteration of times it must be for the better except there be comotions or civil wars which God grant may never happen in this country or Kingdom.[44]

For the period from March 1812 onwards the range of surviving evidence on underground activity in Lancashire and Cheshire becomes considerably wider. This means that a more solid record of events can be constructed, and that the validity of the various sources can be more easily tested by checking them against each other. It happens that as a result of the efforts of Colonel Fletcher and his agents the places about which we have most information for the spring months of 1812 are Bolton and Manchester; but the impulse for the adoption of violent tactics seems to have come initially from Stockport. A distinguishing feature of Stockport was the fact that several steam-powered weaving factories had been established there, and these had become a focus of popular hostility. Discussions during the winter between weavers, manufacturers and magistrates about the level of wages and the effect of steam looms on employment had produced nothing in the way of relief; and two weavers' delegates who had gone to London on the advice of the Rector of Stockport to present their case to the Secretary of State had been politely received by Ryder but had been given 'no kind of satisfaction'.[45] In February rumours were circulating about impending attacks on the weaving factories,[46]

[42] Thompson, *The Making of the English Working Class*, 535; Richard Cobb, *The Police and the People: French Popular Protest 1789–1820* (Oxford, 1970), 6–7.

[43] Walvin, *op. cit.*; Marianne Elliott, 'The "Despard Conspiracy" reconsidered', *Past and Present*, LXXV (1977), 51–3.

[44] MS. diary of William Rowbottom, under January 1812, Oldham Local Interest Centre.

[45] Statements of T. Whittaker, 4 July 1812, H.O. 42/121, and O. Nicholson, 7 October 1812, H.O. 42/128.

[46] J. Lloyd to Viscount Warren-Bulkeley, 11 February 1812; Bent's report headed 17 February; Lloyd to H.O., 26 February 1812, H.O. 42/120.

and at the end of that month or the beginning of March two delegates from Stockport went to attend a weavers' meeting at Bolton. They said that since other means of obtaining redress had failed the weavers must act for themselves, and they produced an oath which was read out to the meeting. Most of those present apparently disapproved of it, but one man agreed to take it and copied it down.[47] During the next week or two the oath began to spread among the Bolton weavers, a small secret committee was formed, and nocturnal meetings began to be held on Bolton Moor.[48] By 19 March an agent named John Stones was attending these meetings and reporting back to the adjutant of the Bolton Local Militia.[49]

Later in March a delegate named Joseph Wright went from Stockport to Manchester to form a secret committee there on the same lines as those established at Stockport and Bolton. We know this from the subsequent statements of Humphrey Yarwood, one of the Manchester weavers whom Wright met and to whom he administered the oath. A small executive committee was set up headed by John Buckley (who appears to have been a dissenting preacher as well as a weaver by trade). A system of tallies was introduced soon afterwards to facilitate confidential communication between the three towns, and it was agreed that each committee should do its best to spread the organization as far as possible.[50] On Sunday 5 April a general meeting of delegates from weaving towns in the Manchester region was held at a public house in Salford. Among those who attended were Stones (as one of the Bolton representatives), Buckley, and delegates from Stockport, Failsworth, Saddleworth, Oldham and Ashton-under-Lyne.[51] The meeting decided that on the following Thursday (9 April) simultaneous attacks should be made on factories at Bolton, Stockport and Manchester, each committee choosing its own target. However, when on Monday the 6th this plan was referred by the Manchester executive committee to representatives from the Manchester districts, it was rejected, and delegates had to be sent to Bolton and Stockport to countermand the operation.[52]

At this point the story is further complicated by the appearance of a fresh strand of activity. On 25 March the loyalist party in Manchester had requisitioned the Borough Reeve for a town meeting to consider an address to the Prince Regent expressing support for the government which, at the expiry of the restricted regency, he had retained in office; and a public meeting was fixed for 8 April.[53] This move was clearly a most provocative one in the current state of the country. Only a few weeks before, the Bolton meeting of 21 February had declared in its address to the Regent:

> Their sufferings have hitherto found some alleviation in the consoling hope, that the period of your Royal Highness's accession to power would be to them the dawn of better days. It is, therefore, with indescribable emotions of alarm and dismay,

[47] Statements of O. Nicholson and J. Lyon, 7 October 1812, H.O. 42/128.
[48] Statements of T. Gregory and R. Waddington, 7 October 1812, *ibid.*
[49] J. Warr to Fletcher, 20 March 1812, enclosed in Fletcher to H.O., 23 March 1812, H.O. 42/121.
[50] Memorandum of conversation with Yarwood, 19 June 1812, H.O. 40/1, fo. 170; Yarwood's statement of 22 June 1812, *ibid.*, fo. 47.
[51] H.O. 40/1, fo. 47 (Yarwood). Cf. Stones' report of 6 April 1812, *ibid.*, fo. 64.
[52] *Ibid.*, ff. 47–8 (Yarwood), 70 (Bent, 7 April).
[53] Scrapbooks of the Rev. W. R. Hay, vol. VI, 1, Chetham's Library, Manchester.

that they have lately heard rumours that it is the intention of your Royal Highness to persevere in that system of policy which has been the cause of all our sufferings.[54]

In Manchester a group of middle-class reformers led by Ottiwell Wood, a wealthy Unitarian, resolved to mount an opposition to the loyalists. Several handbills were printed and circulated, calling on the people to attend the meeting on the 8th and to convert the resolutions into a call for drastic changes in national policy. The most stirring of these handbills was headed 'Now or Never!' and began:

> Those inhabitants who do not wish for an increase of taxes and poor rates – an advance in the price of provisions – a scarcity of work, and a reduction of wages, will not fail to go to the meeting on Wednesday morning next, at the Exchange, and *oppose the 154 persons* who have called you together.[55]

The handbills were circulated outside Manchester as well as within it, and one witness reported: 'It is impossible to conceive the great and sudden effect they produced on the public mind.'[56] In addition, a meeting of the middle-class reformers at the Bridgewater Arms on 6 April invited the meeting of Manchester district representatives, which was being held on the same evening, to send someone to consult with them; and Buckley went over and was asked to help in securing as large an attendance as possible at the public meeting on the 8th.[57]

Realizing now the extent of the opposition and the possibility of trouble, the Borough Reeve and constables called off the meeting at the last moment. But thousands of people nevertheless assembled, and when the Exchange was found to be locked it was broken into and some windows and furniture were smashed. Meanwhile some 3,000 people went to St Ann's Square and adopted the set of resolutions which had been moved by the City radical, Robert Waithman, at the London Common Hall on 26 March.[58] The episode showed how far the frame of mind of the Manchester populace had changed since the 1790s, when mobs had attacked the house of Thomas Walker and destroyed the offices of the radical *Manchester Herald*.[59] Also, the Exchange riot seems to have broken down the inhibitions which had hitherto checked disorder in the surrounding region. Before 8 April there had been little actual violence, apart from an attack on William Radcliffe's warehouse at Stockport on 20 March;[60] but during the next two or three weeks a variety of disturbances took place in south Lancashire and Cheshire.

---

[54] *Liverpool Mercury*, 24 April 1812. Cf. Bent's account of the sentiments of the people of Mellor and its neighbourhood, report headed 18 March, H.O. 40/1, fo. 60.

[55] H.O. 40/1, fo. 169. For two handbills of a comparatively Whiggish tone, dated 2 and 6 April 1812, see Shuttleworth Scrapbook, p. 7, Manchester Reference Library.

[56] *The Times*, 11 April 1812.

[57] H.O. 40/1, ff. 70 (Bent, 7 April), 171 (Yarwood, 19 June).

[58] Hay Scrapbooks, vol. VI, 1; Fletcher to H.O., 11 April 1812, H.O. 40/1, fo. 88. Waithman's resolutions set out a long list of grievances, lamented the retention of the present ministers in office, and urged that they should be replaced by men pledged to correct abuses and to reform parliament (*Cobbett's Political Register*, 28 March 1812, cols. 412–14).

[59] Cf. *Cobbett's Political Register*, 2 May 1812, cols. 547 *et seq.*

[60] Lloyd to H.O., 21 March 1812, H.O. 40/1, fo. 5.

The most common form of outbreak was the food riot. Flour and potato prices, already very high in the early months of the year, had recently risen still further,[61] and there were food riots during April in various parts of England. In the cotton district there was an outbreak in the potato market at Manchester on the 18th, and on the 20th and 21st disturbances occurred at Rochdale, Oldham, Ashton-under-Lyne, Stockport and several smaller places.[62] At much the same period, and in some instances linked with the food-rioting, there were several attempts to destroy factories and machinery. On the 14th a large crowd assembled in the Stockport area, burned the cottage and destroyed the steam looms of Joseph Goodair of Edgeley, and broke the windows of other factory-owners' houses.[63] On the 20th an attack was made on Daniel Burton's steam loom factory at Middleton, the assailants including colliers and others from Hollinwood and Saddleworth who had come from the food riot at Oldham. The factory was guarded and the attack was beaten off, five people being killed and more wounded. On the following day the attack was renewed, after the crowd had called at Oldham in search of arms but had found the militia depot well defended; this time they succeeded in destroying the house and outbuildings of one of Burton's sons, though at the cost of several more lives.[64] On the same day at Tintwistle, in the north-east corner of Cheshire, food was seized from grocery shops and sold off at reduced prices, and attacks were made on machinery – both on carding machines (for combing cotton) and on shearing frames used in the woollen industry.[65] Finally, the most dramatic coup of Lancashire Luddism occurred on the 24th, when the large steam-weaving factory at Westhoughton was destroyed by fire.

This last event was the culmination of a considerable amount of underground activity in the Bolton area, in which Stones appears to have played a leading part. During April oaths were being administered at nocturnal meetings on the moors, and on the night of the 19th a band of Luddites which included (by arrangement between Stones and Adjutant Warr) ten local militiamen with their faces blackened, met and 'twisted in' a local militia serjeant on the road between Bolton and Chowbent. The plan was to attack Westhoughton that night, but by the time the Bolton party reached Chowbent the men who were due to meet them there had dispersed. The successful attack on Westhoughton five days later took the authorities by surprise. The factory was left temporarily undefended as a result of a misunderstanding, and forty or fifty people from Chowbent were able to set fire to it without interference. Colonel Fletcher, who had been away on enclosure business when the firing occurred, made a number of arrests on his return; and these seem to have put a stop to agitation in the Bolton area. At the special assizes at Lancaster in late May and early June three men and one boy were sentenced to death

---

[61] Colonel J. G. Clay (Manchester) to H. O., 23 March 1812, H.O. 42/121; Lomax (Bolton) to Whitbread, 4 April 1812, Whitbread MSS., no. 4212; *Gentleman's Magazine*, LXXXII (1812), pt. I, 303, 399.

[62] Hay Scrapbooks, vol. VI, 5–7.

[63] *Ibid.*, 5; Lloyd to H.O., 16 April 1812, H.O. 40/1, fo. 12.

[64] W. Chippendale to J. Chippendale, 21 April 1812, H.O. 42/122; W. Chippendale to Fletcher, 23 April 1812, H.O. 40/1, ff. 102–5; Hay Scrapbooks, vol. VI, 7.

[65] Prosecution briefs in P.R.O., T.S. 11/370/1160.

for arson at Westhoughton and eleven men were sentenced to transportation for taking or administering unlawful oaths.[66]

These Luddite activities near Bolton do not seem to have been closely connected with proceedings elsewhere in the cotton district. On 20 April there was a delegates' meeting at Ardwick Green on the eastern side of Manchester, attended (according to Bent) by representatives from Saddleworth, Ashton, Newton, Droylsden, Hollinwood, Stockport, Withington, Northenden, Stretford, Urmston, Eccles, Worsley and Astley Green;[67] but no one from Bolton was present, and it would appear that after the abandonment of the combined operation arranged for 9 April the Bolton organization and its Chowbent subsidiary acted independently of the larger organization based in Manchester. It also appears that the attacks on factories at Stockport and Middleton resulted rather from local initiatives than from any centralized plan of operations. Yarwood, who was not actually a member of the Manchester executive committee but was informed of its proceedings by Buckley, said later that he did not know what had occasioned the Stockport disturbances around 14 April;[68] and Bent reported that when the men of the Boardmans Square district of Manchester assembled on the 21st to join the affray at Middleton, they were stopped by their leaders who said that to go there would be a breach of orders. Bent went on to say: 'The Execetive recomands they people to be pacable and not to disturbe the pace on any account those people who does are not of those who is twisted inn their may be a fewe who mix with the other but they are fewe.'[69]

The Manchester executive committee was chiefly occupied during April in spreading the oath and attempting to raise money. Large numbers of people, not only weavers but also spinners and tailors, were sworn in, and a representative from each of the latter trades was added to the committee.[70] But over money serious difficulties arose. Attempts were made to introduce regular subscriptions, and at the delegates' meeting at Ardwick Green on 20 April Bent was appointed general treasurer. But the weavers were able to give very little, and when Buckley called on the spinners and tailors to contribute to the expenses of the executive committee which he headed, they 'refused to pay anything to the weavers', saying that any money subscribed would be paid into the hands of the treasurer at the next general meeting of delegates (which was due to take place at Failsworth on 4 May). Buckley was so incensed by this that he arranged to have the spinners' and tailors' delegates, and Bent, excluded from the Failsworth meeting. The country delegates who attended this meeting did produce some money and offered to deposit it with Buckley, but he said that the sum was too small and told them to take it back and bring more to the next meeting. This was fixed for a month later, but never

[66] Depositions in P.R.O., P.L. 27/9; prosecution briefs in T.S. 11/980/3580 and T.S. 11/1059/4766; H.O. 40/1, ff. 68, 72, 83, 92–3, 98–9; statements of O. Nicholson and others, 7 October 1812, H.O. 42/128; *The Trials of All the Prisoners at the Special Assizes for the County of Lancaster, commencing May 23 1812* (Lancaster, 1812); V. I. Tomlinson, 'Letters of a Lancashire Luddite transported to Australia 1812–1816', *Transactions of the Lancashire and Cheshire Antiquarian Society*, LXXVII (1974), 118 *et seq*.

[67] Bent's report headed 18 April, H.O. 40/1, ff. 106–7. As Bent's place-names are not easy to make out, one or two of these identifications are speculative.

[68] H.O. 40/1, fo. 53.

[69] *Ibid.*, fo. 106.

[70] *Ibid.*, fo. 48 (Yarwood).

took place. The quarrel in Manchester reached a point at which Buckley threatened to give himself up and reveal all he knew unless the spinners handed over the money which he felt to be due to him. Bent reported in mid-May that as a result of the breach the weavers had stopped twisting-in, and Yarwood recorded later that 'the failure in the money concern put an entire stop and end to the business throughout Manchester and environs'.[71]

During May the emphasis switched back to petitioning. There had been some activity of this kind even during April. On the 26th the Manchester magistrates sent to the Home Office a printed handbill addressed to the 'weavers, spinners, mechanics and others' of Chorley. Printed at Preston and dated (in manuscript) 20 April, this announced that signatures were being collected for a petition to the House of Commons. The petition drew attention to the 'unexampled distress' suffered by the working population; to the enormous salaries enjoyed by sinecurists; and to the large sums paid from public funds to refugees from abroad. It then requested the House

> to check and restrain the extravagant expenditure of the public money; which, by occasioning the imposition of enormous taxes, increases the price of the necessaries of life – and to compel his Majesty's Ministers to adopt a line of policy which, by conciliating neutral nations, may effect the revival of trade.

The magistrates considered this handbill to be a cover for some more sinister design, but the petition was in fact presented to the House of Commons on 4 May, and it was followed on the 13th by an almost identical one from Chowbent, carrying nearly 1,900 signatures.[72] In Manchester, it was around the middle of May that the committee of trades reassembled and resumed the attempt (which had been shelved in March) to organize a petition for peace and parliamentary reform.[73] A meeting on the 18th, attended by delegates from several other towns and villages, spent six hours discussing a set of resolutions and a draft petition. Money for printing costs was provided by the Saddleworth and Stalybridge delegates, and Bent was (once again) appointed treasurer.[74] A larger meeting, attended by over 100 people, was held at the Elephant, Tib Street, on the 26th, and twelve resolutions were formally passed. These, which were printed in handbill-form and published in a radical newspaper in London on 3 June, declared *inter alia*:

> That with the exception of a few individuals, our nominal representatives. . . have ceased to be the efficient guardians of our properties, our liberties, and our lives.

> That they have frequently permitted us to be wantonly plunged into unnecessary and ruinous wars . . .

---

[71] *Ibid.*, ff. 49–53 (Yarwood), 133–4 (Bent's report headed 12 May).

[72] Rev. W. R. Hay and Colonel J. Silvester to H.O., 26 April 1812, and enclosure, H.O. 42/122; *Commons Journals*, LXVII, 348–9, 374–5; *Cowdroy's Manchester Gazette*, 23 May 1812.

[73] H.O. 40/1, fo. 172 (Yarwood). According to Bent (*ibid.*, ff. 133–4) there was a possibility that the weavers would be refused representation on this committee, on account of the recent quarrel.

[74] *Ibid.*, ff. 133–4.

That so long, intense, and extensive have been the sufferings of the people, that unless a strong hope of speedy deliverance be immediately infused into the public mind, the most dreadful consequences may be apprehended...

That the only rational ground of hope, is in a speedy, radical, and efficient reform in the Commons House of Parliament.

An address to the Prince Regent and a petition to the House of Commons were to be prepared by a committee of eleven members. The committee met several times, and a general meeting was advertised by handbills for 11 June, to approve the address and petition in their final form.[75] This meeting was to take place at the Elephant, but was switched at the last moment to the Prince Regent's Arms, Ancoats Lane, because of a rumour that the deputy constable of Manchester intended to disrupt it. The meeting was attended by about forty working men, some as representatives of different trades, some as delegates from places outside Manchester, and some, it appears, as individuals who had come in response to the handbill.[76]

Before the meeting a weaver named Samuel Fleming had told Colonel Silvester, one of the Manchester magistrates, that he was being urged to take the oath; and with the sanction of Silvester and Nadin (the deputy constable) he went to the Prince Regent's Arms with the deliberate intention of getting himself twisted in.[77] Leaving the meeting while it was still in progress, he told Silvester that the oath had been administered to him, and Nadin went to the inn with a posse of soldiers and arrested all those in the room. Thirty-eight men were in due course indicted for the administration of an unlawful oath, and were tried at Lancaster assizes in August. The prosecution did its best to establish a connection between the meeting of 11 June and earlier nocturnal meetings in the open air. But the essence of the case against the prisoners rested simply on the testimony of Fleming, and he was flatly contradicted by witnesses for the defence who had been present at the meeting but had left before Nadin's arrival. In accordance with a clear instruction from the judge, the jury returned a verdict of acquittal.[78] A celebratory dinner was held a few days later by the 'Friends of Parliamentary Reform' in Manchester, and was attended by Major Cartwright who had taken a keen interest in the case.[79]

[75] Handbill in P.L. 27/9; *The Statesman*, 3 June 1812; *Report of the Proceedings on the Trial of Thirty-Eight Men, on a Charge of administering an unlawful Oath... at Lancaster, on Thursday, 27th August, 1812. With an Introductory Narrative by John Knight* (Manchester, 1812), 94–5, 122.

[76] From Manchester, in addition to John Knight and William Washington, there were six spinners, three weavers, two turners, two cutters, one joiner, one fustian-dresser, one tin-plate worker, one brick-layer, one broker, one shoemaker, one calico-printer and one tailor; from outside Manchester there were seven weavers, four hatters, one spinner, one sawyer, one bricklayer and one warper. Hay Scrapbooks, vol.

vi, 10; *Trial of Thirty-Eight Men*, pp. ii, 101–3, 106, 111, 123.

[77] N. Milne to H. C. Litchfield, 17 June 1812, H.O. 40/1, fo. 451.

[78] *Trials of Thirty-Eight Men, passim*.

[79] *Cowdroy's Manchester Gazette*, 5 September 1812; Frances D. Cartwright, *Life and Correspondence of Major Cartwright* (2 vols., 1826), II, 34–7. Cartwright, William Roscoe and Thomas Walker all contributed to the costs of the defence: see Walker to J. Shuttleworth, 21 August 1812, Shuttleworth Scrapbook, fo. 8; S. Harrison to his wife, 28 August 1812 (copy), H.O. 42/129.

While the thirty-eight men were awaiting trial money was being collected in Manchester and its neighbourhood to support their families and to meet their legal costs.[80] At the same time a fresh committee was formed to carry on preparations for petitioning, and meetings were openly held both in Manchester and in the country to promote petitions for peace and reform.[81] Agitation of a more militant kind may also have been resumed in some places. There was no resumption of machine-breaking, but there were reports of underground activity in the area to the south-east of Manchester in June. In the middle of the month there was a spate of arms-stealing from private houses in the villages of Godley, Newton, Hyde and Hattersley, and Bent wrote shortly afterwards that the people of that neighbourhood were well supplied with arms and eager to 'make a *start*'.[82] Captain Francis Raynes of the Stirling Militia was instructed towards the end of June to patrol the disturbed area between Stockport, Ashton and Mottram, moving his troops around at night in order to surprise or deter secret meetings. He also employed spies, and in August he was able to make several arrests which broke the solidarity of the disaffected.[83] An act of parliament of 9 July had offered indemnity to anyone who, within the next three months, confessed to having taken illegal oaths and took an oath of allegiance before a magistrate. Following Raynes's arrests there was a rush to take advantage of this act. During the last week in August at least 800 people 'untwisted' themselves before magistrates at Stockport and Hyde;[84] and a considerable number of others did so in various parts of the cotton district during the remaining period of the indemnity.[85]

One fact that emerged from the confessions made to the magistrates was that some at least of the thirty-eight men acquitted at Lancaster in August *had* been connected with secret oath-taking. One of them, James Knott, a hatter from Hyde, took the oath of allegiance himself and admitted that he had twisted in twenty or thirty people. Another, Edmund Newton, spinner, of Hadfield, was alleged by several people to have administered the oath to them; and among those who untwisted themselves at Didsbury were two men who had been key witnesses for the defence at the Lancaster trial.[86] One should not infer from all this that the thirty-eight were wrongly acquitted. It is likely that the meeting at the Prince Regent's Arms *was* a genuine reform meeting, and there is no reason to disbelieve John Knight's statement that he expressed on that occasion

[80] Fletcher to H.O., 30 June 1812, H.O. 42/124; Captain F. Raynes to Major-General T. Maitland, 25 July 1812, H.O. 40/2, fo. 75.

[81] J. Marshall to S. Simons, 29 June 1812, H.O. 42/129; Lloyd to H.O., 30 July 1812, H.O. 42/125; Maitland to H.O., 5 August 1812, H.O. 42/126.

[82] H.O. 40/2, fo. 20; Fletcher to H.O., 30 June 1812, H.O. 42/124.

[83] H.O. 40/2, ff. 31, 93 *et seq.*; F. Raynes, *An Appeal to the Public: containing an Account of Services rendered during the Disturbances in the North of England, in the Year 1812* (1817), 30, 46–7, 57–9.

[84] Maitland to Earl Fitzwilliam, 28 August 1812, Wentworth Woodhouse Muniments [W.W.M.], F.46/51, Sheffield City Libraries; H.O. 40/2, ff. 121, 129; Raynes, *op. cit.*, 82.

[85] E.g. R. A. Farington (Didsbury) to H.O., 13 September 1812, H.O. 42/127; Sir R. Clayton (Adlington) to H.O., 18 October 1812, H.O. 42/128.

[86] Lloyd to H.O., 8 November 1812, enclosing examination of J. Knott, 8 September 1812, H.O. 42/129; C. Prescott to H.O., 20 September 1812, H.O. 42/127; Farington to H.O., 2 October 1812, H.O. 42/128.

his disapproval of 'illegal violence'.[87] It is evident, however, that there was no clear-cut division between those who participated in 'constitutional' reform movements and those who engaged in underground activity;[88] and some people may have regarded the former as a convenient cover behind which money and support could be raised for other purposes. Yarwood recalled a remark which John Bent had made to him after the Manchester weavers had stopped twisting in early in May:

> He said if this business had been, or was to be carried out under the pretence of a petition for peace or parliamentary reform, many persons would contribute under that pretence as would not under any other, and it would be a safer plan too.[89]

Another point that emerged from the renunciation of illegal oaths was that the number of those who had taken such oaths during the spring and early summer had been far from negligible; and it is doubtful whether the view of some historians that oath-taking was a factitious phenomenon attributable to 'spies and their dupes'[90] can be accepted. It does appear that in the Bolton area John Stones acted as an *agent provocateur* and actually used threats to induce people to take the oath,[91] but it also seems clear that oath-taking had started at Bolton (initiated by delegates from Stockport) before Stones became involved.[92] How the oath originated, and at what date, remain uncertain points.[93] Bent, as noted above, had reported that an oath was already in use near Manchester in the latter part of 1811. Almost all the firm-looking evidence concerning oath-taking in Lancashire and Cheshire refers to the spring and summer of 1812, but there are one or two scraps of evidence which seem to tie in with his earlier reports. One is from a distinctly dubious source, Samuel Fleming, the accuser of the thirty-eight men; according to him, a Manchester weaver who urged him to take the oath said that he himself 'had been a-gait of the business of twisting-in before last Christmas'.[94] Possibly more reliable is the statement – undated, but probably assignable to late August – of Thomas Wood of Mottram when abjuring the oath before the Rector of Stockport: he said that he had been twisted in by a Stockport man ten months before.[95]

[87] Examination of J. Knight, 13 June 1812, P.L. 27/9.

[88] Major-General Maitland reported to the Home Office on 20 July and 5 August 1812 (H.O. 42/125 and 126) that the meetings and petitions for peace and parliamentary reform involved men 'notoriously connected' with the late disturbances and the administration of oaths. These were probably not such 'wild statements' as Thomis has suggested (*The Luddites*, 24).

[89] Yarwood's statement of 22 June 1812, H.O. 40/1, fo. 52.

[90] Hammonds, *op. cit.*, 336–8. Darvall went so far as to write (*op. cit.*, 193) that 'only upon the evidence of spies is there any evidence of secret oaths being administered'.

[91] Statements of J. Greenhalgh, 17 July 1812, H.O.

42/132, and of O. Nicholson and P. Gaskell, 7 October 1812, H.O. 42/128.

[92] See above, p. 42.

[93] The authorities believed that the oath had been brought to Bolton by delegates from Nottingham in February 1812 (prosecution brief, King v. John Hurst et al., T.S. 11/980/3580); but this may have been a confusion arising from the visit of the Stockport delegates. Men from Nottingham were said to have visited Stockport in the previous December (Lloyd to Viscount Warren-Bulkeley, 1 January 1812, H.O. 42/119). Bent did report in February that an oath was in use in Nottingham, but the oath which he quoted was not the one that came into use in Lancashire (report headed 17 February, H.O. 42/120).

[94] *Trial of Thirty-Eight Men*, 37.

[95] Raynes, *op. cit.*, 91–2.

There remains the crucial question of what the purpose of the oath was. The oath itself – which was quite distinct from the obviously political ones used by the United Britons a decade earlier[96] – is unhelpful. It merely committed the person taking it to reveal nothing about the membership or proceedings of the 'secret committee' and to pursue any traitors 'to the verge of nature'.[97] Dr Robert Taylor, a Unitarian physician at Bolton who had collected evidence about the disturbances in that area, published a letter in March 1813 denying that they were 'at all connected with political opinions';[98] and it does seem likely that the oath that was introduced at Bolton and Manchester in February–March 1812 was specifically intended to form a secret confederacy for machine-breaking purposes. In Yarwood's words, the aim was 'to destroy steam looms, and to collect money to procure arms to repel force by force if hindered in the execution of their designs'.[99] This interpretation of the oath is supported by the evidence of John Parnell, a prosecution witness at the trial of Thomas Whittaker for administering unlawful oaths. Having been arrested when the military dispersed a meeting near Stockport in mid-April, Parnell confessed to having taken the oath at a meeting of weavers at Gatley Ford on 6 April. According to his account, Whittaker and another man had asked those present whether they wished the steam looms to be stopped, and they had all raised their hands; then Whittaker had read out the oath phrase by phrase, the others repeating it after him. The oath, Parnell said, 'meant to stand by one another and not to tell of one another and the meaning was to destroy steam looms'.[100]

Evidence of a different kind, suggesting that the agitation in the north-west did have revolutionary intentions, comes mainly from spies, or from prisoners who hoped to avoid prosecution or secure lenient treatment by making 'important' disclosures. According to Thomas Whittaker, for example, a Manchester delegate who visited Stockport in late March said that a general rising of the people would take place at an appointed time, standards would be set up in different parts of the kingdom, and every magistrate and military officer would be seized or killed.[101] Bearing more directly on the oath itself there is the testimony of two agents of Nadin who got Yarwood to twist one of them in on 4 May. When they asked him what the aims of the organization were, Yarwood allegedly said that those who took the oath were associating to obtain 'a general reform and a general change'.[102]

Information of this kind may be regarded as suspect; but there is some other evidence

[96] H.O. 42/61, fo. 201; *Journals of the House of Lords*, XLIII, 131–2. There is evidence from both Lancashire and Yorkshire, however, that in 1812, as in 1801, verses 25–7 of the 21st chapter of Ezekiel were sometimes used in conjunction with the oath. See H.O. 40/1, fo. 163; H.O. 42/61, fo. 122; P.R.O., K.B. 8/91, fo. 207.

[97] *Annual Register* (Otridge ed.), 1812, Appendix, 391–2.

[98] *The Statesman*, 27 March 1813; reprinted in *Letters on the Subject of the Lancashire Riots in the Year 1812* (Bolton, n.d.), 5–15. Cf. R. Needham to

Fletcher, 29 June 1812, and Fletcher to H.O., 30 June 1812, H.O. 42/124.

[99] H.O. 40/1, fo. 47. Cf. statement of O. Nicholson, 7 October 1812, H.O. 42/128.

[100] Deposition of J. Parnell, 17 April 1812, K.B. 8/90; prosecution brief, T.S. 11/370/1160.

[101] 'Manchester Delegate's Report before the Stockport Committee about the 25 of March 1812', H.O. 42/121. Cf. H.O. 40/1, ff. 64 (Stones, 6 April 1812) and 70 (Bent, 7 April).

[102] Statements of J. Taylor and T. Whitehead, 7 May 1812, H.O. 42/123.

of a similar tendency which seems less open to objection. Thomas Wood of Mottram, for instance, said that the men who had twisted him in had told him 'that there was to be a revolution, and that all who were not for it, would be killed; and those who were for it, were to take an oath'.[103] It is also worth noting that by his own account – which is far from sensational in tone – Humphrey Yarwood at first imagined that the secret organization was directed simply against power looms, but later became convinced that 'some thing further than the destruction of steam looms or machinery was intended'.[104] The Manchester secret committee appears, at least in the second half of April, to have actually dissociated itself from machine-breaking.[105] Also, one wonders whether the arms-stealing that went on to the east and south-east of Manchester in June can simply be explained in terms of the campaign against power looms – especially in view of the connection (which will be discussed below) between that region and the underground organization at Barnsley.

On balance it seems likely that the oath-bound organization in the north-west did, in some places at least, have a seditious element; and there is *some* evidence that activity of this kind began before the machine-breaking disturbances took place. Other questions remain. For example, were preparations for a rising ever very advanced? And did they extend beyond a merely local insurrection to a more broadly based challenge to the existing state? On the first question, one should note that the authorities in Lancashire were alarmed by rumours of a projected rising in early May. But in view of the information supplied by Yarwood and Bent it is unlikely that these fears had much foundation. There were reports from the Oldham area that a 'general rising' had been fixed for 4 May,[106] but this may have been a misconception arising from the delegates' meeting at Failsworth which had been arranged for that day. As for the second question – whether large-scale revolutionary action was ever seriously planned – one needs before tackling it to put north-western Luddism into a wider context: to consider whether revolutionary intentions were harboured elsewhere, especially in Yorkshire, and whether anything in the nature of a national underground can be supposed to have existed.

In the West Riding of Yorkshire there had been some seditious activity in the opening years of the century, but it appears that the clothdressers or croppers – the occupational group which was to be basically responsible for Yorkshire Luddism – had not been much involved in this. According to a letter written by William Cookson, mayor of Leeds, in August 1802, the secret political meetings that were then being held were attended by 'labouring poor of all descriptions', while the croppers' combination was 'directed steadily to their own immediate concerns'.[107] The croppers were skilled and relatively

---

[103] Raynes, *op. cit.*, 92. Others were more vague about what the oath involved. Some Manchester men said that when they were sworn in 'no information was given to them, as to what must be done, but they were told, "to be ready when called upon"' (Farington to H.O., 13 September 1812, H.O. 42/127).

[104] H.O. 40/1, fo. 51.

[105] *Ibid.*, fo. 133 (Bent).

[106] Chippendale to Fletcher, 23 April 1812 (copy), H.O. 40/1, fo. 104; J. Lees to H.O., 23 April 1812, H.O. 42/122.

[107] Cookson to Fitzwilliam, 16 August 1802, W.W.M., F.45/79.

well-paid artisans, and their chief aim was to prevent the introduction of cloth-finishing machines – gig mills and shearing frames – which threatened to undermine their craft and status. In this they were, for a time, successful. But for several years after 1802 they were involved in a running battle with the larger masters over the statutory regulation of the industry, the workmen wishing to secure the enforcement – and the masters the repeal – of certain Tudor statutes applying to the woollen trade, including an Act of Edward VI's reign which prohibited the use of gig mills. After lengthy investigations, involving the clothworkers in much expensive presentation of evidence to parliamentary committees, the outcome was the repeal in 1809 of the statutes which they had wished to see revived and strengthened. By 1811–12 cloth-finishing machines, especially shearing frames, had reappeared in considerable numbers. They had been introduced in workshops in the Huddersfield district, where the croppers were less well organized than they were in Leeds; and a few factories had been set up in which the machines were installed on a large scale. Other causes of unemployment and distress among the clothworkers in 1811–12 (as among the Lancashire cotton workers) were stagnation of trade and the high price of provisions. It was against this background, and under the influence of the Nottinghamshire example, that machine-breaking tactics were adopted in Yorkshire in the opening months of 1812.[108]

It seems clear that in the period from January to April the disturbances in the West Riding were essentially industrial, being intended to force employers to abandon the objectionable machines. Though the first machine-breaking incident took place at Leeds,[109] most of the early attacks were on quite small workshops in the vicinity of Huddersfield. Then, having succeeded in destroying nearly all the shearing frames which were 'not connected with establishments on a large scale', the Luddites turned their attention to the larger concerns.[110] Successful attacks were made on the Thompson brothers' shearing mill at Rawdon (a few miles north-west of Leeds) on 23 March, and on Joseph Foster's mill at Horbury near Wakefield on 9 April. On 11 April an assault was made on William Cartwright's mill at Rawfolds near Liversedge, but it was resisted and beaten off. A week later Cartwright himself was shot at on the road to Huddersfield, and on the 28th William Horsfall, a prominent owner of shearing frames at Marsden, was actually assassinated. From the evidence which subsequently came to light concerning some of these incidents, it would appear that those involved were mainly croppers, though for the large-scale attacks they may have drawn some support from other working men.[111]

[108] A. J. Randall, 'The Shearmen's Campaign: a Study of the Woollen Industry and the Industrial Revolution 1800–1809', M.A. thesis, University of Sheffield (1972); Hammonds, *op. cit.*, 167–89; Thompson, *The Making of the English Working Class*, 170–9.

[109] *Leeds Mercury*, 25 January 1812.

[110] 'Memorial of the Secret Committee for preventing unlawful depredations on machinery and shearing frames in the town and neighbourhood of Huddersfield', 29 April 1812, H.O. 40/1, fo. 198.

[111] Following some arrests in October 1812, one or two of those who had been involved in Luddite activities agreed to give evidence against their colleagues, and provided most of the information which made possible the prosecution and conviction of several leading Luddites at the York Special Commission in January 1813. Those indicted before this Commission for offences alleged to have been committed before the end of April were all clothdressers. See *Report of Proceedings under Commission of Oyer*

For this early phase of the disturbances, indications of political motivation are relatively slight. An anonymous letter to a Mr Smith, owner of shearing frames at Hill End, Huddersfield, warned in March that 2,782 'sworn heroes' at Huddersfield, together with allies in other parts of the United Kingdom, were ready to rise against the 'tyranious government' and would not lay down their arms until parliament had 'put down all machinery hurtful to the commonality' and had repealed the act making frame-breaking a capital offence.[112] Here the main aims were apparently industrial, though accompanied by a vague threat of rebellion. Another document of the same period explicitly minimized the political aspect. The Huddersfield magistrate, Joseph Radcliffe, received a letter from the 'Solicitor to General Ludd' which stated that 'as soon as obnoxious machienery is stopd or destroyd the Genearal and his brave army will be disbanded, and return to their employment, like other liege subjects'.[113] Against this one has to place the interesting fact that after the attack on Foster's mill at Horbury on 9 April someone found on the road nearby a copy of a printed pamphlet of the United Britons which had been circulating in the West Riding in 1802.[114] This was a clearly seditious publication, and its appearance at Horbury suggests that at least one person who had been involved in the underground movement early in the century was participating in, and trying to influence, the Luddite movement.

After the spring phase of Yorkshire Luddism attacks on clothdressing machinery did not stop altogether;[115] but the disturbances took on a somewhat different character. From late April through the summer the main activity was the seizure of firearms from private houses. Sir Francis Wood, Vice-Lieutenant of the West Riding, reported in June that there had been 'some hundreds of cases', mainly in the neighbourhood of Huddersfield and Birstall and in the area to the west of Wakefield, and he expressed the fear that the general system of terror that was being introduced would end, 'as the same course of outrage ended in Ireland, in open rebellion against the government of the country'.[116] In fact later in the year the robberies were to become more random and diffuse: money, provisions and other articles were stolen as well as weapons, and many of the robbers appear to have been ordinary criminals taking advantage of the alarms created by Luddism.[117] But for a time during the summer the agitation seems to have remained fairly disciplined, though by that stage it was no longer concentrated in a particular

and Terminer and Gaol Delivery, for the County of York...January 1813 (1813) [cited hereafter as *York Special Commission*], xiv–xix.

[112] Crump, *op. cit.*, 229–30. The letter is dated 9 or 10 March.

[113] 'Solicitor to General Ludd' to Radcliffe, 20 March 1812, Radcliffe MSS., 126/7, Rudding Park, Harrogate. The letter is headed 'Nottingham' but appears to have been posted in Huddersfield.

[114] Printed pamphlet headed 'Countrymen', H.O. 42/124; Hay to H.O. 40/1, fo. 423. Cf. the copy sent to Fitzwilliam in July 1802, W.W.M., F.45/71–1.

[115] For incidents at Halifax and Gildersome in September, see H.O. 40/2, ff. 406 and 416.

[116] Wood to F. Lumley, 10 June 1812, Hickleton MSS., A.4/7, Garrowby, York; Wood to Fitzwilliam, 11 and 17 June 1812, H.O. 40/1, ff. 215 and 224. Thomis would appear to be mistaken in asserting (*The Luddites*, 95) that 'Wood had no fear of rebellion arising out of arms thefts'.

[117] Maitland to H.O., 13 September 1812, H.O. 42/127. Some of the later robberies were reported to have been carried out by gangs of men who did not speak the local dialect or were unacquainted with the country (H.O. 40/2, ff. 486, 550 and 623).

branch of the cloth industry. According to evidence which emerged later, the parties which raided private houses for arms in the early summer included not only croppers but working men from other occupations.[118] At the same period oath-taking, which had been adopted by croppers in the Huddersfield district in the spring, appeared in other trades[119] and other areas; and whereas it had originally been used to prevent the discovery of those involved in the campaign of direct action against clothdressing machines and their owners,[120] there is evidence that it acquired a political flavour.

A clothier named John Hinchcliffe of Upper Thong near Holmfirth alleged that in May a local clothdresser named John Schofield had tried to swear him into the 'society of Ludds', and had told him that 'they were wanting to get a body of men within the Liberty of Holmfirth; that they had one at Huddersfield, and wanted to get a body in all places, and then it might be settled in a moment; and every place might do its own, and overturn the Government'.[121] Such a group seems to have come into existence in Halifax, where an agent from Manchester got himself twisted in early in July; those involved included a hatter named John Baines (a veteran Jacobin who allegedly said that 'his eyes had been open twenty-three years') and several shoemakers.[122] There was another group at Barnsley, consisting mainly of linen weavers. Barnsley lay outside the clothdressing area, but the Luddite oath (or a somewhat garbled version of it) was being used there in May. According to Thomas Broughton, the weaver who gave information to the authorities about the Barnsley circle, some 200 people were sworn into it during the summer and the purpose of the oath was 'to form a regular organization in the country to overthrow the tyrannical system of government'.[123] One interesting feature of this group was that it evidently had a connection with south-east Lancashire. On 28 June Broughton went with two of the Barnsley leaders, John Eadon and Craven Cookson, to Salter's Brook on the Yorkshire–Cheshire border to meet a man named James Haigh from Ashton-under-Lyne.[124] It is clear from the Lancashire sources that Haigh was a well-known 'twister': several of those who abjured the oath at Stockport and Hyde in August named him as the man who had sworn them in.[125] Cookson, when arrested and examined, admitted that the meeting at Salter's Brook had taken place, and also that he had visited Ashton and met Haigh there five weeks earlier (though he claimed that the purpose of both journeys had been to inquire about possibilities of employment in

[118] Those indicted for raiding a house at Foolstone on 18 May included four croppers, five labourers and one weaver (*York Special Commission*, pp. xiv–xix, 205).

[119] For example, those from the parish of Halifax who subsequently untwisted themselves before the local magistrate Dr Coulthurst included ten clothdressers, seven clothiers, three coalminers, three wool-spinners and one cordwainer (W.W.M., F. 46/127).

[120] K.B. 8/91, ff. 162 and 182.

[121] *Ibid.*, fo. 43; *York Special Commission*, 89.

[122] *Ibid.*, 115 *et seq.*; prosecution brief, King v. John Baines *et al.*, T.S. 11/813/2673.

[123] *York Special Commission*, 110; Major J. H. Seale to Viscount Sidmouth, 30 June 1812, Sidmouth MSS., 152 M/C 1812/OH, Devon Record Office; deposition of T. Broughton, 26 August 1812, W.W.M., F. 46/122; prosecution brief, King v. John Eadon, T.S. 11/813/2676.

[124] Deposition of T. Broughton, 4 September 1812, K.B. 8/91, fo. 63.

[125] Raynes to Maitland, 10 August 1812, H.O. 40/2, fo. 89; Raynes, *op. cit.*, 73–4, 90–1. Haigh, a Dukinfield weaver, was arrested by Raynes but had secured himself against prosecution by taking the oath of allegiance.

Lancashire).[126] Another Barnsley weaver who was arrested on Broughton's information, William Thompson, said that he had been twisted in by Haigh.[127] A further notable feature of the group at Barnsley was its clear connection with the abortive rising that was to take place eight years later, on the night of 11–12 April 1820, when some 300 men marched from Barnsley to Grange Moor near Huddersfield in the mistaken belief that other insurgents would meet them there. Three of the men whom Broughton named as prominent in the 1812 organization – Cookson, Thompson and Stephen Kitchenman – were to figure in the affair of 1820.[128]

All this evidence does seem to demonstrate the existence, in some places at least, of underground groups with revolutionary aims. The contacts between Barnsley and Ashton also show that there was some co-operation between such groups – and there were reports of similar contacts between Huddersfield and Manchester.[129] But one should not jump to the conclusion that a very extensive revolutionary network existed. Even within the West Riding it is doubtful whether there was any coherent underground system linking the main industrial centres. Thomas Broughton (by then an agent in the pay of the authorities) asserted in a deposition of 26 August that many people had been sworn in at both Leeds and Sheffield, but he added that the Barnsley committee had had no communication with either place until he himself, as secretary, had opened a correspondence with Leeds a week earlier.[130] Leeds featured also in John Bent's reports as a place where large numbers of people were sworn in. He told Fletcher in March that, according to a man named Welch who had visited him from Leeds, the following oath was in use there:

> I do most sollamey promiss and swair that I will be faithful and keep all things intrusted to me on the business now comming on and I furthermore do sware that I will do all in my power to forward the same and that neither hope feer or reward shall induce me to declair the same derecterley or inderectley but rather have my head cut off with both my hands and all my family served the same if any I have so help me god.[131]

E. P. Thompson cites this oath as typical of those 'fabricated by *agents provocateurs*',[132] and it does have a distinctly questionable ring. It is conceivable that there was a substantial revolutionary organization in Leeds, but if so it was very successful in giving the authorities no sign of its existence. The report of a lieutenancy subcommittee on the Leeds district in August stated 'that it is at present uniformly quiet and in the far larger proportion of it uniformly has been so'; the poorer classes had endured great privations

---

[126] Prosecution brief, King v. Eadon and Cookson, T.S. 11/813/2676.
[127] J. Stuart Wortley to H.O., 6 September 1812, H.O. 42/127.
[128] F. K. Donnelly, 'The General Rising of 1820: A Study of Social Conflict in the Industrial Revolution', Ph.D. thesis, University of Sheffield (1975), 239, 249 *et seq.*

[129] Yarwood's statement, 22 June 1812, H.O. 40/1, fo. 49; Fletcher to H.O., 23 June 1812, *ibid.*, fo. 165.
[130] W.W.M., F. 46/122.
[131] Report headed 25 March, H.O. 40/1, fo. 86.
[132] Thompson, *The Making of the English Working Class*, 633 n. The fact that this oath is found in one of Bent's reports is not noted by Thompson (cf. note 149 below).

with 'a fortitude truly heroic and a patience most exemplary'.[133] As for Sheffield, there was a food riot there on 14 April and it appears that a few men – led by John Blackwell, a journeyman tailor who was to play a similar role in a disturbance of April 1820 – gave a seditious turn to the affair by leading a band of youths in an attack on the arms depot of the local militia; 200 weapons were smashed and seventy-eight were stolen. However, General Grey concluded after investigating the incident that it was 'totally unconnected with the proceedings at Leeds, Huddersfield, etc.'; and the town was quiet for the remainder of the summer, apart from a conventional food riot on 18 August.[134] One should add that there were other parts of the West Riding – in particular the area of worsted manufacture centred on Bradford – which showed virtually no symptoms of illegal activity in 1812.[135]

There were allegations, of course, that a conspiracy existed which spread far beyond the West Riding and the Lancashire cotton district. Joseph Thompson (alias Tonge, alias Tipping, alias Obadiah Bellamy), who was capitally convicted of arson and theft at Goodair's cottage at Edgeley, told the chaplain of Chester gaol before his execution that 'there existed a rebellion in the kingdom, widely extended, and well organized';[136] and the same idea appeared in the anonymous letter sent to Mr Smith of Huddersfield in March:

> By the latest letters from our Correspondents we learn that the Manufacturers in the following Places are going to rise and join us in redressing their Wrongs, Viz. Manchester, Wakefield, Halifax, Bradford, Sheffield, Oldham, Rochdale and all the Cotton Country where the brave Mr Hanson will lead them on to Victory, the Weavers in Glasgow and many parts of Scotland will join us the Papists in Ireland are rising to a Man.[137]

All this was rather vague – except for the reference to Joseph Hanson, who had in fact died six months before.[138] John Bent, however, was more specific. According to reports which he made in the spring of 1812, there was a 'Grand Committee' in London with which committees at places such as Leeds and Stockport were in correspondence; delegates, some Irish and some English, travelled frequently between London, the Midlands, the north and Ireland; in Newcastle-under-Lyme and the Potteries more than 7,000 men were sworn in and possessed between them 2,380 guns, pistols and swords; and in London itself some 7,400 people had taken the oath by 7 April and 14,000 (mainly Spitalfields weavers and tailors) by 12 May.[139]

How much substance is there likely to have been in information of this kind? It is

---

[133] B. Dealtry and M. A. Taylor to Fitzwilliam, 14 August 1812, Hickleton MSS., A. 4/7.

[134] Donnelly and Baxter, *op. cit.*, 412–14, 419–20; Grey to H.O., 18 April 1812, H.O. 42/122; Maitland to H.O., 22 August 1812, H.O. 42/126.

[135] Cf. John James, *History of the Worsted Manufacture in England* (1857), 373.

[136] H.O. 40/1, ff. 15 and 339. Cf. Higgin to Fletcher, 15 June 1812 (copy), H.O. 42/124.

[137] Crump, *op. cit.*, 230.

[138] *Cowdroy's Manchester Gazette*, 14 September 1811.

[139] Bent's report headed 17 February, H.O. 42/120; reports headed 25 March, 7 and 15 April, 12 May, H.O 40/1, ff. 86–7, 70, 96 and 133.

possible that there was some movement to and fro between republican circles in Ireland and the Irish population of Lancashire and London, though one doubts whether preparations for rebellion in Ireland were as advanced as Bent's reports indicated.[140] As for widespread connections within the English working class, it is clear that the Nottinghamshire framework knitters, in the course of their campaign to obtain legislative protection after February 1812, established contact with groups of hosiery workers in various parts of England and Scotland and sent a delegate to Ireland;[141] but although this activity could obviously be misconstrued, there was actually nothing subversive about it. There was also an association of handloom weavers, which had been formed in 1809 and included the main Scottish centres, Carlisle, and the Lancashire–Cheshire cotton district. According to Alexander Richmond, who was active in the Scottish branch, the association lasted until 1812, and attempts were made in that year (without success) to introduce the Luddite organization into Scotland. But it is clear from the context that what he meant by 'Luddite' organization was one for pursuing industrial ends by direct action.[142]

With regard to the existence of *revolutionary* combinations, there is reason to question some of Bent's information. Against his account (early in April) of already-established contacts between the underground organizations of Manchester and London,[143] one needs to place Yarwood's statement that after the delegates' meeting of 20 April the Lancashire organization was hoping, if it could collect enough money, to send a delegate to London to *form* a connection there.[144] In London itself there is no doubt that profound popular dissatisfaction existed in 1812,[145] but it seems unlikely that large-scale oath-taking could have occurred there without the authorities getting wind of it.[146] Even the committee of secrecy of the House of Lords, which produced a fairly alarmist report about the Luddite disturbances, had to admit that there was no real evidence of any connection between the disturbed counties and a conspiracy in London.[147] It may well be, however, that there were people in the north who *believed* in such a connection. Thomas Broughton said in his original deposition in June:

> that their intention at present is, when the scheme is sufficiently ripe, to raise a few partial disturbances in this part of the country, to draw off as many troops as possible from the Metropolis, and that then the great rising will take place there.[148]

[140] In July 1814 Bent was still passing on the news, purportedly derived from Irish delegates, that in Ireland 'all things was getting ready' (report headed 4 July, enclosed in Fletcher to H.O., 19 July 1814, H.O. 42/140).

[141] *Records of the Borough of Nottingham* (9 vols., Nottingham, 1882–1956), VIII, 148–9, 151–2; G. Henson to P. Aitken (Glasgow), 22 June 1812, H.O. 42/124; Sir C. Saxton to H.O., 28 June 1812, H.O. 100/167, ff. 242–5.

[142] A. B. Richmond, *Narrative of the Condition of the Manufacturing Population* (1825), 14, 33 n.

[143] H.O. 40/1, fo. 70.

[144] *Ibid.*, fo. 49.

[145] See, for example, Coleridge's account of the conversation he overheard in a public house at the time of Perceval's assassination: E. L. Griggs (ed.), *Collected Letters of Samuel Taylor Coleridge* (6 vols., Oxford, 1956–71), III, 410.

[146] The police magistrates had informants among the Spitalfields weavers: see J. Moser to H.O., 12 February 1812, H.O. 42/120.

[147] *Journals of the House of Lords*, XLVIII, 970–3; Marquess of Lansdowne to Lord Holland, 19 July 1812, British Library, Additional MSS. 51686.

[148] Seale to Sidmouth, 30 June 1812, Sidmouth MSS., 152M/C 1812/OH.

Bent, if he gave his various contacts the same kind of information as he sent to Colonel Fletcher, may have helped to spread misleading ideas about the extent and seriousness of the revolutionary movement.[149] It does appear that some people came to feel that they had been misled. An agent reported in July that the men of Ashton and Stalybridge were much dispirited, having sent delegates to Yorkshire who had been unable to learn of any real communication with London; 'they thought they had been deceived by their leaders who told them, that a number of great men in London had engaged to join them'.[150]

The idea that members of the higher classes, in London or elsewhere, would join the disaffected is one that appears from time to time in the documents on Luddism[151] and requires brief consideration. Some public men such as Burdett did argue that the government, by pursuing policies which caused serious popular distress, was chiefly to blame for the disturbances and that the Luddites ought to be leniently treated.[152] But the leading radicals were generally anxious to dissociate themselves and their cause from any kind of violence. Major Cartwright, in a letter published in the *Nottingham Review* in January 1812, warned that nothing was more likely to strengthen the hands of the 'borough-faction' than a popular resort to force; and Cobbett strongly defended the reformers against anti-Jacobin attempts to connect them with disturbers of the peace:

> The cause of reform has never been attempted to be supported by violence; it has uniformly relied upon the force of reason and law; it is, therefore, infamous in the last degree to endeavour to confound its advocates with those who, from the unhappy circumstances of the times, are led to set both at defiance.[153]

In the north there was one employer – Thomas Hulme, partner in a bleaching firm at Bolton – who was a committed radical[154] and was rumoured to have encouraged the Luddites;[155] but whether he was a potential revolutionary one cannot say. Other middle-class radicals in Lancashire were careful not to be implicated in dubious

[149] E. P. Thompson asserts (*The Making of the English Working Class*, 649) that 'Bent was not a provocateur', but one wonders whether his confidence on this point is justified.

[150] Lieutenant-Colonel G. Hadfield to Major-General W. P. Acland, 14 July 1812, H.O. 40/2, fo. 228.

[151] For example, Stones alleged in his report of 6 April that Waddington, the Bolton delegate who had accompanied him to the meeting at Salford on the 5th, had said that men such as Cochrane, Burdett and Whitbread would join them when the country was ready (H.O. 40/1, fo. 64).

[152] *Parliamentary Debates*, XXIII, 980.

[153] *Nottingham Review*, 3 January 1812; *Cobbett's Political Register*, 2 May 1812, col. 564. By early 1813 there was a small group of ultra-radicals or Spenceans in London, including Arthur Thistlewood and Maurice Margarot, who may have regarded physical-force methods with more favour. (See the reports of James Smith, January–February 1813, H.O. 42/136.) But apart from the fact that a pamphlet by Margarot, *Proposal for a Grand National Jubilee*, was published at Sheffield in 1812 by the radical printer John Crome, there seems to be no evidence of any connection between this group and the northern agitation of that year.

[154] He joined Major Cartwright's Union for Parliamentary Reform in 1812 and was to be a Hampden Club delegate in 1817. See *Life of Cartwright*, II, 380: Henry Hunt, *Memoirs* (3 vols., 1820–2), III, 411.

[155] He was said to have encouraged his workmen to join the Luddites, and to have dismissed those who gave evidence for the Crown at the Lancaster special assizes. See prosecution brief, King v. James Knowles, T.S. 11/380/3580; Fletcher to H.O., 11 June 1812, H.O. 42/124.

activities. Those in Manchester who organized the opposition to the loyalist requisition early in April withdrew from the proceedings when rioting broke out on the 8th, to avoid giving any 'appearance of countenance' to acts of violence.[156] And William Cowdroy, the radical journalist, refused to print the resolutions of the Manchester reform meeting of 26 May in case the proceedings turned out to be less constitutional than they looked.[157]

Crouzet has suggested that there was a revolutionary situation in 1812, but without the revolutionaries to exploit it.[158] In fact, while it is true that revolutionary leaders of sufficient standing to provide the focus and inspiration for a national movement seemed to be lacking, there is evidence that the northern working classes did contain men with revolutionary aims, who began to mobilize in a rudimentary way. The precise relationship between this movement and the machine-breaking disturbances – the extent to which the one shaded into or developed out of the other – remains unclear. The underground groups that were the most obviously political, those at Halifax and Barnsley, cannot be shown to have had any direct involvement in machine-breaking. On the other hand they did use the 'Luddite' oath, and apparently the name itself.[159] The insurrectionary strand seems to have been at its strongest in the early summer, and it is hard to believe that this had no connection with the conflicts of the immediately preceding period. In particular, it seems likely that the confrontations at Rawfolds and Middleton – when the assailants were faced not only by the factory-owners and their men but also by militiamen called in to guard the mills[160] – should have helped to give a political colour to the solidarities and antagonisms that had previously developed. All in all, there do seem to be grounds for questioning the statement recently made by Malcolm Thomis and Peter Holt that Luddism 'remained devoid of any tendencies to develop into a political revolutionary movement'.[161] Still, one may well doubt whether the revolutionary impulse that did occur was at all formidable. It did not apparently get beyond the formation of a few loosely connected conspiratorial groups, patchily supplied with arms.[162] Nor was it very sustained: it weakened during the summer, as the authorities sharpened their techniques of intelligence and control[163] and as commercial prospects began to improve.

The revolutionary strand was to re-emerge once or twice later in the decade, at times of repression: in the Ardwick conspiracy of March 1817 in Lancashire, and in the Folly

[156] Archibald Prentice, *Historical Sketches and Personal Recollections of Manchester* (1851), 50.

[157] Bent's report headed 2 June, H.O. 42/124; *Cowdroy's Manchester Gazette*, 20 June 1812.

[158] Crouzet, *op. cit.*, II, 805. More recently, it has been suggested that the situation in 1812 was particularly dangerous because lower-class disaffection was 'for the first time associated with middle-class disaffection': A. D. Harvey, *Britain in the Early Nineteenth Century* (1978), 292. But the middle-class discontent that was expressed through the campaign against the Orders in Council was very different in character from the lower-class disaffection of the period, and was not associated' with it in any but a chronological sense.

[159] Cf. K.B. 8/91, ff. 63 and 67.

[160] For the role of the military on the second day of the 'Middleton fight', see Samuel Bamford, *Early Days* (2nd ed., Manchester, 1859), 303–6.

[161] M. I. Thomis and P. Holt, *Threats of Revolution in Britain 1789–1848* (1977), 33.

[162] Broughton reported in August that the Barnsley group had no arms but believed that when a 'rupture' took place they could seize those of the military by surprise (W.W.M., F. 46/122).

[163] For the adoption in Yorkshire of the methods used with success in Lancashire and Cheshire, see Hammonds, *op. cit.*, 312–13.

Hall and Grange Moor risings of 1817 and 1820 in the West Riding. But of the two political strands – revolutionary and radical – that were present in the northern agitation of 1812, the radical one was to be much the more widely supported. This strand had been in evidence, at least in Lancashire, since before the Luddite disturbances began. The public address sent from Manchester and Salford to Sir Francis Burdett in the summer of 1810 was signed by nearly 18,000 people;[164] in the winter of 1811–12 there were the moves (described above) at Manchester and Bolton to petition for peace and parliamentary reform; and the renewed attempt by the Manchester committee of trades in the summer of 1812 overlapped with the latter stages of underground agitation in Lancashire and Cheshire. But it was in the period following the disturbances that petitioning gained momentum, owing to the efforts of Major Cartwright and the response which they evoked. He visited Lancashire and Yorkshire in the late summer of 1812 and returned (in the course of a more extensive political tour) early in the next year.[165] In October 1812 a branch of his 'Union for Parliamentary Reform' was founded at Halifax, and within two months 17,000 people there had signed a petition for parliamentary reform.[166] By the following spring similar petitions had been signed by 30,000 people in Manchester and by considerable numbers in Bolton, Rochdale, Oldham, Lees, Ashton-under-Lyne, Stockport, Saddleworth, Leeds, Wakefield, Barnsley, Sheffield and other places.[167] Such activity prepared the way for the Hampden Clubs movement and for the presentation of very numerous petitions from Lancashire and Yorkshire in 1817.[168]

It thus appears that the crisis of 1812 was of some importance in the process whereby discontent in the northern counties acquired a major political dimension. Of course, there was no wholesale shift from industrial to political forms of activity. The growth of popular interest in the latter was no obstacle to the development of trade unionism; and machine-breaking was to recur on some occasions, notably in the cotton industry in 1826.[169] But there was from about 1812 a wider tendency than there had been earlier (either in the radical societies of the 1790s or in the underground movement at the turn of the century) for working men to support political agitation. A final question worth asking about Luddism and politics is what evidence remains concerning the changes of attitude and ideology that lay behind this trend.

Of the ideas that provided legitimation for Luddism, E. P. Thompson has written in a masterly way.[170] The Luddites were driven to adopt violent methods, and felt justified

[164] *Cowdroy's Manchester Gazette*, 30 June, 7 July 1810.

[165] *Life of Cartwright*, II, 37–42, 45–52.

[166] *An Appeal to the Nation by the Union for Parliamentary Reform according to the Constitution. With...the Articles adopted by the local Union at Halifax* (Halifax, 1812), 118–20; *The Statesman*, 15 December 1812. The Huddersfield district was also involved in the movement: see Radcliffe MSS., 126/7A.

[167] Cartwright to Shuttleworth, 24 February 1813,

Shuttleworth Scrapbook, 8; Cartwright to Thomas Holt White, 11 March 1813, Holt White MSS., no. 464, Gilbert White Museum, Selborne.

[168] John Cannon, *Parliamentary Reform 1640–1832* (Cambridge, 1972), 171 n.

[169] Hammonds, *op. cit.*, 126–8. For an outbreak at Huddersfield in February 1816, see documents in H.O. 42/148.

[170] Thompson, *The Making of the English Working Class*, 594–604.

in doing so, partly because the state had abrogated what they saw as its responsibility for protecting the essential interests of the worker by wage-regulation[171] or other paternalist measures. The Stockport delegates who visited Bolton in the early spring of 1812 said that 'since Government would give them no satisfaction it became necessary to take the means into their own hands';[172] and a few weeks later on the other side of the Pennines the 'solicitor to General Ludd' wrote to Joseph Radcliffe: 'The Cloth dressers in the Huddersfield district as spent seven thousand pounds in petition Government to put the laws in force to stop the shear frames and gig mills to no purpose so they are trying this method now.'[173] If machine-breaking was one response to the state's negative attitude, that attitude was likely at the same time to strengthen whatever feelings already existed of alienation from the political system. Such feelings did exist in some degree. A Jacobin tradition dating from the 1790s survived in some places through the first decade of the nineteenth century, being kept alive, according to Colonel Fletcher, by a hard core of men who had 'admired the French Revolution in all its different stages'.[174] A few documents testified to its existence: for example a manuscript handbill headed 'No King No War' which was found on the highway near Bolton in 1807,[175] and a printed list of democratic 'Principles, Maxims, and Primary Rules of Politics' which was sent to the Home Office in May 1811 by an anonymous correspondent at Halifax with the information that it was being 'industriously circulated' in the local workshops.[176] There were one or two similar manifestations in the period of Luddism itself. A handwritten paper found at Huddersfield, addressed to croppers, weavers and the public at large, exclaimed: 'All nobles and Tyrants must be put down, come let us follow the noble example of the Brave Citizens of Paris.'[177] And one might mention again the pamphlet of the United Britons found at Horbury, which called on the people to 'enrol under the sacred Banners of Liberty' and recover their 'imprescriptible Rights'.[178] The Jacobin tradition may have helped to inspire the underground agitation that existed for a time after machine-breaking was checked. But unfortunately (though not surprisingly) little direct evidence exists about the inspiration or objectives of underground political activity at that period. For anything more specific than remarks about the need to remove a tyrannical system of government, one is thrown back on the reports of John Bent. According to his accounts of ideas that were current from the autumn of 1811 onwards, the main argument of those who wanted revolution rather than reform was that the latter would not get rid of the national debt and the high

[171] The men who assembled on Dean Moor near Bolton on the night of 19 April 1812 discussed 'the Act of Queen Elizabeth which empowered the Magistrates to raise Wages to the price of Provisions' (statement of J. Heys, 7 October 1812, H.O. 42/128).

[172] Statement of O. Nicholson, *ibid.*

[173] Radcliffe MSS., 126/7.

[174] Fletcher to H.O., 27 December 1807, H.O. 42/91. According to Fletcher and William Chippendale of Oldham, these men were able to play from time to time on popular discontents arising from the war and

other causes. See Fletcher to H.O., 23 November 1804, H.O. 42/79, 7 March 1805, H.O. 42/82, February 1808, H.O. 42/95, and 25 February 1811, H.O. 42/114; Chippendale to Fletcher, 29 January 1806, H.O. 42/87, and 25 December 1807, H.O. 42/91.

[175] Fletcher to H.O., 27 December 1807, H.O. 42/91.

[176] Anon. to H.O., 17 May 1811, and enclosure, H.O. 42/111.

[177] Crump, *op. cit.*, 229; H.O. 40/1, fo. 228.

[178] H.O. 42/124.

taxation required to service it;[179] and although (as suggested above) there are grounds for distrusting some of his information about revolutionary activity[180] it is not unlikely that such a view should have been in circulation.[181]

As one would expect, it was the radical strand of the northern agitation that has left most evidence about the ideas that informed it. We have noted the support which Burdett's cause had aroused in the Manchester region when he clashed with the House of Commons in 1810; and the resolutions and petitions of Lancashire reform meetings in 1812 had a partly Burdettite flavour.[182] For example, the address and petition submitted to the Manchester meeting of 11 June – which were to have been presented to the Commons by Burdett – mentioned a number of the grievances which he had emphasized in his address to the Regent moved at the beginning of the parliamentary session: the burden of taxation, the multiplication of barracks, the use of *ex officio* informations to control the press. However, Burdett's programme of reform was not fully democratic, and in an important way the Manchester documents went beyond his views. While they asked for an extension of the suffrage 'as far as taxation', they were not echoing Burdett's call for the enfranchisement of those subject to *direct* taxes; they specifically requested 'that each man, not insane nor confined for crime, be entitled to vote for his representative'.[183] It was many years since the working-class demand for manhood suffrage had been thus formally expressed, and the occasion foreshadowed the success of Samuel Bamford and others in substituting this measure for a more restricted proposal at the Hampden Club convention of January 1817.[184]

Another respect in which the nascent (or renascent) Lancashire reform movement of the Luddite period differed from Burdettism – and indeed from most of the radicalism of the 1790s – was the obvious and immediate way in which industrial grievances, and parliament's refusal to redress them, lay behind it. This was explicitly shown in the address published by the Manchester petitioning committee in October 1811. The address was largely based on a pamphlet issued by the weavers of Glasgow, which had inquired why the legislature should so adamantly refuse to interfere on behalf of the weavers when it did interfere in other economic matters – notably through regulations affecting the price of corn. The Manchester address went on to ask, in a paragraph apparently written by John Knight:

179 Report endorsed 10 October [1811], and reports headed 4 and 11 November [1811], H.O. 42/117; reports headed 18 and 19 March [1812], H.O. 40/1, ff. 60 and 61.

180 An additional point worth mentioning in this connection is that in more than one instance when Bent provided details on which the authorities could check – the names of people living in particular localities – these could not be substantiated. See J. H. Smyth to H.O., 26 September 1804, enclosing R. Walker to Smyth, 22 September, H.O. 42/79; Beckett to Fletcher, 2 December 1811, H.O. 79/1, fo. 110.

181 Cobbett, in the *Political Register* for 1810–11, had been discussing the national debt and paper money in the series of articles entitled 'Paper against Gold'.

182 For a comment on the Burdettite style of the Bolton resolutions of 21 February 1812, see Fletcher to H.O., 25 February 1812, H.O. 42/120.

183 *Trial of Thirty-Eight Men*, 96–9; *Sir Francis Burdett's Address to the Prince Regent, as proposed in the House of Commons . . . on the 7th of Jan. 1812* (1812).

184 Samuel Bamford, *Passages in the Life of a Radical* (2 vols., 1844), I, 18–19.

Had you possessed 70,000 votes for the election of members...
application have been treated with such indifference, not to say inattentio.
believe not. Is it not therefore high time to look to your own concerns, to claim.
the constitutional privilege of selecting those men who are to make the laws which
govern you, and direct your exertions?[185]

Similar notions appear in the draft petition to the Commons which was read out at the
Prince Regent's Arms on 11 June 1812. The petition deplored the Commons' refusal,
despite the great rise in the price of provisions, to sanction wage regulations; and it
pointed out that the Combination Act prevented the labourers from 'unitedly attempting
to advance their wages' in proportion to the rise in prices. It also claimed, more
generally, that 'the object of all political institutions ought to be the general good, the
equal protection and security of the person and property of each individual, and
therefore labour (the poor man's only property) ought to be held as sacred as any other'.[186]
The inclusion of such points distinguished this petition from those presented to
parliament in 1793 and from the Burdettite petitions of 1810, and one can discern here
the emergence of a brand of radicalism that was more clearly related to the needs of the
industrial working class than previous political ideologies had been.[187] Thompson, who
interprets Luddism as part of the struggle for the subordination of industrial capitalism
to social priorities, says that 'we must see the years 1811–13 as a watershed, whose streams
run in one direction back to Tudor times, in another forward to the factory legislation
of the next hundred years'.[188] These years are also important, it may be suggested, as
a stage in the process whereby working men came to regard democratic control of the
state as an essential means to the improvement of their condition.

[185] Note 26 above; Hammonds, *op. cit.*, 84–5.

[186] *Trial of Thirty-Eight Men*, 98.

[187] John Knight appears to have played a key role in this development. It is also clear, from the interesting letters which he wrote to his wife while he was awaiting trial in Lancaster Castle, that he was moving towards anti-capitalist views of a still more original kind. See especially his letter of 18 August 1812 (copied by the gaoler), H.O. 42/129.

[188] Thompson, *The Making of the English Working Class*, 603.

21

Chartism

Most recent work on Chartism has been concerned, explicitly or implicitly, with arguments about class. This topic, of course, has had a long-standing association with Chartism: the original theories of Marx and Engels about how classes and class confrontations develop in industrial societies were mainly based on observation of what was happening in England in the 1840s (especially in the north west). In recent decades, a great stimulus to debate about class formation in English history has been given by E.P. Thompson's *The Making of the English Working Class* (first published in 1963). He deals with a period of some 40 years ending in the early 1830s; but Chartism is seen by him as largely a continuation and development of the trends described in his book, and it is clear that if an integral working class did come into existence in the first half of the nineteenth century the Chartist period marked its peak of self-consciousness and united action.

One of the issues raised by E.P. Thompson which applies to the study of Chartism as well as to that of earlier decades is the question of what constitutes the making of a class. According to his definition, 'class happens when some men . . . feel and articulate the identity of their interests as between themselves, and as against other men whose interests are different from (and usually opposed to) theirs'. From a strictly historical-materialist position, he has been criticised for putting too much emphasis on 'consciousness' and for not paying enough attention to the 'objective' (or socio-economic) determinants of class. It has been argued that one cannot properly speak of the 'making' of the English working class in the first half of the nineteenth century, because it was not a proletariat in the full Marxist sense: it was not 'predominantly a labour force operating . . . in factories or other technical complexes'.[2]

Nevertheless, many historians have used conceptions of class that resemble Thompson's. While accepting that Britain's manufacturing

---

[1] A. Wilson, *The Chartist Movement in Scotland* (Manchester, 1970); D. Goodway, *London Chartism, 1838-1848* (Cambridge, 1982); A.F.J. Brown, *Chartism in Essex and Suffolk* (Chelmsford, 1982).

[2] P. Anderson, *Arguments within English Marxism* (London, 1980), p. 45.

economy was still dominated by workshops and hand technology rather than by factories and steam-powered machinery, they have held that in the 1830s most workers employed in industry had developed or were developing a sense of their common interest as against the classes which governed and employed them; and they have also held that Chartism – the movement to establish popular control over parliament and to eliminate social exclusiveness and bias from the representative system – was essentially fuelled by this consciousness.

As for the characteristics of Chartism which are regarded as evidence of this kind of class-consciousness, different historians have focussed on different aspects. Some – including several who could be broadly classified as 'left-wing' – have questioned how far Chartism *was* a developed class movement in the various respects concerned. The present pamphlet will try to give some impression of the directions which scholarly debate has recently taken on these issues; and it will also touch briefly on the controversial question of why working-class radicalism lost much of its impetus and militancy around the middle of the century.

A feature of Chartism which has been particularly stressed as indicating a new degree of working-class unity on a national scale is the movement's relative comprehensiveness, in both geographical and occupational terms. Admittedly, Chartism was much stronger in some areas than others, and most of the areas where it was outstandingly strong – notably the three textile districts of south Lancashire, the West Riding of Yorkshire and the East Midlands – had been centres of popular agitation earlier in the century, at the time of Luddism and the Hampden Clubs. But it is also true that the movement achieved significant strength in several regions which had seen little in the way of organised radicalism before, such as the Black Country, parts of the south west, and above all South Wales; and to demonstrate the movement's national coverage Dorothy Thompson has compiled a list of approximately a thousand places in Britain for which there is evidence of Chartist activity at some time between 1839 and 1848.

In regard to occupational groups, it has been shown in recent studies of Lancashire and London that a striking thing about the personnel of Chartism was the wide range of urban and industrial workers involved.[3] While economic factors only partially account for this, they were certainly of major importance. At a general level, the protracted and widespread economic troubles of 1837-42 created massive hardship and discontent. More specifically, outworkers in textiles – handloom weavers in the cotton industry, linen-weavers and woolcombers in Yorkshire, silk-weavers in

[3] R. Sykes, 'Early Chartism and Trade Unionism in South-East Lancashire' in *The Chartist Experience: Studies in Working-Class Radicalism and Culture, 1830-1860*, ed. J. Epstein and D. Thompson (London, 1982); D. Goodway, *op. cit.*, n. 1 above.

Essex – remained chronically depressed, and in some places such as ↓ Bolton and Barnsley, they continued to be, as in the early nineteenth century, the dominant force in radical politics. At the same time there were many other types of artisan, for instance in the clothing, building and furniture trades, whose position was either deteriorating or highly vulnerable. Several factors were responsible for this: the growth of a mass market for goods of relatively low quality; a downward trend in the prices of manufactured goods, which increased the pressure on employers to reduce unit costs; and a permanent tendency, in a period of high population growth, for the supply of labour to exceed the demand for it. Such factors were responsible for a continuing expansion of the 'dishonourable' or non-unionised sector of the traditional trades such as tailoring and shoemaking: a sector characterised by practices such as 'sweating' (or the intensification of work loads), sub-contracting, and the employment of unapprenticed and semi-skilled labour. In the London trades, it was only in a relatively small sector catering for the West End market that high standards of quality and craftsmanship were maintained, and even men working in this sector felt that their ability to restrict the recruitment of labour, to protect customary working conditions and to maintain wage levels was in danger of being eroded. Artisans in a few trades, such as coachmaking, watchmaking and bookbinding, enjoyed a high level of prosperity and security and generally kept clear of Chartist politics. But a characteristic of Chartism in London – and in Lancashire as well – was the small number of trades which maintained this sort of aloofness.

Also, factory workers played a more significant part in Chartism than they had in previous radical movements, the most obvious example being the cotton spinners of the north west. In the opening decades of the century their long hours of work had been offset by relatively high levels of security and remuneration, but their position was now being weakened by technological change: the introduction of the self-acting mule reduced the level of skill and strength required and devalued their role in the production process. Seeing less prospect than they had earlier of being able to protect their interests by trade-union action, many of them turned – at least temporarily – to political agitation. Another occupational group which should be mentioned is the miners. Formerly, they had been rather insulated from broad working-class movements, but in the late thirties and early forties considerable numbers of them – notably in Wales and the west midlands, where there had been a long history of bitterness in industrial relations – became involved in Chartism. In the Staffordshire miners' strike of August 1842, this involvement seems to have been superficial; though Chartists played an important part in organising the strike, the specific local grievances of the miners were given much more prominence than the pursuit of the Charter. In the South Wales coalfield, on the other hand, Chartist 'missionaries' were remarkably successful in

1838-39 in inducing both miners and ironworkers to participate *en masse* in a genuinely political agitation.[4]

There is a further aspect of Chartism's social inclusiveness that has recently attracted attention: the unprecedented extent to which women were involved.[5] Over a hundred female radical associations are known to have existed in the early years of the movement, and it has been estimated that a third of those who signed the National Petition of 1839 and the petition on behalf of the transported Chartist John Frost in 1841 were women. Moreover, in many towns Chartist organisations by no means confined themselves to political campaigning, but provided a wide range of social and instructive activities which involved whole families, and in which women played a very important part. This strong female contribution was not principally inspired by an urgent desire for women's suffrage. Although a few people, such as R.J. Richardson of Manchester and Goodwyn and Catherine Barmby of Suffolk, were arguing for this in the 1840s, it was not usually given high priority by the Chartists, and most women who participated in the movement seem to have been more anxious to secure votes for their class than for their sex.

What enabled Chartism to embrace so many parts of the country and so many types of working people? One general factor which has already been mentioned is the impact of economic depression. More important in directing large numbers of people to a *political* corrective for their sufferings was the widely shared and cumulative indignation aroused by the government policies of the 1830s. The view that the Reform Act of 1832 was a cheat, and that the Whigs and the middle classes had betrayed the popular support which had helped to secure the Bill's passage, was very prevalent outside the new electorate; and a succession of subsequent measures and events – including coercion in Ireland, the transportation of the Tolpuddle Martyrs and the Glasgow spinners, and above all the Poor Law Amendment Act of 1834 – created the impression that the new regime was systematically oppressive towards working people. The change of government in 1841 did not do much, at least in the short term, to alter this impression. Peel and his Home Secretary, Graham, refused to repeal the New Poor Law, dealt more harshly with Chartist agitators than the Whigs had done, and firmly opposed the enactment of a ten-hour day in factories.

While these external factors help to account for the strong current of opinion that animated Chartism, the cohesion of the movement was strengthened internally by new organisational developments. In its early

[4] D. Philips, 'Riots and Public Order in the Black Country, 1935-1860', in *Popular Protest and Public Order*, ed. R. Quinault and J. Stevenson (London, 1974), pp. 154-56; D. Jones, *The Last Rising: The Newport Insurrection of 1839* (Oxford, 1985).

[5] D. Jones, 'Women and Chartism', *History* (1983); D. Thompson, *The Chartists* (London, 1984), pp. 120-51.

years Chartism relied heavily, for the means of holding it together, on the personality of Feargus O'Connor and the wide circulation of his paper the *Northern Star*. But the 'General Convention of the Industrious Classes' of 1839, whose members were chosen at public meetings up and down the country, and whose existence for a period of six months was financed by money raised almost entirely from the working classes, represented a new level of organisational achievement within popular radicalism. So, to an even greater extent, did the National Charter Association formed in the following year. With its central, paid executive and its network of 'localities' – 400 of them in the peak year of 1842 – the NCA has been described as 'the first independent political party of the working class in history'.[6]

Another feature of these years which has been regarded as particularly indicative of working-class unity is the close association which became apparent in some areas between Chartism and the trade unions. Although there was always a large degree of overlap in terms of leadership and personnel between radical movements and trade societies, it was unusual for the latter to participate directly in campaigns for political reform. But the Chartist period did see a considerable incursion of trade unions, as such, into politics. In Scotland, for example, they played a conspicuous part in Chartist demonstrations and contributed extensively to Chartist funds.[7] In England in the early 1840s a number of them, chiefly in London and Manchester, formed themselves into NCA localities, and trade societies played a crucial part in the general strike of August 1842. The decision to call upon all workers to stop work until the Charter became the law of the land was taken at a meeting of some 200 delegates representing trades in the Manchester area. In the preceding months of depression many wage reductions had been imposed by employers, and attempts to resist them by strike action had been unsuccessful. The obvious need in these circumstances for a united front, and a spreading belief that the Charter offered a common remedy which the various trades could combine in pursuing, produced a moment when distinctions between trade and political concerns seemed immaterial to many people.

It should be noted, however, that the general strike, although widely supported in parts of the north west and the west midlands, was not by any means a national one, and that its failure, together with the economic recovery of the mid-1840s, led to a decline of trade-union involvement in radical politics. An overlap continued to exist between the two movements, and some Chartists – such as W.P. Roberts, who served a

---

[6] J. Epstein, *The Lion of Freedom: Feargus O'Connor and the Chartist Movement, 1832-1842* (London, 1982), p. 220.

[7] A. Wilson, 'Chartism', in *Popular Movements, c. 1830-1850*, ed. J.T. Ward (London, 1970), pp. 126-27.

prison sentence for Chartist activities and then became legal adviser to the new Miners' Association – made important contributions to trade-union development. But the number of trade localities of the NCA fell away, and in 1848, although there was a revival of trades support for political reform in some places (especially London), the unions did not immerse themselves in the campaign for the Charter as widely and forcefully as they had in 1842.[8]

For some historians in the Marxian tradition an important measure of the development of working-class consciousness lies in the extent to which it becomes 'revolutionary'. Recent research has thrown new light on the 'physical force' aspect of Chartism. It has been shown, for instance, in relation to Lancashire in 1839 that the Chartists not only asserted the constitutional right of all citizens to bear arms but availed themselves of this right more extensively than earlier radicals had done.[9] The pike was the weapon that was most easily available and widely possessed, but there were also moves to obtain and distribute fire-arms. In the summer of 1839 there was a widespread belief that a popular resort to force might have some chance of success, and it is conceivable that clashes with police or troops in this climate of opinion might have ignited a 'general rising' in the north west which would have been difficult to control. In Wales, an actual rebellion did occur in November of that year. The Newport Rising was an insurrection on a larger scale than any other in nineteenth-century Britain.[10] Planned with remarkable secrecy in the mining communities of south-east Wales, where working-class solidarities were strengthened by an unusual degree of segregation from the higher classes, the march on Newport involved some 7,000 men, five or six hundred of whom carried guns. The affair showed that the mobilisation of large numbers of working men for revolutionary purposes was not impossible in Britain. At the same time, it showed what obstacles any such operation faced. The insurgents were dispersed by a body of some 30 soldiers firing from the windows of the Westgate Hotel; and the lesson seemed to be that so long as military discipline held firm, untrained and patchily armed rebels had little chance of standing up to regular troops.

There were further insurrectionary episodes in the Chartist period, which historians have investigated. Evidence has been produced to show that the attempted risings at Sheffield, Dewsbury and Bradford in January 1840 were preceded by a considerable amount of underground

[8] On Chartism and the trade unions, see J. Rule, *The Labouring Classes in Early Industrial England, 1750-1850* (London, 1986), chapter 13.
[9] R. Sykes, 'Physical-Force Chartism: The Cotton District and the Chartist Crisis of 1839', *International Review of Social History* (1985).
[10] D. Jones, *op. cit.* n. 4 above; I. Wilks, *South Wales and the Rising of 1839* (London, 1984).

activity, in the north east as well as the West Riding;[11] and David Goodway has argued that London Chartism reached its high point of 'revolutionary potential' in 1848 and that the conspiracy in the summer of that year had greater backing in the metropolis than has usually been supposed. It remains very doubtful, however, whether *mass* support for revolutionary action could have been realistically expected on either occasion. The general strike of 1842 did evoke mass support, and saw a great deal of tumult and defiance of authority. But there was much less confidence than there had been earlier about the possibility of mounting a direct challenge to the military power of the state. The *Northern Star* warned that 'the people had nothing to fight with and would be mown down by artillery if they attempted to fight'; and even G.J. Harney, who had been a strong advocate of insurrection in 1839, took the line in 1842 that physical conflict could only end in defeat.[12]

One could, of course, be a militant Chartist without being a believer in physical force as a practical option. Feargus O'Connor, for example, has often been described – and often was in his own time – as a 'physical force' Chartist. But although he never *ruled out* the possibility of armed conflict (especially if the authorities took the offensive), his basic strategy was one of intimidation. The constitutional rights to hold public meetings and to petition parliament were used in order to assemble people in formidable numbers, to imbue them with a sense of their collective strength, and to try to convince the nation and parliament of the irresistible nature of the demand for reform. O'Connor, influenced by the experience of speaking alongside militants such as J.R. Stephens at Anti-Poor Law meetings, used a violent form of rhetoric; and he countenanced some novel methods of exciting alarm such as the torchlight demonstrations of the autumn of 1838. Yet his menacing expressions were balanced by reservations and conditional clauses which ensured that he stopped short of incitement to the actual use of force, and on a number of crucial occasions – in January 1840 and April 1848, for instance – his influence was exerted to discourage conspiracy and physical aggression. Still, it has been stressed that he *was* a militant in the sense of being thoroughly committed to the full Chartist programme and to the independence of the working-class movement; and (at least until the mid-1840s) he was fiercely opposed to any move which might divert energy from the central political campaign.[13] It was over matters such as these, rather than over the question of 'moral' versus 'physical' force, that the most important divisions among popular radicals occurred.

[11] A.J. Peacock, *Bradford Chartism, 1838-1840* (York, 1969); W.H. Maehl, 'The Dynamics of Violence in Chartism: A Case Study in North-Eastern England', *Albion* (1975).

[12] A.R. Schoyen, *The Chartist Challenge: A Portrait of George Julian Harney* (London, 1958), p. 116.

[13] J. Epstein, *op. cit.* n. 6 above; D. Thompson, *The Chartists*, pp. 96-105.

Some of those who had been prominent in the early years of Chartism, such as William Lovett of the London Working Men's Association, decided after 1839 that a new approach was required. One of the assumptions which lay behind the 'new move' launched in 1840-1 was that Chartism was unlikely to achieve its objects through mass intimidation or physical force; and another was that even if it *were* possible to gain power by these means one could not expect such power to be beneficially used unless, in Lovett's words, 'the social and political superstructure were based upon the *intelligence* and *morality* of the people.'[14] Lovett's plan was to build up a widespread system of popular education financed voluntarily by the working classes and their sympathisers. However, to those Chartists who were still optimistic about the prospects of agitation aimed directly at the achievement of working-class power, this 'new move' seemed diversionary. Its opponents also maintained that it was impracticable in view of the depths of working-class poverty, and that only *after* the people's attainment of political power could any satisfactory system of education be established. Moreover the 'new move' could be seen as reflecting a derogatory view of the current capabilities of working men; and it involved co-operation with middle-class radicals, who were asked for financial assistance. O'Connor's response to Lovett's initiative (which was also a challenge to his own style of leadership) was to treat it as a betrayal of the movement, and when he called on Chartists to choose unequivocally between the National Charter Association and Lovett's National Association for Promoting the Political and Social Improvement of the People, he won overwhelming support, even in London.

The question, raised along with others by the 'new move', of whether or not there should be collaboration with middle-class reformers was one that aroused much discussion during the Chartist period. Early on, middle-class radicals made a significant contribution to the movement. Some of them, in London and Birmingham, helped with the drafting of the People's Charter and the National Petition in 1837-38, and more than half the delegates elected to the Convention of 1839 were classifiable as middle-class. Most of these delegates, however, withdrew from the Convention before long on account of the violent tone adopted by many Chartists in discussing what 'ulterior measures' should be employed if the National Petition were rejected. Thereafter, middle-class participation was much less substantial, though the possibility of collaboration was revived in 1841-42 when the Complete Suffrage Union was launched by the Quaker businessman and philanthropist Joseph Sturge. This initiative was aimed at combining the agitation for radical reform of

[14] *The Life and Struggles of William Lovett*, introduction by R.H. Tawney (London, 1967), p. 203.

parliament with the campaign for free trade. The Anti-Corn Law League had aroused Chartist hostility, partly because of a belief that its ulterior aim was to enable manufacturers to lower wages, and partly because it was seen as a rival for public attention and support. The CSU, by committing itself to universal suffrage and other points of the Charter, did gain a welcome from moderate Chartists such as Lovett, John Collins, Henry Vincent and Robert Lowery: O'Connorites, on the other hand, viewed it with distrust as a middle-class attempt to take over the leadership of popular radicalism. Ultimately, it proved impossible to secure agreement even between the Sturgeites and Lovett, but it was already apparent by the time that failure occurred that O'Connor's hostile line towards the CSU had won the backing of the majority of Chartists.[15]

In due course, after 1848, O'Connor himself and even G.J. Harney were to come round to the view that co-operation with middle-class radicals was essential if any progress was to be made. For most of the 1840s, however, the leaders of what has justifiably been called 'mainstream' Chartism were reluctant to consider alliances with groups outside the working classes which might claim a disproportionate share of influence over the movement.

Another subject which has an important bearing on the question of how far Chartism was a class movement is the nature of its ideology and the extent to which it could be regarded as 'socialist'. It used to be common for historians, especially those of the left, to treat the agitation as a basically economic one, and to regard the Charter itself as a somewhat misleading and anomalous expression of popular discontents whose real sources and remedies lay outside the system of parliamentary representation. G.D.H. Cole went so far as to say that 'the Chartist movement was essentially an economic movement with a purely political programme'; it was 'embryonic Socialism, based on the class struggle, and hostile, above all, to the newly dominant middle-class industrialists'.[16] Recently, however, Gareth Stedman Jones, though himself a socialist historian, has questioned how far Chartism can be described in these terms and has re-emphasised the centrality of politics in the agitation. He has argued that Chartism inherited from earlier radical movements not only its essentially political programme but also its analyses of distress and oppression. There was little hostility, he maintains, towards employers and capitalists as such; the basic causes of exploitation were regarded as political rather

[15] A. Wilson, 'The Suffrage Movement', in *Pressure from Without in Early Victorian England*, ed. P. Hollis (London, 1974).
[16] G.D.H. Cole, *A Short History of the British Working-Class Movement, 1789-1947* (London, 1948), pp. 90, 109.

than as being inherent in the current economic system or mode of production, and what people saw as the crucial dividing line between classes was not one determined by different economic roles but the one established by the Reform Act of 1832 between those who possessed and those who were excluded from political power.

It is true, with certain qualifications, that few Chartists were committed to a socialist reorganisation of society. There were Owenites who did aim at this goal, but in the 1840s they formed a sect of only a few thousand, and its composition was less predominantly working-class than that of Chartism. Since the failure of the Grand National Consolidated Trades Union in 1834, there had been no large-scale revival of popular faith in Owenism as a social solution. There were some people in the late thirties, such as Lawrence Pitkethly of Huddersfield, who combined an explicit commitment to socialism with a commitment to Chartism; and there were other Chartists, such as Bronterre O'Brien, who cherished socialist aims but thought it best to keep them in the background until the political battle had been won.[17] Also, in the early 1850s, under the leadership of Ernest Jones, what remained of the Chartist movement did adopt a brand of socialism which owed much to Continental writers, including Marx and Engels; the Chartist convention of March-April 1851, for instance, listed 'the rapid abrogation of wages-slavery' among the movement's objectives.[18] It remains the case, however, that signs of overt socialism were unusual during the climatic years of the agitation.

There were hardly any proposals to take over the factories and expropriate their owners (as Stedman Jones points out); and even ideas about taking over the land and turning it into 'the people's farm', which had formed a strand in earlier radical thinking, did not play a central part in the movement. The scheme of social improvement which was most popular with Chartists was O'Connor's Land Plan of the mid-1840s. This was inspired by the belief that part of the industrial workforce could be transferred to the desirable lot of independent smallholders, through the purchase of land with money subscribed by the people at large; and it was additionally hoped that such a process would benefit those who remained in industrial employment by relieving the surplus of labour. O'Connor said in the *Northern Star* in April 1843 that his plan had no more to do with socialism than it had with Halley's Comet, and it is clear that he was himself a strong believer in economic individualism.[19]

There is no doubt that Chartist ideology was more radical than socialist; and one may also note that the tradition of radicalism to which it

[17] E. Royle, *Victorian Infidels* (London, 1974), p. 135; M. Beer, *A History of British Socialism* (2 vols., London, 1929), ii. 44.

[18] J. Saville, *Ernest Jones: Chartist* (London, 1952), p. 45.

[19] A.R. Schoyen, *op. cit.* n. 12 above, pp. 148, 180.

belonged was not altogether a working-class one. All the six points of the Charter had been mooted in the 1770s and 1780s by men such as Major Cartwright and the Duke of Richmond, before significant numbers of working men became involved in organised politics. Also, grievances which middle-class as well as working-class reformers had long been attributing to the system of government, such as 'corruption' and excessive taxation, continued to figure prominently in Chartist speeches and manifestoes. However, the key point of the Chartist programme, universal male suffrage, had been very closely associated since the 1790s with *working-class* political movements, and the fact that Chartism was radical rather than socialist did not prevent it from being deeply infused with class feeling.

This feeling was not directed exclusively *against* any single clearly-defined class: social antagonisms were not simplified to that extent. The notion of a conflict of interest between the middle and working classes was often qualified by a recognition that some middle-class groups, such as shopkeepers who depended on the custom of working people, did not fit neatly into such a pattern. Also, of course, there was much resentment against the landowning aristocracy, which was still dominant in governmental circles and which was regarded as blatantly corrupt and parasitic. Nevertheless, it is arguable that in the areas where Chartism was strongest class feeling was directed more intensely against 'capitalists' than against the old ruling class. Political factors contributed to this. Many of the state policies and legislative measures of the 1830s could be seen as promoting or protecting the interests of capitalists: for instance, the stern treatment of trade unionists, the very limited scope of factory legislation, and above all the New Poor Law, which was commonly interpreted as an attempt to coerce people into working for low wages by attaching deterrent conditions to the acceptance of poor relief. When the Chartists complained, as they frequently did, about 'class legislation' they were not thinking simply, or even primarily, about legislation that benefited the landowning aristocracy.

It is also arguable that there was an increasingly widespread and entrenched belief that in economic and social relations as well as in political terms a basic conflict of interest existed between the owners of industrial capital and their workers. The deepening of this conviction was attributable in part to a variety of changes in the structure and organisation of industry, some of which have already been mentioned. It was in the textile factories of Lancashire and Yorkshire that the starkness of the confrontation between capital and labour was most pronounced, and it was, of course, on the basis of his observations in the Manchester area that Engels argued in his book *The Condition of the Working Class in England* (1845) that society was polarising into the two great camps of bourgeoisie and proletariat. But a number of specialised studies have indicated that it was not only in the factory-based textile industries that conflicts between employers and employed were intensifying. In the Birmingham metal trades, for instance, an increasingly competitive market situation, a growth of larger units of production, an extension of the use of steam power, and an erosion of the control exercised by trade societies over workshop practices were combining to undermine the comparatively harmonious class relations which had formerly characterised the town; and a similar sharpening of conflict was apparent in the London handicraft trades as large-scale capitalist employers became more common.[20]

The effect of these industrial developments was reinforced by ideological ones. We have seen that few Chartists, before mid-century, espoused a full socialist analysis; but it is none the less true that what can broadly be called anti-capitalist ideas were widely current. These stemmed partly from the popularisation of the theories of Thomas Hodgskin and others, who had argued in the twenties and thirties that labour alone was the source and measure of value, and that industrial and commercial profits involved an unjustified exaction from the class which actually produced the country's wealth. A corollary of the spread of such ideas was a strong reaction against political economy. Doctrines derived, somewhat selectively, from 'classical' economists such as Adam Smith and Ricardo were much used in the early nineteenth century to justify policies which maximised freedom and incentives for the capitalist, while conveying the message that there was no real conflict of interest between capital and labour. Also, Malthus's ideas were used to justify a poor-law policy which restricted the granting of relief and tried to discourage irresponsible procreation by the poor. In the 1830s, such doctrines were frequently criticised and denounced in the popular radical press as specious attempts to legitimise and disguise class-interest and exploitation; and the debate did a great deal to accentuate the division between the outlook of the middle classes (including that of middle-class radicals, who often subscribed to political economy) and the outlook of working men.

These various factors – political, industrial and ideological – were helping to give a variety of workers a common sense of participation in a *general* struggle between capital and labour. Indeed it was sometimes explicitly stated that this was the essential contest in which Chartists were engaged. 'Ours is the conflict of labour against capital', said the Manchester conference of the National Charter Association in its address of 17 August 1842.[21] Such statements did not mean that the *abolition* of

[20] C. Behagg, 'An Alliance with the Middle Class: The Birmingham Political Union and Early Chartism, in *The Chartist Experience* (*op. cit.* n. 3 above); D. Goodway, *op. cit* n. 1 above.

[21] M. Jenkins, *The General Strike of 1842* (London, 1980), p. 273.

capitalism was intended; but they did reflect the fact that hostility to capitalists and 'steamlords' was a very powerful animating feature of Chartism, and they also implied that a basic aim of the movement was to establish, via the attainment of the Charter, proper *defences* for labour against exploitation. This would be effected partly through the elimination of 'class legislation', but it would also be done by more positive means, for major causes of oppression were located in the workings of a capitalist system which was allowed to operate *without* legislative controls. While the precise measures that would be required to provide satisfactory protection for labour against capital were not often specified in detail, there was broad agreement that steps should be taken to limit the destructive effects of uncontrolled competition in producing unemployment, low wages, and excessive hours of work. All Chartists favoured factory legislation, many favoured taxes or other controls on the introduction of machinery, and some favoured statutory arrangements for the fixing of wages. Also, it was believed that a parliament controlled by the mass of the people would be able to remove a whole range of specific grievances which resulted from the domination of capital over labour in particular industries, from the customary docking of wages in Black Country coalmines to excessive rents for stocking-frames in the Nottingham hosiery trade.

The overall problem of how far Chartism was a class movement can be regarded as involving two rather separate questions. One is how far the Chartists themselves were class-conscious; and the other is how far and how deeply, such a consciousness permeated the working classes in general. On the first question, some scholars who have reservations about the class nature of Chartism have drawn attention to the common ground that existed between this movement and others of a different social composition. Essays written about Lovett, Lowery and Vincent have emphasised those elements within Chartism – beliefs in education, temperance, free trade, financial retrenchment, the destruction of aristocratic and Anglican privilege – which overlapped with or foreshadowed the Liberalism of the mid-Victorian period.[22] But a much greater volume of recent work has been devoted to the aspects of Chartism which *distinguished* it from middle-class radicalism and Liberalism; and these aspects do seem more characteristic of the Chartist mainstream. Other historians have stressed the internal divisions – between the various occupational groups involved, skilled and less skilled, traditional and modern – which made working-class support for the movement very heterogeneous. Yet in spite of the variety of grievances that motivated the

---

[22] B. Harrison and P. Hollis, 'Chartism, Liberalism and the Life of Robert Lowery', *English Historical Review* (1967); B. Harrison, 'Teetotal Chartism', *History* (1973); D. Large, 'William Lovett', in *Pressure from Without* (*op. cit.* n. 15 above).

component groups, it seems clear that the majority of activists had a strong sense of the interdependence, at least at a political level, of working-class interests.

However, *relatively* comprehensive though the movement was, Chartism never came very close to embracing the whole of the working classes. Rural areas were hardly involved at all, and even in industrial parts of Britain mass participation was in some places patchy and ephemeral: on Tyneside, for example, it only lasted for a few weeks in the summer of 1839. It is possible, of course, that many of those who did not participate, or only participated briefly, nevertheless shared an ongoing sense of common interest with other working men and of antagonism towards the higher classes. It has been suggested that the lack of involvement of agricultural labourers in Chartism was due more fundamentally to the problems of mounting agitation in the countryside rather than to any lack of class feeling or of sympathy with Chartist goals.[23] On the other hand, it appears that for many of the working people who did participate at times in the movement, it was only for brief periods that commitment to the pursuit of a collective class interest overrode differences of locality, occupation and status and took priority over sectional concerns. There were some people, certainly, whose whole existence was suffused with an awareness of class. But for many others, although the sense of belonging to a class might be intermittently important, it was often overlaid by the sense of belonging to some smaller grouping such as a trade society or religious congregation, the thrust of whose activities would not necessarily coincide with that of class-based agitation.

The extent of active class consciousness achieved in the summer of 1839 and in August 1842 was exceptional; and after 1848 the solidarity and militancy of the peak years of Chartism gave way to a period of comparatively temperate and fragmented working-class activity, marked by a greater reliance on trade unionism. The abruptness and magnitude of the changes have been played down by some historians and should not be exaggerated, but it cannot be denied that a notable shift took place. the reasons for it have provoked much discussion, and they should be at least briefly considered.[24]

Perhaps the most obvious factor that weakened the momentum of Chartism was repeated failure. To mobilise mass support, the movement needed to generate a widespread belief that success was possible. The

---

[23] R. Wells, 'Rural Rebels in Southern England in the 1830s', in C. Emsley and J. Walvin (ed.), *Artisans, Peasants and Proletarians* (London, 1985).

[24] For a fuller study of the debate, see N. Kirk, *The Growth of Working-Class Reformism in Mid-Victorian England* (London, 1985), chapter 1.

events of 1839 – the confusion over 'ulterior measures', the half-hearted and largely abortive attempt to stage a political strike or 'national holiday', and the swift suppression of the Newport Rising – seriously damaged its capacity to do this; and the defeat of the general strike in 1842 damaged it further. In 1848, the impact of failure was even more crushing. There has been much discussion about how far the Kennington Common demonstration of April 10 really was a 'fiasco', and how far its portrayal as such was a myth attributable to anti-Chartist propaganda.[25] But whatever misrepresentations there were, the fact remains that the authorities, aided by the press, inflicted on the popular reform movement the most important psychological defeat of the century. The event marked, as John Belchem has said, the bankruptcy of a long tradition of 'mass platform' agitation;[26] and it must have led many besides O'Connor to feel that the working classes could no longer realistically hope to achieve their own enfranchisement without the help of other social groups.

In addition to the evaporation of confidence in the possibility of success, another outstanding reason for the decline of Chartism – and a factor which operated both after 1842 and after 1848 – was economic recovery. In recent decades there has been something of a reaction among historians against an earlier tendency to consider that variations in the level of popular agitation could be explained essentially in terms of economic fluctuations. That earlier tendency was epitomised in the 'social tension chart' which W.W. Rostow compiled on the basis of data concerning wheat prices and movements of the trade cycle;[27] and the reaction against such 'economic reductionism' is to some extent a healthy one, since popular agitation has a complex range of causes and its chronology cannot be matched exactly to changes in economic variables. Yet the fundamental importance of the trade cycle should not be neglected. The fact that popular campaigns for political reform were very difficult to mount or sustain except in times of more than usual hardship was unanimously recognised by contemporaries. Harney, to give just one example, wrote in the *Northern Star* on 2 September 1848: 'When trade is good, political agitation is a farce'. Marx and Engels writing the *Communist Manifesto* in 1847-48, believed that there was a tendency under industrial capitalism for cyclical crises to become progressively more severe and to 'put on its trial, each time more threateningly, the existence of the entire bourgeois society'. In fact, although the crisis of 1847-48 was hardly less

---

[25] H. Weisser, *April 10: Challenge and Response in England in 1848* (Lanham, Maryland, 1983), pp. 291-97.

[26] J. Belchem, 'Feargus O'Connor and the Collapse of the Mass Platform', in *The Chartist Experience* (*op. cit.* n. 3 above).

[27] W.W. Rostow, *The British Economy of the Nineteenth Century* (Oxford, 1948), pp. 123-25.

catastrophic than that of 1842, moderation of cyclical fluctuations in the
ensuing years meant that the country did not experience appalling
depressions of the kind which, since the end of the French wars, had
periodically impelled masses of people into urgent political activity.

A third factor of importance in accounting for the movement's decline
was the change that occurred in the attitudes and policies of the governing
and propertied classes. To a large extent, this change can be regarded as a
result of Chartism, and as evidence of its partial success. The movement,
and the alarms created by it, did much to focus attention on social
problems and to instil a new determination into efforts to tackle them.
These efforts partly took the form of practical Christian philanthropy on a
local basis, which was doubtless motivated by genuine compassion as well
as by a conscious or unconscious desire to alleviate discontent and reduce
the starkness of class divisions. Also, a liberalisation of state policies
became apparent in the course of the 1840s. Significant manifestations of
this trend were the repeal of the Corn Laws in 1846, the Factory Act of
1847, the Public Health Act of 1848, which at last gave some legislative
substance to public concern about urban sanitation, and the Industrial
and Provident Societies Act of 1852, which gave co-operative societies
legal recognition and protection for their funds. A basic assumption of
Chartist analysis was that until the people gained control of the political
system no real improvement in their position was possible. But when
improvement began to take place *without* democratic reform, the thrust of
the Chartist case was greatly weakened.[28]

Two other theories about the decline of Chartism are worth
mentioning. One, put forward by T.R. Tholfsen, is that there was a
tendency for working-class culture to become assimilated to the culture of
the middle classes: as working people came to attach increasing value to
moral and intellectual improvement, the area of consensus between the
two cultures broadened and class antagonisms abated. Yet although such
a convergence may have occurred in the mid-Victorian period, one feels
that this may have been more a consequence than a cause of the decline of
combative working-class radicalism. The Chartists of the 1840s prided
themselves on their independence of middle-class tutelage, and so long as
their hopes of political success were kept alive there were not many signs
that the culture of politically-conscious working people was being
assimilated to what Tholfsen calls 'a culture characterised by middle-
class hegemony'.[29]

The other theory focuses on changes of a structural kind within
manufacturing industry, and in particular on the role of the labour
aristocracy. The most ambitious version of this theory is the one advanced
by John Foster on the basis of research on Oldham. He attributes the

---

[28] T.R. Tholfsen, *Working-Class Radicalism in Mid-Victorian England* (London, 1976).

political stabilisation of the mid-nineteenth century partly to a liberalisation of bourgeois attitudes; but the other factor he particularly stresses is the emergence, in Oldham's cotton and engineering industries, of a privileged grade of pacemakers and taskmasters whose high wages and status depended not so much on their distinctive skills as on close co-operation with management. He thus argues that changes in industry and in the structure of the workforce account for a growing 'collaborationism' among the elite of the working class and for the decline of a united working-class consciousness. Various criticisms have been made of Foster's theory. It has been argued, for example, that pacemaking and sub-contracting were by no means new phenomena in the mid-nineteenth century. Similarly but more generally, it has been argued that an aristocracy of labour had always existed in industry, and that it is hard to identify, at the national level, any change in its character and influence that could account for the mid-century change in the nature of working-class politics.[30]

Another hypothesis of a more general kind, however, may be more helpful in explaining in industrial terms both the working-class militancy which reached its peak in the late thirties and early forties, and the onset of a more moderate phase around 1850. According to this interpretation, to which several writers have contributed, the first half of the century was a period of disruptive transition in the methods and relations of production. Various categories of workers were involved in struggles to protect themselves against basic threats to their status, independence and even livelihood: outworkers fought against mechanisations and drastically falling piece-rates, artisans against the infringement or abrogation of the customary practices of their trades, factory workers and others against loss of control over the labour process. This background of industrial flux and insecurity helped to produce a period of unusual militancy in working-class politics, as workers clutched at the possibility that political power could be used to arrest or reverse the processes which were eroding their respective positions. Clearly, the working-class radicalism of the Chartist period cannot be explained wholly in these terms. It was partly inspired by more positive aims, such as a desire to assert the dignity of working men by establishing an equality of political rights. Yet one suspects that for most working men who took part in radical agitation motives of self-defence, not only against 'class legislation' but also against the damaging effects of industrial trends, were of great underlying importance. It is worth noting that the places where Chartism retained its vitality longest, well into the 1850s, were towns such as Bradford and

---

[30] J. Foster, *Class Struggle and the Industrial Revolution* (London, 1974); G. Stedman Jones, *Languages of Class: Studies in English Working-Class History, 1832-1982* (Cambridge, 1983), chapter 3.

Halifax where handworkers in the woollen and worsted trades were still holding out as best they could against the advance of mechanisation.

It can be argued further that in most sections of industry by around 1850 the battles of the first half of the century had been more or less lost, and a consolidation of industrial capitalism was visibly taking place. Conflict between capital and labour did not by any means come to an end, but the framework of labour relations in which it continued was a narrower and more institutionalised one. Meanwhile in the political sphere there was a spreading recognition of the fact that the establishment of working-class supremacy, however desirable, was not practicable in existing circumstances, and there was a reversion to an idea that had sometimes been articulated earlier in artisan circles: that working men deserved representation as an 'interest', along with other interests. The role of skilled and unionised workers in these shifts of emphasis in the working-class movement was, of course, very important. They did not constitute to any great extent a *new* aristocracy of labour; but there was a change in their approach resulting from the stabilisation of economic conditions and from a growing belief that in both the economic and the political fields there were prospects of improvement which did not depend on a full-blooded challenge to the existing distribution of power. An implication of the general interpretation we have been outlining – and it is an implication that is now accepted by a variety of historians – is that one must reject, or indeed reverse, the notion in the *Communist Manifesto* that the working class tends to become more militant as it becomes more proletarianised. Militancy, it is argued, is more naturally associated with the traumas and dislocations of the early stages of industrialisation than with a more mature and settled phase of industrial capitalism. In circumstances of the latter kind, a strong sense of class may continue, and solidarity may increase at some levels as the labour movement develops a greater degree of national organisation. But the strategies on which the working classes rely for the advancement of their interests do not usually involve those of massive confrontation.

22

Bentham and Marx [1]

On the monument over Karl Marx's grave in Highgate Cemetery there is a text taken from the *Theses on Feuerbach*: 'The philosophers have only interpreted the world in various ways. The point, however, is to change it'. Bentham, of course, has no grave: he sits in a glass-fronted box a few miles to the south of Highgate; and he died in 1832, thirteen years before the theses on Feuerbach were jotted down in the young Marx's notebook. But he would have agreed profoundly with the observation quoted on Marx's monument. And among the philosophers who *have* 'changed the world' – or significantly altered its development – Marx and Bentham can both be included.

Ghita Ionescu, a Romanian political exile who became professor of political science at Manchester, published a book five or six years ago called *Politics and the Pursuit of Happiness*, in which he argued that for 130 years or so the world had been dominated by two ideologies: Marxism on the one hand and Benthamism or utilitarian liberalism on the other. 'No other ideology', Ionescu wrote, 'has ever enjoyed such a long continuity or such a universal impact as these two'. Since Ionescu's book was written – and particularly in the last few months – amazing things have happened, and the death of Marxism has been widely proclaimed. Indeed, in a recent issue of *Private Eye* there was a picture of the Marx monument in Highgate Cemetery carrying the inscription 'OK, so we all make mistakes'. Whether that leaves us in a situation where 'Bentham rules' is something I will return to later on. But what I should like to do in this lecture is to compare their respective interpretations of society and to examine various affinities and links and contrasts between them. I shall concentrate more on Bentham than on Marx, partly because I have done more work on him myself, and partly because he is less well known. And that being the case I shall start if I may with a few words of introduction about Bentham, with apologies to those who know a lot about him already. What almost everyone knows about him, I think, if they have heard of Bentham at all, is

[1] Draft of Inaugural Lecture to have been given by John R. Dinwiddy, 14 May 1990.

two things: one is that he coined or popularised, the phrase 'the greatest happiness of the greatest number' – and the other is that his body is preserved in this rather curious way at University College.

On the latter point, a word or two of explanation may be called for. As a result of directions given in his will, Bentham's body was publicly dissected after his death, and the skeleton was then reassembled, clothed (with additional padding) in one of his suits, and seated in a chair in a glass-fronted box. He thought that the techniques used by the Maoris for preserving human heads could usefully be adapted in Europe: as memorials to the dead, preserved heads (or as he called them auto-icons) would be more satisfactory than any statue could be because they would be more realistic. And he believed that the auto-icons of famous men would be an inspiration to later generations. He was a vain man himself, as well as an eccentric one – and he hoped that after his death a club would be got up (like the Pitt Club or the Fox Club) to commemorate him and propagate his ideas. 'When Bentham has ceased to live,' he wrote, 'whom will the Bentham Club have for its chairman? Whom but Bentham himself. On him will all eyes be turned – to him will all speeches be addressed.' There is in fact a Bentham Club at University College – and at its annual dinner the box is wheeled in and Bentham presides from a corner of the room. One should add, though, that the attempt of Southwood Smith (a doctor and friend of Bentham, who was to become one of the great public health reformers of the nineteenth century) to preserve Bentham's head was not at all successful. What he did (as he recorded in a subsequent letter) was to draw off the fluids by placing the head under an air pump over sulphuric acid. But this process not only drew off the fluids, but also drained all expression from the face. The result was quite hideous, and the head is now kept in a box in a basement of University College. The head one sees on the auto-icon is a wax model taken from a bust of Bentham sculpted in his own lifetime.

Shifting now to the second thing that most people have heard of in relation to Bentham: his 'principles of utility' or 'greatest happiness principle' was the principle that all actions and policies and institutions should be judged by how far they contribute to (or detract from) the happiness of the community, the greatest happiness of the greatest number. He considered that this criterion of morality was preferable to any other, largely because it was more concrete – because it provided an external, non-mystical standard or basis for moral judgements; and that sort of basis was not provided, he thought, by other moral codes which were supposedly derived from natural law, or divine ordnance, or intuitive moral sense. These latter modes of argument were in his view devices for giving a specious reinforcement to what were really subjective judgements or appeals to authority. So when someone said that certain actions or rules of behaviour were right because they were in accordance with natural law, or because they were divinely ordained, or because they appealed to man's ingrained moral sentiments, all that person was in fact saying was that he himself approved of such actions or rules, or that they had been approved of by other people whose opinion or authority he respected. Another crucial thing about Bentham's principle of utility was that it was not just the basic principle of moral philosophy: it was also intended and treated by him as an instrument of reform. It provided a yardstick by which existing institutions of all kinds could be judged in terms of their social benefits and social costs.

It was not, of course, a really novel idea: many political thinkers had stated more or less explicitly that the happiness of the community was the purpose or *raison d'être* of government. Also, as a yardstick, the principle of utility was not by any means without problems. It raised very serious questions about how, if at all, happiness could be measured, and how the happiness of one person could be compared or summed with that of another. Bentham believed, however, that in spite of all the problems associated with it, the principle of utility provided a less arbitrary criterion for political and social judgements than any other, and one that was more likely than any other to command general assent: and throughout his career he tried as systematically as he could to apply this principle in assessing existing institutions and practices and seeing how far they needed to be reformed.

What he was most interested in reforming, for most of his life, was the law. Trained for the legal profession as a young man, he was appalled by the state of the English legal system: by the complexity and obscurity of the law, and by the way in which the legal system seemed to be geared to the interests of lawyers rather than to the interests of the public. In response to an English judge who claimed in 1792 that no man was so low as not to be within the law's protection, Bentham said that in fact recourse to the law was so expensive that it was beyond the reach of ninety-nine people out of every hundred. And the fundamental reason for this was that judges and lawyers always had an interest in making the law so complicated and inaccessible that only they themselves could find their way around it. What was needed, in Bentham's view, was to put a stop to this form of exploitation and to remove the uncertainties that characterised the current legal system. What was needed was systematic codification: the creation of a comprehensive and intelligible code of laws which would be devoted in every detail to the aim of maximising the general happiness.

As well as being a law reformer, Bentham was also in the last twenty years or so of his life, a committed reformer in politics. He was one of those rather unusual people who become more radical as they get older, rather than more conservative. He was frustrated by the unresponsiveness of existing governments to his proposals for legal reform: and in his sixties be became a strong believer in democracy, as the only likely means of ensuring that governments did actually pursue the greatest happiness of the greatest number, instead of the interests of what he called the 'ruling few'.

The next question I want to look at is what Marx – who began writing or publishing a decade or so after Bentham's death – thought or wrote about Bentham. Marx had two modes of writing, though they sometimes got rather conflated: one was intended to be objective and 'scientific', the other was subjective and polemical. When he was in his scientific mode, he was very willing to recognise and affirm that the capitalist stage of human history was an enormously constructive one – constructive above all in building up the forces of production to previously unimagined levels; and he was also willing to recognise (when he was in this mode) that those thinkers who had formulated the ideology which helped the capitalist system to establish itself had made important advances in the realm of ideas.

The chief passage in which Marx – and Engels – considered Bentham in this sort of light comes in their joint work, *The German Ideology*, written in 1845-6 (but not actually published until 1932, a hundred years after Bentham's death). In this passage Marx and Engels examine the evolution of the conception of human relations as essentially relations of mutual usefulness and exploitation. They see this theory of human nature and behaviour as having been developed especially by the French Enlightenment thinkers such as Helvetius and Holbach, who held that human beings are egoistic and driven by self-interest and that all relationships can be analysed in terms of people 'using' one another. What Bentham did (Marx and Engels go on to say) was to take this rather abstract, generalised theory of human nature or psychology, and give it what they called 'positive economic content' by fusing this French Enlightenment theory with English political economy, the 'classical' economic theories developed in Britain during the period of commercial and industrial growth in the late eighteenth and early nineteenth centuries. Bentham's version of utilitarianism was thus seen as closely linked to a particular emerging mode of production, and as providing what was in the context of that time a cogent and appropriate rationale for bourgeois capitalism. This is described by Marx and Engels as a notable 'advance', a notable 'achievement'.

Underlying Marx's recognition of the constructive aspect of the bourgeois phase of history there was, of course, a deep moral revulsion against the human devastation caused by capitalism. Marx regarded it as his role not only to analyse capitalism in a scientific fashion, revealing both the secrets of its achievements and the trends within it that were leading towards its collapse; but also to arouse indignation against the system and to help to generate a revolutionary consciousness, thereby advancing the process whereby capitalism would be superseded. He had, therefore, a polemical and moralistic mode of writing which he often used against the bourgeoisie and against bourgeois theorists; and he was particularly venomous in attacking bourgeois theorists when he felt that their ideas were being used not so much to advance and justify the victory of capitalism over feudalism, but to prolong the life of capitalism by providing it with ideological buttressing or apologetics. By the time he came to write the first volume of *Capital* in the 1860s, Marx had come to see Bentham in this sort of light; and in this volume Bentham comes in for sustained and vehement abuse. He is famously described, for example, as 'the arch-philistine, Jeremy Bentham, the insipid, pedantic, leather-tongued oracle of the commonplace bourgeois intelligence of the nineteenth century'. And Marx goes on to say in a footnote: 'Bentham is a purely English phenomenon . . . at no time and in no country has the most trivial banality ever before strutted about with such appalling self-satisfaction . . . Had I the courage of my friend Heinrich Heine, I should call Mr. Jeremy a genius in the way of bourgeois stupidity.'

What was it about Bentham that Marx objected to so much? The particular passage of abuse that I have just quoted from was directly provoked by Bentham's view of the so-called 'wages fund' – by his view that the level of wages, in a country with a given population, is determined by the amount of capital available for the payment of labour. This was a view that Marx regarded as erroneous, and also as characteristic of bourgeois or capitalist apologetic – since it carried the implications that labour could not increase its share of social wealth and could not expect wages to rise above subsistence level. This was not, however, the most fundamental issue on which Marx disagreed with Bentham. What he above all disliked was Bentham's conception – or what he took to be Bentham's conception – of human nature, and the emphasis he placed on *interest* as the motivating force in human behaviour. As we shall see, Marx did not fully understand Bentham's ideas about psychology: but the basic view he attributed to him was that human beings are thoroughly selfish. In another passage in *Capital* – on the classical theory of exchange as involving mutual advantage, benefit to both parties – Marx says that this theory reflects the ideas and values of Jeremy Bentham, in that 'each of the pair is only concerned with his own interest. The power which brings them together, which makes them enter into relation with one another, is self-interest, and nothing more. Every one for himself alone, no one with any concern for another.' It was Marx's view that Bentham regarded his egoistic interpretation of human psychology as universally valid – and that Bentham had totally failed to realise that this interpretation was specific to a particular historical epoch (the capitalist one). Bentham, Marx says (and I quote), 'assumes the modern shopkeeper, and above all the modern English shopkeeper to be the normal man. Whatever seems useful to this queer sort of normal man and his world, is regarded as useful in itself.' So Marx treats Bentham in *Capital* as the exponent of a simplistic and unhistorical theory which is merely a validation or attempted validation of bourgeois egoism.

I shall return later to Bentham's views about human nature and how they compared with those of Marx; but a question I want to ask at this point is how far Bentham's social and political thought really fitted the interpretation of him as an archetypal bourgeois apologist? And a point that needs to be made at the outset in this connection is that Marx did not known Bentham's writings terribly well. Something the two men had in common was that they both wrote prose that was on the whole very difficult to read. Bentham's style was indeed described by Cobbett as 'puzzling and tedious beyond mortal endurance', and another early nineteenth-century critic referred to it as 'the Sanscrit of modern legislation'. Marx, understandably, instead of struggling with Bentham's English, preferred to read him in the French editions which were produced by Bentham's friend and interpreter, Etienne Dumont. These French editions presented a somewhat simplified version of Bentham's thought. It is also significant that they were based on Bentham's writings of the late eighteenth century, before he had become a thoroughgoing radical in politics.

Had Marx read the later, fully radicalised, Bentham, he would still no doubt have regarded him as an essentially bourgeois kind of reformer – but he might have recognised none the less that their respective theories had a certain amount in common. This was particularly true in the area one might call the social psychology of politics. One of the most interesting respects in which Bentham anticipated Marx was in his perception that people's behaviour and ideas and beliefs are largely conditioned by their social situations. John Stuart Mill, in a famous essay on Bentham which he wrote after the latter's death, praised him for having drawn attention to 'selfish interest in the form of class-interest', and for having identified the phenomenon which Bentham called 'interest-begotten prejudice' – for showing, in other words, how a ruling class or elite will develop (to a large extent unconsciously) beliefs and ideas that suit and support their own collective interests. Bentham admitted that one could not always predict how an *individual* would think and behave from examining his or her situation. But he considered that the behaviour of groups was almost invariably determined by their self-regarding interests – and that the larger the group was the more confidently this rule could be applied.

Bentham also anticipated in a quite striking way the modern Marxist notion of cultural or ideological hegemony – a notion particularly associated with Antonio Gramsci, who argued in the inter-war period that the survival of capitalism was due not principally to coercion, but rather to the more subtle means whereby the ruling class influenced and conditioned people's attitudes and values, and induced the workers to accept and consent to the system that exploited them. Marx and Engels themselves had expressed some ideas that foreshadowed this notion of hegemony. They had, for example, written in the 1840s that the class which controlled the means of material production also controlled the means of intellectual production, and that the ruling ideas of each age were the ideas of its ruling class. Bentham actually got a good deal closer to the theory that Gramsci subsequently developed. He was initially interested in the devices used by the legal profession to mystify and delude the public and enable lawyers to fleece the community. But in due course he came to feel that the whole governing class was using its control over the church, the universities and most of the press to exercise what he called a 'delusive influence' over the people at large. The purpose of this delusive influence was to induce them to accept and even respect the existing mode of government and distribution of power; or, as Bentham himself puts it, 'to engage the people to submit to be sold, oppressed and plundered'. In another passage in the same work (his *Constitutional Code* written in the 1820s), Bentham said that the conceptions, judgements and even languages of the mass of the population had been placed 'almost completely under the guidance, and almost, as it were, at the disposal' of the aristocracy; and he showed how loyalism and deference were inculcated, by ceremonial display, and by the rhetorical use of terms like 'dignity', 'honour', 'glory', and by a variety of fictions and fallacies.

I have been suggesting that in some respects Bentham's ideas were not as distant from Marxian ways of thinking as one might have expected from reading Marx's attacks on him. There were other important aspects of Bentham's thought, however, that did conform pretty closely to the interpretation of his philosophy as essentially bourgeois. One such aspect is the anti-aristocratic thrust of his political and economic analysis. He called the British political system a mixed despotism of monarch and aristocracy, and maintained that the ruling few used their political power to 'drain all pockets into their own' – to raise money from the population at large through taxation, and to share out the proceeds among themselves in the form of salaries, sinecures, pensions and so on. At the economic level, Bentham shared with Ricardo the view that the aristocracy was basically parasitic, in that it lived off rent – off its ownership of land – without actually contributing anything to the production of wealth. So there was a real conflict of interest, in his opinion, between the aristocracy on the one hand and the rest of the community on the other – a conflict that was far more real than any conflict of interest between capital and labour, employers and employed. He believed that employers and workers had a shared interest in economic growth: in a high rate of capital accumulation, which would mean a high demand for labour and a rising trend in real wages. He was certainly a believer in what Marx called capitalism.

He did not believe in *unfettered* capitalism and laissez-faire: he was aware of the costs as well as the benefits of a capitalist system, and he thought that its social ill-effects should be counteracted by a fair amount of state intervention for purposes of social protection and welfare; for example, in areas such as public health; provision for the poor; maintaining stores of food as a safeguard against famine; promoting schemes of social insurance; enforcing safety regulations in mines and factories; and even restricting industrial pollution. Compared with other 'classical' economists, he was unusual in the range of responsibilities that he thought the government should undertake. Still, he did believe that free enterprise and market forces were the most effective mechanisms for producing growth and prosperity; and he thought that the most important way in which the state could contribute to economic prosperity was by ensuring that property was secure.

His concern for the security of property was sharpened, no doubt, by the French Revolution; and it is significant that although he attacked the aristocracy's control of political power in England, he was not prepared to attack its property rights in any fundamental way. He was afraid that once the security of one form of property was weakened or destroyed, other forms would also be endangered. He recognised that some systems of property distribution might be more conducive to happiness than others; and it is important to note at this point that there were elements within his own philosophy which pointed in the direction of egalitarianism. For instance, he said that in assessments of general or collective happiness, the happiness of any one person 'high or low, rich or poor', should count for as much as that of any other person. He was also one of the earliest people to give clear expression to the principles of what later came to be called the diminishing marginal utility of money: that is, the principle that the better off one is, the less one will normally derive in terms of additional happiness from a given quantity or unit of additional income. The implication of this principle is that the more equal the distribution of wealth or income, the greater the overall sum of happiness that will be derived from the wealth available. Bentham thought that there was a natural tendency as civilisation advanced for property to become more widely diffused – and he pointed out that not many generations earlier European societies had been sharply divided into a small class of landowners and a multitude of serfs. He thought that governments could assist the diffusion of property in a very cautious way by measures relating to the laws of inheritance, but that any attempt at a major shift from the existing distribution of property to a more egalitarian one would be terribly dangerous to social order and economic prosperity. He wrote in 1795:

> A revolution in property! It is an idea big with horror . . . It involves the ideas of possessions disturbed, of expectations thwarted: of estates forcibly ravished from the living owners, of opulence reduced to beggary, of the fruits of industry made the prey of rapacity and dissipation.

From the economic point of view, of course – as that last phrase about the fruits of industry indicates – Bentham's concern about the security of property was a concern about the need for incentives. The less confident people were that they would be able to hold on to the wealth they acquired, the less incentive there would be to economic enterprise. This seemed to Bentham a very powerful argument against any attempt to introduce socialism or community of goods. Under such a system, he maintained, coercion would become necessary in order to maintain production; 'the gentle motive of reward', as he put it, would have to be replaced by the 'doleful motive of punishment'.

Utilitarianism and socialism should not be regarded as necessarily incompatible. There was one interesting figure in the early nineteenth century who actually tried to combine them, and who provided something of a link between Bentham and Marx. He was an Irishman called William Thompson – a landowner in County Cork, a man of great eccentricity and kindness, known for rambling in the Irish countryside with a tricolor flag attached to his walking stick, for his devotion to animals and his pioneering concern for the rights of women. Bentham too (besides being notably eccentric) was much concerned about the interests of women and about those of animals. (If you buy something from the Body Shop these days, it will be given to you in a bag made of recycled paper carrying a statement against animal testing and a quotation from Bentham which says: 'The question is not, can they reason? Nor, can they talk, but can they suffer?')

One way and another, Thompson and Bentham had much in common. Thompson was impressed by Bentham's writings (initially in fact by those on education) and got in touch with him. Bentham invited him to stay at his house in London, which he did for several months in 1822-3. Shortly afterwards, in 1824, Thompson published an enormous, turgid and fascinating book called *An Inquiry into the Principles of the Distribution of Wealth most Conducive to Human Happiness*. The introduction contained a warm tribute to Bentham, who was said to have contributed even more to moral science than Bacon had to physical science: and Thompson's commitment to the greatest happiness principle was explicitly stated on the first page of the first chapter. Working from Bentham's premises, Thompson arrived at markedly different conclusions about the organisation of society. He laid particular emphasis on the principle of the diminishing marginal utility of wealth, which Bentham himself expounded in a work published in 1822, at very much the time when he and Thompson were in contact with each other. Thompson expressed the principle in his book as follows:

> Such is the effect on happiness of the continued addition of successive equal portions of wealth that every succeeding portion diminishes in effect. Of 1,000 portions of the matter of wealth, the first 100 are necessary to repel hunger and thirst and to support life . . . the effect of [a] second hundred in intensity of

enjoyment is so infinitely beneath that produced by the first 100, as to be incapable of any comparison. Every hundred added is less and less productive of absolute increase of happiness to the possessor.

Where Thompson diverged from Bentham was over the interpretation and relative importance of security on the one hand and equality on the other. Bentham considered that both these things were desirable, but that there was usually a tension or competition between them – and that for the sake of the general happiness and prosperity it was more important that property should be secure than that it should be equally divided.

Underlying Bentham's views about the security of property and the need for incentives was the assumption that it was the capitalist who played the crucial part in the generation of wealth and the capitalist whose efforts needed to be encouraged and stimulated. Thompson accepted that, given human nature as it then was, incentives might be necessary in order to maximise production. But incentives, he asked, for whom? In Thompson's view it was the labourer rather than the capitalist who was the real producer of wealth; and he argued that the existing system of private property offered very little security or incentive to the real producer, the working man, since the major part of the produce of his labour was taken away from him in the shape of profits and rent. The most effective stimulus to exertion and production would be to allow every labouring man to enjoy the full fruits of his own labour; and this would involve creating a situation in which the workers themselves controlled the means of production and competed with one another, within a system analagous to market socialism.

This was not for Thompson the ideal form of social organisation. His ideal was a system which did *not* rely on selfishness and competition: a system in which production and consumption were collectively organised, in which people worked for the community rather than for themselves, and in which happiness was maximised through an equal distribution of goods. He appreciated that this system would require a profound change in social attitudes and values. He was vague about how the shift from one system to another could be brought about, but thought that Robert Owen's communitarian experiments were important moves in the right direction. He believed that there was a fundamental benevolence in human nature which would assert itself once the competitive conditions which promoted selfishness were removed.

In the summer of 1845 Marx stayed for six weeks with Engels in Manchester; they spent most of the time in the delightful medieval library of Chetham's Hospital, reading English works on political economy. It was at this time that Marx read Thompson's book on the distribution of wealth, and he was later to cite the book in a number of his own writings. It is extremely hard to know how much he was actually influenced by it – and how Thompson's influence on Marx compared with that of other

English socialists whom Marx also read, such as Thomas Hodgskin. It is worth mentioning, though, that the terms 'surplus value' and 'mode of production' are both used in Thompson's book and may have been picked up there by Marx – and indeed these *concepts* were articulated by Thompson in ways that anticipated certain aspects of Mark's economic and historical analyses. Leaving aside the question of possible influences, what the two men shared most fundamentally was an optimism about the possibility of changing human nature. Thompson was of course classifiable in Marx's terms as a 'utopian' socialist – a term implying several characteristics that Marx criticised. The Utopian socialists – as defined in the *Communist Manifesto* and elsewhere – were socialists who believed that they could achieve their ends through moral argument and peaceful persuasion, and did not recognise the need for class conflict and revolutionary action; they were socialists who concentrated more on describing their ideal form of society than on looking realistically at how it could be achieved.

Although Marx criticised the Utopian socialists and emphatically distinguished his own approach from theirs, he did himself have a vision of what future communist society would be like; and although he never tried to describe this society in detail, there are a number of passages scattered through his works which indicate, sometimes in very evocative terms, the outline of what he had in mind. It was, indeed, a most inspiring vision. The material basis of full communism, as envisaged by him, would be an economy of abundance – a society freed from the pressures of economic scarcity.

Scarcity, in Marx's view, was the real cause of social or class conflict. He believed that on the basis of capitalism, achieved both through the vast increases in productivity resulting from industrialisation and technological progress, and through the social organisation and regulation of the forces of production which capitalism had done so much to build up, it would be possible to satisfy everybody's needs and to remove the sources of contention. Also, as a result of increasing mechanisation, it would be possible to reduce very substantially the proportion of people's time that they had to devote to the production of the material goods that society needed. Marx says, in a famous passage at the end of the third volume *Capital*, that as the 'realm of necessity' contracts, the 'realm of freedom' will expand – the realm of freedom being the area of life in which people will be able to engage in truly creative and satisfying activities and fulfil their potential as human beings. So in spite of his attacks on Utopianism, Marx himself did look forward to a qualitative transformation change in human life and human relations. He thought that conflict and alienation – man's alienation from his fellow-men and the stunting of his human capacities – were rooted in certain economic and social circumstances, and that once those circumstances were radically changed, alienation would be transcended, and human beings would live together in harmony and co-operation, while at the same time developing themselves fully as individuals. This was the sort of vision that was encapsulated in phrases like the one in the *Communist Manifesto* which says that the class conflicts of bourgeois society all give way to 'an association in which the free development of each is the condition for the free development of all'.

How did these views of Marx about the future of society compare with those of Bentham? Bentham's general view on the matter can best be expressed in his own words in a passage I would like to quote at some length from *Essays on the Influence of Place and Time in Matters of Legislation*. (It was written in the 1780s, before his style had become really convoluted.)

> Perfect happiness belongs to the imaginary regions of philosophy, and must be classed with . . . the philosophers stone. It may be possible to diminish the influence of, but not to destroy, the sad and mischievous passions. The unequal gifts of nature and of fortune will always create jealousies: there will always be opposition of interests, and consequently rivalries and hatred. Among the higher as well as the lower classes, there will be desires which cannot be satisfied, inclinations which must be subdued . . This faithful picture . . . is more worthy of regard than the deceptive exaggerations which excite our hopes for a moment, and then precipitate us into discouragement . . . Let us seek only for what is attainable . . . We shall never make this world the abode of perfect happiness: when we shall have accomplished all that can be done, this paradise will yet be . . . only a garden; but this garden will be a most delightful abode, compared with the savage forest in which men have so long wandered.

Bentham had a fair degree of optimism about the possibilities of social improvement, but no belief in perfectibility. He thought that improvement could chiefly be brought about through legislation: legislation aimed at minimising conflict between individuals in pursuit of their own individual goals, and aimed at providing a secure environment in which this pursuit could be carried on. His ideas about legislation were closely bound up with his ideas about human nature. Marx, as we have seen, interpreted Bentham as regarding human beings as thoroughly selfish. And indeed Bentham did consider that people are bound to seek in the first place their *own* happiness, in the sense that people do what they want to do: they do what they think, in the circumstances, will give them most satisfaction. Looking at things from the point of view of society, on the other hand (rather than from the individual's point of view) Bentham says (as we have seen) that the aim should be the greatest happiness of the greatest number: this is the criterion of right and wrong.

There appears to be some difficulty about reconciling his notion of psychology with his notion of ethics. If one assumes that for the individual the only possible motive for action is the maximising of his own happiness, how can one expect him to promote the happiness of others? How can one expect him to act in accordance with an ethical principle which lays down that the greatest happiness of the greatest number is the object to be aimed at? In answer to this question Bentham said that one can not expect anyone to promote the happiness of others to the exclusion of his own happiness. But one can, through wise legislation, ensure that people pursue their own happiness in ways which either do not damage, or actually promote, the happiness of others. This was to be done primarily through legal sanctions – through the creation of laws which imposed punishments for anti-social behaviour, and thus made it in the individual's *interest* not to damage the happiness of others. Also, Bentham attached a certain amount of importance to *social* or moral sanctions. He thought that for most people the 'love of reputation' was an important motive, and that if a climate of opinion could be fostered in which harmful behaviour was disapproved of and beneficient action praised, this would have a salutary effect on people's conduct. And he thought that by means of what he called *indirect* legislation – which included forms of propaganda and public instruction – the climate of opinion could be influenced in the right directions, the pressure exerted by society's opinion could be strengthened, and people could be diverted from inclinations and activities which might have socially harmful effects.

Bentham thought, too, that people had sympathies which led them to take pleasure in the happiness of others and to be hurt by other people's pain. The role of sympathy in his psychological theory – which was particularly prominent in his later writings – was something that Marx was apparently unaware of. Bentham did consider that all actions are motivated by interest, and having an interest in something means to expect to derive from it some pleasure or avoidance of pain; but he did not mean that human beings are necessarily *selfish* in the usual sense of the word. He used the word 'interest' in a very broad sense, to cover not only 'self-regarding' interest, but also what he called 'social' or 'extra-regarding' interest. One can have an interest in promoting the welfare of others – not just or not necessarily because one hopes to derive some benefit or advantage for oneself in return: one can also have an interest – a genuinely *social* interest – in acting benevolently and giving happiness to others, because one derives pleasure from acting in this way (without any ulterior motive).

As society progressed, Bentham thought that the force of social interests and motives would tend to strengthen: as people became more educated and enlightened, and more aware of each other's needs and of the beneficial effects of reciprocal concern, they would increasingly come to feel a spontaneous care for other people's welfare. Nonetheless, Bentham never believed that social interests and motives would actually come to predominate over self-regarding ones. He thought that people would always tend to conform to what he called 'the principle of self-preference'. Indeed he thought that this principle was not a bad thing: in his opinion each individual should normally be regarded as the best judge of his own happiness, of what gave him pleasure. A greater sum of overall happiness was likely to result from allowing each person to pursue his own happiness in his own way (short of interfering with that of others): more happiness would be likely to result from this situation than would be likely to result from each person concerning himself with other people's happiness.

Although he thought that the possibilities of improving human behaviour were considerable, Bentham did not – unlike Thompson and Marx – have any optimistic belief in the possibility of *transforming* it. Direct comments on socialism in Bentham's writings are infrequent – but there is one, written in the 1780s, which expresses directly his scepticism about the possibility of human nature being radically changed under a socialist system. He wrote:

> The prospects of benevolence and concord which have seduced so many ardent minds, are under this system, only the chimeras of the imagination . . . In the division of labour . . . who would be content with his lot and not esteem the burthen of his neighbour lighter than his own? . . . And in the division of property, how impossible to satisfy everyone, to preserve the appearance of equality, to prevent jealousies, quarrels, rivalries, preferences . . . What an apparatus of penal laws would be required, to replace the gentle liberty of choice, and the natural reward of the cares which each one takes for himself. This system could only be maintained by political or religious slavery.

This picture may be unduly black; but it seems to me broadly true that in the last hundred and fifty years visions like Marx's, of socialism combined with harmony and freedom, have nowhere been realised, and that attempts to realise them have ended badly. The brand of socialism which to my mind has retained some validity is the revisionist or social democratic brand, which was largely developed in *reaction* to Marx and Marxism, and which one associates with names such as Bernstein and Crosland: a brand of socialism which focuses not on class conflict, revolutionary action and the complete socialisation or collectivisation of property and economic activity, but rather on achieving a redistribution of wealth and opportunities through progressive taxation and state-supported educational and social services.

In Bentham's philosophy there are elements which point, if not quite in the same direction, at least towards a brand of liberalism which attempts to combine the benefits of individual enterprise and freedom of choice with an active concern for social protection and welfare. Followers of his in the nineteenth century contributed not only to extensive reforms of the English legal system, but also to important social reforms in fields such as public health and factory legislation. As we have seen, his concern about the security of property made him extremely cautious about measures for redistributing wealth. But the economist and mathematician, F.Y. Edgeworth, drew attention in the 1870s to the passages in Bentham's work where the concept of the diminishing marginal utility of money was first clearly expounded, and went on to show how this concept could provide the basis of a rationale for progressive taxation. Two or three decades later the New Liberals and Fabians who were constructing an ideology that would help to lay the foundations of the welfare state, regarded Bentham as one of their principal mentors. And Bentham's interest in the measurement of utility, and his belief that policy decisions should be determined as far as possible by the calculation and comparison of different 'sums' of happiness, made him the acknowledged progenitor of twentieth-century theories of cost-benefit analysis and welfare economics.

Most of these ideas, though not quite as unfashionable as Marxism, have been exposed to much criticism in the 1980s by thinkers of the New Right who trace their intellectual ancestry back to Adam Smith rather than to Bentham. But the 1990s may conceivably see a swing back to the sort of mix between spontaneity and interventionism that has been associated with the Benthamite tradition.

Index

Page numbers in bold type refer to complete essays.

on aristocracy 275, 427, 428
auto-icon 422
and Bolívar 302-3, 343
and Brougham 290, 297, 352, 353
Brougham on 309-10, 353
and Burdett 116, 287, 289-90
and Burke 253-5, 268, 271
on capitalism 427-8, 430
Carlyle on 357
and Cartwright 57, 287-9
Catholic Emancipation 282
and Cobbett 289
codification of law 278, 292, 298,
    300-1, 305, 306, 307, 308, 310, 311,
    345-6, 347-8, 349, 350, 351-2, 353,
    364, 366, 369, 423
and common law 305, 349, 350, 368
conversion to democracy 210, 273-6,
    423-4
and the Crown 281-2
'delusive influence' 427
diminishing marginal utility of money
    428-9, 435
dominant minority 261
and Dumont 293, 307-8, 309
Dumont as editor etc, of works 291,
    293, 294, 296, 297-9, 302, 304, 305,
    307, 339, 340, 342, 343, 344, 358
eccentricity 341, 353, 422, 429
Edinburgh Review and 352-7
education of the people 285, 433
egocentricity 309-10
on ethics and utility **315-37**, 355-6,
    357, 432-3
on Fox 9
France and 306, 346-8
and Francis Place 290
freedom of the press 279
on French Revolution 283-4
Geneva and 307-8
Germany and 306, 346, 348
Greece and 307
on happiness 432, 434
household suffrage 280, 285, 290
India and 307, 308-9, 352
on international law 336
and James Mill 273, 274, 275, 276,
    287, 308
jogging 309, 341
J. S. Mill on 265, 289, 312, 426
and Judge Ashhurst 200, 204
later years 309-10
Latin America and 275-6, 302-4, 343,
    352

law reform 278-9, 292, 296, 297, 312,
    353, 423
and legal profession 278-9, 353, 423,
    427
legislation 292, 304, 317-18, 322, 325,
    328-31, 333, 334, 337, 343, 356-7,
    432, 433
and Locke 286
Madame de Staël and 306, 313, 360
and Marx **421-35**
and Mexico 276
and natural law 233, 296, 299, 343,
    422-3
and natural rights 283, 288, 306
New Poor Law 311-12, 361
Pannomion **363-9**
Panopticon scheme 280, 292, 307-8,
    309, 356
parliamentary reform 273, 274, 275,
    276, 279, 287, 297
and physical force 286-7, 297
political radicalism **273-90**, 344
on poor relief 311, 428
Portugal and 300
and property 284, 428-9, 430, 434,
    435
on punishment 321-2, 352, 353
and religion 298-9, 330
republicanism 282
Roebuck on 312-13
ridicule of 340-1, 342-3, 353
and Romilly 290, 297, 348, 352, 353
and Scott 340
secret ballot 273, 280, 288, 297, 354
on self-interest 284, 325, 425, 433
on self-preference 322-4, 433-4
and sinecures 274, 276, 292-3, 427
and socialism 429, 434
and sovereignty 356-7
Spain and 275-6, 286, 299-301, 343-4
style 295-6, 297-8, 341-3, 353, 426
on sympathy 325, 433
on taxation 275, 427
universal suffrage 281, 285, 286, 289,
    290, 297, 353-4
utilitarianism 229, 230, 299, 306, 310,
    334, 336, 354-5, 357, 424
utility principle **315-37**, 422-3, 435
on wealth 428-9, 435
women and the vote 288
and women's interests 429
writings 291-2, 293-4, 310-11
mentioned 96, 102, 142, 144, 203, 256,
    259

peace negotiations 13
and reform 81, 82
reform motion (1797) 2, 51
and Waithman 76, 77
and Wyvill 52, 59
mentioned 32, 46, 256
Grigby, Joshua 32
Grimké, Thomas 346
'Guienne, chevalier de' 155

Habeas Corpus Act 26, 42, 80, 150, 167, 178
Haigh, James 392-3
Halévy, Elie 60, 262, 273, 274, 281, 310
Hall, Charles **87-107**
and Cobbett 105
Effects of Civilization . . . 88, 89-98, 99
on Malthus 97-8
and Marxism 105
on property 92, 103-4
as Utopian socialist 105-7
Hallam, Henry 229
Hamburger, Joseph 286
Hamilton, Lord Archibald 12
Hammond, Anthony 348
Hammond, Barbara 125, 371-2
Hammond, J.L. 125, 371-2
Hampden Club 54, 80, 117, 119, 290, 400
Hampden Clubs 80, 116, 118, 214, 216, 398
Hanson, Joseph 394
Hanway, Jonas 136
Harcourt, Duc d' 161
Hardinge, Sir Henry 132, 134, 138
Hardy, Thomas 11, 41-2, 66, 189, 193
Harney, George Julian 222-4, 226, 227, 228, 409, 411, 417
Harrington, James 118
Hart, H.L.A. 363
harvests 190, 194, 375
Harvey, D.W. 82
Hastings, Warren 238
Hayward, Abraham 348
Hazlitt, William 9, 118, 185, 212, 294, 356, 357-8
headgear, radical 209, 224-5
Hegel, G.F.W. 346
Hennell, Mary 105
Henry IV, king of England 118, 163
Henson, Gravener 120, 122
Hermosilla, José Gomez 344
Hetherington, Henry 224
Hey, Richard 206
Heywood, Samuel 21, 22, 27, 29
Higgins, Godfrey 58
Hill, Lord 133, 134

Hill, Serjeant 149
Hinchcliffe, John 392
historic rights theory 169
Hobbes, Thomas 173
Hobhouse, Sir John Cam 5, 8, 9, 132, 133, 134, 139, 166
Hodgskin, Thomas 104, 105, 217, 357, 414, 431
Hodgson, Richard 189
Holdsworth, Sir William 163
Holland, Lord
on Burdett 123, 147
on Cartwright 59-60
and Fox's *History . . .* 12, 19, 23, 24
and reform of Parliament 76
Roscoe letter 47
and Waithman 80, 81
mentioned 56
Holland House group 165, 212, 293
hosiery workers 120-1, 371, 395
household suffrage, approved/proposed by:
Bentham 280, 285, 290
Burdett 116, 400
Cartwright 57, 287
Fox 2
Philip Frances 38
Waithman 78
Wyvill 37, 50
Howard, Henry 22
Hulme, Thomas 396
Hume, David 282-3
Hume, Joseph
and army commissions 140
and flogging in the army 132, 133, 134, 141, 144, 147
Fox and 24-5, 26
and Fox dinners 11-12
Hall and 102
on happiness 96
as historian 20-1, 24-5
and military expenditure 139
on Poor Law 311-12
and property 92, 245-6
and Somerville 141
on 'usefulness' 229, 249
Hume, L.J. 280, 322, 325-6
Humphreys, James 348
Hunt, F.K. 143
Hunt, Henry, 'Orator'
on Burdett/Burdettites 117, 120
and flogging in the army 132, 133, 134, 144
and Fox 5
hat worn 209